Cottrell-Brashear Family Linage

Ancestors of Taylor Cosby Cottrell, Jr.

Cottrell-Brashear Family

Taylor Cosby Cottrell, Sr.
Circa 1935

Estella Zalame Brashear
Circa 1958

Jo Ann Cottrell
Bowling Green, Kentucky
Circa 1960

T.C. Cottrell
Plattsburg AFB, New York
Circa 1987

Cottrell-Brashear Family Linage

Ancestors of Taylor Cosby Cottrell, Jr.

Researched and Written By

T.C. Cottrell

T.C. Cottrell
2016

First Printing: 2016

ISBN: 978-0-578-17932-2

T.C. Cottrell
867 Jamestown Drive
Rockledge, Florida 32955

Website: www.tcottrell.com

Email: tccottrell@earthlink.net

Dedication

To my family past and present for information passed down through the generations of my Cottrell, Brashear, Lashbrook, and Taylor lines, but especially to my wife who is the true genealogist in my combined family linage. She held onto a treasure trove of photographs, notes, and original clippings until the Author became interested in his family's origin. Without her love of family history, and her steadfast purpose to preserve the Author's linage, regardless of his interest at the time, this book could not have become a reality.

Contents

Acknowledgements

The real credit for the research contained in this book goes to the author's family who initially gathered family history from living relatives, kept copies of obituaries from local and regional newspapers, and wrote memories of their childhood. Credit also goes to the author's immediate family who held on to boxes of photographs and written notes while the author had little interest in genealogy.

Additional credit goes to the genealogists who painstakingly read microfilm, line by line and page by page, before the advent of computers and searchable databases. Credit also goes to the LDS Church for their mission of capturing records throughout the world and generously making them available completely free for public use.

The author is not a genealogist. However, he has come to love genealogy and has found great joy in standing on the shoulders of the giants that came before him – the real genealogists and historians that held on to, and recorded, the historical documents that are the sources for this publication.

Preface

Relationship references throughout this book center on the author, Taylor Cosby Cottrell, Jr., also known as T.C. Cottrell, who was born in Bowling Green Kentucky in June of 1944. He attended College High School, a training school for Western Kentucky University, graduating in 1962. After being awarded a Bachelor's Degree from Western Kentucky University he entered the U.S. Air Force in 1968.

For the next 20 years he served in the U.S. Air Force as a pilot, and later as an instructor and command pilot. During 1972 he flew combat missions into both North and South Vietnam. Before retiring in 1988 he received a Master's Degree from the State University of New York, in Plattsburgh.

In the fall of 1988 he moved to Florida to begin a second career spanning over 27 years with a multi-national corporation providing support and services to government customers throughout the world. In the spring of 2016 he ended his second career and now finds the time to pursue his primary interests including photography, writing, and genealogy.

Introduction

This publication is organized into four sections. Section One contains information on the Author's paternal line (Cottrell) and related family. Section Two contains information on the author's maternal line (Brashear) and related family. Section Three contains surname maps showing the locations of events where the specific location is known. Section Four contains photographs and documents of interest that are either in the possession of the author or in the public domain. The author's research extends well beyond the 4th generation on most lines but is not included in detail in this book for brevity and because in many cases the reliability of the sources may be relatively low.

The level of detail in the narratives depends on the information available through research and on the author's intent on providing a life summary that is both accurate and interesting. Information on living people is intentionally limited or omitted entirely.

A brief overview of the origin of the Cottrell-Brashear and related lines follow.

Cottrell Paternal – The author's Cottrell line likely originates from England. However, the earliest Cottrell ancestor in the author's research is Richard Cottrell, the author's 6th great-grandfather. Richard's descendants are listed below:

- Richard Cottrell who was born 1662 in New Kent County, Virginia and died on 16 March 1715 in New Kent County, Virginia.
  - Richard Cottrell who was born in 1687 in St. Peter's Parish in New Kent County, Virginia and died on 13 October 1715 in Middlesex County, Virginia.
    - Richard Cottrell who was born on 17 December 1710 in New Kent County, Virginia and died on 12 March 1792 in Henrico County, Virginia.
      - Peter Cottrell who was born on 1 September 1760 in Henrico County, Virginia and died on 25 July 1816 in Henrico County, Virginia.
        - William Cottrell who was born on 13 June 1785 in Henrico County, Virginia and died on 7 January 1838 in Henrico County, Virginia.

The remaining author's Cottrell line and family members, including William's family, is covered in detail in Section 1, Chapters 1-4.

Cosby Paternal – The author's Cosby line is believed to originate in England. The earliest Cosby ancestor reasonably confirmed by the author is David Cosby, the author's 6th great-grandfather. The author's Cosby descendants are listed below:

- David Cosby who was born in 1703 in England and died in September 1770 in Louisa County, Virginia.
  - David Cosby who was born in 1728 in Louisa County, Virginia and died in September 1804 in Goochland County, Virginia.
    - Jeremiah David Cosby who was born on 11 October 1761 in Goochland County, Virginia and died circa 1813 in Pawhatan County, Virginia.
      - William Winifred Cosby who was born circa 1780 in Pawhatan County, Virginia and died circa1821 in Virginia.
        - Jefferson M Cosby who was born in 1806 in Pawhatan County, Virginia and died on 25 December 1880 in Chesterfield County, Virginia.

The author's remaining Cosby line and family members, including Jefferson's family, is covered in Section 1, Chapter 5.

Lashbrook Paternal – The author's Lashbrook line originates in England. Common variations included Lashbrook, Lashbrooke, and Lashbrooks. The earliest confirmed Lashbrook ancestor in the author's research is William Lashbrook, the author's 5th great-grandfather. Lashbrook was spelled differently in many sources, sometimes even within the same family unit. Lashbrook descendants are listed below:

- William Lashbrook who was born on 17 October 1717 in Devon, England; died on 24 November 1760 in Prince William County, Virginia.
  - William Lashbrook who was born in 1748 in Dumfries, Prince William County, Virginia and died before 6 August 1816 in Bullitt County, Kentucky.
    - James B. Lashbrook who was born on 15 March 1775 in Jefferson County, Kentucky and died on 10 October 1823 in Daviess County, Kentucky.
      - Norris Lashbrook who was born on 8 July 1809 in Bullitt County, Kentucky and died on 6 October 1846 in Daviess County, Kentucky.

The author's remaining Lashbrook line and family members, including Norris's family are covered in Section 1, Chapters 6-7.

Taylor Paternal – The author's Taylor line is a difficult line to research because the surname Taylor is a very common name and there multiple Taylor lines living in Kentucky in the 1700s and 1800s. The author believes that George Taylor, who was born in 1738 in Augusta in Rockbridge County, Virginia, is his 5th great-grandfather. The author's Taylor descendants are listed below:

- George Taylor who was born in 1738 in Augusta, Rockbridge County, Virginia and died on 31 January 1801 in Crab Creek, Montgomery County, Virginia.
  - John Taylor who was born on 23 July 1764 in Pulaski, Pulaski County, Virginia and died on 26 September 1845 in Pulaski, Pulaski County, Virginia.
    - John R. Taylor who was born in 1795 and died before 1 June 1840. According to Nellie Cottrell John was one of the first settlers of Louisville, Kentucky, called Yellow Banks.
      - Jefferson M. Taylor who was born 8 February 1823 in Jefferson County, Kentucky and died 30 January 1892 in Daviess County, Kentucky.

The author's remaining Taylor line and family members, including Jefferson's family are covered in Section 1, Chapter 8.

Brashear Maternal – The author's Brashear line is well researched and documented in *A Brashear(s) Family History*, a multi-volume set of excellent research works published by Charles Brashear. The name Brashear was spelled differently included Brashear, Brashears, Brasseur, and Brashier. It was frequently spelled differently for the same individual on several source documents and sometimes even spelled differently within the same record. The Brashear line originates in France. The earliest Brashear ancestor reasonably confirmed by the author is Robert Brasseur/Brashear the Huguenot, born around 1598 in France. Robert was the author's 8th great-grandfather. The author's Brashear descendants are listed below:

- Benjamin (Benois) Brasseur who was born circa 1620 in France and died in December 1662 in Calvert County, Maryland.
  - Robert Brashier III who was born circa 1646; died in 1712.

- Samuel Brashear Sr. who was born in 1673 in Maryland and died in August 1740 in Maryland.
  - Samuel Brashear Jr. who was born on 12 February 1696/97 and died before 1 November 1773 in Prince George County, Maryland.
    - Ignatius (Nacy) Brashear who was born on 17 April 1734 in Prince George County, Maryland and died on 5 October 1807 in Shepherdsville, Bullitt County, Kentucky.
      - Levi Brashear who weas born on 14 November 1773 in Maryland and died in 1828 in Nelson County, Kentucky.

The author's remaining Brashear line and family members, including Levi's family are covered in Section 2, Chapters 1-3.

Crutchfield Maternal – The author has been unable to determine the origin of the Crutchfield line with any degree of accuracy. The earliest ancestor identified in the author's research is William D. Crutchfield, the author's 3rd great-grandfather, who was born in 1751. The author's Crutchfield descendants are listed below:

- William D. Crutchfield who was born in 1751 and died on 27 March 1807 in Boyle County, Kentucky.
  - Richard D. Crutchfield who was born in n1782 in Richmond, Henrico County, Virginia and died on 7 April 1843 in Danville, Boyle County, Kentucky.

The author's remaining Crutchfield line and family members, including Richard's family are covered in Section 2, Chapter 4.

Campbell Maternal – Like the Taylor line, the Campbell line is difficult to research due to the multitude of Campbell lines spreading from Virginia throughout the United States. However, the origin of the author's Campbell line is reasonably confirmed to be Scotland. The earliest ancestor identified by the author was Henry Campbell, the author's 5th great-grandfather who was born around 1706 in Scotland. The author's Campbell descendants are listed below:

- Henry Campbell who was born in 1706 in Pgrtshire, Scotland and died on 7 December 1772 in Amherst County, Virginia.
  - Joel Campbell who was born circa 1748 in England and died on 7 April 1832 in Amherst County, Virginia.

- Wiley Campbell who was born on 8 July 1772 in Amherst County, Virginia and died 2 February 1842 in Amherst County, Virginia.
  - John Sale Campbell who was born on 25 April 1803 in Amherst County, Virginia and died 1 November 1892 in Warren County, Kentucky.

The author's remaining Campbell line and family members, including John's family are covered in Section 2, Chapters 5-6.

Penner Maternal – The origin of the author's Penner line is also difficult to research because there were multiple Penner lines in Kentucky during the 1700's and common first names were prevalent through Warren County, Kentucky. The earliest Penner ancestor confirmed by the author was Peter Penner, the author's 4th great-grandfather who was born in 1731. Peter's descendants are listed below:

- Peter Penner who was born in 1731 and died in 1796.
  - John Penner who was born in 1769 in Virginia and died on 1 October 1833 in Warren County, Kentucky.
    - Peter Penner who was born on 5 October 1795 in Montgomery County, Virginia and died on 18 April 1869 in Warren County, Kentucky.

The author's remaining Penner line and family members, including Peter's family are covered in Section 2, Chapter 7.

Cottrell Ancestor Chart

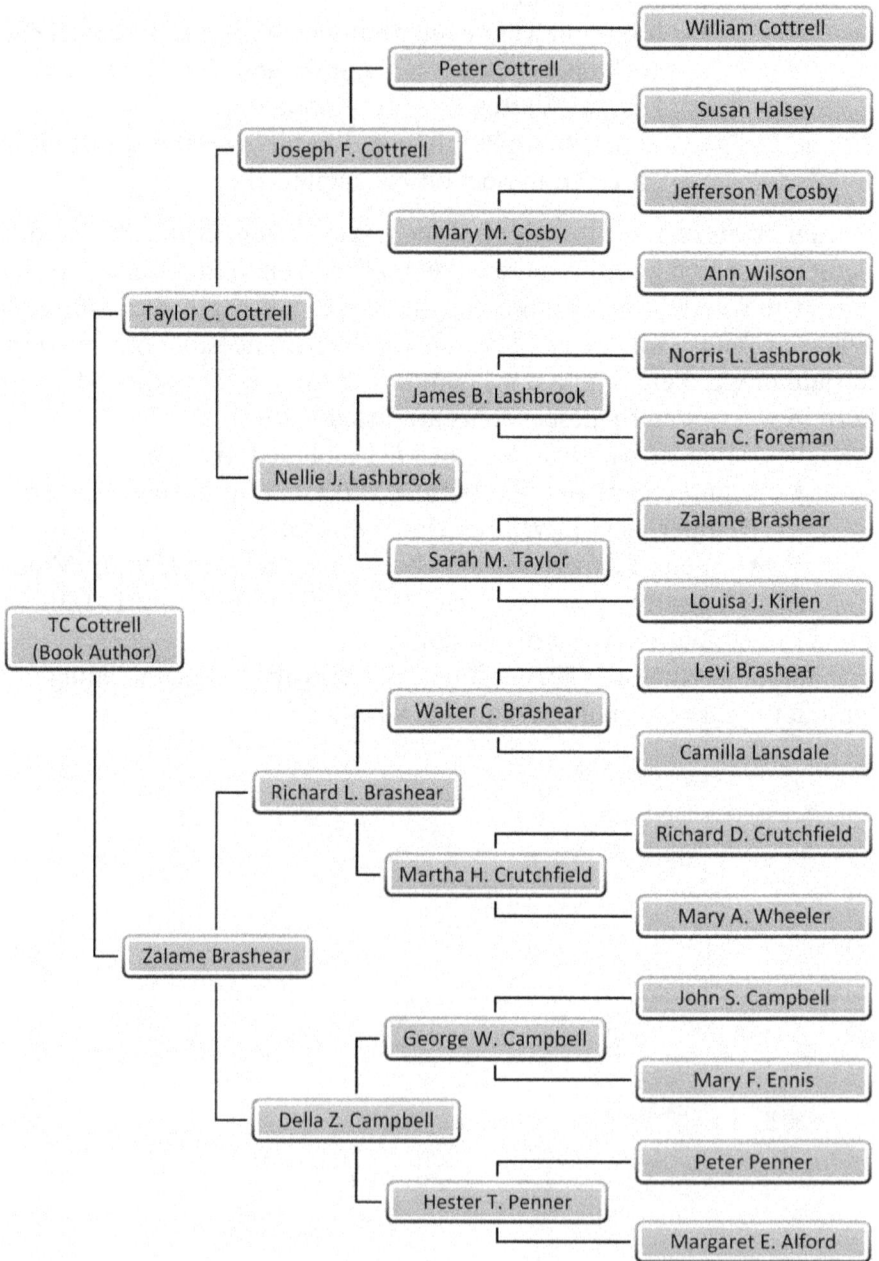

- TC Cottrell (Book Author)
  - Taylor C. Cottrell
    - Joseph F. Cottrell
      - Peter Cottrell
        - William Cottrell
        - Susan Halsey
      - Mary M. Cosby
        - Jefferson M Cosby
        - Ann Wilson
    - Nellie J. Lashbrook
      - James B. Lashbrook
        - Norris L. Lashbrook
        - Sarah C. Foreman
      - Sarah M. Taylor
        - Zalame Brashear
        - Louisa J. Kirlen
  - Zalame Brashear
    - Richard L. Brashear
      - Walter C. Brashear
        - Levi Brashear
        - Camilla Lansdale
      - Martha H. Crutchfield
        - Richard D. Crutchfield
        - Mary A. Wheeler
    - Della Z. Campbell
      - George W. Campbell
        - John S. Campbell
        - Mary F. Ennis
      - Hester T. Penner
        - Peter Penner
        - Margaret E. Alford

Section 1 - Cottrell Paternal Linage

Paternal Ancestor Chart

Cottrell, Cosby, Lashbrook, Taylor

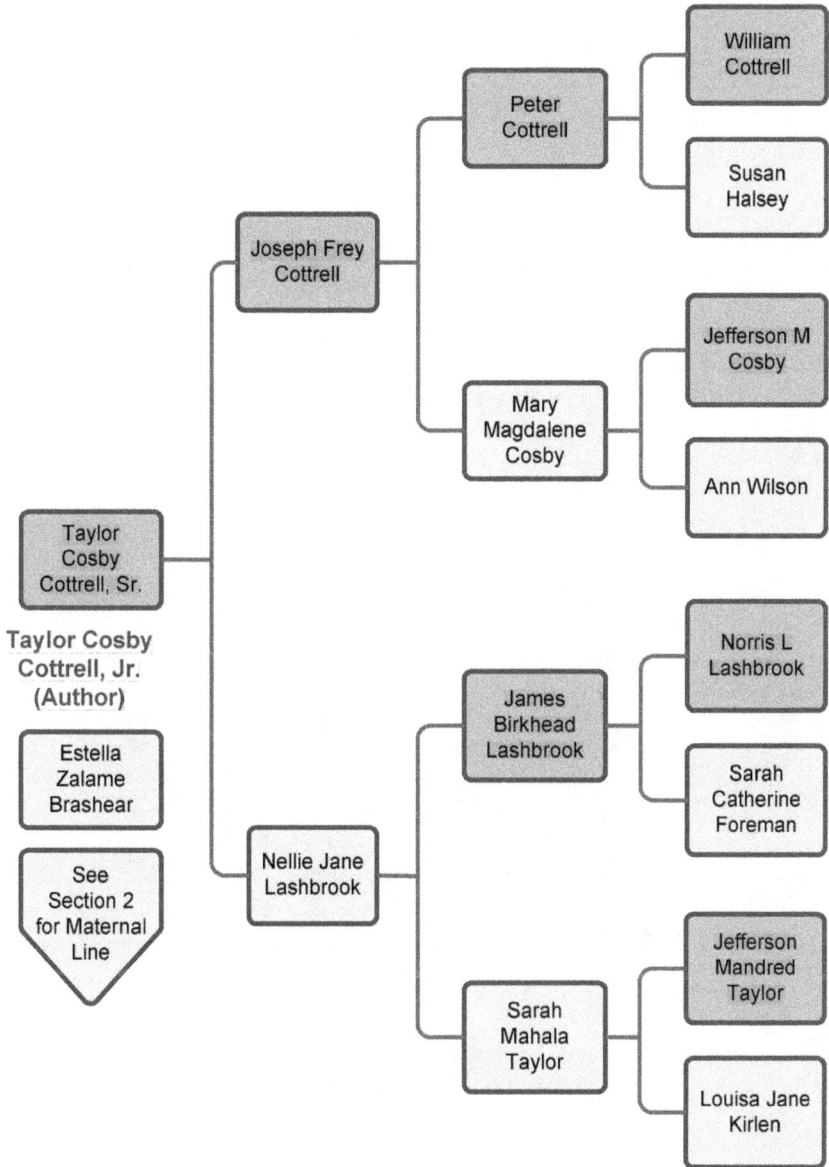

```
                                                        ┌─── William Cottrell
                                     ┌─── Peter Cottrell ┤
                                     │                   └─── Susan Halsey
              ┌── Joseph Frey Cottrell┤
              │                      │                          ┌─── Jefferson M Cosby
              │                      └─── Mary Magdalene Cosby ──┤
Taylor Cosby ─┤                                                 └─── Ann Wilson
Cottrell, Sr. │
              │                                  ┌─── Norris L Lashbrook
              │                 ┌── James Birkhead Lashbrook ──┤
              │                 │                └─── Sarah Catherine Foreman
              └── Nellie Jane Lashbrook┤
                                │                          ┌─── Jefferson Mandred Taylor
                                └─── Sarah Mahala Taylor ──┤
                                                           └─── Louisa Jane Kirlen
```

Taylor Cosby Cottrell, Jr. (Author)

Estella Zalame Brashear

See Section 2 for Maternal Line

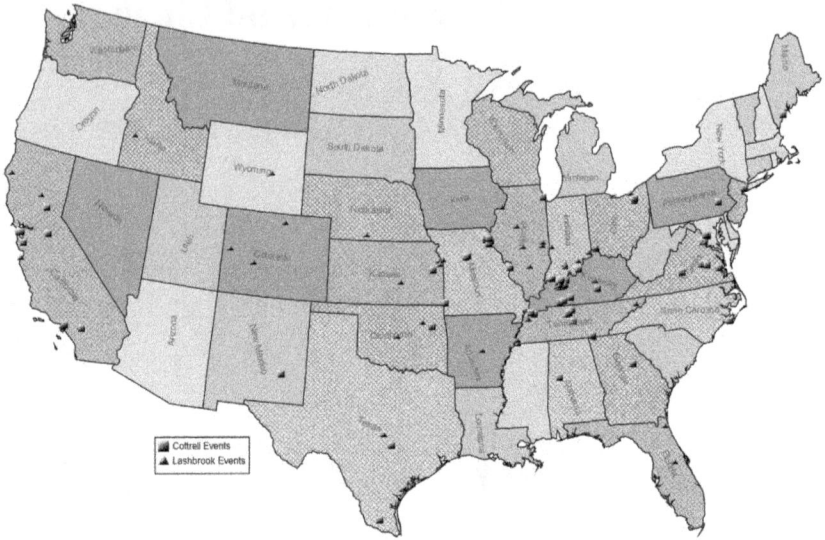

Cottrell and Lashbrook Event Locations

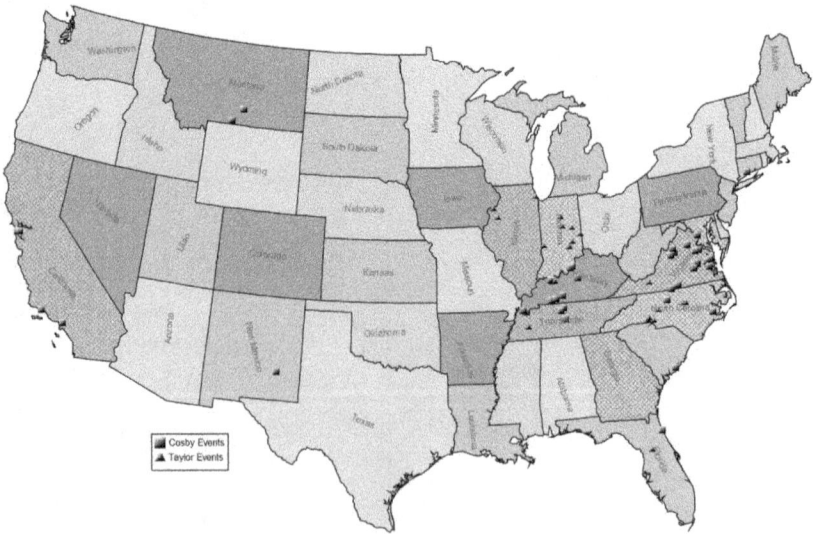

Cosby and Taylor Event Locations

Chapter 1 – William Cottrell Family

2nd Great-grandfather of Taylor Cosby Cottrell, Jr.

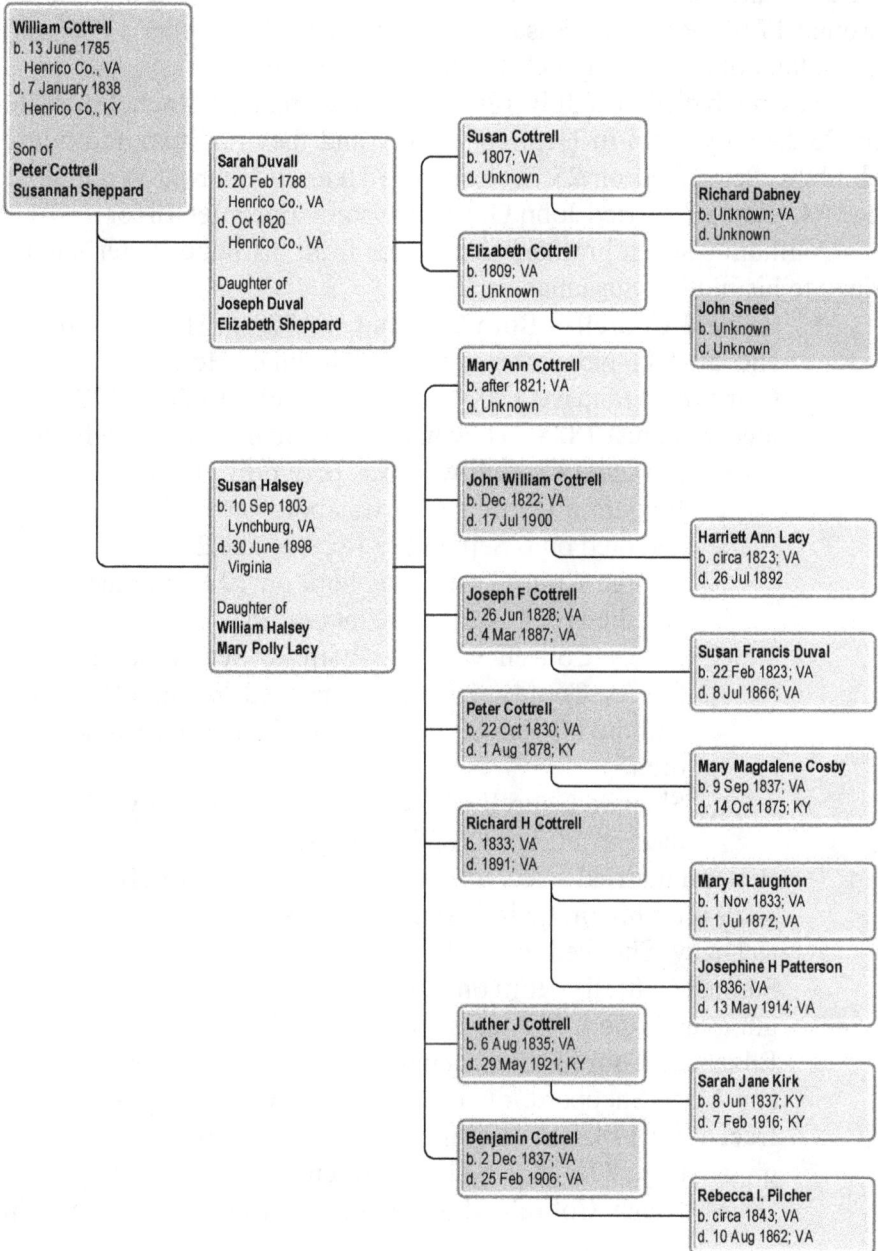

William Cottrell
b. 13 June 1785
  Henrico Co., VA
d. 7 January 1838
  Henrico Co., KY

Son of
Peter Cottrell
Susannah Sheppard

Sarah Duvall
b. 20 Feb 1788
  Henrico Co., VA
d. Oct 1820
  Henrico Co., VA

Daughter of
Joseph Duval
Elizabeth Sheppard

Susan Halsey
b. 10 Sep 1803
  Lynchburg, VA
d. 30 June 1898
  Virginia

Daughter of
William Halsey
Mary Polly Lacy

Susan Cottrell
b. 1807; VA
d. Unknown

Richard Dabney
b. Unknown; VA
d. Unknown

Elizabeth Cottrell
b. 1809; VA
d. Unknown

John Sneed
b. Unknown
d. Unknown

Mary Ann Cottrell
b. after 1821; VA
d. Unknown

John William Cottrell
b. Dec 1822; VA
d. 17 Jul 1900

Harriett Ann Lacy
b. circa 1823; VA
d. 26 Jul 1892

Joseph F Cottrell
b. 26 Jun 1828; VA
d. 4 Mar 1887; VA

Susan Francis Duval
b. 22 Feb 1823; VA
d. 8 Jul 1866; VA

Peter Cottrell
b. 22 Oct 1830; VA
d. 1 Aug 1878; KY

Mary Magdalene Cosby
b. 9 Sep 1837; VA
d. 14 Oct 1875; KY

Richard H Cottrell
b. 1833; VA
d. 1891; VA

Mary R Laughton
b. 1 Nov 1833; VA
d. 1 Jul 1872; VA

Josephine H Patterson
b. 1836; VA
d. 13 May 1914; VA

Luther J Cottrell
b. 6 Aug 1835; VA
d. 29 May 1921; KY

Sarah Jane Kirk
b. 8 Jun 1837; KY
d. 7 Feb 1916; KY

Benjamin Cottrell
b. 2 Dec 1837; VA
d. 25 Feb 1906; VA

Rebecca I. Pilcher
b. circa 1843; VA
d. 10 Aug 1862; VA

William Cottrell was born on 13 June 1785 in Henrico County, Virginia.[1] He was the son of Peter Cottrell and Susannah Sheppard. His father Peter was born on 1 September 1760 in Henrico County, Virginia and his mother Susannah Sheppard was also born in Virginia around 1758. Peter and Susannah married on 3 November 1778[2] and had a total of at least eight children including William.

Susannah died on 7 July 1807. Peter then married Rachel Carlisle on 23 January 1808 in Henrico County and they had two additional children. Peter died on 25 July 1815 in Henrico County, Virginia, at age 54. Rachel married John O. Mosley sometime after 1816.

William's seven brothers and sisters from his father Peter's marriage to his mother Susannah included:

- Richard Cottrell – Born 26 October 1779 in Henrico County and died 11 November 1829 in Virginia. He married Anna Clark on 8 January 1800. Anna was born 10 June 1777 and died 9 August 1828. They had at least five children including:
    o Margaret Cottrell who was born on 12 October 1800.
    o Benjamin Cottrell who was born on 15 January 1803 and died on 6 September 1828, at age 25.
    o George Cottrell who was born on 10 September 1804 and died on 4 April 1841, at age 36.
    o Nancy Cottrell who was born 26 September 1815 in Shelby County, Kentucky, married William S. Floyd, and died 9 January 1885. They had at least nine children.
    o Shepard Cottrell who was born on 27 January 1817 and died on 11 April 1838. Age 21.
  Richard married a second time to Doeshy Elliott in September 1829 after his first wife's death in 1828. She was also known as Dicey. She died in 1863.[3]
- Samuel Cottrell – Born on 7 June 1781 in Henrico County, Virginia and died 3 August 1858 in Virginia. He married Elizabeth Cottrell, the daughter of Charles Waddell Cottrell and Mary Sheppard, on 1 December 1803. She was born 19 December 1782 in Virginia and died 30 March 1853 in Virginia, at age 70. They had at least ten children including:
    o Nancy Cottrell who was born on 18 November 1804 in Virginia.

- o Unidentified Cottrell who was born on 22 June 1806 in Virginia.
- o Mary Cottrell who was born 22 August 1808 and died 14 August 1853 in Daviess County, Kentucky.
- o Charles Cottrell who was born on 26 December 1810 in Virginia and died on 5 April 1882, at age 71.
- o Samuel Cottrell who was born on 18 July 1813 in Henrico County, Virginia and died in September 1873 in Henrico County, at age 60.
- o Elizabeth Cottrell who was born on 22 June 1815 in Virginia.
- o Martha Cottrell who was born in 1817 and died on 15 July 1853.
- o Emaby C. Cottrell who was born on 20 September 1819 in Virginia.
- o Benjamin Preston Cottrell who was born in 1821 in Henrico County, Virginia and died 31 March 1856 in Henrico County. He married Ann Octavia Drewry in 1845. She was born in 1825 in King William County and died in 1901 in Richmond. They had at least four children.
- o Josephine S. Cottrell who was born on 8 July 1825 in Virginia. She married Luzbyth H. Wade and they had at least eight children.[4]

- Peter Cottrell, Jr. – Born on 23 February 1783 in Henrico County and died on 1 March 1827 in Henrico County, at age 44. He married Sally Ellis, the daughter of William Ellis, on 29 November 1804. She was born around 1783. They had at least seven children including:
  - o Lucy Cottrell who was born on 6 January 1805 in Virginia.
  - o John Cottrell who was born on 13 October 1806 in Virginia.
  - o Maria Cottrell who was born on 26 September 1808 in Virginia.
  - o Sarah Cottrell who was born in June 1811 in Virginia. She married Daniel Mathews and they had at least seven children.

- o Peter Cottrell who was born on 9 May 1817 in Virginia and died in October 1822 in Virginia, at age 5.
- o Reuben Cottrell who was born on 10 November 1819 in Virginia.
- o Caroline Cottrell who was born on 18 July 1823 in Virginia.[5]
- ▪ Elizabeth A. Cottrell – Born on 23 May 1787 in Henrico County, Virginia. She married William Hutchinson on 24 November 1803. He was born circa 1790 in Virginia.[6] They had at least one child including:
  - o Joseph Hutchinson who was born in 1831 in Virginia.[7]
- ▪ Abel Cottrell – Born on 5 January 1790 in Henrico County, Virginia and died on 8 July 1852 in Lewis County, Missouri. He was buried in the Cottrell Cemetery in Lewis County. He married Rosa Jane Thornton on 27 April 1810 in Shelby County, Kentucky.[8] She was born in 1776 in Virginia and died sometime after 1860. She was also buried in the Cottrell Cemetery in Lewis County.[9] They had at least two children including:
  - o Peter Cottrell who was born on 2 February 1813 in Shelby County, Kentucky and died on 8 October 1855 in Lewis County, Missouri. Peter married Susan A. Stipes and they had at least six children.[10]
  - o James P. Cottrell who was born on 5 October 1818 in Shelby County, Kentucky and died on 26 July 1890 in Lewis County, Missouri. He married Martha Elizabeth Stipes and they had at least eight children.[11]
- ▪ Reuben Cottrell – Born on 4 April 1792 near Richmond, Virginia and died on 29 May 1862 in Daviess County, Kentucky, at age 70. He was buried in Macedonia Baptist Church Cemetery in Habit, Kentucky.[12] He married Sarah Homer Patman, the daughter of John Patman and Elizabeth Smith, on 16 March 1811 in Henrico County. She was born on 10 March 1794 in Virginia and died before 1862 in Daviess County.[13] They had at least eleven children including:
  - o Elizabeth Smith Cottrell who was born on 15 January 1812 in Virginia and died on 13 March 1873 in Hancock County, Kentucky, at age 61. She was buried in

the Union Baptist Church Cemetery in Hancock County. She married twice, first to a Dulin with whom she had at least two children and then to Hardin Haynes Ellis with whom she had at least five children.

o Cyanah H. Cottrell who was born on 23 January 1814 in Virginia and died in 1886 in Daviess County, Kentucky, at age 72. She married John Hazelrigg and they had at least ten children.

o Cynthia Shepard Cottrell who was born 19 February 1816 in Shelby County, Kentucky and died before 1850. She married Jefferson Cox. They had at least one child.

o Susannah B. Cottrell who was born on 30 December 1817 in Shelby County and died on 18 June 1853 in Daviess County, at age 35. She married John Leven Kirk and they had at least seven children.

o Samuel S. Cottrell who was born 16 May 1820 in Shelby County and died 9 January 1859 in Shelby County, at age 38. He married Elizabeth Stone. They had at least six children.

o Noel L. Cottrell who was born on 11 May 1822 in Shelby County and died on 17 April 1887 in Daviess County, at age 64.

o Miranda Barnwell Cottrell who was born on 4 July 1824 in Shelby County and died on 22 May 1904 in Owensboro, Kentucky, at age 79. She was buried in Macedonia Baptist Church Cemetery in Dermot, Kentucky. She married James Morrison Birkhead and they had at least eight children.

o John Patmon Cottrell who was born on 15 January 1827 in Shelby County and died on 12 September 1862 in Daviess County, at age 35. He was buried in Elmwood Cemetery in Owensboro. He married Laura Ann Birkhead. They had at least four children.

o Usebia N. Cottrell who was born on 17 November 1829 in Shelby County. She was not mentioned in her father's will thus she likely died young.

- o Calvin E. Cottrell who was born on 12 July 1831 in Shelby County and died on 20 April 1906 in Daviess County, at age 74. He was buried in Elmwood Cemetery in Owensboro. He married Mary E. Jones and they had at least five children.
  - o Virginia Cottrell who was born on 25 December 1834 in Daviess County and died on 27 October 1916 in Owensboro, Kentucky. She was buried in Elmwood Cemetery in Owensboro, at age 81. She married John Perry Fugua and they had at least two children.[14]
- Joseph Sheppard Cottrell – Born on 3 August 1795 in Henrico County, Virginia. He married Lucy Bryant on 5 January 1815 in Shelby County, Kentucky and they had at least one child including:[15]
  - o Elizabeth J. Cottrell who was born on 15 November 1824 and died on 2 August 1889.[16]

William's siblings from his father Peter's marriage to his stepmother Rachel Carlisle included:

- Susannah Cottrell – Born on 23 November 1808 in Virginia. She married Jefferson Wilkerson on 29 April 1823 in Henrico County.[17]
- John Jefferson Cottrell – Born 7 June 1810 in Virginia and died 8 September 1810 in Virginia.[18]

William Cottrell Family Timeline

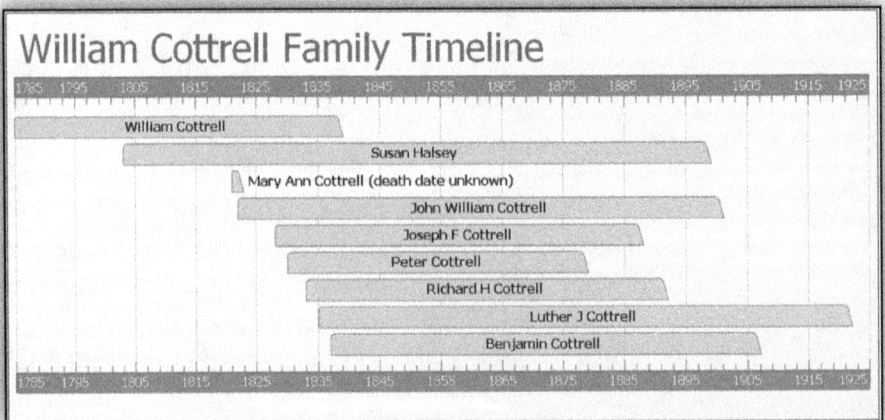

William married Sarah Du-Val on 1 December 1806 in Henrico County.[19] Sarah, also known as Sally, was born on 20 February 1788 in Henrico County. She was the daughter of Joseph DuVal and had at least one brother, Stephen DuVal who was born on 3 December 1782 in Pawhatan County, Virginia and died on 30 July 1851 in Chesterfield County, Virginia. It is interesting to note that Steven married William's second wife Susan Halsey after William's death.[20]

Susan Halsey

Upon the probate of his father's will on 17 April 1816 William received one sixth of his father's property including all the Negros excepting his Brother Abel's boy George. He also received over 100 acres of land lying on the Tuckahoe Creek, where he was living in 1816. William and his brothers Richard, Samuel, Peter, Abel, Reuben, and Joseph also received a share in his father's saw mill.[21]

William and Sarah had at least two children including Susan Cottrell and Elizabeth S. Cottrell before Sarah died in October 1820 in Henrico County, Virginia, at age 32.[22]

William then married Susan Halsey, the daughter of William Halsey and Mary Polly Lacy, on 25 September 1821 in Henrico County.[23] Susan was born on 10 September 1803 in Lynchburg, Virginia.[24] They had seven children before

William Cottrell
Hollywood Cemetery
Richmond, VA

William died at his home on 7 January 1838 in Henrico County, at age 52.[25]

Susan then married Steven DuVal, son of Joseph DuVal, on 19 October 1843 in Chesterfield County, Virginia.[26] Stephen was born on 3 December 1782 in Pawhatan County, Virginia and had previously been married to Lucy Johnson who died in 1842.

Steven had at least eight children before his marriage to Susan Halsey including Samuel Sheppard DuVal, Sarah Ann DuVal, Edwin Joseph DuVal, Benjamin Johnson DuVal, Lucy Jane DuVal, Stephen Obediah DuVal, and Mary Ellen DuVal. Steven and Susan had one child together, Seth Alexander DuVal, who was born on 7 January 1846 in Richmond, Virginia.[27]

Susan appeared on the census of 1850 in the household of her husband Stephen in Chesterfield County. Stephen DuVal, age 69 was listed along with Susan, age 63, William, age 21, and Seth, age 5. Also listed in the household was Richard Cottrell, age 17, Luther Cottrell, age 15, and Benjamin Cottrell, age 13. His real estate was valued at $11,500.[28]

Susan Halsey Frith
Hollywood Cemetery
Richmond, VA

According to his stepson Luther Cottrell, Stephen loved chestnuts and peanuts so much that he always had one or the other in his pocket and ate them so frequently that the direction of his riding could be determined by the trail of hulls he dropped.

It was said that Stephen built Bosher's Dam on the James River and used water from the river to run a nail manufactory and that he owned the first iron foundry in Virginia. Steven DuVal died on 30 July 1851 in the evening at his home in Cedar Grove in Chesterfield County, at age 68. He was buried in Cedar Grove in the family burying ground.[29]

Susan then married William F. Frith on 7 July 1854 in Goochland County, Virginia.[30] William was born in 1800 in Chesterfield

County.[31] Susan was listed on the 1860 census in the household of her husband William in Goochland County. William Frith, age 60 was listed along with Susan, age 57, Francis E., age 38, Ellen C., age 21, Indeanna A., age 19, William Moody, age 19, and Seth A. DuVal, age 14. Susan had a personal estate valued at $4,000. Her husband's real estate was valued at $12,000 while his personal estate was valued at $24,000; both wealthy sums in 1860.[32]

William Frith died in October 1887 and was buried on 5 October in Hollywood Cemetery in Richmond Virginia in Section 3, Lot 8.[33] Susan died on 30 June 1898 in Virginia at age 94. She was buried in Hollywood Cemetery in Richmond in Section I, and Lot 32.[34]

Susan Cottrell (circa 1807)

Daughter of William Cottrell & Sarah DuVal
Great-grandaunt of Taylor Cosby Cottrell, Jr.

Susan Cottrell was born circa 1807 in Henrico County, Virginia. She was the daughter of William Cottrell and Sarah DuVal.[35] Susan married Richard Dabney on 1 April 1828 in Henrico County. Richard was born around 1803 in Virginia.[36] Richard was listed on the 1840 census in Henrico County. Susan may have been the female age 20 to 29. The census also listed a total of five slaves and one additional white female age 60 thru 69 whose identity is unknown.[37].

Elizabeth Sarah Cottrell (1809-1881)

Daughter of William Cottrell & Sarah DuVal
Great-grandaunt of Taylor Cosby Cottrell, Jr.

Elizabeth Sarah Cottrell was born on 12 March 1809 in Henrico County, Virginia. She was the daughter of William Cottrell and Sarah DuVal.[38] Elizabeth married John Sneed on 17 April 1830 in Henrico County. John was born on 5 December 1798.[39] It is likely that Sarah had at least three unidentified additional children. Elizabeth died on 3 August 1881, likely in Hanover County, Virginia. She was buried in the Snead Cemetery in Hanover County.[40] John died on 10 February 1885 in Hanover County and was also buried in the Snead Cemetery.[41]

Children of Elizabeth Sarah Cottrell and John Sneed.

- Jona E. Snead - Born about 1834.[42]

- Alonzo Boardman Snead - Born in 1838 in Virginia, died in 1912, buried in Berea Baptist Church Cemetery in Rockville in Hanover County, Virginia.[43] Alonzo married Louisa W. George on 2 December 1860 in Friendship in Goochland County, Virginia. Louisa was born in 1838 in Friendship. She was the daughter of William and Susan W. George.[44] Alonzo served in Company E., 15th Virginia Infantry from 11 December 1864 until paroled on 9 April 1865. Louisa died in 1900 in Virginia. She was also buried in Berea Baptist Church Cemetery. Alonzo and Louisa had at least the following children:
  o Anna Boardman Snead – Born on 25 April 1862 in Goochland County, Virginia, married Charles Anderson Bowles on 28 May 1884, and died on 15 April 1946 in Short Pump in Henrico County, Virginia. She was buried in Berea Baptist Church Cemetery in Rockville, Virginia. Her cause of death was cerebral hemorrhage.[45]
  o Joseph Malcom Snead – Born on 30 May 1866 in Virginia. He married Hattie M. Deitrick on 29 October 1897 in Henrico County. Joseph died on 27 June 1954 in Henrico County, Virginia. He was buried in Berea Baptist Church Cemetery in Rockville.[46]
  o Otie Lee Snead – Born on 27 April 1868 in Virginia, married James Henry Scott on 29 September 1891 in Henrico County, Virginia, and died on 26 April 1949 in Rockville, Virginia. They were both buried in Berea Baptist Church Cemetery in Rockville.[47]
  o Lemuel A. Snead – Born circa 1872 in Henrico County, Virginia, married Lizzie E. Wood on 31 January 1900 in Richmond, Virginia.[48]
- Robert J. Snead - Born around 1842. Enlisted in Company C, Virginia 15th Infantry Regiment on 18 July 1861 in Grove Wharf, Virginia. Died on 22 January 1862 at the Williamsburg, Virginia Hospital.[49]
- Betsey A.H. Snead - Born around 1843 in Virginia.[50] No additional information is known.
- Edwin Shook Snead - Born on 27 September 1846 in Hanover County, Virginia. He died on 1 November 1932 in Rockville,

Virginia. Edwin was buried in Berea Baptist Church Cemetery in Rockville, Virginia.[51] Edwin married Rosaline Victoria Johnson on 1 January 1868 in Goochland County, Virginia.[52] Rosaline died on 20 June 1923 and was also buried in Berea Baptist Church Cemetery next to her husband Edwin.[53] Edwin and Rosaline had at least the following children:

- o Robert William Snead – Born on 11 January 1870, married Mary Lee Smither, and died on 21 November 1968. He was buried in Berea Baptist Church Cemetery in Rockville, Virginia.[54]
- o Lillie Snead – Born on 23 December 1877, married Lucian Leslie Tinsley, and died on 3 October 1969. She was buried with her husband Lucian in Berea Baptist Church Cemetery in Rockville, Virginia.[55]
- o Daisy Snead – Born on 14 November 1881, married Clinton L. Johnson, and died on 30 January 1975 in Richmond. She was buried in Berea Baptist Church Cemetery in Rockville.[56]

- John H. Snead - Born around 1854 in Virginia. Listed in 1870 census in the household of John and Elizabeth as John H. Snead, age 16. May have been their child.

Mary Ann Cottrell (after 1821)

Daughter of William Cottrell & Susan Halsey
Great-grandaunt of Taylor Cosby Cottrell, Jr.

Mary Ann Cottrell was born after 1821 in Henrico County, Virginia. She was the daughter of William Cottrell and Susan Halsey. No additional information is known.[57]

John William Cottrell (1822-1900)

Son of William Cottrell & Susan Halsey
Great-granduncle of Taylor Cosby Cottrell, Jr.

John William Cottrell was born in December 1822 in Henrico County, Virginia. He was the son of William Cottrell and Susan Halsey.[58] John married Harriet Ann Lacy, the daughter of Fleming Lacy and Elizabeth H. Richards, on 4 March 1844 in Goochland County, Virginia. Harriet was born circa 1823 in Manikin, Virginia.[59]

According to Minnie Jane Cottrell, the records of Goochland County Virginia show John William "owned a great deal of land, and was considered wealthy."[60] He appeared on the census of 1850 in Goochland County, as John W. Cottrell, age 27, listed as head of household along with Harriet A., age 27, George C., age 5, and Henry L., age 2. His real estate was valued at $1,300.[61]

John was listed as a farmer on the census of 1860 in Goochland County, as Jno. W. Cottrell, age 36 along with Harriet A., age 36, George C., age 14, Henry L., age 11, Rosa B., age 8, Stewart H., age 5, Willie, age 3, and Susan E., age 1. Real estate was valued at $15,000 and personal estate was valued at $2,000.[62]

He appeared on the census of 1870 as a farmer in Goochland County, as John W. Cottrell, age 47, along with Harriet A., age 47, Rosa B., age 19, Stewart N., age 15, William A., age 14, and Susan R., age 11. Also listed was Susan Frith, age 64 and three black individuals who could not read or write. Real estate was valued at $9,100 and personal estate was valued at $1,039.[63]

John was listed as a farmer on the census of 1880 in Goochland County, as J.W. Cottrell, age 57 along with his wife Harriet A., age 57, daughters Rosa B., age 29 and Susie, age 20 and sons Henry L., age 32, and Willie O., age 23.[64] Harriet Cottrell, John's wife, died on 26 July 1892.[65]

John was a farmer on the census of 1900 in Goochland County. He was

John William Cottrell		
1850	Goochland County, VA	Coal Miner
1860	Goochland County, VA	Farmer
1870	Goochland County, VA	Farmer
1880	Goochland County, VA	Farmer
1900	Goochland County, VA	Farmer

listed as John W. Cottrell, age 77 along with his son Henry L., age 52, and daughters Rosa B., age 49 and Susie R., age 39.[66] John died on 17 July 1900, at age 77.[67]

Children of John William Cottrell and Harriet Ann Lacy:[68]

- George C. Cottrell – Born circa 1845 in Virginia, likely on 12 January 1845 and died sometime after the 1860 census in Kentucky, likely on 9 November 1910. It is believed that George served in Company A, Virginia 24th Infantry Regiment of the

Confederacy and that he was buried in Pewee Valley Cemetery in Oldham County, Kentucky.[69]

- Henry Leon Cottrell – Born in February 1848 in Manikin, Goochland County, Virginia and died on 8 February 1923 in Dover, Goochland County, Virginia. His cause of death was stomach cancer. He was buried in Dover Forest, his home place in Manikin, Virginia. Henry never married. His death certificate indicated he was an "old bachelor" and "altogether a single man."[70]

- Rosa Belle Cottrell – Born on 28 March 1851 and died 23 November 1935 in Dover, Goochland County, Virginia. Her cause of death was old age. She was a school teacher, lived for some time in the home of her brother Henry Leon, and never married. She was described as very sweet and spiritual in her life. Many friends and relatives, as well as colored friends, attended her funeral. At her funeral a colored woman, who was a teacher and had been taught by Rosa, sang "I want to be an Angel and with the Angels stand A crown upon my forehead, A harp within my hand."[71]

- Stewart Hollins Cottrell – Born on 17 October 1853 in Goochland County, Virginia and died on 28 January 1930 at 12:30 in the afternoon in Goochland County, Virginia. His cause of death was heart disease. He married Harriett Alexanna Bowles in 1876. Harriett was born on 18 August 1855 and Died on 4 November 1910. They are buried together in Bowles Cemetery in Cardwell, Goochland County, Virginia. Stewart and Harriett had at least four children including:
  o Sarah A. Cottrell - Born on 10 August 1880, married William Cabell Alvis, and died on 15 May 1979 in Richmond. She was also known as Sadie. Cause of death was Pneumonia. She was buried in the Alvis Family Cemetery in Goochland County, Virginia.[72]
  o Ira Baughan Cottrell - Born on 10 June 1883, married Roberta Francis Wiley, and died on 11 April 1947 in Oilville in Goochland County, Virginia. Cause of death was heart disease. He was buried in the Bethel United Methodist Church Cemetery in Oilville.[73]

- o Stuart C. Cottrell - Born on 21 August 1890 in Cardwell, Virginia, married Edna Withers Kent on 25 May 1920 in the District of Columbia, Died on 21 April 1935 in Cardwell in Goochland County, Virginia. He was buried in Bowles Cemetery in Cardwell.[74] Edna then married Lewis Harrison Tilman on 1 January 1940 in Westhampton, Virginia. Edna died on 26 October 1977 in Richmond, Virginia.[75]
- o Anna B. Cottrell - Born on 22 December 1892, married Edward Lange and died on 17 April 1966 in Baltimore, Maryland.[76] She was buried in the Baltimore National Cemetery along with her husband Edward in Section K, Site 804.[77]

- William O. Cottrell – Born circa 1857 in Virginia and died sometime after 1880, likely on 4 January 1885 in Goochland County, Virginia. William was also known as Willie.[78]

- Susan R. Cottrell – Born in July 1860 in Goochland County, Virginia and died on 29 March 1914 in Manikin in Goochland County. Her cause of death was heart failure. Susan was buried in a home cemetery in Manikin, Virginia. She was also a school teacher and lived for some time with her brother Henry Leon along with her sister Rosa Belle. Susan never married.[79]

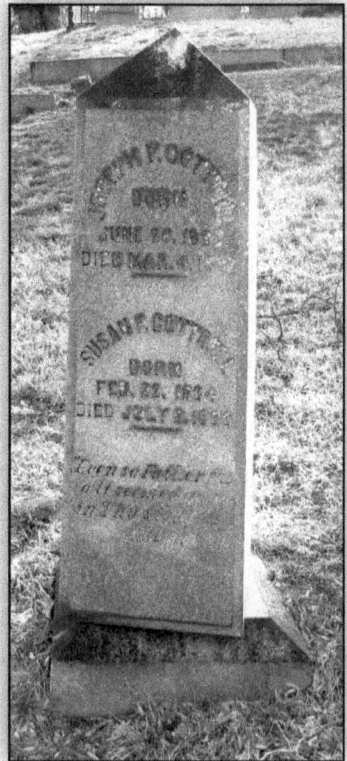

Joseph & Susan Cottrell
Hollywood Cemetery
Richmond, VA

Joseph F Cottrell (1828-1887)

Son of William Cottrell & Susan Halsey
Great-granduncle of Taylor Cosby Cottrell, Jr.

Joseph F. Cottrell was born on 26 June 1828, in Henrico County, Virginia. He was the son of William Cottrell and Susan Halsey.[80] Joseph married Susan Francis Duval, daughter of Stephen DuVal and Lucy Johnson on 25 March 1857 in Henrico County. Susan was born on 22 February 1834 in Virginia and was Joseph's step-sister.[81]

Joseph entered military service on 20 August 1864 in Richmond, Virginia, as a Private in Company 3rd, Virginia 3rd Co. Howitzers Light Artillery Battery. He listed his occupation as a coal dealer at the time of his enlistment.[82] His wife Susan died on 8 July 1866 in Henrico County, Virginia, at age 32. She

Joseph F. Cottrell		
1870	Henrico County, VA	Coal Dealer
1880	Richmond (Ind. City), VA	Coal Merchant

was buried in Hollywood Cemetery in Richmond, Virginia, in Section I, Lot 32.[83]

Joseph appeared on the census in 1870 as a coal dealer in Henrico County, in the household of William Weisinger as Joseph Catrell, age 42. His daughters Katy, age 15, Mary, age 12, and Emma, age 10 were also listed.[84]

In 1880 he was living at 810 Main Street in Richmond. He was also listed on the 1880 census in Richmond (Independent City), Virginia, enumerated on 18 June 1880 listing Joseph F. Cottrell, age 51 and widowed along with his daughters Mary, age 21 and Emma, age 19.[85]

Joseph died on 4 March 1887 in Richmond, Virginia, at age 58. He was buried at Hollywood Cemetery in Richmond, in Section I, Lot 32.[86]

Children of Joseph F. Cottrell and Susan Francis Duval:

- Katy Cottrell – Born in 1855 in Henrico County, Virginia. No additional information is known.[87]
- Mary L. Cottrell – Born in 1858 in Henrico County, Virginia and died in 1910 in Virginia. She was buried in Hollywood Cemetery, Richmond, Virginia in Section I, Lot 32.[88]

- Emma Jane Cottrell – Born on 22 July 1860 in Henrico County, Virginia and died on 23 April 1952 in Richmond, Virginia, at age 91 at her home. Her cause of death was arteriosclerosis. She was buried on 25 April 1952 in Hollywood Cemetery in Section I, Lot 32.[89]

Peter Cottrell (1830-1878)

Son of William Cottrell & Susan Halsey
Great-grandfather of Taylor Cosby Cottrell, Jr.

Peter Cottrell was born on 22 October 1830 in Henrico County, Virginia. He was the son of William Cottrell and Susan Halsey. Information on the Peter Cottrell Family, and Peter's life history, along with that for his wife Mary Magdalene Cosby and their seven children is covered in detail Section 1, Chapter 2, Peter Cottrell Family.[90]

Richard H. Cottrell (1833-Likely 1891)

Son of William Cottrell & Susan Halsey
Great-granduncle of Taylor Cosby Cottrell, Jr.

Richard H. Cottrell was born in 1833, in Henrico County, Virginia. He was the son of William Cottrell and Susan Halsey. Richard was listed on the census of 1850 in the household of Stephen DuVal in Chesterfield County, Virginia, as Richard Cottrell, age 17 and attending School.

He married Mary Roberts Laughton on 25 May 1853 in Goochland County, Virginia. Mary was born circa 1835 in New Jersey.[91]

Richard was listed on the census of 1860 as a blacksmith in Chesterfield County, enumerated on 4 August 1860. Rich. H. Cottrell, age 25 was listed along

Richard H. Cottrell		
1840	Chesterfield County, VA	Unknown
1850	Chesterfield County, VA	Unknown
1860	Henrico County, VA	Farmer
1870	Daviess County, KY	Coal Miner

with Mary, age 25, Clara, age 5, Nora, age 3, and Mary, age 1.[92] It is likely Mary died on 3 July 1872 in Richmond and is buried in Hollywood Cemetery.

Richard then married Josephine Hesselline Patterson, the daughter of Thomas Patterson and Susan Thomas on 18 January 1882. Josephine was born in 1834 in Caroline County, Virginia. She died on 13 May 1914 in Roanoke, Virginia and was buried in Hollywood Cemetery in Richmond, Virginia on 14 May 1914. Richard died sometime before February 1906, possibly on 26 January 1891. Richard may also have enlisted in the Confederacy in Company I, Virginia 6th Infantry Regiment on 9 May 1861 in Manchester, Virginia.[93]

Children of Richard H. Cottrell and Mary Roberts Laughton:

- Clara Cottrell – Born in November 1855 in Henrico County, Virginia and died 23 August 1929 in the District of Columbia at age 73. She married James Baird, who had previously been married and was widowed, around 1902. They apparently had no children. She was buried in Hollywood Cemetery in Richmond Virginia.[94]
- Nora A. Cottrell – Born 18 February 1857 in Virginia and died 17 October 1944 in Lynchburg, Virginia. She married William Davidson Diuguid around 1880. William was born on 10 September 1851 in Lynchburg City, Virginia and died on 11 November 1927 in Lynchburg City. Nora and William were buried in Spring Hill Cemetery in Lynchburg, Virginia.[95] Nora and William had at least five children including:
  - Laughton Davidson Diuguid – Born on 5 October 1881 and died on 31 May 1905 in Lynchburg. He was buried in Spring Hill Cemetery in Lynchburg.[96]
  - Mary Sampson Diuguid – Born on 29 May 1883 in Lynchburgh, Virginia and died on 25 August 1968 in Lynchburg. Mary never married. She traveled to Belgium in 1928, returning to the port of New York on the Lapland on 8 October 1928. She was buried in Spring Hill Cemetery in Lynchburg.[97]
  - Infant Child – Died at one-day old in 1885 and was buried in Spring Hill Cemetery.
  - Garnett B. Diuguid – Born on 31 May 1888 and died on 17 November 1925. He was buried in Spring Hill Cemetery.
  - Infant Child - Died 1 hour and 30 minutes after birth in 1893 and was buried in Spring Hill Cemetery.

- Emily C. Cottrell – Born on 20 October 1862 in Virginia; died 2 March 1940 in Virginia. Her cause of death was a cerebral hemorrhage. She was buried in Hollywood Cemetery in Richmond, Virginia. Emily married; her husband's last name was Pryor. In 1920 she was widowed and living with her sister Clara Baird in Washington, DC.[98]

Luther J. Cottrell (1835-1921)

Son of William Cottrell & Susan Halsey
Great-granduncle of Taylor Cosby Cottrell, Jr.

Luther J. Cottrell was born on 6 August 1835, in Henrico County, Virginia. He was the son of William Cottrell and Susan Halsey.[99] Luther appeared in the census of 1850 in the household of Stephen DuVal in Chesterfield County, Virginia as Luther Cottrell, age 15 and attending school.[100]

A bond for the marriage of Luther J. Cottrell and Sarah Jane Kirk was signed on 11 December 1854 in Owensboro, Daviess County, Kentucky, by Luther and James Birkhead in the sum of one hundred dollars. Luther married Sarah Jane Kirk, the daughter of John Leven Kirk and Susannah B. Cottrell, on 11 December 1854 in Daviess County, at her father's home.[101] Sarah was born on 8 June 1837 in Daviess County.[102]

An abstract from Virginia records, published in the Virginia Genealogical Society Quarterly, listed Luther J. Cottrell and Benjamin Cottrell, children of William Cottrell in a 160-acre land warrant, assumed to be after 1858 since Benjamin's age was listed as 21.[103]

Luther was a tobacco dealer and farmer on the 1870 census in

Luther J. Cottrell		
1840	Chesterfield County, VA	Unknown
1850	Chesterfield County, VA	Unknown
1870	Daviess County, KY	Tobacco Dealer
1880	Daviess County, KY	Tobacco Dealer
1900	Daviess County, KY	Farmer
1910	Daviess County, KY	Farmer
1920	Daviess County, KY	N/A

Daviess County, Kentucky. He was listed as Luther J. Cotterell, age 34 as head of household with a residence valued at $4,000 and personal estate valued at $600. Sarah J, age 32 was listed as keeping house. Children included Mary S., a female, age 12, William, a male, age 14, and Albert J., a male, age 9.[104]

On the 1880 census in Daviess County, enumerated on 7 June 1880, Luther J. Cottrell, age 45 was listed as a boarder in the home of William Frasher. His wife Sarah J., age 41 was also listed.[105]

In 1890 he was a tobacco buyer living at 733 6th Street in Louisville, Jefferson County, Kentucky.[106] He was listed on the census of 1900 in Daviess County, as Luther J. Cottrell, age 64 and renting a farm listed on farm schedule 83. His wife Sarah J., age 62 was listed as being born in June 1837, in Kentucky, having been in present marriage 45 years, and being the mother of three children with two children living. Luther's son, Albert A. Cottrell, age 40, was listed as being born in May 1860 in Kentucky and working as a farm laborer. His grandson Paul Johnson, age 22, born in October 1877, was also listed as working as a farm laborer.[107]

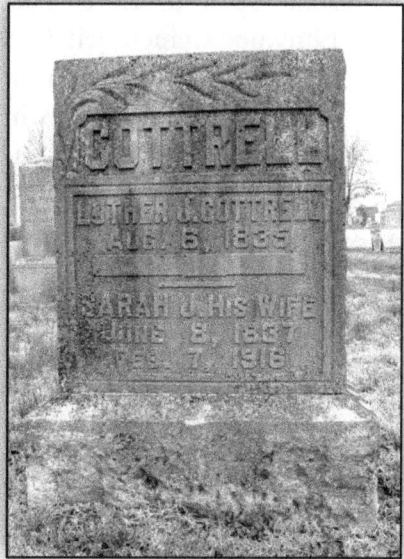

Luther and Sarah Cottrell
Elmwood Cemetery
Owensboro, KY

The 1910 census in Daviess County, enumerated on 7 May 1910, listed L.J. Cottrell, age 74, as head of household, and owning a farm listed on farm schedule 202, free of mortgage. He was also identified as a survivor of the confederate army. His wife, Sarah, age 72, was listed as having had 3 children with one living.[108]

Sarah Jane died on 7 February 1916 at her residence at 605 Clay Street in Owensboro, Daviess County, Kentucky. Her cause of death was acute bronchitis following a week's illness of pneumonia. She was buried in Elmwood Cemetery in Owensboro, Kentucky. Sarah was universally known as "Aunt Jane" in Owensboro and was one of the pioneer residents at the time of her death.[109]

Luther was listed on the 1920 census in Daviess County, enumerated on 2 January 1920, as L. J. Cottrell, age 85 and widowed along with J. W., age 63 who was also widowed. J. W. was listed as Luther's brother. However, it is likely this was actually J. William, his son and had been incorrectly listed on the census.[110]

Luther died on 29 May 1921 in Daviess County, at age 85. He was buried in Elmwood Cemetery in Owensboro, Kentucky, in the Cottrell Family Plot in Section E-2.[111]

Children of Luther J. Cottrell and Sarah Jane Kirk:

- Mary Susan Cottrell – Born 4 June 1856 in Kentucky; died 22 June 1878 in Owensboro, Kentucky. She was buried in Elmwood Cemetery in Owensboro, Kentucky.[112] Mary married William Stanton Johnson on 2 November 1875 in Daviess County, Kentucky. William was born on 4 June 1856 and died on 22 June 1878. They had at least one child including:

  Mary Susan Johnson
  Elmwood Cemetery
  Owensboro, Kentucky

  o Paul Judson Johnson who was born on 22 October 1877 in Kentucky married, his wife's name was Eura. They had at least four children including Marguerite Johnson, born around 1903 in Kentucky, Jay W. Johnson, born on 15 March 1905 in Daviess County, Kentucky and died on 13 February 1989 in Owensboro, Hettie Louise Johnson who was likely born on 31 March 1988 in Kentucky, and Herman S. Johnson who was likely born on 29 March 1909 in Kentucky and died on 4 April 1970 in Hillsborough, Florida. Paul died in 1960 and his wife Eura died in 1975. They were buried in Odd Fellows Cemetery in Morganfield, Kentucky.

- John William Cottrell – Born 7 February 1858 in Daviess County, Kentucky and died 29 May 1921 at City Hospital in Owensboro, Kentucky. His cause of death was obstruction of the bowels. He was buried in Elmwood Cemetery in Owensboro, Kentucky in Section E-2.[113]
- Albert J. Cottrell – Born 7 May 1860 in Daviess County, Kentucky and died 22 June 1903 in Daviess County, Kentucky. He was buried in Elmwood Cemetery in Owensboro, Kentucky in the Cottrell Family Plot in Section 2.[114]

Benjamin J. Cottrell (1837-1906)

Son of William Cottrell & Susan Halsey
Great-granduncle of Taylor Cosby Cottrell, Jr.

Benjamin Cottrell was born on 2 December 1837 in Henrico County, Virginia. He was the son of William Cottrell and Susan Halsey. Benjamin was listed on the census of 1850 in the household of Stephen DuVal in Chesterfield County, Virginia, as Benjamin Cottrell, age 13 and attending school.[115]

Around 1856 Benjamin moved to Richmond after attending a military school in Lynchburg, Virginia and started a coal business as an

Benjamin J Cottrell

agent for brothers who were working the mines near Clayton. For many years his place of business was on the southeast corner of Eighth and Main Streets in Richmond. After moving his business several times, he finally settled in an office at 201 South Ninth Street.[116]

An abstract from Virginia records, published in the Virginia Genealogical Society Quarterly listed Luther J. Cottrell and Benjamin

Cottrell, children of William Cottrell in a 160-acre land warrant, assumed to be after 1858 since Benjamin's age was listed as 21.[117]

Benjamin was listed as a coal merchant on the census of 1860 in the household of Elizabeth Ann (Parsons) Pilcher in Henrico County, Virginia, as Benjamin Cottrell, age 22.[118] He married Rebecca Imogen Pilcher, daughter of John A. Pilcher and Elizabeth Ann Parsons around 1861. Elizabeth was

Mariah Elizabeth Pace

born circa 1843 in Henrico County, and died on 10 August 1862 in Henrico County shortly after their daughter Rebecca Imogene was born.[119]

Benjamin served in the Twenty-fifth Virginia Regiment, Cavalry in 1863 as a non-commissioned officer in the Confederacy. He then married Mariah Elizabeth Pace, the daughter of George D. Pace and Lucindia Hutchin on 24 December 1863 in Richmond, Virginia with the ceremony performed by Rev. Doctor J.B. Jeter. Mariah was born on 21 May 1840 in Middlesex County, Virginia. She also went by the name of Bettie and Maria.[120]

Benjamin appeared on the census of 1870 in Richmond County, Virginia as Benjamin Cottrell, age 32 along with Maria, age 29, Virginia L., age 5, Olive, age 3, and Benjamin, age 6/12 and born in January. Real estate value was listed as $1,200 and personal estate was valued at $500.[121]

He was a wood and coal dealer on the 1880 census in Richmond, Virginia, enumerated on 1 June 1880. Ben Cottrell, age 42 was listed along with his wife M.E., age 39, daughters R.J., age 18, Virginia, age 15, Olive, age 13, Estella, age 7, and Etta, age 3. His son Ben H, age 10 and his mother Susan H. Fritch, age 77 were also listed. A black servant cook was also in the household.[122]

Benjamin and his wife Mariah were living at 11 West Cary Avenue in Richmond, when he was listed on the 1900 census, enumerated on 11 June 1900. He was listed as Banjamin Cottrell, age 62 along with his wife Mariah E., age 59, daughters Virginia Lee, age 35, Olive, age 33, and Marietta B., age 22. His niece Emma J., age 44, and single, was also listed.[123]

Benjamin died on 25 February 1906 in Richmond at age 68 at 10:00 in the morning in his home at 11 West Cary Street after an illness of nearly three months. His cause of death was the result of "some strange, almost inexplicable, tubercular trouble, which developed very suddenly and made alarming headway." Funeral services

Benjamin Cottrell		
1840	Chesterfield County, VA	Unknown
1850	Chesterfield County, VA	Unknown
1860	Henrico County, VA.	Coal Merchant
1870	Richmond (Ind. City), VA	Coal Dealer
1980	Richmond (Ind. City), VA	Coal Dealer
1900	Richmond (Ind. City), VA	Coal Dealer

were held on 26 February 1906 at Calvary Baptist Church in Richmond. He was buried in Hollywood Cemetery in Richmond.[124]

Mariah Cottrell died on 26 March 1918 in Richmond, at age 76. She was buried with her husband Benjamin in Hollywood Cemetery in Richmond.[125]

Children of Benjamin Cottrell and Rebecca Imogen Pilcher:

- Rebecca Imogene Cottrell – Born on 9 July 1862 in Richmond, Virginia and died 3 August 1950 at St. Lukes Hospital in Richmond, Virginia, at age 88, after a seven-day hospital stay. Her cause of death was arteriosclerosis. Funeral services were held on 5 August 1950 at the Sutherland-Brown Funeral Home in Richmond at 11:00 in the morning. She was buried in Riverview Cemetery in Richmond. Rebecca married Tom T. Wilhoyte circa 1882. Tom was born in December 1852 in Kentucky and died before 1910. In 1900 he was a dry goods clerk. [126] Rebecca and Tom had at least one child including:
  - o Edward Douglas Wilhoyte - Born on 13 November 1886 in Kentucky and died on 1 April 1929 in Brook Hill in Henrico County, Virginia. He was buried on 2

April 1929 in Riverview Cemetery in Richmond, Virginia. Edward was listed as widowed on this death certificate.[127]

Children of Benjamin Cottrell and Mariah Elizabeth Pace:

- Virginia Lee Cottrell – Born on 17 November 1864 in Henrico County, Virginia and died on 8 July 1949 in Richmond, Virginia at age 84. Her cause of death was heart failure. In 1900 Virginia was a school teacher. In 1926 she traveled to Bermuda with her sister Olive returning on 14 August of that year. She also traveled with Olive to Honolulu, Hawaii in February 1930. She lived for a time with her sister Olive and never married. She was buried in Hollywood Cemetery in Richmond.[128]

- Olive Cottrell – Born on 7 November 1866 in Henrico County, Virginia and died on 29 September 1951 in Richmond, Virginia at age 84 at 9:00 in the morning at her residence on Hanover Avenue. She lived for a time with her sister Virginia and never married. In February 1928 she traveled to Bermuda with her sister Virginia. In 1930 she traveled with her sister Virginia to Honolulu, Hawaii. Her cause of death was cancer. She was buried on 29 September 1951 in Hollywood Cemetery in Richmond, in Section G, Lot 6.[129]

Benjamin Howard Cottrell

- Bernice Cottrell – Born 11 July 1868 in Richmond, Henrico County, Virginia and died 11 August 1869 in Richmond, at age 1. Her cause of death was Cholera Infantum. She was buried in Hollywood Cemetery in Richmond.[130]

- Benjamin Howard Cottrell – Born on 6 January 1870 in Henrico County, Virginia and died on 30 May 1961 in Richmond Virginia at age 91 at his residence on Hanover Avenue at 9:10 in the evening. His cause of death was a cardiac stand still. He was buried in Riverview Cemetery in Richmond. Benjamin married Lelia Pace Dowell, the daughter of James R. Dowell and Margaret A. Sewell, on 18 October 1893 at Park Place Church in Richmond, Virginia with the ceremony performed by Rev. Young. Lelia was born on 1 August 1872 in Virginia. In 1920 Benjamin was the president of a coal company in Virginia and in 1930 he was working as a coal merchant. Benjamin and Lelia had at least 10 children between 1894 and 1910 all of whom were born in Virginia. Lelia Pace died on 4 February 1941 in Richmond. Her cause of death was cerebral hemorrhage. She was buried on February 5th at Riverview Cemetery in Richmond.[131] Their children included:

- o Benjamin Cottrell - Born on 6 October 1894 in Richmond, Virginia. When he registered for the WWI draft in 1917 he was employed as a Civil Engineer for the Southern Railway System and had served for four years as a 2nd Lt. in the Cadets at the Virginia Polytechnic Institute and State University in Blacksburg, Virginia. He married Mable Shirley Horne on 17 November 1927. Benjamin died on 23 July 1988 in Richmond and was buried in Hollywood Cemetery in Richmond.[132] Mable died on 18 March 1867 in Virginia and was also buried in Hollywood Cemetery.[133]
- o Philip Rutherford Cottrell – Born on 18 April 1896 in Richmond, Virginia. When he registered for the WWI draft in 1918 he was living in Eubank, Kentucky and was employed as a material inspector for the Southern Railway System. He married Lucille Beatrice Motz on 27 January 1923 at The Church of the Transfiguration in New York City. Lucille was born in 1900 in Hamilton County, Ohio. Philip died on 18 April 1978 in Broward County, Florida.[134]
- o Virginia Lee Cottrell - Born on 27 January 1898 in Richmond, Virginia and married Henry Carl Messerschmitt on 26 September 1920 at the Immanuel Baptist

Church in Richmond with the ceremony performed by the Rev. John M. Pilcher. Virginia died on 23 November 1976 in Virginia and was buried in the Hollywood Cemetery in Richmond.[135] Henry died on 10 January 1994 in

Virginia Lee Cottrell
Hollywood Cemetery
Richmond, Virginia

Virginia, at age 103 and was also buried in the Hollywood Cemetery next to his wife Virginia.[136]

- o Margaret Halsey Cottrell - Born on 11 March 1900 in Richmond, Virginia and married Robert Welford Phillips on 15 November 1921 in Richmond. Margaret died on 20 June 1994 in Richmond, at age 94.[137] Robert died on 6 February 1968 in Richmond and was buried in Hollywood Cemetery.[138] They had at least four children including Robert Welford Phillips who was born on 31 July 1924 and died on 14 July 2009[139], Lelia Dowell Phillips who was born on 30 September 1925, married Robert Ryland Toone, and died on 3 December 2005[140], Howard Cottrell Phillips who was born 10 March 1931[141], and Mary B. Phillips who was born circa 1938.
- o James Dowell Cottrell - Born on 17 September 1901 in Richmond, Virginia and married Zenovia Guthrie on 28 November 1928 in Morehead City in Carteret County, North Carolina. James died on 30 August 1989 in Virginia and was buried in Forest Lawn Cemetery in Norfolk, Virginia.[142] Zenovia died on 25 August 1986 in Virginia and was also buried in Forest Lawn Cemetery.[143] They had at least two children including Virginia Lee Cottrell who was born on 17 November 1864 and died on 8 July 1949 in Richmond, and Benjamin G. Cottrell who was born around 1935 in Virginia.

o William George Cottrell - Born on 14 May 1903 in Richmond. His wife's name was Louise, and he died in 1955 in Chattanooga, Tennessee.[144]

o Mariah Elizabeth Cottrell – Born 4 May 1906 in Richmond, married John Haden Hankins on 7 December 1943, and died 8 January 1994, likely in Virginia.[145]

o Robert Dowell Cottrell - Born in 1907 in Virginia and likely died before 1920 because he was not listed on the census. It is likely that Robert was actually J. Robert Dowell, a cousin that Benjamin and Lelia took in and took care of as a son.[146]

o Joseph Howard Cottrell - Born on 7 July 1908 in Richmond, Virginia and married Marie Louise Walz on 10 December 1938 at Grace Covent Church in Richmond with the Rev. John Newton Thomas officiating. Marie was born in Lexington, Virginia on 7 March 1907. She was given in marriage by her mother Minnie Frances Schmidt and wore her mother's wedding gown of duchess lace. Joseph

Joseph Howard & Marie W. Cottrell
Maury Cemetery
Richmond, Virginia

died in on 27 July 1975 at Johnston-Willis Hospital in Richmond and was buried in Hollywood Cemetery in Richmond in Section 18, Lot 57.[147] Marie died on 21 October 1994 in Virginia and was also buried in Hollywood Cemetery.[148]

o Mildred Cottrell - Born on 24 March 1910 in Richmond, Virginia and died 6 August 1946 at the home of her sister at 2015 Park Avenue in Richmond. Her cause of death was bronchial pneumonia. Funeral services were held at Sutherland-Brown Funeral Home in Richmond at 4:00 in the afternoon. She was buried in Riverview Cemetery in Richmond.[149] She never married.

- Estelle Wallwork Cottrell – Born 1 August 1872 in Richmond, Virginia; died 27 February 1946 in Chesterfield County, Virginia at age 73 at 6:20 in the evening. Funeral services were held on 1 March 1946 at Joseph W. Bliley Funeral Home in Richmond. She was buried the same day in Riverview Cemetery in Richmond. She married James Garland Hening, the son of William Henry Hening and Olivia Campbell, on 7 November 1894 in Richmond. James was born on 13 October 1868 in Pawhatan County, Virginia and died on 21 January 1953 in Richmond. He was buried on 23 January 1953 in Riverview Cemetery in Richmond. In 1920 Estelle and James traveled to Havana, Cuba. In 1938 they traveled to Rio De Janerio, Brazil. Estelle and James had at least one child:
  - o James Garland Hening, Jr. – Born 25 November 1897 in Henrico County, Virginia and died 16 January 1982 in Richmond. He married Clarice Shackelford Hening on 4 June 1941 in Bruington in Chesterfield County, Virginia. According to their marriage record Clarice's father was Benjamin Cabell Hening and her mother was Peachy Shackelford. Clarice was born 6 December 1898 and died 5 July 1986 in Gloucester, Virginia. She was buried in Greenwood Memorial Park in Goochland County, Virginia. James Jr. had his body donated to the Virginia State Anatomical Program in Richmond.[150]
- Marietta Butterfield Cottrell – Born in June 1877 in Henrico County, Virginia and died 14 August 1906 in Richmond, Virginia at age 29. Marietta never married.[151]

Seth Alexander DuVal (1846)

Son of Stephen DuVal & Susan Halsey
Great-granduncle of Taylor Cosby Cottrell, Jr.

Seth Alexander DuVal was born on 7 January 1846 in Richmond, Virginia, eight miles southwest on the James River. He was the son of Stephen DuVal and Susan Halsey. [152] He appeared on the census of

1850 in the household of Stephen DuVal in Chesterfield County, Virginia, as Seth, age 5.[153] He was listed on the census of 1860 in the household of William F. Frith in Goochland County, as Leth A. Daval, age 14.[154]

Seth remained on the old homestead until late in the Civil War when he enlisted in Company I, Tenth Regiment of the Virginia Confederate Cavalry Volunteers in December 1863. He remained in service until the close of the war.[155] During his service he served under General William Lee who was the son of Robert E. Lee. He took part in several major engagements and was detailed as a scout for General Early following the battle of Haw Shop. He received his parole at Appomattox Court House.[156]

Seth married Mary Alice Haynes, daughter of Samuel Haynes and Mary Ann Barnhill, on 10 October 1867. Mary was born on 9 October 1850 in Masonville, Kentucky. It was said that her mother Mary Barnhill, an old settler of Daviess County, was a relative of Daniel Boone.[157]

Seth appeared on the census of 1870 in Daviess County, Kentucky, as Seth A. Duvall, age 24 along with Mary A., age 20, Samuel S., age 2, and George, age 11/12. Real estate was valued at $4,000 and personal estate was valued at $2,300. He was a farmer in October 1870 and owned a large farm of 146 acres which he purchased from his father-in-law. The entire 146 acres was under cultivation except for a few acres of timber. He raised tobacco, corn, wheat, hay, oats and stock. He was a member of the Democratic Party and was a Baptist.[158]

Seth was listed on the 1880 census agricultural schedule of Masonville Precinct, Daviess County, as owner of a farm that included 60 acres of improved land and 58 acres of unimproved land. The total value including land, buildings, machinery and livestock was $2,425 dollars. Livestock included five horses and two milk cows which produced 400 pounds of butter the previous year. The farm included four additional cattle and four calves, one of which died. The farm also included 19 swine and 13 chickens which produced 160 eggs. During the previous year 15 acres of land were used to produce 300 bushels of Indian corn and 5 acres produced 44 bushels of wheat.[159]

He appeared on the population schedule census of 1880 in Daviess County, as Seth A. Duvall, age 34 along with his wife Mary A., age 29, sons Samuel, age 11 and Benj. A., age 6, nephew Charles Cottrell, age

16, father-in-law Samuel Haynes, age 72 and mother-in-law Mary A. Haynes, age 69.[160]

In 1885 Seth and Mary Alice moved to Kansas because they were seeking a climate for Seth's health. They lived for some time in Altamont where Seth established the first bank in the area before they settled on a farm about four miles north of Edna, Kansas. In the fall of 1909 he returned to Virginia for a short visit with friends and relatives.[161] His wife Mary Alice died on 4 July 1909 in Edna, Kansas. She was buried at Elm Grove Cemetery in Edna, Labette County, Kansas.[162]

Seth was listed in the 1910 census in the household of his son, Samuel Stephens DuVal in

Seth Alexander DuVal		
1850	Chesterfield County, VA	N/A
1860	Goochland County, VA.	Unknown
1870	Daviess County, KY	Farmer
1980	Daviess County, KY	Farmer
1910	Labette County, KS	Retired Farmer
1920	Labette County, KS	None
1930	Okmulgee County, OK	None

Labette County, as Seth A., age 64 and widowed. In the 1920 census he was listed in the household of his son, Samuel Stephens DuVal in Labette County, as Seth A., age 74.[163] In 1922 he moved to Oklahoma to be with his granddaughter Mrs. E.D. Glass.[164] In 1930 he was listed on the census in the household of his granddaughters' husband, Earl D. Glass in Okmulgee County, Oklahoma, as S.A. Duvall, age 84.[165]

Seth's name, with a birth date, but no death date, is recorded on the Gravestone of his wife Mary Alice DuVal in Elm Grove Cemetery in Edna, Labette County, Kansas. It is likely he is buried there and that his death date was never added to the marker.[166]

Children of Seth Alexander DuVal and Mary Alice Haynes:

- Samuel Stephens DuVal – Born on 10 October 1868 in Daviess County, Kentucky near Masonville. Samuel married Daisy May Robbins in 1890. Daisy was born on 16 May 1870 in Knoxville, Illinois. Samuel and Daisy moved first to Labette County, Kansas in 1920. They later moved to Oklahoma in 1925 where Samuel engaged in the dairy business. Daisy died on 31 August, 1958 in Okmulgee County, Oklahoma, at age 88. Samuel and Daisy had at least three children including:
  - o Ruby DuVal – Born on 25 March 1890 in Fontenac, Kansas and married Earl D. Glass on 6 June 1907 in

Oklahoma County, Kansas. She was employed as a public school teacher in 1930.[167] They had at least two children including Earl D. Glass who was born on 27 November 1909 in Kansas near Altamont, and Arline O. Glass who was born on 27 December 1911, also in Kansas near Altamont.[168]

o Paul Alexander DuVal - Born on 17 July 1895 in Edna, Kansas and died 18 February 1970 in Tulsa, Oklahoma. He was buried in the Newton School Cemetery in Wright County, Missouri.[169] Paul married Garna E. Newton on 12 March 1922. Paul was employed by the Board of Education and registered for the WWII Draft in Tulsa, Oklahoma in 1942. Garna died on 26 November 1981 in Missouri and was also buried at the Newton School Cemetery.[170] They had at least one child including Paul Newton DuVal who was born in 1937 in Tulsa County, Oklahoma and died in 1984 in Missouri. He was also buried in the Newton School Cemetery in Missouri.

o Kathleen A. DuVal – Born on 4 September 1903 in Edna, Kansas. She married Roy T. Scott in 1919, likely in Labette County, Kansas. Kathleen was a railroad agent in Newton County, Missouri in 1930.[171] They had at least one daughter Paul Helen, born circa 1922.

- George Aretus DuVal – Born in May 1870 in Daviess County, near Masonville and died in 1873 in Daviess County.[172]
- Benjamin A. DuVal – Born on 17 January, 1874 in Daviess County, Kentucky and died on 5 January 1913 in Kansas, at age 38. He was buried in the La Harpe Cemetery in La Harpe in Allen County, Kansas. He married Stella Bicknell, who was the daughter of Austin and Anna Bicknell in 1896. Stella was born on 10 March 1877 in Kansas and died on 21 August 1909 in Kansas, at age 32 She was also buried at La Harpe Cemetery in La Harpe in Allen County, Kansas.[173] Benjamin was a merchant in 1900 and a mail carrier for a railroad in 1910. Benjamin and Stella had at least five children including:

  o Theodore A. DuVal – Born on 25 February 1897 in Kansas and died on 3 February 1905 in Kansas, likely in Barton City, at age 7. He was buried in La Harpe Cemetery in Allen County, Kansas.[174]

o Pearl A. DuVal - Born in September 1898 in Kansas. She was not listed in the 1910 census with her father thus is it is likely she died before 1910 in Kansas, likely in Barton City.

o Thelma C. DuVal - Born in 1904 in Kansas, likely on 4 January 1904. She likely married a Basham and likely died on 3 May 1985 and was buried in Eldorado Cemetery in Jackson County, Oklahoma.[175]

o Mary Alice DuVal – Born around 1906 in Kansas.[176] She was living in the home of her grandfather Austin M. Bicknell on the 1925 Allen County, Kansas census. She was listed as single and working as a servant in the home of Errett Newby on the 1930 census in Oklahoma City, Oklahoma.

o China Ann DuVal – Born in 1908 in Kansas. She likely died in 1972. She likely married William Claude Gifford and is likely buried in Arapaho Cemetery in Custer County, Oklahoma.[177]

Chapter 2 – Peter Cottrell Family

Great-grandfather of Taylor Cosby Cottrell, Jr.

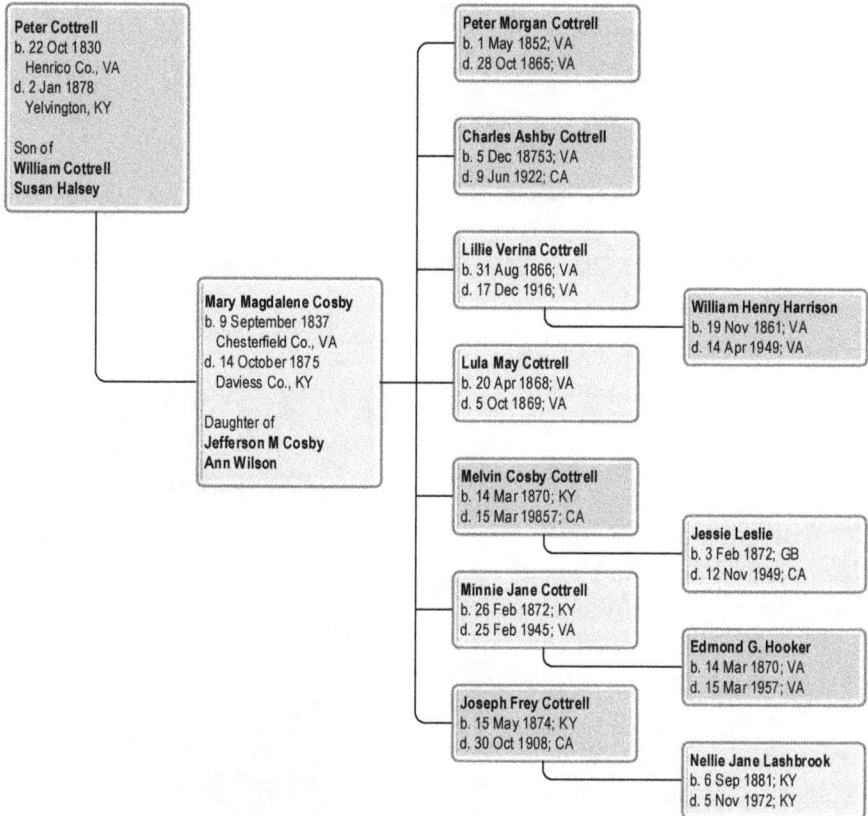

Peter Cottrell
b. 22 Oct 1830
  Henrico Co., VA
d. 2 Jan 1878
  Yelvington, KY

Son of
William Cottrell
Susan Halsey

Mary Magdalene Cosby
b. 9 September 1837
  Chesterfield Co., VA
d. 14 October 1875
  Daviess Co., KY

Daughter of
Jefferson M Cosby
Ann Wilson

Peter Morgan Cottrell
b. 1 May 1852; VA
d. 28 Oct 1865; VA

Charles Ashby Cottrell
b. 5 Dec 18753; VA
d. 9 Jun 1922; CA

Lillie Verina Cottrell
b. 31 Aug 1866; VA
d. 17 Dec 1916; VA

William Henry Harrison
b. 19 Nov 1861; VA
d. 14 Apr 1949; VA

Lula May Cottrell
b. 20 Apr 1868; VA
d. 5 Oct 1869; VA

Melvin Cosby Cottrell
b. 14 Mar 1870; KY
d. 15 Mar 19857; CA

Jessie Leslie
b. 3 Feb 1872; GB
d. 12 Nov 1949; CA

Minnie Jane Cottrell
b. 26 Feb 1872; KY
d. 25 Feb 1945; VA

Edmond G. Hooker
b. 14 Mar 1870; VA
d. 15 Mar 1957; VA

Joseph Frey Cottrell
b. 15 May 1874; KY
d. 30 Oct 1908; CA

Nellie Jane Lashbrook
b. 6 Sep 1881; KY
d. 5 Nov 1972; KY

Peter Cottrell was born on 22 October 1830 in Henrico County, Virginia. He was the son of William Cottrell and Susan Halsey.[1] He had at least six brothers and sisters including Mary Ann Cottrell, John William Cottrell, Joseph F. Cottrell, Richard H. Cottrell, Luther J. Cottrell, and Benjamin Cottrell. He also had at least two half-sisters including Susan Cottrell and Elizabeth Cottrell. His siblings are covered in detail in Section 1, Chapter 1, William Cottrell Family.

Peter married Mary Magdalene Cosby, daughter of Jefferson M. Cosby and Ann Wilson, on 2 January 1861 in Chesterfield County, Virginia.[2] Mary Magdalene was also known as Rosa and Polly.

Peter Cottrell Family Timeline

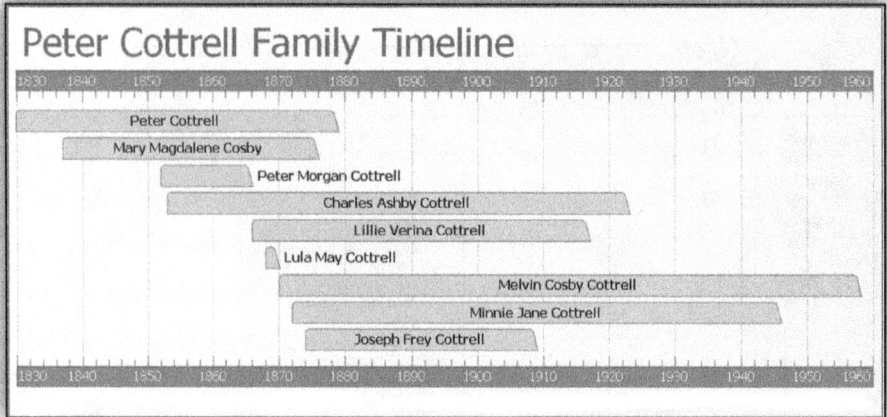

Timeline (1830–1960):
- Peter Cottrell
- Mary Magdalene Cosby
- Peter Morgan Cottrell
- Charles Ashby Cottrell
- Lillie Verina Cottrell
- Lula May Cottrell
- Melvin Cosby Cottrell
- Minnie Jane Cottrell
- Joseph Frey Cottrell

Peter began military service on 30 June 1861 in Laurel Hill, Virginia, when he enlisted in the Confederate States Army. He was transferred to Captain John F. Wren's Company, subsequently Company B of the 40th Battalion of Virginia Cavalry C.S.A. on 23 June 1862 and was promoted to Corporal in the Confederate States Army on 8 September 1862.[3] He was later promoted to Sargent of Company B, 24th Regiment Virginia Cavalry on 8 August 1864 and was listed on the Company B Muster Roll for September and October of that year. This is the last file where the War Department, Adjutant General's Office, shows him present.

Peter Cottrell

Peter's name appeared on a list of men in a Prisoners of War hospital, belonging to the Army of Northern Virginia, on 9 April 1865. This list contained men who had been surrendered at Appomattox

Court House on 9 April, 1865, by General Robert E. Lee, to Lieutenant General U.S. Grant, commanding Armies of the United States. Peter was paroled at the Huguenot Springs Hospital on 22 April, 1865 and his military records indicate he reached at least the rank of 2nd Lieutenant in Company F, 23rd Regiment Virginia Infantry of the Confederate States Army.[4]

Peter was a coal miner on the census of 1870 in Daviess County, Kentucky where he was listed as age 39 and head of household with a personal estate valued at $100. Rosa,

Peter Cottrell
Elmwood Cemetery
Owensboro, KY

a female, age 31, was listed as keeping house. Lillie V., a female age 3, and males Chas A., age 6 and Melvin, age 3 months were also listed. Of additional interest is that his home was located next door to his brother Luther J. Cottrell.[5]

Peter died on 2 January 1878 in Yelvington, Daviess County, Kentucky, at age 47.[6]   He was buried on 2 January 1878 at Elmwood Cemetery in Owensboro, Kentucky between his son Joseph F. Cottrell and his wife Rosa Cottrell in the Cottrell Family Plot in Section E-2.[7]

Mary Magdalene Cosby (1837-1875)

Wife of Peter Cottrell
Great-grandmother of Taylor Cosby Cottrell, Jr.

Mary Magdalene Cosby was born on 9 September 1837 in Chesterfield County, Virginia.[8]   She was the daughter of Jefferson M. Cosby and Ann Wilson.[9] Mary was also known as Rosa and Polly.[10] She appeared on the census of 1850 in the household of Jefferson M. Cosby in Chesterfield County, Virginia, as Mary, age 12 and attending school. It is assumed, although not proved, that this Mary is the Rosa listed as 20 on the 1860 census who was actually born in 1837.[11] She had at least five brothers and sisters from her father's first marriage on 31 January 1826 to her mother Ann Wilson in Pawhatan County, Virginia. Her brothers and sisters included:

- Philip Lafayette Cosby – Born on 4 January 1827 in Pawhatan County and died on 4 June 1911 in Burkville in Nottoway County, Virginia, at age 84.[12] Philip married Eliza Charlotte Atkinson on 8 June 1854.[13] They had at least three children including Thomas J. Cosby who was born around 1855 and died on 14 November 1887[14], Ira Lafayette Cosby who was born on 28 February 1858 and died on 8 April 1934[15], and an unnamed daughter who was born and died in October 1860.[16] Elizabeth died sometime before 1863.[17] Philip

Mary Magdalene Cosby

then married Virginia Ann (Crump) Howard on 3 March 1863.[18] They had at least two additional children including Philip V. Cosby who was born on 16 June 1864,[19] and an unnamed son who was born on 26 April 1866 and died in September 1867, at age 1.[20]

- Branch E. Cosby – Born in 1831 in Virginia[21] and died before 1900. Branch married Mary S. Walker on 16 October 1856.[22] They had at least three children including Florence Cosby who was born on 17 July 1857 and died on 14 December 1935[23], Howel Hunter Cosby who was born on 4 May 1859 and died on 20 December 1897[24], and Nancy L. Cosby who was born in 1861.[25] Mary died between 1862 and 1869. Branch then married Adeline Howard on 27 April 1872.[26] They had at least four additional children including Rosa Russell Cosby who was born on 10 September 1872 and died on 30 January 1963[27], Mary Dawson Cosby who was born on 13 April 1873 and died in November 1956, Maud Camp Cosby who was born on 15 December 1878 and died on 21 May 1958[28], and Vera Branch Cosby who was born on 3 February 1883[29]. Adeline died on 22 January 1914 in Hardin County, Kentucky.[30]

- Judith Ann Cosby – Born in 1834 in Virginia and died before April 1940.[31] Judith married James Moseley Stratton on 28 March 1855.[32] They had at least two children including Lorenza Dow Stratton who was born in June 1857 and died in 1928[33], and Martha Ninaver Stratton who was born in 1861[34]. James died in 1903 in Goochland County, Virginia.[35]
- Robert Dabney Cosby – Born in 1838 in Virginia and married Luo Courtney in 1858.[36]
- Sarah J. Cosby – Born in 1839 in Virginia and died after 1910. She married Daniel W. Stratton around 1858.[37] They had at least three children including Ivin Maud Stratton who was born in 1859[38], Walter H. Stratton who was born on 28 January 1861 and died on 15 January 1931[39], and Nettie Lou Stratton who was born on 17 January 1865 and died on 12 June 1961.[40]

Mary's mother Ann Wilson died sometime before 1840 in Virginia. Mary's father Jefferson then married Nancy Harris on 26 October 1840 in Goochland County, Virginia.[41] They had at least seven additional children (Mary's half-brothers and half-sisters) including:

- Monterey Cosby who was born on 12 November 1846 and died on 15 December 1934.[42] Monterey married Beverly Farrar Morrissett in 1869. This was his second marriage and he had at least two children from his first wife Judith Delany.[43] Monterey and Beverly had at least five children including Allen Lynnwood Morrissett who was born on 9 February 1872 and died on 23 March 1960[44], Irvin Morrissett who was born on 30 November 1874 and died on 2 May 1907[45], Wellington Morrissett who was born on 7 March 1875 and died on 6 June 1919[46], Vivian Morrissett who was born on 8 September 1877 and died on 11 November 1961[47], and Pearl Morrissett who was born on 7 September 1879 and died on 27 October 1965[48]. Beverly died on 5 July 1922 in Danville, Virginia, at age 89.[49]

- Luther Calvin Cosby – Born on 1 March 1853 in Chesterfield County and died on 12 March 1941 in Midlothian in Chesterfield County, at age 88.[50]   Luther married Annie Jewett Watkins on 28 April 1887.[51] They had at least two children including Calvin Watkins Cosby who was born on 7 November 1887 and died on 20 January 1948[52], and Irving Handcock Cosby who was born on 18 May 1889 and died on 5 November 1971[53]. Annie died sometime before April 1930 in Chesterfield County.[54]

- Richard Hamilton Cosby – Born on 3 November 1853 in Chesterfield County and died on 12 May 1926 in Chesterfield County, at age 72.[55] He married Sarah Elizabeth Cosby around 1885. She was the daughter of Ludwell Williams Cosby and Rebecca Wilson. They had no children. Sarah Died sometime before January 1920.[56]

- Charles Monroe Cosby – Born on 22 August 1855 in Chesterfield County and died on 13 November 1940 in Midlothian, Virginia.[57] Charles married Maggie Florence Jackson on 30 December 1887.[58] They had at least three children including Jefferson Judson Cosby who was born on 28 July 1889 and died on 24 November 1957[59], Bernard Jackson Cosby who was born on 23 September 1891 and died on 29 July 1918[60], and Florence Sadie Cosby who was born on 10 August 1893 and died on 4 May 1974.[61] Maggie died on 11 August 1950 in Richmond, Virginia, at age 87.[62]

- Lelia Mataline Cosby – Born in February 1859 in Chesterfield County and died on 29 September 1930 in Danville, at age 71. She married Joseph Goodman Puryear on 26 February 1884.[63] They had at least six children including Benjamin Puryear who was born and died between 1885 and 1900, Elma Wyllie Puryear who was born on 27 November 1886 and died on 22 February 1984[64], Georgie W. Puryear who was born on 18 November 1888, Benson Jefferson Puryear who was born on 22 November 1890, Ethel G. Puryear who was born in January 1893, and Samuel Sumpter Puryear who was born on 26 August 1895 and died on 5 July 1981.[65]

- Nannie Lee Cosby – Born on 10 October 1864 in Chesterfield County and died on 15 February 1934 in Danville, at age 69. She married Charles Edgar Harris on 15 May 1887.[66] They had at least three children including Edgar Starr Harris who was born on 8 May 1889 and died in January 1975[67], Randolph C. Harris who was born on 12 April 1891 and died on 28 August 1957, and Urna Alma Harris who was born on 18 November 1893 and died on 19 December 1947. Charles died on 20 May 1945 in Danville, Virginia at age 80.[68]

- John Stuart Cosby – Born on 17 March 1867 in Chesterfield County and died on 6 April 1940 in Midlothian, at age 73.[69] He married Jannett Jewett in 1904. They had at least one child, Stuart Shelby Cosby who was born on 2 August 1905 and died on 15 July 1981.[70] Jannett died on 5 February 1941 in Midlothian, at age 67.[71]

Mary's father Jefferson M. Cosby died on 25 December 1880 in Chesterfield County, Virginia. His cause of death was chronic diarrhea.[72] Her step-mother Nancy Harris died on 10 March 1905 in Chesterfield County, at age 84. She was buried in Midlothian, Virginia, at the old family burying ground.[73]

Mary married Peter Cottrell, son of William Cottrell and Susan Halsey, on 2 January 1861 in Chesterfield County, Virginia.[74]

She appeared on the census of 1870 in the household of Peter Cottrell in Daviess County, Kentucky, enumerated on 1 June 1870. Peter Cottrell, age 39, was listed as head of household with a personal estate valued at $100. Rosa, a female,

Mary Magdalene Cosby
Elmwood Cemetery
Owensboro, KY

age 31, was listed as keeping house. Lillie V., a female age 3, and males Chas. A, age 6, and Melvin, age 3 months were also listed. Of additional interest is that his home was located next door to Peter's brother Luther J. Cottrell.[75]

Mary died on 14 October 1875 in Daviess County, Kentucky, at age 38.[76] She was buried in Elmwood Cemetery in Owensboro, next to her husband Peter in the Cottrell Family Plot.[77]

Peter Morgan Cottrell (1862-1865)

Son of Peter Cottrell and Mary Magdalene Cosby
Granduncle of Taylor Cosby Cottrell, Jr.

Peter Morgan Cottrell was born on 1 May 1862 in Goochland County, Virginia.[78] He was the son of Peter Cottrell and Mary Magdalene Cosby. Peter died on 28 October 1865 in Goochland County, Virginia, at age 3.[79]

Charles Ashby Cottrell (1863-1922)

Son of Peter Cottrell and Mary Magdalene Cosby
Granduncle of Taylor Cosby Cottrell, Jr.

Charles Ashby Cottrell was born on 5 December 1863 in Manikin, Goochland County, Virginia.[80] He was the son of Peter Cottrell and Mary Magdalene Cosby.[81] He appeared on the census of 1870 in the household of Peter Cottrell in Daviess County, Kentucky, as Chas. A. Cotterell, age 6.[82] He was listed on the census of 1880 in the household of his uncle, Seth Alexander DuVal in Daviess County, Kentucky, as Charles Cottrell, age 16 and single.[83] He was on the census of 1900 at Tuolumne County, California. An unnamed Carlon was listed as head of household. Charles was listed as age 36, single, and an employee as a farm laborer in the household.[84]

Charles was registered to vote in 1901 in the Altaville Precinct, while living at Angels Camp, Calaveras County, California.[85] Charles and his brother Melvin Cottrell went to Redlands, California after the death of their brother Joseph on 31 October 1908 and accompanied Joe's body

Charles Ashby Cottrell		
1870	Daviess County, KY	In School
1980	Daviess County, KY	Farm Laborer
1900	Toulumne County, CA	Farm Laborer
1910	Calaveras County, CA	Gold Mine Millman
1920	Calaveras County, CA	Gold Mine Millman

on the train which left Redlands, California on 3 November and arrived in Owensboro, Kentucky on 7 November 1908.[86]

He was listed on the census of 1910 in Calaveras County, California. Janetta M. Crooks was listed as head of household. Charles, age 46 and single, was listed in the household as a lodger.[87]

Charles was a Millman in a gold mine when he appeared in the census of 1920 at Calaveras County, enumerated on 7 January 1920. Janetta M. Crooks was listed as head of household. Charles was listed in the household as single and a boarder.[88] He was found on a passenger list of United States citizens sailing on the S.S. Sonoma on 6 June 1921 departing San Francisco, California for Honolulu, Hawaii.[89]

Charles died on 9 June 1922 in Nevada City, California, at the age of 58. He was buried in Pine Grove Cemetery in Nevada City.[90]

Lillie Verina Cottrell (1866-1916)

Daughter of Peter Cottrell and Mary Magdalene Cosby
Grandaunt of Taylor Cosby Cottrell, Jr.

Lillie Verina Cottrell was born on 31 August 1866 in Goochland County, Virginia. She was the daughter of Peter Cottrell and Mary Magdalene Cosby.[91] Lillie appeared on the census of 1870 in the household of Peter Cottrell in Daviess County, Kentucky, as Lillie V. Cotterell, age 3.[92] She was listed as a cousin, Lillie Cotrell, age 13 and single in the household of Jno. R. Chapman in the 1880 census.[93]

Lillie married William Henry Harrison on 24 February 1886 in Manchester, Virginia.[94] William was born on 19 November 1861 in Woodberry Mills, Pawhatan County, Virginia. He was a bricklayer and contractor in the building industry.

Lillie was listed in the 1900 census in the household of William in Chesterfield County, Virginia; enumerated on 8 June 1900 listing William H. Harrison, age 37 along with his wife Lilla, age 32, sons J. Ashby, age 12, Dillard H., age 11, and William L., age 8 and daughters Mary C., age 9,

William Henry Harrison		
1900	Chesterfield County, VA	Bricklayer
1910	Chesterfield County, VA	Bricklayer
1920	Richmond (Ind. City), VA	Bricklayer
1930	Richmond (Ind. City), VA	Bricklayer

Linda W., age 3, and Florence V., age 7/12.[95] Lillie appeared on the census of 1910 in the household of William in Chesterfield County,

Virginia; enumerated on 26 April 1910 listing William H. Harrison, age 49 along with his wife Lellie V., age 44, daughters Mary, age 20, Linda, age 15, Florence, age 10, Virginia, age 7, and Elizabeth, age 1 and sons William L., age 18 and William H., age 4.[96]

Lillie died on 17 December 1916 at St. Elizabeth's Hospital in Richmond, Virginia. Her cause of death was ophthalmic goiter, also known as Grave's disease. She was buried on 18 December 1916 in Maury Cemetery in Richmond, Virginia.[97]

William was living with his son Williams Ludwell Harrison in Richmond, Virginia in 1930.[98] He died on 14 April 1949 in Huntington, West Virginia, at age 87.[99]

Children of William Henry Harrison and Lillie Verina Cottrell:[100]

- James Ashby Harrison – Born 22 June 1887 in Chesterfield County, Virginia and died 30 April 1917 in Richmond, Virginia at 3:10 in the morning at age 29.[101] His cause of death was tuberculosis. James was buried on 1 May 1917 in Maury Cemetery in Richmond.[102]
- Roland Halsey Harrison – Born 19 June 1888 in Chesterfield County, Virginia and died 22 March 1905 in Swansboro, Chesterfield County. She was buried in Maury Cemetery.[103]
- Mary Cosby Harrison – Born 23 December 1889 in Chesterfield County, Virginia and died 30 April 1923 in Roanoke, Virginia at 11:00 in the morning at age 33. Her cause of death was pulmonary tuberculosis. Mary is buried in Evergreen Burial Park in Roanoke, Virginia. She married Cecil Eggleston Cosby, son of Emmett Lloyd Cosby and Annie E. Simms on 1 July 1916 in Richmond, Virginia. Cecil was born on 27 June 1889 in Virginia. Cecil and Mary had at least one child including:
  - Varina Cottrell Cosby - Born on 27 December 1917 in Roanoke, Virginia and died on 11 May 1918 from Whooping Cough. She was buried in Evergreen Burial Park in Roanoke.[104]
- Williams Ludwell Harrison – Born 6 January 1892; died 23 April 1963 in Huntington, Cabell County, West Virginia. He married Estelle Bruce Lester, on 15 September 1920 in Richmond, Virginia, at age 71. Williams was a veteran of WWII

and a civil engineer on a steam railway. Williams and Estelle had at least two children including:

- o Nancy Bruce Harrison – Born on 21 March 1929 in Richmond. She likely married Jack P. Davis in 1948.
- o Williams Ludwell Harrison, Jr. – Born on 18 October 1930 in Henrico County, Virginia, married Colleen O'Neil Ferguson in 1953.[105]

- Andrew J. Harrison – Born 19 November 1893 in Manchester, Chesterfield County, Virginia; died 16 April 1896 in Chesterfield County, Virginia, at age 2.[106]
- Lillie Varina Harrison – Born 20 December 1895 in Chesterfield County, Virginia and died 30 December 1895 in Chesterfield County, Virginia, 10 days after her birth.[107]
- Linda Walton Harrison – Born 6 January 1897 in Chesterfield County, Virginia and died 8 November 1975 in Sarasota, Manatee County, Florida, at age 78. She was buried in Silver Spring, Maryland. She married after the 1930 census. Her last name was Meyers on her Death Record.[108]
- Florence C. Harrison – Born 8 October 1899 in Chesterfield County, Virginia and died 21 January 1919 in Richmond, Virginia, at age 19.[109]
- Virginia Dare Harrison – Born 15 July 1902 in Manikin in Chesterfield County, Virginia and died 13 August 1934 at the University Hospital in Charlottesville, Virginia, at age 32. Her cause of death was post-operative shock, circulatory failure, and pulmonary tuberculosis. She was buried in Maury Cemetery, Richmond.[110] Virginia Dare and her sister Elizabeth were patients in the Catawba Sanitarium in 1930. Catawba Sanatorium was founded in 1908 and was a public institution for the treatment of tuberculosis. It was known as one of the most organized and best equipped institutions of its kind. It remained open until late 1940 and later became the Catawba Hospital.[111]
- William Henry Harrison, Jr. – Born 27 Jun 1905; died 1 April 1991 in Virginia, at age 85. He was buried on 3 April 1991 in Hollywood Cemetery in Richmond, Virginia in Pavilion Section, Lot 112.[112] William was a civil engineer for the railroad

and was later listed on the census as a "rodman on a steam railway". He married Martha Lillian Hall on 3 March 1925 in Richmond.[113] She divorced Alan on 16 April 1979, died on 22 August 1992, and was buried in Maury Cemetery in Richmond.[114] William then married Martha Dyson Baker in Richmond. Martha died on 13 July 1997 and was buried in Hollywood Cemetery in Richmond.[115] William and his first wife Martha Hall had at least one child including:

- o Gene Dare Harrison - Born 22 December 1925 in Henrico County and married Alan Richard Knopp, the daughter of William August Knopp and Elva Letita Rodgers 3 Marcy 1950. They divorced 16 April 1979.

- Elizabeth Cottrell Harrison – Born 13 March 1909 in Chesterfield County, Virginia and died 20 December 1934 in Catawba, Virginia, at age 25. Funeral services were held on 22 December 1934 in Richmond, Virginia at 3:30 in the afternoon at her home on Dundee Avenue. She was buried on 22 December 1934 in Maury Cemetery.[116] Elizabeth and her sister Virginia Dare were patients in the Catawba Sanitarium in 1930. The Sanatorium was founded in 1908 and was a public institution for the treatment of tuberculosis. It was known as one of the most organized and best equipped institutions of its kind.[117]

Lula May Cottrell (1868-1869)

Daughter of Peter Cottrell and Mary Magdalene Cosby
Grandaunt of Taylor Cosby Cottrell, Jr.

Lula May Cottrell was born on 20 April 1868 in Goochland County, Virginia. She was the daughter of Peter Cottrell and Mary Magdalene Cosby.[118] She died on 5 October 1869 in Goochland County, Virginia, at age 1.[119]

Melvin Cosby Cottrell (1870-1957)

Son of Peter Cottrell and Mary Magdalene Cosby
Granduncle of Taylor Cosby Cottrell, Jr.

Melvin Cosby Cottrell was born on 14 March 1870 in Owensboro, Daviess County, Kentucky. He was the son of Peter Cottrell and Mary

Magdalene Cosby.[120] Melvin was listed on the census of 1870 in the household of Peter Cottrell in Daviess County, Kentucky, as Melvin Cotterell, age 3 months.[121] He was listed on the census of 1880 in the household of his uncle, Branch E. Cosby in Spencer County, Indiana, as Meldm Cottrel, age 9 and attending school.[122]

Melvin married Jessie Leslie, daughter of Theodore Leslie and Ann Cowie around 1894.[123] Jessie was born on 3 February 1872 in Ordiquhill, Banff, Scotland.[124]

Melvin Cosby Cottrell

In 1908 Melvin was registered to vote in the Third Ward, Ninth Precinct as a Democrat, while living at 513 20th Street, Oakland, Alameda County, California.

Melvin and his brother Charles Ashby went to Redlands, California after the death of their brother Joseph Cottrell on 31 October 1908 and accompanied Joe's body on the train which left Redlands on 3 November and arrived in Owensboro, Kentucky on 7 November 1908.[125]

Melvin was listed on the census of 1910 in Elkhart County, Indiana. He was living at 412 Franklin in Elkhart City at the time of the census. Melvin Cottrell, age 40 was listed as head of household along with his wife Jesse, age 36. He was renting a home and out of work on the day of the census. Jesse was listed as the mother of two children, none of which were living.[126]

In 1916 Melvin was registered to vote in the Tenth Precinct as a Democrat, while living at 3934 Army in San Francisco, California.[127] In 1920 he was registered to vote in the Thirty Seventh Precinct still as a Democrat but living at 640 Madrid in San Francisco.[128]

He was a veteran of WWI on the census of 1920 in San Francisco County, California where he was listed on the census as Melvine Cottrell, age 49 along with his wife Jessie, age 34. Jessie was listed as a Naturalized citizen with the year of immigration to the United States unknown.[129]

Melvin and Jessie lived at 656 Madrid Street in San Francisco, California on 12 January 1920. He was a member of Steamfitters Union Local 38 of San Francisco.[130] He was registered to vote in 1930 in the Fifty Fifth Precinct, this time as a Republican, and living at 640 Madrid in San Francisco.[131]

Melvin Cottrell, age 60 was listed in the 1930 Census in San Francisco County, California on 12 April 1930 as owning his own home valued at $2,200, and having a radio set. His wife Jessie, age 58 was also listed.[132] In 1935 Melvin and Jessie visited his sister,

Melvin Cosby Cottrell		
1870	Daviess County, KY	N/A
1880	Spencer County, IN	In School
1910	Elkhart County, IN	Odd Job Laborer
1920	San Francisco County, CA	Shipyard Steam Fitter
1930	San Francisco County, CA	Refinery Steam Fitter
1940	Alameda County, CA	Shipyard Steam Fitter

Minnie J. Hooker, in Richmond, Virginia. It was their first visit to Virginia since Melvin went West in 1887.[133]

Melvin and Jessie were listed on the 1940 census in Oakland, Alameda County, California, living at 3023 Fibert Street. Melvin was listed as Melvin Cottrell, age 70 along with his wife Jessie, age 68. There were three additional persons listed in the household including Melvin McAds, brother-in-law, Marie McAds, sister, and Helen McAds, niece. Melvin McAds, and his wife Marie McAds were also living in the household. The relationship listing is obviously incorrect although the wife was listed as a niece, which was incorrect as Marie was born after Melvin's parents were deceased. It is likely that she was Jessie's sister.[134]

Jessie died on 12 November 1949 in Oakland, California, at age 77. Funeral services were held on 14 November 1949 in Oakland at the East 14th Street Chapel of the Grant D. Miller Mortuaries, Inc., at 2:00 in the afternoon. Her ashes were interred on 14 November 1949 at Chapel of the Chimes Columbarium and Mausoleum in Oakland.

Melvin died on 15 March 1957 in Oakland, California 9:10 AM while in route to Kaiser Foundation Hospital. His cause of death was coronary thrombosis. Funeral services were held on 18 March 1957 at 14th Street Chapel of Grant Miller Mortuaries in Oakland at 10:00 in the morning. He was cremated on 18 March 1957 in Oakland with Grant Miller Mortuaries handling the arrangements. Final internment was in the Chapel of the Chimes Columbarium and Mausoleum in Oakland next to his wife.[135] Melvin and Leslie had no children.

Minnie Jane Cottrell (1872-1945)

Daughter of Peter Cottrell and Mary Magdalene Cosby
Grandaunt of Taylor Cosby Cottrell, Jr.

Minnie Jane Cottrell was born on 26 February 1872 in Yelvington, Daviess County, Kentucky. She was the daughter of Peter Cottrell and Mary Magdalene Cosby.[136] Minnie appeared on the census of 1880 in the household of John Leven Kirk in Daviess County, as Minnie Cottrell, age 8. She was listed as a boarder and attending school.[137]

She moved to Manchester, Virginia which later became South Richmond, around 1888.[138] She

Minnie Jane Cottrell

married Edmond Goodman Hooker, son of Edmond Anderson Hooker and Margaret Elizabeth Harrison, on 17 July 1889 in Manchester, Virginia. Edmond was born on 12 May 1867 at Henley's Store near Fine Creek Mills in Pawhatan County, Virginia. He was a bricklayer by trade.[139]

Minnie appeared on the census of 1900 in the household of her husband Edmond in Chesterfield County, Virginia; enumerated on 8 June 1900. E.G. Hooker, age 32 was listed along with his wife Minnie J., age 28, son Edmond C., age 8, and daughter Margarette E., age 8/12. Edmund was listed as owning his home, which was mortgaged at the time.[140]

She was listed on the census of 1910 in the household of her husband Edmond in Richmond, Virginia; enumerated on 23 April 1910. Edmond Hooker, age 41 was listed as head of household living on Hull Street along with his wife Minnie, age 32. His sons Edmond, age 18 and Edmond A., age 8 along with his daughters Margaret, age 10 and

Dorcas G., age 1 were also listed. He owned his farm, which was listed on farm schedule 4, free of mortgage.[141]

Minnie appeared on the census of 1920 in the household of her husband Edmond at 3115 Hull Street in Richmond; enumerated on 12 January 1920. Edmond G. Hooker, age 51 was listed along with his wife Minnie J., age 47, son Edmond, age 19, and daughters Margaret E., age 20 and Dorcas G., age 11.[142]

Edmond died on 14 February 1921 in Richmond, at age 53 at 5:40 in the afternoon. His cause of death was chronic intestinal nephritis. He was buried on 16 February 1920 in Maury Cemetery in Richmond in the E.G. Hooker family plot.[143]

Minnie was listed on the census of 1930 in Richmond, Virginia, enumerated on 10 April 1930 as Minnie J. Hooker, widowed, age 58 and head of household. Her son Edmond, age 29 and daughter Dorcas, age 21 were also listed. She owned her home which was valued at $8,000.[144]

Edmond Hooker & Minnie Cottrell
Maury Cemetery
Richmond, Virginia

Minnie was the historian of the Elliott Grays Chapter of the United Daughters of the Confederacy in 1933. In April she also served as the general chairperson for arranging a musical and dramatic entertainment at the Soldier's Home. The Melodramatic Pageant of the War Between the States was the title of the production and the veterans of the home were the special guests of the chapter.[145]

She was listed on the census of 1940 in Richmond still living at 3115 Hull Street. The census listed Minorva J. Hooker, age 68 and widowed along with her daughter Dorcas G., age 34 and single.

Minnie served as president of the Fonticello Woman's Christian Temperance Union for 25 years and was elected president of the WCTU on 15 September 1938. She was also appointed as a delegate to the State Convention of the WCTU in 1938. She was active in the affairs of the Daughters of the American Revolution, the Daughters of

1812, and the Elliott Grays' Chapter of the United Daughters of the confederacy. She was a charter member of the Weathford Memorial Baptist Church.[146]

Minnie died on 25 February 1945 in Richmond, Virginia, at age 72 early in the day at her residence on Hull Street. Her cause of death was cerebral hemorrhage. Funeral services were held on 27 February 1945 at Weathford Memorial Baptist Church in Richmond, at 11:00 in the morning.[147] She was buried on 27 February 1945 at Maury Cemetery in Richmond, in the E.G. Hooker family plot next to her husband Edmond.[148]

Children of Minnie Jane Cottrell & Edmond Goodman Hooker:

- Raymond Cottrell Hooker – Born 21 May 1891 in Manchester, Chesterfield County, Virginia and died on 30 Jun 1970 in Richmond, Virginia at age 79 at 1:00 in the afternoon after having just phoned into the hospital. His cause of death was heart disease. He was buried on 30 June 1979 in Maury Cemetery in Richmond.[149] Raymond graduated in May 1912 from the Medical University of Virginia in Charlottesville, Virginia and served as a physician and surgeon in New York and later in Richmond.[150] He briefly served in the Medical

Esther Maud Cheatham

Corps of the Unites States Army serving first at Camp Greenleaf in Georgia in January 1918 and then at Camp Dix in New Jersey in April 1918. He married Esther Maud Cheatham, the daughter of William M. Cheatham and Sallie B. Lester, on 12 June 1918 in the home of Esther's parents outside Richmond.[151] They had at least four children including:

  o Two unnamed children died at birth, one in 1920 and the other in 1921.[152]

- o Raymond Cottrell Hooker Jr. - Born on 24 February 1925 in Richmond, married Mary Elizabeth Wilburn on 7 July 1951, and died on 31 January 1995 in Richmond. He was a veteran of World War II and served a two-year stint in the United States Navy during the war. He graduated from the Medical College of Virginia in 1953 and joined his father's medical practice and continued his father's practice until he retired in 1984.[153]
- o Esther Jane Hooker – Born 25 January 1929 in Richmond, married Thomas Peirson Stratford on 6 June 1953 and died 16 April 2012 at St. Mary's Hospital in Richmond. She graduated with honors from Meredith College in Raleigh, North Carolina in December 1943. She later attended the University of Pennsylvania Graduate School and taught 5th grade for several years.[154]

Esther Maude died on 16 June 1936 in her home in Richmond at age 42 from a cerebral hemorrhage. She was buried in Maury Cemetery in Richmond.[155] After Esther's death Raymond married Fannie Edna Beal, the daughter of Robert C. Nesbit and Margaret Ann Belk, on 9 August 1938. The ceremony was performed by Raymond's brother-in-law Dr. John L. Slaughter, the pastor of the First Baptist Church in Birmingham, at the Woodland Heights Baptist Church in Richmond.[156] Following the wedding Raymond and Fannie traveled to France for their honeymoon returning to the port of New York on the Aquitania from Cherborg, France on 13 September 1938. It was said that Dr. Hooker loved to practice medicine and that he worked all the time. He normally started his day at 6:00 in the morning and frequently didn't get back home until 2:00 in the morning. He ate all his meals at the office and had a cook upstairs. There were no children from this union. Fannie was born on 5 August 1902 in Union County, North Carolina and died on 5 March 1993 at Chapel Hill, Orange County, North Carolina at age 90. She was buried at Bethlehem United Methodist Church Cemetery in Union County, North Carolina.[157]

- Margaret Elizabeth Hooker – Born 2 Sep 1899 in Chesterfield County, Virginia and died in November 1976 in Boulder, Colorado at age 77. She was buried in the Fort Logan National Cemetery in Denver, Colorado.[158] Margaret attended and graduated from the Southern Baptist Theological Seminary in Louisville, Kentucky on 7 June 1922. This is likely where she met her future husband. She married John Lawrence Slaughter on 12 September 1923 in Richmond, Virginia. John was born on 28 August 1897 in Fannin in Rankin County, Mississippi. Her husband John was later called to ministry in the Baptist church in 1942.[159] Margaret's husband John died on 29 May 1979 in Boulder, Colorado at age 81 at his home after a brief illness. He was buried at Fort Logan National Cemetery, in Denver, Colorado with his wife Margaret.[160] They had at least two children including:

  o John L. Slaughter who was born on 22 September 1924, married Mary Ann Morris on 5 June 1948, and likely died in Florida.

  o Jane La Rogue Slaughter who was born on 7 July 1930 and married Firmon E. Hardenbergh in 1959. Jane died on 14 September 2009 in Alabama.[161] She was buried with her husband Firmon E. Hardenbergh in the Alabama National Cemetery in Montevallo in Shelby County, Alabama.[162]

Edmond Anderson Hooker
Maury Cemetery
Richmond, Virginia

  Jane and Firmon had at least four children including two daughters and two sons.

- Edmond Anderson Hooker – Born 20 February 1901 in Chesterfield County, Virginia and died 27 April 1989 in Richmond,

Virginia at age 88. He was buried in Maury Cemetery in Richmond, in the E.G. Hooker family plot.[163] He graduated from Richmond College with a Bachelor of Science degree on 11 June 1924 and was working as an office clerk in a manufacturing company in 1930 and as the Assistant Treasurer of Atlantic Life Insurance Company in 1942. He married Ernestine Cary Hatcher on 19 June 1937 in Richmond, Virginia.[164] The ceremony was performed by John L. Slaughter. Ernestine was born on 14 February 1900 in Surry County, North Carolina and died on 6 April 1997 in Richmond at age 97. She was the daughter of Ernest Selden Hatcher and Charlotte Elizabeth Dick. She was buried next to her husband in Maury Cemetery in Richmond.[165] Edmond served in the U.S. Navy from 5 October 1942 until he was released from the service on 10 March 1949. Number of children, if any, is unknown.

- Peter Cosby Hooker – Born 26 March 1903 in Chesterfield County, Virginia and died 12 April 1904 in Swansboro, Virginia in the home of his parents. Funeral services were held on 13 April 1904 at 11:00 in the morning at his parent's home. He was buried on 13 April 1904 in Maury Cemetery in Richmond.[166]

- Jane Halsey Hooker – Born 7 January 1907 in Chesterfield County, Virginia and died 24 February 1907 in Swansboro, Virginia at 11:00 in the morning at the home of her parents. Her funeral was held at her residence in Swansboro at 11:00 in the morning. She was buried on 26 February 1907 in Maury Cemetery.[167]

- Dorcas Goodman Hooker – Born 11 November 1908 in Chesterfield County, Virginia and died 1 February 1977 in Richmond, Virginia at age 68. She was buried in Forest Lawn Cemetery in Richmond.[168] In 1937 she traveled to Havana, Cuba returning to the port of New York on 15 July of the same year. In 1940 she was employed as a state highway department clerk. She married Albert William Herthel on 8 November 1947 at 11:00 in the morning in Wetherford Memorial Baptist

Church in Richmond, Virginia. Albert was born on 21 November 1895 in Floyd County, Indiana. He was the son of Willie L. and Nanie Herthel.[169] Dorcas was dressed in water-lily blue and carried a colonial bouquet of brides' roses and gardenias. She was given in marriage by her brother Dr. Raymond C. Hooker. Her sisters Es-

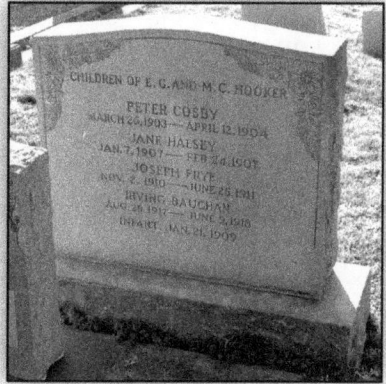

Hooker Children
Maury Cemetery
Richmond, Virginia

ter Jane and Helen served as attendants. They were dressed in flame taffeta and carried colonial bouquets of flame chrysanthemums and yellow roses. Winfrey Wade served as best man and Edmond Hooker and Richard Hargers were ushers. A wedding breakfast was held immediately following the wedding at the home of Dr. and Mrs. Hooker. Albert was employed by Reynolds Metals Company in Richmond in 1942 when he registered for the WWII Draft. He was living in Richmond at the time. Albert died on 18 November 1972 in the Eastern State Hospital in Richmond, at age 76. His cause of death was myocardial failure with arteriosclerotic heart disease. He was buried in Forest Lawn Cemetery in Richmond, Virginia. Number of children, if any, is unknown.

- Hooker - Born 21 January 1909 in Virginia and died 21 January 1909 in Richmond, Virginia. Unnamed child, unknown sex, likely a stillbirth. The child was buried in Maury Cemetery in Richmond, Virginia.[170]
- Joseph Frye Hooker – Born on 2 November 1910 in Richmond, Virginia and died on 25 Jun 1911 in Richmond in the evening at the residence of his parents at 3115 Hull Street. Funeral services were held on 26 June 1911 at 5:00 in the afternoon at the residence of his parents in Richmond. He was buried on 26 June 1911 in Maury Cemetery in Richmond.

- Irving Baughan Hooker – Born on 29 August 1917 in Richmond in Chesterfield County, Virginia and died on 9 June 1918 at 3:00 in the afternoon in Richmond, Virginia. His cause of death was acute utero-colitis. He was buried on 11 June 1918 in Maury Cemetery in Richmond.[171]

Joseph Frey Cottrell (1874-1908)

Son of Peter Cottrell and Mary Magdalene Cosby
Granduncle of Taylor Cosby Cottrell, Jr.

Joseph Frey Cottrell was born on 15 May 1874 in Yelvington, Daviess County, Kentucky. He was the son of Peter Cottrell and Mary Magdalene Cosby. Information on the Joseph Frey Cottrell Family, and Joseph's life-history, along with that for his wife Nellie Jane Lashbrook and their son is covered in Section 1, Chapter 3, Joseph Cottrell Family.[172]

Chapter 3 – Joseph Frey Cottrell Family

Great-grandfather of Taylor Cosby Cottrell, Jr.

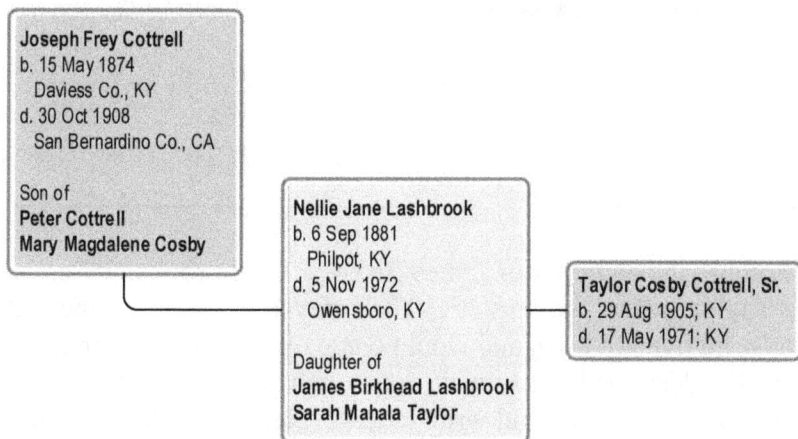

Joseph Frey Cottrell
b. 15 May 1874
   Daviess Co., KY
d. 30 Oct 1908
   San Bernardino Co., CA

Son of
Peter Cottrell
Mary Magdalene Cosby

Nellie Jane Lashbrook
b. 6 Sep 1881
   Philpot, KY
d. 5 Nov 1972
   Owensboro, KY

Daughter of
James Birkhead Lashbrook
Sarah Mahala Taylor

Taylor Cosby Cottrell, Sr.
b. 29 Aug 1905; KY
d. 17 May 1971; KY

Joseph Frey Cottrell was born on 15 May 1874 in Yelvington, Daviess County, Kentucky. He was the son of Peter Cottrell and Mary Magdalene Cosby.[1] He had at least six brothers and sisters, each of which is covered in detail in Section 1, Chapter 2, Peter Cottrell Family. Joe went to the home of Mr. and Mrs. John Tyler Harrison to live after the death of his father in 1878.[2] He was listed on the census of 1880 in Daviess County, Kentucky, enumerated on 16 June in the household of John T. Harrison as Joseph, age six and attending school.[3]

He graduated from the Western Normal School in

Joseph Frey Cottrell

1890. Joseph wrote his name as Joe F. Cottrell, Philpot, Kentucky along with the Date of May 4th, 1896 in his bible. He dated Nellie Jane

Joseph Frey Cottrell Family Timeline

| 1874 | 1884 | 1894 | 1904 | 1914 | 1924 | 1934 | 1944 | 1954 | 1964 | 1974 |

Joseph Frey Cottrell

Nellie Jane Lashbrook

Taylor Cosby Cottrell, Sr.

| 1874 | 1884 | 1894 | 1904 | 1914 | 1924 | 1934 | 1944 | 1954 | 1964 | 1974 |

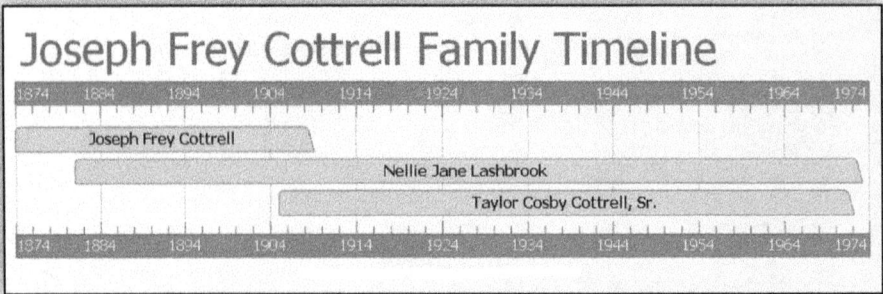

Lashbrook, the daughter of James Birkhead Lashbrook and Sarah Mahala Taylor, when she was 18. They stayed at home on these dates because he lived in town and would come out to her home on a bicycle that Nellie described as a bicycle that "wasn't built for two". He would call her over the phone and write letters. Nellie said this was "not too exciting, but romantic just the same."[4]

Joseph held membership in the Masons in Owensboro Kentucky.[5] He taught school in the fall and the winter and then went to Bowling Green to Western Teachers College until he graduated with a law degree. After graduation he practiced law in Owensboro, Kentucky. He studied law in the office of Miller & Todd in 1904 and was elected city prosecutor for Owensboro in 1905 on the Democratic ticket. The election of Joe caused the law firm of Cottrell & Kirk to dissolve after a partnership of about five years.[6]

A bond in the sum of $100 was signed on 6 September 1904 in Owensboro, Kentucky for the marriage of Joseph Frey Cottrell and Nellie Jane Lashbrook. The bond was signed by Joe F. Cottrell and James Weir, Jr. Joseph married Nellie on 6 September 1904 in Daviess County with the services conducted at home by the pastor of Macedonia Church, Rev. J.B. Hocker. Witnesses were Ambrose Taylor and Eulah Brooks.[7] Nellie had at least six brothers and sisters, each of which is covered in detail in Section 1, Chapter 7, James Lashbrook Family.

Around 1907 Joseph moved to New Mexico for his health. It is likely that he was already experiencing symptoms of tuberculosis. He was there approximately one month before Nellie and his one-year-old son Taylor joined him. They lived in a 4 room unfurnished house, except that the bedroom and kitchen were furnished. Nellie's doctor told her the high altitude was affecting her heart so they all returned to Kentucky after an additional seven week stay. During their time in Roswell Nellie said it snowed 18 inches. She said a prairie dog colony was located next door and on the other side of the property the only neighbor lived about a block away. Their neighbor loaned them a horse and buggy one Sunday and they drove out to an irrigation plant 20 miles away where Joseph killed a jack rabbit and shot a duck.

Joseph moved back west to Redlands California on 12 October 1908 and lived there for approximately three weeks until he moved into "The Settlement" where he remained until his death. The Settlement was a sanatorium camp that had been established in 1901 for needy consumptives in any stage of their disease of Tuberculosis. It was located on 40 acres of rolling land about three miles from Redlands at an elevation of 1500 feet. All patients lived in tents which contained ordinary conveniences. A wooden building with a dining-room, kitchen, store-room, and a bath was also located on the property along with a pavilion which served as an assembly and amusement room for the patients.[8]

Joseph died on 30 October 1908 at "The Settlement", in Redlands, San Bernardino County, California, at age 34 at 2:00 in the morning. His cause of death was Pulmonary Tuberculosis.[9]

Joseph was described as one of the best known and most highly respected citizens of Owensboro and a young man of sterling character and a fearless and efficient officer of the law in an article published in an Owensboro newspaper on 31 October 1908 following his Death. The article was titled "Was Loved Official - Resolutions Adopted upon Death of Joe F. Cottrell." The article stated "Whereas, a telegram having been received announcing the death of Joseph F. Cottrell, who departed this life on October 30th, 1908, whose death, we sincerely mourn, therefore, be it,

Resolved-First, that he was a true, faithful and loved official of our city, whose death has brought upon us a sorrow and sadness which will scarcely be removed during our short space of life.

But we are comforted with a well-grounded hope that in life eternal he will receive that welcome plaudit of 'Well done thou good and faithful servant, enter into the joy of their God.'

Resolved-Second. That in the death of Joseph Cottrell, the city loses a worthy official and true Christian, and his wife and son a kind and generous husband and father.

Resolved-Third. That the sympathy of the police force and court officials be extended to his family, and we commend them to Him, the Great Comforter, who will reunite them when the 'Son of Righteousness cometh from over the Seas.'

Resolved-Fourth. That a copy of these resolutions be spread on the police court docket and a copy be furnished the family, and the same be published in the two daily papers.

Committee-Judge Yewell Haskins, George P. Meisenheimer, Thomas L. Ellis, R.P. Thornberry."[10]

The City Council of Owensboro met on 3 November 1908 and elected Martin Yewell to succeed Joe Cottrell as City Prosecutor.[11]

Joseph's body was shipped from Redlands California to Owensboro Kentucky on 3 November 1908 and arrived in Owensboro in the evening of the 7th of November on the Illinois Central Railroad. His brothers Charles and Melvin accompanied his body on the train. After arrival in Owensboro his body was taken to his late residence on Daviess Street.[12]

Funeral services were held on 9 November 1908 in the afternoon at his residence in Owensboro. The funeral was "very largely attended by the many friends of the deceased." He was buried by the side of his Father, Peter Cottrell in

Joseph Frey Cottrell
Elmwood Cemetery
Owensboro, Kentucky

Section 2 of the Elmwood Cemetery in Owensboro on 9 November 1908.[13]

Nellie Jane Lashbrook (1881-1972)

Wife of Joseph Frey Cottrell
Grandmother of Taylor Cosby Cottrell, Jr.

Nellie Jane Lashbrook

Nellie Jane Lash-brook was born on 6 September 1881 in Phil-pot, Daviess County, Kentucky. She was the daughter of James Birk-head Lashbrook and Sarah Mahala Taylor.[14] She had at least six broth-ers and sisters, each of which is covered in detail in Section 1, Chapter 7, James Birkhead Lash-brook Family. When Nellie was two years old she found some beans and put one in her nose, then climbed on a gate and called to her mother to tell her what she had done. Her mother tried to get the bean out, but was unable. Later, in the night she took Nellie to a doctor in Masonville where the bean was removed. This was a story she told often and in her telling it was obvious it was one of her fond memories of childhood.[15]

Her first move came in 1884 when she was 3 years old. She re-membered it being night when they got to their new home near Macedonia Baptist Church in Daviess County, Kentucky along with their cows, horses, pigs, chickens, dog, cat, and furniture. She said everything seemed out of place and she cried to go home.[16]

Nellie's closest friend growing up was Virginia, who was the youngest daughter of one of the sisters of her mother Sara. They lived on a joining farm and Virginia and Nellie were "almost inseparable".

There was a red gate between their farms where they met when they couldn't go to each other's houses. They would climb up on the fence and "give this call A-WEE, A-WEE, A-WEE-O, A-WEE, A-WEE, IVY-I-O."[17]

When Nellie was 7 years old she had a pet lamb called Jo. The lamb was spurned by his mother and was supposed to be a runt. Nellie got a kick out of watching the lamb drink out of his bottle. The faster he drink out of his bottle, the faster his tail would shake. He grew until she had to feed him thru the fence to keep him from butting her down. Later they took him to the market and sold him.[18]

While remembering her childhood Nellie said "winter would come and we had big fire in the fireplace and popcorn. Our legs would get too hot, and our back too cold and when the fire got too low, fresh wood would be put on and, if there was snow it would almost put the fire out, and we'd be cold again, pretty soon there was a nice fire and then we'd be warm and off to bed we would go, no fire in room, but under tons of quilts and blankets and we could see our breath, and have cold noses."[19]

When Nellie was 8 years old they had a hired hand that apparently had epileptic fits and spells. One night he went "round and round" and would have fallen on Nellie except her father and brother, Taylor caught him. She was scared because he was shaking all over and frothed at the mouth. Nellie's brother Leon didn't seem to like playing with his brother Forman and Nellie together, so she gave him her glass slipper to play with.[20]

Their buggy horse was a big sorrel named John Henry. He was a very gentle horse. When Nellie was 9 years old her father bought a new horse that was rawboned, had a long neck, and was also supposed to be gentle. Nellie decided to ride him to Dermott after the mail about a mile away. Her trip was successful until they got thru the lot gate on returning home and the horse saw the stall door. He made a "bee line" and she had to grab the top of the barn door and let the horse go into the barn to keep from being bumped off.[21]

Nellie was baptized around 1892 in Dermott, Daviess County, Kentucky, in a big pond.

When Nellie and her friend Virginia were 12 years old Virginia's mother, who Nellie called Aunt Sis, died. Virginia had 5 brothers and an older sister Lizzie. Virginia and Nellie corresponded for many years and remained close friends. They spent many hours together playing games of the times. Nellie recalled that one night she spent the night with Virginia and they tried some of the old time sayings, one was to boil eggs, cut them into halves, take out the yolk, fill the white half with salt, eat it, get into bed backwards, and not say a word to anyone or take a drink of water. She recalled that just as they got into bed it begun to rain real hard and since they couldn't say a word she whistled which got them tickled and they almost convulsed in laughter. She said of course that much salt and no water and they "naturally dreamed of it and whenever they dreamed they dreamed of a boy giving them a drink." She dreamed that night of being at one end of a long porch and could see a man at the other end with a bucket of water and a small dipper, but couldn't make out who he was, for as she walked toward him he moved away.[22]

Nellie's family raised turkeys. One of her household duties when she was 14 was to find the turkey's nests. She would hide behind bushes to watch for them because if they saw her "they would go in another direction."

Sarah Mahala Taylor
Nellie Jane Lashbrook

She was thrown from a horse while taking sewing supplies to her mother to make burial clothes for a neighbor's child who had died just after birth. The fall broke her ankle. She was unable to put weight on the foot for 6 weeks. During the time she was laid up she "made a lifelong friend", Joseph Cottrell. She said he was "the only sweetheart I ever had."[23]

Nellie was ill with typhoid in 1899 before she turned 18 in September. While she was near death from Typhoid, lightning from a severe electrical storm struck a wire fence near her home and she received a shock from the strike. The Doctor thought she was passing away because she could not speak due to the effects of the lightning but she "knew what they were saying". After that she said she started to get better.[24]

Nellie dated Joseph Cottrell when she was 18. They stayed at home on these dates because he lived in town and would come out on a bicycle that she described as "wasn't built for two". He would call her over the phone and write letters. Nellie said this was "not too exciting, but romantic just the same."[25] She was listed on the census of 1900 in the household of her father, James Birkhead Lashbrook in Daviess County, Kentucky, as age 18 and in school.[26]

Nellie married Joseph, son of Peter Cottrell and Mary Magdalene Cosby, on 6 September 1904 in Daviess County, Kentucky with the services conducted at home by the pastor of Macedonia Church, Rev. J.B. Hocker. Witnesses were Ambrose Taylor and Eulah Brooks.[27]

Nellie and Joseph lived in Roswell, Chaves County, New Mexico around 1907, in a 4 room unfurnished house, except that the bedroom and kitchen were furnished. Joseph had moved to New Mexico around 1907 for his health, likely because he was suffering from tuberculosis. He was there approximately one month before Nellie and their one-year-old son Taylor joined him. Nellie's doctor told her the high altitude was affecting her heart so they all returned to Kentucky after an additional 7 week stay.

When Nellie traveled to New Mexico with her son Taylor they traveled by train. The trip took 4 days. They missed their train in Oklahoma City, Oklahoma and had to spend a night there. During her seven week stay in Roswell she said it snowed 18 inches. A prairie dog colony was located next door and on the other side the only neighbor lived about a block away. The neighbor loaned Nellie and her husband her horse and buggy one Sunday and they drove out to the irrigation plant 20 miles away. While there her husband Joseph killed a jack rabbit and shot one duck.[28]

Joseph moved back west to Redlands, California on 12 October 1908 and lived there until he moved into "The Settlement", a sanatorium camp for people suffering from tuberculosis, where he died on 30 October 1908.[29] Nellie lived with her mother Sarah Mahala Lashbrook on Miller Mill Road in Daviess County, Kentucky after the death of her husband.

She was listed on the census of 1910 in the household of her mother, Sarah in Daviess County, Kentucky, as age 28 along with her son Taylor C. Cottrell, age 4.[30] She was listed on the census of 1920 as a clothes maker and head of the household, age 38, and widowed. She owned her own home free of mortgage and was living with her son, Taylor C. Cottrell, age 14 who was attending school. The Whittinghill family, father, mother, and three children, were listed as renters in her home.[31]

Nellie received a telegram announcing the birth of her granddaughter Jo Anne Cottrell on 16 July 1928 from her son T.C. Cottrell, Sr. He asked her to "send bed at once" in the telegram. Her answer was written on the face of the telegram. It read "Congratulations. Heart full of love. Shipping bed today. Mother."[32]

She was listed on the 1830 census as living with her mother Sarah at 571 Saint Ann Street as Nellie Jane Cottrell, age 40 and widowed.[33]

Nellie lived with her brother Dudley Lashbrook in Russellville, Kentucky after his wife Sallie died. She took care of Dudley's daughter and was later appointed her guardian around 1934 and apparently served as her guardian until Dudley married Sophie Herman. Nellie was still living in Russellville in 1935. In 1936 she started collecting and dressing antique dolls. She designed and made clothes for many of the dolls, some of which dated back to the late Century. The clothing was meticulously made to match their time period, even down to the laced shoes.[34]

In 1936 Nellie lived in Bowling Green, Kentucky, in a house she bought from Mrs. W.A. Lee for $6,500. The deed indicated that payment of $1,000 in cash was paid at the time of signing and that the remainder was due in four promissory notes with the first payment of $500 being due in 1937, the second and third payments of $1,000 being due in 1938 and 1939, and the fourth payment of $3,000 being due on or before 12 December 1940.[35]

Nellie was issued what is believed to be her last Kentucky Driver's License in July of 1937. It remained valid until 31 July 1938. She was listed on the 1940 census as Nellie Cottrell, age 58 and widowed and living at 1530 State Street.[36]

Nellie's talent in designing and making clothes for period dolls and, if needed, restoring their bodies, was mentioned in an article in the Park City Daily News, a local Bowling Green newspaper, on 10 September 1950. The article indicated she had been doing this type work for years. Around 1951 Nellie started whittling wooden dolls while she was confined to the bed with a broken leg. This hobby continued until she was no longer able to whittle due to her age and health, around 1970.[37]

On 27 August 1961 an article was published in the local newspaper describing Nellie's hobby of whittling and dressing dolls. Her doll collection was also featured in the article. Among the collection were many wooden dolls which she had

Carved Wooden Doll – Named Wyatt Earp
Designed, carved, & dressed by Nellie Cottrell
Painted by Zalame Cottrell

made and dressed as well as a large collection of china dolls. She dressed these dolls from the "skin out", and if they had stuffed bodies even included a corset for support like they would have worn during the period they were from.[38]

In early 1971 the heirs of Foreman K. Lashbrook, Nellie's brother, transferred ownership of a portion of Lot 16, Section I in Elmwood Cemetery, Owensboro, Kentucky to Nellie. The Ownership transfer was signed by James Small Lashbrook, Frances Small Lashbrook, Jessie Small Lashbrook, and Margaret R. Lashbrook, wife of James S. Lashbrook.[39]

Nellie's health declined after she fell and broke her hip. After a short hospital stay she was moved to a local Nursing Home in Bowling Green, Kentucky where she remained until after her son Taylor Cosby Cottrell's death in 1971. In 1972 she was moved to a nursing home in Fordsville in Ohio County, Kentucky where she remained until her death later in the year. Her health continued to decline and she never fully recovered after breaking her hip.

She was taken to the Daviess County Hospital in Owensboro for treatment for Pneumonia and died in the Owensboro Daviess County Hospital, at age 91 at 3:20 in the afternoon on 5 November 1972. Her cause of death was listed as Pneumonia as the primary cause with Debilitation from Parkinson's and Congestive Heart Failure as secondary causes.[40]

Nellie Jane Lashbrook
Elmwood Cemetery
Owensboro, Kentucky

Funeral services were held on 7 November 1972 at Elmwood Cemetery in Owensboro, at 1:00 in the afternoon with graveside arrangements handled by Glenn Funeral Home and the graveside service with Rev. Jerry Oakley officiating. Her Grandson, TC Cottrell, was unable to attend her funeral because he was stationed overseas and flying combat missions in support of the Vietnam War at the time. Nellie was buried in Elmwood Cemetery in Owensboro in Section I, Lot 16, in the Lashbrook Family Plot.[41]

Zalame Cottrell, Nellie's daughter-in-law, purchased a marker on 2 October 1973 to match the marker of Nellie's brother Foreman K. Lashbrook. The marker was placed on her grave on the first anniversary of her death.[42]

Taylor Cosby Cottrell, Sr. (1905-1971)

Son of Joseph Frey Cottrell and Nellie Jane Lashbrook
Father of Taylor Cosby Cottrell, Jr.

Taylor Cosby Cottrell, Sr. was born on 29 August 1905 in Dermott, Daviess County, Kentucky. He was the son of Joseph Frey Cottrell and Nellie Jane Lashbrook.[43] Information on the Taylor Cosby Cottrell, Sr. Family, and Taylor's life-history, along with that for his wife Della Zoleme Campbell and their two children is covered in detail in Section 1, Chapter 4, Taylor Cosby Cottrell, Sr. Family.

Chapter 4 – Taylor Cosby Cottrell, Sr. Family

Father of Taylor Cosby Cottrell, Jr.

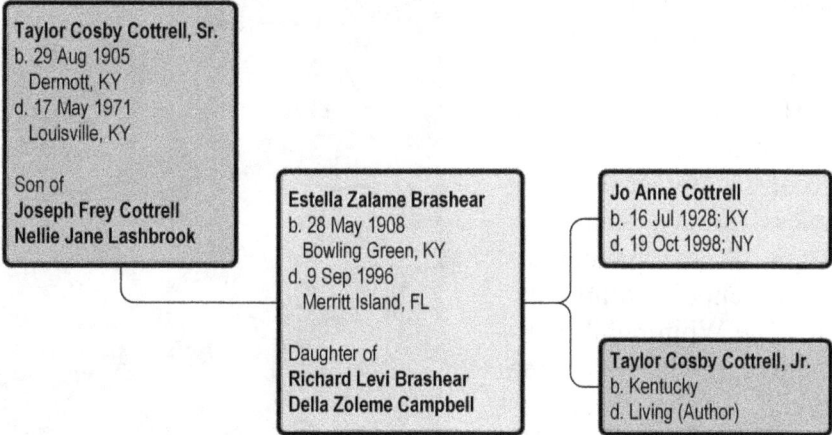

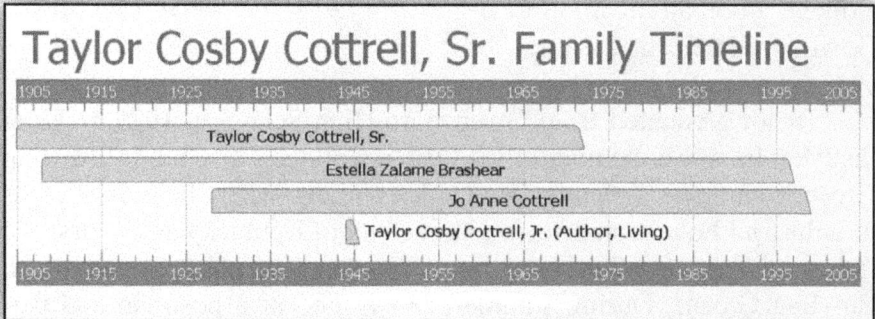

Taylor Cosby Cottrell, Sr.
b. 29 Aug 1905
 Dermott, KY
d. 17 May 1971
 Louisville, KY

Son of
Joseph Frey Cottrell
Nellie Jane Lashbrook

Estella Zalame Brashear
b. 28 May 1908
 Bowling Green, KY
d. 9 Sep 1996
 Merritt Island, FL

Daughter of
Richard Levi Brashear
Della Zoleme Campbell

Jo Anne Cottrell
b. 16 Jul 1928; KY
d. 19 Oct 1998; NY

Taylor Cosby Cottrell, Jr.
b. Kentucky
d. Living (Author)

Taylor Cosby Cottrell, Sr. Family Timeline

| 1905 | 1915 | 1925 | 1935 | 1945 | 1955 | 1965 | 1975 | 1985 | 1995 | 2005 |

Taylor Cosby Cottrell, Sr.

Estella Zalame Brashear

Jo Anne Cottrell

Taylor Cosby Cottrell, Jr. (Author, Living)

| 1905 | 1915 | 1925 | 1935 | 1945 | 1955 | 1965 | 1975 | 1985 | 1995 | 2005 |

Taylor Cosby Cottrell Sr. was born on 29 August 1905 in Dermott, Daviess County, Kentucky; a small town located about five miles from Owensboro.[1]   He was born at home in the same bed in which his mother Nellie Jane had been born in 1881.[2] Taylor was the son of Joseph Frey Cottrell and Nellie Jane Lashbrook.[3]

In 1906 Taylor lived with his father and mother in Roswell in Chaves County, New Mexico for about 7 weeks until moving back to Kentucky with his mother.[4] He attended grade school near Owensboro in Daviess County, Kentucky and was living with his grandmother and mother on Miller Mill Road in Daviess County, Kentucky on 20 April

1910 when he was listed on the census in the household of his grandmother, Sarah Mahala Lashbrook as Taylor, age 4 along with his mother Nellie Cottrell.[5]

He was listed on the 1920 census in the household of his mother Nellie in Daviess County, Kentucky, as age 14 and having attended school within the year. The Whittinghill family, father, mother, and three children, were listed as renters in their home.[6] He was a member of the Ogden College football team in Bowling Green that same year.[7]

Taylor Cosby Cottrell, Sr.

Taylor graduated from Owensboro High School in 1923.[8] Later that year he was a member of the Ogden College "Y" Club in Bowling Green, Kentucky.[9] He attended Ogden College where he took courses in Industrial Education from the University of Kentucky and courses in Industrial Arts and Teaching from Western Kentucky University in Bowling Green. During summers he worked as a postman and part time in garages.[10]

He was a member of Ogden College's Triangle Club in 1924 and was also a member of the Order of DeMolay, Commandery Number 23 on 21 January 1926.[11]

Taylor married Estella Zalame Brashear, daughter of Richard Levi Brashear and Della Zoleme Campbell, on 16 April 1927 in Gallatin, Sumner County, Tennessee. The ceremony was performed by J.W. McCormach, Justice of the Peace.[12] In June 1927 he and his wife Zalame lived in Kyrock in Edmondson County, Kentucky where he was employed by the Old Kentucky Rock Asphalt Company as Chief Chemist.[13] The asphalt mined and prepared by the Old Kentucky Rock Asphalt Company was stored in and distributed from Bowling Green.

The asphalt was also known as Kyrock and was manufactured from the mid-1920s through the late 1950s. It was used in over half of the states in the U.S. and in a number of foreign countries to surface highways, airport runways, warehouse floors, and tennis courts.[14]

Shortly after moving to Kyrock Taylor, by then known as T.C., and his wife Zalame made their first craft project together. He started making pieces of furniture from empty dynamite powder boxes and Zalame painted them and then painted original designs on them. Their projects and designs were later featured in American Home Magazine, a national publication that featured articles about homes, home decorating, and frequently included instructions for creating craft and art objects for the home.[15]

T.C. sent a telegram to his mother on 16 July 1928 to announce the birth of her granddaughter Jo Anne Cottrell. He asked his mother to "send bed at once". Her answer was written on the face of the telegram and read "Congratulations. Heart full of love. Shipping bed today. Mother."[16]

In the fall of 1929 T.C. was employed by the DuPont Company in Old Hickory Tennessee. After starting work for DuPont, T.C. and Zalame initially lived in a one room location with a kitchen for Joanna's milk. They later rented a house and rented one sleeping room in the house to the Deputy Sheriff and then later to a couple from Kyrock with whom they shared food. DuPont built additional houses for employees and they got one and rented one of the bedrooms to Doug Smith who was from Bowling Green.[17]

T.C. was an operator at a cellophane plant on 16 April 1930.[18] He was listed on 1930 census in Davidson County, Tennessee, enumerated on 16 April 1930, as Taylor C., age 24, head of household, and renting a home at 404 Hadley Avenue in Old Hickory, Tennessee with a value of $15,000. His wife Zalame, age 22 and his daughter Jo Anne, age 1 year, 9 months were also listed. Four lodgers were also living in the home.[19]

Later in 1930 he moved to the DuPont facilities in Richmond Virginia and helped start the new DuPont Spruance Cellophane Plant outside Richmond. The plant was named in honor of rayon pioneer William Spruance. The plant initially produced cellophane and later Cordura rayon and during World War II expanded to a wartime peak of over 4,000 workers at the Spruance site.[20]

TC and Zalame lived on 49th Street in Richmond in a rented house until the owner went bankrupt in the spring of 1931. Later that year they lived on Petersburg Turnpike in Petersburg, Virginia in a cottage near the DuPont Plant and then in a large house in Petersburg with the cottage owner's Mother, Mrs. Davis, and according to Zalame, a ghost. She frequently related stories of waking in the middle of the night and finding what appeared to be a Civil War Soldier standing at the foot of their bed. In the fall they lived on Forest Hill Avenue in Richmond in a downstairs apartment.[21]

In 1934 T.C. moved his family to Russellville Kentucky because of health issues and because Dudley Lashbrook, his mother's brother, wanted T.C. to manage the shop in his Ford Agency. T.C. only weighed 138 pounds at the time. T.C. and Zalame initially lived rent free in the old Price Home in Russellville Kentucky. They had the whole down stairs apartment and had a maid and cook so Zalame could work at the Ford Agency. Dudley later sold the home and they rented a house in Russellville.[22]

In 1936 he was employed by the Louisville Kentucky Service Division of Ford Motor Company

LASHBROOK MOTOR CO.
RUSSELLVILLE, KY.

TOURING	$436.28
RUNABOUT	415.80
COUPE	569.50
TUDOR	577.75
FORDOR	629.32
T-CHASSIS	346.50
RUNABOUT, with P-U Body	436.28
* * * * * * * * * * *	
TRUCK	$371.50
TRUCK, with body	429.50
TRUCK, with platform body	424.50
TRUCK, with stake body	441.00
TRUCK, with closed cab	458.10
TRUCK, with closed cab and body	515.80
TRUCK, with closed cab and platform body	511.10
TRUCK, with closed cab and stake body	527.60
STARTER ON TRUCK—ADD	$ 50.00

Sales Card
Lashbrook Motor Company
Circa 1934

as a traveling Service Representative and then Mechanic Instructor for locations covering Kentucky, Tennessee, and Indiana.[23] In 1938 he worked for the Ford Agency in Murfreesboro in Rutherford County, Tennessee. He and Zalame were living in Murfreesboro at the time.[24]

In 1939 they were living at 1530 State Street in Bowling Green, Kentucky and T.C. was working as an instructor at Western Trade School in Bowling Green. Western Trade School had been established the same year and T.C. was one of the initial instructors. Later that year he bought a part ownership in the Taylor Ford Dealership, part of the Elkton Motor Company, in Eklton, Kentucky. Zalame went back to live with his mother while T.C. was in Eklton. According to Zalame, in the spring of 1940 T.C. told her that she and Jo Anne had to come to Elkton and that she had to do the bookkeeping at the dealership and if she would not come, he was thru.[25]

While in Elkton they lived in a house owned by Jefferson Taylor Lashbrook, a brother of T.C.'s mother. After moving into Jefferson's house they had their furniture and antiques that had been in storage in Louisville moved into the house.[26] T.C. was a part owner and mechanic in a garage in May 1940 and

Taylor Cosby Cottrell, Sr.		
1910	Daviess County, KY	N/A
1920	Daviess County, KY	Student
1930	Davidson County, TN	Cellophane Plant Operator
1940	Todd County, KY	Garage Mechanic

was listed on the 1940 census in the household of Jefferson Taylor Lashbrook in Todd County, Kentucky, as T.C. Cottrell, nephew, age 34.[27]

By 1940 T.C. had become interested in a new mechanical field, that of aircraft repair and maintenance. In 1941 he moved to Outlaw Field in Clarksville Tennessee and worked long hours and studied at night to acquire both aircraft mechanic and engine mechanic ratings. He became manager of the Gill-Dove Airport where he was in charge of the maintenance and hangers as well as the over-all supervision of the airport. He was also a deputy sheriff at the time and carried a gun to protect the airfield.[28]

In 1941 T.C. was 5 foot 11 and one half inches tall, weighed 185 pounds, and had gray hair.[29] He was awarded an Airman Certificate granting him Ratings of Aircraft Engines Mechanic and Aircraft Mechanic in December 1941 in Elkton, Todd County, Kentucky.[30] In 1942 he was employed by Embry-Riddle in Union City, Obion County, Tennessee.[31]

In August that year they lived in Martin, Weakley County, Tennessee where they initially slept on the floor in the office at the airport until they found a two-bedroom apartment. After an attack of bed bugs, they moved into the home of a local widow that was recommended by a banker. Zalame said the woman was "really cracked."[32] T.C. was awarded a Ground Instructor Certificate granting him Ratings of Engines and Aircraft in August 1942.[33]

T.C. began military service on 3 August 1943 at Camp Forrest, Franklin County, Tennessee, as a Private in the Enlisted Reserve Corps of the Army as a Flying Instructor.[34] T.C. and Zalame lived in Union City in Obion County, Tennessee on 3 August 1943 where he became the Director of the Ground School on 1 October 1943 at the 67th AAF Flying Training Detachment; Army Air Forces contract Pilot School.[35] T.C. received a letter of commendation from Major Parsons in October 1943 for "outstanding improvement in ground school operation during the past several months". The commendation further cited that under his leadership the ground school had achieved the number one position in the entire Army Air Forces Eastern Flying Training Command.[36] He ended military service on 19 April 1944 and was released from the 67th AAF Flying Training Detachment, Union City, Tennessee and from duties as the Director of their Ground School on 19 Apr 1944, concurrent with his separation from the Army.[37]

Cottrell Family Home – Circa 1960
1530 State Street, Bowling Green, Kentucky

In April 1944 T.C. and Zalame were living in the Antilla Hotel in Coral Gables in Miami-Dade County, Florida where they remained during portions of April and May while waiting for the Embry Riddle Air Training School to get organized.[38] In May of 1944 gasoline rations were requested by T.C.'s employer so he could return his family to Kentucky from Miami because the doctor had recommended Zalame return home due to illness and because they he had been unable to obtain housing at a rate they could afford particularly since they had a daughter and Zalame was expecting another child soon.[39] Later in 1944 TC was employed by the Blue Grass Airlines as the Supervisor of Maintenance until the company went out of business. They also had maintenance shops in Ashland and Paducah Kentucky and after May 1944 at the Warren County Airport in Bowling Green, Kentucky.[40] By 1946 Bluegrass

Airlines was providing statewide service with links to seven cities with regularly scheduled weekday flights. The airline was logging over 900 miles daily. They attributed their initial success to progressive maintenance.

On 8 April 1945 T.C. was confirmed in the Episcopal Church at Christ Episcopal Church, Bowling Green, Kentucky.[41] He was again employed by Western Trade School in Bowling Green as an Automotive Instructor in Early 1946. An article published in the Kentucky Vocational School News in 1949 praised T.C. for his dedication to his job as a Master Mechanic Teacher and stated that "T.C. contacts all the garage owners and managers in the vicinity of Bowling Green to place his students and when he places them - they stick! Lately, garage-men have been placing orders with him...This keeps the automotive department of the school on its toes to see who will be the next student to be placed on the job, for each boy is only referred to employment after T.C. says the student is ready."[42]

Zalame and T.C. produced and sold tin and wood items starting in 1950. T.C. made lamps from oil cans and crafted tin shades for the lamps and then wired them. Zalame painted the lamps. T.C. even made an air compressor from a water tank and a refrigerator motor so Zalame could use air spray paint when she painted a background on the articles they made.[43] T.C. had a workshop in the basement of his home where he created both wood and tin items using available material like tin from food containers and wood from cigar boxes. Many of

Napkin Box
Made from cigar box wood by TC Cottrell
Design created and painted by Zalame Cottrell

their joint projects were featured in The American Home magazine starting as early as 1950.[44]

In July of 1951, T.C. was appointed as a Lay Reader in the Episcopal Church in Bowling Green and Russellville under the supervision of the Reverend Hugh C. McKee, Jr. by Bishop Charles Clingman of Kentucky. The period of service for this appointment extended for one year until 8 July 1952. In 1952 he was employed by Bowling Green Manufacturing Company as Chief Inspector of Plant II.[45] In November of 1952, he was re-appointed as a Lay Reader in Christ Church for a period extending until 12 November 1953.[46]

T.C. left a will in 1952, leaving his estate to his wife Zalame B. Cottrell and appointing her as the Executrix of his estate and guardian of his infant child Taylor Cosby Cottrell, Jr. The will appointed his daughter Jo Anne Cottrell to serve as both Executrix and guardian in the event his wife failed to qualify.[47] He was also named in the will of his wife on the same date where she left her estate to her husband and designated him as the Guardian for her infant son. Her will also designated her daughter to serve in both capacities in the event her husband was unable or subsequently died.[48]

T.C. completed a course in Modern Business Practice offered by the Department of Business and Government through the Community College Division on 12 December 1961 at Western Kentucky State College in Bowling Green, Kentucky.[49]

T.C. spent many hours in the basement of their home creating woodwork projects and taught his son to use both power and hand tools for both woodwork and metalwork. They both became interested in Amateur Radio in the 1960s and both secured General Class Amateur Radio Licenses. T.C.'s call sign was WA4OPS (Old Pipe Smoker) and his son Taylor's was WA4FLF (Frisky Little Fellow). T.C. was a member of the Kentucky Colonels Amateur Radio Club in Bowling Green and served as president of the club in the early 1960s. In later years they spent many hours communicating through this medium after T.C.'s son joined the Air Force following graduation from college.[50]

T.C. was promoted to Quality Manager in April 1964 and in his new duties covered both Bowling Green Manufacturing Company plants.[51] He continued to hold membership in Vesper Lodge Number 71 in Elkton, Kentucky as a Master Mason and apparently maintained his membership in this lodge even after he had permanently moved to Bowling Green.[52] T.C. retired from Bowling Green Manufacturing Company on the 1st of January 1971.[53] On the 14th he was hired as a consultant for Colt Industries, Holley Carburetor Division under the direction of Art Zaske.[54]

In May of 1971, he visited his daughter Joanna in New York City while on a business trip to New Jersey. He left on Tuesday, the 11th, after only one day of retirement, and returned on Friday the 14th. This was the last time he saw or talked to Joanna before his death. He called his son Taylor before leaving and again just after he returned on Friday. During this second phone call he talked about what fun he had with Joanna and how they had bonded for the first time in years. This had been a special time for them both.[55]

T.C. died on 17 May 1971 in Louisville, Jefferson County, Kentucky, at age 65.[56] He was pronounced DOA at St. Joseph Infirmary in Louisville. The death was certified at 8:55 in the morning. He was on a business trip to

Gold-plated pocket watch with Mason Emblem
Carried by TC Cottrell for many years

New York and had a heart attack at Standifield Airport.[57] His cause of death was cardio pulmonary arrest. Funeral services were held on 19 May 1971 at Christ Episcopal Church in Bowling Green, Warren County, Kentucky, at 10:00 in the morning with Rev. Howard Surface officiating. Family attending the funeral included his mother Nellie Jane Lashbrook Cottrell, his wife Zalame Brashear Cottrell, his daughter JoAnne Cottrell, his son Taylor Cosby Cottrell, Jr., and his wife, and their son, T.C.'s only grandchild. Pall Bearers included Harold Evans, Robert Westerfield, Jack Hawkins, Marvin Smeathers, Larry Kries, Jim Jones, Delton Duke, and Ralph Holman. Over 160 friends and relatives signed the funeral book. There were 40 flower arrangements and over 45 people from the Warren County Plant of Holly Carburetor donated to a memorial fund to the Kentucky Heart Association in T.C.'s name.[58]

A close friend of his son wrote a touching poem in memory of T.C.'s life. The poem read:

In Memoriam T.C. Cottrell, Sr.

The briefcase sits in the corner empty now of any documents of worries of business full of memories of past deals and speculated pay raises and promotions.

The chair lounges by the radio set whose mike will no more feel his hand nor hear his mouth voice NATO phonetics calling others miles away to the fraternity of man.

The dining table has one less setting one less chair for the cat to scratch more room for the guests to sit more pain and less joy for the remaining diners.

The double bed cries out in desire for the other body to crush its springs in peaceful sleep beside his mate who soaks her pillow with so many tears of mourning caused by his going.

The family and friends weep silently yet loudly at his sudden demise at the loss of him, of his step over the threshold, of his voice of love and parental advice and understanding.[59]

TC was buried on 19 May 1971 in Fairview Cemetery in Bowling Green, Warren County, Kentucky at 11:30 in the morning with Gerard-Bradley Funeral Chapel in charge of arrangements.[60] Taylor C. Cottrell, Sr., WA4OPS, was listed in the "Silent Keys" area of the August 1971 issue of QSL, an Amateur Radio Magazine.[61]

Taylor Cosby Cottrell
Fairview Cemetery
Bowling Green, Kentucky

Estella Zalame Brashear (1908-1996)

Wife of Taylor Cosby Cottrell, Sr.
Mother of Taylor Cosby Cottrell, Jr.

Estella Zalame Brashear was born on 28 May 1908 in Bowling Green, Warren County, Kentucky. She was the daughter of Richard Levi Brashear and Della Zoleme Campbell.[62] She had three brothers and sisters, each of which are covered in detail in Section 2, Chapter 3, Richard Levi Brashear Family.

Zalame appeared on the census of 1910 in the household of her father, Richard Levi Brashear in Warren County, Kentucky, as Zaleam, age one year and four months and attending school.[63] She was listed on the 1920 census in the household of her mother, Della Zoleme Brashear in Warren County, Kentucky, as Zalame, age 11, at home and attending school.[64]

Estella Zalame Brashear

In 1923 she completed Business Writing using the Zaner Method of Arm Movement at Bowling Green Public Schools in Warren County, Kentucky.[65] She was baptized on 19 April 1924 at Christ Episcopal Church in Bowling Green on Easter evening by Rev. W. Elliston Cole. Witnesses were her mother Della and sister Kathleen.[66]

Her Bowling Green High School Attendance Report when she was 15 showed she was absent twice during the year and tardy seven times. She received an A in all subjects except for Deportment and Ancient History in which she received a B in each.[67]

She was confirmed in Christ Episcopal Church on 26 October 1924 in Bowling Green, by Bishop Charles E. Woodcock.[68]

Zalame completed the Leslie Method of Writing Penmanship in 1925 at South-Western Publishing Company in Cincinnati, Hamilton

County, Ohio. Although the certificate issued by South-Western Publishing Company was issued in Ohio, it is probable that Zalame actually
took this course by correspondence.[69]   Her Bowling Green High
School Attendance Report at age 17 showed she was absent four times
during the year and tardy 77 times, which was more than half the days
in the year. She received an A in two subjects, a B in two, and a C in
the remaining two. She completed a penmanship course in August
1926 at Bowling Green Business University in Bowling Green, Kentucky.[70]

Zalame married Taylor Cosby Cottrell Sr., son of Joseph Frey Cot-
trell and Nellie Jane Lashbrook, on 16 April 1927 in Gallatin, Sumner
County, Tennessee with the ceremony performed by J.W. McCormach,
Justice of the Peace.[71]

She graduated on 30 May 1927 from Bowling Green High School
with a High School Diploma and was then employed as a student
teacher at the Bowling Green Business University in September the
same year.[72]

She and her husband T.C. moved to Kyrock, Kentucky around
1927. Shortly after moving there they made their first craft project together when T.C. made pieces of furniture from empty dynamite power
boxes and Zalame painted them and then painted original designs on
them.[73]

After starting work for the DuPont Company in late 1929 T.C. and
Zalame initially lived in a one room location that had a kitchen for Joanna's milk. They later rented a house and rented one sleeping room to
the Deputy Sheriff and then later to a couple from Kyrock and shared
food. DuPont built more houses for employees and they got one and
rented one bedroom to Doug Smith from Bowling Green.[74]

Zalame was listed on the census of 1930 in the household of Taylor
Cosby Cottrell, Sr. in Davidson County, Tennessee; enumerated on 16
April 1930. Taylor C., age 24, was listed as head of household, and
renting a home with a value of $15,000. His wife Zalame, age 22 and
his daughter Jo Anne, age 1 year, 9 months were also listed. Four lodg-
ers were also listed as living in the home.[75]

In April 1930 they lived at 404 Hadley Avenue in Old Hickory,
Davidson County, Tennessee.[76]   Later that year they lived on 49th
Street in Richmond, Virginia, in a rented house until the owner went
bankrupt in the spring of 1931. They then lived on Petersburg Turnpike

in Petersburg, Virginia, in a cottage near the DuPont Plant. In the summer of 1931 they moved to the upstairs of a large house with the cottage owner's Mother, Mrs. Davis. Zalame said a ghost also lived with them in the house. She claimed to have seen this ghost several times standing at the end of their bed. In the fall of 1931 they lived on Forest Hill Avenue in Richmond, Virginia, in a downstairs apartment.[77]

In 1934 they moved to Russellville in Logan County, Kentucky so T.C. could work for the Lashbrook Motor Company. Zalame worked for the company as a bookkeeper. They initially lived rent free in the old Price Home in Russellville where they had the whole down stairs apartment and had a maid and cook so Zalame could work at the Ford Agency. Dudley Lashbrook, one of T.C.'s mother's brothers later sold the home and they rented a house.[78]

In March 1938 they had moved to Murfreesboro in Rutherford County, Tennessee. By 1939 they had moved back to Bowling Green, Kentucky and were living at 1530 State Street while T.C. was working as an instructor at Western Trade School.[79]

They then moved to Elkton in Todd County, Kentucky where T.C. started work for the Elkton Motor Company. Zalame was also employee by the company as the bookkeeper in March 1939. By the fall of 1939 Zalame was living in Bowling Green with T.C.'s mother Nellie Cottrell where she lived until the spring of 1940 when she moved back to Elkton to be with her husband. Joanna attended the Training School while they were in Bowling Green.[80]

According to Zalame, in the spring of 1940 T.C. told her that she and Jo Anne had to come to Elkton and that she had to do the bookkeeping at the dealership and if she would not come, he was thru. They lived in a house owned by Jefferson Taylor Lashbrook, a brother of T.C.'s mother. While there they had their furniture and antiques, which had been in storage in Louisville, moved to Elkton.[81]

Zalame also ran an antique shop out of her home while continuing to work at the Taylor Ford Dealership as bookkeeper. Her business card titled Zalame's Antiques, listed china, glassware, and furniture.[82]

She was listed on the census of 1940 in the household of Jefferson Taylor Lashbrook in Todd County, Kentucky, as Zalame, niece, age 31.[83]

In August 1942 Zalame and T.C. had moved to Tennessee and lived in Martin in Weakley County. They initially slept on the floor in the office at the airport until they found a two-bedroom apartment. After an attack of bed bugs, they moved into the home of a local widow that was recommended by their banker. Zalame said the woman was "really cracked."[84]

Zalame executed a power of attorney in Union City, Tennessee on 9 April 1943 appointing her mother Della Z. Brashear as her Attorney-in-Fact to negotiate and enter into a settlement, accept payment and issue receipts and releases, of all her interest in and to the Walter C. Brashear estate as well as the estates of Jennie Brashear, Dora Brashear and William L. Brashear. The power of attorney was made because there was a controversy existing between the heirs Jennie, Dora, and William as to the correct and proper distribution of the proceeds of Walter Brashear's estate.[85]

In 1944 Robert L. Brashear, Zalame's brother, distributed a one-fourth share of the remaining money from the sale of the Brashear Lands in Kentucky, assumed to be lands originally owned by Walter Curren Brashear, to Zalame. Robert issued checks to Zalame, Kathleen Brashear (her sister), and to Richard H. Brashear (her other brother) to cover portions of their inheritance from the William Helm Brashear estate.[86]

In April 1944 they lived in the Antilla Hotel in Coral Gables in Miami-Dade County, Florida where they remained during portions of April and May while waiting for the Embry Riddle Air Training School to get organized.[87] Zalame continued to paint articles as a hobby from 1928 until she and her husband returned to Bowling Green in late May 1944 where she started studying seriously and making her own designs. As of September 1950, Estella Zalame Brashear was also known as Zeleme.[88] Her business card from around 1950 read "Zeleme's Handicraft Shop". The phone number at the State Street address in Bowling Green was 240-R. The card listed Lamp Globe Decorating, Lamp Shades, Wiring, Peasant Furniture Decorating, and Tole Giftware.[89]

Zalame designed and painted "Peter Hunt" folk art on a truck which had been passed down from her Campbell relatives. According to Zalame the trunk had belonged to Mary Frances Ennis, Zalame's Great-grandmother, who was the wife of John Sale Campbell. According to family lore it traveled on the wagon train with Mary's family when they migrated from Virginia to Kentucky in 1805. It was said that Mary Frances stored her most prized possessions in the trunk.

Zalame and T.C. produced and sold tin and wood items starting around 1950. T.C. made lamps from oil cans and tin shades for the lamps and then wired them. Zalame then painted the lamps. He even made an air compressor from a water tank, refrigerator motor, and some other things so Zalame could use air spray paint

Antique Trunk
Owned by Mary F. Ennis, wife of John Sale Campbell
Peter Hunt folk ark designed and painted
by Zalame Cottrell

when she put background on the articles. From as early as 1950 Zalame created patterns for Toll painting on objects such as tin ware, glass, and trunks.[90] Her patterns, including detailed instructions and drawings, were published in The American Home magazine.[91]

Zalame was named in her husband's will dated 12 November 1954 in Warren County, Kentucky, as executor with T.C. leaving his estate to her and appointing her as the Executrix of his estate and guardian of his infant child Taylor Cosby Cottrell, Jr.. The will appointed his daughter Jo Anne Cottrell to serve as both Executrix and guardian in the event his wife failed to qualify. [92]

Zalame also left a will on the same date in Bowling Green leaving her estate to her husband and designating him as the Guardian for her infant son. The will also designated her daughter to serve in both capacities in the event her husband was unable or subsequently died.[93]

Zalame attended her 30th High School Reunion and Alumni Banquet on the 15th of May, 1957. The banquet was held in the High School Banquet Hall and was attended by 28 additional members of her senior class.[94]

Zalame received her share of her inheritance from the estate of her aunt Georgia Campbell on 17 Feb 1959. The Brashear family property on the Louisville Road north of Bowling Green, approximately one-half mile north of the Emory G. Dent Bridge, was sold around 1960.

The transaction was handled by the Martin Realty Company with proceeds going to the owners of the property who were Zalame, her sister Kathleen, and her brother Richard.[95]

She was a member of the Jaggers Astronomical Society in Bowling Green in 1960 and was serving as president of the society when an article about a pending meteor shower appeared in the Park City daily news. She was quoted extensively in the article about meteors and how meteor showers occur. She also held membership in the Kentucky Guild of Artists and Craftsmen as a charter Craftsman member in 1961.[96]

Zalame was notified of the death of her husband on 17 May 1971. She purchased 140 square feet of land in Fairview Cemetery, Bowling Green, Kentucky the same day. The deed described the cemetery plot as Lot 16, Section R, Plat 1. It was large enough for four people and was located in Fairview Cemetery Number One in Bowling Green. T.C. was buried in this plot on 19 May 1971 at approximately 11:30 in the morning.[97]

Zalame left a will on 25 May 1971 in Bowling Green, Warren County, Kentucky, leaving her estate, half to her son and half to her daughter, and appointing her son to serve as Executor.[98]

Several photographs of Zalame weaving at her looms were featured in the 14 April 1972 issue of the Park City Daily News, a local newspaper. She started weaving around 1953 and initially learned everything from scratch. She bought a large loom and then her husband built several additional smaller table looms. She was instructed by a neighbor who taught at Western Kentucky University. She purchased a two-bedroom home at 868 Nutwood Avenue on 22 March 1973 and moved in shortly thereafter, probably in late May 1973.[99]

One of her weaving patterns called the Union Cross-Roads pattern was featured in "Kentucky's Bicentennial Calendar 1975". The calendar was produced and sold by the Kentucky Guild of Artists and Craftsmen.[100]

Kathleen Brashear, Zalame's sister, appointed her as her Attorney-in-Fact with full power to act in her name in all of her affairs on 18 October 1974.[101] On 29 October 1974 Zalame signed a contract for the sale of Lots 34 and 35, lake front property located near Port Oliver in Allen County, Kentucky. The sale was handled by the Warren County Realty Company. The property included a small two-bedroom vacation cottage and 198 feet of lake front property where T.C. and Zalame had spent many weekends relaxing from daily life challenges. It had served as their "getaway" vacation home.[102]

An article in the Park City Daily News on 27 February 1977 described Mrs. Cottrell's love of weaving. She made her own patterns and was a juried weaver in both the Kentucky and Southern Kentucky Guilds of Artists and Craftsmen. She indicated in the article that she was planning to raise cotton in her yard and have a friend spin it for weaving. At the time of the article she had nine floor looms and numerous other types of looms, many built by her husband.[103]

In June of 1977 Zalame received a Certificate of Commemoration from the Governor of Kentucky in appreciation for her participation in the Governor's Conference on Aging in May, and in recognition of contributions and loyalty to the Commonwealth of Kentucky.[104] In early 1978, Zalame wove miniature coverlets in snowflake and snowball patterns in wine, medium blue, gold, and brown colors. The warp for these coverlets was set to 60 threads to the inch which allowed superb scale and detail. She sold these coverlets through her Son's miniature business, Cottrell Limited Editions.[105]

A photograph of Zalame demonstrating how to use a loom was included in the chapter on weaving in a book titled The Traditional Arts and Crafts of Warren County, Kentucky, published by the Bowling Green-Warren County Arts Commission in 1980.

Her sister Kathleen H. Brashear left a will on 15 July 1982 which appointed Zalame as Co-Executor of her estate along with the family Attorney William J. Parker. The will bequeathed Kathleen's home on High Street in Bowling Green to Zalame along with a cherry chest that matched her bed (both of which were made by her Great-Grandfather Campbell), a marble top table, blue candlesticks, and a corner cupboard. Zalame also was to receive a painting by Kathleen's Aunt Mildred, a Hepplewhite table, a family portrait, a hand-painted trunk, the Brashear and Campbell Coat of Arms, two cane bottom chairs, an amethyst water set, a Shaker table and glass case on table, a red chair which was painted for her mother, and several painted pictures. Others were also named in the will for smaller items. The remainder of the estate was to be divided equally between Kathleen's nephew Richard Brashear and Zalame.[106]

A photograph of Zalame holding a family valentine was featured in the 14 February 1986 issue of the Park City Daily News, a Bowling Green, Kentucky newspaper. The valentine was hand cut by William Pitt Brashear in 1835 and included four circular sections with hand-drawn doves with flowers. It also contained a verse written by Pitt to his intended. Unfortunately, Pitt, a rising young attorney, died young, before he was able to marry his intended.[107]

Zalame was the informant for the death of her sister Kathleen Hope Brashear on 5 August 1986 at 1019 High Street in Bowling Green, Warren County, Kentucky; at 1:00 in the afternoon.[108] Kathleen had died peacefully in her favorite chair before Zalame dropped by her home for a visit. The final settlement and discharge of co-executors William J. Parker and Zalame B. Cottrell in the estate of Kathleen H. Brashear, filed on 8 May 1987, was approved by the Warren District Court on 16 June 1987.[109]

Zalame left a new will on 1 November 1988 in Bowling Green, Warren County, Kentucky; leaving her estate, half to her son Taylor Cosby Cottrell, Jr. and half to her daughter, Jo Anne Cottrell and appointing her son to serve as Co-Executor with William J. Parker.[110] In early 1990 her health declined to the point that she was becoming lost when driving to the store. Her neighbor called her son Taylor who was living in Florida and expressed concern over her continued ability to live alone. Zalame apparently had also been seeing things in her house that she had described as "little buggy-eyed owls" and had taken to keeping a pistol nearby for protection. Her son traveled to Kentucky and was able to convince Zalame to issue a power of attorney to him to assist her in moving to Florida. She initially moved into the home of her Son in Florida but her mental state continued to decline leading to confusion and significant memory lapse.[111]

On the 22nd of March, 1990, Zalame experienced mild tremors. She was taken to the nearest emergency room and went into a full seizure in the arms of her son. She was experiencing a heart attack when they arrived at the hospital. She was stabilized in the emergency room. After a brain scan confirmed she had a massive hemorrhage in her brain, and thus would likely not recover, her son signed consent to withhold extraordinary measures which had been her expressed wishes not to be kept alive on a machine.[112]

After a short hospital stay she was transferred to a nearby Nursing Home after no improvement. At the time of her transfer she was unable to walk, unable to feed herself, and did not appear to know those around her or understand where she was. She lived in this medical center from March 1990 until 1995 with several trips to the nearby hospital emergency room for treatment of various issues. During this time, she appeared to be happy and was described by the staff as one of their favorite residents. However, she had little memory of who or where she was and seldom recognized her family during frequent visits. She was transferred by her son to a Merritt Island nursing home on 13 February 1995 due to increasingly poor care at the original nursing home.[113]

In September 1996 her health suddenly declined further after she likely experienced a series of strokes. Her son was with her when she died on 9 September 1996 at Merritt Manor Nursing Home, Merritt Island, Brevard County, Florida, at age 88; at 1:30 in the morning.[114]

Her body was transferred from a local funeral home in Florida to the J.C. Kirby and Son Funeral Chapel in Bowling Green, Kentucky where visitation was held from 6:00 to 8:00 in the evening on the 10th of September 1996. Initial handling and forwarding of her remains was by Wylie-Baxley Funeral Home in Merritt Island, Florida.[115] Floral tributes at her funeral included a casket spray of red roses from her family; a basket of summer flowers from her son's friends at work; a basket of fresh flowers; a saddle of fall silk flowers; a vase of pink, white, purple carnations, iris, and daisies; and red roses in a vase.[116]

Estella Zalame Brashear
Fairview Cemetery
Bowling Green, Kentucky

Funeral services were held graveside on 11 September 1996 at 10:00 in the morning. She was buried in Fairview Cemetery in Bowling Green following the graveside service. A close friend of her Son, who was one of his High School classmates, saw her funeral notice in the local newspaper and showed up at the Cemetery and volunteered to help carry her casket to the burial plot.[117]

Jo Anne Cottrell (1928-1998)

Daughter of Taylor C. Cottrell, Sr. and Estella Zalame Brashear
Sister of Taylor Cosby Cottrell, Jr.

Jo Anne Cottrell was born on 16 July 1928 in Kyrock, Edmondson County, Kentucky, at 2:00 in the afternoon. She weighed 7 pounds at birth. She was the daughter of Taylor Cosby Cottrell Sr. and Estella Zalame Brashear.[118]

Jo Anne Cottrell

Jo Anne was listed on the census of 1930 in the household of her father, Taylor Cosby Cottrell Sr., living at 404 Hadley Avenue in Old Hickory in Davidson County, Tennessee, as Jo Anne, age 1 year, 9 months. On 1 April 1935 she was living with her parents in Russellville in Logan County, Kentucky.[119]

In March 1938 she was living with her Grandmother Nellie Jane Cottrell in Bowling Green, Kentucky while her mother and father were setting up a new home in Murfreesboro, Tennessee. According to a postcard from her mother, her parents were to come to Bowling Green on Sunday the 13th of March to take her, and their dog Joy, back to Murfreesboro.[120]

In 1939 she was living at 1530 State Street in Bowling Green. In the city directory of that year she was listed as a student.[121] In 1940 she was listed on the census in the household of Jefferson Taylor Lashbrook in Todd County, Kentucky, as Jo Anna, cousin, age 5.[122]

Jo Anne wrote a poem titled "Queen of All Lands" when she was 12 years old and in the seventh grade in a local school in Elkton, Kentucky. The poem was published in an unidentified Todd County

Newspaper and also appeared in Allan M. Trout's "Greetings", a popular column which appeared daily in the Courier-Journal, a newspaper located in Louisville, Kentucky.

The poem read:

"I'm glad to be an American, I'm glad as can be; and a part of a country that is a land of the free; I'm proud of the Stars and Stripes, and for what they stand--Freedom of speech and election, and everything in our land.

For boys and girls, a home was found, where they would be happy, safe, and sound--The settlers fought hardships, Indians and starvation, to make peace, homes and civilization.

Times go on, and America still stands--Long live America, queen of all lands!"[123]

Jo was baptized on 19 February 1943 in Union City, Obion County, Tennessee, in the St. James Episcopal Church by Rev. L.A. Wilson. Baptism sponsors were Mrs. W.D. McAnulty and Mrs. G.G. Lobdell both friends of her parents.[124] She was confirmed as an Episcopalian on 21 February 1943 in Union City, in the St. James Episcopal Church by E.P. Dandridge, Bishop Coadjutor of Tennessee.[125]

In 1944 Jo Anne held a tea at her home in Bowling Green "in honor of her house guest, Miss Louise Boone of Elkton." The newspaper article said the "lace-covered tea table was attractively decorated with yellow chrysanthemums and yellow candles in crystal holders." There were more than 32 guests attending the tea that included family and friends.[126]

Jo Anne graduated from Western Teachers College High School in Bowling Green on 12 May 1946.[127] Later in 1948 she shared with a close friend that she wanted to be a great writer and planned to use the name of "Camille Cottrell."[128]

Jo Anne was employed in a hospital in Lexington, Fayette County, Kentucky in 1949 where she edited a newsletter. She was employed as a psychiatric aid at Norton infirmary on 10 September 1950 in Louisville, Jefferson County, Kentucky.[129] The house that became the infirmary was initially a protestant hospital, Louisville's first, named for a well-loved local Episcopal priest and missionary who died in 1881. Next to the hospital was a school of nursing, Kentucky's first.

Around 1951 Jo Anne moved to Chicago, Illinois where she worked as a copy writer for Marshall Fields and Montgomery Ward.[130] She was named in the will of her mother on 12 November 1954 designating her to serve as executrix of her will and guardian of her brother Taylor Cosby Cottrell, Jr. in the event her husband was unable or subsequently died.[131]

Jo Anne met Lawrence A. Sloan while living in Chicago and they became engaged. Lawrence obtained a marriage license on 14 September 1955 in Chicago in Cook County, Illinois and they were married on 17 September 1955 at the Chapel of the Holy Grail in Chicago with the Rev. Mr. James Patton officiating. She wore a "street length dress of brown wool with champagne accessories at her wedding". Her attendant was a close friend from Chicago. Mr. Sloan's best man was also a close friend from Chicago. Jo Anne's mother, father, and young brother traveled to Chicago by train and attended the wedding.[132] They stayed in a hotel on one of the top floors with a fire escape outside the window and left the window open because there was no air conditioning in the hotel.

Jo Anne divorced Lawrence on 12 October 1962 in Winston County, Alabama after enduring an abusive relationship that had continued since their marriage.[133] She moved to 162 Columbia Heights in Brooklyn Heights, New York around 1963. Her business card indicated she did free-lance copy service and retail fashion sales promotion catalogs. She also stopped using her married name and returned to using Cottrell.[134]

In the late 1960's Joanna moved from Brooklyn Heights to 105 Bank Street in Greenwich Village in lower Manhattan, New York where she remained for the rest of her life. There she met Ernest Graham Pilley, son of Jeffee A. Pilley and Juditeth Grunway. They lived together until Ernie became gravely ill and moved back to North Carolina in 1994.[135]

Joanna's father visited her at her apartment in New York during a business trip the week of 11 May 1971. This was his first and only visit while she lived in New York. It was a bonding time for them both and Joanna always remembered the time they spent together as a special time.[136]

Jo Anne was a Free-Lance Copywriter in January 1974. Her business card for her 105 Bank Street address in the Village, in Manhattan indicated she handled newspaper, catalogues, and direct mail. She was also known as Joanna Cottrell.[137]

Between 1984 and 1988 she traveled to Puerto Plata in the Dominican Republic at least annually each year.[138] Joanna and a lifelong friend went to Jones Beach on Long Island nearly every weekend until her friend died in 1989. They would wake before dawn and take a taxi to Penn Station, then take the train to Long Island, and then take a bus to the beach. They would spend the entire day at the beach. Her friend said she had a perpetual image of Joanna, walking down toward the shore, towel trailing behind her, a blissful look on her face, thermos of wine in hand.[139]

Joanna traveled to Puerto Plata in the Dominican Republic in April of 1991 and again in May of 1992.[140] Later in 1992 she left a will that made provisions for her "long-time companion, Ernest Graham Pilley" through transfer of her rent controlled apartment and all monies remaining from her inheritance from her mother. She later changed this will to leave all proceeds to her brother.[141]

Joanna served on a jury for the Supreme Court of the State of New York for 5 days starting 29 March 1993. In May she received another summons for juror duty. The summons indicated she had been deferred three times since Jan 23 1992. There was no record of the disposition of this summons.[142]

In early September 1994, after a long illness and hospitalization due in part to Alcoholism, Drug Addiction, and Emphysema, Ernie Pilley moved out of Joanna's apartment and moved to North Carolina to be with his sisters. He died two weeks later on 13 September 1994 in Durham, North Carolina. He was buried in Maplewood Cemetery located in Durham. His gravestone indicated he had served as a Corporal in the Army during World War II.[143]

On 23 October 1997 Joanna signed a Guardianship Designation appointing her brother as her guardian in the event she was unable to care for herself. The document granted him full financial, medical, and social care decision making. She also signed a Health Care Proxy appointing her brother as her proxy for medical decisions. The document confirmed her desire that artificial nutrition and hydration be withdrawn or withheld as indicated in her Living Will which she also signed on the same date.[144] Her living will indicated that if she was in a terminal condition, permanently unconscious, or minimally conscious with irreversible brain damage she did not want cardiac resuscitation, mechanical respiration, tube feeding, or antibiotics and that she did want maximum pain relief.[145]

In the spring of 1998, a longtime friend, called Joanna to arrange a visit but Joanna told her she was "too busy to work her in on such short notice". According to her neighbors this was around the time Joanna started withdrawing from contact with the outside world. Her last checkbook showed visits to four different doctors between May and August 1998. Her handwriting significantly changed during this time. It is surmised from this, and information from neighbors, that she may have known or suspected she was ill. This may have been an additional factor in her heavy drinking in her last months of life.[146]

Jo Anne died on 19 October 1998 at 105 Bank Street in New York city, at age 70; at 10:56 in the evening. Her immediate cause of death was complications of chronic alcoholism. Other significant conditions contributing to death were hypertensive and atherosclerotic cardiovascular disease.[147]

On 22 October 1998 Joanna's cat Clementine died after being in intensive care since Joanna's death. Clementine had been taken to a local Feline Health Clinic after Joanna's death as requested in her will. Clementine was cremated at the request of Joanna's brother.[148]

Neighbors of Joanna relayed the events that led up to her death to her brother after he arrived in New York to make final arrangements following her death. Her downstairs neighbor had noticed a water leak from the ceiling of his apartment and when he and other neighbors knocked on her door she told them she was on the floor and could not get up. They entered her apartment from the roof garden and found her lying on the floor, very weak and extremely dehydrated. She refused to allow them to call for medical assistance. The boyfriend of her neighbor stayed with her and talked to her for some time after they got her in bed. They went downstairs and after considering the situation decided to call for medical help. Before calling they returned to Joanna's apartment and found she had died. They called the police who responded and because it was an unattended death the police impounded the apartment until a medical examiner could confirm the death was from natural causes. One of the policemen contacted Joanna's brother to notify him of his sister's death.[149]

Joanna's brother and his wife traveled to New York the next day and remained there for a short period of time to arrange for transport of her body to Kentucky for burial and to start the process of handling of her estate with the assistance of a lawyer that Joanna had used to prepare her will. They remained in New York until after her estate was probated and then traveled to Bowling Green, Kentucky to make final arrangements for her burial.[150]

Her estate was probated on 23 October 1998 at Surrogate's Court, New York, New York County, New York.[151] An obituary was printed in The Villager, a local newspaper where Joanna wrote a pet column.

It listed her as an animal lover and indicated she had written the column titled "Pet Talk" for over 6 years. Her column "dealt not only with dogs, cats, birds, and hamsters" but even discussed the return of sea horses to the Hudson River.[152]

Final arrangements were handled by J.C. Kirby and Son Funeral Chapel at 832 Broadway, Bowling Green, Kentucky. She was buried on

Joanna Cottrell
Fairview Cemetery
Bowling Green, Kentucky

26 October 1998 at Fairview Cemetery in Bowling Green, with Redden's Funeral Home, Inc. in charge of transfer of remains to J.C. Kirby Funeral Home who was in charge of arrangements.[153]

After Joanna's funeral her brother returned to New York for a short period of time to arrange for closure of her apartment. Her brother was confirmed by the Surrogate's Court of the County of New York to be the executor of her estate on 29 October 1998.[154] A celebration and toast for Joanna, who was called "Our Lady of the Pets", was held on Tuesday the 3rd of November at the Cowgirl Restaurant at the corner of 10th and Hudson.

On 21 April 1999 Joanna's attorney, who had been retained by her brother to handle the legal matters in settling her estate, filed her final list of assets with the Surrogate's Courte of the State of New York. [155]

Taylor Cosby Cottrell, Jr. (1944)

Son of Taylor C. Cottrell, Sr. and Estella Zalame Brashear
Living Author of this Book

    The life story of Taylor, also known as T.C., who is the author of this book, is not included because he was living at the time of the book's publication. However, a short biography for T.C. Cottrell, Jr. can be found in the Preface.

Chapter 5 – Jefferson M. Cosby Family

2nd Great-grandfather of Taylor Cosby Cottrell, Jr.

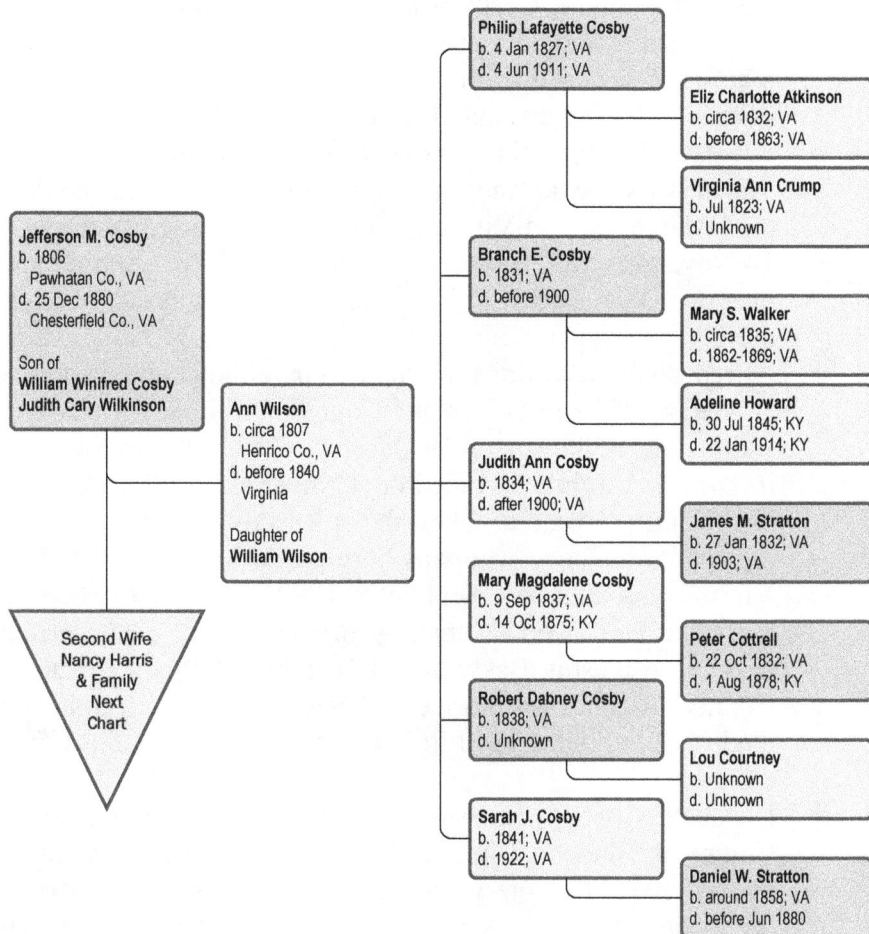

Philip Lafayette Cosby
b. 4 Jan 1827; VA
d. 4 Jun 1911; VA

Eliz Charlotte Atkinson
b. circa 1832; VA
d. before 1863; VA

Virginia Ann Crump
b. Jul 1823; VA
d. Unknown

Jefferson M. Cosby
b. 1806
   Pawhatan Co., VA
d. 25 Dec 1880
   Chesterfield Co., VA

Son of
**William Winifred Cosby
Judith Cary Wilkinson**

Branch E. Cosby
b. 1831; VA
d. before 1900

Mary S. Walker
b. circa 1835; VA
d. 1862-1869; VA

Ann Wilson
b. circa 1807
   Henrico Co., VA
d. before 1840
   Virginia

Daughter of
William Wilson

Adeline Howard
b. 30 Jul 1845; KY
d. 22 Jan 1914; KY

Judith Ann Cosby
b. 1834; VA
d. after 1900; VA

James M. Stratton
b. 27 Jan 1832; VA
d. 1903; VA

Mary Magdalene Cosby
b. 9 Sep 1837; VA
d. 14 Oct 1875; KY

Peter Cottrell
b. 22 Oct 1832; VA
d. 1 Aug 1878; KY

**Second Wife
Nancy Harris
& Family
Next
Chart**

Robert Dabney Cosby
b. 1838; VA
d. Unknown

Lou Courtney
b. Unknown
d. Unknown

Sarah J. Cosby
b. 1841; VA
d. 1922; VA

Daniel W. Stratton
b. around 1858; VA
d. before Jun 1880

Jefferson M. Cosby was born in 1806 in Pawhatan County, Virginia. He was the son of William Winifred Cosby and Judith Cary Wilkinson. His father William was born around 1780 in Pawhatan County, Virginia and his mother Judith was born circa 1780 also in Virginia. They married on 22 October 1798 in Pawhatan County. Judith's father was Thomas Wilkinson.

William's father was Jeremiah David Cosby who was born on 11 October 1761 in Goochland County, Virginia. William also went by the name of blind David. He was a fiddle player and in one of the times he was playing for a dance he was blinded. This apparently happened when he was shot by a Mr. Gilliam by accident. Jeremiah David died around 1813 in Pawhatan County, Virginia. [1] Jefferson had at least six brothers and sisters including:

- Ludwell Williams Cosby who was born around 1800 in Pawhatan County and died in June 1869 in Pawhatan County. He married Rebecca Wilson on 20 October 1825. Rebecca was born in 1804 in Pawhatan County and died in March 1861 in Pawhatan County. They had at least seven children.

- Mahala Cosby who was born around 1808 in Virginia and died on 4 March 1864 in Virginia. She married James Turnley on 14 November 1832. James was born in 1808 in Virginia and died on 4 March 1864 in Virginia. They had at least five children.

- Alfred Cosby who was born in 1813 in Virginia and died on 4 November 1881 in Goochland County, Virginia. He married Judith Ann Wilkinson on 19 December 1837. Judith was born in 1813 in Virginia and died on 4 November 1881 in Goochland County, Virginia. They had at least four children.

- Agatha Ann Cosby who was born on 26 November 1815 in Virginia and died on 1 September 1899 in Virginia. She was buried in Hollywood Cemetery in Richmond. She married Richard Augustus Bass on 9 December 1840 in Pawhatan County. Richard was born on 22 March 1815 in Virginia and died on 2 February 1860 in Virginia. They had at least four children.

- Elizabeth Cosby who was born around 1820 in Pawhatan County and died on 7 July 1893 in Richmond. She was buried in Hollywood Cemetery. She married William H. Wilkinson on 14 January 1839. William was born in 1820 in Pawhatan County and died on 7 July 1893 in Richmond. They had at least five children.

- John Calvert Cosby who was born around 1820 and died before 1850 in Virginia. [2]

Jefferson married his first wife Ann Wilson on 31 January 1826 in Pawhatan County. [3] She was the daughter of William and Susan Wilson and was born around 1807 in Virginia. She also went by the name of Nancy. She died sometime before 1840 in Virginia. [4]

Jefferson and Ann had at least six children including Philip Lafayette Cosby, Branch E. Cosby, Judith Ann Cosby, Mary Magdalene Cosby, Robert Dabney Cosby, and Sarah J. Cosby.[5]

After Ann's death Jefferson married Nancy Harris on 26 October 1840 in Goochland County, Virginia.[6] Nancy was born on 2 October 1820 in Virginia and was the daughter of Richard Harris.[7] Jefferson and Nancy also had at least six children including Monterey Cosby, Luther Calvin Cosby, Richard Hamilton Cosby, Charles Monroe Cosby, Lelia Mataline Cosby, Nannie Lee Cosby, and John Stuart Cosby.[8]

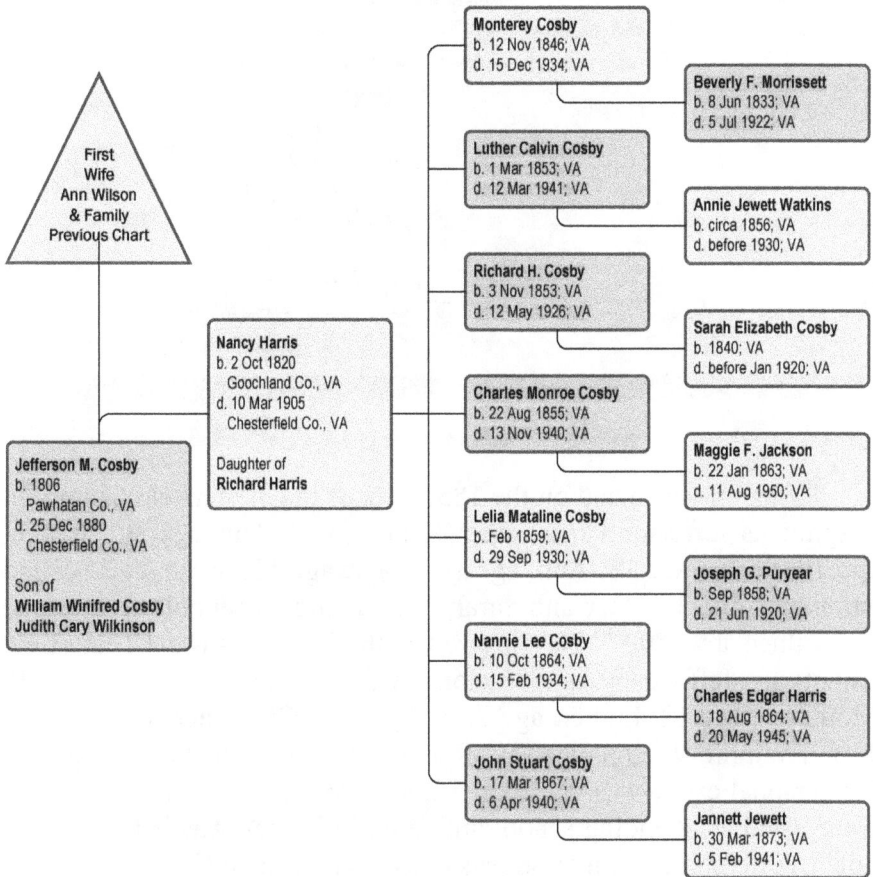

First
Wife
Ann Wilson
& Family
Previous Chart

Jefferson M. Cosby
b. 1806
    Pawhatan Co., VA
d. 25 Dec 1880
    Chesterfield Co., VA

Son of
**William Winifred Cosby
Judith Cary Wilkinson**

Nancy Harris
b. 2 Oct 1820
    Goochland Co., VA
d. 10 Mar 1905
    Chesterfield Co., VA

Daughter of
Richard Harris

Monterey Cosby
b. 12 Nov 1846; VA
d. 15 Dec 1934; VA

Beverly F. Morrissett
b. 8 Jun 1833; VA
d. 5 Jul 1922; VA

Luther Calvin Cosby
b. 1 Mar 1853; VA
d. 12 Mar 1941; VA

Annie Jewett Watkins
b. circa 1856; VA
d. before 1930; VA

Richard H. Cosby
b. 3 Nov 1853; VA
d. 12 May 1926; VA

Sarah Elizabeth Cosby
b. 1840; VA
d. before Jan 1920; VA

Charles Monroe Cosby
b. 22 Aug 1855; VA
d. 13 Nov 1940; VA

Maggie F. Jackson
b. 22 Jan 1863; VA
d. 11 Aug 1950; VA

Lelia Mataline Cosby
b. Feb 1859; VA
d. 29 Sep 1930; VA

Joseph G. Puryear
b. Sep 1858; VA
d. 21 Jun 1920; VA

Nannie Lee Cosby
b. 10 Oct 1864; VA
d. 15 Feb 1934; VA

Charles Edgar Harris
b. 18 Aug 1864; VA
d. 20 May 1945; VA

John Stuart Cosby
b. 17 Mar 1867; VA
d. 6 Apr 1940; VA

Jannett Jewett
b. 30 Mar 1873; VA
d. 5 Feb 1941; VA

In October 1847 Jefferson received payment from New York Life Insurance Company for the loss of his slave, Isaac, who was a miner at the pits in Clover Hill, Virginia.[9] The Clover Hill Coal Pits were later the site of a disastrous explosion in 1867 where 30 whites and 39 colored were killed.

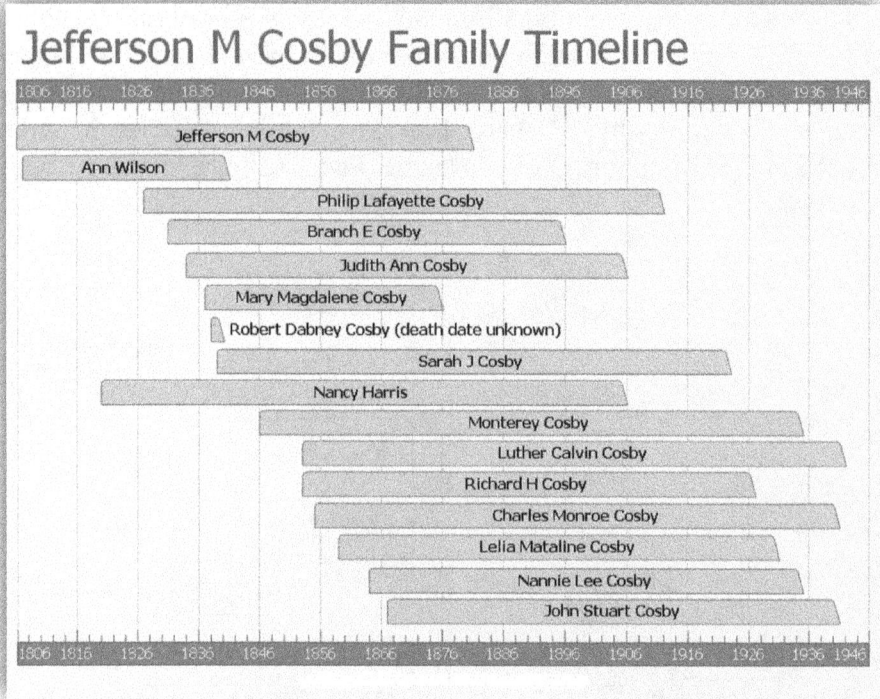

Jefferson M Cosby Family Timeline

Jefferson was listed on the 1850 census in Chesterfield County in Virginia as Jefferson Cosby, age 49 along with Ann, age 30, Branch, age 19, Philip, age 18, Ann, age 16, Mary, age 12, Sarah, age 10, and Monterey, age 3. Mary and Sarah were attending school. Real estate was valued at $1,800.[10] He appeared on the 1860 census in Chesterfield County, as Jeff Cosby, age 59 along with Ann, age 38, Rosa, age 20, Monterey, age 12, Luther, age 7, R.H., age 6, Chas., age 4, Likia, age 1, and Winnie Wilson, age 50. Real estate was valued at $3,000 and his personal estate was valued at $2,000. Monterey, Luther, and R.H. were listed as attending school and Winnie Wilson was listed as "idiotic". Jefferson's occupation was listed as machinist.[11]

In 1870 Jefferson was listed on the census in Chesterfield County, as Jefferson Cosby, age 69 along with Nancy, age 40, Monterey, age 21, Luther C., age 18, Richard, age 16, Charles, age 13, Lillie, age 12,

Nannie, age 7, and John, age 4. Real estate was valued at $1,688 and personal estate was listed as $848. His occupation on the 1870 census was farmer.[12]

In 1880 he was listed on the census in Chesterfield County, as Jefferson Cosby, age 79 along with his wife Ann, age 60, sons Luther C., age 28, Richard H., age 25, Charles M., age 22, and John S., age 14 and his daughters Lelia M., age 21 and Nannie L., age 16. His widowed daughter Sarah J. Stratton,

Jefferson M. Cosby		
1850	Chesterfield Co., VA	Farmer
1860	Chesterfield Co., VA	Machinist
1870	Chesterfield Co., VA	Farmer
1880	Chesterfield Co., VA	Farmer

age 38 along with his grandsons Ivin M. Stratton, age 21 and Walter H. Stratton, age 19, and his granddaughter Nettie L. Stratton, age 14 were also listed. His occupation was listed as farmer.[13]

Jefferson died on 25 December 1880 in Midlothian, Chesterfield County, Virginia. His cause of death was chronic diarrhea.[14] His wife Nancy was listed on the 1900 census in the household of her son Charles Monroe Cosby in Chesterfield County as Nancy, age 80 and widowed.[15] Nancy died on 19 March 1905 in Chesterfield County, at age 84. Funeral services were held on 11 March 1905 in Midlothian, Chesterfield County, Virginia at the gravesite on the family burying ground at 3:00 in the afternoon.[16]

Philip Lafayette Cosby (1827-1911)

Son of Jefferson M. Cosby and Ann Wilson
Great-granduncle of Taylor Cosby Cottrell, Jr.

Philip Lafayette Cosby was born on 4 January 1827 in Pawhatan County, Virginia. He was the son of Jefferson M. Cosby and Ann Wilson. Philip also went by the name of Tumby.[17] He was listed on the 1850 census in Chesterfield County, Virginia, in the household of his father Jefferson as Philip, age 18. He was employed as a carpenter at the time.[18] He married Elizabeth Charlotte Atkinson, who was born circa 1832 in Virginia, on 8 June 1854 in Chesterfield County.[19]

Philip was listed on the 1860 census in Chesterfield County, as Phillip L. Cosby, age 28 along with Eliza C., age 28, Thos. J., age 5, and Ira J., age 2. Real estate was valued at $700 with a personal estate value of $1,200. He was employed as a mechanic at the time.[20]

Children of Philip Lafayette Cosby and Elizabeth C. Atkinson:

- Thomas J. Cosby – Born circa 1855 in Pawhatan County, Virginia; died on 14 November 1887 in Chesterfield County, Virginia. Cause of death was typhoid fever. Location of burial is unknown. Thomas married Bettie E. Crump on 12 February 1880 in Manchester, Virginia.[21]

- Ira Lafayette Cosby – Born on 28 February 1858 in Virginia; died on 8 April 1934 in Richmond, Virginia at age 76. Cause of death was influenza and pneumonia. He was buried at Bethel Church Cemetery in Midlothian, Chesterfield County, Virginia on 10 April 1934. Ira was a machinist by trade.[22] He married Lina B. Duncan on 3 November 1886 in Newbern County, North Carolina. Lina, also known as Angelina, was born on 28 January 1864 in North Carolina.[23] Lina died on 5 January 1944 in Midlothian, Chesterfield County, Virginia at age 79 and was buried at Bethel Church Cemetery in Midlothian.[24] They had at least five children including:

  o Philip Ransome Cosby - Born on 15 January 1888 in Newbern, North Carolina, married Olivia Blackburn around 1911, and died on 31 October 1969 at Rockingham Memorial Hospital in Harrisonburg, Virginia. He was buried in Edgewood Cemetery in Weyers Cave in Augusta County, Virginia.[25] Philip and Olivia had at least four children including Philip Ransome Cosby, Jr. who was born on 22 April 1917 in Rockingham County, Virginia, William Wilson Cosby who was born on 29 June 1919 in Grottoes, Virginia and died on 23 July 2008 in Waynesboro, Virginia, Francis Blackburn Cosby who was born on 19 October 1920 in Rockingham County and died on 22 September 1913 in Santa Barbara, California, and Carroll Duncan Cosby who was born on 12 May 1926 in Grottoes, Virginia and died on 6 April 1974 at the University of Virginia Hospital in Charlottesville, Virginia.[26]

  o Duncan Ralph Cosby - Born on 22 January 1892 in Weyers Cave, North Carolina. He married in 1929. His wife's name was Lucile. When he registered for the WWI Draft in 1917 he was employed as a miller.

He was living in Harrison County, Virginia at the time. Duncan died on 1 August 1991 in Harrisonburg, Virginia. He was buried in Port Republic Cemetery in Rockingham County, Virginia.[27]

o Ira Lafayette Cosby - Born on 17 September 1895 in New Bern County, North Carolina and married Lillie Leith around 1919. He was living in Grottoes in Augusta County, Virginia when he registered for the WWII Draft in 1942. Ira died in January 1984 likely in Baltimore, Maryland.[28]

o Elizabeth Charlotte Cosby - Born on 3 April 1898 in North Carolina and died on 18 June 1978 in DeKalb, Georgia. Elizabeth married Stewart Fleming Carver.[29]

o Margaret Virginia Cosby – Born on 19 October 1903 in New Bern, North Carolina. She married Walter Lenton Fowler on 31 December 1930. They divorced on 11 April 1947 in Richmond. The divorce record indicated the divorce was contested by Walter and that Margaret did not receive any alimony as the result. Margaret died on 7 June 2001 in a nursing home in New Hanover County, Virginia. She was buried in Bethel Baptist Church Cemetery in Midlothian, Virginia.[30]

▪ Unnamed Daughter – Stillborn in October 1860 in Chesterfield County, Virginia. Burial location is unknown.[31]

Elizabeth died prior to 1863 in Virginia.[32] Philip then married Virginia Ann Crump Howard on 3 March 1863 in Pawhatan County, Virginia. Virginia Ann was born in July 1823 in Chesterfield County and also went by the name of Jennie.[33] Virginia had been previously married and had four children with her first husband Thomas Howard including Rosa Ann Howard, Thomas J. Howard, John L. Howard, and Edward C. Howard.[34]

Philip was listed on the 1870 census in Pawhatan County, Virginia as P.L. Cosby, age 39 along with Virginia A., age 42, Thos. J., age 15, Ira L., age 12, and P.V., age 7. Real estate was valued at $2,000 with personal estate valued at $1,000.[35] In 1880 Philip appeared on the census in Pawhatan County as Philip L. Cosby, age 51 along with his wife Virginia A., age 52 and son Philip V., age 15. Also listed was a step son Edward C. Howard, age 26. Both Philip and his wife Virginia were listed on the 1900 census in Nottoway County, Virginia with Philip being listed as age 71 and Virginia, age 76.[36]

Philip Lafayette Cosby		
1850	Chesterfield Co., VA	Carpenter
1860	Chesterfield Co., VA	Mechanic
1870	Pawhatan Co., VA	Farmer
1880	Pawhatan Co., VA	Farmer
1900	Nottoway Co., VA	Farmer

Children of Philip Lafayette Cosby and Virginia Ann Crump:

- Philip Virginus Cosby – Born on 16 June 1864 in Pawhatan County, Virginia[37] and died 10 February 1941 in Burkeville in Nottoway County. He was buried in Burkeville. Philip married May Belle Smith in 1885. May Belle died in 1945 and is buried in Sunset Hill Cemetery in Burkeville in Nottoway County, Virginia.[38] Philip died on 4 June 1911 in Burkeville in Nottoway County, at age 84. He is buried in Sunset Hill Cemetery in Burkeville.[39] Virginia died in 1912 and is also buried in Sunset Hill Cemetery. They had at least six children including:
  - o Lula May Cosby – Born on 25 February 1886 in Virginia, married James Sterling Gunn on 21 February 1917, and died on 8 February 1980 in Richmond. Her cause of death was cardiac arrest and a complete heart block. She was buried in Sunset Hill Cemetery in Burkeville, Virginia.[40] James was born in 1896 and died in 1971. He was also buried in Sunset Hill Cemetery. They had at least one child, James Sterling Gunn, Jr., who was born on 19 January 1919 and died on 16 August 1987. James, Jr., was buried in Mount Calvary Cemetery in Richmond.
  - o Oscar Livingston Cosby – Born on 10 September 1889 in Richmond. He was employed by the Norfolk and Western Railway in Williamson, West Virginia when he registered for the WWII Draft in 1942.
  - o Hattie Frances Cosby – Born on 20 August 1892 in Chesterfield County, Virginia and married C.H. Hines on 16 December 1913.[41]

- o Bessie Bass Cosby – Born on 28 November 1895 in Virginia, married Aubrey Sidney Bass, and died on 28 January 1966 in Richmond. Aubrey was born on 26 September 1885 and died on 9 August 1971. They were both buried in Maury Cemetery in Richmond.[42]
- o Phyllis Virginius Cosby – Born on 20 January 1898 in Virginia, married Calvin W. Cosby on 26 July 1917, and died on 25 April 1981 in in the Richmond Metropolitan Hospital in Richmond, Virginia. She was buried in Sunset Hill Cemetery in Burkeville, Virginia with Woody Funeral Home in Richmond handling the arrangements.[43]
- o Ralph Leroy Cosby - Born on 15 September 1899 in Nottoway, Virginia and married Mary Michaels Boisseau on 16 November 1940. He was described as medium height with a medium build, brown eyes and dark hair when he registered for the WWI Draft in 1918. He was employed as a civil engineer at the time. Ralph died on 17 February 1998 in Henrico County, Virginia. He was buried in Sunset Hill Cemetery in Burkeville.[44]
- Unnamed Son – Born on 26 April 1866 in Pawhatan County, Virginia and died in September 1867 in Pawhatan County, Virginia. Location of burial is unknown.[45]

Branch Cosby (1831-before 1900)

Son of Jefferson M. Cosby and Ann Wilson
Great-granduncle of Taylor Cosby Cottrell, Jr.

Branch E. Cosby was born in 1831 in Virginia. He was the son of Jefferson M. Cosby and Ann Wilson.[46] He was listed in the 1850 census in Chesterfield County, Virginia, in the home of his father Jefferson, as Branch E, age 19 and working as a carpenter.[47] Branch married Mary S. Walker, the daughter of John and Luvenia Walker, on 16 October 1856 in Chesterfield County.[48] Mary was born circa 1835 in Virginia. She also went by the name of Millie and may also have been called Mollie. Branch was listed in the 1860 census in Chesterfield County as B.E. Cosby, age 29 and a Baptist Minister. Also listed in the household were M.S., age 24, Florence, age 3, H.H., age 1, and Geo. Walker, age 18. [49]

Children of Branch E. Cosby and Mary S. Walker:

- Florence Cosby – Born on 17 July 1857 in Virginia and died on 14 December 1935 in Richmond, Virginia at age 78. Cause of death was coronary thrombosis. She is buried in Maury Cemetery in Richmond.[50] Florence married M.F. Hughes around 1878. Florence was listed as widowed on her death certificate, therefore her husband died before her.
- Howell Hunter Cosby – Born on 4 May 1859 in Virginia and died on 20 December 1897 in Virginia at age 38. He was buried in Maury Cemetery in Richmond. He married Cora Hanson in 1885. Cora was the daughter of E.H. Hanson and Cecelia Nunnally and was born on 13 October 1866 in Chesterfield County, Virginia. She died on 13 February 1944 in Richmond. Howell, Cora, and Ennis are buried together in Maury Cemetery in Richmond, Virginia.[51] Howell and Cora had at least one child:
  - Ennis Branch Cosby – Born on 25 March 1895 and died on 26 December 1916 in Richmond. His cause of death was pneumonia. He was was a printer by trade and married Bertha O. Coalter. They had at least one child, Hunter Coalter Cosby. Ennis was buried in Maury Cemetery in Richmond.
- Nancy L. Cosby – Born in 1861 in Virginia. Date and location of death is unknown.[52] It is possible that she married George A. Ryan on 26 December 1883 in Spencer County, Indiana. If this is correct Nancy died on 22 December 1901 in Grandview, Indiana, at age 41 and they had at least five children including Albert Ryan, Mary Ryan, Grover Ryan, Onida Ryan, and George C. Ryan.

Mary likely died in January 1870 in Chesterfield County, Virginia of Consumption as indicated on 1870 US Federal Census Mortality Schedule where she was listed as Mollie S. Cosby, age 32.[53]

In 1870 Branch was teaching school when he appeared on the census in the household of John Walker in Chesterfield County, Virginia as Branch E. Cosby, age 41.[54]

Branch married Adeline Howard, daughter of John Howard and Nancy Johnson, on 27 April 1872. She was born on 30 July 1845 in Daviess County, Kentucky.[55] Branch was listed as a preacher on the 1880 census in Spencer County, Indiana as Branch E. Cosby, age 49 along with his wife Addie, age 34, son Howel H., age 21, and daughters Framee, age 22, Nancy L., age 19, Mary D., age 7, Rosa, age 3, and Maud, age 1. His nephew Meldm Cottrel (the correct spelling should have been Melvin Cottrell), age 9 was also listed in the household.[56]

Branch E. Cosby		
1850	Chesterfield Co., VA	Carpenter
1860	Chesterfield Co., VA	Minister
1870	Chesterfield Co., VA	Teacher
1880	Spencer Co., IN	Preacher

Children of Branch E. Cosby and Adeline Howard:

- Rosa Russell Cosby – Born on 10 September 1872 in Kentucky. She married Arway Nation Cottrell on 1 January 1902 in Daviess County, Kentucky at the home of her step-father John Howard. Rosa was working as a dressmaker in her home in April of 1930. She died on 30 January 1963 in Los Angles, California at age 90 and is buried at Rose Hills Memorial Park in Whittier, California in Terrance Lawn Garden, Section 1, Lot 827, Grave 836. Her husband Arway died on 26 January 1969 in Los Angeles and is buried next to Rosa at Rose Hills Memorial Park.[57] They had at least two children including:
    - o Cosby Monon Cottrell – Born on 7 February 1905 in Kentucky, married Florence Elizabeth Manson before 1940, and died on 19 December 1968 in Los Angeles, California. He was buried in Rose Hills Memorial Park in Whittier, California.[58]
    - o Maude Cottrell – Born on 5 August 1907, married Roland O. Wagner on 23 March 1967, and died on 1 February 1988 in Los Angeles. She was buried in Rose Hills Memorial Park in Whittier, California.[59]
- Mary Dawson Cosby – Born 13 April 1873 in Kentucky and died on 22 November 1956 in Depauw in Harrison County, Indiana at age 83. She was buried in Lexington Cemetery in Lexington, Kentucky. She also went by the name of Mamie

and Mayme.[60] She married Ramer Beatty Curtis on 3 February 1911 in Daviess County, Kentucky. Ramer was born on 6 February 1880 in Fayette County, Kentucky likely in Lexington, and died on 21 January 1965 in Corydon in Harrison County, Indiana. He was the son of John James Curtis and Sarah Malinda Curtis. When he registered for the WWI Draft in 1918 he was described as medium height with a stout build, grey eyes and brown hair. He was employed as a blacksmith and was living in Utica in Daviess County at the time. He was buried in Lexington Cemetery in Lexington, Kentucky.[61] Mary and Ramer had at least two children:

- o Carlton Jay Curtis – Born on 3 October 1912 in Hardin County, Kentucky and died in 1960. Carolton married Anna E. Ginter on 4 May 1937 in Clark County, Indiana. He was buried in Lexington Cemetery in Lexington in Fayette County, Kentucky.[62]
- o Edward H. Curtis – Born on 3 October 1916 and died on 28 September 1978. He was buried in Hancock Chapel United Methodist Cemetery in Harrison County, Indiana.[63]
- Maude Camp Cosby – Born on 15 December 1878 in Indiana; died on 21 May 1958 in Los Angeles, California. She married Clifton Slade Howard circa 1904. Clifton died on 17 August 1943 in Los Angeles. Maude and Clifton were buried in Grand View Memorial Park in Glendale in Los Angeles County. They had at least one child including:
  - o Adaline Howard who was born on 30 December 1914 in Daviess County, Kentucky[64] and attended Los Angeles High School and was employed as a Costume Designer in Los Angeles in 1936. In her 1932 high school yearbook she was listed with a pastime of sketching, and aspiration to become an artist, and noted as a collector of elephants.[65]
- Vera Branch Cosby – Born on 3 February 1883 in Newtonville, Indiana; died on 14 November 1961 in Breckinridge, Kentucky. Vera married Allan Lee Alsop on 6 January 1907 in Daviess County, Kentucky.[66] Allen was born on 23 March 1887 and died on 15 October 1963 in Breckinridge, Kentucky.

He was a manager in a tobacco company in Jefferson County, Kentucky in 1920. Vera and Allen had at least one child:

- o Florence Alsop – Born on 25 October 1907 in Gas City, Indiana and died in January 1979. She was living with her father in Daviess County, Kentucky in 1910. In 1920 she was living with her father in Jefferson County, Kentucky. Her birth year is questionable as the Social Security Applications and Claims Index lists date of birth as 25 October 1908.[67]

Branch died sometime before 1900. The location and date is unknown. Adeline was listed on the 1900 census in Daviess County, Kentucky, in the home of her father John Howard, as Adiline Cosby, age 59 and widowed. Her daughters Mary, age 28, Rosy, age 23, Maude, age 21, and Vera, age 18 were also listed in the household.[68]

In 1910 Adiline was listed as head of the household on the census in Daviess County, as Addie Cosby, age 64. Her daughter Mamie, age 37, was also listed in her household. She was living next door to her son-in-law Arway Cottrell and his wife Rosa at the time.[69]

Adeline died on 28 March 1913 in Hardin County, Kentucky. She was buried in Utica Baptist Church Cemetery in Daviess County.[70]

Judith Ann Cosby (1834-after 1900)

Daughter of Jefferson M. Cosby and Ann Wilson
Great-grandaunt of Taylor Cosby Cottrell, Jr.

Judith Ann Cosby was born in 1834 in Virginia. She was the daughter of Jefferson M. Cosby and Ann Wilson. She was listed on the 1850 census in Chesterfield County, Virginia in the household of her father Jefferson, as Ann, age 16.[71]

Judith married James Moseley Stratton on 28 March 1855 in Chesterfield County, Virginia. James was born on 27 January 1832 in Cumberland County, Virginia and died in 1903 in Goochland County. He was also known as Moses.[72] He served in Company C, 23rd Virginia Infantry Regiment and was buried in the Dover Baptist church Cemetery in Manakin, Virginia.

She appeared on the 1870 census in Chesterfield County, Virginia in the household of Sarah Stratton, age 28 along with her husband

James and several other Stratton adults and children. James was listed as age 36 and Judith was listed as age 35.[73]

She appeared on the 1880 census in the household of her husband James in Goochland County. James was listed as Moses Stratton, age 47 along with Judith A., age 46 and a daughter Martha A., age 19.[74] In 1900 she was listed in the household of her husband James, as Judith A., age 65. Her son Lorenza D., age 43, daughter-in-law Jennie, age 46, grandsons Normon R., age 16 and William M., age 12, and grand-daughter Ninna M., age 10 were also listed.[75] Judith died after 1900. James died in 1903 in Goochland County, Virginia. They were both buried at Dover Baptist Church Cemetery in Manakin, Goochland County, Virginia.[76]

Children of Judith Cosby and James Stratton:

- Lorenza Dow Stratton – Born in June 1857 in Virginia; died in 1928 in Virginia. Lorenza married Jennie Dunard on 4 December 1878 in Goochland County, Virginia. She was also known as Jenetta. Jennie was born in 1853 in Virginia. Lorenza was a salesman in 1900 and a grocery store salesman in 1910. His wife Jennie died on 26 February 1912 in Virginia at age 58. They were both buried in Dover Baptist Church Cemetery in Manakin, Goochland County, Virginia.[77] They had at least three children including:
    - o Normon R. Stratton – Born on 8 December 1884 in Virginia and died on 10 July 1915 in Manakin, Virginia. He was buried in Dover Baptist Church Cemetery in Manakin in Goochland County, Virginia.[78]
    - o William Moseley Stratton – Born on 20 June 1886 in Virginia and died on 20 February 1909 in Manakin, Virginia. He was buried in Dover Baptist Church Cemetery in Manikin, Virginia.[79]
    - o Ninna M. Stratton who was born on 2 April 1890 in Manakin, Virginia, married John Daniel Ripley on 15 December 1909 in Washington, D.C. John was the son of George W. Ripley and Mary Carter. He was born on 21 March 1887 and died on 30 September 1949 in Lynchburg, Virginia. He was described as medium height with a stout build, blue eyes, and dark hair when

he registered for the WWI draft in 1917. He was a telegraph operator at the time. Ninna died on 27 April 1960 in Lynchburg. They were both buried in Spring Hill Cemetery in Lynchburg. They had at least one child, John Daniel Ripley who was born on 14 May 1915 and died on 11 May 2012.[80]

- Martha Ninaver Stratton – Born in 1861 in Virginia. Martha married Lewis B. Stratton on 22 March 1883 in Goochland County, Virginia. Lewis was born in 1859.[81]

Mary Magdalene Cosby (1837-1875)

Daughter of Jefferson M. Cosby and Ann Wilson
Great-grandmother of Taylor Cosby Cottrell, Jr.

Mary Magdalene Cosby was born on 9 September 1837 in Chesterfield County, Virginia. She was the daughter of Jefferson M. Cosby and Ann Wilson. Information on Mary and her Family, and Mary's life history, along with that for her husband Peter Cottrell and their seven children is covered in detail in Section 1, Chapter 2, Peter Cottrell Family.[82]

Robert Dabney Cosby (1838-??)

Son of Jefferson M. Cosby and Ann Wilson
Great-granduncle of Taylor Cosby Cottrell, Jr.

Robert Dabney Cosby was born in 1838 in Virginia. He married Lou Courtney in 1858. Lou was also born around 1838 in Virginia. No additional information is known about Robert or Lou.[83]

Sarah J. Cosby (1841-1922)

Daughter of Jefferson M. Cosby and Ann Wilson
Great-grandaunt of Taylor Cosby Cottrell, Jr.

Sarah J. Cosby was born on 19 July 1841 in Virginia. She was the daughter of Jefferson M. Cosby and Ann Wilson. She was listed in the 1850 census in the household of her father Jefferson in Chesterfield County, Virginia as Sarah, age 10 and attending school. Sarah was also known as Sally.[84] She married Daniel Witt Stratton who was born in Virginia, around 1858. They had at least three children including Ivin

Maud Stratton, Walter H. Stratton, and Nettie Lou Stratton.[85] Sarah
was listed on the 1870 census in Chesterfield County, Virginia as Sarah, age 28 and head of the household along with Maud, age 12, Walter,
age 10, and Nettie B., age 3. Sarah's husband Daniel died before 1880,
date and location of death unknown.[86]

Children of Sarah and Daniel Witt Stratton:

- Ivin Maud Stratton – Born in 1859 in Virginia. He was living
  in the home of his grandfather Jefferson on the 1800 census in
  Chesterfield County, Virginia listed as Ivan M. Stratton, age
  21, single and working as a laborer on the farm. Date and location of death is unknown.[87]
- Walter H. Stratton – Born on 28 January 1861 in Virginia and
  died on 15 January 1931 at Johnston-Willis Hospital in Richmond Virginia, at age 69. He was buried in Hollywood
  Cemetery in Richmond, Virginia in Section 5, Lot 54. Walter
  was a farmer by trade and apparently never married.[88]
- Nettie Lou Stratton – Born on 17 January 1865 in Virginia and
  died on 12 June 1961 at Resthaven Nursing Home in Richmond, Virginia, at age 96. Her cause of death was cerebral
  hemorrhage. She was buried in Hollywood Cemetery in Richmond, Virginia. Nettie married Lucian Shelby Bass, son of
  William Upshur Bass and Sallie E. Redford, in 1888. Lucian
  was born on 14 December 1865 in Virginia and was a merchant
  in the Marine Corps in April of 1910 and a retail merchant in a
  general store in April 1930. They apparently had no children.
  Lucian died on 7 January 1950 in Midlothian, Virginia, at age
  84 and was buried in Hollywood Cemetery in Richmond, Virginia in Section 5, Lot 54.[89]

Sarah was listed as living with her father Jefferson M. Cosby on
the 1880 census as Sarah J. Stratton, age 38, and widowed.[90] She was
listed in the household of Lucian Shelby Bass on the 1910 census in
Chesterfield County, Virginia as Sally S. Stratton, mother-in-law, age
68 and widowed.[91] Sarah was listed on 1920 in Chesterfield County,
in the household of Shelby L. Bass, as Sallie Stratton, mother-in-law,
age 78 and widowed.[92] Sarah died in September 1922, likely in Virginia, and is buried in Hollywood Cemetery in Richmond, Virginia in
Section 5, Lot 54.[93]

Monterey Cosby (1846-1934)

Daughter of Jefferson M. Cosby and Nancy Harris
Great-grandaunt of Taylor Cosby Cottrell, Jr.

Monterey Cosby was born on 12 November 1846 in Chesterfield County, Virginia. She was the daughter of Jefferson M. Cosby and Nancy Harris.[94] She was listed on the 1850 census in Chesterfield County in the household of her father Jefferson, as Monterey, age 3 and in the 1860 census of her father in Chesterfield County, as Monterey, age 12 and attending school.[95] In 1869 Monterey married Beverly Far-rar Morrissett, son of John F. Morrissett and Nancy Ann Winfree. Beverly was born on 8 June 1833 in Chesterfield County and had previously married Judith Delany in 1858 before marrying Monterey in 1869. Beverly and Judith had two children Mary R. Morrissett and John H. Morrissett.[96]

Monterey was listed on the 1870 census of Chesterfield County, in the household of her father as Monterey Morrissett, age 21 along with her husband.[97] She was listed on the 1880 census in the household of her husband Beverly in Pittsylvania County, Virginia, as Monterey, age 32 along with daughters Mary R., age 20, Vivian, age 2, and Pearl, age 8/12. Sons Jno. H., age 19, Allen, age 8, Wellington, age 7, and Irvin, age 5 were also listed.[98]

In 1900 she was living with her husband at 771 Grove Street in Danville, Virginia. She was listed on the 1900 census in the Independent City of Danville in the household of her husband Beverly, as Monterey, age 52 along with sons Allen L., age 28, Wellington, age 26, Irving, age 25, and daughters Vivian, age 22 and Pearl, age 20.[99]

Monterey's family was still living at the same address in Danville in 1910 when she appeared on the census as Monterey C., age 63 along with daughters Vivian, age 32 and Pearl, age 30.[100] Beverly became a member of the Danville, Virginia police force in 1876 and was later recognized in an article in the Richmond Times Dispatch in 1918 as the oldest policeman in Virginia having been on the force for the past 40 years. He retired from the Danville police force in 1922.[101]

Children of Monterey Cosby and Beverly Morrissett:

- Allen Lynwood Morrissett – Born on 9 February 1872 in Chesterfield County, Virginia and died on 23 March 1960 in

Greensboro in Guilford County, North Carolina, at age 88 at the home of his daughter Mrs. Hilda Linehan following several years of declining health. Cause of death was chronic brain syndrome due to circulatory disturbance. His funeral was held at the Hanes-Lineberry Chapel. He was buried in Green Hill Cemetery in Danville, Virginia with graveside services at 5:15 in the afternoon.[102] Allen married Janie Booker Dallas on 7 July 1904 in Rockingham County, North Carolina. Janie was born on 24 April 1880 in North Carolina. Allen was a pressman for a newspaper in 1920 and a pressman in a print shop in April 1930.[103] Janie Booker Morrissett died on 4 August 1961 in Greensboro, North Carolina, at age 81 at her home at 816 Lexington Avenue. Funeral services were held at the Hanes-Lineberry Chapel with the Rev. Dwight Mullis officiating. She was also buried in Green Hill Cemetery in Danville, Virginia.[104] They had at least three children including:

- o Cosby Linwood Morrissett – Born on 6 April 1905 in Virginia, married Alma Stanley Qualls on 5 September 1931, and died on 6 November 1983 in Greensboro, North Carolina. He was buried in Pine Hill Cemetery in Burlington, Alamance County, North Carolina.[105] When he registered for the WWII Draft in 1942 he was living in Winston-Salem, North Carolina and working for the Piedmont Engraving Company.
- o Hilda V. Morrissett – Born on 14 November 1908 in Danville, Virginia, married Joseph J. Linehan around 1928, and died on 18 July 1993 in Greensboro. She was listed as widowed on her death certificate and was buried in Green Hill Cemetery in Danville, Virginia.[106]
- o Charlotte R. Morrissett – Born on 10 March 1915 in Elon College in Alamance County, North Carolina. She married Irvin Paylor Quate on 23 April 1938 in Guilford County, North Carolina. He was the son of D.M. Quate and Mytle C. Quate. Irvin was born on 18 October 1913 in Guilford County, and died on 14 October 1962 in Greensboro. Charlotte died on 17 December 1990 in James Island in Charleston County,

South Carolina. She was buried in Guilford Memorial
Park in Greensboro, North Carolina in Section 11.[107]

- Irvin Morrissett – Born on 30 November 1874 in Virginia; died
  on 2 May 1907, at age 32. He was buried in Green Hill Cemetery in Danville, Virginia. Irvin worked as a lab accountant
  in 1900 and never married.[108]

- Wellington Morrissett – Born on 7 March 1875 in Virginia and
  died on 6 June 1919 in Virginia, at age 44. He apparently died
  from a pulmonary disease. He was buried in Green Hill Cemetery in Danville, Virginia. His marital status in unsure. His
  death record lists him as single, yet his cemetery marker lists
  him as "Father Wellington Morrissett". At least one book on
  the Cosby Family lists him as having married Maggie Crawley
  in 1893, but he is listed as single on the 1900 census living with
  his father. He was a job printer in 1900 and in 1918 when he
  registered for the draft for World War I he was living in Norfolk, Virginia and working as a printer for S.B. Turney and
  Sons.[109]

- Vivian Morrissett – Born on 8 September 1877 in Danville,
  Virginia and died on 11 November 1961 in Danville, Virginia,
  at age 84. Her cause of death was congestive heart failure complicated by severe malnutrition. Funeral services were held at
  Townes Memorial Chapel. She was buried in Green Hill Cemetery in Danville, Virginia. Vivian never married and in later
  years lived with her sister Pearl in Danville.[110]

- Pearl Morrissett – Born on 7 September 1879 in Danville, Virginia and died on 27 October 1965 in Memorial Hospital in
  Danville, Virginia. Her cause of death was uremia due to congestive heart failure. Funeral services were held at Townes
  Memorial Chapel. She was buried in Green Hill Cemetery in
  Danville, Virginia. Pearl never married and in later years lived
  with her sister Vivian in Danville.[111]

Beverly died on 5 July 1922 in Danville, Virginia, at age 89. He
was buried in Green Hill Cemetery in Danville with a great number of
citizens and virtually the entire police force participating. Monterey
died on 15 December 1934 in Danville at age 88 and was also buried
in Green Hill Cemetery in Danville.[112]

Luther Calvin Cosby (1853-1941)

Son of Jefferson M. Cosby and Nancy Harris
Great-granduncle of Taylor Cosby Cottrell, Jr.

Luther Calvin Cosby was born on 1 March 1853 in Chesterfield County, Virginia. Luther was the son of Jefferson M. Cosby and Nancy Harris.[113] He was listed on the 1860 census in Chesterfield County in the home of his father Jefferson as Luther, age 7 and in the 1870 census in Chesterfield County in the home of his father as Lucher C., age 18 and attending school.[114] In 1880 he was still living with his father and was listed in the census in Chesterfield County as Luther C., age 28 and single.[115]

Luther married Annie Jewett Watkins on 28 April 1887 in Chesterfield County, Virginia. Annie was the daughter of John Watkins and Emily Ramsey Jewett and was born on 7 April 1853 in Virginia. Her mother was born in England.[116] Luther was listed on the 1900 census in Chesterfield County as Luther C. Cosby, age 47 and head of the household along with his wife Annie J., age 47 and sons Calvin W., age 12 and Irvin H., age 11.[117] In 1910 he was listed on the census in Chesterfield County as Luther C. Cosby, age 53 along with his wife Anna J., age 54 and sons Calvin, age 23 and Irvin, age 21. His mother-in-law Emily R. Watkins, age 70 and widowed was also living in their household.[118]

In 1920 Luther was listed on the census in Chesterfield County as Luther C., age 67. His wife Annie W., age 64 along with his son Irving H., age 30 and daughter-in-law Eunice N., age 29 were also listed.[119] In 1930 Luther was listed in the census in Chesterfield County in the home of his son Irving Handcock Cosby as Luther C, age 79 and widowed.[120]

Luther Calvin Cosby

1860	Chesterfield Co., VA	Unknown
1870	Chesterfield Co., VA	None
1880	Chesterfield Co., VA	Farm Laborer
1900	Chesterfield Co., VA	Carpenter
1910	Chesterfield Co., VA	Farmer
1920	Chesterfield Co., VA	Farmer
1930	Chesterfield Co., VA	N/A

Children of Luther Cosby and Annie Watkins:

- Calvin Watkins Cosby – Born on 7 November 1887 in Midlothian, Virginia and died on 20 January 1948 in Resthaven

Nursing Home in Midlothian, at age 60. His cause of death was cardiac arrest brought on by terminal pneumonia and cirrhosis of the liver. He was buried at Mount Pisgah Methodist Church Cemetery in Midlothian.[121] Calvin married Phyllis Virginius Cosby on 26 July 1917 in Burkeville in Nottoway County, Virginia.[122] She was the daughter of Phillip V. Cosby and May Smith and was born on 29 January 1898 in Nottoway County.[123] Calvin was described as medium height, medium build with blue eyes and brown hair when he registered for the WWI draft in 1917. He was the manager of Percy J. Straws in Richmond at that time and was living in Midlothian. Calvin and Phyllis divorced on 25 June 1928 in Richmond with the cause of the divorce listed as cruelty and desertion.[124] Calvin worked as a clerk in a grocery store in 1930 and in 1942 was working at the L.S. Bass Store in Midlothian.[125] Phyllis Virginius died on 25 April 1981 in the Richmond Memorial Hospital and was buried in Sunset Hill Cemetery in Burkeville, Virginia.[126] Calvin and Phyllis had at least two children including:

- o Annie May Cosby – Born around 1919 in Virginia.[127]
- o Fay Louise Cosby – Born on 4 December 1920 in Chesterfield County, Virginia and married Charles S. Scott on 30 March 1942 in Portsmouth, Virginia.[128]

- Irving Handcock Cosby, Sr. – Born on 18 May 1889 in Midlothian, Virginia and died on 5 November 1971 in Midlothian, at age 82. He was buried at Mount Pisgah Methodist Church Cemetery in Midlothian.[129] Irving was described as being medium height with a slender build, blue eyes, and light hair when he registered for the WWI draft in 1917. He was living living in Midlothian. He was employed as a police and game warden for the county of Chesterfield at the time. Irving married Irma V. Enroughty before 1920. She was born around 1900 in Pawhatan County, Virginia and was the daughter of James Winston Enroughty and Lena Bell Jordan and was apparently also known as Eunice or Emma. They had at least two children including:
  - o Irving Hancock Cosby Jr. – Born on 12 June 1920 in Chesterfield County, Virginia, married Rachel Estelle Turner on 13 June 1942, and died on 20 May 1994 in

Virginia. He was buried in Dale Memorial Park in Chesterfield, Virginia in Section 3, Cross Garden.[130] Irving was a county constable in 1930 and in 1942 was employed by the Etchison Hat Company in Midlothian.[131] Erma died in 1987 in Midlothian and was buried at Mount Pisgah Methodist Church Cemetery in Midlothian.[132]

o Calvin Thomas Cosby who was also known as Thomas Winston Cosby – Born on 28 February 1927 in Chesterfield County, married Elsie Mae Waters on 19 November 1949, and died on 5 November 1986 in Chesterfield County. His cause of death was from a small bowel obstruction. He served in the Coast Guard. He was buried in Providence United Methodist Church Cemetery in Chesterfield.[133]

Annie Watkins Cosby died on 13 November 1928 in Midlothian, Virginia, at age 75. Her cause of death was cerebral hemorrhage. She was buried in Mount Pisgah Methodist Church Cemetery in Chesterfield County, Virginia.[134] Luther Cosby died on 12 March 1941 in Midlothian, at age 88. Funeral services were held at Winfree Memorial Baptist Church in Midlothian and he was buried in Mount Pisgah Methodist Church Cemetery in Midlothian.[135]

Richard Hamilton Cosby (1853-1926)

Son of Jefferson M. Cosby and Nancy Harris
Great-granduncle of Taylor Cosby Cottrell, Jr.

Richard Hamilton Cosby was born on 3 November 1853 in Chesterfield County, Virginia. Richard was the son of Jefferson M. Cosby and Nancy Harris.[136] Richard was listed on the 1860 census in the home of his father Jefferson in Chesterfield County as R.H., age 6 and attending school.[137] In the 1870 census in Chesterfield County he was listed in the household of his father as Richard, age 16.[138] In the 1880 census he was still living in the home of his father in Chesterfield County and was listed as Richard H., age 25 and single.[139] Around 1885 he married Sarah Elizabeth Cosby, daughter of Ludwell Williams Cosby and Rebecca Wilson. Sarah was born around 1841 in Virginia.[140]

Richard was listed on the 1900 census in Chesterfield County, Virginia as Richard H., age 44 along with his wife Lizzie, age 56. He was listed as owning his home, free of mortgage. According to the census they had not had any children in the 15 years of their marriage. There was no occupation listed for Richard.[141] He was a

Richard Hamilton Cosby		
1860	Chesterfield Co., VA	Unknown
1870	Chesterfield Co., VA	Farm Laborer
1880	Chesterfield Co., VA	Farm Laborer
1900	Chesterfield Co., VA	Unknown
1920	Chesterfield Co., VA	Grocery Store Salesman

farmer by trade in early years. Sarah Died sometime before the 1920 census. In 1920 Richard was listed as a cousin in the household of Shelby L. Bass as Richard H. Cosby, age 65, and widowed.[142] He was employed at the time as a grocery store salesman.

Richard died on 12 May 1926 in Chesterfield County, at age 72. His cause of death was cancer of the stomach. He was buried in Hollywood Cemetery in Richmond, Virginia in Section 5, Lot 54. Richard and Sarah had no children.[143]

Charles Monroe Cosby (1855-1940)

Son of Jefferson M. Cosby and Nancy Harris
Great-granduncle of Taylor Cosby Cottrell, Jr.

Charles Monroe Cosby was born on 22 August 1855 in Midlothian in Chesterfield County, Virginia. He was the son of Jefferson M. Cosby and Nancy Harris.[144] He was listed on the 1860 census in Chesterfield County in the household of his father Jefferson as Chas., age 4.[145] He was listed on the 1870 census in the household of his father in Chesterfield County as Charles, age 13 and attending school.[146] On the 1880 census in Chesterfield County he was listed in the household of his father as Charles M., age 22, single, and working as a farm laborer.[147]

Charles married Maggie Florence Jackson on 30 December 1887 in Chesterfield County, Virginia. Maggie was the daughter of Richard H. Jackson and Harriett McGhee and was born on 22 January 1863 in Richmond, Virginia.[148]

Charles was listed on the 1900 census in Chesterfield County as Charles M. Cosby, age 44 along with his wife Florence, age 37, sons

Judson J., age 10 and Bernard J., age 9. His daughter Florence S., age 6 was also listed along with his mother Nancy, age 80 and widowed.[149] In the 1910 census in Chesterfield County he was listed as Charles M. Cosby, age 52 along with his wife Florence L., age 47, sons Jeff J., age 20 and Bernard, age 18, and his daughter Florence S., age 16.[150] On the 1920 census in Chesterfield County he was listed as Charles M. Cosby, age 64 and owning

Charles Monroe Cosby		
1860	Chesterfield Co., VA	N/A
1870	Chesterfield Co., VA	None
1880	Chesterfield Co., VA	Farm Laborer
1900	Chesterfield Co., VA	Farmer
1910	Chesterfield Co., VA	Farmer
1920	Chesterfield Co., VA	Farmer
1930	Chesterfield Co., VA	Farmer

a mortgaged farm on farm schedule 113. His wife Maggie F., age 56 and son Jefferson J., age 30 were also listed in the household.[151]

In the 1930 census in Chesterfield County, Charles was listed as head of household along with his wife Maggie F., age 67, son Judson J., age 42, daughter-in-law Darcy D., age 30, and grandson Bernard J., age 6. They were living on Middleton Pike at the time.[152]

Children of Charles Monroe Cosby and Maggie Florence Jackson:

- Jefferson Judson Cosby – Born on 28 July 1889 in Midlothian, Chesterfield County, Virginia; died on 24 November 1957 at Veterans Administration Hospital in Richmond, Virginia, at age 68. His cause of death was carcinoma of the hypopharynx with metastases. He was buried at Bethel Baptist Cemetery, Midlothian County, Virginia.[153] Judson worked in the lumber manufacturing business for many years and in later life was a farmer. When he registered for the WWI Draft in 1917 he was described as medium height with a slender build, brown eyes and brown hair. He was employed as a lumberman at the time and living in Midlothian, Virginia. He married Daisy Dell Everett on 12 October 1921 in Midlothian at the home of her Uncle, S.R. Sanders at 1819 Hanover Avenue. Daisy was also known as Darcy.[154] Jefferson was a veteran of WWI and was listed as unemployed when he registered for the draft for World War II in 1942. Daisy died on 14 August 1882 at her home in Pender County, North Carolina, at age 84. She was buried in Bethel Baptist Church Cemetery in Virginia.[155] Jefferson and Daisy had at least one child including:

- o Bernard Jackson Cosby – Born on 24 January 1924 in Midlothian, married Joan McGlothlin on 1 February 1947, and died on 24 October 1985 at General Hospital in Wilmington, North Carolina. He was buried in Sea Lawn Memorial Park in Hampstead in Pender County, North Carolina.[156]

- Bernard Jackson Cosby – Born on 23 September 1891 in Midlothian in Chesterfield County, Virginia and died on 29 July 1918 in France at age 26. His cause of death was from wounds received while serving as a Private during World War I while a member of Company B., 165th Infantry. When Bernard registered for the WWI Draft in 1917 he was described as tall with a slender build, blue eyes, and red hair. He was living in Midlothian at the time and was working as a farmer. Funeral Services were held on 26 June 1921 at Bethel Baptist Church in Midlothian, Virginia. Bernard was buried in the Bethel Baptist Church Cemetery following the funeral.[157]

- Florence Sadie Cosby – Born on 10 August 1893 in Midlothian, Chesterfield County, Virginia and died on 4 May 1974 in Richmond, Virginia, at age 80. She married Emmett Donald Farmer in 1918. Emmett was born on 28 April 1888 in Richmond. He died on 23 March 1929 at a local hospital in Richmond, Virginia, at age 40. After the death of her husband Emmett, Florence married James Green Oliver on 10 March 1946. James was born on 23 March 1885 in Chase City, Virginia and died on 27 October 1978 at age 93.[158] Florence and Emmett had at least two children including:

- o Emmett Donald Farmer – Born on 12 January 1919 in Richmond, married Susan Baugh James on 10 March 1945, and died on 14 April 2010 in Richmond. Burial location is unknown.[159]
- o Monroe Newton Farmer – Born on 11 August 1923 in Richmond, married June Audrine Tribbett on 14

October 1944, and died on 3 December 1992 in Norfolk, Virginia. He was a Midshipman in 1944 and
attended the United States Merchant Marine Academy in New York. Following his graduation, he was
commissioned an ensign in the U.S. Merchant Ma-
rines. He was buried in Eastern Shore Chapel
Cemetery in Virginia Beach, Virginia.[160]

Charles died on 13 November 1940 in Midlothian, Chesterfield
County, Virginia, at age 85. His cause of death was heart failure. Fu-
neral services were held at Winfree Memorial Baptist Church in
Midlothian. He was buried at Bethel Church Cemetery in Chesterfield
County.[161] Maggie died on 11 August 1950 in Richmond, Virginia, at
age 87. Her cause of death was arterial sclerosis. She was buried at
Bethel Church Cemetery in Midlothian in Chesterfield County.[162]

Lelia Mataline Cosby (1859-1930)

Daughter of Jefferson M. Cosby and Nancy Harris
Great-grandaunt of Taylor Cosby Cottrell, Jr.

Lelia Mataline Cosby was born in February 1859 in Chesterfield
County, Virginia. She was the daughter of Jefferson M. Cosby and
Nancy Harris. She was listed on the 1860 census in the household of
her father Jefferson in Chesterfield County, as Lilia, age 1.[163] She was
on the 1870 census in her father's household in Chesterfield County, as
Lillie, age 12 and attending school. In 1880 she was listed in the census
of Chesterfield County, in the household of her father as Lelia M, age
21 and single.[164]

Lelia married Joseph Goodman Puryear on 26 February 1884. Joseph was born in September 1858 in Halifax County, Virginia. He was
the son of Benson Jefferson Puryear and Elizabeth Dickerson Hall.[165]
Lelia was listed on the 1900 census in the household of her husband
Joseph in Pittsylvania County, Virginia as Lelia M., age 41 along with
daughters Elma W., age 13, Georgie W., age 11, and Ethel G., age 7.
Sons Benson J., age 9 and Sumpter S., age 4 were also living in the
household.[166] Joseph was a tobacconist in June of 1900.

Lelia was on the 1910 census in Danville Independent City, Virginia in the household of her husband Joseph, listed as Lela M., age 49
along with her sons Benson J., age 19 and Sumpter S., age 14, and

daughter Ethel W., age 17. In 1920 she was listed on the census in Campbell County, Virginia in the home of Richard Puryear as Lelia M. Puryear, age 57. Her husband, listed as J.G., age 63 was also in the household.[167]

Children of Lelia Mataline Cosby and Joseph G. Puryear:

- Benjamin Puryear – According to "My Wife's Family", written by Noah Bradley, Lelia and Joseph had a son named Benjamin who was born and died between 1885 and 1900.[168]
- Elma Wyllie Puryear – Born on 27 November 1886 in Virginia and died on 22 February 1984 in Leewood Nursing Home in Annandale, Fairfax County, Virginia, at age 97.[169] Cause of death was arteriosclerotic cardiovascular disease. Demaine Funeral Homes in Alexandria, Virginia handled final arrangements. She was cremated at Lee's Crematory in Washington, DC. Elma married Spencer Samuel Haithcock on 30 June 1908 in Danville, Virginia. Samuel was the son of Spencer S. Haithcock and Lucy Ann Shanks.[170] Elma and Samuel were divorced on 20 April 1931 in Virginia.[171] They had at least two children including:
  o Howard Spencer Haithcock – Born on 12 March 1909 in Savannah, Georgia, married Margaret Wilson on 16 February 1935 in Richmond, Virginia, divorced on 19 May 1942 in Richmond, and died on 19 September 2002 in Asheville in Puncombe County, North Carolina. Margaret was the plaintiff in the divorce decree and the cause of divorce was listed as desertion. Howard was buried in Saint Alban's Memorial Grove in Annandale, Fairfax County, Virginia.[172]
  o Katherine Louise Haithcock – Born during 1910 in Georgia.[173]
- Georgie W. Puryear – Born on 18 November 1888 in Virginia. Georgia married Edgar R. Norwood on 14 September 1906 in Halifax, Virginia. She was listed in the 1900 census of her father Joseph in Pittsylvania County, Virginia as Georgie W, age 11 and attending school. No additional information on either Georgie or Edgar is known.[174]

- Benson Jefferson Puryear – Born on 22 November 1890 in Danville, Virginia. He was listed on the 1900 census of Pittsylvania County in the household of his father as Benson J, age 9 and attending school. Benson registered for the draft while living in Bernalillo County, New Mexico in 1917. He was described as medium height, slender build with blue eyes and brown hair at the time and was living in Albuquerque and working for a dry goods store. He was also listed as married and having served in the Virginia National Guard. No additional information is known.[175]
- Ethel Goodman Puryear – Born on 13 January 1893 in Danville, Virginia. She was listed in the 1900 census of Pittsylvania County in the home of her father as Ethel G. She was living at 631 North 4th Avenue in Phoenix, Arizona while employed as a nurse in 1930. No additional information is known.[176]
- Sumpter Stuart Puryear – Born on 26 August 1895 in Pittsylvania County, Virginia; died on 5 July 1981 in Floyd County, Georgia, at age 85.[177] He was buried in Myrtle Hill Cemetery in Rome in Floyd County, Georgia. He married Etta Staub on 11 December 1920 in Fulton, Georgia. She was also known as Marietta Staub and was the daughter of John Christen Stub and Katherine Murray. Etta died on 12 August 1972 in Floyd County, Georgia and was also buried in Myrtle Hill Cemetery in Rome. They had at least one child:
  - Marietta Puryear – Born on 14 March 1926 in Georgia, married, husband's last name Near, and died on 22 October 2008, likely in Georgia. She was buried in Myrtle Hill Cemetery in Rome in Floyd County, Georgia with Daniels Funeral Home handling the arrangements.[178]

Joseph died on 21 June 1920 in Danville, Pittsylvania County, Virginia, at age 64. His cause of death was heart disease. He was buried in Green Hill Cemetery in Danville, Virginia.[179] Lelia died on 29 October 1930 in Memorial Hospital in Danville, at age 71. Her cause of death was heart failure. She was also buried in Green Hill Cemetery in Danville.[180]

Nannie Lee Cosby (1864-1934)

Son of Jefferson M. Cosby and Nancy Harris
Great-grandaunt of Taylor Cosby Cottrell, Jr.

Nannie Lee Cosby was born on 10 October 1864 in Chesterfield County, Virginia. She was the daughter of Jefferson M. Cosby and Nancy Harris.[181] She was listed on the 1870 census of Chesterfield County in the household of her father Jefferson as Nannie, age 7.[182] She was on the 1880 census of Chesterfield County in the home of her father as Nannie L., age 16 and single.[183]

She married Charles Edgar Harris on 15 May 1887 in Caswell, North Carolina.[184] Charles was born on 10 August 1864 in Pittsylvania County, Virginia. He was a coal dealer by trade.

Nannie Lee was listed on the 1910 census in the home of her husband Charles in Pittsylvania County, Virginia as Nannie L., age 44 along with her son Randolph C., age 19, daughter Uma A., age 17, and mother Asenith, age 78 and widowed. Her son Edger S., age 20 and his wife Lucy L., age 23 and their son Edgar R., age 1 8/12 were also listed in the household. [185]

In 1920 they were on the census in Pittsylvania County living at 664 Jefferson Street in Danville. Charles was listed as head of household, age 55 along with his wife Nannie L., age 55, son Randolph C., age 28, daughter-in-law Mamie P., age 24, daughter Urna A., age 24, and mother Asraneth, age 89.[186]

Children of Nannie Lee Cosby and Charles Edger Harris:

- Edgar Starr Harris – Born on 8 May 1889 in Danville in Pittsylvania County, Virginia and died on 12 January 1975 in Memorial Hospital in Danville, Virginia. He was buried in Green Hill Cemetery in Danville.[187] Edgar married Lucy E. Phillips on 15 September 1909 in Danville. She was born on 24 March 1887 and was the daughter of P.P. Phillips and Lucy Davis. Edgar was described as medium height and stout build with brown eyes and black hair when he registered for the WWI draft in 1917 while living in Danville. He was employed by the Danville City Plumbing Department at the time. In 1942 when he registered for the WWII draft he was employed by the Harris Coal Company in Danville. Lucy died on 25 August

1962 in Danville at the Roman Eagle Memorial Nursing Home. She was also buried in Green Hill Cemetery in Danville.[188] They had at least four children including:

- o Edgar Randolph Harris – Born on 26 June 1909 in Danville, Virginia, married Anna Mary Bing on 25 July 1934 in Lynchburg, Virginia. Anna was born on 28 September 1910 in Free Union, Virginia and was the daughter of Henry Bing and Clara Via. They had at least one child, Winified D. Harris who was born about 1938 in Virginia. Edgar died on 27 January 1996 in Clemmons in Forsyth County, North Carolina in a Nursing Home. He was buried in Mountain View Cemetery in Danville.[189]

- o Georgia Winfred Harris – Born on 27 June 1914 in Danville, Virginia and died on 15 October 1936 in Danville in Pitts County. She was listed as a pianist and single on her death certificate. She was buried in Green Hill Cemetery in Danville.[190]

- o Grace Estelle Harris – Born on 3 May 1919 in Pittsylvania, Virginia, married Charles Alexander Womack, Sr., on 2 October 1941 in Danville, Virginia, and died on 19 January 1994 in Danville. Charles was born in Martinsville, Virginia on 18 July 1917. He was the son of Charles T. Womack and Lena Robins, and was employed by the Virginia Carolina Electric Supply Company at the time of their marriage. Charles founded Womack Electric Supply which developed into a chain of stores throughout Virginia and North Carolina. He was also known for his philanthropic work. Grace and Charles had at least five children including Charles A. Womack, Jr., Robin Womack, David Womack, Kay Womack, and Jil Womack. Charles died on 1 June 2005 in Danville. Charles and Grace were both buried in Mountain View Cemetery in Danville.[191]

- o Edgar Starr Harris who was born on 18 May 1925 in Virginia. He enlisted in the U.S. Army on 4 June 1946 at the age of 21 and married Ethel Lucy Fowlkes shortly thereafter on 8 June 1946 in Caswell, North Carolina. [192] Ethel was born on 6 February 1926 in Pelham Caswe, North Carolina and died in September 1993. She was the daughter of James Hester Fowlkes and Neva E. Duncan.[193]

- Randolph Cosby Harris – Born on 12 April 1891 in Danville, Virginia and died on 28 July 1957 at 18 Elizabeth Street, Port of Spain, Trinidad, at age 66. His cause of death was uremia, mesenteric thrombosis and heart block. He was returned to the United States for burial by Pan American Airways on 3 August 1957.[194] He was buried in Forest Hill Cemetery in Glen Ellyn, DuPage County, Illinois.[195] He registered for the draft for WWI on 5 June 1917 while working as a bookkeeper in Danville, Virginia. He was described as tall with a medium build, brown eyes, and dark red hair at the time. Randolph married Mary Maimee Celestine Phillips in August 1919. Mary Maimee was born around 1894. Randolph registered for the WWII draft in 1942. He was living in Oak Park in Cook County, Illinois at the time and was employed by the United States Tobacco, Company in Chicago. Mary Maimee died on 8 June 1968 and was buried in Forest Hill Cemetery in DuPage County, Illinois.[196] Randolph and Mary Maimee had at least two children including:
  - o Randolph Cosby Harris Jr. – Born on 7 July 1921 in Danville in Pittsylvania County, Virginia and married Joyce Marjorie Hayes. Joyce was born in on 19 June 1927 and died on 9 May 2008. She was the daughter of William A. Hayes and Viola C. Dauer. Randolph died on 10 September 2011 in Glen Ellyn, Illinois, at the age of 90. Joyce was born on 19 June 1927 and died on 9 May 2008. She had previously been married to Robert Donald Feeheley in 1949. Randolph was a Captain in the US Air Force during World War II. He was buried in Abraham Lincoln National Cemetery in Elwood in Will County, Illinois in Section C4-063, Row D, Site 19 along with his wife Joyce.[197]
  - o George Philip Harris – Born in 1923 in Illinois, killed in action on 12 December 1944 while piloting a B-26

Bomber during World War II. He was a First Lieutenant in the U.S. Army Air Forces in the 449th Bomber Squadron, 322nd Bomber Group, Medium. He received a Purple Heart and Air Medal and was listed on the World War II Honor Roll. His monument is located in Henri-Chappelle American Cemetery and Memorial in Arrondissement de Verviers in Liege, Belgium in Plot G, Row 5, Grave 2.[198]

- Urna Alma Harris – Born on 18 November 1893 in Danville, Virginia and died on 19 December 1947 in Colony in Amherst County, Virginia, at age 55. Her cause of death was coronary disease. Her date of birth is somewhat in question as it was listed as 18 November 1893 on her gravestone and 29 November 1892 on her death certificate. She was buried in Green Hill Cemetery in Danville, Virginia. She was listed on the 1910 census in the household of her father in Pittsylvania County as Urna A., age 17, single and attending school. In 1920 she was living with her father at 664 Jefferson Street in Danville, Virginia. Urna never married.[199]

Nannie Lee died on 15 February 1934 in Danville in Pittsylvania County, Virginia, at age 69 at her home on West Main Street. Funeral services were held at Mount Vernon Church in Danville, Virginia. She was buried in Green Hill Cemetery in Danville.[200] Charles died on 20 May 1945 in Danville, at age 80. His cause of death was acute myocarditis. He was also buried in Green Hill Cemetery in Danville.[201]

John Stuart Cosby (1867-1940)

Son of Jefferson M. Cosby and Nancy Harris
Great-granduncle of Taylor Cosby Cottrell, Jr.

John Stuart Cosby was born on 17 March 1867 in Chesterfield County, Virginia. John was the son of Jefferson M. Cosby and Nancy Harris.[202] He was listed on the 1870 census in the household of his father Jefferson M. Cosby as John, age 4.[203] He appeared on the 1880 census in the household of his father in Chesterfield County as John S., age 14, single, and at school.[204]

John married Jannett Jewett on 27 July 1904 in Caswell County, North Carolina. Jannett was born on 30 March 1873 in Midlothian,

Virginia. She was the daughter of George H. Jewett, who was born in England, and Bettie Cole who was born in Virginia.[205]

John was a carpenter in April 1910. He was listed on the 1910 census in Chesterfield County, Virginia as John S. Cosby, age 43 along with his wife Jeanette J., age 34 and their son Stewart, age 5.[206] In 1920 he was

John Stuart Cosby		
1870	Chesterfield Co., VA	None
1880	Chesterfield Co., VA	In School
1910	Chesterfield Co., VA	Carpenter
1920	Chesterfield Co., VA	Railroad Machinist
1930	Chesterfield Co., VA	Railroad Inspector

listed on the census in Chesterfield County as a machinist on the railroad. His wife Janetta, age 45 and son Stewart, age 14 were also listed.[207]

In 1930 he was a railroad inspector when he appeared on the census in Chesterfield County as John S. Cosby, age 63 along with his wife Jeanetta J., age 56 and son Stewart S., age 24.[208] In 1940 he was listed on the census in Chesterfield County as John S. Cosby, age 73 along with his wife Janette, age 60 and son Stuart, age 34. He was still working and was listed as a Railroad Shop Foreman.[209]

Children of John Stuart Cosby and Jannett Jewett:

- Stuart Shelby Cosby – Born on 2 August 1905 in Virginia; died on 15 July 1981 in the VA Medical Center in Richmond, Virginia, at age 75. His cause of death was congestive heart failure coupled with a seizure disorder. He was buried at Mount Pisgah Methodist Church Cemetery in Midlothian, Virginia.[210] Stuart was listed in the household of his father in 1910 in Chesterfield County as Stewart, age 5. In 1920 he was listed as Stewart, age 14 and attending school. In the 1930 census in Chesterfield County he was listed as Stewart S, age 24 and single. In 1940 he was still living with his parents in Chesterfield County and was listed as a Finisher in a Hat Factory. He enlisted in the Army on 12 March 1942 at Camp Lee in Virginia as a Private. Stuart married Eron M. Fore, daughter of Julian Fore and Alice McMahon, on 19 November 1942 in Richmond, Virginia.[211] Eron was born on 5 July 1906 and died on

15 March 1999 in Henrico County, Virginia. She was also buried at Mount Pisgah Methodist Church Cemetery in Midlothian.[212]

John died on 6 April 1940 at his home in Midlothian in Chesterfield County, Virginia, at age 73,. His cause of death was coronary thrombosis. Gravesite Masonic funeral services were held on 8 April 1940 in Midlothian. He was buried at Mount Pisgah Methodist Church Cemetery in Midlothian.[213]

Jannett died on 5 February 1941 at 6:30 in the evening in Midlothian, at age 67. Her cause of death was heart disease. She was also buried at Mount Pisgah Methodist Church Cemetery.[214]

Chapter 6 – Norris L. Lashbrook Family

2nd Great-grandfather of Taylor Cosby Cottrell, Jr.

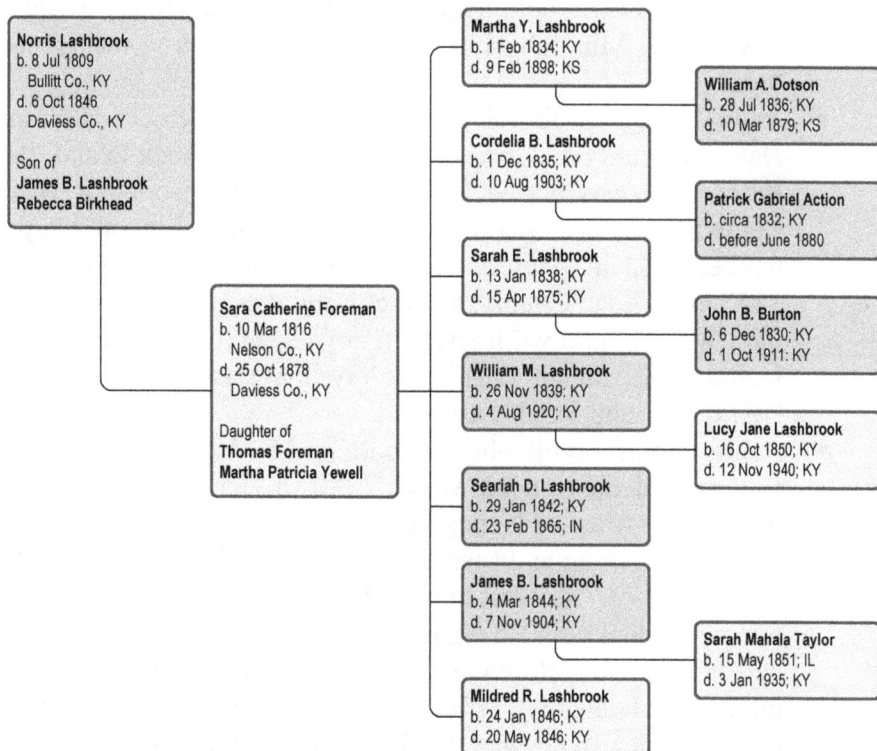

Norris Lashbrook
b. 8 Jul 1809
  Bullitt Co., KY
d. 6 Oct 1846
  Daviess Co., KY
 	
Son of
James B. Lashbrook
Rebecca Birkhead
	Martha Y. Lashbrook
	b. 1 Feb 1834; KY
	d. 9 Feb 1898; KS

	William A. Dotson b. 28 Jul 1836; KY d. 10 Mar 1879; KS
	Cordelia B. Lashbrook b. 1 Dec 1835; KY d. 10 Aug 1903; KY
	Patrick Gabriel Action b. circa 1832; KY d. before June 1880

Sara Catherine Foreman
b. 10 Mar 1816
  Nelson Co., KY
d. 25 Oct 1878
  Daviess Co., KY
 	
Daughter of
Thomas Foreman
Martha Patricia Yewell
	Sarah E. Lashbrook
	b. 13 Jan 1838; KY
	d. 15 Apr 1875; KY

	John B. Burton b. 6 Dec 1830; KY d. 1 Oct 1911: KY
	William M. Lashbrook b. 26 Nov 1839: KY d. 4 Aug 1920; KY
	Lucy Jane Lashbrook b. 16 Oct 1850; KY d. 12 Nov 1940; KY
	Seariah D. Lashbrook b. 29 Jan 1842; KY d. 23 Feb 1865; IN
	James B. Lashbrook b. 4 Mar 1844; KY d. 7 Nov 1904; KY
	Sarah Mahala Taylor b. 15 May 1851; IL d. 3 Jan 1935; KY
	Mildred R. Lashbrook b. 24 Jan 1846; KY d. 20 May 1846; KY

     Norris L. Lashbrook was born on 8 July 1809 in Bullitt County, Kentucky. He was the son of James B. Lashbrook and Rebecca Birkhead. His father James was born on 15 March 1775 in Jefferson County, Kentucky and was the son of William Lashbrook and Epha Effy Etherlridge both of whom were born in Prince William County, Virginia and died in Bullitt County, Kentucky. His mother Rebecca Birkhead was born on 10 February 1777 in Shenandoah County, Virginia and died on 11 October 1838 in Daviess County, Kentucky. She was the daughter of Jesse Abraham Birkhead and Mary Crume both of whom were born in Virginia and died in Kentucky.[1] Norris had at least five brothers and sisters including:

- John Lashbrook who was born in 1803 in Adams Fork in Henry County, Kentucky and died on 27 June 1874 in Daviess County. He married Rebecca Burton who was the daughter of Allen Burton and Rebecca Hamner on 31 January 1827 in Ohio

County, Kentucky. Rebecca was born on 7 February 1798 in
Mercer County, Kentucky and died on 8 May 1870 in Daviess
County. They had at least six children Amanda M. Lashbrook,
James A. Lashbrook, Bassett B. Lashbrook, John Wesley
Lashbrook, Minorah H. Lashbrook, and Sarah Anne Lash-
brook.

- John Wesley Lashbrook who was born on 9 October 1806 in
Daviess County and died on 3 March 1864 in Rock Island, Illinois. He was buried at the Confederate Prisoner of War
Cemetery in Rock Island. He married Sarah Wright on 2 September 1833 in Daviess County. Sarah died on 10 October
1847 in McLean County, Kentucky and was buried in the William Wright Family Cemetery. They had at least four children
including Elizabeth Lashbrook, Syrilda Lashbrook, Alax J.
Lashbrook, and Sarah Lashbrook.

- James B. Lashbrook who was born on 15 May 1812 in Bullitt
County and died on 22 March 1880 in Harlen County, Ne-
braska. He Married Nancy Foreman who was the daughter of
Thomas Foreman and Martha Patrica Yewell on 14 July 1839
in Owensboro. She was born in 1809 in Nelson County, Kentucky and died on 9 November 1846 in Daviess County. They
had at least two children including Elizabeth Lashbrook and an
unidentified daughter. After Nancy's death he married Huldah
Adosia Bolen, who was the daughter of Elijah Bolen, on 23
October 1859 in Daviess County. She was born on 5 March
1833 in New York and died on 12 January 1922 in Bonner
Springs, Kansas, at age 88. They had at least four children including John B. Lashbrook, James Lawrence Lashbrook,
Matilda Florence Lashbrook, and Charles Wesley Lashbrook.

- Serilda Lashbrook who was born in 1820 in Bullitt County.
She married Edmund W. Frazier on 3 August 1837 in Daviess
County. He was born in 1817 and died on 30 November 1853
in Daviess County. They had at least five children including
Sanders Frazier, Albert Frazier, Lucy A. Frazier, W. Blanton
Frazier, and Smantha Martha Frazier.

- Achilles Asa Lashbrook who was born on 2 July 1820 in Bullitt
County and died on 20 November 1881 in McLean County,

Kentucky. He was buried in Salem Methodist Cemetery in Daviess County. He married Martha Ann Johnson, who was the daughter of Rebecca Bennett, on 1 April 1841 in Ohio County, Kentucky. She was born on 26 January 1824 in Kentucky and died on 12 May 1874 in Daviess County. She was also buried in the Salem Methodist Cemetery. They had at least eight children including Sarah A. Lashbrook, James Phillip Lashbrook, William Edmund Lashbrook, John Samuel Lashbrook, America Gardner Lashbrook, Surelda Frances Lashbrook, Rosey L. Lashbrook, Alice Elizabeth Ann Lashbrook, and Martha J. Lashbrook.[2]

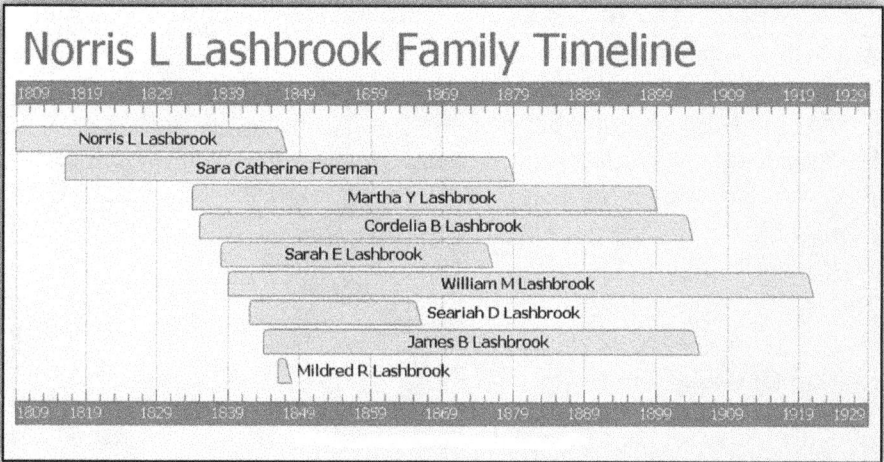

Norris married Sara Catherine Foreman, who was the daughter of Thomas Foreman and Martha Patricia Yewell on 11 March 1833 in Nelson County, Kentucky.[3] Sara's father Thomas was born on 20 October 1786 in Pennsylvania and died on 24 May 1838 in Nelson County, Kentucky. Her mother Martha was born on 24 October 1789 in Culpeper County, Virginia and died in 1864 in Virginia. Thomas and Martha married in Nelson County, Kentucky on 23 March 1806.[4] Sara Catherine was born on 10 March 1816 near Bardstown in Nelson County. She also went by the name of Kitty.[5] Sarah had at least two siblings including Nancy Foreman who was born in 1809 in Nelson County, Kentucky and died on 9 November 1846 in Daviess County,

Kentucky and Emily Foreman who was born in 1822 in Nelson County and died in 1863 in Ohio County, Kentucky.[6]

After their marriage Norris and Sara Catherine settled on their farm near the Bethabara Church in Masonville Precinct. They were both members of the Methodist Episcopal Church.[7] Norris witnessed the probate of the estate of his mother Rebecca when the Court issued Letters of Administration to his brother John on 12 November 1838.[8] Norris was one of the pioneers of Daviess County and was described as an earnest Christian and a good husband, father and neighbor and a very intelligent man, of good judgement.[9]

Norris and Sara had at least seven children including Martha Yewell Lashbrook, Cordelia Bean Lashbrook, Sarah Elizabeth Lashbrook, William Martin Lashbrook, Seariah Deering Lashbrook, James Birkhead Lashbrook, and Mildred Rebecca Lashbrook. Norris died on 6 October 1846 in Daviess County, at age 37. He was buried at Lashbrook Family Cemetery in Browns Valley in Daviess County.[10] His estate was probated on 9 November 1846 in Daviess County.[11]

Sarah Catherine Foreman

Sarah then married George A.R. Wilhite, also spelled Wilhoyte, on 5 December 1848 in Daviess County.[12] George was Catherine's cousin. Catherine had six additional children with George, all of whom died as infants.[13] Sara was listed on the 1850 census in the household of George A.R. Wilhite in Daviess County as Cathrn, age 24 along with Martha Lashbrook, age 6, Cordelia Lashbrook, age 14, Elizth. Lashbrook, age 12, Wm. M. Lashbrook, age 10, Leah Lashbrook, age 8, James Lashbrook, age 6, and Benjm Wright, age 18. The ages of both George and Sara listed them as approximately 10 years younger than they were in 1850.[14] In 1860 Sara was listed on the census in the household of her husband in Daviess County, as Catherine, age 44 along with Wm. M.

Lashbrooks, age 20, Sarah D. Lashbrooks, age 18, and James B. Lashbrook, age 16.[15]

Family lore, according to Nellie Jane Lashbrook, was that Catherine's son Sariah Lashbrook's horse was shot out from under him and he was captured and taken to Camp Chase, a prison in Ohio. Dysentery broke out in prison and he took ill and was so sick that his mother Catherine went to see him. It was said that she had to take a boat from Owensboro, Kentucky to Evansville, Indiana and then on to Camp Chase. When she reached Camp Chase, Sariah begged her to "ask him out of prison" to die. According to family lore, Catherine traveled to Washington, partially by horseback, to see President Lincoln to seek the release of her son so he could die at home. When she arrived the butler wouldn't let her in, but it was said the President happened by and motioned for her to come in. He shook hands with her and asked about her mission. An aged father was also at the gate with a letter asking for his son to be released. Lincoln was said to have granted both requests.

However, when she got back Sariah was dead.[16] In this case family lore was at least partially incorrect as is several published works listing his death as Camp Case. According to his service record, as well as Camp Morton camp records reviewed at the National Archives, list him as a prisoner of war at Camp Morton, rather than Camp Chase, and record his death at Camp Morton in Indianapolis, Indiana.[17]

Sara was listed on the 1870 census in the household of her husband George in Daviess County as Catherine, age 54 along with Jas. B. Lashbrook, age 26. Real

Sarah Catherine Foreman
Macedonia Baptist Church Cemetery
Philpot, Kentucky

estate value was listed as $3,800 and personal estate value was listed as $1,250.[18]

Sara died on 25 October 1878 in Daviess County, at age 62. She was buried in Macedonia Baptist Church Cemetery in Daviess County, next to her son Seariah.[19] Date and location of death of George Wilhoyte is unconfirmed but was likely 31 January 1888 at his residence near Bethabara, Kentucky. It is also likely he was buried in Bethabara Baptist Church Cemetery in Daviess County.[20]

Martha Yewell Lashbrook (1834-1898)

Daughter of Norris L. Lashbrook and Sara Catherine Foreman
Great-grandaunt of Taylor Cosby Cottrell, Jr.

Martha Yewell Lashbrook was born 1 February 1834 in Daviess County, Kentucky. She was the daughter of Norris L. Lashbrook and Sara Catherine Foreman.[21] She was listed on the 1850 census in Daviess County in the home of George A.R. Wilhite, her step-father, as Martha Lashbrook, age 16.[22]

Martha married William A. Dotson on 25 March 1853. William was born on 28 July 1836 in Leitchfield in Grayson

Martha Yewell Lashbrook

County, Kentucky. In 1859 William entered the ministry of the M.E. Church and although born and raised under southern influence he remained loyal to the M.E. Church and stood firmly in support of the Union.[23]

Martha was listed on the 1860 census in the home of her husband William in Campbell County, Kentucky as Martha, age 26. Her daughter Sara was also listed as S.E., age 5.[24]

She was found on the 1870 census in McCracken County, Kentucky in the home of her husband William as Martha, age 35 along with Sarah E., age 13, Willie S., age 8, Edward E., age 5, and Florance C., age 1.[25]

The 1885 Kansas census indicated that Martha and her children moved to Kansas from Colorado so they likely lived for a short time in Colorado after leaving Kentucky before arriving in Kansas.[26] William died on 10 March 1879 in Newton in Harvey County, Kansas. William's cause of death was congestion of the lungs.

Funeral services were held for William on 11 March 1879 in the M.E. Church in Newton. His remains were escorted from his residence to the church and from there to the cemetery by the Masons of the city. He was buried in Greenwood Cemetery in Newton.[27]

Children of Martha Yewell Lashbrook and William A. Dotson:

- Sarah E. Dotson – Born on 30 November 1855 in Grayson County, Kentucky. The last known location for Sarah was the 1870 census in McCracken County, Kentucky.[28]
- William Simpson Dotson – Born on 14 February 1862 in Grayson County, Kentucky; Died on 7 March 1922 in Newton in Harvey County, Kansas, at age 60. He was buried in Greenwood Cemetery in Newton.[29] In 1880 he was working in a hardware store and in 1885 in a grocery store.[30] William married Mary Ellen Scott in 1886. Mary was born on 17 January 1869 in Ohio.[31] She was the daughter of Isiah Scott and Harriet Minerva Sinks. By 1900 they had moved to Newton. Mary Ellen likely died 3 June 1954 in Newton and is buried in Greenwood Cemetery.[32] William and Mary Ellen had at least three children including:
  o William Harrison Dotson – Born on 3 May 1888 in Newton, Kansas, married Carrie Adele Strittmater, and died on 5 July 1969 in Hildago County, Texas. William registered for the WWI draft on 5 June 1917 while living in Newton, Kansas. He was employed as a wholesale merchant at the time and was described as short, medium build with brown eyes and brown hair. In 1925 he was an owner of a produce business. He was buried in Mission Burial Park South in San Antonio in

Bexar County, Texas.[33] William and Carrie hat at least two children including William Francis Dotson and Robert Scott Dotson.

- o Katheryn Mary Dotson – Born on 5 August 1895 in Newton, Kansas, married John A. Murray, and died on 6 October 1975 in Houston, Texas. She was a music teacher in 1915 and a school teacher in 1920. She was buried in Memorial Oaks Cemetery in Houston, Texas on 7 October 1975.[34]
- o John Irving Dotson – Born on 2 February 1900 in Kansas, married Gladys Graybill in 1921, and died on 4 April 1953 in Kansas.[35] John was Mayor of Wichita, Kansas in 1941 and served as City Commissioner for three terms. John and Gladys had at least two children including John Graybill Dotson and Scott Irving Dotson. John and Gladys were both buried in Greenwood Cemetery in Newton, Kansas.
- Edward T. Dotson – Born on 1 July 1864 in Kentucky; Died on 13 October 1887 in Newton in Harvey County, Kansas, at age 23. He was buried in Greenwood Cemetery in Newton. Edward never married.[36]
- Florance C. Dotson – Born in September 1869 in Kentucky; Died on 25 November 1934 in San Diego, California, at age 66. Florance married Walter Lytle Hulick in 1895.[37] Walter was born on 21 September 1871 in Batavia in Clermont County, Ohio. He was the son of Erastus Hulick and Amanda Lytle.[38] Walter died 31 May 1955 also in San Diego.[39] They had at least two children including:
  - o Alice Hulick – Born on 18 February 1896 in Kansas, married James Lavallee, and died on 28 March 1984 in San Diego. Alice and James traveled to London, England arriving in London on the Ship Iberia on 16 April 1960. Alice was buried in Cypress View Mausoleum and Crematory in San Diego, California in the North Building, Bronze Corridor.[40]
  - o Ernest Oliver Hulick who was born on 1 November 1905 in Kansas, married, wife's name was Helen, and died on 19 October 1975 in San Diego.[41] Helen was

born around 1907 in Oklahoma. Ernest was buried in Cypress View Mausoleum and Crematory in San Diego, California in the North building, Bronze Corridor.[42]

Martha was listed on the 1880 census in Harvey County, Kansas as Martha Dotson, age 46, keeping house, and widowed. Her sons Willie, age 17 and Edward, age 15 were listed as single and her daughter Flora C., age 11 was listed as attending school.[43] She was found on the 1885 census in Harvey County as M.Y. Dotson, age 51 and widowed along with W.S. Dotson, age 23, E.G. Dotson, age 20, and F.C. Dotson, age 16.[44] She was on the 1895 Harvey County census as Martha Y. Dotson, age 61 along with Flora C., age 25.[45]

Martha died on 9 February 1898 at her residence on West Seventh Street in Newton, Harvey County, Kansas, at age 64. Her cause of death was pneumonia brought on by the grippe. Funeral services were held at the M.E. Church in Newton. She was buried in Greenwood Cemetery in Newton.[46]

Cordelia Bean Lashbrook (1835-1903)

Daughter of Norris L. Lashbrook and Sara Catherine Foreman
Great-grandaunt of Taylor Cosby Cottrell, Jr.

Cordelia Bean Lashbrook was born on 1 December 1835 in Daviess County, Kentucky. She was the daughter of Norris L. Lashbrook and Sara Catherine Foreman.[47] She was listed on the 1850 census of her step-father George A.R. Wilhite in Daviess County, as Cordelia Lashbrook, Age 14.[48] She married Patrick Gabriel Action, the son of Bartemus Action and Sarah Ann Sallie Robey, on 22 March 1853 in Daviess County.[49] Patrick was born around 1832 in Kentucky.[50]

Cordelia was listed on the 1860 census in the household of her husband Patrick in Ohio County, Kentucky as Cordelia, age 28 along with Sarah C., age 5, and John W., age 2. Two other Acton families were listed in adjacent dwelling numbers on the census.[51] She appeared on the 1870 census in Ohio County in the household of her husband Patrick as Cordelia, age 34 along with Sarah C., age 14, and Wm. L., age 10/12, born in August. Real estate was valued at $2,000 and personal property was valued at $1,000. Children that were previously listed on the 1860 census, John W. Acton and Cicero M. Action were not listed so it is likely they both died prior to 1870.[52]

Children of Cordelia Bean Lashbrook and Patrick Gabriel Acton:

- Sarah Catherine Acton – Born on 2 September 1855 in Ohio County, Kentucky and died on 20 July 1919 in Sulphur Springs in Ohio County, Kentucky, at age 63. Her cause of death was cerebral hemorrhage. She was buried in Sunnydale Cemetery in Ohio County, Kentucky.[53] Sarah married Robert Newton Duke on 14 June 1990 in Ohio County. Robert was the son of William Duke and Julia Ann Neely and was born on 18 June 1848 in Kentucky.[54] Robert died on 9 March 1925 in Sunnydale in Ohio County, at age 76. He was buried in Sunnydale Cemetery.[55] Sarah and Robert had at least two children including:
  - o Ernest D. Duke – Born on 9 May 1885 in Ohio County, married Fannie M. Berry on 27 January 1914, and died on 27 May 1928 in Sunny Dale, Kentucky. Fannie was born in 1893 and died on 10 March 19654. They were buried together in Sunnydale Cemetery in Narrows, in Ohio County.[56]
  - o Elizabeth B. Duke - Born on 29 May 1894 in Kentucky and died on 12 February 1901.[57]
- John William Acton – Born on 8 November 1857 in Ohio County, Kentucky. He was not listed on the 1870 census so it is likely his death occurred prior to 1870.[58]
- Cicero M. Acton – Born in 1860 in Ohio County, Kentucky. He was not listed on the 1870 census so it is likely his death occurred prior to 1870.[59]
- William Lee Acton – Born on 28 August 1869 in Ohio County, Kentucky; Died on 5 July 1931 at his home on Bolivar Street in Owensboro in Daviess County, Kentucky at age 61. His cause of death was heart disease.[60] Funeral services were held at the Third Baptist Church in Owensboro and he was buried in Elmwood Cemetery in Owensboro.[61] William married Lillian S. Lee on 24 April 1901 in Owensboro. He was a house carpenter and building contractor by trade. William and Lillian apparently had no children.[62]

Patrick died before the 1880 census, date and location of death is unknown. Cordelia was listed on the 1880 census in Daviess County,

Kentucky as Cordelia Acton, age 44, widowed, and the step-daughter in the household of George Wilhoyte. William L. Acton, age 10 was listed as George's grandson.[63] After the death of her husband, Cordelia lived with her daughter Mrs. Robert Duke.[64]

Cordelia died on 10 August 1903 at her home in Narrows in Ohio County, Kentucky, at age 67. Funeral services were held on 12 August 1903 at her home in Narrows. Her son William traveled from Owensboro, Kentucky to attend her funeral. She was buried in Sunnydale Cemetery in Ohio County.[65]

Sarah Elizabeth Lashbrook (1838-1875)

Daughter of Norris L. Lashbrook and Sara Catherine Foreman
Great-grandaunt of Taylor Cosby Cottrell, Jr.

Sarah Elizabeth Lashbrook was born on 13 January 1838 in Daviess County, Kentucky. She was the daughter of Norris L. Lashbrook and Sara Catherine Foreman.[66] She was listed on the census of 1850 in the household of her step-father George A.R. Wilhite in Daviess County, as Elizth., age 12.[67] Sarah married John Bassett Burton, son of James A. Burton and Susan Ward on 12 May 1859 in Daviess County. John was born on 6 December 1830 in Ohio County, Kentucky. [68]

Sarah was listed on the 1860 census in Daviess County in the household of her husband John as S.E. Barton, age 21. Florence Barton, age 6/12 and Jno. Lashbrooks, age 26 were also listed.[69] She was listed on the 1870 census in the household of her husband John in Daviess County as Sarah E., age 31. James N., age 2 was also listed. John's estate was valued at $4,000 with personal property valued at $2,000.[70]

Children of Sarah Elizabeth Lashbrook and John Bassett Burton:

- Florence Burton – Born on 28 March 1860 in Daviess County and died on 20 November 1868 in Daviess County, at age 8. She was buried in the John A. Burton Family Cemetery in Masonville in Daviess County.[71]
- Electa Burton – Born on 27 February 1862 in Daviess County and died on 20 November 1868 in Daviess County, at age 6.

She was buried in the John A. Burton Family Cemetery in Masonville.[72]

- Joseph S. Burton – Born on 8 December 1863 in Daviess County and died on 23 November 1868 in Daviess County, at age 4. He was buried in the John A. Burton Family Cemetery in Masonville.[73]

- Susan C. Burton – Born on 26 July 1866 in Daviess County and died on 24 November 1868 in Daviess County, at age 2. She was buried in the John A. Burton Family Cemetery in Masonville.[74]

- James Martin Burton – Born on 25 August 1868 in Daviess County and died on 14 May 1886 in Daviess County, at age 17. In 1880 James was listed on the census as ill with Rheumatism. He was buried in the John A. Burton Family Cemetery in Masonville.[75]

- Samuel E. Burton – Born on 24 April 1872 in Daviess County; Died on 26 March 1965 in Daviess County. He was buried in Rosehill Cemetery in Owensboro in Daviess County, Kentucky.[76] Samuel married Ella J. Ellis on 24 January 1893 in Daviess County. Ella was born on 25 November 1873 in Daviess County.[77] Ella died on 28 May 1923 in Masonville in Daviess County, at age 49. She was buried in Rosehill Cemetery in Owensboro.[78] Samuel and Ella had at least two children including:
  - o Florence V. Burton – Born on 7 June 1895 in Daviess County and married Paul Adams Kirk on 30 December 1914. Paul was born on 16 April 1893 and died on 15 February 1954. Florence died on 6 August 1983 in Kentucky. They were both buried in Rosehill-Elmwood Cemetery in Owensboro. They had at least two children including Hugh Jackson Kirk and Pauline Ellis Kirk.[79]
  - o Hugh Bassett Burton – Born on 2 November 1896 in Daviess County and married Anna Reade Cruse in 1925. Anna was born on 26 April 1897 and died on 2 May 1957. Hugh died on 17 November 1992 in Colorado Springs, Colorado.[80] They were both buried in Rosehill-Elmwood Cemetery in Owensboro. They had

at least one child including Grace Cruse Burton who was born in 1922 in Daviess County.[81]

Sarah Elizabeth died on 15 April 1875 in Daviess County, at age 37. She was buried in the James A. Burton Family Cemetery in Masonville.[82]

John was listed on the 1880 census in Daviess County as John Bassett Burton, age 49 along with two sons Martin, age 11, and Samuel, age 8. Martin was listed as suffering from Rheumatism.[83]

John married Emma D. Hunter on 13 January 1881 in Daviess County.[84] Emma was born on 4 November 1845 in Nelson County, Kentucky. She was the daughter of Sanford Hunter.[85]

John was listed on the 1900 census in Daviess County, as Jack A. Burton, age 69 along with his wife Emaline D., age 52 and sons Emit B., age 16, and Hunter, age 14. Mary Hunter, age 17 was also listed.[86] In 1910 he was listed on the census in Daviess County, as J.B. Burton, age 80 along with his wife E.S., age 61 and son L.H., age 24.[87] John held membership in the Masonic lodge and was a devout member of the Baptist church.[88]

Children of John Bassett Burton and Emma D. Hunter:

- John B. Burton, Jr. – Born on 18 April 1882 in Daviess County, Kentucky and died on 16 November 1882 in Daviess County, Kentucky. He was buried in the James A. Burton Family Cemetery in Masonville, Daviess County.[89]
- Emmett Byrd Burton – Born in 18 August 1883 in Daviess County, Kentucky. He was described as medium height and medium build with brown eyes and brown hair when he registered for the draft in 1918 while living in Owensboro, Kentucky. Emmett died in March 1958 in Pinellas, Florida.[90]
- Ludwell Hunter Burton – Born on 28 August 1885 in Daviess County, Kentucky. His mother was living in his home in Whitesville in Daviess County in 1920. When he registered for the WWI Draft in 1918 he was described as tall, with a medium build, blue eyes and brown hair. He was living in Utica in Daviess County and working as a farmer at the time. In 1942 when he registered for the draft for World War II he was living in Boonville in Warrick County, Indiana. His aunt Marguerite Miller, age 78 was also living in his home in 1920.[91] Ludwell

married around 1918 and that his wife's name was Mary. She had previously been married and had at least three children from her previous marriage including Clara M. Gasser, James E. Gasser, and Charles Gasser. Ludwell and Mary had at least two children including Margret Burton who was born about 1922 and Anna Bell Burton who was born about 1926. An application for Social Security was filed in 1942. Date and location of death is unknown.

John died on 1 October 1911 at his home in Masonville, Daviess County, Kentucky, at age 80. His cause of death was heart trouble following several years of ill health. Funeral services were held in his home in Masonville with a large number of friends and relatives in attendance. He was buried in the James A. Burton Family Cemetery in Masonville.[92] Emma moved into the home of her son Ludwell near Owensboro around 1920 and was listed on the Daviess County census as Emma L. Burton, age 74.[93] Emma died on 8 August 1930 in Masonville. She was buried in Rosehill Cemetery in Owensboro.[94]

William Martin Lashbrook (1839-1920)

Son of Norris L. Lashbrook and Sara Catherine Foreman
Great-granduncle of Taylor Cosby Cottrell, Jr.

William Martin Lashbrook was born on 26 November 1839 in Daviess County, Kentucky. He was the son of Norris L. Lashbrook and Sara Catherine Foreman.[95] He was listed on the census of 1850 in the household of his step-father George A.R. Wilhite in Daviess County, as Wm. M. Lashbrook, age 10.[96]

On the 1860 census in Daviess County he was still living in the household of his step-father and was listed as Wm. M. Lashbrooks, age 20 and working as a farm hand.[97]

William began military service on 29 September 1861 in C.T. Noel's Company, Wheeler's Confederate Cavalry. He was in the battles of Murfreesboro, Tennessee; Perryville, Kentucky; the battle of Chichamauga, Tennessee; Missionary Ridge, Dug Gap on Taylor's Ridge, Kenesaw Mounty, Georgia; Peach Tree Creen, Georgia; Bentonville, North Carolina; and various other skirmishes including a twenty-five days' skirmish in the mountains of Eastern Kentucky, on a retreat after the battle of Perryville. He ended military service on 25

May 1865 after the close of the Civil War and returned to Daviess County.[98]

On 2 February 1869 a bond for the marriage of William and Lucy Jane Bean was signed in Owensboro, Kentucky, by William and Thos. W. Birkhead in the sum of one hundred dollars. William married Lucy who was the daughter of Henry H. Bean and Martha Yewell Birkhead on 2 February 1869 in Daviess County at the home of Geo. Wilhite with the marriage performed by W.M. Lashbrook.[99] After their marriage they settled near Bethabara Church in Daviess County.[100]

William and Lucy were members of the Baptist church. William was a farmer in 1870 when he was listed on the census in Daviess County as Wm. Lashbrook, age 30. His real estate was valued at $6,000 and his personal estate was valued at $1,600. Lucy, age 20 was listed in the household along with Morris, age 1.

In 1877 William purchased a farm located just southwest of Masonville. The farm was described as a fine farm of 128 acres, 80 of which were under cultivation at the time of the article. He raised tobacco, corn, wheat and hay, and horses and cattle. He was a Mason and belonged to the John J. Daviess Lodge, No. 389. He was also a member of the Sugar Grove Church.[101]

William was listed on the 1880 census in Daviess County, as William Lashbrook, age 40. His wife Lucy, age 30 along with sons Norris, age 10, George, age 8, Thomas, age 6, Henry, age 2, and Babe, age 6/30 were also listed in the household. Two boarders were also listed in the household.[102]

He was also listed on the 1880 agricultural schedule of Masonville Precinct in Daviess County as owner of a farm that included 63 acres of improved land and 60 acres of unimproved land. The total value including land, buildings, machinery and livestock was $2,600. Livestock included six horses and two milk cows which produced 150 pounds of butter the previous year. The farm included 2 additional cattle which were purchased the previous year, one which was sold and one which was slaughtered. The farm included 20 swine and 20 chickens which produced 200 eggs. During the previous year 19 acres of land were used to produce 700 bushels of Indian corn and 6 acres produced 96 bushels of wheat. Additional crop produced 8,660 pounds of tobacco. Five acres of land held 50 apple trees which produced 60 bushels of apples. Fifty cords of lumber, valued at $50 were cut from the land in 1879.[103]

William was listed on the 1900 census in Daviess County as William M. Lashbrook, age 60 along with his wife Lucy J., age 51. His sons George W., age 28, Henry, age 22, and Yeiser, age 20, all single, were listed as farm laborers. Yeiser was listed as attending school. William's daughter Katie B, age 14 and single was listed as attending school.[104]

William was listed on the 1910 census in Daviess County as W.M. Lashbrook, age 70 and owning a farm free of mortgage which was

William Martin Lashbrook		
1850	Daviess County, KY	Farmer
1860	Daviess County, KY	Farm Hand
1870	Daviess County, KY	Farmer
1880	Daviess County, KY	Farmer
1900	Daviess County, KY	Farmer
1910	Daviess County, KY	Farmer
1920	Daviess County, KY	Farmer

listed on farm schedule 180. His wife, L.J., age 60 was also listed as well as his son Yeiser, age 25, who was working as a laborer on the farm. They lived on Hartsfield Road at the time.[105]

William left a will in Daviess County, on 13 May 1917, witnessed by J.W. Ellis and Sam. E. Burton. The will appointed his wife Lucy as his executor and stated she was to receive his entire estate to provide for maintenance and support until her death and then the proceeds remaining were to be divided equally among his children.[106]

He was listed on the 1920 census in Daviess County, as William M. Lashbrook, age 80 along with his wife Lucy J., age 70. A single orphan Mack Williams, age 13 was also listed in the household. His place of birth as well as the places of birth of his parents was listed as unknown.[107]

Children of William Martin Lashbrook and Lucy Jane Bean:

- Norris Lawrence Lashbrook – Born on 15 November 1969 in Daviess County, Kentucky and died on 26 November 1935 in Owensboro, Kentucky, at age 66. His cause of death was acute pneumonia. Funeral services were held on 27 November 1935 at First Baptist Church in Owensboro. He was buried in Rosehill Cemetery in Owensboro.[108] A bond for the marriage of Norris and Emma Lorena Williams was signed on 14 March 1892 in Owensboro, by Norris and Nick Hope in the sum of one hundred dollars. Norris and Emma married on 15 March

1892 at the home of Sullivan Williams in Daviess County. The ceremony was performed by E.J. Maddox in the presence of M. Haynes, C.R. Williams, M.P. Hope, and Nicholas Hope.[109]

In 1902 Norris entered the ministry as a Baptist minister and for the following 33 years until the time of his death he served as minister of, and worked in, churches in Daviess, Ohio, and McLean counties in Kentucky.[110] Emma died on 12 August 1943 in Masonville, Kentucky, at age 78.

Norris and Lorena Lashbrook
Rosehill Cemetery
Owensboro, Kentucky

Her cause of death was chronic myocardium. Funeral services were held on 13 August 1943 at Delbert J. Glenn Funeral Home in Owensboro. She was buried in Rosehill Cemetery, in Owensboro. [111] They had at least one child:

- o Lawrence Carland Lashbrook – Born on 12 September 1893 in Masonville, married Pattie Moorman Thomas on 24 September 1919, then married Beulah Birch Waldrop around 1972 after Pattie died in 1968. Lawrence died on 7 July 1989 in Owensboro. Lawrence was initially reported as killed in action in France in 1918 but the report was incorrect. He had been severely wounded five or six miles north of Cateau-Thierry when he was "knocked cold". He was put on a truck and taken to a town near Paris where he was operated on that evening. He was later taken to Vichy, France where he stayed for three months and one day. He was on his way to the front when the armistice was signed. He returned home from the war as a wounded veteran on 6 August 1919.[112]

- ▪ George W. Lashbrook – Born on 21 January 1872 in Masonville in Daviess County, Kentucky and died on 12 December

1956 in Owensboro, at age 84. He was buried in Rosehill Cemetery in Owensboro.[113] He married Chloe Belle Sharon on 4 February 1904 in Beda in Ohio County, Kentucky.[114] George was a laborer at a saw mill in 1910 and a bookkeeper in a lumber mill in 1920.[115] In 1930 he was a bookkeeper in a planning mill.[116] Chloe Belle died on 7 December 1961 in Daviess County, at age 80 and was buried in Rosehill Cemetery in Owensboro.[117] George and Chloe had at least one child:

- o Helen Rachel Lashbrook – Born on 2 August 1911 in Masonville, married Edward W. Wemes who was likely born on 9 August 1907 and died in October 1973. Helen died in on 12 February 2000 in Owensboro.[118]

- Thomas Jefferson Lashbrook – Born on 16 June 1874 in Daviess County, Kentucky and died on 13 August 1965 in at age 91.[119] He was buried in Rosehill Cemetery in Owensboro. He married Cordelia Millicent Bruner, the daughter of Rev Robert Tab Bruner and Rebecca Leora Hale on 30 March 1899 at the residence of R.T. Bruner in Daviess County. The ceremony was performed by R.T. Bruner in the presence of W.L. Acton, E.E. Bruner, James Berry, and others.[120] Cordelia died on 27 February 1960 in Daviess County, at age 81. She was buried in Rosehill Cemetery in Owensboro.[121] Thomas and Cordelia had at least five children including:

  - o Harry Eugene Lashbrook – Born on 6 October 1901 in Daviess County, married Beulah Birch Waldrop on 18 February 1926, and died on 14 February 1972 in Daviess County. Beulah was born on 11 February 1905 in McMinnville, Tennessee and died on 28 August 1996 at Carmel Home on Old Hartford Road in Owensboro. They had at least one child, Harry Eugene Lashbrook, Jr., who was born on 24 March 1928 and died on 9 April 1984. Harry and Beulah were buried in Rosehill-Elmwood Cemetery in Owensboro.[122]

  - o Walter H. Lashbrook – Born on 11 June 1903 in Daviess County, never married, and died on 17 January 1918 in Masonville in Daviess County. The contributing cause of his death was influenza. He was buried in Rosehill-Elmwood Cemetery.[123]

- o Robert William Lashbrook who was born on 28 September 1906 in Daviess County, married Muriel Arline Cook on 18 June 1930, and died on 20 July 1984 in Nashville, Tennessee.[124] Muriel was born on 16 July 1906 in Kentucky and died on 26 October 2003 in Athens in Limestone County, Alabama, at age 97.
- o Frank Ford Lashbrook who was born on 17 May 1908 in Daviess County, married Lilliam Emogene Baird on 30 May 1936, and died on 15 November 1969 in Newbern, Tennessee. Lilliam was born on 7 February 1916 in Daviess County and died on 3 February 2004 at Hartland Villa in Lewisport in Daviess County, at age 97. She was the daughter of Albert C. Baird and Salley T. Stiles. Frank and Lilliam were buried in Rosehill-Elmwood Cemetery.[125]
- o Earl Thomas Lashbrook who was born on 12 March 1910 in Daviess County, and died on 8 April 1994 in Utica, Kentucky.[126]
- Henry Lashbrook – Born on 17 December 1877 in Daviess County, Kentucky; Died on 4 October 1955 in Daviess County, at age 77. He was buried in Rosehill Cemetery in Owensboro, Kentucky.[127] Henry married Carrie Elnora Bruner, daughter of Rev. Robert Tab Bruner and Rebecca Leora Hale, on 24 October 1900 in Daviess County, with the marriage performed by Carrie's father R.T. Bruner at their home in Owensboro in the presence of Norris Lashbrook, E.E. Bruner, and James Berry.[128] Carrie Elnora was born on 3 December 1872 in Daviess County and died on 22 October 1950 in Philpot in Daviess County, at age 77. Her cause of death was cancer of the lung.

Henry Lashbrook

She was buried on 24 October 1950 in Rosehill Cemetery in Owensboro.[129] Henry and Carrie had at least five children including:

- o Leadrew Bruner Lashbrook – Born on 29 September 1901 in Daviess County, married Thelma Guidmar Westerfield on 27 January 1923, and died on 10 March 1935 in Owensboro. Thelma was born on 4 December 1901 in Ohio County and died on 13 July 2000 at Bon Harbor Nursing Home in Owensboro. They had at least three children including Anna Nadine Lashbrook, Jean Marie Lashbrook, and Earl Donald Lashbrook. Leadrew and Thelma were buried in Rosehill-Elmwood Cemetery in Owensboro.[130]
- o Catherine Lashbrook – Born on 21 February 1905 in Masonville, likely married Weldon Hudson on 6 December 1924, then married Wiley French around 1955 after Weldon's death in 1947. Catherine, also spelled Katherine, died on 21 October 1960 in Cisney in Wayne County, Illinois.[131]
- o Martin Truman Lashbrook - Born on 20 May 1907 in Daviess County, and died on 29 March 1968 in Daviess County.[132]
- o Roy Bean Lashbrook – Born on 8 July 1909 in Daviess County, married Corinne Victoria Schupbach around 1937, and died on 5 May 1994 in Oklahoma City, Oklahoma. He was buried in Chapel Hill Memorial Gardens Cemetery in Oklahoma City.[133]
- o Earnest Gardner Lashbrook – Born on 19 April 1914 in Daviess County, married Hazel Wood Whittaker on 30 March 1940, and died on 24 August 2000 at Carle Arbours Nursing Home in Savoy, Champaign County, Illinois. He was buried in Rosehill-Elmwood Cemetery in Owensboro.[134]

- ■ Yeiser Lashbrook – Born on 25 May 1880 in Daviess County, Kentucky; Died on 18 December 1867 in Daviess County Hospital in Owensboro, Kentucky, at age 87 after an illness of three weeks. Funeral services were held on 20 December 1967 at Haley-McGinnis and Owensboro Funeral Home with services conducted by the Rev. Ralph Williams, pastor of Sugar Grove Baptist Church. He was buried in Rosehill Cemetery in Owensboro.[135] He married Ida Bell Holbrook on 1 February 1911 in Ohio County, Kentucky. Ida was born on 2 February 1889 in Kentucky.[136] Ida Bell died on 2 February 1972 in Utica in Daviess County, at age 83. She was buried in Rosehill Cemetery in Owensboro in section T, lot 132.[137] Yeiser and Ida Bell had at least two children including:

- o Lodford Freeman Lashbrook who was born on 25 July 1913 in Masonville and married Margaret Elizabeth Moreland on 23 December 1940. He was described as 67 inches in height and weighing 141 pounds when he enlisted in the Army in 1941. He died on 31 October 2000 in Owensboro;[138]
- o Austin Morris Lashbrook who was born on 6 June 1919 in Daviess County, and died in July 1973 in Boise in Ada County, Idaho.[139] Yeiser was chosen to serve as a juror in 1936 for a murder trial in Owensboro which resulted in a verdict of guilty and subsequent public hanging of the defendant named Bethea. This hanging is acknowledged as the last public execution in America.[140]

- Foreman Lashbrook – Born on 14 September 1882 in Daviess County, Kentucky and died on 15 May 1883 in Daviess County. He is buried in the Masonville United Methodist Church Cemetery, in Masonville in Daviess County, Kentucky.[141]
- Lashbrook (Infant Daughter) – Born and died on 28 July 1884 in Daviess County, Kentucky. She is buried in the Masonville United Methodist Church Cemetery, also known as the Salem Methodist Church Cemetery, in Masonville, Kentucky.[142]
- Catherine Bean Lashbrook – Born on 26 February 1886 in Daviess County, Kentucky and died on 3 September 1961 in Daviess County, at age 75. She is buried in Rosehill Cemetery in Owensboro, Kentucky.[143] She was also known as Katie Bee Lashbrook. She married James Walter Burton on 24 November 1909 at the home of Norris Lashbrook in Daviess County with the marriage performed by Norris in the presence of Emmet Burton and Yeiser Lashbrook.[144] James was born in 1884 in

Daviess County and died on 2 April 1959 in Daviess County, at age 75. He is buried in Rosehill Cemetery in Owensboro.[145] Catherine and James had at least six children including:

- o Mary Lucille Burton, who was born on 7 January 1911 in Daviess County, Kentucky, married Junious G. Pantle, who was the son of Ernest Pantle and Jemina Pentle, on 3 August 1935 in Daviess County, and died on 4 January 1998 in Owensboro. They had at least one child, Robert B. Pantle.

- o Edith Elba Burton who was born on 12 February 1914 in Daviess County, married Christian Adam Pantle around 1935, and died on 8 January 2002 in Daviess County. Christian was born on 23 February 1906 in Owensboro and died on 27 August 1980 in Owensboro. He was they son of Ernst Gottfried Pantle and Gemima Pantle. They were both buried in Rosehill-Elmwood Cemetery in Owensboro.

- o Nellie Marguerite Burton, who was born on 20 December 1916 in Daviess County and died on 11 December 1917 in Masonville in Daviess County. She was buried in the James A. Burton Cemetery in Masonville. Her death certificate indicated she was single.

- o William Washington Burton, who was born on 11 March 1919 in Masonville, married Eunice Stevens in 1947, and died on 1 July 1998 in Napier, New Zealand. William and Eunice had at least three children including Kelvin Blair Burton, Pascall Lashbrook Burton, and Meryl Burton.

- o Joseph Kenneth Burton, who was born on 12 March 1923 in Daviess County, married Barbara Jean Wimp on 4 March 1949, and died on 13 October 2002 in Utica, Kentucky. Joseph enlisted in the Army on 24 April 1943 while living in Indiana. Barbara was born on 16 September 1931 in Daviess County and died on 23 September 2001 in Utica, Kentucky. She was the daughter of Ira Turner Wimp and Eva Wimp. Joseph and Barbara had at least one child, Phillip Lee Burton. They were both buried in Rosehill-Elmwood Cemetery.

o Carroll Rodman Burton, who was born on 7 October 1927 in Daviess County and enlisted in the Army on 24 January 1946 while living in Louisville, Kentucky.[146]
- Martin D. Lashbrook – Born on 14 September 1889 in Daviess County, Kentucky and died on 12 February 1890 in Daviess County. He is buried in Masonville United Methodist Church Cemetery, also known as the Salem Methodist Church Cemetery, in Masonville, Kentucky.[147]
- Flora M. Lashbrook – Born on 28 September 1891 in Daviess County, Kentucky and died on 2 February 1892 in Daviess County, at age 1. She is buried in Masonville United Methodist Church Cemetery.[148]

William died on 4 August 1920 in Masonville at age 80. His cause of death was acute nephritis. He was buried on 4 August 1920 in Rosehill Cemetery in Owensboro, Kentucky.[149]

His estate was probated on 6 August 1920 in Owensboro; proved by the oaths of J.W. Ellis and Sam. E. Burton, with James Weir, Clerk of Daviess County, presiding.[150]

Lucy was listed on the 1930 census in Daviess County as Lucy Lashbrook, head of household, age 79 and widowed. She owned her home on Hartford Road at the time. Mac. Williamson, age 25 and single was listed as a lodger/servant in her home. He was also working on a farm that he owned.[151]

Lucy died on 12 November 1940 in Masonville in Daviess County, at age 90. Funeral services were held on 13 November 1940 in Sugar Grove Baptist Church in Fordsville at 2:00 in the afternoon with the Rev. J.H. Chissom officiating and her grandsons serving as pallbearers. She was buried in Rosehill Cemetery in Owensboro.[152]

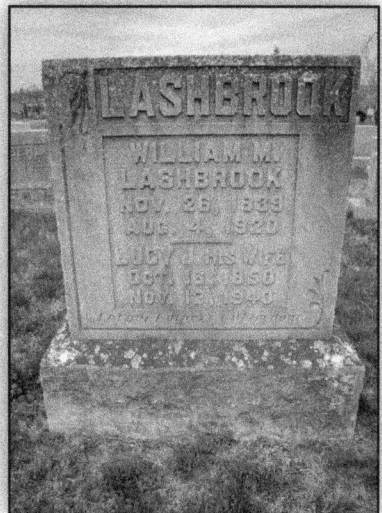

William & Lucy Lashbrook
Rosehill Cemetery
Owensboro, Kentucky

Seariah Deering Lashbrook (1842-1865)

Son of Norris L. Lashbrook and Sara Catherine Foreman
Great-granduncle of Taylor Cosby Cottrell, Jr.

Seariah Deering Lashbrook was born on 29 January 1842 in Daviess County, Kentucky. He was the son of Norris L. Lashbrook and Sara Catherine Foreman.[153] He was listed on the 1850 census in Daviess County in the household of his step-father George A.R. Wilhite, as Leah, age 8.[154] He was listed on the 1860 census as Sarah D., age 18.[155] Both the 1850 and 1860 census listed him as female. It is assumed that Leah, and Sarah D. Lashbrook were Seariah Deering since he was listed on neither census and the birth year of all three match. He was also known as Sariah D. Lashbrook.

He began military service on 5 October 1861 in Russellville, Logan County, Kentucky where he enlisted as a Private in Company A of the 1st Cavalry Regiment of Kentucky, also known as Captain Noel's Company, Wheeler's Confederate Cavalry.[156]

The First Regiment of the Kentucky Cavalry was formed in March 1863 by the consolidation of the 1st (Helm's) Regiment Kentucky Cavalry and the 3rd Regiment Kentucky Cavalry. The men of this company appear to have served in the 1st (Helm's) Regiment of the Kentucky Cavalry prior to the consolidation.[157]

According to his service record he was paid $300 on 22 March 1864 to compensate him for the loss of his horse which was "killed in action" at Beech Gore, Tennessee on 12 January 1863. He was wounded and captured at the battle of the Sacotchee Valley in Tennessee on the Sacotchee River in a charge at Snake Creek Gap on the 9th of May 1864. He was then taken to Camp Morton in Indianapolis Indiana and arrived there on 22 May 1864.[158]

The ledger of prisoner accounts for Camp Morton shows that he was paid $15 on the First of December 1864 and an additional $5 on the Fifth, Tenth, and Fifteenth of December 1864.[159]

Family lore, according to Nellie J. Lashbrook, was that Sariah's horse was shot from under him and he was captured and taken to Camp Chase, a prison near Chicago, Illinois. Dysentery broke out in the prison and he took ill and was so sick that his mother Catherine Lashbrook went to see him. She had to take a boat from Owensboro to Evansville, Indiana and then on to Camp Chase.

When she reached Camp Chase, Sariah begged her to "ask him out of prison" to die. It was said that Sariah's mother then traveled to Washington, partially by horseback to see President Lincoln to seek the release of her son so he could die at home. According to family lore when she arrived at the residence the butler wouldn't let her in, but the President happened by and motioned for her to come in. He shook hands with her and asked about her mission. An aged father was also at the gate with a letter asking for his son to be released. It was said that Lincoln granted both requests. However, when she got back to the prison Sariah was dead.[160]

Seariah Deering Lashbrook
Macedonia Baptist Church Cemetery
Daviess County, Kentucky

In this case family lore was at least partially incorrect. His actual service record, reviewed by the author at the National Archives in Washington, D.C., indicate the actual location where he was being held and died was not Camp Chase. He was actually being held at Camp Morton. Camp Morton was a similar camp located in Indianapolis, Indiana. Their records document him as a prisoner of war and record his death at the camp with cause of death listed as chronic diarrhea. The incorrect death location was not only passed down through family lore, but has also been incorrectly documented in several published works dealing with the Lashbrook Family.

Seariah's actual death occurred on 23 February 1865 at Camp Moron at age 23 while in prison as a Confederate prisoner of war. Camp Morton records indicate he was buried in grave number 1452, in Green Lawn Cemetery in Indianapolis, Indiana.[161] Green Lawn was a cemetery frequently used for prisoners who died at Camp Morton.

According to family lore, Sariah was given "quite a large funeral procession". His horse, with the saddle empty, was also in the procession.[162] It is unclear when his body was moved from Green Lawn Cemetery but his final resting place is in the Macedonia Baptist Church Cemetery in Daviess County, Kentucky.[163]

James Birkhead Lashbrook (1844-1904)

Son of Norris L. Lashbrook and Sara Catherine Foreman
Great-granduncle of Taylor Cosby Cottrell, Jr.

James Birkhead Lashbrook was born on 4 March 1844 in Daviess County, Kentucky. He was the son of Norris L. Lashbrook and Sara Mahala Taylor.[164] Information on the James Birkhead Lashbrook Family and James' life-history, along with that for his wife Sara Catherine Forman and their seven children is covered in detail in Section 1, Chapter 7, James Birkhead Lashbrook Family.

Mildred Rebecca Lashbrook (1846-1846)

Daughter of Norris L. Lashbrook and Sara Catherine Foreman
Great-grandaunt of Taylor Cosby Cottrell, Jr.

Mildred Rebecca Lashbrook was born on 24 January 1846 in Masonville, Daviess County, Kentucky. She was the daughter of Norris L. Lashbrook and Sara Catherine Foreman.[165] Mildred died at noon on 20 May 1846 in Masonville, Kentucky at age 3 months and 26 days. She was buried by the side of her Grandmother Rebecca Birkhead Lashbrook on 21 May 1846 in the Lashbrook Family Cemetery in Browns Valley in Daviess County, Kentucky.[166]

Chapter 7 – James Birkhead Lashbrook Family

Great-grandfather of Taylor Cosby Cottrell, Jr.

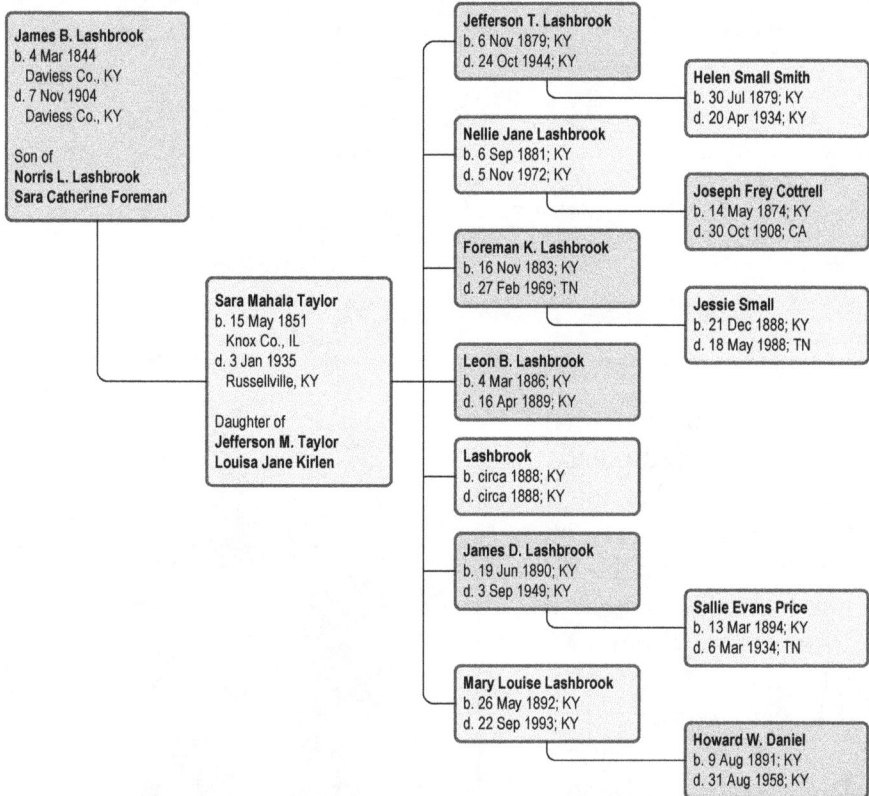

James B. Lashbrook
b. 4 Mar 1844
  Daviess Co., KY
d. 7 Nov 1904
  Daviess Co., KY

Son of
Norris L. Lashbrook
Sara Catherine Foreman

Sara Mahala Taylor
b. 15 May 1851
  Knox Co., IL
d. 3 Jan 1935
  Russellville, KY

Daughter of
Jefferson M. Taylor
Louisa Jane Kirlen

Jefferson T. Lashbrook
b. 6 Nov 1879; KY
d. 24 Oct 1944; KY

Helen Small Smith
b. 30 Jul 1879; KY
d. 20 Apr 1934; KY

Nellie Jane Lashbrook
b. 6 Sep 1881; KY
d. 5 Nov 1972; KY

Joseph Frey Cottrell
b. 14 May 1874; KY
d. 30 Oct 1908; CA

Foreman K. Lashbrook
b. 16 Nov 1883; KY
d. 27 Feb 1969; TN

Jessie Small
b. 21 Dec 1888; KY
d. 18 May 1988; TN

Leon B. Lashbrook
b. 4 Mar 1886; KY
d. 16 Apr 1889; KY

Lashbrook
b. circa 1888; KY
d. circa 1888; KY

James D. Lashbrook
b. 19 Jun 1890; KY
d. 3 Sep 1949; KY

Sallie Evans Price
b. 13 Mar 1894; KY
d. 6 Mar 1934; TN

Mary Louise Lashbrook
b. 26 May 1892; KY
d. 22 Sep 1993; KY

Howard W. Daniel
b. 9 Aug 1891; KY
d. 31 Aug 1958; KY

James Birkhead Lashbrook was born on 4 March 1844 in Daviess County, Kentucky. He was the son of Norris L. Lashbrook and Sara Catherine Foreman.[1] He had at least six brothers and sisters. Additional information on his parents and siblings is covered in detail in Section 1, Chapter 6, Norris L. Lashbrook Family.

James was listed on the 1850 census in Daviess County, in the household of his step-father George A.R. Wilhite as James Lashbrook, age 6.[2] He was listed on the 1860 census in Daviess County, in the household of George A.R. Wilhite as James B. Lashbrooks, age 16.[3] In 1870 James was listed on the Daviess County, census as Jas. B. Lashbrook, age 26 in the household of his step-father George Wilhite along with his mother Catherine.[4]

James Birkhead Lashbrook Family Timeline

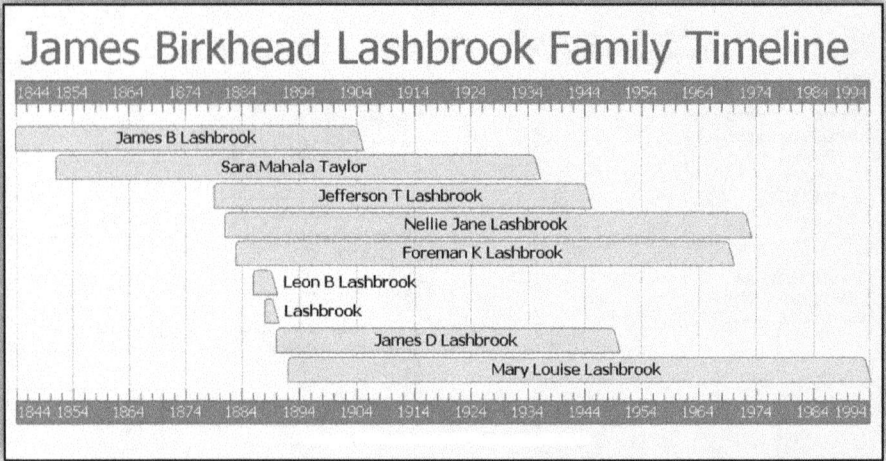

| 1844 1854 | 1864 | 1874 | 1884 | 1894 | 1904 | 1914 | 1924 | 1934 | 1944 | 1954 | 1964 | 1974 | 1984 1994 |

James B Lashbrook
Sara Mahala Taylor
Jefferson T Lashbrook
Nellie Jane Lashbrook
Foreman K Lashbrook
Leon B Lashbrook
Lashbrook
James D Lashbrook
Mary Louise Lashbrook

James kept a journal where he recorded poetry, expenses, and other interesting items. As an example he wrote in his journal that he bought a 173-pound hog from J.M. Taylor on January 17th, 1884. Later entries during the year listed boarders S.D. Chissom and George Cottrell at $3 per week. He kept a ledger of expenses during late 1875 and early 1876. Some of the items listed included ammuni-

James Birkhead Lashbrook

tion – 45 cents; quart of Brandy – 80 cents; soda – 10 cents; leather for bridal – 50 cents; Doctor Bill - $3.30; pair of shoes - $5; horse in livery – 25 cents; and a watch chain – 75 cents. It was interesting to note that his ledger showed a quart of Brandy nearly every month with price varying from 20 cents to 80 cents. He also accepted a pistol as payment of a $4 dept. [5]

He also wrote lines of poetry throughout his journal which the author assumes to be his own creation. One example seemed to be a love poem which appeared to be titled "Lines."

> *And her face is lily clear, lily shaped and dropped in duty.*
> *To the law of its own beauty, and forehead fair and saintly,*
> *Which thru blue eyes under shine, like meek prayers before a shrine.*
> *Man for the field and woman for the hearth,*
> *Man for the sword, and for the needle she;*
> *Man with the head, and woman with the heart:*
> *Man to command and woman to obey.*[6]

Another short poem found in his journal on the same page, provides a glimmer into his thoughts on love. The poem, which was seemed to be titled "Love is not Love" although the title may have also been the first line as shown below.

> *Love is not love*
> *Which alters, when its alteration finds.*
> *Or bends with the remover to remove,*
> *Oh, no! It is an ever fixed mark,*
> *That looks on temptations and is never shaken"*[7]

James married Sarah Mahala Taylor, the daughter of Jefferson Mandred Taylor and Louisa Jane Kirlen, on 15 November 1877 in Daviess County at her father's home. Their marriage bond was signed by James and W.W. Hays. The marriage was performed by the Rev. J.W. Dawson. Sarah was born on 15 May 1851 in Galesburg, Knox County, Illinois.[8] She also went by the name of Sallie. She had at least fourteen brothers and sisters, each of which are covered in detail in Section 1, Chapter 8, Jefferson Mandred Taylor Family. Sarah was listed on the 1860 census in

Sarah Mahala Taylor

Daviess County, in the household of Jefferson Mandred Taylor as Sarah M., age 9.[9] She appeared on the 1870 census in the home of her father Jefferson as Sarah, age 17.[10]

According Nellie Lashbrook her father took frequently helped soldiers during the Civil War that had become lost and separated from their company in the dense woods by guiding them to join their company before the home guards caught them. She said he was too young at the time to "join up" and guessed he was serving by helping the lost soldiers find their way.

On 30 October 1878 James wrote in his journal that he sold 9 ½ pounds of butter for $1.64 1/3 cents; 3 1/2 dozen eggs for 38 1/2 cents; and 4 pairs of socks for $1.20.[11] He was listed on the 1880 census in Daviess County, as James Lashbrook, age 36 and married. His wife was listed as Sally M., age 29, married and keeping house. His son Taylor, age 6 months was also listed in the household.[12]

James wrote in his journal that he killed a sow for meat the first Monday in December 1883. Journal entries in March 1886 recorded boarding fees received from George Burton of $2 per week covering March and April.[13] He was listed on the 1900 census in Daviess County as James B. Lashbrook, age 56 and owning a farm free of mortgage with the farm listed on farm schedule 25. His wife Sarah M., age 48 along with his sons J.T., age 20, Foreman K., age 16, and Dudley J., age 9 were also listed, with his sons all attending school. His daughters Nellie J., age 18 and Mary L., age 8 were also listed as single and in school.[14]

James and Sarah had at least seven children including Jefferson Taylor Lashbrook, Nellie Jane Lashbrook, Foreman Kerlin Lashbrook, Leon B. Lashbrook, an unnamed daughter, James Dudley Lashbrook, and Mary Louise Lashbrook.[15]

James died on 7 November 1904 in Daviess County, at age 60 at his home in Dermot. His cause of death was complication of diseases.[16] He was buried on 8 November 1904 in Elmwood Cemetery in Owensboro, Kentucky in the Lashbrook Family Plot in Section 5.[17]

Sarah was listed on the 1910 Census in Daviess

James Birkhead Lashbrook		
1850	Daviess County, KY	N/A
1860	Daviess County, KY	Farm Hand
1870	Daviess County, KY	Farm Hand
1880	Daviess County, KY	Farmer
1900	Daviess County, KY	Farmer

County, as Sarah M. Lashbrook, head of household, age 58, widowed, and owning her own farm mortgage free. Her sons Taylor, age 30, single and Dudley, age 19 and single were both listed as farmers. Her daughter Mary L., age 17 was listed as single and in school. Her daughter Nellie Cottrell, age 28 and widowed and Nellie's son Taylor C. Cottrell, age 4 were also listed in her home. Sara's mother, Louisa J. Taylor, was listed as living on a nearby farm.[18] The 1920 Census in Daviess County, listed Sara Lashbrook as head of household, age 68 and widowed. She owned her own home free of mortgage. Richard R. Hayes was also listed in the same dwelling as head of household and married to Sarah E. Hayes. Richard was listed as a laborer in a shoe factory.[19]

James B. and Sarah Lashbrook
Elmwood Cemetery
Owensboro, Kentucky

Sarah was listed on the 1930 Census in Daviess County as Sarah, age 70. She was head of the household, widowed, and owned her home that was valued at $8,000. Her daughter Nellie, age 40 and widowed was also listed as living in her household.[20] Sarah died on 3 January 1935 in Russellville in Logan County, Kentucky, at age 83. She was buried in Elmwood Cemetery in Owensboro, Kentucky next to her husband James.[21]

Jefferson Taylor Lashbrook (1879-1844)

Son of James Birkhead Lashbrook and Sarah M. Taylor
Granduncle of Taylor Cosby Cottrell, Jr.

Jefferson Taylor Lashbrook was born on 6 November 1879 in Philpot in Daviess County, Kentucky. He was the son of James Birkhead Lashbrook and Sarah Mahala Taylor.[22] He was listed on the 1880 census in the household of his father James in Daviess County, as Taylor, age six months.[23] He was listed on the 1900 census in Daviess County, in the household of his father as J.T., age 20. Jefferson was listed on the 1910 census in Daviess County, in the household of his mother, Sarah, as Taylor, age 30.[24]

Jefferson married Helen Smith Hall, daughter of William Conley Hall and Katherine F. Smith on 18 April 1910.[25] Helen was born on 30 July 1879 in Bowling Green in Warren County, Kentucky. She was the daughter of William Conley Hall and Katherine Frazier Smith.[26] In 1918 when Jefferson registered for the draft he was living in Owensboro and working as a traffic manager for Rapin Sugar Feed Company.[27] In 1920 he was a telegraph operator. Jefferson was listed on the 1920 census in Daviess County, as Jefferson, age 39 along with his wife Helen, age 40. William L. Action and Lillian S. Action were listed as renters in his home.[28] Around 1927 Jefferson and Helen moved to Elkton, Kentucky where he "conducted" the Ford agency in Elkton.[29] By 1930 he was working as an automotive salesman.

In the 1930 census in Daviess County he was listed as Taylor, age 40 along with his wife Helen, age 40. His wife's father William Hall, age 70 and his wife's mother Katherine Hall, age 71 were also living in the household.[30]

Helen died on 20 April 1934 at 2:30 in the afternoon in Elkton in Todd County, Kentucky, at age 54. Her cause of death was cerebral hemorrhage. She was buried in Fairview Cemetery in Bowling Green, Kentucky on 21 April 1934.[31] Her husband Jefferson was appointed as the administrator of her will in the Todd County Court on 2 June 1934. Helen and Jefferson had no children.

In the 1940 census Jefferson was listed as head of the household in Todd County, Kentucky as J.T. Lashbrook. Also living in the household were his nephew T.C. Cottrell, Age 34 and T.C.'s wife and daughter Zalame, age 31 and Joanna, age 5.[32] In May 1940 Jefferson was the president of a motor company in Elkton. He moved back to Owensboro before his death and lived for a short time in the home of his sister Mary Louise Lashbrook. He was destitute and the only significant possession he owned was a diamond ring which he gave to Mary Louise before his death.[33]

Jefferson Taylor Lashbrook		
1880	Daviess County, KY	N/A
1900	Daviess County, KY	In School
1910	Daviess County, KY	Farmer
1920	Daviess County, KY	Telegraph Operator
1930	Todd County, KY	Auto Salesman
1940	Todd County, KY	Motor Co. President

Jefferson died on 24 October 1944 at the City-County Hospital in Owensboro, at age 64. His cause of death was kidney related issues. Funeral services were held on 25 October 1944 at the Delbert J. Glenn Funeral Home in Owensboro with the Rev. A.F. Cagle, pastor of the Third Baptist Church, officiating. He was buried later in the day in Fairview Cemetery in Bowling Green in Cemetery 1, Section N, Site N-44e.[34]

Nellie Jane Lashbrook (1881-1972)

Daughter of James Birkhead Lashbrook and Sarah Mahala Taylor
Grandmother of Taylor Cosby Cottrell, Jr.

Nellie Jane Lashbrook was born on 6 September 1881 in Philpot, Daviess County, Kentucky. She was the daughter of James Birkhead Lashbrook and Sarah Mahala Taylor.[35] Information on Nellie Jane Lashbrook's life-history, along with that for her husband Joseph Frey Cottrell and her son T.C. Cottrell is covered in detail in Section 1, Chapter 3, Joseph Frey Cottrell Family and Section 1, Chapter 4, Taylor Cosby Cottrell, Sr. Family.

Foreman Kerlin Lashbrook (1883-1969)

Son of James Birkhead Lashbrook and Sarah Mahala Taylor
Granduncle of Taylor Cosby Cottrell, Jr.

Foreman Kerlin Lashbrook was born on 16 November 1883 in Daviess County, Kentucky. He was the son of James Birkhead Lashbrook and Sarah Mahala Taylor.[36] He was listed on the 1900 census in the household of his father James in Daviess County, as Foreman K., age 16.[37] In 1910 he was listed as a boarder on the census in Crittenden County, Arkansas in what was likely a boarding house as Fourman Lashbrook, age 25, employed as a Real Estate Agent. There were 27 other boarders listed in the house.[38]

A bond for the marriage of Foreman Kerlin Lashbrook and Jessie Small was signed on 14 July 1910 in Owensboro in Daviess County, Kentucky by F.K. Lashbrook and J.Y. Small. Foreman married Jessie on 14 July 1910 in Owensboro. The ceremony was performed by C.C. Carroll in the presence of W.W. Wells and J. Lashbrook.[39] Jessie was born on 21 December 1888 in Daviess County. She was the daughter of Jerry Y. Small and Alice Moseley.[40]

Foreman was employed as an abstractor for several companies including the Memphis Rhodes Abstract Company and the Marion Bank in 1918. When he registered for the WWI Draft he was described as medium height with a slender build, brown eyes and dark hair with slight balding. He was living in Memphis at the time. In 1920 he was employed in general business as an abstractor. On the 1920 census in Shelby County, Tennessee, Foreman was listed as Frelan K. Lashbrook, age 36. His wife Jessie S., age 30, daughter Frances S., age 2 10/12, and Claire L., age 2/12 were also listed.[41]

He was listed on the Shelby County, Tennessee 1930 census as F.K. Lashbrook, age 42, along with his wife Jessie, age 40,

Foreman Kerlin Lashbrook

daughter Francis, age 12, and son James, age 9. They were living in a home, valued at $20,000 at 1050 Roland in Memphis when the census was taken. The Thomas Barrett family, including wife and daughter, were also listed as living in the home.[42]

In 1933 Foreman and Jessie were living at 700 North Parkway in Memphis.[43] In 1954 they were living at 824 Young Avenue and Foreman was working as a Salesman.[44]

Foreman Kerlin Lashbrook		
1900	Daviess County, KY	In School
1910	Crittenden County, KY	Real Estate Agent
1920	Shelby County, TN	Abstractor
1930	Shelby County, TN	Insurance Agent
1940	Shelby County, TN	Cab Driver

In 1940 he was listed as F.K. Lashbrook, age 56 on the census in Shelby County, Tennessee along with his wife Jessie, age 40, daughter

Francis, age 12, and son James, age 9. They were living at 1824 Young in Memphis as the time and Foreman was employed as a cab driver.[45]

Children of Foreman Kerlin Lashbrook and Jessie Small:

- Frances Small Lashbrook – Born on 26 February 1917 in Tennessee and died on 14 May 2006 in Southaven in DeSoto County, Mississippi, at age 89. Funeral services were held on 16 May 2006 at Forest Hill Midtown Funeral Home, in Memphis, Tennessee. Burial was in Forest Hill Cemetery Midtown in Memphis.[46] Frances married Robert Edward Felix sometime before 1960.[47] Robert was born on 14 May 1923 and served in the Navy from 14 May 1993 until he was released from service on 1 October 1945.[48] He was the son of Charles A. Felix. Frances and Robert had at least four children before they divorced sometime after 1960. Robert married again before he died on 5 September 1993 in Memphis.[49] He was also buried in Forest Hill Cemetery.

- Claire Louise Lashbrook – Born on 18 February 1919 in Tennessee and died on 9 July 1920 in Owensboro in Daviess County, Kentucky, at age 1. Her cause of death was enterocolitis. She was buried in Elmwood Cemetery in Owensboro, in the Lashbrook Family Plot in Section I, Lot 16.[50]

- James Small Lashbrook – Born on 2 July 1920 in Memphis in Shelby County, Tennessee and died on 7 May 1991 in Little Rock in Pulaski County, Arkansas, at age 70. He was buried in Forest Hill Cemetery Midtown in Memphis, Tennessee.[51] In 1930 James was working for a tire company as a tire splicer.[52] He enlisted in the Army as a Warrant Officer at Fort Oglethorpe, Georgia on 5 February 1943.[53]

Forman Kerlin Lashbrook
Elmwood Cemetery
Owensboro, Kentucky

He married Margaret Rice between 1943 and 1954. Margaret was born on 15 February 1925. In 1969 James and Margaret lived at 464 South Reece in Memphis. Margaret died on 5 July 1985 in Memphis. She was buried next to her husband James in Forest Hill Cemetery, Midtown in Memphis, Tennessee.[54]

Foreman died on 27 February 1969 at Memphis Baptist Hospital in Memphis, at age 85 following a long illness. Funeral services were held on 3 March 1969 at Elmwood Cemetery in Owensboro, Kentucky with the graveside services conducted by the Rev. Gerald Lord, associate pastor of Third Baptist Church. He was buried in Elmwood Cemetery in Owensboro in the Lashbrook Family Plot.[55]

Jessie died on 18 May 1988 in Memphis, at age 99.[56] She was buried in Forest Hill Cemetery Midtown in Memphis, Shelby County, Tennessee in Section 33.[57]

Leon B. Lashbrook (1886-1889)

Son of James Birkhead Lashbrook and Sarah Mahala Taylor
Granduncle of Taylor Cosby Cottrell, Jr.

Leon B. Lashbrook was born on 4 March 1886 in Daviess County, Kentucky. He was the son of James Birkhead Lashbrook and Sarah Mahala Taylor.[58] According to Nellie Jane Lashbrook, Leon's sister, didn't seem to like his brother Foreman playing with him so she gave him her glass slipper to play with. Leon had meningitis for six weeks, probably just prior to his death.[59] He died on 16 April 1889 in Daviess County, at age 3. The Lashbrook Family Bible listed his age at death as 3 years, 1 month, and 12 days.[60]

Lashbrook, Unnamed Daughter (1888-1888)

Daughter of James Birkhead Lashbrook and Sarah Mahala Taylor
Grandaunt of Taylor Cosby Cottrell, Jr.

An unnamed daughter was born to James Birkhead Lashbrook and Sarah Mahala Taylor around 1888, She died the same year.[61] Although this may have been a still birth no record has been found. Cause of death and burial location is also unknown.

James Dudley Lashbrook (1890-1949)

Son of James Birkhead Lashbrook and Sarah Mahala Taylor
Granduncle of Taylor Cosby Cottrell, Jr.

James Dudley Lashbrook was born on 19 June 1890 in Daviess County, Kentucky. He was the son of James Birkhead Lashbrook and Sarah Mahala Taylor. He was also known as Dudley.[62] He appeared on the census in Daviess County, in 1900 in the household of his father, as Dudley J., age 9.[63] He graduated from Owensboro High School in 1908 and attended the University of Kentucky in Lexington in Fayette County, Kentucky after high school graduation.[64] He was listed on the 1910 census in Daviess County, in the household of his mother Sarah, as Dudley, age 19.[65]

Dudley was described as medium height, medium build, with brown eyes and light brown hair when he registered for the World War I

James Dudley Lashbrook

Draft in 1917. He was living in Louisville, Kentucky at the time and employed as an Internal Revenue Officer working for the IRS.[66] He moved to Russellville in Logan County, Kentucky in 1919 and established a Ford agency together with Mr. Matt Hargen. He was the owner of the Lashbrook Motor Company, distributors of Ford Farm implements and the Logan County agent for the Standard Oil Company in June 1919.[67] In 1920 he was listed on the census in Logan County as a lodger in the household of Millie V. Morrison, as James D. Lashbrook, age 29 and single.[68]

Dudley married Sallie Evans Price, daughter of Vernon Dixon Price and Bettie Evans, on 6 July 1921. Sallie was born on 13 March 1894 in Logan County.[69] In 1930 James was listed as the head of household on the census in Logan County, as James D. Loshbrook, age

38. His wife Sallie E., age 36 and daughter Sarah E., age 7 were also listed in his household.[70]

Dudley and Sallie had one child, a daughter, who was born on 1 October 1922 in Logan County. She married and had three children.

Sallie died in the evening of 6 March 1934 in a hospital in Nashville in Davidson County, Tennessee, where she had been confined for more than six weeks. Her cause of death was sepsis. Her remains were brought to Russellville immediately after her death and lay in state at her home on Ninth street while hosts of friends of the family visited the home. Funeral services were conducted at the First Baptist Church where she had been a faithful and devout member all of her. Her pastor the Rev. C.B. Jackson, assisted by

Maple Grove Cemetery
Russellville, Kentucky

Rev. Edward F. Coffman, conducted the service which was attended by a large number of relatives and friends. She was buried at Maple Grove Cemetery in Russellville, Kentucky.[71]

Dudley married Sophie Hermon around 1938. Sophie was born on 14 January 1890 in Daviess County, Kentucky.[72] She was the daughter of John Preston and Belle Taylor. She had previously been married and was a member of the First Presbyterian Church, the Daughters of the American Revolution, and the Logan County Library Board. She was also an accomplished musician who studied organ and piano in Chicago. She had

Sophie Hermon

moved to Logan County in the 1930s as a social worker and had been in charge of the welfare office in Russellville. She was the first woman to serve on a grand jury in Daviess County and was a Democrat who loved to talk politics and take part in campaigns.

She was described as "tall and imposing in appearance" in her obituary. It said "august" might be a better adjective. It also described her as "sharp of tongue and quick of wit" which made her a formidable citizen when she set forth on a crusade.[73] The author remembers many visits to her home in Russellville. Her home was filled with limited edition prints of wildlife, primarily birds, by a Ray Harm, an American artist best known for his paintings of wildlife. She also had many figurines and of animals, especially dogs. Sophie left some of her collection of dog figurines to the author. She also had a Hammond organ in her living room and occasionally would play songs from the Episcopal Church Hymnal.

Sophie Lashbrook Home
Russellville, Kentucky
Photograph taken by author in 2011

In 1940 Dudley was listed on the census in Logan County, as J. D. Lashbrook, age 49. His wife Sophie Lashbrook, age 49 and daughter Sarah E. Lashbrook, age 17 were also listed. Dudley's brother-in-law John Herman, age 44 was also listed in the household.[74] Dudley was known for "the great civic pride which motivated his business and personal relationships in Logan County.

He was living on East 9th Street in Russellville when he registered for the WWII Draft in 1942. Dudley listed himself as "self-employed" at the time. His telephone number in Russellville on the draft registration was listed as 269.[75]

Dudley was considered one of the most progressive leaders of the community in which he resided. He served on the City Council of Russellville and as the president of the Russellville Chamber of Commerce.

He was also a charter member of the Rotary Club of Russellville and had served as its president. He was an elder in the Presbyterian Church and served in several of the highest positions in the Synod.[76]

Dudley left a will on 21 May 1949 that provided for his wife Sophie and daughter Sarah Kries. It appointed them as Joint Executrices of the will. The will was later probated in the Logan County Court on 7 September 1949 following Dudley's death on 3 September 1949 in Russellville, Kentucky, at

James Dudley Lashbrook		
1900	Daviess County, KY	In School
1910	Daviess County, KY	Farmer
1920	Logan County, KY	Garage Owner
1930	Logan County, KY	Ford Dealer
1940	Logan County, KY	Auto Dealer

age 59. His cause of death was a coronary occlusion due to coronary arteriosclerosis.[77] An editorial in the local newspaper, the News-Demmorrat, said the following:

> *"Death of a loved one is always a tragedy to those left behind, whether it be a peaceful closing of a long life, a sudden snapping of a young life with all its bright future ahead, or an untimely cessation of a life at the height of its career, with its purposes only half-finished. In the death of James Dudley Lashbrook, at the height of his usefulness to his fellowmen, we feel Russellville has lost a man it can ill afford to spare. A successful businessman, Mr. Lashbrook had turned his talents and devoted his time to service of his community. It was his belief Russellville should progress. Progressive himself, he had in mind a like program for the town he had chosen for his home. His growth he hoped to see reflected in his home town, and to that end he spent his last efforts. Russellville sorrows over the loss of one whose death cut short a fulfillment of these purposes. He will be missed."[78]*

Funeral services were handled by Richardson Funeral Home, with Rev. Thomas A. DeVore officiating. Pallbearers were the elders of the Presbyterian Church. Honorary pallbearers were represented by three employees of the Lashbrook Motor Company and by three employees of the Standard Oil Agency. The funeral was attended by a large number of friends and relatives from out of town. He was buried on 5 September 1949 in Elmwood Cemetery in Owensboro in the Lashbrook Family Plot in Section 5.[79]

Sophie died on 22 September 1973 in the Logan County Hospital in Russellville, at age 83. Funeral services were held on 24 September at 10:00 in the morning at the Sanders Funeral Home with the Rev.

James Dudley & Sophie Lashbrook
Elmwood Cemetery
Owensboro, Kentucky

Scott Phillips officiating. Burial followed in Elmwood Cemetery in Owensboro next to her husband in the Lashbrook Family Plot. Pallbearers were Earl Spurlock, Roy Mays, Carl Page, Shirley Pillow, William G. Fuqua and Wilford Duncan.[80]

Mary Louise Lashbrook (1892-1993)

Daughter of James B. Lashbrook and Sarah M. Taylor
Grandaunt of Taylor Cosby Cottrell, Jr.

Mary Louise Lashbrook was born on 26 May 1892 in Daviess County, Kentucky. She was the daughter of James Birkhead Lashbrook and Sarah Mahala Taylor. She also went by the name of Louise.[81] She was listed on the 1900 census in Daviess County in the household of her father James, as Mary L, age 8. In 1910 she was listed in the household of her mother Sarah in Daviess County, as Mary L., age 17 and attending school.[82]

Mary Louise Lashbrook

Mary married Howard W. Daniel, son of Stonewall Jackson Daniel and Gertrude Howard on 18 May 1915 in Daviess County.[83] His father Stonewall was born on 17 August 1865 in Daviess County, Kentucky and died on 30 July 1941 in Daviess County. He was the son of Isaiah C. Daniel and Sarah Catherine Nuckols[84] His mother Gertrude was in February 1870 in Daviess County and died on 9 May 1954 in Owensboro. Stonewall and Gertrude were both buried in Rosehill Elmwood Cemetery in Owensboro.[85] Their son Howard was born on 9 August 1891 in Daviess County.[86]

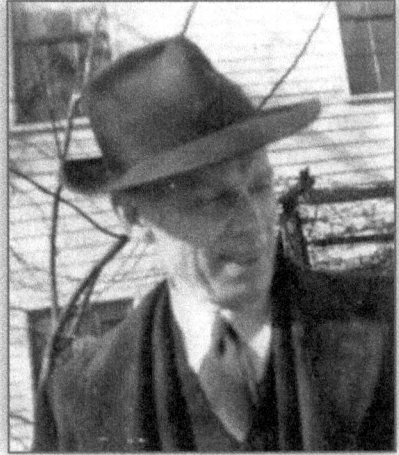
Howard W. Daniel

Mary was listed on the 1930 census in Daviess County, in the household of her husband Howard W. Daniel, as Louise, age 37. Her daughter Mary, age 14 was also listed as attending school.[87]

Howard W. Daniel Home
Owensboro, Kentucky

In 1940 she was listed on the census in Daviess County, in the household of her husband Howard, as Mary, age 47 along with their daughter Mary Lenore, age 24. Howard was a farmer by trade and owned a large farm on Pleasant Valley Road near Owensboro.[88]

During the war Howard secured an order from the government that allowed him to raise Hemp on the farm. The only people that the government would allow to work with the Hemp were German POWs. When it was time to plant and harvest the Hemp, POWs were brought from Breckenridge County, Kentucky to perform the

Howard W. Daniel		
1900	Daviess County, KY	N/A
1910	Daviess County, KY	In School
1920	Daviess County, KY	Farmer
1930	Daviess County, KY	Farmer
1940	Daviess County, KY	Farmer

harvesting and planting. Howard apparently told people in the area that the Hemp was used to smoke as well as to make ropes.[89]

Children of Mary Louise Lashbrook and Howard W. Daniel:

- Mary Lenore Daniel – Born on 25 February 1916 in Daviess County, Kentucky and died on 31 January 2011 in the Owensboro Medical Health System in Owensboro, at age 94. Funeral services were held on 4 February 2011 at Gleen Funeral Home and Crematory in Owensboro. She was buried in Owensboro Memorial Gardens in Daviess County, on 4 February 2011.[90] Mary was also known as Lenore. She was editor of the college year book at Georgetown College in 1937. She graduated that year from Georgetown College in Scott County, Kentucky and returned to Owensboro where she was later a member of the faculty of the Daviess County High School. She married Marvin Jewel Smeathers, son of Jerome

Mary Lenore Daniel

Houston Smeathers and Merle Scott on 21 May 1943 in San Antonio in Bexar County, Texas at the First Baptist Church with the immediate families present.[91] Mary wore a dusty blue street length dress, with navy accessories, and a corsage of Sweetheart roses. Marvin was born on 2 April 1915 in Maceo in Davies County, Kentucky. He was the son of Jerome Houston Smeathers and Merle Scott. His father Jerome was born on 31 March 1876 in Kentucky and Died on 18 January 1953. He was the son of Harold Smeathers and Sarah Thornsberry. His mother Merle was born on 1 December 1885 in Daviess County and died on 11 December 1972 in Owensboro. Lenore and Marvin moved back to Owensboro in late 1944 or early 1945 and lived on a farm adjacent to her mother and father. Lenore taught at the Davies County High School until she began her family and her role as a homemaker and farm wife. They had two children, a son and a daughter. Marvin served in the military during the war. He began military service on 15 May 1942 at

Marvin J. Smeathers

Fort Benjamin Harrison in Indiana and was stationed at Kelly Field in San Antonio in Bexar County, Texas when he married Mary. He was active in civic affairs and later served as president of the Daviess County Lions Club and Harvesters Club and was a 4-H Club member and leader. He served as president and director of the Daviess County Farm Bureau and chairman of the Red Cross. He also served as treasurer of the TPA and playground fund of Macco School. He was a strong supporter of the Yellow Creek Baptist Church and was a former deacon.[92] Marvin died on 19 November 1990 at Mercy Hospital in Owensboro, Daviess County, at age 75. Funeral services were held on 21 November 1990 at Glenn Funeral Home in

Owensboro. He was buried in Owensboro Memorial Gardens in Owensboro.[93]

The author remembers visits to the farms of both Louise and Lenore which were located on Pleasant Valley Road just outside Owensboro, Kentucky. He especially remembers the road to the farms along the Ohio River and riding in a farm truck to the fields to see the cows of which there were many. When his family visited Lenore he played with his two cousins. There was a large barn on Howard's farm that was usually filled with tobacco leaves that hung from rafters in the barn. There was also a large pond that contained that was used by the livestock. It contained Bass, Bluegill, and some very large catfish. The author remembers fishing there in the hope of catching something "big". There were also ducks and geese that were aggressive and chased the author when he got too close. His Great-grandmother Louise frequently warned him that they would bit if he didn't leave them alone. The author spend many hours exploring both properties but was never allow to stray very far from either home. The house where Louise and Howard lived was a stately property with large columns supporting a porch roof that was two stories tall. The home was filled with furniture that was likely passed down from past generations.

Howard died on 31 August 1958 in Daviess County, at age 67. The family bible stated 67 years and 22 days.[94] Funeral services were held on 1 September 1958 in Owensboro at the Third Baptist Church, with Delbert J. Glenn Funeral Home handling the arrangements and Rev. T.L. McSwain and Rev. Neil Wilson officiating. He was buried in Elmwood Cemetery in Owensboro, in Section 6.[95]

Howard W Daniel & Mary L. Lashbrook
Elmwood Cemetery
Owensboro, Kentucky

Louise was the oldest member of Third Baptist Church just prior to her death in 1993. She was a former member of the Women's Missionary Union and Rosehill Homemakers. She had also served as president of the Daviess County Homemakers Club and taught in the primary Sunday school department of the Third Baptist Church for many years.[96]

Mary Louise died at her home at 1942 Pleasant Valley Road in Owensboro on 22 September 1993, at age 101. Visitation was held at the Gleen Funeral Home in Owensboro on 24 September from 2:00 to 6:00 in the afternoon, and after 9:00 in the morning on 25 September. Funeral services were held on 25 September 1993 at the Glenn Funeral Home at 10:00 AM. She was buried on 25 September 1993 in Elmwood Cemetery in Owensboro, in Section 6.[97]

Chapter 8 – Jefferson Mandred Taylor Family

2nd Great-grandfather of Taylor Cosby Cottrell, Jr.

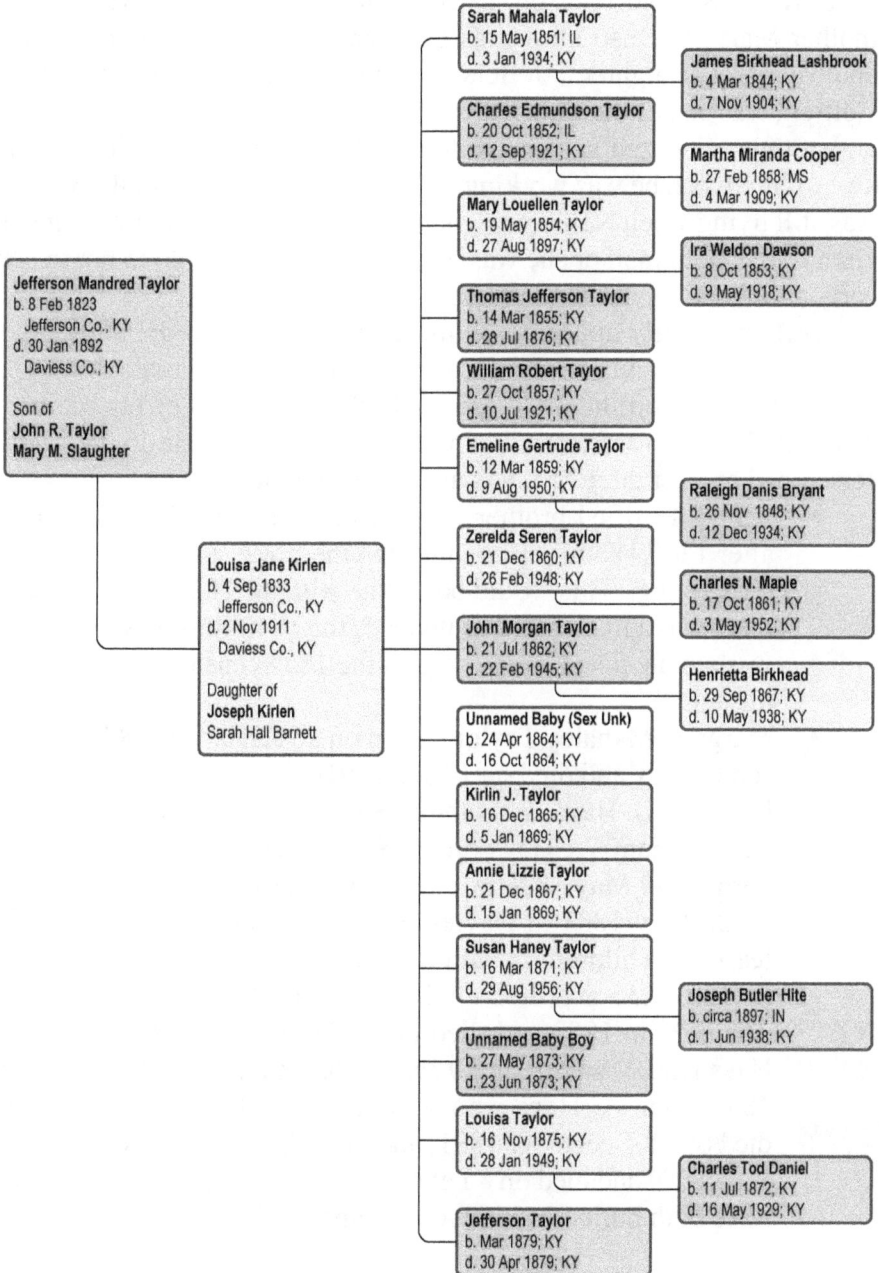

Jefferson Mandred Taylor
b. 8 Feb 1823
  Jefferson Co., KY
d. 30 Jan 1892
  Daviess Co., KY

Son of
John R. Taylor
Mary M. Slaughter

Louisa Jane Kirlen
b. 4 Sep 1833
  Jefferson Co., KY
d. 2 Nov 1911
  Daviess Co., KY

Daughter of
Joseph Kirlen
Sarah Hall Barnett

Sarah Mahala Taylor
b. 15 May 1851; IL
d. 3 Jan 1934; KY

James Birkhead Lashbrook
b. 4 Mar 1844; KY
d. 7 Nov 1904; KY

Charles Edmundson Taylor
b. 20 Oct 1852; IL
d. 12 Sep 1921; KY

Martha Miranda Cooper
b. 27 Feb 1858; MS
d. 4 Mar 1909; KY

Mary Louellen Taylor
b. 19 May 1854; KY
d. 27 Aug 1897; KY

Ira Weldon Dawson
b. 8 Oct 1853; KY
d. 9 May 1918; KY

Thomas Jefferson Taylor
b. 14 Mar 1855; KY
d. 28 Jul 1876; KY

William Robert Taylor
b. 27 Oct 1857; KY
d. 10 Jul 1921; KY

Emeline Gertrude Taylor
b. 12 Mar 1859; KY
d. 9 Aug 1950; KY

Raleigh Danis Bryant
b. 26 Nov 1848; KY
d. 12 Dec 1934; KY

Zerelda Seren Taylor
b. 21 Dec 1860; KY
d. 26 Feb 1948; KY

Charles N. Maple
b. 17 Oct 1861; KY
d. 3 May 1952; KY

John Morgan Taylor
b. 21 Jul 1862; KY
d. 22 Feb 1945; KY

Henrietta Birkhead
b. 29 Sep 1867; KY
d. 10 May 1938; KY

Unnamed Baby (Sex Unk)
b. 24 Apr 1864; KY
d. 16 Oct 1864; KY

Kirlin J. Taylor
b. 16 Dec 1865; KY
d. 5 Jan 1869; KY

Annie Lizzie Taylor
b. 21 Dec 1867; KY
d. 15 Jan 1869; KY

Susan Haney Taylor
b. 16 Mar 1871; KY
d. 29 Aug 1956; KY

Joseph Butler Hite
b. circa 1897; IN
d. 1 Jun 1938; KY

Unnamed Baby Boy
b. 27 May 1873; KY
d. 23 Jun 1873; KY

Louisa Taylor
b. 16 Nov 1875; KY
d. 28 Jan 1949; KY

Charles Tod Daniel
b. 11 Jul 1872; KY
d. 16 May 1929; KY

Jefferson Taylor
b. Mar 1879; KY
d. 30 Apr 1879; KY

Jefferson Mandred Taylor was born on 8 February 1823 in Jefferson County, Kentucky.[1] He was the son of John R. Taylor who was born in 1795 and Mary M. Slaughter who was born in 1802 in Louisville, Kentucky and died on 20 November 1893 in Louisville. His mother Mary was also known as Lena and was the daughter of John and Margaret Slaughter. Jefferson's father John, according to Nellie Cottrell, was one of the first settlers of Louisville, called Yellow Banks at that time. She said he was "a stern looking man and we all stood in awe of him when he was working."[2] However, since it is unlikely John was still living when Nellie was young she was either remembering her Grandfather Jefferson or she was remembering stories told to her in her early childhood by her mother about John.

Jefferson likely appeared on the census of 1830 in the household of his father, John, in Jefferson County, Kentucky, as a male 5-9.[3] He was likely listed on the 1840 census in the household of his mother, Mary M. Taylor in Jefferson County, Kentucky, as a male 15-19.[4] Jefferson had at least three brothers and sisters including:

- An unidentified brother who was born around 1825 and died after 1840. Family lore indicated there was another child who died young. This would be in-line with the 1830 census where there was a male listed as under 5, the 1840 census where there was a male listed as 10-14, and the 1850 census where he was missing.
- Margaret Mahaley Taylor - Born on 26 January 1828 in Jefferson County and died on 14 June 1910, at age 82 at the home of her son J.D. Hays on Anthony Street in Owensboro. She married William W. Hays on 17 September 1854. William was born on 30 May 1826 in Jefferson County, Kentucky and died on 20 May 1883 in Daviess County, at age 56. They had at least five children including James D. Hays who was born on 31 July 1855 and died on 4 April 1941, Charles J. Hays who was born in 1858 and died on 14 December 1897, Joseph T. Hays who was born on 30 June 1862 and died on 4 September 1890, John A. Hays who was born on 20 October 1864 and died on 18 December 1891, and Will S. Hays who was born in June 1870 and died on 8 February 1902. Margaret and William were both buried in Elmwood Cemetery in Owensboro.

- Joseph Elijah Taylor – Born on 26 March 1838 in Jefferson County and died on 27 February 1905 in Wabash County, Indiana, at age 66 in his home in the city of Wabash. His cause of death was lagrippe inflicted with gastritis. He was buried at South Park Cemetery in Greensburg in Decatur County, Indiana. Joseph enlisted into military service on 19 October 1861 and served in Company F, 26 Regiment of the Kentucky Infantry Volunteers for 3 years. He was disabled by Chronic Diarrhea and Piles in 1861 but mustered back into Company F in the Union Army at Camp Andrew in 1862. He was reduced to ranks by order of Captain R.E. Hacket with a charge of cowardice in front of the enemy at Nashville, Tennessee on 28 February 1865 and ended military service in July at Salisbury, North Carolina when he was mustered out of the Army. Later in 1865 Joseph entered Methel College in Logan County, Kentucky where he spent a year followed by the Bible College of Kentucky University at Lexington. Elijah married Lucy Emma Gibbony on 16 May 1872 in Lexington, Kentucky. Lucy was born on 19 April 1851 in Kentucky. She was the daughter of Edward Gibbony of Lexington, Kentucky and Julia A. Smither also of Lexington. She died on 19 December 1936 in Peru in Miami County, Indiana, at age 85. Her cause of death was diabetes. He established the first permanent Christian Church in Owensboro and served the ministry throughout many locations in Indiana and Kentucky. Joseph and Lucy had at least one child including Drucilla C. Taylor who was born on 12 October 1873 and died on 3 October 1949.

Jefferson was a carpenter and cabinet maker. He also mended musical instruments. According to Nellie Cottrell, Jefferson's Great-granddaughter, he made a violin out of curly maple and repaired one he called Able. He also used his skills as a cabinet maker to make all of their furniture out of birds-eye maple.[5]   He was also a miller and loved fine guns. Jefferson's obituary indicated he was born in Jefferson County, Kentucky and moved to Illinois in his early manhood returning to Daviess County in 1847.[6]   However, by 1850 he was located in Nelson County as confirmed by the census that year.

A bond for the marriage of Jefferson and Louisa Jane Kirlen was signed on 11 August 1849 in Jefferson County, Kentucky by Jefferson

Jefferson Mandred Taylor Family Timeline

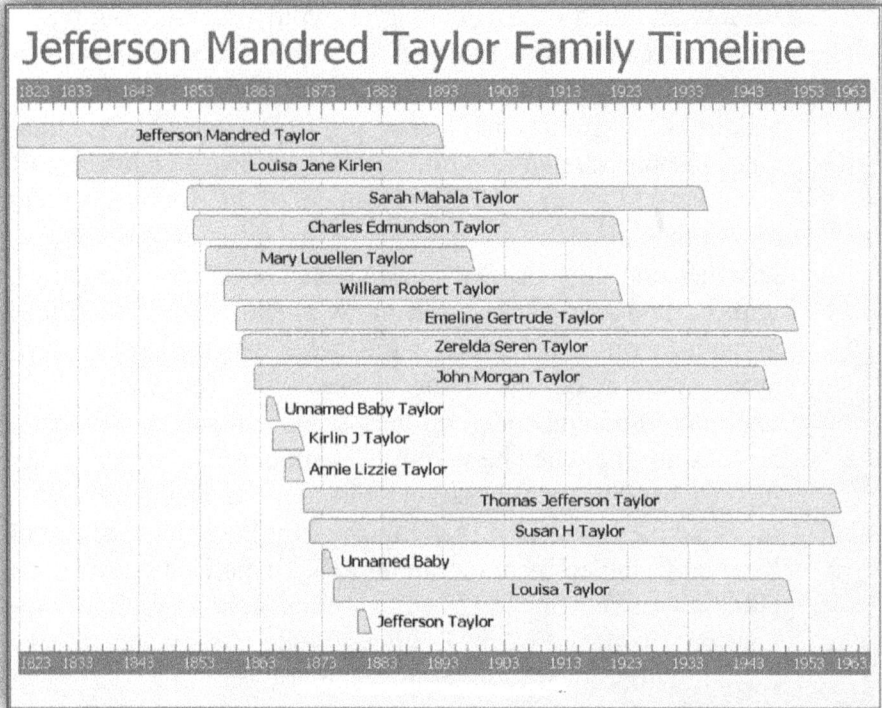

| | 1823 | 1833 | 1843 | 1853 | 1863 | 1873 | 1883 | 1893 | 1903 | 1913 | 1923 | 1933 | 1943 | 1953 | 1963 |

- Jefferson Mandred Taylor
- Louisa Jane Kirlen
- Sarah Mahala Taylor
- Charles Edmundson Taylor
- Mary Louellen Taylor
- William Robert Taylor
- Emeline Gertrude Taylor
- Zerelda Seren Taylor
- John Morgan Taylor
- Unnamed Baby Taylor
- Kirlin J Taylor
- Annie Lizzie Taylor
- Thomas Jefferson Taylor
- Susan H Taylor
- Unnamed Baby
- Louisa Taylor
- Jefferson Taylor

M. Tailor (correct spelling Taylor) and James W. Kerlin with consent in writing by the oath of James W. Kerlin which was based on written consent from her mother Sarah Shake the previous day. Jefferson married Louisa Jane Kirlen, daughter of Joseph Kirlen and Sarah Hall Barnett, on 11 August 1849 in Jefferson County. The ceremony was performed by William P. Barnett (Louisa's uncle). Jefferson obtained the marriage license the same day

Jefferson Mandred Taylor

but the certificate was not signed until the 13th. Their surnames were spelled Tailor and Kirlin on the certificate.[7]

Louisa was born on 4 September 1833 in Jefferson County, Kentucky. She was the daughter of Joseph Kirlen and Sarah Hall Barnett. Her father Joseph was born in Virginia and her mother Sarah was born on 29 July 1809 in Kentucky. Louisa's father died in 1839 when she was very young. In 1846 her mother married Adam Shake. According to family lore, based on recollections of Nellie Cottrell, Louisa didn't like Adam and during the marriage ceremony stood by her mother holding to her dress and cried out loud.

Louisa had three brothers and sisters including Mary Wilkes Kirlen who was born in 1832 in Kentucky, married George Washington Shake, and had at least one child Joseph

Louisa Jane Kerlin

Adam Shake, James W. Kirlen who was born around 1834 in Kentucky, and Joseph B. Kirlen who was born around 1837 in Kentucky. She also had at least one half-sister, Tabitha Shake, who was born from her mother's marriage to Adam Shake.[8]

In 1850 Jefferson was listed on the Nelson County, Kentucky census as Jefferson Taylor, age 27 along with L. Taylor, age 17. He appeared on the Illinois State Census of 1855 in Adams County, Illinois, as Jefferson M. Taylor, between the ages of 30 to 40, along with one white female 20 to 30 years of age (likely his wife Louisa), two white females under 10 (likely Sarah Mahala and Mary Louellen), and one white male under 10 (likely Charles Edmundson). Livestock was valued at $270.[9]

He was listed on the 1860 census in Daviess County as J.M. Taylor, age 36 with real estate valued at $500 and a personal estate valued at $4,000. Louisa, age 25, Sarah M., age 9, Charles E., age 7, Mary L., age 5, Thomas J., age 3, and Wm R., age 1 were also listed in his household. Charles E. and Mary L. were listed as attending school and Louisa was listed as a domestic lady.[10] Family lore was that Jefferson often gave ammunition and guns to soldiers that came through during the Civil War. It was said he would guide lost soldiers thru the dense woods to "join their company before the home guards found them."[11]

According to family lore Jefferson and Louisa started housekeeping together with a large mantle clock, which was operated by two weights. It had to be re-wound each day using a key that was stored inside the clock behind the door. The clock was a "Seth Thomas" clock and remained on their mantle until it was passed down to Jefferson's daughter Sarah Mahala Lashbrook and then to the Cottrell family from Sarah's daughter Nellie Cottrell. According to family lore based on stories told to Nellie Cottrell, Jefferson's Granddaughter, he often gave guns and ammunition to soldiers that passed through their land. He would tell her Grandmother Louisa to fix something to eat and leave it in the cellar and he would later slip the food to the soldiers. One time she

Mantel Clock
belonged to Jefferson and Louisa Taylor

boiled a ham, baked lots of bread pretending it was for their family because they did not trust their tenants to not notify the home guards. They apparently went to great lengths to avoid detection by the home guards and on one occasion after preparing the food Louisa and a neighbor named Mrs. Green left while Jefferson slipped into the cellar and took the food to the soldiers. When Louisa and Mrs. Green returned and went to get the food for dinner they came out of the cellar and told the tenants that their dogs had eating all the food and they would have to cook another dinner. Jefferson also went to great lengths to avoid detection from the home guards by storing his guns and ammunition in the woods. When it rained he would take Louisa, who was only 6 years old at the time, out into the woods to get the guns and ammunition. Jefferson would stay out of sight where he couldn't be seen by the home guards and wait for her to bring him the guns and ammunition. Louisa recalled she was scared of the lightening and the dark night.[12]

Jefferson was listed on the 1870 census in Daviess County as Jefferson M. Taylor, age 47 along with Louisa, age 36, Sarah M., age 17, Charles E., age 16, Mary L., age 14, Thomas J., age 11, Wm R., age 9, Emily G., age 7, Zerilda, age 6, John M., age 4, and Susan, age 6 months. His real estate was valued at $3,000 and his personal estate was valued at $400.[13] In 1880 he was listed on the census in Daviess County as Jefferson Taylor, age 56. Also listed was his wife Louisa, age 46; sons William, age 22 and John M., age 17; and daughters Emma, age 21, Zerelda, age 18, Susan, age 10, and Louisa, age 6.[14]

Jefferson and Louisa had 15 children including Sarah Mahala Taylor, Charles Edmundson Taylor, Mary Louellen Taylor, Thomas Jefferson Taylor, William Robert Taylor, Emeline Gertrude Taylor, Zerelda Seren Taylor, John Morgan Taylor, Kirlin Jo Taylor, Annie Lizzie Taylor, Susan M. Taylor, Louisa Taylor, Jefferson Taylor, and two unnamed babies (one of who was a son).[15]

Jefferson died on 30 January 1892 in Daviess County, Kentucky. His cause of death was la grippe. Funeral services were held on 31 January 1892 at the Macedonia Baptist Church Cemetery in Daviess County with the Rev. W.H. Dawson officiating.[16] He was buried in the Macedonia Baptist Church Cemetery which was located a little Northwest of the church as the junction of Settle Road and State Road 1456. Graves in the original Macedonia Church Cemetery were later moved to a new location across the road from the church in 1996.[17]

Jefferson Mandred Taylor		
1850	Nelson County, KY	Carpenter
1860	Daviess County, KY	Miller
1870	Daviess County, KY	Miller
1880	Daviess County, KY	Flower Miller

Louisa was listed on the 1900 census in Daviess County, Kentucky as Louisa J. Taylor, age 66, head of household, and owning her own farm listed on farm schedule 24, free of mortgage. Her son William A., age 41 was listed as working on the farm as a farm laborer. Louisa was listed as having been the mother of 15 children, 8 of which were still living at the time. She appeared on the census of 1910 in Daviess County as Louisa J. Taylor, age 77, not working, but living on a farm owned free of mortgage listed on farm schedule 49. She was living near her daughter Sarah M. Lashbrook at the time.[18]

Louisa died on 2 November 1911 in Dermot in Daviess County, at age 78. Her cause of death was heart failure.[19] She was buried at Macedonia Baptist Church Cemetery next to her husband. Her grave was later moved with the rest of the graves when the cemetery was moved to a new location across the street from the Macedonia Baptist Church.[20]

Jefferson M. and Louisa Jane Taylor
Macedonia Baptist Church Cemetery
Daviess County, Kentucky

Sarah Mahala Taylor (1851-1935)

Daughter of Jefferson M. Taylor and Louisa Jane Kirlen
Great-Grandmother of Taylor Cosby Cottrell, Jr.

Sarah Mahala Taylor was born on 15 May 1851 in Galesburg, Knox County, Illinois. She was the daughter of Jefferson Mandred Taylor and Louisa Jane Kirlen.[21] Information on Sarah and her Family, and Sarah's life history, along with that for her husband James Birkhead Lashbrook and their seven children is covered in detail in Section 1, Chapter 7, James Birkhead Lashbrook Family.

Charles Edmundson Taylor (1852-1921)

Son of Jefferson Mandred Taylor and Louisa Jane Kirlen
Great-Granduncle of Taylor Cosby Cottrell, Jr.

Charles Edmundson Taylor

Charles Edmundson Taylor was born on 20 October 1852 in Illinois. His gravestone lists his birth year as 1854. However, the family bible record lists the year as 1852 and his sister Mary Lou was born in 1854. Thus the author believes the bible record to be correct. Charles was the son of Jefferson Mandred Taylor and Louisa Jane Kirlen.[22] He appeared on the census of 1860 in Daviess County, Kentucky in the household of his father Jefferson, as Charles E., age 7 and attending school.[23]

In 1870 he was listed in the household of his father in Daviess County, as Charles E., age 16 and in school. Charles also went by the name of Dick.[24]

A bond for the marriage of Charles and Martha Miranda Cooper was signed on 14 April 1876 in Owensboro, Kentucky by C.E. Taylor and J.B. Lashbrooks. Charles married Martha on 16 April 1876 at the home of Joseph King in Daviess County. The ceremony was performed by J.D. Arnold.[25] Martha was the daughter of Thomas Cooper and was born on 27 February 1858 in Lee's Summit in Jackson County, Missouri.[26]

In 1880 he was listed on the census in Daviess County, as Charles E., age 26. His wife Mattie M., age 22 was also listed as well as two sons Charles M., age 3 and Marion A., age one.[27] He appeared on the 1900 census in Daviess County, as C.E. Taylor, age 42 along with his wife Mattie M., age 42. She was listed as being the mother of 8 children, 7 of which were living. His son Marion A., age 21, daughter

Mercedes, age 19, daughter Celeste, age 17, son Arnold C., age 15, daughter Louisa G., age 13, and son William, age 11 were also listed.[28]

Children of Charles E. Taylor and Martha M. Cooper:

- Charles Mandred Taylor – Born on 29 December 1876 in Daviess County, Kentucky and died on 22 June 1957 in Owensboro, Kentucky, at age 80. He is buried in Macedonia Baptist Church Cemetery in Daviess County.[29] Charles married Cora Allice Nelson, daughter of William Henry Nelson and Cecelia Masterson Pagan on 17 April 1899. Cecelia was born in December 1850 in Kentucky.[30] Cora died on 21 July 1925 in Bloomington

Charles Mandred Taylor
Macedonia Baptist Church Cemetery
Daviess County, Kentucky

in McLean County, Illinois, at age 46. She is buried in Macedonia Baptist Church Cemetery in Daviess County.[31] Charles then married Ora Hale on 9 February 1929 in Daviess County. Ora was born on 1 July 1881 in Daviess County. Charles and Ora did not have any children. Ora died on 21 September 1949 in Daviess County, at age 68. She is buried in Macedonia Baptist Church Cemetery in Daviess County.[32] Charles and Cora had one child:

  o Lena Todd Taylor – Born on 20 October 1905 in Philpot in Daviess County and died on 28 January 1994 in Owensboro, at age 88. She was buried in Rosehill-Elmwood Cemetery in Owensboro.[33] Lena married John Truman Heltsley on 8 January 1929. John was born on 15 December 1906 in Ohio County, Kentucky and died on 5 August 1967 in Owensboro. John was also buried in Rosehill-Elmwood Cemetery.[34]

- Ambrose Marion Taylor – Born on 2 February 1879 in Daviess County, Kentucky and died on 15 February 1968 at hillcrest Nursing Home in Philpot in Daviess County, Kentucky at age

89 after a 2 1/2-month illness. Funeral services were held at James H. Davis Chapel in Daviess County. Burial followed in Macedonia Baptist Church Cemetery in Daviess County.[35] Ambrose married Katheryne M. Moreland on 11 January 1905 in Daviess County. The ceremony was performed by Rev. W.H. Dawson. She was also known as Katie.[36] Ambrose was a mail carrier on a rural route in 1910. He was also a farmer by trade and owned a farm throughout most of his life.[37] Ambrose and Katheryne had

Ambrose M. Taylor & Katheryne Moreland
Macedonia Baptist Church Cemetery
Daviess County, Kentucky

no children. Katheryne died on 21 March 1967 at Hillcrest Nursing Home in Daviess County, at age 87. She was buried in Macedonia Baptist Church Cemetery.[38]

- Mercedes Taylor – Born on 17 November 1880 in Daviess County, Kentucky and died on 30 July 1967 at Owensboro-Daviess County Hospital in Owensboro, Kentucky, at age 86 after a 10-week illness. She was buried at Rosehill Cemetery in Owensboro, Kentucky.[39] Mercedes married Robert M. Robinson on 26 February 1912 in Daviess County. Robert was born on 16 August 1889 in Maceo, Daviess County.[40] Robert died on 5 January 1967 in Owensboro-Daviess County Hospital from complications of injuries suffered in an automobile accident on 31 December 1966. Funeral services were held on 6 January 1967 at Delbert J. Glenn Funeral Home in Owensboro. He was buried at Rosehill Cemetery in Owensboro, on 6 January 1967.[41] They had at least four children including:

  o W.H. Robinson – Stillborn on 18 November 1913 in Maceo in Daviess County. He was buried the next day in Yelvington, Kentucky.[42]

  o Evelyn Taylor Robinson – Born on 11 November 1914 in Maceo in Daviess County and died on 20 October 2001 in Prospect in Jefferson County, Kentucky. She

was buried on Rosehill-Elmwood Cemetery in Owensboro.[43] She married Herschel Curtis Craig who was
born on 4 May 1913 in McLean County, Kentucky and
died on 20 October 2002 in Prospect. He was buried
alongside Evelyn in Rosehill-Elmwood Cemetery.[44]

o Bobby F. Robinson – Born on 20 November 1916 in
Maceo in Daviess County and died on 14 March 2002
in Owensboro. She was buried in Rosehill-Elmwood
Cemetery in Owensboro.[45] She married Raymond Rus-
sell Burdette who was born on 20 October 1911 in
Daviess County and died on 23 January 1989 in Ow-
ensboro. He was also buried in Rosehill-Elmwood
Cemetery with his wife Bobbie.[46]

o Frank E. Robinson – Born on 14 February 1919 in Maceo in Daviess County and died on 25 August 2007 in
Madison in Jefferson County, Indiana. He was raised
in Owensboro, graduated from Owensboro High
school, and attended Western Kentucky University in
Bowling Green. He was a graduate of Embry-Riddle
School of Aeronautics. He married Ina Mae Wicker on
22 February 1942 in Whitesburg, Kentucky. Ina was
born on 24 April 1915 and died on 1 July 2005. Frank
developed an air strip on his farm and owned and operated Robinson Flying Service. During World War II he
taught flight instruction. He was active in several Baptist churches and was the author of more than 100
Gospel tracts that have been distributed worldwide.[47]

- Unidentified Taylor child born and died between 1881 and
1899 (1900 census indicated Martha was the mother of 8 children with 7 living).[48]

- Celeste P. Taylor – Born on 16 November 1882 in Daviess
County, Kentucky and died on 9 August 1973 in Owensboro
in Daviess County, Kentucky, at age 90. She was buried in
Rosehill Cemetery in Owensboro, Kentucky.[49] Celeste mar-
ried Isaac Newton Norris on 26 May 19143 in Daviess
County.[50] Isaac was born on 4 June 1885 in Daviess County.[51]
He was a mechanist in a carriage factory in 1920 and a foreman
in a furniture factory in 1940. In 1945 he was a cabinet maker.

Isaac died on 19 December 1945 in at Pap's Restaurant on East Fifth Street in Owensboro, at age 60. His cause of death was a heart attack which was determined from information from family and people that saw him "drop dead". He was buried in Rosehill Cemetery in Owensboro on 20 December 1945.[52] Celeste and Isaac had at least two children including[53]:

- o Dixie M. Norris – Born on 24 October 1915 in Daviess County, Kentucky.[54] It is likely she married William Flake Bruner. If this is correct then Dixie died on 23 January 1978 in Daviess County, Kentucky.[55]
- o Samuel Newton Norris – Born on 21 July 1921 in Daviess County, Kentucky and died on 19 November 2002 in Owensboro. He was buried in the Owensboro Memorial Gardens in Owensboro.[56]

- Arnold Chrisman Taylor – Born on 31 January 1885 in Daviess County, Kentucky and died on 19 August at the General hospital in Gastonia, North Carolina, at age 96. He was buried at Stanley Cemetery in Gaston County, North Carolina.[57] Arnold moved to Stanley Creek, North Carolina in early 1900 to become the new depot agent for the Brevard Station.[58] He married Ada Elnora Yelton Ensley in 1908.[59] Ada was born on 8 August 1885 in Rutherford County, North Carolina.[60] In 1910 Arnold was a depot agent for a steam railroad, likely the S.A.I.R.R. Company for whom he worked in 1918.[61] He was described as medium height and medium build with dark eyes and dark hair when he registered for the draft in 1918. Ada died on 27 September 1937 in Stanley in Gaston County, North Carolina. She was buried at Stanley Cemetery.[62] Arnold then married Mae Sudie Abernethy after the death of his first wife Ada. Mae was born on 10 August 1905 in North Carolina. Mae died on 13 February 1992 in Gastonia, at age 86. She was buried at Stanley Cemetery.[63] Arnold and Ada had at least four children including: [64]

- o Arnold Chrisman Taylor, Jr. Born on 22 August 1909 in Gaston County, North Carolina and died on 31 December 1997 in a Nursing Home in Stanley in Gaston County. He was listed as widowed on his death record.[65] Additional information is unknown.

- o Flay Morrison Taylor – Born on 21 December 1911 in North Carolina and died on 23 August 1969 in Apex in Wake County, North Carolina. He was buried in Raleigh Memorial Park in Raleigh in Wake County. Flay married Margaret Lyles.[66] She was born on 7 November 1907 in Cabarrus County, North Carolina and died in Raleigh on 19 January 2006. She was buried next to her husband Flay in Raleigh Memorial Park.[67]
  - o Merle Virginia Taylor – Born on 30 January 1915 in Gaston County, North Carolina.[68]
  - o Mildred Elnora Taylor – Born on 15 June 1919 in Gaston County, North Carolina.[69]
- Louise G. Taylor – Born on 2 January 1886 in Daviess County, Kentucky and died on 4 December 1971 in Daviess County, at age 85. She was buried at Macedonia Baptist Church Cemetery in Daviess County. Louise never married.[70]
- William Dick Taylor – Born on 20 October 1889 in Owensboro, Kentucky and died in May 1970 in Indiana, at age 80. He was buried at Union Cemetery in Eaton in Delaware County, Indiana.[71] William married Mildred Abbott in 1920.[72] She was born on 3 January 1906 in Indiana. They lived in Chicago in 1935. By 1940 they had moved back to Indiana. They apparently had no children. Mildred died in January

Louise G. Taylor
Macedonia Baptist Church Cemetery
Daviess County, Kentucky

1974 in Indiana and was buried in Union Cemetery in Eaton in Delaware County, Indiana.[73]
- Cooper Ellis Taylor – Born on 17 March 1903 in Owensboro, Kentucky and died on 27 June 1986 in the General Hospital Raleigh in Wake County, North Carolina, at age 83. He was buried in North Carolina.[74] Cooper married Catherine Elizabeth Carroll on 21 December 1929 in Pitt County, North Carolina. The ceremony was performed by William H. Covert,

a Baptist Clergyman. Catherine was born on 8 August 1901 in Pitt County, North Carolina.[75] In 1930 Cooper was the branch manager for Candys Peanut and in 1940 he was a wholesale farm tools sales manager.[76] Cooper and Catherine had at least two children, one of whom was John Carroll Taylor who was born on 13 April 1942 in Mecklenburg County, North Carolina and died on 8 November 2013 in Greenville, Virginia, at age 71. Their other child was living at the time of the writing of this book and is thus not included.[77] Catherine died on 19 November 1973 in Raleigh, at age 72.[78]

Martha died on 4 March 1909 in Daviess County, at age 51. She was buried at Macedonia Baptist Church Cemetery in Daviess County, located a little Northwest of the church at the junction of Settle Road and State Road 1456. Graves in the cemetery were moved to a new location across the road from the church in 1996.[79]

Charles Edmundson Taylor		
1860	Daviess County, KY	In School
1870	Daviess County, KY	In School
1880	Daviess County, KY	Farmer
1900	Daviess County, KY	Farmer
1910	Daviess County, KY	Farmer
1920	Daviess County, KY	Farmer

Charles was listed on the 1910 census in Daviess County, as Charles E. Taylor, age 56 along with his daughters Mercedes, age 28, Celeste, age 26, and Louisa, age 21. His son Cooper E., age 7 was also listed. Charles owned a farm free of mortgage that was listed on farm schedule seven.[80]

Charles left a will on 24 January 1913 in Owensboro, Kentucky leaving his estate to his children to be held in trust by his trustee until his youngest child arrived at the age of twenty-one and then to be sold and converted into money and divided equally among his remaining children. There were conditions in the remaining four pages that covered his two unmarried daughters Celeste and Louise to ensure they were adequately provided for. There were also conditions dealing with withholding funds if the trustee felt his youngest son, upon arriving at the age of twenty-one, was not sufficiently capable of judiciously handling his share.[81]

Charles appeared on the 1920 census in Daviess County as Charles E. Taylor, age 66 along with his daughter Louise, age 27 and his son

Cooper E., age 16. They were living on Litchfield Road in Daviess County at the time.[82]

Charles died on 12 September 1921 in Owensboro, Kentucky, at age 68. His cause of death was complications of kidney disease. He was buried on 13 September 1921 in the original Macedonia Baptist Church Cemetery located next to the Macedonia Baptist Church in Daviess County, Kentucky, which was located a little Northwest of the church at the junction of Settle Road and State Road 1456.[83] His estate was probated on 14 September 1921 in Owensboro by the recording of his will.

Charles E. Taylor and Martha M. Cooper
Macedonia Baptist Church Cemetery
Daviess County, Kentucky

His grave was moved to a new location across the road from the Macedonia Baptist Church in 1996 along with the other graves in the cemetery after the church decided to use the land for other purposes.[84]

Mary Louellen Taylor (1854-1897)

Daughter of Jefferson Mandred Taylor and Louisa Jane Kirlen
Great-Grandaunt of Taylor Cosby Cottrell, Jr.

Mary Louellen Taylor was born on 19 May 1854 in Kentucky. She was the daughter of Jefferson Mandred Taylor and Louisa Jane Kirlen.[85] She was listed on the 1860 census in the household of her father Jefferson in Daviess County, Kentucky, as Mary L., age 5 and attending school.[86] In 1870 she was listed on the census of her father in Daviess County, as Mary L., age 14.[87]

Mary married Ira Weldon Dawson, son of Joseph McCann Dawson and Elizabeth Miller, on 23 December 1875 in Daviess County.[88] Ira was born on 8 October 1853 in Daviess County.[89] In 1880 she was listed on the census in Daviess County, in the household of her husband

Ira W. Dawson as Mary L., age 26. Their daughter Lizie C., age 3 and son Taylor, age 10/12 were also listed in the household.[90]

Children of Mary Louellen Taylor and Ira Weldon Dawson:

- Elizabeth E. Dawson – Born on 4 June 1877 in Daviess County, Kentucky and died on 7 July 1933 in Dermot in Daviess County, at age 56.[91] Cause of death was cancer. She was buried on 8 July 1933 in Rosehill Cemetery in Owensboro. Elizabeth married Eula J. Brooks on 28 November 1901 in the home of Ira Dawson, in the presence of John M. Taylor and Doctor C.T. Daniel. Eula was born on 1 July 1874 in Ohio County, Kentucky.[92] Elizabeth and Eula apparently had no children. Eula died on 11 November 1946 at

Mary Louellen Taylor

  the Owensboro-Daviess County Hospital in Owensboro, at age 72. His cause of death was cardiovascular renal disease. He is buried in Macedonia Baptist Church Cemetery.[93]
- Charles Taylor Dawson – Born on 22 July 1879 in Daviess County, Kentucky and died on 9 May 1924 in Owensboro, at age 44. He married Katherine Robinson on 25 December 1904 in Vigo County, Indiana. Katherine was born in 1887 in Missouri. No additional information considered reliable has been found.[94]
- Nancy Virginia Dawson – Born on 28 December 1881 in Daviess County, Kentucky and died on 16 March 1972 in Daviess County, at age 90. She was buried in Rosehill Cemetery in Owensboro.[95] Nancy married Otto Ira Emrich in 1906. Otto was born on 17 January 1881 in Hancock County, Kentucky.[96] Otto Died on 6 January 1978 in Philpot, Kentucky. He was buried

in Rosehill Cemetery in Owensboro.[97] Nancy and Otto had at least two children including:

- o Ray Vivian Emrich – Born on 17 January 1907 in Kentucky and died on 13 February 2003 in Daviess County. She was buried in Rosehill-Elmwood Cemetery in Owensboro.[98] Rae married Miller Haynes Taylor who was born on 22 February 1932 in Daviess County and died on 14 October 1936 in Daviess County. Miller was also buried in Rosehill-Elmwood Cemetery next to his wife Ray.[99]
- o Charles Weldon Emrich – Born on 19 July 1911 in Kentucky and died on 27 October 1990 in Palm Beach, Florida. He was buried in Pinecrest Cemetery in Lake Worth in Palm Beach County. His gravestone also lists Catherine T. Emrich, born on 18 December 1915 and died on 24 December 1984.[100] According to Florida Marriage Records Charles married Lydia Margaretta Eurich after Catherine's death on 10 January 1986 in Palm Beach County.[101]

- William Carmie Dawson – Born on 20 December 1885 in Daviess County, Kentucky and died on 17 October 1967 at St. Anthony Hospital in Terre Haute in Vigo County, Indiana, at age 81. Funeral Services were held at Ryan Funeral Home in Terre Haute, Indiana. He was buried in Highland Lawn Cemetery in Terre Haute, Indiana in Section 1.[102] William married Ada Cook on 26 April 1912 in Marion County, Indiana. Ada was born in 1885 in Terre Haute, Indiana. William was a druggist by trade and worked for years as a pharmacist in Terre Haute. Ada died in 1981 in Indiana and is buried in Highland Lawn Cemetery in Terre Haute in Vigo County, Indiana, with her husband in Section 1.[103] William and Ada had at least one child: [104]

- o William Robert Dawson – Born on 21 May 1917 in Terre Haute in Vigo County, Indiana and died on 19 February 1999 in the Union Hospital Emergency Room in Terre Haute. He was buried in Highland Lawn Cemetery in Terre Haute with military graveside rites by Veteran of Foreign Wars Post 872. William married

Rosa Lee Brown who died on 22 April 1997. He served in the Army Air Force from 1942 to 1946.[105]

- Felix Ira Dawson – Born on 1 June 1886 in Daviess County, Kentucky and died on 8 April 1962 in Owensboro-Daviess County Hospital in Owensboro, at age 75. Funeral services were held at Delbert J. Gleen Mortuary in Owensboro. He is buried in Rosehill Cemetery in Owensboro.[106] Felix married Aurora Irene Martin on 11 August 1912. Aurora was born on 2 December 1890 in Daviess County. Aurora died on 17 December 1968 in Daviess County, Kentucky, at age 78.[107] She is buried in Rosehill Cemetery in Owensboro. Felix and Aurora had at least six children including:[108]

  o Arnold Marion Dawson – Born on 10 July 1914 in Daviess County and died on 26 June 1969 in Van Nuys in Los Angeles County, California. He was buried in Rosehill-Elmwood Cemetery in Owensboro.[109]

  o Carlin Ford Dawson – Born on 7 December 1915 and died on 8 January 1976. He was buried in Maplewood Cemetery in Anderson in Madison County, Indiana in Section 24. Carlin married. His wife's name was Gaynell. She was born on 12 May 1918, died on 30 September 2007 and is buried next to her husband Carlin in Maplewood Cemetery.[110]

  o Minnie Lou Dawson – Born on 21 May 1918 in Daviess County, Kentucky and died on 19 September 1995. She was buried in Owensboro Memorial Gardens. Minnie married twice; first to James Harlan Park and then to William B. Belford. Both James and William are buried in Owensboro Memorial Gardens.[111]

  o Virginia M. Dawson – Born on 25 November 1920 in Daviess County, Kentucky.[112]

  o Edna Elizabeth Dawson – Born on 15 January 1926 in Daviess County, Kentucky and died on 21 July 2011. Her husband's last name was Meserve.[113]

  o Mary Helen Dawson – Born on 1 September 1927 in Philpot in Daviess County, Kentucky and died on 10 November 2007. Mary married. Her husband's last name was Taylor. She was buried in Rosehill-Elmwood Cemetery in Owensboro.[114]

- Miller Kerlin Dawson – Born on 20 December 1889 in Philpot in Daviess County, Kentucky and died on 9 December 1948 in Owensboro-Daviess County Hospital in Owensboro.[115] Miller married Margaret Forest Jones on 17 March 1914 in Daviess County. Margaret was born on 29 March 1893 and died on 5 May 1974 in Owensboro, at age 81[116]. She was buried in Rosehill Cemetery in Owensboro.[117] Miller and Margaret had at least three children including:
  - Kathryn Elizabeth Dawson – Born on 22 April 1915 in Philpot in Daviess County, Kentucky and died on 1 December 1999.[118] Kathryn married Clifton Long on 10 August 1936 in Detroit in Wayne County, Michigan.[119]
  - Roy Jones Dawson – Born on 1 December 1917 in Daviess County and died on 26 July 1959 in Owensboro. He was buried in Rosehill-Elmwood Cemetery in Owensboro. Roy married Bonnie A. Trail.[120] She was born on 6 April 1919 in Ohio County, Kentucky and died on 20 June 1978 in Owensboro. She was also buried in Rosehill-Elmwood Cemetery next to her husband Roy.[121]
  - Thurman Miller Dawson – Born on 10 April 1927 in Philpot in Daviess County, Kentucky and died on 29 May 1993 in Kentucky.[122]
- John Mandrid Dawson – Born on 3 June 1894 in Daviess County, Kentucky and died on 21 November 1985 in Hillcrest Nursing Home in Owensboro, Kentucky. He is buried in Rosehill Cemetery in Owensboro.[123] John married Nellie Ellen Easton on 31 March 1920 in Daviess County.[124] Nellie was born on 14 June 1897 in Daviess County. John and Nellie had at least two children including:
  - Royce Edmund Dawson – Born on 26 August 1925 in Daviess County, Kentucky and died on 2 December 2012.[125]
  - Morris Elton Dawson – Born on 12 April 1927 in Daviess County, Kentucky and died on 24 August 2007 in

Owensboro. He was buried in Rosehill-Elmwood Cemetery in Owensboro.[126] Morris married Lillian Morgan who was born on 8 April 1917 in Fremont County, Iowa and died on 17 August 2014 in Owensboro. She was also buried in Rosehill-Elmwood Cemetery next to her husband Morris.[127]

Nellie died on 23 April 1927 at City Hospital in Owensboro, Kentucky, at age 29. She was buried in Rosehill Cemetery in Owensboro.[128] John then married Lenora Hite on 27 November 1929 in Daviess County.[129] She was born on 26 March 1903 in Daviess County. In 1932 John was elected as the first board chairman of the Daviess County Board of Education.[130] Lenora died on 2 September 1936 at City Hospital in Owensboro, Daviess County. She

Ira Dawson, Mary L. Taylor, Mary C. Emrich
Macedonia Baptist Church Cemetery
Daviess County, Kentucky

was buried in Rosehill Cemetery in Owensboro.[131] In 1938 John began a 27-year employment with the Green River Electric Corporation when he was placed in charge of right-of-way procurement for the company.[132] John married his third wife, Nina Marie in 1938. Nina was born on 20 June 1901 in Kentucky and died on 3 January 1957 in Daviess County at age 55. She is buried in Rosehill Cemetery in Owensboro.[133] John Retired as member relations director of Green River Electric Corporate in 1965. He was honored by Green River Electric in early 1985 at a member meeting with a Pioneer Award, an award that is presented to individuals who have made significant and lasting contributions to early development and advancement of rural electrification programs.[134]

Mary died on 27 August 1897 in Daviess County, at age 43. Funeral services were held on 28 August 1897 at Macedonia Baptist

Church in Daviess County with the Rev. W.H. Dawson conducting the service. She was buried on 28 August 1897 at Macedonia Cemetery in Daviess County.[135] Her grave was moved to the new location across the road from the church in 1996 along with the other graves in the cemetery.

Ira was listed on the 1900 census in Daviess County, as Ira Dawson, age 46 along with his daughters Lizzie C., age 22 and Virginia N., age 18 and sons William C., age 16, Felix I., age 13, Miller C., age 10, and John M., age 5.[136] Ira married Mary Catherine Emrich, daughter of John Emrich and Elizabeth Schmidt, in 1902. Mary was born on 17 December 1858 in Kentucky. Ira was listed on the 1910 census in Daviess County as Ira Dawson, age 56 along with his wife Mary, age 51 and sons Miller, age 20 and John, age 15.[137]

Ira died on 9 May 1918 in Philpot, Daviess County, Kentucky, at age 64. Funeral services were held on 10 May 1918 at Macedonia Baptist Church in Daviess County, with services conducted by Revs. N.F. Gabbert and John Barker. He was buried in Macedonia Baptist Church Cemetery.[138]

Mary Catherine died on 15 August 1951 in Philpot in Daviess County, at age 92. Her cause of death was arteriosclerosis. She was also buried in Macedonia Cemetery in Daviess County.[139]

Thomas Jefferson Taylor (1855-1876)

Son of Jefferson Mandred Taylor and Louisa Jane Kirlen
Great-Granduncle of Taylor Cosby Cottrell, Jr.

Thomas Jefferson Taylor was born on 14 October 1855 in Daviess County, Kentucky. He was the son of Jefferson Mandred Taylor and Louisa Jane Kirlen.[140] Thomas was listed on the 1860 census in Daviess County, in the household of his father Jefferson, as Thomas J., age 3.[141] He appeared on the 1870 census in the home of his father in Daviess County, as Thomas J., age 11.[142]

Thomas died on 28 July 1876 in Daviess County, at age 20 on the Taylor farm located on the north fork of Panther Creek and Miller's Road near Owensboro. He was "thrown and dragged rapidly and ruthlessly through woods and up and down a rugged winding path for the distance of a mile. According to his obituary "…his mother risked her life by seizing the broken reins and holding on to the terrified mule until his foot came loose. She then took hold of his hands and called him by name. He was unresponsive. She held his hands "while his lips quivered, his breast heaved, and he breathed his last."[143]

He was described as being of "good physical constitution from early youth, and being well developed in body and mind, naturally industrious and energetic, and of such an even, quiet temperament, with no dissipated or profane habits, that meet him when, and wherever you would, his face lit up with a smile, and he seemed only to think of his duty in making others happy. He was a dutiful, affectionate son, a kind loving brother, and from his youth up, was a good companion and agreeable associate, airways acting from true principle and with pure motivation and possessed of those traits of generosity and judicious youth and genuine man." He was buried in Macedonia Baptist Church Cemetery in Daviess County, Kentucky.[144]

William Robert Taylor (1857-1921)

Son of Jefferson Mandred Taylor and Louisa Jane Kirlen
Great-Granduncle of Taylor Cosby Cottrell, Jr.

William Robert Taylor was born on 27 October 1857 in Daviess County, Kentucky. He was the son of Jefferson Mandred Taylor and Louisa Jane Kirlen.[145] William was listed on the 1860 census of Daviess County, in the home of his father Jefferson, as Wm. R., age 1.[146] He was listed on the 1870 census in Daviess County, in his father's home as Wm. R., age 9.[147] In 1880 he was listed on the census in Daviess County, in the household of his father Jefferson as William, age 22 and single. He was working as a laborer in a mill at the time.[148] William was listed on the 1900 census in Daviess County, in the home of his mother Louise, as William A., age 41 and single. William never married. He died on 10

William Robert Taylor

July 1921 in Owensboro, Daviess County, at age 63. His cause of death was heart disease. He is buried in Macedonia Baptist Church Cemetery, in Owensboro.[149]

Emeline Gertrude Taylor (1859-1950)

Daughter of Jefferson M. Taylor and Louisa Jane Kirlen
Great-Grandaunt of Taylor Cosby Cottrell, Jr.

Emeline Gertrude Taylor was born on 12 March 1859 in Daviess County, Kentucky. She was the daughter of Jefferson Mandred Taylor and Louisa Jane Kirlen.[150] Emeline was listed on the 1870 census in Daviess County, in the home of her father Jefferson, as Emily G., age 9.[151] She was listed in the home of her father on the 1880 census in Daviess County, as Emma, age 21 and single.[152]

Emma married Raleigh Danis Bryant on 5 January 1882 in Daviess County. The cere-

Emeline Gertrude Taylor

mony was performed by R.S. Fleming in the presence of J.J. Hunter and C.E. Taylor.[153] Raleigh was born on 26 November 1848 in Daviess County.[154] In 1900 Emma was listed on the census in Daviess County, in the home of her husband Rolla D. Bryant, along with their daughters Hortense, age 17, Harriet, age 7, and Ruth, age 3, and sons Hugh, age 15, William, age 9, Samuel J., age 5, and James R., age 1. Raleigh owned his farm which was listed on farm schedule 161, free of mortgage.[155]

In 1910 Emma was listed on the census in the home of her husband in Daviess County, as Emma, age 50 along with their sons Hugh M., age 24, William E., age 19, Samuel J., age 15, and James R., age 11. Their daughters Harriett L., age 17 and Ruth M., age 13 were also living in the home.[156] In 1920 Emma was listed in the census of Daviess

County, in the home of her husband R.D. Bryant, as Emaline, age 60. Their sons Sam J., age 24 and James R., age 19 were also listed.[157]

Children of Emeline Taylor and Raleigh Bryant:

- Hortence Bryant – Born in October 1882 in Dermot, Daviess County, Kentucky and died on 19 January 1949 in Richmond, Virginia, at age 66. She is buried in Rosehill Cemetery in Owensboro.[158] A bond for the marriage of Hortence Bryant and James Authur Kirk was signed on 19 October 1904 in Daviess County, by J.A. Kirk and R.D. Bryant. Hortense married James on 19 October 1904 in Daviess County, in the home of Hortense's father R.D. Bryant. The ceremony was performed by J. Denham Hocker with Dr. C.J. Daniel and Dr. E. McCornish serving as witnesses.

Hugh Mandred Bryant
Macedonia Baptist Church Cemetery
Daviess County, Kentucky

  James was born on 2 April 1881 in Daviess County.[159] James died on 3 September 1934 in Kentucky, at age 53. He is buried in Rosehill Cemetery in Owensboro, Kentucky.[160] Hortense and James had at least one child:
  - Elizabeth C. Kirk – Born around 1906 in Kentucky. Living with her parents in 1930 in Kansas City in Jackson, Missouri. She was listed as single on the census and working as a public school teacher.[161]
- Hugh Mandred Bryant – Born on 15 December 1884 in Daviess County, Kentucky and died on 1 December 1916 in Daviess County, at age 31. His cause of death was Urania poisoning complicated by Bright's Disease. He is buried in Macedonia Baptist Church Cemetery in Daviess County. Hugh never married.[162]

- William Ellis Bryant – Born on 6 November 1892 in Owensboro, Kentucky and died on 24 June 1947 at the New Century Hotel in Dawson Springs in Hopkins County, Kentucky, at age 54. His cause of death was a heart attack. He was buried on 1 July 1947 in Kentucky.[163] William married Emma Mae Hatcher in 1920. Emma was born on 13 April 1902 in Warren County, Kentucky. William was a general food salesman in 1930 and Chief of Police for Paducah, Kentucky in 1947.[164] Emma died on 14 May 1952 at Riverside Hospital in Paducah, at age 50 following an automobile crash. She was buried on 16 May at Maplelawn Cemetery in Paducah.[165] William and Emma had at least one child:
  - Mary J. Bryant – Born circa 1923 in Kentucky, likely in McCracken County. Listed with her mother and father on the 1940 census living at 361 Wallace Lane in Paducah, Kentucky.[166]
- Harriette Bryant – Born on 20 December 1892 in Daviess County and died on 17 December 1986 in Owensboro, Kentucky.[167] She married Charles Cadwallader Lewis who was born on 12 May 1875 in Owensboro. Charles died on 3 March 1948 at Owensboro-Daviess County Hospital in Owensboro. He was buried in Rosehill Cemetery in Owensboro. Harriett and Charles apparently had no children.[168]
- Samuel Jefferson Bryant – Born on 9 September 1894 in Daviess county and died on 17 January 1958 in Kentucky, at age 63. He was buried at Rosehill Cemetery in Owensboro.[169] Samuel married Martine M. Norton in 1916. Martine was born on 12 October 1895 in Daviess County. Martine died on 10 December 1988 in Owensboro, Kentucky, at age 93. She was buried in Rosehill Cemetery in Owensboro.[170] Samuel and Martine had at least two children:[171]
  - Elizabeth L. Bryant – Born on 12 September 1921 in Daviess County, Kentucky and died on 19 February 2011 in Daviess County. She was buried in Rosehill-Elmwood Cemetery in Owensboro. Elizabeth also went by the name of Betty.[172] She married Estel Kerrick who was the son of Miles and Lillie Kerrick. He was born in

1923 and died on 27 July 1994. He was buried in Rose-hill-Elmwood Cemetery next to his wife.[173]

o Dorothy Jean Bryant – Born on 3 March 1925 in Leba-non Junction, Kentucky and died on 10 December 2002 in Kentucky. She was buried in Cave Hill Cemetery in Louisville in Jefferson County, Kentucky. Dorothy married. Her husband's last name was Muir.[174]

▪ Ruth M. Bryant – Born in January 1897 in Daviess County, Kentucky. She was listed on the 1900 and 1910 census in Da-viess County in the home of her father Raleigh. No additional reliable information is known about Ruth.[175]

▪ James Raleigh Bryant – Born on 22 February 1900 in Daviess County. James was listed on the 1910 and 1920 census in Da-viess County in the home of his father Raleigh.[176] He registered for the draft for World War I on 12 September 1918 while living in Owensboro and attending school.[177] No additional reliable information is known about James.

Raleigh died on 12 December 1934 in Owensboro, Kentucky, at age 86. His cause of death was heart disease. He was buried on 14 December 1934 in Rosehill Cemetery in Owensboro.[178]

Emma died on 9 August 1950 in Owensboro, Kentucky, at age 91. Her cause of death was heart disease. She was buried in Rosehill Cem-etery in Owensboro, Kentucky on 11 August 1950.[179]

Zerelda Seren Taylor (1860-1948)

Daughter of Jefferson Mandred Taylor and Louisa Jane Kirlen
Great-Grandaunt of Taylor Cosby Cottrell, Jr.

Zerelda Seren Taylor was born on 21 December 1860 in Daviess County, Kentucky. She was the daughter of Jefferson Mandred Taylor and Louisa Jane Kirlen.[180] She appeared on the census of 1870 in Da-viess County, in the home of her father Jefferson, as Zerilda, age 6.[181] In 1880 she was in the census of her father in Daviess County as Zerelda, age 18 and single.[182]

Zerelda married Charles N. Maple the son of William Maple and Almarinda Coe on 15 August 1894 in Jefferson County, Kentucky.[183] Charles was born on 17 October 1861 in Jefferson County.[184] In 1900 she was listed on the census of her husband Charles N. Maple in Jefferson County as Zerelad, age 36. Charles owned his own farm which was listed on farm schedule 71, free of mortgage.[185] In 1910 Zerelda was listed on the census of Jefferson County, in the home of her husband Charles, as Zerelda, age 48. Their son William, age 3 was also listed.[186] In 1920 she was listed as Zerelda Seren, age 58 on the census of Jefferson County, along with her husband Charles N. Maple and son William M., age 13.[187]

Zerelda Seren Taylor

In 1930 she was listed on the census in Jefferson County as Zerelda, age 68 along with her husband Charles N. Maple, age 68 and their son W. Mandred, age 23. They were living on a farm on Cooper Chapel Road at the time.[188] The 1940 census of Jefferson County, listed Charles N. Maple as head of household along with his wife Cerelda, age 78.[189]

Children of Zerelda Seren Taylor and Charles N. Maple:

- William Mandred Maple – Born on 23 April 1906 in Kentucky and died on 18 June 1984 in Louisville in Jefferson County, Kentucky. He was buried in Pennsylvania Run Cemetery in Louisville.[190] William was listed as a farmer on both the 1930 and 1940 census. William married Evelyn Coe in 1932. She was born on 26 June 1909 in Kentucky. William and Evelyn apparently had no children.[191] Evelyn died on 17 December 1909 in Jefferson County, at age 78. She is buried in Pennsylvania Run Cemetery in Louisville, Kentucky.[192]

Zerelda died on 26 February 1948 in Louisville, Kentucky, at age 87. Her cause of death was cerebral embolism. She was buried on 28 February 1948 in Pennsylvania Run Cemetery in Louisville.[193]

Charles died on 3 May 1952 in Louisville, at age 90 in the morning at his home on Maple Road. His cause of death was cardio vascular hypertension due to advanced age. He was buried on 5 May 1952 in Pennsylvania Run Cemetery in Louisville.[194]

John Morgan Taylor (1862-1945)

Son of Jefferson Mandred Taylor and Louisa Jane Kirlen
Great-Granduncle of Taylor Cosby Cottrell, Jr.

John Morgan Taylor was born on 21 July 1862 in Daviess County, Kentucky. He was the son of Jefferson Mandred Taylor and Louisa Jane Kirlen.[195] He was listed on the census of 1870 in the household of his father Jefferson in Daviess County, as John M., age 4.[196] In 1880 he was listed on the census in the household of his father in Daviess County, as John M., age 17 and attending school. He was suffering with rheumatism at the time.[197]

John Morgan Taylor		
1870	Daviess County, KY	N/A
1880	Daviess County, KY	In School
1900	Daviess County, KY	Farmer
1910	Daviess County, KY	Farmer
1920	Daviess County, KY	Farmer
1930	Daviess County, KY	N/A
1940	Daviess County, KY	N/A

John married Henrietta Birkhead, the daughter of Thomas Wesley Birkhead and Mary Ann Nelson, on 13 January 1887 at the home of Thomas Birkhead in Daviess County. The ceremony was performed by B.P. Swindler with F.D. Stow and Ira Dawson serving as witnesses.[198] Henrietta was born on 29 September 1867 in Kentucky.[199] In 1900 John was working as a Poor House Keeper when he appeared on the census in Daviess County as John M., age 36. His wife Henrietta, age 33 and son Roy B., age 3 were also listed. An adopted son, Virgil Lee Cook, age 13 was also living in the household as well as two servants Frank Omer and Clare Gardner.[200]

John Morgan Taylor & Henrietta Birkhead
Rosehill Cemetery
Owensboro, Kentucky

In 1910 John was listed on the census of Daviess County as John M., age 45 and owning a farm listed on farm schedule 30, free of mortgage. His wife Henrietta, age 43 was listed as well as their son Roy, age 12 and attending school. Frank Stevens, a servant, also lived in the home and was attending school.[201]

In 1920 John was living on Litchfield Road when he was listed on the census in Daviess County, as Morgan G. Taylor, age 54. His wife Henrietta, age 53, his son Roy, age 23, and his daughter-in-law Frances, age 20 was also listed. A lodger, Lucile Bristow, age 14 was also living in the household. [202] Lucile was adopted by John sometime before the 1930 census. John appeared on the 1930 census in Daviess County as John M., age 65 along with his wife Henrietta, age 63 and adopted daughter Lucile Bristow, age 31. He owned his home which was valued at $8,000 and had a radio set. His farm was listed on farm schedule 195.[203]

Children of John Morgan Taylor and Henrietta Birkhead:

- Virgil Lee Cook (adopted son) – Born in December 1896 in Kentucky. He was listed in the household of John Morgan Taylor and Henrietta Birkhead on the 1900 census in Daviess County as Virgil Lee Cook, an adopted son, age 13 and attending school.[204]
- Roy Birkhead Taylor – Born on 19 December 1896 in Owensboro in Daviess County and died on 17 February 1960 in Owensboro in Daviess County, at age 63.[205] His cause of death was a myocardial infraction. He was buried in Rosehill Cemetery in Owensboro on 18 February 1960. Roy married Minnie Frances King, the daughter of James Lewis King and Cora Ann Kirk, on 26 May 1915 in Spencer County, Indiana. When he registered for the WWI Draft in 1918 he was described as medium height, medium build with gray eyes and light brown hair. He was living in Owensboro at the time and listed himself as self-employed. Roy worked as an oil well driller in the 1930s and 1940s.[206] They apparently had no children. Minnie Frances died on 9 December 1956 in Daviess County, at age 50. She is buried next to her husband Roy in Rosehill Cemetery in Owensboro.[207]

- Lucile Bristow (adopted daughter) – Born around 1903 in Kentucky. She was listed as a lodger in the household of John Morgan Taylor and Henrietta Birkhead on the 1920 census in Daviess County. However, on the 1930 census in Daviess County she was listed as Lucile Bristow, age 27, single, and an adopted daughter in the household of John. Thus it is assumed that John adopted her sometime between 1920 and 1930.[208].

Henrietta died on 10 May 1938 at 11:00 in the morning in Philpot in Daviess County, at age 70. Her cause of death was bronchial asthma. She was buried on 11 May 1938 in Rosehill Cemetery in Owensboro.[209]

In 1940 John was listed on the census in Daviess County, as J. Morgan Taylor, age 76 and widowed. His son Roy B., age 43 and daughter-in-law Frances, age 40, and Roy's mother-in-law Cora King, age 63 were also living in the household at the time.[210]

John died on at 2:00 in the afternoon on 22 February 1945 at 2004 Circle Avenue in Owensboro, at age 82. His cause of death was chronic myocarditis. He was buried on 23 February 1945 in Rosehill Cemetery in Owensboro.[211]

Unnamed Baby Taylor (1864-1864)

Son of Jefferson Mandred Taylor and Louisa Jane Kirlen
Great-Granduncle/aunt of Taylor Cosby Cottrell, Jr.

An unnamed baby Taylor was born to Jefferson Mandred Taylor and Louisa Jane Kirlen on 24 April 1864 in Daviess County, Kentucky and died on 16 October 1864 in Daviess County. The baby was listed in Louisa's bible as "one that died without a name".[212]

Kirlin Jo Taylor (1865-1869)

Daughter of Jefferson Mandred Taylor and Louisa Jane Kirlen
Great-Grandaunt of Taylor Cosby Cottrell, Jr.

Kirlin Jo Taylor was born on 16 December 1865 in Daviess County, Kentucky. She was the daughter of Jefferson Mandred Taylor and Louisa Jane Kirlen. She died on 5 January 1869 in Daviess County, at age 3.[213]

Annie Lizzie Taylor (1867-1869)

Daughter of Jefferson Mandred Taylor and Louisa Jane Kirlen
Great-Grandaunt of Taylor Cosby Cottrell, Jr.

Annie Lizzie Taylor was born on 21 December 1867 in Daviess County, Kentucky. She was the daughter of Jefferson Mandred Taylor and Louisa Jane Kirlen. She died on 15 January 1869 in Daviess County, at age 1.[214]

Susan Haney Taylor (1871-1956)

Daughter of Jefferson Mandred Taylor and Louisa Jane Kirlen
Great-Grandaunt of Taylor Cosby Cottrell, Jr.

Susan Haney Taylor was born on 16 March 1871 in Taylors Mills in Daviess County, Kentucky. She was the daughter of Jefferson Mandred Taylor and Louisa Jane Kirlen. She was also known as Gussie.[215] She was listed on the 1870 census in Daviess County, in the home of her father Jefferson as Susan, age 6/12.[216] In 1880 she was listed in the census in Daviess County, in the household of her father as Susan, age 10 and attending school. She was also known as Susie.[217] She married Joseph Butler Hite in Indiana around 1897.[218] Joseph was born on 19 November in 1864. He was the son of Thomas Taylor Hite and Nancy Cook.[219]

Susan was listed on the 1900 census in Daviess County in the home of her husband Joseph as Susie H. Hite, age 30. Their son Orion, age 2 was also listed.[220] In 1910 she was listed on the census in the home of her husband J.B. Hite in Daviess County as S.H. Hite, age 40. Their sons O.M., age 12, J.D., age 6 and L.W., age 1 were also listed.[221] Susan was listed on the 1920 census in Daviess County,

Susie H. Taylor and Joseph B. Hite
Macedonia Baptist Church Cemetery
Daviess County, Kentucky

in the home of her husband Joseph as Susie H., age 49. Their sons Douglas J., age 16 and Leslie W., age 10 were also listed.[222]

In 1930 Susan was listed on the census in Daviess County with her husband Joe as Susie H., age 60. Their son Douglas, age 26 and widowed along with their grand-daughter Anna S., age 3 11/12 were also living in the household.[223]

Children of Susan Haney Taylor and Joseph Butler Hite:

- Orion Maxwell Hite – Born on 15 February 1898 in Daviess County, Kentucky and died on 5 April 1986 in Daviess County. He is buried in Mount Hope Cemetery in Logansport in Cass County, Indiana. Orion married Ruth Hope Ford on 4 December 1920 in Kokomo in Cass County, Indiana. Ruth died on 18 July 1951 and is buried next to her husband in Mount Hope Cemetery in Logansport, Indiana. They had at least three children including:
  - Joseph Hite – Born on 30 August 1921 in Indiana and died on 20 August 1985 in San Diego.[224]
  - Owen Eugene Hite – Born on 2 February 1932 in Logansport County, Indiana and died on 16 November 1996, likely in Logansport. He was buried in Mount Hope Cemetery in Logansport in Cass County, Indiana.[225] Owen married Ruth Hope on 4 December 1920 in Kokomo, Indiana. Ruth was born on 1 April 1904 and died on 18 July 1951. She was also buried in Mount Hope Cemetery next to her husband Owen.[226]
  - Donald Lee Hite – Born on 9 March 1938 in Indiana and died on 15 October 1991. He was buried in Memorial Gardens Cemetery in Poplar Bluff in Butler County, Missouri.[227]
- Douglas Joseph Hite – Born on 7 January 1904 in Daviess County, Kentucky and died on 10 July 1969 in Hollywood in Broward County, Florida.[228] Douglas married Nannie Louise Hardesty on 5 January 1925 in Daviess County. They had one child:
  - Anna Sue Hite – Born on 14 April 1926 in Owensboro, Kentucky and died on 16 January 1989.[229]
- Leslie Ward Hite – Born on 3 February 1909 and died on 2 July 1963. He is buried in Rosehill Cemetery in Owensboro, Kentucky. He married Marie Harris. Marie was the daughter

of Eugene Harris and Willie Malone Moore. She was born on 21 December 1911 in Todd County, Kentucky and died on 8 May 1979 in Daviess County. She is buried next to her husband in Rosehill Cemetery in Owensboro, Kentucky.[230]

Joseph died on 1 June 1938 in Owensboro, Kentucky. He is buried in Macedonia Baptist Church Cemetery in Owensboro.[231]

Susan was listed on the 1940 census in Daviess County the home of her son Joseph Hite, age 36, as Susie H., Mother, age 70 and widowed. Her son's wife Ferris, age 24 and their son Joseph, age 6 were also listed in the home.[232] Susan died on 29 August 1956 in Daviess County. She is buried in Macedonia Baptist Church Cemetery in Owensboro, Kentucky next to her husband Joseph.[233]

Unnamed Baby Taylor (1873-1873)

Son of Jefferson Mandred Taylor and Louisa Jane Kirlen
Great-Granduncle of Taylor Cosby Cottrell, Jr.

An unnamed baby boy was born on 27 May 1873 in Daviess County, Kentucky. He was the son of Jefferson Mandred Taylor and Louisa Jane Kirlen. He died on 23 June 1873 in Daviess County. The baby was listed in Louisa's bible as "a son was born May the 17 73 died without a name June 23 73."[234]

Louisa Taylor (1875-1949)

Daughter of Jefferson Mandred Taylor and Louisa Jane Kirlen
Great-Grandaunt of Taylor Cosby Cottrell, Jr.

Louisa Taylor was born on 16 November 1875 in Daviess County, Kentucky. She was the daughter of Jefferson Mandred Taylor and Louisa Jane Kirlen.[235] She was also known as Louise. She was listed on the 1880 census of Daviess County, in the home of her father Jefferson as Louisa, age 6.[236] Louisa married Charles Todd Daniel around 1895.[237] Charles was born on 11 July 1872 in Daviess County. He was the son of Isiah Daniel and Katherine Nichols.[238] She was listed on the 1900 census in Daviess County, in the home of her husband C. Daniel as Louise Daniel, age 25. Their daughters Ruth, age 3 and Mildred, age 1 were also listed.[239]

In 1910 she was listed on the census in Daviess County, Kentucky in the home of her husband Charles T. Daniels as Louise, age 33 along with their daughters Ruth K., age 13, Mildred, age 11, and Kathrine, age 5. Their son Charles T. Daniels, Jr., age 9 was also listed.[240] In 1920 she was listed on the census in Daviess County, in the home of her husband Charles as Louise, age 44. Their children Ruth K., age 23, Mildred E., age 21, Charles T., age 19, Kathryn L., age 14, and Karlin K., age 9 were also listed in the household.[241] Charles died on 16 May 1929 in Calhoun in Mclean County, Kentucky. His cause of death was cerebral hemorrhage. He is buried in Macedonia Baptist Church Cemetery in Daviess County, Kentucky.[242]

In 1930 Louise was listed in the census in Daviess County, as Louise, age 55 and widowed. Her son Karlin, age 19 and single was also listed.[243] Louise was listed on the 1940 census in Jefferson County, Kentucky as Louise, age 60, widowed and head of household along with her daughter Ruth, age 40 and Karlin, age 29. They were living at 1324 Third Street in Louisville, Kentucky at the time.[244]

Children of Louisa Taylor and Charles Tod Daniel:

- Ruth K. Daniel – Born around 1897 in Kentucky. The last confirmed location for Ruth was the 1940 census when she was living with her mother in Daviess County, Kentucky.[245]
- Mildred Emma Daniel – Born on 22 October 1898 and died on 25 May 1983. She is buried in Forest Hill Cemetery Midtown in Memphis, Shelby County, Tennessee.[246] She married Roy Marcellus Robinson. They divorced after a 20-year marriage. Mildred's second husband was Lawrence L. McCall. Mildred and Roy had at least two children including:
  - William Karlin Robinson – Born on 26 October 1922 in Memphis, Tennessee and died on 21 September 1998 at Sty. Francis Hospital in Memphis. He was buried in the Memphis Funeral Home and Memorial Gardens in Shelby County, Tennessee.[247]
  - Elizabeth Ann Robinson – Born on 4 July 1926 in Memphis, Tennessee and died on 11 September 2012 in DeSoto County in Mississippi. She was buried in Forest Hill Cemetery-South in Memphis.[248] She married Roy William Sipes who was born on 11 February

1922 and died on 10 March 2012. He was also buried in Forest Hills Cemetery.[249]

- Charles Todd Daniel, Jr. – Born 5 September 1900 in Daviess County, Kentucky and died on 30 August 1970 in Owensboro, Daviess County, Kentucky.[250] He was described as medium height, stout build with gray eyes and blonde hair when he registered for the draft in 1918. He is buried in Rosehill Cemetery in Owensboro, Daviess County, Kentucky. It is likely that Charles married Esther Smeathers who was born on 30 July 1903 and died on 20 March 1990 and they had at least one child:
  - George Clayton Daniel – Born on 19 December 1928 in Daviess County and died on 28 January 1964 in Owensboro. He was buried in Rosehill-Elmwood Cemetery.[251] George married Anna Lee King who was born on 9 October 1930 in Webster County, Kentucky and died on 1 August 1998 in Indianapolis, Indiana. She was also buried in Rosehill-Elmwood Cemetery next to her husband George.[252]
- Kathryn L. Daniel – Born around 1906 in Kentucky. The last confirmed location for Kathryn was the 1930 census when she was living with her father in Daviess County, Kentucky.[253]
- Karlin K. Daniel – Born around 1911 in Kentucky. The last confirmed location for Karlin was the 1940 census when he was living with his mother in Daviess County, Kentucky.[254]

Louisa died on 28 January 1949 in Huntington, Cabell County, West Virginia, at age 70 years, 2 months, and 11 days. She is buried in Macedonia Baptist Church Cemetery in Daviess County.[255]

Jefferson Taylor (1879-1879)

Son of Jefferson Mandred Taylor and Louisa Jane Kirlen
Great-Granduncle of Taylor Cosby Cottrell, Jr.

Jefferson Taylor was born on 25 March 1879 in Daviess County, Kentucky. He was the son of Jefferson Mandred Taylor and Louisa Jane Kirlen. He died on 30 April 1879 in Daviess County, Kentucky.[256]

Section 2 - Cottrell Maternal Linage

Maternal Ancestor Chart

Brashear, Crutchfield, Campbell, Penner

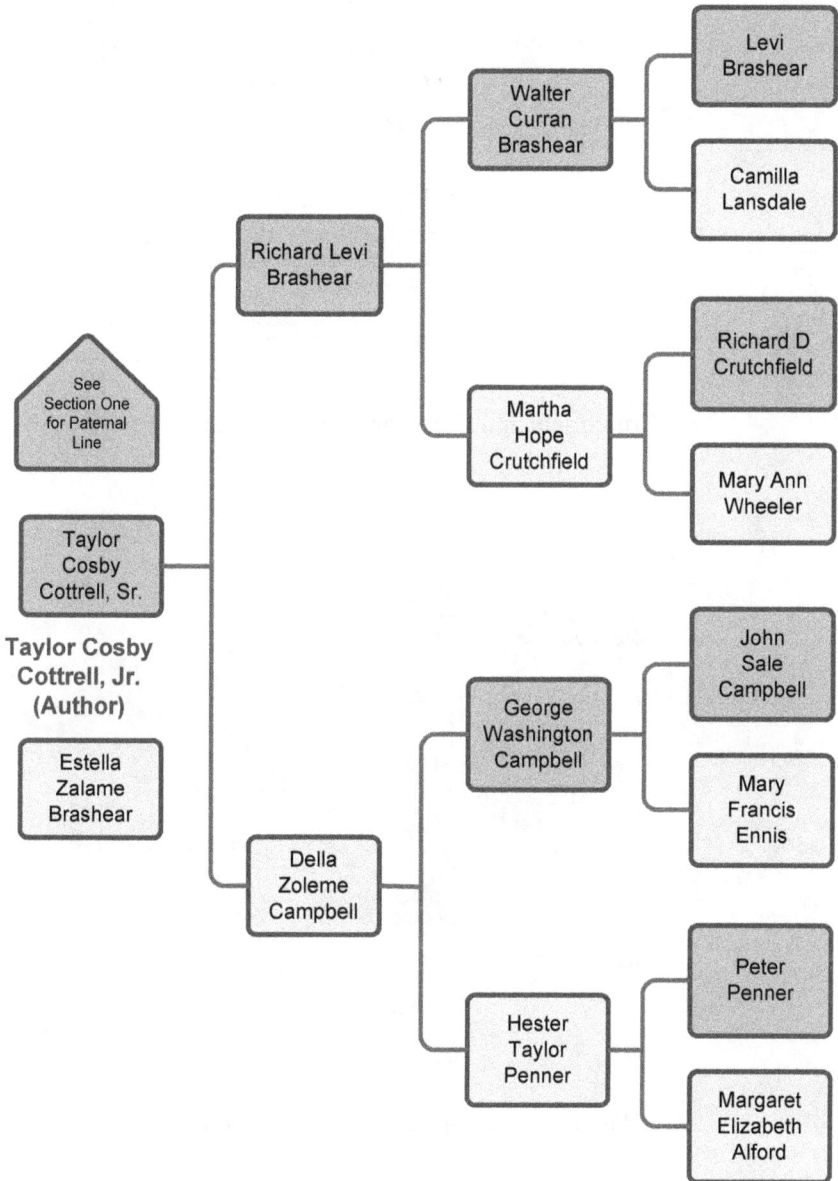

See Section One for Paternal Line

Taylor Cosby Cottrell, Sr.

Taylor Cosby Cottrell, Jr. (Author)

Estella Zalame Brashear

Richard Levi Brashear

Walter Curran Brashear

Levi Brashear

Camilla Lansdale

Martha Hope Crutchfield

Richard D Crutchfield

Mary Ann Wheeler

Della Zoleme Campbell

George Washington Campbell

John Sale Campbell

Mary Francis Ennis

Hester Taylor Penner

Peter Penner

Margaret Elizabeth Alford

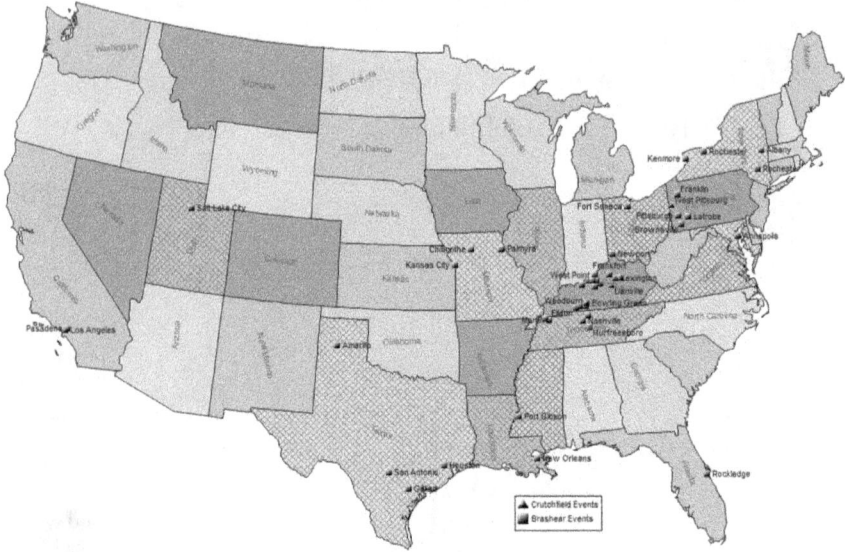

Crutchfield and Brashear Event Locations

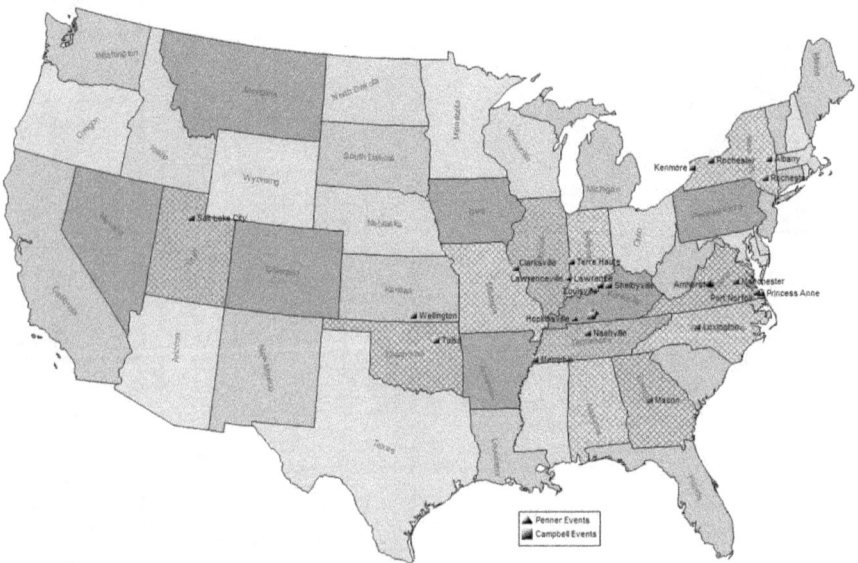

Penner and Campbell Event Locations

Chapter 1 – Levi Brashear Family

2nd Great-grandfather of Taylor Cosby Cottrell, Jr.

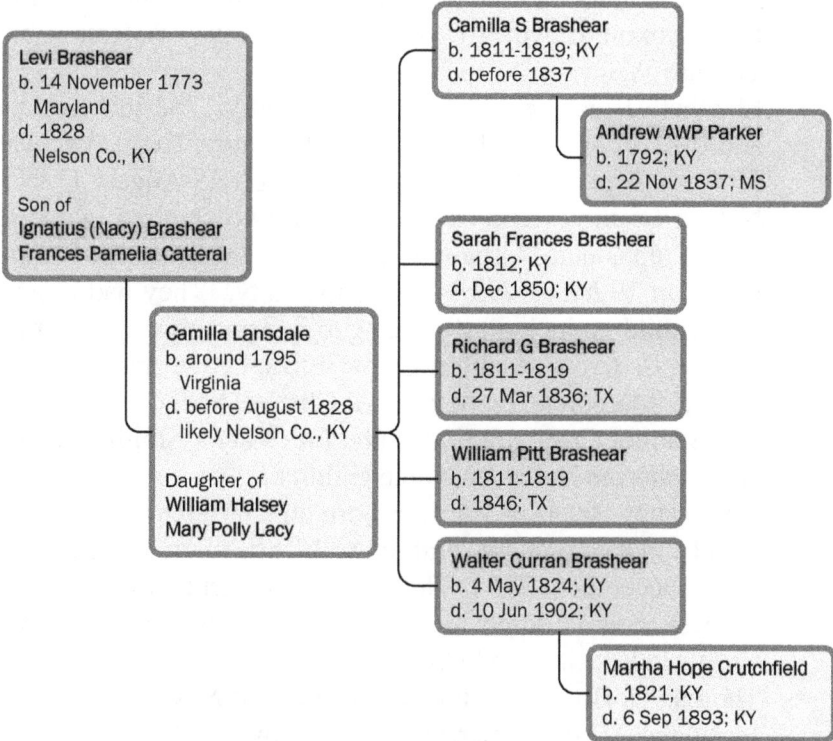

Levi Brashear
b. 14 November 1773
 Maryland
d. 1828
 Nelson Co., KY

Son of
Ignatius (Nacy) Brashear
Frances Pamelia Catteral

Camilla Lansdale
b. around 1795
 Virginia
d. before August 1828
 likely Nelson Co., KY

Daughter of
William Halsey
Mary Polly Lacy

Camilla S Brashear
b. 1811-1819; KY
d. before 1837

Andrew AWP Parker
b. 1792; KY
d. 22 Nov 1837; MS

Sarah Frances Brashear
b. 1812; KY
d. Dec 1850; KY

Richard G Brashear
b. 1811-1819
d. 27 Mar 1836; TX

William Pitt Brashear
b. 1811-1819
d. 1846; TX

Walter Curran Brashear
b. 4 May 1824; KY
d. 10 Jun 1902; KY

Martha Hope Crutchfield
b. 1821; KY
d. 6 Sep 1893; KY

Levi Brashear was born on 14 November 1773 in Prince Georges, Maryland. He was the son of Ignatius (Nacy) Brashear and Frances Pamelia Catteral.

Levi's father Ignatius was born on 17 April 1734 in Prince George County, Maryland, died on 5 October 1807 in Shepherdsville in Bullitt County, Kentucky, and was buried at Old Crow Brashear Cemetery in Shepherdsville.[1] He was also known as Nacy.

Levi's mother Frances was born on 14 April 1736 and died on 31 December 1804, at age 68. Nacy and his wife Frances moved to Brownsville, Fayette County, Pennsylvania around 1778. In 1784 they settled in Bullitt County, Kentucky. Nacy was of Huguenot descent.[2]

Levi moved to Nelson County, Kentucky with his parents around 1807 and was a trader between Louisville, Kentucky and New Orleans, Louisiana.[3]

Levi had at least fourteen brothers and sisters including:

- Mary Brashear who was born on 5 March 1760 in Maryland and died before 1822. She married Levin Wilcoxon on 11 February 1780 and they had at least four children including Walter B. Wilcoxon, Lloyd Wilcoxon, Ignatius Nancy Wilcoxon, and Thomas Wilcoxon.[4]
- Elizabeth Brashear who was born 12 July 1762 in Maryland and died 12 October 1826 in Bullitt County, Kentucky. Her first marriage was to Christian Crepps on 25 August 1785 in Nelson County, Kentucky. They had two children including John Crepps and Margaret Crepps. She then married Samuel Crow on 29 May 1793 in Nelson County. They had at least seven children including Nancy Crow, Ann Crow, Basil Crow, Samuel J. Crow, Matilda Crow, Eliza Crow, and Margaret Crow.[5] Margaret Crepps married Charles Anderson Wickliffe and Samuel Crow married Catherine Waters Smith. Samuel and Catherine had at least nine children.
- Ann Nancy Brashear who was born on 23 March 1763 in Maryland and died on 6 November 1829.[6] She married Basil Crow on 10 December 1796 in Nelson County, Kentucky. They had at least three children including Maria Brashear Crow, Ann Crow, and Basil Catryl Crow, Jr.
- Thomas C. Brashear who was born on 10 November 1764 in Maryland. Thomas married Nancy Brown. They had at least six children including Otho Brashear, Thomas Brashear, Mathew Brashear, Archibald Brashear, Mary Brashear, and John C. Brashear.
- Samuel Brashear who was born on 12 October 1766 in Maryland and died before 1776.
- Ignatius Brashear, Jr., who was born on 28 March 1768 in Prince George County, Maryland and died on 21 May 1827 in Bullitt County, Kentucky. He married Mary F. Orme on 24 March 1796 in Louisville. They had at least seven children including Nancy Brashear, Robert H. Brashear, Lucy C. Brashear, Ruth Caroline Brashear, America Brashear, and Dennis Brashear.[7]
- Robert Brashear who was born on 31 August 1769 in Maryland. He married Elizabeth Beall Harrison.

- Archibald Edmonston Brashear who was born on 2 November 1771 in Maryland and died before 1776.
- Dr. Walter Brashear who was born on 11 February 1776 in Maryland and died on 23 October 1860 in Louisiana. He married Margaret Barr. They had at least one child, Margaret Brashear.[8]
- Joseph Brashear who was born on 9 December 1778 in Maryland and died on 30 October 1845. He married Elizabeth Nobel in 1798. Joseph and Elizabeth had at least eight children including Mortimer M. Brashear, Amanda A. Brashear, William W. Brashear, Levi L. Brashear, Moray J.C. Brashear, Flavilla M. Brashear, Alexander P.A. Brashear, and Elizabeth R. Brashear.[9]
- Dennis Brashear who was born on 15 August 1780 in Maryland. He married Lucinda McDowell.
- Pamela Brashear who was born in 1781 in Maryland. She married twice, first to Rev. John P. Trotter and second to Charles Alexander.
- Mary Eliza Brashear who was born in 1781. She married Joseph Sullivant.
- Ruth Brashear who was born on 13 September 1782 and died in June 1861.[10] She married John Hackley on 8 November 1810 in Nelson County, Kentucky.

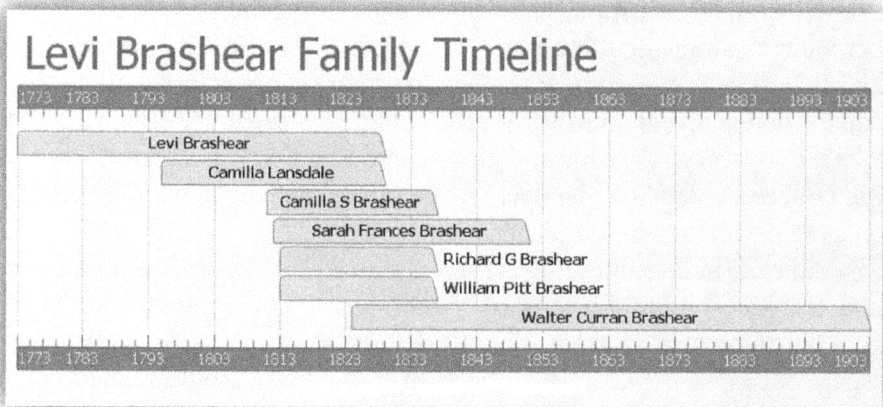

Levi Brashear Family Timeline

	1773 1783 1793 1803 1813 1823 1833 1843 1853 1863 1873 1883 1893 1903
Levi Brashear	
Camilla Lansdale	
Camilla S Brashear	
Sarah Frances Brashear	
Richard G Brashear	
William Pitt Brashear	
Walter Curran Brashear	

Levi married Camilla Lansdale on 8 May 1809 in Bardstown in Nelson County, Kentucky.[11] Camilla was born circa 1773 in Virginia.[12]

Levi and Camilla had at least five children including Camilla S. Brashear, Sarah Frances Brashear, Richard G. Brashear, William Pitt Brashear, and Walter Curran Brashear.[13] Levi appeared on the census of 1820 with a total of 16 slaves.

Levi died in 1828 in Nelson County, Kentucky.[14] Date and location of the death of his wife Camilla is unknown. However, Camilla died before 18 August 1828 as evidenced that she was listed as deceased in a Circuit Court Document in Nelson County, Kentucky.[15] Location of death was likely Nelson County, Kentucky.

Camilla S. Brashear (Circa 1811-1848)

Daughter of Levi Brashear and Camilla Lansdale
   Great-Grandaunt of Taylor Cosby Cottrell, Jr.

Camilla S. Brashear was born between 1811 and 1819 in Lexington in Fayette County, Kentucky. She was the daughter of Levi Brashear and Camilla Lansdale.[16] In 1825 Camilla was enrolled as a student in the first class of the Science Hill School in Shelbyville, Kentucky. The school was founded in 1825 and soon became widely-known and drew patronage from most of the states of the Union.[17]

Camilla wrote her sister Sarah Frances on 11 September 1830 from Port Gibson, Mississippi. This was one of many letters to her sister. In her letter she indicated that Port Gibson was a very healthy place to live and shared her concern over the health of her relatives in Kentucky because of an alarming number of cases of congestive fever. She said she was getting very religious and also shared that she was currently reading Gibbons History of the decline and fall of the Roman Empire which was eight volumes in length.[18]

A bond, in the sum of $50, for the marriage of Camilla S. Brashear and Andrew William Porter Parker was signed on 1 September 1831 in Bowling Green in Warren County, Kentucky by A.W.P. Parker and A.R. Macey.[19] Andrew was born in 1792 in Lexington in Fayette County, Kentucky.[20]

Children of Camilla S. Brashear and A.W.P. Parker:

- Corilla Parker – Born on 1 July 1832 in Lexington, Kentucky and died on 28 December 1913 at 1:00 in the afternoon in Boyle County, Kentucky, at age 81. Her cause of death was chronic intestinal nephritis. She was buried on 30 December 1913 in Bellevue Cemetery in Danville, Kentucky.[21] Corilla married William Drake Irvine, son of John Glover Irvine and Emeline Drake, on 30 December 1851 in Lexington, Kentucky.[22] William was born on 16 June 1829 in Walnut Hills in Fayette County, Kentucky.[23] He registered for the Civil War Draft in July 1863 while living in Boyle County. His occupation was listed as farmer. William died on 12 November 1895 in Boyle County. He was buried Bellevue Cemetery with his wife.[24] Corilla and William had at least 12 children including:
  - William Porter Irvine – Born on 4 October 1852 in Danville in Boyle County, Kentucky and died on 1 November 1938 in Kentucky, at age 86. He was buried in Bellevue Cemetery in Danville in Section 1, Lot 17. William never married.[25]
  - Emaline Irvine – Born on 17 May 1854 in Danville and died on 7 July 1876 in Kentucky, at age 22. She also went by the name of Emma.[26]
  - Camilla Lansdale Irvine – Born on 8 June 1856 in Danville and died at 4:25 in the afternoon on 1 December 1922 in Jessamine County, Kentucky, at age 66. Her cause of death was from stomach problems. She was buried on 3 December 1922 in Bellevue Cemetery in Danville. Camilla married Melanethan Young in 1883, likely in Jessamine County.[27] He was the son of Robert Young and Josephine Henderson. He was born on 20 January 1849 in Kentucky and died at 7:30 in the evening on 9 February 1924 in Fayette County. He was buried on 12 February in the Lexington Cemetery in Fayette County.[28] Melanethan's will was probated on 18 February 1924 in the Jessamine County Court. In his will he left specific sums of money to several young men including a colored boy who was the son of John Young. He also left funds to the Presbyterian Mission

Church at Camp Nelson, Kentucky and stock to be controlled by the deacons of the Presbyterian Church at Nicholasville, Kentucky for mission work. Additional funds were left to the West Lexington Presbytery. A memorial tablet with the proper inscription in memory of the services rendered in Presbytery missions by himself and his wife Camilla Young was to be placed in the Presbyterian Mission Church at Camp Nelson.[29]

o John Glover Irvine – Born on 7 September 1858 in Danville and died on 6 April 1930 in Cave Hill, Arkansas, at age 71. He was buried in Bellevue Cemetery in Danville in Section A, Lot 104. John married Betty Flanagan in January 1885. She died in 1912 and he then married Virginia Reppert Flanagan. around 1885. John had at least four children including John Boyd Irvine who died in an accident in Florida, Dorothy Irvin Pope who died suddenly sometime before 1930, and two daughters who were still living at the time of his death, Mrs. M. L. McGraw of Danville and Mrs. Harry S. Voris of McVeigh, Kentucky. Burial services were held in the home of his daughter Mrs. M. L. McGraw at 10:00 in the morning followed by burial with Dr. M.M. Allen presiding.[30]

o Alexander Macy Irvine – Born on 15 November 1860 in Danville and died on 24 January 1919 in Kentucky at age 58. He was buried in Bellevue Cemetery in Danville in Section E, Lot 55. Alexander married Alma Craig in 1888.[31] Alma was born on 28 June 1860 in Boyle County and died on 21 July 1940 in Danville, at age 80. She was buried in Bellevue Cemetery in Section E, Lot N1/2 55.[32]

o Robert Ogden Irvine – Born on 9 December 1861 in Danville and died on 28 December 1867 in Boyle County, Kentucky at age 6. He was buried in Bellevue Cemetery in Section 2, Lot 24.[33]

o Mary Belle Irvine – Born on 4 April 1864 in Danville and died on 7 April 1908 in Kentucky at age 44. She was buried in Bellevue Cemetery. It appears she never married.[34]

o Charles Howard Irvine – Born on 11 November 1866 in Danville and died on 28 December 1944 in Boyle County, Kentucky. He was buried in Bellevue Cemetery.[35] Charles married Hannah Simons in January 1910. Hannah was born on 30 March 1871 in Madison County, Kentucky and died on 11 May 1952 in the McDowell Memorial Hospital in Danville, at age 81. She was buried in the Bellevue Cemetery.[36]

o Lelia B. Irvine – Born on 3 April 1869 in Danville and died on 20 November 1960 in Boyle County, Kentucky at age 91. She was buried in Bellevue Cemetery in Section 4, Lot 33. She apparently never married.[37]

o Harry Beverly Irvine – Born on 24 August 1871 in Danville and died on 24 October 1895 in Kentucky at age 24. He was buried in Bellevue Cemetery in Section 1, Lot 17. Harry apparently never married.[38]

o Clara Hopewell Irvine – Born on 26 October 1873 in Danville and died on 6 Marcy 1878 in Kentucky at age 4. She was buried in Bellevue Cemetery in Section 3, Lot 541.[39]

o Andrew Todd Irvine – Born on 6 June 1878 in Danville and died on 30 December 1924 in Danville, at age 46. He was buried in Bellevue Cemetery in Danville in Section 1, Lot 17.[40] Andrew was registered for the WWI Draft on 12 September 1918.[41] He was listed as Insane on the registration and was described as medium height, medium build with gray hair and brown eyes. He was also found on the 1910 and 1920 census as a patient in the Eastern State Hospital for the Insane in Lexington in Fayette County, Kentucky.[42]

▪ Camile Parker – Born around 1834[43] and died before April 1848.[44] Locations of Birth, Death, and Burial unknown.

▪ Alexander Irvine Parker – Born around 1836[45] and died before April 1848.[46] Locations of Birth, Death, and Burial unknown.

Andrew died on 22 November 1837 in Port Gibson in Claiborne County, Mississippi at the residence of his brother Dr. James P. Parker.

He was buried in Wintergreen Cemetery in Port Gibson, in Section B, Lot 40 with Masonic honors.[47] His estate was probated on 25 December 1837 in Claiborne County Probate Court. James P. Parker was appointed by the court to administer his brother Andrew's Estate. The courts also appointed five men to jointly inventory and appraise the goods and Estate of Andrew because he died intestate. The final appraisal listed a total value of $1060.50 which included one gold watch and chain, a looking glass, a large number of books, a pair of saddle bags, one clock, a copy of the United States Constitution, a secretary, a pair of andirons, and half interest in a gun trunk.[48]

An insolvent notice on Andrew's estate was published in the Port Gibson Herald and Correspondent on 7 April 1848. Andrew's brother James P. Parker, testified in the Probate Court on 24 September 1849 that Corilla, the only child and sole distribute of Andrew's Estate, was a nonresident of Mississippi and was currently residing in Kentucky.[49]

A notice was published in the Port Gibson Herald and Correspondent each week from 28 September to 21 December

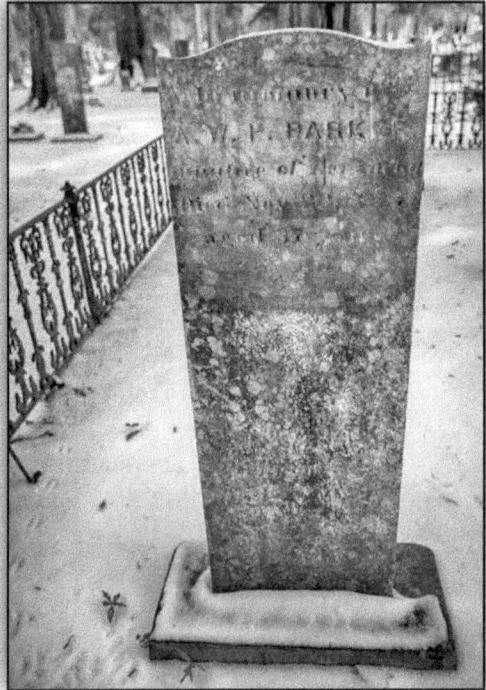

A.W.P. Parker
Wintergreen Cemetery
Port Gibson, Mississippi

1849 advertising for claimants to the Estate of Andrew W.P. Parker to appear before the Probate Court of the County of Claiborne on the fourth Monday and the 24th day of December 1849 when the final accounting of the Estate would be published. The notice specifically listed Corilla M. Parker, who was one of the daughters of Andrew.

However, there was no mention of Camilla in any of the newspaper publishing or court documents thus it is likely that she proceeded him in death sometime before 1837.[50]

Sarah Frances Brashear (Circa 1812-1850)

Daughter of Levi Brashear and Camilla Lansdale
Great-Grandaunt of Taylor Cosby Cottrell, Jr.

Sarah Frances Brashear was born circa 1812. She was the daughter of Levi Brashear and Camilla Lansdale.[51] She married Jonathan Clark Temple on 16 October 1834 in Nelson County, Kentucky. He was born in 1812 and was the son of Benjamin and Eleanor Eltings Clark.[52] Sarah died in December 1849 in Warren County, Kentucky.[53] Jonathan was listed on the 1850 census in Warren County, Kentucky as J.C. Temple, age 38 along with James R. Temple, age 10 and Walter R. Temple, age 8.[54]

Children of Sarah Frances Brashear and Jonathan C. Temple

- James Richard Temple – Born circa 1840 in Kentucky.[55] It is likely that James married Mary McCoy on 24 April 1867 in Spencer County, Indiana.[56] It is also likely that James and Mary, along with eight children (two daughters and six sons) were living in Indiana as evidenced by the 1880 census.[57] On 30 June 1885 it is likely that James and Mary along with six children were living in Hernando County, Florida as evidenced by the 1885 census.[58] This tracks with the information found for his brother Walter R. Temple in the disabled volunteer soldiers records. James was consistently listed as a physician including on what appears to be his gravestone located in Fairview Cemetery in Memphis, Texas. James died on 2 August 1906 in Memphis in Hall County, Texas. He was buried in Fairview Cemetery, South Section, in Memphis in Plot D-48-7.[59] Based on this information James and Mary had at least the following children:
  - Fannie Temple – Born around 1861 in Kentucky. Census transcription in error in 1870 census listed Fannie as Frank. Census image clearly shows

Frances. In 1880 she was listed as Fannie.[60] Additional information is unknown.

o Warner R. Temple – Born on 2 January 1864 in Kentucky and died on 1 October 1887. He was buried in Tucker Hill Cemetery in Hernando County, Florida.[61]

o Robert Temple – Born around 1866 in Kentucky.[62] Possibly died on 2 February 1929 in Los Angeles, California.

o Charlie Brashear Temple – Born 25 February 1868 in Kentucky and died 15 October 1910 in Memphis in Hall County, Texas. Buried in Fairview Cemetery, in Memphis in Hall County. Charlie married Ella Tucker who was born 14 February 1870 and died 25 June 1948. She was also buried in Fairview Cemetery.[63] They had at least three children including James H. Temple who was born 5 February 1892 and died 25 September 1913, William J. Temple who was born 25 September 1900 and died 29 December 1965, and Mary Ella Temple who was born 3 June 1910 and died 26 February 1916.

o William James Temple – Born 27 September 1872 in Kentucky and died 16 June 1893. He was buried in Fairview Cemetery, in Memphis, Texas.[64] He was also known as Willie. He registered for the WWI Draft on 12 September 1918 while living in Bell County, Texas. He was described as tall with a medium build, black eyes and black hair. He was employed as a mechanic in Temple, Texas at the time.[65]

o Max Gatewood Temple – Born on 28 October 1878 in Indiana and died 1 September 1941 in Anaheim in Orange County, California.[66] He was buried in Melrose Abbey Memorial Park in Anaheim.[67] Max registered for the WWI Draft on 12 September 1918 while living in Memphis, Texas. He married sometime after 1918. His wife's name was Myrtle. She was born in 1882 in Memphis in Hall County,

Texas and died in 1939, likely in Anaheim, California. She was also buried in Melrose Abbey Memorial Park.[68] They had at least two children including Blanche Temple who was born about 1903,[69] and Maxine Temple who was born on 28 January 1904.[70]

o Lucy Blanche Temple – Born on 28 October 1878 in Indiana and died on 13 October 1976 in Orange County, California at age 97. She was buried in Fairhaven Memorial Park in Santa Ana in Orange County. Blanche married Cornelius T. Palmer who was born on 8 November 1879 died on 27 November 1927 in Orange County. He was described as medium height with a medium build, blue eyes and brown hair when he registered for the WWI Draft in 1918. He was living in Memphis in Hall County, Texas at the time and was working for Western Union as a telegrapher. Cornelius was also buried in Fairhaven Memorial Park.[71]

- Walter R. Temple – Born circa 1842 in Kentucky.[72] The next reliable information on Walter was found in the records for disabled volunteer soldiers. The record indicated that Walter had enlisted on 15 September 1861 in Cincinnati, Ohio and was discharged in January 1862 with hemorrhoids identified as a disability. He apparently re-enlisted in August 1864 and remained in service as a physician with the U.S. Navy until 1 October 1865. He was listed as widowed with the name of his nearest living relative being his brother James R. Temple who was residing in Brooksville, Florida at the time.[73]

Jonathan then married Elizabeth Wallace Page, daughter of Henry and Jane B. Deane, on 13 November 1851 in Logan County, Kentucky.[74] It is likely that Elizabeth was born on 2 July 1820 in Calra in Cumberland County, Virginia. It is also likely that Jonathan died in 1851 in Logan County, Kentucky a few weeks after his marriage to Elizabeth, and that Elizabeth died in June 1872 in Chillicothe, Missouri.[75]

Richard G. Brashear (before 1819-1836)

Son of Levi Brashear and Camilla Lansdale
Great-Granduncle of Taylor Cosby Cottrell, Jr.

Richard G. Brashear was born between 1811 and 1819. He was the son of Levi Brashear and Camilla Lansdale.[76] Richard served as first sergeant of a volunteer company that originated in Bardstown in Nelson County, Kentucky during the Texas War of Independence. The company left Bardstown in the fall of 1835. By March of that year they were on the San Antonio River about 85 miles southeast of San Antonio. On 6 March 1836 their commander Colonel Fannin surrendered the company to portions of Santa Anna's Army. On the 26th of March, Santa Anna ordered his commanding officers to shoot the prisoners. The next day Richard was one of several hundred prisoners who attempted to flee after the first volley, but he was killed as he crossed the San Antonio River.[77]

Richard died on 27 March 1836 in Goliad, Texas, in the "Fannin Massacre" during the Texas Revolution. His cause of death was a gunshot from enemy soldiers. He is buried at Presidio la Bahia, in Goliad in Goliad County, Texas.[78]

William Pitt Brashear (before 1819-1846)

Son of Levi Brashear and Camilla Lansdale
Great-Granduncle of Taylor Cosby Cottrell, Jr.

William Pitt Brashear was born between 1811 and 1819. He was the son of Levi Brashear and Camilla Lansdale.[79] William migrated early to Texas and was a soldier in the Texas Revolution. In 1835 William, who also went by the name of Pitt, met and fell in love with Catherine Malone of Bardstown, Kentucky. He expressed his love and devotion to her through an intricate valentine he hand-cut from parchment. The valentine had numerous cutouts and included an original poem as well as drawings of birds and flowers.

The valentine was passed down through the Brashear family and is in the possession of the author's younger daughter. The poem read as follows:

Lady! auspicious fortune has foretold
Thy name and mine shall e'er entwine;

And if thou art not unkind and cold,
Thou wilt receive this valentine.

Lady! hast seen the rainbow bright,
Come out and sit upon the cloud?
E'ere so does hope, dispel the night
That hung around me like a shroud.

Hast thou not seen a budding flower,
By this rude storm, all trodden down?
Even so is love, in one short hour,
It dies beneath a dark'ning frown.

Thou Catherine take this emblem faint,
Of the warm heart already thine.
My heart, my soul, I cannot paint,
Will thou accept my valentine?

Valentine – Handmade by William Pitt Brashear – circa 1835
Approximately 10x16 inches

He was listed in the 1840 Citizens of Texas tax roles in Jackson County and was granted 640 acres on bounty warrant on 16 May 1836 and 10 December 1836.[80]

After the battle of San Jacinto on 21 April 1836, and while Santa Anna was a prisoner at Velasco, William attempted to gain entry into the prison to kill Santa Anna in revenge for Fannin's Massacre where his brother Richard Brashear had been killed. However, General Houston, in anticipation of some such attempt by those who hated Santa Anna, had him surrounded constantly with a strong guard. William made one attempt to see Santa Anna but when the guards found his pistol during a search he was turned away.[81]

In 1839 he went to Lavaca County to look into land. He frequently traveled alone to examine tracts of land many miles from the security of the settlement in which he was staying even when warned of the danger of Comanche warriors in the area. While on one of the trips alone he was chased by a band of Indians. He escaped on his half-bred Mexican house named "Get out." William died in 1846 in Texas.[82]

Walter Curran Brashear (1824-1902)

Son of Levi Brashear and Camilla Lansdale
  Great-Grandfather of Taylor Cosby Cottrell, Jr.

Walter Curran Brashear was born in May 1824 near Bardstown in Nelson County, Kentucky. He was the son of Levi Brashear and Camilla Lansdale.[83] Information on the Walter Curran Brashear Family, and Walter's life history, along with that for his wife Martha Hope Crutchfield, and their nine children is covered in detail in Section 2, Chapter 2, Walter Curran Brashear Family.

Chapter 2 – Walter Curran Brashear Family

Great-grandfather of Taylor Cosby Cottrell, Jr.

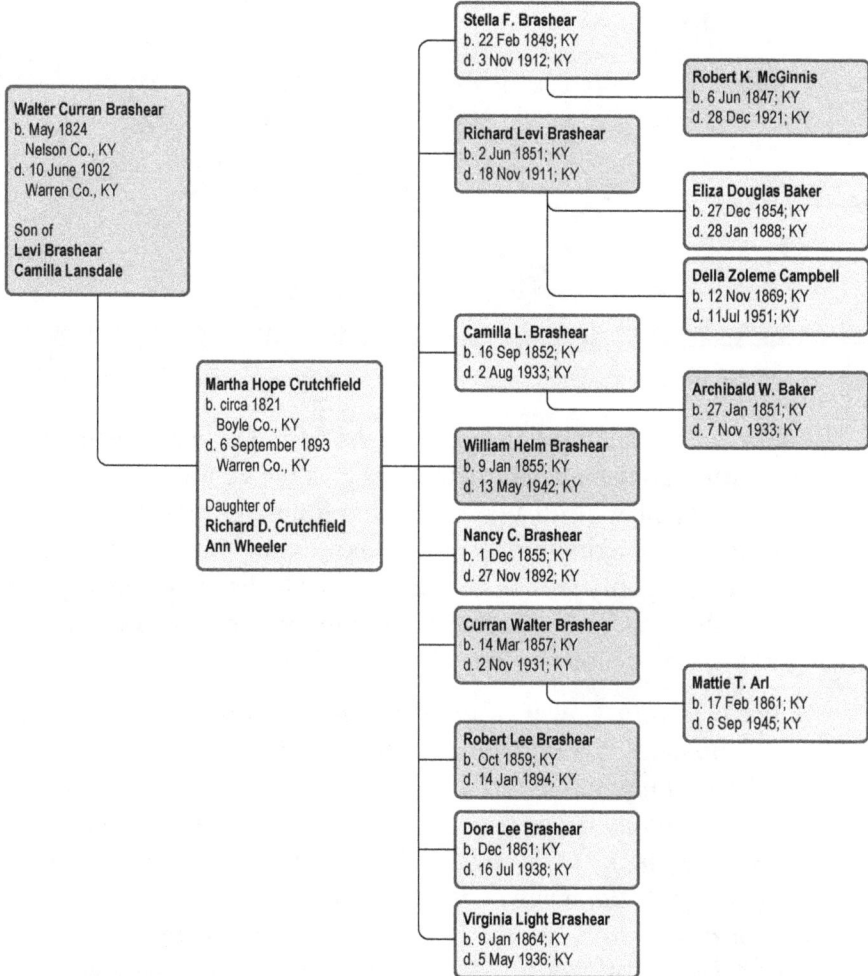

Walter Curran Brashear
b. May 1824
  Nelson Co., KY
d. 10 June 1902
  Warren Co., KY

Son of
Levi Brashear
Camilla Lansdale

Martha Hope Crutchfield
b. circa 1821
  Boyle Co., KY
d. 6 September 1893
  Warren Co., KY

Daughter of
Richard D. Crutchfield
Ann Wheeler

Stella F. Brashear
b. 22 Feb 1849; KY
d. 3 Nov 1912; KY

Robert K. McGinnis
b. 6 Jun 1847; KY
d. 28 Dec 1921; KY

Richard Levi Brashear
b. 2 Jun 1851; KY
d. 18 Nov 1911; KY

Eliza Douglas Baker
b. 27 Dec 1854; KY
d. 28 Jan 1888; KY

Della Zoleme Campbell
b. 12 Nov 1869; KY
d. 11 Jul 1951; KY

Camilla L. Brashear
b. 16 Sep 1852; KY
d. 2 Aug 1933; KY

Archibald W. Baker
b. 27 Jan 1851; KY
d. 7 Nov 1933; KY

William Helm Brashear
b. 9 Jan 1855; KY
d. 13 May 1942; KY

Nancy C. Brashear
b. 1 Dec 1855; KY
d. 27 Nov 1892; KY

Curran Walter Brashear
b. 14 Mar 1857; KY
d. 2 Nov 1931; KY

Mattie T. Arl
b. 17 Feb 1861; KY
d. 6 Sep 1945; KY

Robert Lee Brashear
b. Oct 1859; KY
d. 14 Jan 1894; KY

Dora Lee Brashear
b. Dec 1861; KY
d. 16 Jul 1938; KY

Virginia Light Brashear
b. 9 Jan 1864; KY
d. 5 May 1936; KY

Walter Curran Brashear was born in May 1824 near Bardstown in Nelson County, Kentucky. He was the son of Levi Brashear and Camilla Lansdale.[1] Walter's parents died when he was young and he was raised by his Uncle Alexander Massey who lived in Russellville in Logan County, Kentucky.[2] Walter had at least four brothers and sisters including Camilla S. Brashear, Sarah Frances Brashear, Richard G. Brashear, and William P. Brashear, each of whom are covered in detail, along with his parents, in Section 2, Chapter 1, Levi Brashear Family.

Walter Curran Brashear Family Timeline

1821	1831	1841	1851	1861	1871	1881	1891	1901	1911	1921	1931	1941	1951

Martha Hope Crutchfield

Walter Curran Brashear

Stella F Brashear

Richard Levi Brashear

Camilla L Brashear

Nancy Crutchfield Brashear

William Helm Brashear

Curran Walter Brashear

Robert Lee Brashear

Dora Lee Brashear

Virginia Light Brashear

1821	1831	1841	1851	1861	1871	1881	1891	1901	1911	1921	1931	1941	1951

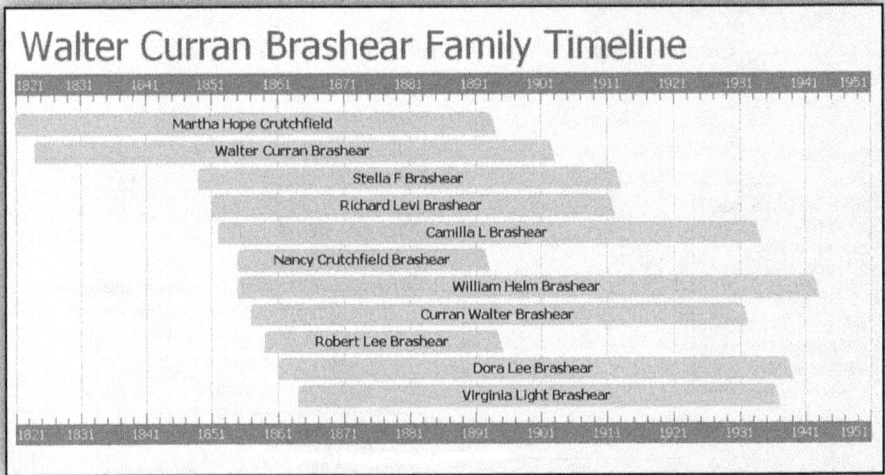

Walter served an apprenticeship in the office of the *Green River Gazette* before purchasing and then serving as the editor of the paper.[3]

On 19 November 1846 Walter wrote a long and very sad letter to Ben. C. Grinder in Lexington, Kentucky expressing that he was "under the influence of gloomy feelings". He also said he had not been to town in a long while because he had been pouring over law books.[4] In discussing power and death he wrote the following.

> *"What is wealth, power, a great manna, the approbation of men, compared with a life of toil, strife, bickering, envy, jealousy, and mountainous evils consequent upon a struggle to gratify ambitious desires, and what are our most cherished hopes, but so many of those fabled apples, which turn to ashes upon the lips? Yea, what is life itself but a page in the infinite volume of eternity, upon which is written, but trouble and death? Death! A reality which maketh high and low tremble."*[5]

Walter apparently corresponded with his future wife Martha Crutchfield over many months. On 27 December 1846 he wrote a long letter to Martha and detailed his concern that she understood that if she married him she would be sharing the "discomforts, inconveniences and privations of a thinly populated and frontier state." He warned her of his poverty and the hardships she would endure and said, "I mean it literally, not comparatively. Consider then for a moment the duties devolving upon the wife of a man without servants or the means of procuring them – duties to which you have never been accustomed, very drudgery."[6]

In January 1847 Walter was living in Warren County, Kentucky with one of his sisters near Bowling Green.[7] He corresponded with Martha Crutchfield on 4 March 1847 to confirm his planned arrival date in Danville, Kentucky on the 19th of April and agreed

Walter Curran Brashear

that their wedding would be a private one that could be arranged after his arrival.[8] Walter wrote a final letter to Martha on Thursday, the 15th of April, letting her know he was ill with chills, but hopeful that the chills would break and he would be able to make a start at the trip to Danville in a day or two, and, by hard riding, still be able to reach Danville by Monday the 19th of April.[9]

A bond for the marriage of Walter and Martha Hope Crutchfield was signed on 29 April 1847 in Boyle County, Kentucky, by W.C. Brashear and John F. Warren. Walter married Martha, who was the daughter of Richard D. Crutchfield and Anne Wheeler, around April 1847

Martha Hope Crutchfield

in Danville. Martha was born around 1821 in Boyle County.[10] Her father Richard was born in 1782 in Richmond, Virginia and was the son of William D. Crutchfield and Agnes D. Sevier.[11] Her mother Anne was born in 1791 in Fort Cumberland, Maryland and was also known as Elizabeth.[12] Her father died on 7 April 1843 in Danville and her mother died on 112 June 1831 in Boyle County, Kentucky. Both her parents were buried in Bellevue Cemetery in Danville.[13] Martha had at least seven brothers and sisters including:

- Elizabeth Jane Crutchfield who was born on 14 November 1814 in Boyle County, married Dr. Robert Russell McKinney on 19 July 1832 in Danville, and died on 6 August 1868. Robert was born on 11 May 1810 in Stanton in Lincoln County, Kentucky and died on 25 September 1876 in Fayetteville in Fayette County, Tennessee. He was a medical doctor. They had at least nine children including Joel McKinney, Martha Cordelia McKinney, John V. McKinney, Charles D. McKinney, Elvira McKinney, Dr. Henry Clay McKinney, Robert R. McKinney, Jennie F. McKinney, and Mary McKinney.[14]
- Emmeline Crutchfield who was born in 1816, married Jonathan R. Nichols in November 1846, and died before 1870 in Boyle County. Jonathan was born in 1824 in Kentucky and died in 1880 in Boyle County. He worked as a cabinet maker and in later life as an undertaker. They had at least nine children including James C. Nichols, Jennie Nichols, Sallie M. Nichols, Agnes Nichols, Walter B. Nichols, Alice Nichols, Estelle Nichols, J. Boyle Nichols, and John M. Nichols.[15]
- Sarah Crutchfield who was born around 1824 in Boyle County and was working as a teacher in August 1870 while living in the home of Ralph Georgi in Fayette County, Kentucky.[16]
- Agness C. Crutchfield who was born on 21 March 1825 in Danville, married Jonathan B. Nichols in February 1846, and died on 17 April 1856 in Mercer County, Kentucky. Her cause of death was apoplexy. Jonathan was born in 1824 in Danville and died on 25 April 1896 in Danville. He was the County Court Clerk in Boyle County in 1870. They had at least three children including William S. Nichols, Richard G. Nichols, and Reed S. Nichols. Agness and Jonathan were both buried in Bellevue Cemetery in Danville.[17]
- Rachel A. Crutchfield who was born in 1830 in Boyle County, Kentucky.[18]

- Richard Ann Crutchfield who was born on 26 August 1831 in Kentucky, married Ralph Georgi on 5 June 1860 in Boyle County, and died at 1:00 in the morning on 9 April 1923 in Lexington in Fayette County, Kentucky. Her cause of death was listed as old age.[19] Ralph was born in 1833 in Germany and was a professor of music when they married. Ralph died on 2 November 1898 in Lexington.[20] His cause of death was cystitis. Richard and Ralph were buried in Lexington Cemetery in Lexington, Kentucky. They had one child, Anna Georgi who was born around 1861 in Kentucky and died on 2 October 1941 at Good Samaritan Hospital in Lexington. Her cause of death was complications from a fractured hip coupled with old age. She was also buried in Lexington Cemetery.[21]

In 1859 Walter purchased 100 acres of land on Beech Bend (a bend in the Barron River) Northwest of Bowling Green.[22] In 1860 he was working as a butcher when he was listed on the census in Warren County as Wm. C. Brashears, age 35. Martha, age 34, Stella F., age 11, Richard L, age 9, Camilla, age 8, Wm. H., age 6, Nancy, age 5, Curran, age 3, and Robt., age 11 months were also listed in his household. His real estate was valued at $3,000 and his personal property was valued at $2,712.[23]

Anna Georgi

Walter registered for the draft for the Civil War in February 1864 while living in Bowling Green. He reported his occupation as a farmer on the registration.[24] He was confirmed in the Episcopal Church on 3 April 1867 at Christ Episcopal Church in Bowling Green, by R. Rev. G.D. Cummings.[25] Martha was also confirmed by Rev. Cummings on the same date. Walter was elected to the Vestry of the church for the Ecclesiastical year on 12 April 1868.[26]

Cabin on Beach Bend Property
Likely the first home of Walter Curren Brashear
Watercolor Painting, signed and dated 1902
Original owned by the Author

In 1870 he was listed on the census in Warren County, as Walter Brashear, age 46 along with Martha, age 45, Stella F., age 21, Richard L., age 19, Camila L., age 17, William H., age 15, Nancy W., age 13, Curran, age 12, Robert, age 10, Dora, age 8, and Virginia, age 6. His real estate was valued at $2,500 and personal estate was valued at $1,000.[27]

He was elected again to the Vestry of Christ Episcopal Church in Bowling Green for the Ecclesiastical year on 21 April 1878.[28] Walter was listed on the 1880 census in Warren County as Walter C. Brashear, age 55. His wife Martha, age 55, sons Richard L., age 28, William, age 24, and Robert, age 20 along with his daughters Camilla, age 26, Nancy, age 22, Dora, age 19, and Virginia, age 16 were also listed in the household.[29]

Walter was also listed on the 1880 agricultural schedule of Subdivision Number 228 in Warren County, as the owner of a farm with 70 acres of improved land and 12 acres of unimproved land. Total value including land, buildings, machinery and livestock was listed as $2,501. Walter was paid for 20 weeks of hired labor the previous year and the value of farm productions were $1,540. Livestock included three horses, three mules, and three milk cows which produced 360 pounds of butter the previous year. He sold one cow and slaughtered an additional cow during 1879. The farm included 21 sheep which produced 13 lambs. One sheep was slaughtered, one died of disease, and fifty-six pounds of fleece were produced during the previous year. The farm also included 92 swine and 150 chickens which produced 208 eggs during 1879. During the previous year 35 acres of land were used to produce 1,100 bushels of Indian Corn and 3 acres produced 51 bushels of wheat. Additional crop produced included 150 bushels of potatoes. There were also 4 acres containing 200 apple bearing trees and one acre which produced 50 pounds of grapes that were valued at $600. Twenty pounds of honey was also produced from hives located on the farm and 33 cords of lumber, valued at $155, were cut from the land in 1879.[30]

Walter was elected to the Vestry of Christ Episcopal Church in Bowling Green for another Ecclesiastical year on 10 April 1882.[31] In 1884 he inherited property in Warren County, which was called "Knob Orchard" after the death of his brother Robert Brashear.[32]

Martha died on 6 September 1893 in Warren County.[33] She was buried in Fairview Cemetery in Bowling Green in Cemetery 1, Section C, Site C-247.[34]

Walter remained active in the local church and was elected to the Vestry for another year term on 19 April 1897.[35] In 1900 he was listed on the census in Warren County, as Walter C. Brashear, age 76. Also listed in the household was his son William, age 40 and daughters Dora, age 27 and Virginia, age 25. Three other individuals were listed in the household, two of which were servants.[36]

Walter left a will on 24 December 1900 in Warren County, which indicated his home, farm, and sufficient stock to properly work it were to go to his son William H.

Walter Curran Brashear		
1860	Warren County, KY	Butcher
1870	Warren County, KY	Farmer
1880	Warren County, KY	Farmer
1900	Warren County, KY	Farmer

Brashear and daughters Dora and Jennie L. Brashear, so long as they "remain single and can get along harmoniously together." He indicated the reason he was leaving his property to his younger children was that his three older children, Stella F. McGinnis, Richard L. Brashear, and Camilla L. Baker were already being provided with comfortable homes. He made specific provisions in the will for his son Curran, leaving property in Bowling Green known as the "McNeel Place" to him. He also made provisions for his grandson Robert L. Brashear. He named his son William Helm Brashear as his executor.[37]

In a codicil to the will dated 15 May 1902 he added that any money remaining after payment of his depts. Was to be divided between his six heirs, excluding Curran Brashear, because "the portion I have allotted him is already more than one seventh of the estate."

He wrote a second codicil to his will on the same date, 15 May 1902, stating that the Knob Orchard referenced in the will had been sold and that two hundred and fifty dollars accruing from the last two payments from the sale was to be paid to his son R.L. Brashear to be used "exclusively in aiding him to acquire a thorough knowledge of Electrical Engineering if he shows any disposition to take such a course, or aptitude for it."[38]

Walter died on 10 June 1902 in Bowling Green, at age 78.[39] He was buried on 11 June 1902 in Fairview Cemetery in Bowling Green, in Cemetery 1, Section C, Site C-247.[40] Chas. W. B. Hill officiated at the ceremony.[41] His estate was probated on 23 June 12902 in the Warren County Court, proved by the oaths of D.B. Campbell and J.A. Graham with Virgil Garvin, Clerk of

Walter and Martha Brashear
Fairview Cemetery
Bowling Green, Kentucky

Warren County Court presiding.[42]

Stella F. Brashear (1849-1912)

Daughter of Walter C. Brashear and Martha Hope Crutchfield
Grandaunt of Taylor Cosby Cottrell, Jr.

Stella F. Brashear was born on 22 February 1849 in Warren County, Kentucky. She was the daughter of Walter Curran Brashear and Martha Hope Crutchfield.[43] She was listed on the 1860 census in Warren County, in the household of her father Walter as Stella F. Brashears, age 11 and attending school.[44] In the 1870 Warren County census she was living in the household of her father and was listed as Stella F., age 21.[45]

Stella F. Brashear

Stella married Robert K. McGinnis, son of Jesse Smith McGinnis and Elizabeth P. Bowles, on 11 December 1878 in Warren County, Kentucky.[46] Robert was born on 6 June 1847 in Boyle County, Kentucky.[47] In 1870 he was working as a bookkeeper in a mill and living in the household of D.B. Campbell.[48] In the 1880 census Stella was listed in the household of Robert K.

Robert K. McGinnis

McGinnis as his wife Stella, age 30. Their son Walter, age 5/12 was also listed in the household. Robert was a book maker at the time.[49]

In 1900 Stella was listed in the census in the household of her husband Robert, in Warren County, as Stella F., age 51. Robert owned his home free of mortgage and was working as a bookkeeper in a bank.[50] Stella was listed on the 1910 census in Warren County, in the household of her husband as Stella, age 61.[51]

Children of Stella F. Brashear and Robert K. McGinnis:

- Walter Brashear McGinnis – Born on 24 December 1879 and died on 1 September 1943 at City Hospital in Bowling Green, Kentucky.[52] Funeral services were held at Christ Episcopal Church in Bowling Green. He was buried in Chillicothe in Livingston County, Missouri.[53] Walter married Minnie C. Myers, daughter of William E. and Nancy Myers on 1 January 1902 in Hamilton in Livingston County, Missouri.[54] Walter and his wife lived most of their lives in

Walter Brashear McGinnis

Missouri and Kentucky. He held various jobs throughout his career including serving as an agent for a tea and coffee company in 1910[55], day laborer work in 1920[56], manager of Beech Bend Park near Bowling Green, Kentucky in 1940, and a night clerk in the Park City Motel in Bowling Green, at the time of his death. Minnie was listed on the 1940 census in Warren County, with Walter.[57] She was also listed as the informant on Walter's death record thus she was still living in 1943 at the time of his death. No additional reliable information is known about her. They apparently had no children.

Stella died on 3 November 1912 in Bowling Green, Kentucky. Her cause of death was acute nephritis.[58] She was buried on 4 November 1912 in Fairview Cemetery in Bowling Green.[59]

Robert married Sallie Bohannon sometime after 1913. Sallie was born on 16 September 1871 in Warren County.[60] Robert was listed on the 1920 census in Warren County, as Robert, age 72 along with his wife Sallie, age 46.[61]

Robert died on 28 December 1921 in Bowling Green, Kentucky, at age 74. His cause of death was pneumonia.[62] He was buried on 29 December 1921 in Fairview Cemetery.[63] His estate was probated on 24 January 1922 in the Warren County Court in Bowling Green.[64]

Sallie died on 12 June 1952 in Warren County, Kentucky, at age 80. Her cause of death was coronary arteriosclerotic heart disease with myocardial failure.[65] She was also buried in Fairview Cemetery.[66]

Richard Levi Brashear (1851-1911)

Son of Walter C. Brashear and Martha Hope Crutchfield
Grandfather of Taylor Cosby Cottrell, Jr.

Richard Levi Brashear was born on 2 June 1851 in Warren County, Kentucky. He She was the son of Walter Curran Brashear and Martha Hope Crutchfield.[67] Information on the Richard Levi Brashear Family, and Richard's life history, along with that for his wives Eliza Douglas Baker and Della Zoleme Campbell and Richard and Della's four children is covered in detail in Section 2, Chapter 3, Richard Levi Brashear Family.

Camilla Lansdale Brashear (1852-1933)

Daughter of Walter C. Brashear and Martha Hope Crutchfield
Grandaunt of Taylor Cosby Cottrell, Jr.

Camilla Lansdale Brashear was born on 16 September 1852 in Warren County, Kentucky. She was the daughter of Walter Curran Brashear and Martha Hope Crutchfield.[68] She was listed on the 1860 census in Warren County, in the household of her father Walter as Camila Brashears, age 8 and attending school.[69] In 1869 she was baptized at Christ Episcopal Church in Bowling Green, Kentucky by Rev. J.M. Curtis with Walter L. Brashear as witness.[70] She was confirmed on 30

April of the same year at Christ Church in Bowling Green by the R. Rev. G.D. Cummings.[71]

In 1870 she was listed on the census in Warren County in the home of her father as Camilla L., age 17.[72] In 1880 she was found on the census of her father in Warren County, as Camilla, age 26 and single.[73]

She married Archibald W. Baker, son of Larkin F. Baker and Mary Eliza Lucas in 1881 in Warren County.[74] Archibald was born on 27 January 1851 in Warren County.[75] On 19 April 1983 he was confirmed at Christ Episcopal Church in Bowling Green, Kentucky by the Rt. Rev. T.U. Dudley.[76]

In 1900 she was listed on the census in the household of her husband Archie in Warren County, as Camilla, age 47 having been married for 19 years with no children.[77] In 1910 she was on the census in Warren County, living with her husband Arch, as Camilla L, age 57 along with Arch's nephew

Camilla Lansdale Brashear

Walter C. Brashear, age 22.[78] In 1920 they were living on a farm on Beech Bend Road near Bowling Green, where they were listed on the 1920 census as Arch W. Baker, age 68 and Camilla, age 67.[79] The 1930 census in Warren County, listed them as Arch W. Baker, age 79 and his wife Camille, age 78.[80]

Camilla died on 2 August 1933 at Beech Bend outside Bowling Green, at age 80. Her cause of death was paresis which started around 1929.[81] She was buried on 3 August 1933 in Fairview Cemetery in Bowling Green, on the Baker lot in Cemetery 1, Section B, Site B-19.[82]

Archibald died on 7 November 1933 in Bristow, Kentucky, at age 82. His cause of death was cerebral hemorrhage.[83] He was buried in

Fairview Cemetery in Bowling Green, on the Baker lot in Section B, Site B-19.[84]

William Helm Brashear (1855-1942)

Son of Walter C. Brashear and Martha Hope Crutchfield
Granduncle of Taylor Cosby Cottrell, Jr.

William Helm Brashear was born on 9 January 1855 at Beech Bend in Warren County, Kentucky. He was the son of Walter Curran Brashear and Martha Hope Crutchfield.[85] He was listed on the 1860 census in Warren County, in the household of his father Walter as Wm. H. Brashears, age 6.[86] In 1870 he was listed on the census in Warren County, in the home of his father Walter as William H., age 15.[87] In 1880 William was licensed to practice law by the Warren Circuit Court in Bowling Green, Kentucky. He also appeared on the 1880 census as a lawyer in the household of his father as William, age 24 and single.[88]

In the 1900 census he was listed in the household of his father in Warren County, as William, age, age 40 and single. He was working as a farmer at the time.[89] In 1902, following the death of his father Walter, William and his sisters Dora Brashear and Virginia Brashear received possession of the Beech Bend property just outside Bowling Green. The property had been in the Brashear family since the Civil War.[90] They built a dance pavilion on the property and turned it into "Beech Bend Park". The park had actually been founded by William as a picnic park in 1898. In May 1908 the park opened to the public after the dance pavilion had been "enlarged and encircled with a veranda and otherwise furnished with all conveniences proper to accommodate the public." The pavilion had a hard wood floor and was soon to be a "most popular resort for the society set of Bowling Green."[91] William was a poet and in 1905 published a book titled "The Varied Voices from the Muse of Beech Bend."

In 1910 William was listed on the census in Warren County, as William H. Brasher, age 52 along with his sisters Dora, age 38 and Virginia, age 36. He owned his own farm, mortgage free, which was listed on farm schedule 13. His occupation was listed as farmer.[92]

The Electric Railway Journal, dated 9 August 1913, indicated in the Construction section that W.H. Brasher of Bowling Green "projected the construction for a 3-mile electric railway from Bowling

Green to Beech Bend Park." The article stated that either a power plant would be built or arrangements made for electricity with the Bowling Green Railway. It was also said that the Bowling Green Railway might purchase and operate the line when it was completed.[93]

William was listed on the 1920 census in Warren County, as William H. Breshear, age 55. His sisters Dora, age 38 and Virginia L., age 36, both single, were also listed in the household.[94] In 1930 he was listed on the census in Warren County, as William Brashear, age 71 along with his sisters Jennie, age 63 and Dora, age 61, both single. They were living on Beech Bend Pike at the time and he owned his own farm, listed on farm schedule 18, free of mortgage.[95]

In 1934 William purchased a 7 percent convertible obligation Series A, investment in Associated Gas and Electric Company in the state of New York from the Public National Bank and Trust Company.[96] He was listed in the 1938 Bowling Green City Directory as living on Route 1 in Warren County with $1,800 personal property and owning 143 acres of land.[97] In 1940 he was listed on the census in Warren County as William H. Brashear, age 75 along with his nephew Walter B. McGinnis, age 60. Walter's wife Melba, age 65 and daughter Dollene, age 20 were also living in the household. William was listed as owner and operator of Beech Bend Park at the time. William never married.[98]

William died on at 8:10 in the evening on 13 May 1942 at his home at Beech Bend in Warren County, at age 87. He had been in poor health for several months

William Helm Brashear		
1860	Warren County, KY	N/A
1870	Warren County, KY	In School
1880	Warren County, KY	Lawyer
1900	Warren County, KY	Farmer
1910	Warren County, KY	Farmer
1920	Warren County, KY	Farmer
1930	Warren County, KY	Farmer
1940	Warren County, KY	Farmer

but had been seriously ill for the last 10 days prior to his death. His cause of death was Cardiac Asthma.[99] His body was moved to the Gerard mortuary on College and Tenth streets in Bowling Green following his death. Funeral services were held at Gerard Mortuary at 2:00 in the afternoon with the Rev. G.W. Buchholz, Jr., rector of Christ Episcopal Church in charge of the services. Pallbearers were Walter McGinnis, Walter C. Brashear, Claude L. Brashear, William B. Brashear, Robert L. Brashear, and Campbell Garvin. It is interesting to note that the cost of the funeral was $353 and that the minister was given $10 for conducting the service. William was buried in Fairview Cemetery in Bowling Green, in Cemetery 1, Section C, Site C-247.[100]

There were several noteworthy items listed on the settlement summary produced by Potter-Matlock Trust Company following the death of Walter B. McGinnis who had served as the administrator of William's estate. These included $2,960.80 for the sale of produce and livestock from Beech Bend Park, $3,010.30 from the sale of personal property, and $291.61 from the sale of corn to Charles Garvin who later purchased the Beech Bend Property.[101]

Over the years under the ownership of the Garvin family Beach Bend changed from what had been a community gathering place on the bend in the river to a large amusement park. The first ride was a pony ride, followed by a roller skating rink, dance hall, bowling center and swimming pool. Shortly after WWII mechanical rides were added to the park beginning with a Ferris wheel that was purchased from the Chicago World's Fair. Racing began about the same time with motorcycles. A dragstrip was added around 1950. Around 1960 a campground was added with more than 1,000 spaces and was, for a time, billed as the world's largest.[102]

Nancy Crutchfield Brashear (1855-1892)

Daughter of Walter C. Brashear and Martha Hope Crutchfield
Grandaunt of Taylor Cosby Cottrell, Jr.

Nancy Crutchfield Brashear was born on 1 December 1855 in Warren County, Kentucky. She was the daughter of Walter Curran Brashear and Martha Hope Crutchfield.[103] She was listed on the 1860 census in Warren County, in the home of her father Walter as Nancy Brashears, age 5.[104] She appeared on the 1870 census in the home of her father in Warren County, as Nancy W., age 13.[105] She was confirmed on 5 May 1878 at Christ Episcopal Church in Bowling Green, by the Rt. Rev. T.U. Dudley.[106] She appeared on the census in 1880 in the home of her father in Warren County, as Nancy, age 22 and single.[107] She never married.

Nancy died on 27 November 1892 in Warren County, at age 36. Her cause of death was Typhoid Fever. She was buried in Fairview Cemetery in Bowling Green, in Cemetery 1, Section C, Site C-247.[108]

Curran Walter Brashear (1857-1931)

Son of Walter C. Brashear and Martha Hope Crutchfield
Granduncle of Taylor Cosby Cottrell, Jr.

Curran Walter Brashear was born on 14 August 1857 in Bowling Green in Warren County, Kentucky. He was the son of Walter Curran Brashear and Martha Hope Crutchfield.[109] He was listed on the 1860 census in Warren County, in the home of his father Walter as Curran Brashears, age 3.[110] He was baptized on 5 November 1868 at Christ Episcopal Church in Bowling Green by Rev. J.M. Curtis. His parents served as baptismal sponsors.[111]

He was listed on the 1870 census in the home of his father in Warren County, as Curran, age 12.[112] On the 1880 Warren County Census he was listed in the household of L.A. Hasdell as C.W. Brashear, age 22 and a clerk in store.[113]

A bond for the marriage of Curran Walter Brashear and Mattie T. Arl was signed on 17 October 1883 in Warren County, by Curran and Jos Rice. Curran married Mattie, who was the daughter of John Arl and Sophie Wagner on 17 October 1883 in Bowling Green, with Robert Brashear and Mrs. Joe Twaits as witnesses.[114] Mattie was born on 17 February 1861 in Bowling Green.[115]

Curran was listed on the 1900 census in Warren County, as Curren W. Brashear, head of household, age 42 and owning his home free of mortgage. His wife Mattie, age 39 was listed as having had 6 children, with 6 living. Their daughters Corrine, age 15, Mildred H., age 10 and sons Walter C., age 12, Curren A., age 7, Claud L., age 5, and William B., age 2 were also listed in the household.[116]

Upon the death of his father in 1902 Curren inherited the property in Bowling Green known as the "McNeel Place", rent free. According to his father's will, his father had paid a bank debt on the property of $225 in 1890, which would have been worth $360 in 1900. In the will his father stated that the lot was "a large one, and if in the future, seventh street should be opened up to Park St., which will sometime doubtless be done, is susceptible of being divided into four good build lots upon which cottages may be erected by the father or any of his children for rent or to be occupied by one or more of the family who may desire to do so."[117]

Curran was listed on the 1910 census in Warren County, as Curren W. Brashear, age 52 along with his wife Mattie, age 49. His daughters Corrine, age 25 and Mildred H., age 20 and sons Walter C., age 22, Arl, age 17, Claud, age 15, and William B., age 12 were also listed. Corrine and Mildred were working as a seamstress in a dressmaking establishment while Arl owned his own plumbing shop. Claud and William were listed as attending school and Curren was listed as a plumber in his own shop on the census. Mattie was listed as the mother of 7 children, with six living. Therefore, there was likely a seventh child whose name, sex, and date of birth and death is unknown.[118]

Curran Walter Brashear		
1860	Warren County, KY	N/A
1870	Warren County, KY	In School
1880	Warren County, KY	Clerk
1900	Warren County, KY	Plumber
1910	Warren County, KY	Plumber
1920	Warren County, KY	Plumber
1930	Warren County, KY	Plumber

On the 1920 census in Warren County, Curren was listed as Curren W. Brashear, age 62. His wife Mattie A., age 58 and sons Claud, age 25, William, age 22, and Curren A., age 27 were also listed. Claud and William were working as plumbers and Curren A. was working as a plumbing salesman.[119]

Children of Curren Walter Brashear and Mattie T. Arl:

- Corinne Brashear – Born on 9 August 1884 in Warren County, Kentucky and died on 11 January 1968 in Warren County, age 83.[120] She was buried in Fairview Cemetery in Bowling Green. She was a designer of gowns in 1930 and lived for a time in Chicago. She was listed in the history of Warren County's dressmaking as "among Bowling Green's most successful modesties."[121] She never married.
- Walter Crutchfield Brashear – Born on 12 August 1887 in Bowling Green, Kentucky and died on 30 March 1955 at his home at 710 East 10th Street in Bowling Green, at age 67. His cause of death was cerebral apoplexy and sequela from which he had suffered for 5 years.[122] He was buried in Fairview Cemetery in Bowling Green. Walter married Mary D. Burton on 19 February 1915 in Warren County.[123] She was born on 1 February 1890 in Kentucky.[124] Walter owned and managed Walter Brashear Plumbing and Heating Company, which was

incorporated in 1938 and was located at 334 East 8th Street in Bowling Green.[125] Mary died on 25 July 1968 in McCracken County in Kentucky, at age 78. She was buried in Fairview Cemetery in Bowling Green.[126] Walter and Mary had at least one child: [127]

- o Camilla Brashear – Born on 20 January 1918 in Bowling Green, Kentucky and died on 25 October 2006 in McCracken County, Kentucky, likely in Paducah.[128] It appears likely that Camilla married twice, first to Robert W. Hougland who she divorced prior to 1974 and then to Joseph M. Shellman on 29 June 1974 in Madison County, Kentucky.[129] Camilla was buried in Mount Kenton Cemetery in Paducah with her second husband Joseph who was born on 1 June 1920 in Paducah and died on 26 February 2009 in Paducah.[130]

- Mildred H. Brashear – Born on 7 December 1890 in Warren County, Kentucky and died on 9 April 1920 in Bowling Green, at age 29. Here cause of death was pulmonary tuberculosis.[131] She was buried on 11 April 1920 in Fairview Cemetery in Cemetery 1, Section C, Site C-247.[132] Mildred was baptized on 25 May 1902 at Christ Episcopal Church in Bowling Green by Chas. W.B. Bill with Mrs. Cora Cooksey and Mrs. Madison McGinnis serving as witnesses.[133] She was confirmed on 15 March

Mildred H. Brashear

1903 at Christ Episcopal Church by the Rt. Rev. T.U. Dudley.[134] In 1910 she was working as a seamstress in a dressmaking establishment while living with her father.[135] Mildred married Nathaniel M. Gilmore, son of James W. and Ann S. Gilmore sometime before 1917.[136] Nathaniel was born on 26 April 1889 in Gallatin, Tennessee and worked as a tele-graph operator for the L.N. Railroad Company and later was a veterinary stocks doctor in 1920.[137] They apparently had no children. Nathaniel married Lucy F. Weguilar in 1930. They had at least three children including, Frances W. Gilmore, David N. Gilmore and Hal M. Gilmore. Nathaniel died on 27 April 1966 in Warren County, at age 77.[138]

- Curran Arl Brashear – Born on 27 June 1892 in Bowling Green, Warren County, Kentucky and died on 7 January 1955 at Memorial Hospital in Houston in Harris County, Texas, at age 62. His cause of death was pulmonary Edema due to Circulatory Failure.[139] He was buried on 8 January 1955 in Forest Park Cemetery in Houston.[140] In 1910 Curran was living with his father and was listed on the census as single.[141] When he registered for the World War I Draft in 1918 he was listed as married and was described as medium height, slender build, with blue eyes and brown hair.[142] On 25 June 1918 he began military service as a private. His military service ended on 19 December 1918 with an honorable discharge.[143] In 1920 he was living with his father and was listed as divorced on the census.[144] No additional information is available on what was apparently his first wife. In 1926 he married Helen Cummings, who was the daughter of James E. Cummings and Ruth Coon. Helen was born on 5 August 1901 in Ohio.[145] Sometime prior to 1930 they moved to Houston, Texas. They apparently had no children. Helen died on 12 February 1979 in Shuffield Nursing Home in Houston, at age 77. She was buried at Rest Haven Cemetery in Brady in McCullouch County, Texas.[146]
- Claude Lane Brashear – Born on 15 August 1894 in Bowling Green, Kentucky and died on 22 January 1988 at Greenwood Leflore Hospital in Greenwood in Leflore County, Mississippi, at age 93. He was buried on 23 January 1988 at Odd Fellows Cemetery in Leflore County.[147] He was described as slender with blue eyes and brown hair in June 1917 when he registered for the draft. He was living with his father at the time at 627 Fairview Avenue in Bowling Green.[148] Claude married Kathryn L. Murphy on 15 June 1921 in Warren County, Kentucky. The ceremony was performed by Father Thomas J.

Hayes at the Roman Catholic church in Bowling Green with William Dougherty and Madge Murphy as witnesses.[149] Kathryn, also known as Katie, was the daughter of William and Jennie Murphy and was born on 23 February 1897 in Rockfield in Warren County.[150] Katie died on 29 January 1985 in Greenwood in Leflore County, Mississippi, at age 87. Her funeral was held in Greenwood, on 31 January 1985.[151] Claude and Katie had at least three children including: [152]

- o Corinne Hope Brashear – Born on 1 March 1922 in Bowling Green, Kentucky and died on 18 September 2014 in Greenwood in Mississippi. She was buried in the Odd Fellows Cemetery in Greenwood. She was also known as "Tootie". She retired from Greenwood Leflore Hospital in 1986 to take care of her ailing parents.[153]
- o Harold Lane Brashear – Born on 4 November 1923 in Warren County, Kentucky and died on 14 October 1994.[154] He enlisted as a Private in the U.S. Army on 17 June 1943 in Louisville and ended military service on 25 March 1946.[155]
- o David A. Brashear – Born on 1 December 1932 in Warren County, Kentucky.[156]

- William Bottom Brashear – Born on 20 June 1897 in Bowling Green, Kentucky and died on 20 July 1965 at City Hospital in Bowling Green, at age 68. His cause of death was carcinoma of the lung and congestive heart failure which had an onset approximately one year prior to his death.[157] He was buried in Fairview Cemetery in Bowling Green.[158] He was described as medium height, medium build with blue eyes and light brown hair when he registered for the draft in 1818. He was working for his father as a plumber at that time and was living at 627 Fairview Avenue in Bowling Green.[159] William worked as a plumber for most of his life. In 1930 he was living with five other men at the Elks Club on Main Street in Bowling Green.[160] William never married.

Curren Walter died on 2 November 1931 at City Hospital in Bowling Green, at age 74. His cause of death was cancer of the esophagus.

He was buried in Fairview Cemetery in Bowling Green, in Section N, Site N278e.[161]

Mattie was listed on the 1940 census in Warren County, as Mattie A. Brashear, age 79 and widowed. Her daughter Corinne Brashear, age 54 and son Wm. B. Brashear, age 42 were also listed.[162]

Mattie died on 6 September 1945 in her home at 627 Fairview Avenue in

Curran W. and Mattie A. Brashear
Fairview Cemetery
Bowling Green, Kentucky

Bowling Green, at age 84. Her cause of death was cardio vascular renal disease. She was buried on 8 September 1945 in Fairview Cemetery in Section N, Site N278e.[163]

Robert Lee Brashear (1859-1894)

Son of Walter C. Brashear and Martha Hope Crutchfield
Granduncle of Taylor Cosby Cottrell, Jr.

Robert Lee Brashear was born in October 1859 in Warren County, Kentucky. He was the son of Walter Curran Brashear and Martha Hope Crutchfield.[164] He was listed on the 1860 census in the household of his father in Warren County, as Robt. Brashears, age 11 months.[165] He was baptized on 5 November 1868 at Christ Episcopal Church in Bowling Green, by Rev. J.M. Curtis with his parents serving as sponsors.[166] He was listed in the 1870 census in Warren County, in the home of his father at Robert, age 10.[167] He was found on the 1880 census in the home of his father in Warren County, as Robert, age 20. He was working as a farmer at the time.[168] He apparently never married.

Robert died on 14 January 1894 in Warren County, at age 34. He was buried in Fairview Cemetery in Bowling Green in Cemetery 1, Section C, Site C-247 with the Rev. Virginias O. Gee officiating.[169]

Dora Lee Brashear (1861-1938)

Daughter of Walter C. Brashear and Martha Hope Crutchfield
Grandaunt of Taylor Cosby Cottrell, Jr.

Dora Lee Brashear was born in December 1861 in Warren County, Kentucky. She was the daughter of Walter Curran Brashear and Martha Hope Crutchfield.[170] She was baptized on 5 November 1868 at Christ Episcopal Church in Bowling Green, Kentucky by Rev. J.M. Curtis with her parents serving as sponsors.[171] She was listed on the 1870 census in the household of her father Walter in Warren County, as Dora, age 8.[172] She was confirmed on 26 October 1879 at Christ Episcopal Church by the Rt. Rev. T.U. Dudley.[173]

Dora Lee Brashear

In 1880 she was listed on the census in Warren County, in the home of her father as Dora, age 19 and single.[174] She was found on the 1900 census in Warren County, in the home of her father, listed as Dora Brashiar, age 27 and single.[175]

In 1902 Dora and her sister Virginia and brother William received possession of the Beech Bend property near Bowling Green from their father Walter Curren Brashear following his death. The property had been in the Brashear family since the Civil War.[176]

After the death of her father Dora moved into the home of her brother William where she was found on the census in 1910 in Warren County, as Dora Brasher, age 38 and single.[177] In 1920 she was listed on the census in Warren County, with her brother William, as Dora Breshear, age 38 and single.[178] They were living on the Beach Bend Pike at the time. In 1930 she was found on the census living with her brother William in the same home on the Beach Bend Pike as Dora Brashear, age 61.[179]

Dora died at 1:15 in the afternoon on 16 July 1938 at the home of her brother William on Beech Bend Road near Bowling Green, at age 76. Her cause of death was an intestinal obstruction. She was buried on 17 July 1938 in Fairview Cemetery in Bowling Green, in Cemetery 1, Section C, Site C-247.[180]

Virginia Light Brashear (1864-1936)

Daughter of Walter C. Brashear and Martha Hope Crutchfield
Grandaunt of Taylor Cosby Cottrell, Jr.

Virginia Light Brashear was born on 9 January 1864 in Warren County, Kentucky. She was the daughter of Walter Curran Brashear and Martha Hope Crutch-field.[181] Virginia was baptized on 5 November 1868 at Christ Episcopal Church in Bowling Green, by Rev. J.M. Curtis with her parents serving as sponsors.[182] She was listed on the 1870 census in Warren County in the household of her father Walter as Virginia, age 6.[183] She was confirmed on 26 October 1879 at Christ Episcopal Church in Bowling Green by the Rt. Rev. T.U. Dudley.[184]

In 1880 she was listed on the census in Warren County, in the household of her father

Virginia Light Brashear

as Virginia, age 16 and single.[185] She was listed on the 1900 census in Warren County in the home of her father as Virginia Brashiar, age 25 and single.[186]

In 1902 Virginia and her sister Dora and brother William received possession of the Beech Bend property near Bowling Green from their father Walter Curren Brashear following his death. The property had been in the Brashear family since the Civil War.[187]

After the death of her father, Virginia moved into the home of her brother William where she was found on the census in 1910 in Warren County.[188] She was listed as Virginia Brasher, age 36 and single.

In 1920 she was listed in the census in Warren County, as Virginia Breshear, 36 and single.[189] On the 1930 census of Warren County she was listed in the home of her brother William as Jennie Brashear, age 63 and single.[190] Virginia never married.

Virginia died on 5 May 1936 at 2:18 in the afternoon in the Beech Bend Neighborhood of Warren County, at age 72 years, 3 months, and 27 days. Her cause of death was cerebral hemorrhage. Her death certificate listed her as a housekeeper and indicated she owned her own home. Her sister Corrine was the informant on her death certificate. Virginia was buried on 8 May 1936 in Fairview Cemetery in Section C, Site C-247.[191]

Virginia and Dora Brashear
Fairview Cemetery
Bowling Green, Kentucky

Chapter 3 – Richard Levi Brashear Family

Grandfather of Taylor Cosby Cottrell, Jr.

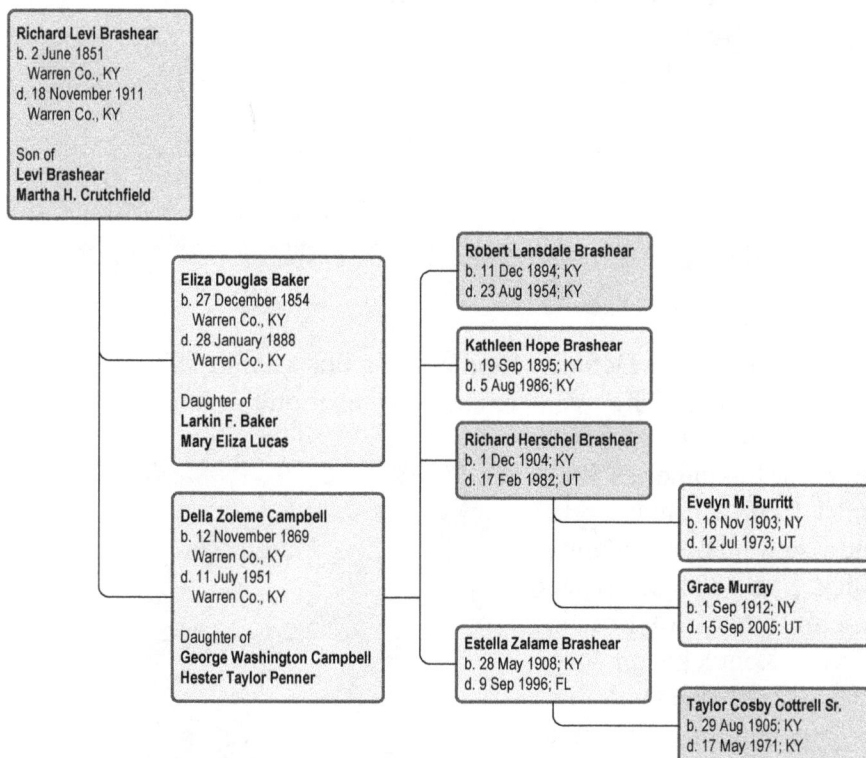

```
Richard Levi Brashear
b. 2 June 1851
  Warren Co., KY
d. 18 November 1911
  Warren Co., KY

Son of
Levi Brashear
Martha H. Crutchfield
```

```
Eliza Douglas Baker
b. 27 December 1854
  Warren Co., KY
d. 28 January 1888
  Warren Co., KY

Daughter of
Larkin F. Baker
Mary Eliza Lucas
```

```
Della Zoleme Campbell
b. 12 November 1869
  Warren Co., KY
d. 11 July 1951
  Warren Co., KY

Daughter of
George Washington Campbell
Hester Taylor Penner
```

```
Robert Lansdale Brashear
b. 11 Dec 1894; KY
d. 23 Aug 1954; KY
```

```
Kathleen Hope Brashear
b. 19 Sep 1895; KY
d. 5 Aug 1986; KY
```

```
Richard Herschel Brashear
b. 1 Dec 1904; KY
d. 17 Feb 1982; UT
```

```
Estella Zalame Brashear
b. 28 May 1908; KY
d. 9 Sep 1996; FL
```

```
Evelyn M. Burritt
b. 16 Nov 1903; NY
d. 12 Jul 1973; UT
```

```
Grace Murray
b. 1 Sep 1912; NY
d. 15 Sep 2005; UT
```

```
Taylor Cosby Cottrell Sr.
b. 29 Aug 1905; KY
d. 17 May 1971; KY
```

Richard Levi Brashear was born on 2 June 1851 in Bowling Green, in Warren County, Kentucky. He was the son of Walter Curran Brashear and Martha Hope Crutchfield.[1] He had eight brothers and sisters including Stella F. Brashear, Camilla Lansdale Brashear, William Helm Brashear, Nancy Crutchfield Brashear, Curran Walter Brashear, Robert Lee Brashear, Dora Lee Brashear, and Virginia Light Brashear. Additional information on Richard Levi's parents and brothers and sisters can be found in Section 2, Chapter 2, Walter Curran Brashear Family.

Levi was listed on the census of 1860 in Warren County in the home of his father Walter, as Richard L., age 9 and attending school.[2] In 1870 he was found on the census of his father in Warren County, Kentucky, as Richard L., age 19.[3]

Levi Brashear Family Timeline

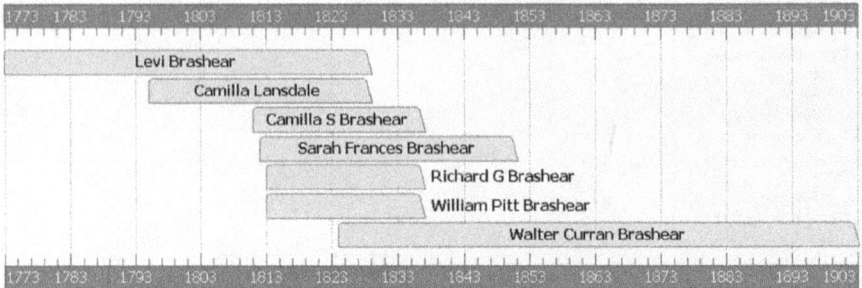

1773	1783	1793	1803	1813	1823	1833	1843	1853	1863	1873	1883	1893	1903

Levi Brashear
Camilla Lansdale
Camilla S Brashear
Sarah Frances Brashear
Richard G Brashear
William Pitt Brashear
Walter Curran Brashear

Richard was a Democrat and cast his first vote in 1872 for Horace Greeley.[4] In 1880 he was listed as a gardener on the census in Warren County, Kentucky in the home of his father as Richard L., age 28 and single.[5] He also went by the name of Dick. In 1884 he located one-mile north of Bowling Green, Kentucky on forty-one acres of fine land.[6]

A bond for the marriage of Richard Levi Brashear and Eliza Douglass Baker was signed on 25 September 1884 in Warren County, Kentucky. Richard married Eliza, who was the daughter of Larkin F. Baker and Mary Eliza Lucas, on 25 September

Richard Levi Brashear

1884.[7] Her father Larkin was born on 22 February 1822 in Tennessee and died on 30 October 1873 in Warren County, at age 51. Her mother Mary was born on 29 June 1822 in Warren County and died on 30 January 1884 in Warren County. They were both buried in Fairview

Cemetery in Bowling Green. Eliza had eight brothers and sisters including the following:

- Margaret A. Baker who was born on 18 December 1841 in Warren County and died on 19 July 1918 in Warren County. She married in 1861. Her husband's last name was Shaffer.[8]
- Matilda F. Baker was born on 23 June 1843 in Warren County and died on 1 February 1906 in Warren County. She married William B. Rock and they had one child William Baker Rock.[9]
- Mary L. Baker who was born on 14 December 1844 in Warren County and died on 27 July 1903. She married Jno. M. Wilkins around 1864.[10]
- Georgiana H. Baker was born in 1849 in Warren County.[11]
- Archibald W. Baker was born on 27 January 1851 in Warren County. He married Camilla Lansdale Brashear, the daughter of Walter Curran Brashear and Martha Hope Crutchfield, in 1881 in Warren County. He died on 7 November 1933 in Bristow in Warren County.[12]
- William D. Baker was born on 10 October 1854 in Warren County and died on 12 November 1932 in Warren County. He married Annie Langley around 1891. They had at least two children including Larkin Langley Baker and Joseph H. Baker.[13]
- Emaline Hyde Baker was born on 15 January 1858 in Bowling Green and died on 1 October 1903 in Bowling Green. She married Andrew Jackson Ragland in 1877.[14]
- Joseph Lucus Baker was born on 16 September 1861 in Warren County and died on 23 July 1898 in Warren County.[15]

Eliza also had three half-siblings who were listed as children of Larkin Baker in Kentucky Birth Records. Since there was no mother listed it is assumed their mother(s) were some of Larkin's slaves. Eliza's half-siblings included:

- Fanny Baker who was born in 1856 in Warren County.[16]
- Henry Baker who was born on 7 April 1859 in Warren County.[17]
- Bunch Baker who was born on 10 November 1859 in Warren County.[18]

Richard and Eliza Baker had one of the first telephones in Warren County. There were no telephone poles so the wires were run on the fence. His phone number was 82 which he kept until the dial system was instituted.[19]

Eliza died on 28 January 1888 in Warren County, Kentucky, at age 33. She was buried on 31 January 1888 in Fairview Cemetery in Bowling Green, Warren County, Kentucky in Section B, Site B-19 with the Rev. Virginias G. Gee officiating.[20]

Richard Levi Brashear Home – Circa 1913

A bond for the marriage of Richard Levi Brashear and Della Zoleme Campbell was signed on 10 January 1893 in Warren County, Kentucky by Richard L. Brashear and George W. Campbell binding them to the Commonwealth of Kentucky in the sum of One Hundred Dollars in the event the marriage did not take place. Richard married Della, who was the daughter of George Washington Campbell and Hester Taylor Penner, on 11 January 1893 at G.W. Campbell's home in Bowling Green.[21]

Della was born on 12 November 1869 in Bowling Green. She had at least nine brothers and sisters including Laura Bell Campbell, Josephine Elizabeth Campbell, John Sales Campbell, Ellen Mitchell Campbell, Pernie Underwood Campbell, Mildred Ann Campbell, Wade Hampton Campbell, Julya Estella Campbell, and Georgia Ennis

Campbell. Additional information for her parents and siblings can be found in Section 2, Chapter 6, George Washington Campbell Family.

Richard and Della were the first commercial florists in Bowling Green. They had three greenhouses but still had to order flowers from other florists from as far away as Chicago to meet the local demand. One of the greenhouses was a violet house where double sweet violets were raised. The middle house was the

Della Zoleme Campbell

busiest because this was where roses were grown. The lower house mostly had Mums which were started outside and then transplanted to the house to bloom for Thanksgiving.[22]

Richard was listed on the 1900 census in Warren County, Kentucky as Richard L. Brashear, age 48 along with his wife Della, age 30. Their son Robert L., age 6 and daughter Kathline H., age 4, along with Ella E. Alexander, a servant age 15, were also listed in the household. His occupation was listed as a Gardner.[23] He was baptized on 14 October 1900 at Christ Episcopal Church in Bowling Green as an adult along with his wife Della by Rev. Joseph J. Cornish.[24]

A fair was held annually at Covington Woods at the end of Magnolia and Nutwood Streets in Bowling Green. One year Richard took the top of his surrey and decorated it with huge lily pads to participate in the parade during the fair. Kathleen stood by her mother and held pick lotus blossoms while her brother Robert sat on the front seat with Richard.[25]

In 1910 he was listed on the census in Warren County as Richard L. Brashear, age 58 with a farm and house owned free of mortgage. His wife Della, age 38 was listed as having a total of four children with four living. His son Robert, age 16 was listed as single and working as a farm laborer. His daughter Cathleen, age 14 was listed as attending school. His son Richard, age 5 was also attending school. His daughter Zaleam, age one year and four months, was also listed as having been in school.[26]

Richard and Della had four children Robert Lansdale Brashear, Kathleen Hope Brashear, Richard Herschel Campbell Brashear, and Estella Zalame Brashear.[27]

Richard Levi Brashear		
1860	Warren County, KY	N/A
1870	Warren County, KY	None
1880	Warren County, KY	Gardner
1900	Warren County, KY	Gardner
1910	Warren County, KY	Farmer

Richard died on 18 November 1911 in Warren County, Kentucky, at age 60 at his home. His cause of death was Bright's disease with paralysis following a stroke after "several months of great suffering." Funeral services were held at Christ Episcopal Church in Bowling Green with services conducted by the rector, Rev. C.P. Parker with Charles Garvin, Charles Spalding, John C. Young, George and Alex Jenkins, A.E. Blewett, C.W. Younger, Henry L. Parks, and William Baker acting as pallbearers. He was buried on 19 Novem-

Richard Levi Brashear
Fairview Cemetery
Bowling Green, Kentucky

ber 1911 in Fairview Cemetery in Bowling Green in Cemetery 1, Section A, Site A-86 after his body had initially been placed in the Ogden vault waiting interment.[28]

Della was listed on the 1920 census in Warren County as Della Brashear, age 49, and widowed. Her occupation was listed as a general farmer. Her son Robert, age 26 was listed as a mechanic and her daughter Kathleen, age 24 was listed as a teacher in City School and single. Her son Richard, age 15 and other daughter Zalame, age 11 were also listed and attending school.[29]

In 1930 Della was listed on the census in Warren County as Della, age 59 and widowed. Her son Robert L., age 36 was listed as a Civil Engineer in private practice and single. Her daughter Kathleen, age 35 was listed as a Teacher in City School and also single.[30] In 1935 a tornado struck the Brashear property, damaged the residence, uprooted trees, and destroyed the greenhouses on the property.[31] In 1938 Della was listed in the Bowling Green City Directory as living on Route 1 in Warren County and owning 32 acres of land.[32] In 1940 the same property was listed as being in Bristow on US 31W.

Della Zoleme Brashear
Fairview Cemetery
Bowling Green, Kentucky

Della was listed on the 1940 Warren County census as Mrs. Della Brashear, age 68 along with her son Robert, age 46 and daughter Kathleen, age 44.[33] In 1942 a war ration book, numbered 240774-51, was issued in the name of Della Zalame Brashear. The book had been secured in her name by her daughter Kathleen. It listed Della as 72 years old, weighing 113 pounds, five feet five inches in height, and having blue eyes and grey hair.[34]

Della died on 11 July 1951 at her home on the Louisville Road just outside Bowling Green, at age 81. Her cause of death was coronary thrombosis.[35] She was buried on 13 July 1951 in Fairview Cemetery in Cemetery 1, Section A, Site A-86.[36]

Robert Lansdale Brashear (1894-1954)

Son of Richard Levi Brashear and Della Zoleme Campbell
Uncle of Taylor Cosby Cottrell, Jr.

Robert Lansdale Brashear was born on 31 January 1894 in the Brashear Home on the Louisville Road just North of Bowling Green in Warren County, Kentucky. He was the son of Richard Levi Brashear and Della Zoleme Campbell.[37] He was baptized on 10 April 1898 at Christ Episcopal Church in Bowling Green on Easter Sunday by Rev. Joseph J. Cornish with Andrew Jackson Ragland and Emmaline Hyde Ragland serving as sponsors. His sister Kathleen Hope Brashear was baptized on the same day.[38]

Robert was listed on the 1900 census in Warren County in the home of his father Levi as Robert, age six.[39] His sister Kathleen, in recollections of her childhood remembered that she and Robert and several other children were invited to a birthday party one summer for Edward Covington. They played "Jennie put the kettle on and let's all take tea" and "Drop the handkerchief." They were given "little glass lanterns filled with hard candy as favors."[40]

Robert Lansdale Brashear

In his youth Robert found a Civil War canon ball and a projectile on the Baker Hill property which was next to the Brashear farm. He placed the cannon ball in the greenhouse water tank behind his home and threw the projectile in the pond to keep them out of the way of the children. He and his sister Kathleen spend many hours hunting for "minney balls" from the Baker property located adjacent to the Brashear farm. The Baker property had once been a Civil War Fort and remnants of past battles were frequently found on nearby farms. They used the minney balls for sinkers on their fishing lines.[41]

Robert received his early education in city schools and the old St. Columbus Academy.[42] St. Columbus was founded in 1863 and was conducted under the auspices of the Sisters of Charity of the Roman Catholic Church.

Robert was listed on the 1910 census in Warren County in the household of his father as Robert, age 16 and single. He was working as a farm laborer at the time.[43] In 1917 he registered for the draft for World War I while living in Bowling Green. He reported he was employed in the tobacco industry and was listed on the draft registration as medium height, medium build with blue eyes and brown hair and having lost one foot in June 1917. It was said that he lost the foot while climbing a fence with a loaded gun.[44]

Robert was listed on the 1920 census in Warren County in the home of his mother Della, as Robert, age 26, single, with an occupation of a mechanic.[45] In August 1926 he entered a picture in a national contest sponsored by the Popular Science Magazine. He was listed in the January 1927 issue as one of 50 winners of $5 for his picture. In 1930 he was listed on the census in the home of his mother in Warren County as Robert L., age 36 and single. He was a Civil Engineer in private practice at the time.

Bee Hives
Located on Brashear Property
Photograph taken in 1931

In 1931 Robert had a photograph of his bee hives, which were located behind the Brashear farm on the Louisville Road just outside Bowling Green turned, into a postcard. At the time he had a total of 10 bee hives.[46] During the 1930s Robert worked as a civil engineer at 914 ½ State Street in Bowling Green. During this time, he was the engineer for the Student Union Building at Western State College, the Southern Bell Plant, the J.E. Bohannon and Company tobacco warehouses, and the Sears Robuck Company building.[47]

Robert was listed on the 1940 census in Warren County in the home of his mother Della as Robert, age 46 and single.[48] He served as the trustee for the Brashear lands that

Robert Lansdale Brashear		
1900	Warren County, KY	N/A
1910	Warren County, KY	Farm Laborer
1920	Warren County, KY	Mechanic
1930	Warren County, KY	Civil Engineer
1940	Warren County, KY	Civil Engineer

were sold in 1942 and distributed the inherited portions to the five children of his grandfather Walter Curren Brashear.[49] After the death of Walter Brashear McGinnis in 1943, Robert cared for Walter's German shepherd "Rex" until Rex died on the evening of 16 January 1944 at 16 years of age.[50]

Robert was appointed by the Warren County Court Administrator on 16 July 1951 to serve as the administrator of the estate of his mother Della Z. Brashear.[51] He left a will that same year leaving one half of his estate to his sister Kathleen H. Brashear so long as she remained single, or one third if she was married with the remaining one half or two thirds respectively split between his sister Zalame Brashear Cottrell and his brother Richard H. Brashear. He stated that the reason he was leaving the greater portion of his estate to his sister Kathleen was "because of her singleness

Robert Lansdale Brashear
Fairview Cemetery
Bowling Green, Kentucky

and age and because of her greater liability to become dependent in her later years" and not because of less affection for his brother and sister.[52] He added a codicil to the will on 17 February 1953 that specifically left his bonds or stocks to his sister Kathleen H. Brashear.[53]

Robert was confirmed on 21 June 1953 at Christ Episcopal Church in Bowling Green by Bishop Charles Clingman.[54] Roberet never married and was a civil engineer in private practice at the time of his death.[55]

Robert died on 23 August 1954 in the Bowling Green Warren County Hospital in Bowling Green at age 60 following a short illness. His cause of death was ruptured aorta aneurism due to dissecting aneurism of abdominal aorta. Funeral services were held on 25 August 1954 at Christ Episcopal Church in Bowling Green with the Rev. Courtney Carpenter of Elizabethtown officiating.[56] The flower list included 69 names.[57] The organist was Mrs. O.A. Matteri. Pallbearers were Dan Amos, Gill Neel, Bud Lowe, Jess Spalding, Jack Russell, Tom Adkisson, Charlie Davis, Edgar Boyd, Dr. A.W. Farnsworth, S.C. Lawson, Pete Lawson, and J.M. Horton.[58] He was buried on 25 August 1954 in Fairview Cemetery in Bowling Green, in Cemetery 1, Section A, Site A-86.[59]

Kathleen Hope Brashear (1895-1986)

Daughter of Richard Levi Brashear and Della Zoleme Campbell
Aunt of Taylor Cosby Cottrell, Jr.

Kathleen Hope Brashear was born on 19 September 1895 in Bowling Green in Warren County, Kentucky. She was the daughter of Richard Levi Brashear and Della Zoleme Campbell.[60] She was baptized on 10 April 1898 at Christ Episcopal Church in Bowling Green on Easter Sunday by Rev. Joseph J. Cornish with Andrew Jackson Ragland and Emmaline Hyde Ragland serving as sponsors. Her brother Robert Lansdale Brashear was baptized on the same day.[61]

She was listed on the 1900 census in the household of her father Richard in Warren County as Kathline H., age 4.[62] She

Kathleen Hope Brashear

was enrolled in College Street School in Bowling Green in 1902.[63] In recollections of her childhood, Kathleen remembered that she and Robert and several other children were invited to a birthday party one summer for Edward Covington. They played "Jennie put the kettle on and let's all take tea" and "Drop the handkerchief". They were given "little glass lanterns filled with hard candy as favors." Kathleen and Robert also spent many hours hunting for "minie balls" from the Baker property located adjacent to the Brashear farm. The Baker property had once been a Civil War Fort and reminants of past battles were frequently found on nearby farms. They used the minie balls for sinkers on their fishing lines.[64]

In 1906 she attended classes at St. Columbia's Academy, a Catholic day and boarding school run by the Sisters of Charity of Nazareth from 1866 until 1912.[65] She was confirmed on 31 January 1909 at Christ Episcopal Church in Bowling Green by Chas. E. Woodcock.[66] In 1910 she was listed on the census in Warren County in the home of her father as Cathleen, age 14 and attending school.[67] On 27 July 1917 she was awarded an Advanced Certificate for teaching in a public school by Western Kentucky State Normal School in Bowling Green.[68]

She taught school in the Rays Branch Seminary in 1915 and 1916. According to Kathleen this was the school where "all of the Campbell children attended school." The school obtained its water from a nearby spring. It was also known as the Rays Branch School and was located near Rays Branch Creek near the Campbell Road which was north of Bowling Green.

In 1920 she was listed on the census in the home of her mother in Warren County as Kathleen, age 24 and single.[69] She was a teacher in City School in 1920 and was employed by the Board of Education of Bowling Green as a teacher at a salary of $87 monthly in 1923.[70] In 1925 her salary had increased to $90 monthly.[71] By 1926 it had raised to $95 monthly.[72] She was listed on the census of 1930 in Warren County in the household of her mother as Kathleen, age 35 and single.[73] In 1935 her salary as a teacher in Bowling Green had risen to $110 monthly.[74] After many years as a member of the Center Street Faculty, Kathleen accepted the position of Warren County Attendance Officer and visiting teacher.[75] In 1940 she was listed on the census in Warren County in the home of her mother as Kathleen, age 44 and single.[76]

War ration book 240773-51 was issued in her name on 6 May 1942. She secured this book at the same time that she also secured

Rays Branch School
Rays Branch near Bowling Green
Photograph taken in 1876

ration books on her mother Della and brother Robert. The book listed Kathleen as 46 years old, weighing 139 pounds, five feet three inches in height, and having grey eyes and brown hair.[77]

Kathleen held membership in the Delta Chapter of the Kentucky Delta Kappa Gamma Society as chairperson of the social committee between 1962 and 1965.[78] She enjoyed creating decorated Easter eggs, bunny rabbits, and chickens each Easter. Her creations were described in a 1963 newspaper article titled "Miss Brashear Enjoys Fancy Cooking Hobby". "For the fancy periscopic eggs, molds dusted with corn starch are filled with sugar to which the right amount of water has been added. They are then allowed to stand until sufficiently hard to allow handling, usually overnight. When they have reached the right stage a window is cut in the end and the inside is removed with a spoon to make the hollow into which the miniature chickens and rabbits, little flowers and other bits of scenic decoration are combined for a perfect picture. Once the scene is set, the window is covered with cellophane and sealed with fancy icing decorations."[79]

In 1965 a baby tornado blew down a water tank on the Brashear property, the former home of Kathleen. She said she had hoped this would be good fortune and allow her to recover a Civil War canon ball that had been laced in the tank years ago by her brother Robert. She recalled that her family had found many souvenirs of the Civil War around the Baker Hill fortification, some of which were given to the Kentucky Building Museum by members of the family.[80]

On the 7th of April 1965 Kathleen received a notice to take depositions at the law office of Marshall Funk on 10th street in Bowling Green, Kentucky. The depositions were to deal with Warren Circuit Court Civil Action Number 12 for the Board of Education of Bowling Green, plaintiff versus the Board of Trustees of the Teachers' Retirement System of the Schools of Bowling Green. She was listed as one of the trustees.[81]

Kathleen left a will on 15 July 1982 in Warren County bequeathing her home on High Street in Bowling Green to her sister Zalame Brashear Cottrell along with the cherry chest that matched her bed (both of which were made by her Great-Grandfather Campbell), her marble top table, blue candlesticks, and a corner cupboard (if her sister wanted the cupboard). Her sister was also to receive a painting by Kathleen's Aunt Mildred, a Hepplewhite table, a family portrait, a hand-painted trunk, the Brashear and Campbell Coat of Arms, two cane bottom chairs, an amethyst water set, a Shaker table and glass case on table, a red chair which was painted for her mother, and several painted pictures. Zalame's two children were also provided for in the will by leaving her flat silver to Joanna Cottrell and her Noritake china and a Cuckoo Clock (which was never to be sold but passed on in the family) to Cosby (Taylor Cosby Cottrell, Jr.). She also left her Early American glassware to her nephew Richard Brashear, Jr. Other household items were to be made available to the family and any remaining items to be sold with the proceeds divided between her sister Zalame and her nephew Richard Brashear, Jr. Her sister Zalame, along with her attorney William J. Parker were appointed as Co-Executors.[82]

Kathleen was honored as the oldest active parishioner of Christ Episcopal Church in Bowling Green at the coffee hour after she celebrated her 90th birthday in 1986. The Sunday bulletin indicated she "was baptized and confirmed at Christ Church when it was down on College Street before the present church was built in 1912". She taught Church School for many years and taught every class from Kindergarten through High School. She was active in other areas of the parish and was a member of St. Margaret's Guild. Many members of the church remembered her making cupcakes, cookies, and prize eggs for the Church School Easter Egg Hunts. She taught school for 29 years and was Director of Pupil Personnel (and first Truant Officer) for 21 years in the city schools. She was a regular attendant at the 8:00 AM services at Christ Church. The article in the bulletin closed by indicating that "Our parish has been enriched by her presence all these years, and we ask God's continued blessings upon her in the future."[83]

Kathleen died on 5 August 1986 at her home at 1019 High Street in Bowling Green, at age 90.[84] She

Kathleen Hope Brashear
Fairview Cemetery
Bowling Green, Kentucky

was found at 6:00 PM by her sister Zalame and pronounced dead at 6:15 PM. Her cause of death was congestive heart failure. Funeral services were held on 8 August 1986 at Christ Episcopal Church in Bowling Green, Kentucky.[85] She was buried on 8 August 1986 in Fairview Cemetery in Section A, Site A-86.[86]

Final settlement and discharge of co-executors William J. Parker and Zalame B. Cottrell were filed on 8 May 1987 and approved by the Warren District Court on 16 June 1987.[87]

Richard Herschel Campbell Brashear (1904-1982)

Son of Richard Levi Brashear and Della Zoleme Campbell
Uncle of Taylor Cosby Cottrell, Jr.

Richard Herschel Campbell Brashear was born in Bowling Green, Kentucky on 1 December 1904. He was the son of Richard Levi Brashear and Della Zoleme Campbell.[88] He was baptized on 23 April 1905 at Christ Episcopal Church in Bowling Green on Easter Sunday by Rev. Wm. K. Marshall with Percy Mottley, Archie Baker, and Mrs. Camilla Baker serving as sponsors. The baptismal record listed his name as Richard Campbell Brashear.[89]

Richard was listed on the census of 1910 in Warren County in the home of his father Levi as Richard, age 5 and attending school.[90] In 1920 he was

Richard Herschel Brashear

listed on the census in Warren County in the household of his mother Della, as Richard, age 15, at home and attending school.[91]

Richard married Evelyn M. Burritt circa 1925 in Rochester in Monroe County, New York.[92] Evelyn was born on 16 November 1903

in Hilton in Monroe County, New York.[93]   She was the daughter of
John William Burritt and Myrtle B. Cheney. Her father John was born
on 21 May 1877 in New York, died in December 1965, likely in New
York, and was buried in Parma Union Cemetery in Parma in Monroe
County, New York.[94] Her mother was born in 1884 in New York and
died in 1963. Myrtle was buried with her husband John in Parma Union
Cemetery.[95] Evelyn had at least three brothers and sisters including:

- Luther Collamer Burritt who was born on 13 August 1906 and
  died on 2 October 1984. Luther married sometime after 1940.
  His wife's name was Dorothy. Luther and Dorothy were buried in Parma Union cemetery in Monroe County, New York.
- Ruth Beatrice Burritt who was born on 23 September 1912 in
  New York and died on 12 January 1997 in San Diego.[96] She
  married Richard Charles Edic. Ruth and Richard were buried
  in Alpine Cemetery in Alpine in San Diego County, California.[97]
- John Burton Burritt who was born on 25 December 1916 in
  Hilton in New York and died on 31 January 1989.[98]

Evelyn was listed as
living with her husband
Richard in the Rochester,
New York City Directory
in 1926.[99]   Richard traveled to the Canal Zone in
1926, departing for Cristobal in the Canal Zone on
15 December 1926 on the
S.S. Cartago and arriving
back in the United States
at the Port of New Orle-
ans, Louisiana on 21
December 1926 just two
days before his son Rich-
ard Herschel Brashear, Jr.,
was born in Rochester,
New York.[100]

Evelyn M. Burritt

In 1930 Richard and Evelyn lived in Kenmore Village in Erie
County, New York at 3049 Delaware Avenue. Richard was working

as a mechanical engineer for the electric company at the time. He was listed on the 1930 census in Erie County, New York as Richard Brashear, age 25 along with his wife Evelyn, age 26 and son Richard, age 3.[101] In 1936 he was working for the New York Telephone and Telegraph Company while living at 626 Shepard in Kenmore in Eerie County. By 1938 they had moved to Albany, New York.[102] On the 1940 census of Albany County, New York he was listed as Richard H. Brashear, age 38 along with his wife Evelyn, age 38 and Son Richard H. Jr., age 5.[103]

In July 1942 Richard made a trip to Geneva, New York to see about an experiment for the Naval Station. He

Richard Herschel Brashear		
1910	Warren County, KY	In School
1920	Warren County, KY	Mechanical Engineer
1930	Erie County, NY	Telephone Engineer
1940	Albany County, NY	Mechanical Engineer

indicated in a letter to his mother that "It was most discouraging, we are having trouble getting material and the boys they hire to work now days are the laziest and dumbest I have seen in my life". He indicated that travel was very limited due to not having enough gasoline for trips and that they will only get 4 gallons a week in the future and that he had done no fishing to speak of because of the gas shortage and that he hadn't even had his boat in the water.[104]

In the late 1950s Richard and Evelyn were living in Albany, New York when Richard's nephew Cosby (the author of this book) visited. Cosby remembers Richard taking him to their mountain cabin on a lake in the Catskill Mountains where there was a bear rug on the floor next to the bed. Richard recalled times where bears and deer would come up next to the cabin and related that he had killed the bear from which the rug was made just outside the front door of the cabin several years before. A large buck's head with a wide spread of antlers also hung over the fireplace. Richard related that the deer had also been killed near the cabin.

Richard and Evelyn moved to Salt Lake City, Utah after his retirement from the Telephone Company for which he had worked for many years. It is assumed the move was to be near his son Richard, Jr., who was living in Salt Lake City and working as a Research Physicist at the time.

Children of Richard H. Brashear and Evelyn M. Burritt:

- Richard Herschel Brashear – Born on 23 December 1926 in Rochester in Ulster County, New York; Died on 24 February 2002 in Salt Lake City, Utah, at age 75. His cause of death was cancer and a long standing history of heart disease. In his obituary his grandson was quoted as saying "My grandpa sits in his boat, telling me

Richard Herschel Brashear, Jr.

about the past…and when he dies, I will really be sad without the stories he tells, but for now I can enjoy them." [105] He was buried on 27 February 2002 in Mount Calvary Catholic Cemetery in Salt Lake City, Utah in Plat D, Section 6, Lot 7, Grave/Crypt 5a.[106] He was also known as Dick, Jr. Richard graduated from Baldwin High School in New York and received a Bachelor of Arts Degree in physics from the University of Vermont where he also did graduate work in physics and electrical engineering. He also attended Columbia University in New York and the University of Japan in Tokyo. [107] He was married in St. Mary's Church in Kingston, Ulster County, New York on 4 November 1956.[108] His wife Evelyn, who was likely born in New York, was still living at the time of the writing of this book thus further identification has not been included. Richard was employed as a research physicist in missile control systems for Sperry Gyroscope Company at the time of their marriage.[109] They later moved to Salt Lake City where Richard worked for Unysis for 37 years as an Electrical Engineer before his retirement. They had five children (three sons and two daughters), all of whom were living at the time of the writing of this book thus further information has not been included.

Evelyn died on 12 July 1973 in Salt Lake City at age 69, following a prolonged illness.[110] She was buried on 14 July 1973 in Mount Calvary Catholic Cemetery in Salt Lake City in Plat D, Section 6, Lot 7, Grave 4.[111] Richard then married Grace Lillian Murray Cummings on 15 November 1974 in Salt Lake City.[112] Family lore was that Grace and Richard had become close during the time that Evelyn had been ill and that Grace had helped care for Evelyn, perhaps as a Hospice Volunteer. Grace Murray was born on 1 September 1912 in New York. She was the daughter of David James Murray and Elizabeth Klein. She also went by the name of Pat and was called "The Angel Lady". She had previously married Kenneth James Cummings in 1934 in Colorado Springs in El Paso County, Colorado. Richard and Grace were listed in the City Directory as living at 5237 Hillsden Drive in Salt Lake City on 16 November, 1974.[113]

Richard died on 17 February 1982 in Salt Lake City at his home.[114] He was buried with a graveside service on 20 February 1982 in Mount Calvary Catholic Cemetery in Salt Lake City in Plat D, Section 6, Lot 7, Grave 3 with Rev. Charley conducting the service.[115]

Grace died on 15 September 2005 at her home in Utah, at age 93. Funeral services were held on 17 September 2005 at 5600 South Vine Street in Murray City with burial in the Murray City Cemetery.[116]

Richard H. and Evelyn M. Brashear
Mount Calvary Catholic Cemetery
Salt Lake City, Utah

Estella Zalame Brashear (1908-1996)

Daughter of Richard Levi Brashear and Della Zoleme Campbell
Mother of Taylor Cosby Cottrell, Jr.

Estella Zalame Brashear was born on 28 May 1908 in Bowling Green in Warren County, Kentucky. She was the daughter of Richard Levi Brashear and Della Zoleme Campbell. She was also known as Zalame.[117] Information on Zalame and her Family, and Zalame's life history, along with that for her husband Taylor Cosby Cottrell, Sr., and their two children is covered in detail in Section 1, Chapter 4, Taylor Cosby Cottrell, Sr. Family.

Chapter 4 – Richard D Crutchfield Family

2nd Great-grandfather of Taylor Cosby Cottrell, Jr.

Richard D. Crutchfield
b. 1782
　Henrico Co., KY
d. 7 Apr 1843
　Boyle Co., KY

Son of
William D. Crutchfield
Agnes D. Sevier

Elizabeth Jane Crutchfield
b. 14 Nov 1814; KY
d. 26 Feb 1875; TN

Robert Russell McKinney
b. 11 May 1810; KY
d. 25 Sep 1876; KY

Martha Hope Crutchfield
b. circa 1821; KY
d. 6 Sep 1893; KY

Walter Curran Brashear
b. May 1824; KY
d. 10 Jun 1902; KY

Sarah Crutchfield
b. circa 1824; KY
d. after 1870

Agness C. Crutchfield
b. 21 Mar 1825; KY
d. 17 Apr 1856; KY

Jonathan B. Nichols
b. 4 May 1824; KY
d. 10 Jun 1902; KY

Anne Wheeleer
b. 1791
　Fort Cumberland, MD
d. after 1860
　Boyle Co., KY

Daughter of
Henry Wheeler

Emma M. Crawford
b. Nov 1836; KY
d. 1909; KY

Emmeline Crutchfield
b. circa 1827; KY
d. 1909; KY

Johnathan R. Nichols
b. circa 1824; KY
d. 1898; KY

Rachel A. Crutchfield
b. 1830; KY
d. unknown

Richard Ann Crutchfield
b. 26 Aug 1831; KY
d. 9 Apr 1923; KY

Ralph Georgi
b. 1833; Germany
d. 2 Nov 1898; KY

Ann Crutchfield
b. 1836; KY
d. unknown

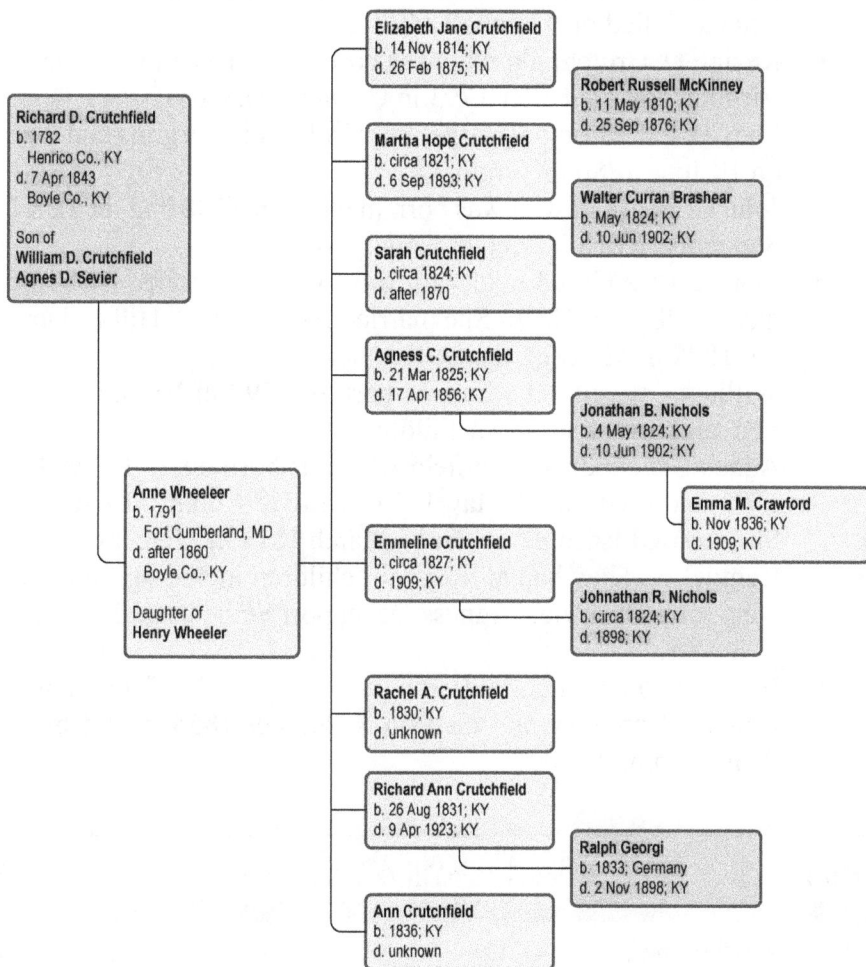

Richard D. Crutchfield was born in 1782 in Richmond in Henrico County, Virginia. He was the son of William D. Crutchfield and Agnes D. Sevier.

Richard's father William was born in 1751 and died on 27 March 1807 in Boyle County, Kentucky. His mother Agnes was born in Virginia and died on 11 June 1831 in Boyle County, Kentucky.[1] William and Agnes moved to Danville, Kentucky before 1797 where William bought 80 acres of land from George Caldwell on 28 November 1797.[2] Will and Agnes were both buried in Bellevue Cemetery in Danville in

Boyle County, Kentucky.[3] Richard had at least eight brothers and sisters including:

- Joanna Crutchfield who was born on 18 December 1775 in Virginia and died on 13 June 1849.[4]
- Keziah D. Crutchfield who was born on 18 December 1775 in Virginia and died after 1793 in Champaign, Ohio.[5]
- Lucy B. Crutchfield who was born in 1784 in Virginia and died on 10 June 1880 in Virginia.[6]
- John Crutchfield who was born in October 1788 and died on 7 September 1818 in Mercer County, Kentucky.[7]
- Martha Jane Crutchfield who was born in October 1788 and died on 28 May 1867. She married Alexander P. Hill in January 1808 in Mercer County, Kentucky.[8]
- William Crutchfield who was born in 1790 in Virginia, married, and had at least two children.[9]
- Agnes Davenport Crutchfield who was born on 23 December 1793 and died on 24 May 1873 in Boyle County, Kentucky. She married Isaac Sevier on 17 March 1814 in Mercer County, Kentucky. They had at least four children including, Jane Sevier, John D. Sevier, Agness Davenport Sevier, and Elizabeth T. Sevier.[10]
- Benjamin F. Crutchfield who was born in 1797 in Mercer County, Kentucky and died on 4 October 1855 in Pittsburg, Pennsylvania.[11]

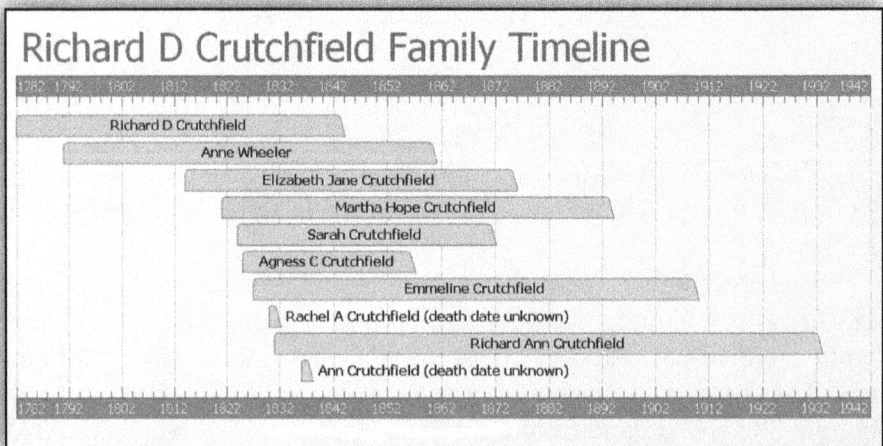

Richard D Crutchfield Family Timeline

Richard married Anne Wheeler on 17 July 1807 in Mercer County, Kentucky. Anne was born in 1791 in Fort Cumberland, Maryland. She was the daughter of Henry Wheeler and was also known as Elizabeth.[12] On 27 January 1816 Richard bought a 5-acre lot from pioneer James Brown in Danville, Kentucky on Dillehay and Fackler streets. Three years later he added another 29 acres to the property. The long yard ran back several hundred feet from Fourth Street and approached through a growth of sugar maples and other native trees.[13]

Anne Wheeler

The Crutchfield home was originally a two story mansion and during the Civil War was used, for a time, as a military hospital. Richard was one of the original subscribers to an Academy Fund in Danville that was formed for the benefit of the College of Kentucky in January 1818. He pledged $100 to the fund.[14]

Richard and Anne had a total of at least ten children including Elizabeth Jane Crutchfield, Emmeline Crutchfield, Martha Hope Crutchfield, Sarah Crutchfield, Agness C. Crutchfield, Rachel A. Crutchfield, Richard Ann Crutchfield, and Ann Crutchfield.[15]

Richard was listed on the 1820 census in Mercer County, Kentucky as Richard Crutchfield. The census listed a total of 11 free white persons, 5 of which were under 16 and 4 of which were over 25 and a total of 6 slaves living in the household.[16]

It is likely that he was listed on the 1830 census in Shaker in Mercer County transcribed as Rich. Butchfield. It is believed this transcription was an error as the last name appears to be Crutchfield. The transcription lists a total of 18 free white persons and 9 slaves.[17]

Richard was listed on the 1840 census in Danville in Mercer County as Richd. D. Crutchfield. The census listed a total of 13 free white persons, 11 of which were under 20 and a total of 9 slaves in the household.[18]

Richard died on 7 April 1843 in Danville, Kentucky. He was buried on 2 May 1843 in Bellevue Cemetery in Danville in Section 2, Lot 2.[19] An administrator bond was posted in the sum of $10,000 in the Circuit Court of Boyle County on 12 June 1843 appointing David A. Rufree, James P. Crutchfield, and Robert Rufree as administrators of his estate.[20]

Anne was listed on the 1850 census in Boyle County enumerated on 8 August 1850, as Ann Crutchfield, age 59 along with Sarah Crutchfield, age 26, Rachel A. Crutchfield, age 20, and Ann Furr, age 14. Real estate was valued at $3,000. On the 1850 Boyle County Slave Schedule Anne was listed as owning a total of 7 slaves ranging in ages from 8 to 48 and including 4 males and three females.[21]

On the 1860 Slave Schedule in Boyle County Ann Crutchfield was listed as owning three slaves, two females and one male.[22] She was listed on the 1860 population schedule census in Boyle County as Ann Crutchfield, age 69 along with Sally Crutchfield, age 34, Alice Graham, age 14, John Graham, age 11, Gral Graham, age 7, and Virgil Garrison, age 6. Real estate was valued at $3,200 and personal estate was listed as $1,000.[23]

Anne died sometime circa 1860 in Danville in Boyle County, Kentucky.

Elizabeth Jane Crutchfield (1814-1868)

Daughter of Richard D. Crutchfield and Anne Wheeler
Great-grandaunt of Taylor Cosby Cottrell, Jr.

Elizabeth Jane Crutchfield was born on 14 November 1814 in Boyle County, Kentucky. She was the daughter of Richard D. Crutchfield and Anne Wheeler.[24] Elizabeth married Dr. Robert Russell McKinney on 19 July 1832 in Danville. Robert was born on 11 May 1810 in Lincoln County, Kentucky.[25]

Elizabeth appeared on the census of 1850 in the household of her husband Robert McKinney, age 40 in Lincoln County, Tennessee, as Elizabeth, age 36 along with Joel, age 16, Martha, age 12, John, age 10, Charles, age 8, Henry Clay, age 6, Elvira, age 4, and Robert, age 2. Real estate was valued at $4,000.[26]

She was listed on the 1860 census in Lincoln County in the home of her husband R.R. McKinney as Elizabeth, age 44. Children in the household included Joel, age 25, Charles, age 17, Every, age 13, Robert, age 11, Jane, age 8, and Mary, age 6. Robert was listed as a physician and Joel was listed as a grocery merchant. Real estate was valued at $6,000 and personal estate was valued at $6,400. Joel's personal estate was valued at $2,000.[27]

Children of Elizabeth Jane Crutchfield and Robert R. McKinney:

- Joel McKinney – Born in 1834 in Tennessee, likely in Lincoln County and died on 14 January 1892 in Fort Smith in Sebastian County, Arkansas.[28] Buried in Mount Airy United Methodist Church Cemetery in Hamblen County, Tennessee. He married Nancy A. Thompson on 2 September 1857 in Jefferson County, Tennessee.[29] Death and burial information on Nancy is unknown. Joel and Nancy had at least six children including[30]:

  o Benjamin Edward McKinney – Born on 9 November 1858 in Hamblen County, Tennessee and died on 31 May 1914 in Hamblen County. He was buried in Mount Airy United Methodist Church Cemetery in Hamblen County. Benjamin married Nancy A. Thompson in Hamblen County, Tennessee on 9 November 1958.[31]

  o Sarah A. McKinney – Born around 1863 in Tennessee.[32]

  o Martha H. McKinney – Born around 1866 and likely died between the 1870 and 1880 census.[33]

  o Mary E. McKinney – Born around 1866 in Tennessee.

  o Margaret A. McKinney – Born around 1868 in Tennessee.[34]

  o Rachel F. McKinney – Born on 27 September 1873 in Tennessee and died on 2 October 1952. She was buried in Mount Airy united Methodist Church Cemetery in Hamblen County. She married Joseph Day on 31 January 1892.[35]

  o Joel Elisha McKinney – Born on 7 May 1877 in Tennessee and died on 13 February 1958 in Knoxville in

Knox County, Tennessee. He was buried in Mount Airy United Methodist Church Cemetery.[36]

- Martha Cordelia McKinney – Born in 1839 in Tennessee, likely in Lincoln County.[37] Martha was listed on the 1850 census with her family in Lincoln County as Martha, age 12.[38] No additional information is known.
- John V. McKinney – Born on 4 December 1840 in Tennessee, likely in Lincoln County and died on 22 November 1923 in East Lake in Hamilton County, Tennessee. He was buried in Forest Hills Cemetery in Chattanooga in Hamilton County, Tennessee.[39] John married Mary Dana Kelso. Mary died on 22 September 1905 in Chattanooga, Hamilton County, Tennessee. She was buried in Forrest Hill Cemetery.[40] John and Mary had at least six children including[41]:
  - o Robert Jefferson McKinney – Born on 17 June 1870 in Tennessee and died on 22 September 1934 in Chattanooga, Tennessee. He was married and his wife's name was Sallie. He also went by the name of Jeffie. He was buried in West View Cemetery in Sweetwater, Tennessee.[42]
  - o Reuben D. McKinney – Born around 1874 in Tennessee and died on 5 March 1926 in Tuscaloosa, Alabama. He was a lumberman and was married and lived in Montgomery, Alabama at the time of his death. He also went by the name of Reubie.[43]
  - o Henry T. McKinney – Born on 22 November 1877 in Lincoln County, Tennessee and died on 1 February 1937 in Chattanooga, Tennessee. Buried in Forest Hills Cemetery.[44]
  - o James Kelso McKinney – Born on 8 April 1879 in Lincoln County, Tennessee and died on 11 September 1945 in Chattanooga, Tennessee.[45]
  - o John Vardaman McKinney – Born on 19 October 1882 in Tennessee and died on 4 January 1939 in Chattanooga in Hamilton County, Tennessee.[46]
  - o Dana Charles McKinney – Born on 26 July 1884 in Tennessee and died on 7 March 1960. He married Kathryn Simmons and they had at least one child,

Henry Kelso McKinney. In 1933 they lived on Lookout Mountain Road in Chattanooga.[47] Charles and Kathryn were both buried in Forest Hills Cemetery in Chattanooga.[48]

o Odell Marion McKinney – Born on 24 November 1887 in Fayetteville in Lincoln County, Tennessee[49] and died in 1947 in Pinellas County, Florida. Odell was buried in Forest Hills Cemetery in Chattanooga, Tennessee.[50]

- Charles D. McKinney – Born circa 1842 in Tennessee, likely in Lincoln County.[51] Listed on the 1860 census in Lincoln County with his family as Charles McKinney, age 17 and attending school.[52] No additional reliable information is known about Charles.

- Elvira McKinney – Born circa 1846 in Tennessee, likely in Lincoln County.[53] She was listed on the 1850 census in the home of Robert McKinney as Elvira Clay, age 4.[54] On the 1860 census in Lincoln County she was listed in the home of Robert as Every McKinney, age 13. Her brothers Henry and Robert were also listed on these census records with a last name of Clay in 1850 and McKinney in 1860. Either the 1850 census record was in error, or she was adopted by Robert McKinney between the 1850 and 1860 census.[55] No additional reliable information is known about Elvira.

- Dr. Henry Clay McKinney – Born on 12 December 1847 in Tennessee, likely Lincoln County and died on 15 June 1919 in Kerens in Navarro County, Texas, at age 71.[56] Cause of death was blood poison. He was buried in Jimmerson Cemetery in Navarro County. Henry was listed on the 1850 census in the household of Robert McKinney as Henry Clay, age 6 and in later records with a last name of McKinney. His brother Robert and sister Elvira were listed on the 1850 census with last names of Clay and on the 1860 census with last names of McKinney. Either the 1850 census record was in error, or Henry was adopted. Since his name at the time of his death was "Henry Clay McKinney" it seems most likely that he was adopted between 1850 and 1860.[57] It appears that Henry may have married twice. First, to Henrietta where he was listed on the 1880 census in Navarro County, Texas with five children including:

- o Lizze McKinney – Born around 1871 in Tennessee.[58] She was living with her father on the 1880 census in Navarro County, Texas and was listed as Lizze, age 9.
- o George McKinney – Born around 1874 in Tennessee.[59] He was living with his father on the 1880 census in Navarro County, Texas and was listed as George, age 6.
- o Pearl McKinney – Born in September 1877 in Tennessee.[60] She was living with her father on the 1900 census in Navarro County, Texas and was listed as Pearl, age 22.
- o Arthur D. McKinney – Born in June 1879 in Tennessee and likely died on 18 October 1937 in Navarro County, Texas. He likely married Mary M. McConnico and they had at least one child including Arthur D. McKinney, Jr. Arthur and Mary were both buried in Oakwood Cemetery in Corsicana in Navarro County, Texas.[61]
- o Ernest McKinney – Born around 1878 in Tennessee.[62]

A stepson Twosy Hines was also listed on the 1880 census.[63] By 1900 Henry had married his second wife Rebecca H. Sawyer and was listed on the 1900 census in Navarro County, Texas with an additional daughter:[64]

- o Orris Elanor McKinney – Born on 2 August 1882 in Texas and died on 4 May 1964 in Wichita Falls in Wichita County, Texas. She married Jessie E. Simmons and they had at least one child including Jessie E. Simmons, Jr.

Rebecca was still living at the time of his death. Additional information on Rebecca is unknown.

- Robert R. McKinney – Born circa 1848 in Tennessee, likely in Lincoln County.[65] He was listed on the 1850 census in Lincoln County as Robert Clay, age 2 and on the Lincoln County census in 1860 as Robert McKinney, age 11 and attending school. His brother Henry and sister Elvira were listed on the 1850 census with last names of Clay.[66] They were listed on the 1860 census with last names of McKinney.[67] Either the 1850 census was in error or they were adopted between 1850 and 1860.

- Jennie McKinney – Born circa 1851 in Lincoln County, Tennessee and died on 2 September 1914 in Fayetteville in Lincoln County, at age 63.[68] She was buried in Rose Hill Cemetery in Fayetteville in Lincoln County.[69] Jennie married Abednego S. Thomas on 7 November 1871.[70] He was born in 1841 and preceded Jennie in death in 1903. Abednego was also buried in Rose Hill Cemetery.[71] They apparently had no children.
- Mary Kercheval McKinney – Born on 12 March 1855 in Fayetteville in Lincoln County, Tennessee and died in Fayetteville on 25 August 1940, at age 85. She was buried in Rose Hill Cemetery in Fayetteville.[72] Mary married John Knight Williams on 7 November 1882 in Lincoln County.[73] John was born on 28 February 1853 in Alabama. John died on 6 November 1926 in Fayetteville and was buried in Rose Hill Cemetery.[74] John and Mary had at least one child:
  - Abednego Thomas Williams – Born on 14 August 1883 and died on 27 November 1970. He was buried in Rose Hill Cemetery in Fayetteville, Tennessee.[75] Abednego married Margaret Carter on 22 November 1911 in Lincoln, Tennessee.[76] Margaret was the daughter of Nelson Pierce Carter and Orra Lee. She was born on 16 March 1948 in Lincoln County and died on 4 June 1948 in Lincoln County. She was buried next to her husband Abednego in Rose Hill Cemetery.[77] Abednego and Margaret hat at least one child, Orra Carter Williams who was born on 8 February 1917 in Fayetteville, Tennessee and died on January the 1st in 1989. She married William North Pitner on 9 February 1946 in Lincoln County. They were both buried in Mount Hope Cemetery in Franklin in Williamson County, Tennessee.[78]

Elizabeth died on 26 February 1875, likely in Lincoln County, Tennessee. She was buried in Old Fayetteville City Cemetery in Fayetteville, Lincoln County, Tennessee.[79]

Robert died on 25 September 1876 in Fayetteville in Fayette County, Tennessee. Burial location is unconfirmed but it seems reasonable that it was in Old Fayetteville City Cemetery.[80]

Martha Hope Crutchfield (1821-1893)

Daughter of Richard D. Crutchfield and Anne Wheeler
Great-grandmother of Taylor Cosby Cottrell, Jr.

Martha Hope Crutchfield was born circa 1821 in Danville in Boyle County, Kentucky. She was the daughter of Richard D. Crutchfield and Anne Wheeler.[81] Information on Martha and her Family, and Martha's life history, along with that for her husband Walter Curran Brashear and their nine children is covered in detail in Section 2, Chapter 2, Walter Curran Brashear Family.

Sarah Crutchfield (1824-after 1870)

Daughter of Richard D. Crutchfield and Anne Wheeler
Great-grandaunt of Taylor Cosby Cottrell, Jr.

Sarah Crutchfield was born circa 1824 in Boyle County, Kentucky. She was the daughter of Richard D. Crutchfield and Anne Wheeler. Sarah appeared on the census of 1850 in the home of her mother Anne in Boyle County, Kentucky as Sarah, age 26.[82] On the 1870 census in Fayette County, Kentucky she was living in the household of her sister Richard Ann's husband Ralph Georgi, listed as Sarah Crutchfield, age 42.[83] Additional information is unknown.

Agness C. Crutchfield (1825-1856)

Daughter of Richard D. Crutchfield and Anne Wheeler
Great-grandaunt of Taylor Cosby Cottrell, Jr.

Agness C. Crutchfield was born on 21 March 1825 in Danville in Boyle County, Kentucky. She was the daughter of Richard D. Crutchfield and Anne Wheeler.[84] A bond for the marriage of Agness C. Crutchfield and Jonathan Ball Nichols was signed on 17 February 1846 in Boyle County by Jon B. Nichols and A.J.M. Shorty. Agness married Jonathan in Boyle County, Kentucky.[85] He was born in 1824 in Danville. Agness was listed on the 1850 census in the household of her husband Jonathan in Boyle County as Ann C., age 25 along with William S., age 2. Laws Hipperdaw, age 26 and a Bar Keeper were also listed in the household. Real estate was valued at $2,500.[86]

Variations in the spelling of the Nichols name, both in translation and even within individual documents, coupled with the large number of Nichols located in the Danville, and Boyle County area, have led to mistakes in both published works as well as the interpretation of original documents. In the case of the Crutchfield related Nichols lines this is compounded by the marriages of Agness to Jonathan B. Nichols and her sister Emmeline to Jonathan R. Nichols. Multiple sources were examined and used, rather than relying on individual sources, to determine the information that follows.

Children of Agness C. Crutchfield and Jonathan Ball Nichols:

- William S. Nichols – Born on 29 September 1848 in Danville in Boyle County, Kentucky and died on 3 February 1912 in Perryville in Boyle County, Kentucky, at age 63. His cause of death was prostatic hypertrophy.[87] He was buried on 6 February 1912 in Bellevue Cemetery in Danville.[88] William married Margaret Moore, the daughter of Dance M. Moore and Margaret Johnstone, circa 1881. Margaret was also known as Maggie and was born on 28 September 1860 in St. Louis, Missouri. Her father was born in Scotland.[89] Maggie died on 3 September 1938 in Midway in Woodford County, Kentucky, at age 77 years, 11 months, and 6 days. She was also buried in Bellevue Cemetery.[90] William and Maggie had at least five children including[91]:
  - Maria Nichols – Born in May 1883, likely in Boyle County.[92] She was listed on the 1900 census in the home of her father in Boyle County as Maria, age 17 and single.
  - Emma Nichols – Born in May 1885, likely in Boyle County.[93] She was listed on the 1900 census in the home of her father in Boyle County as Emma, age 15.
  - Daniel Moore Nichols – Born on 4 September 1887 in Brod Head in Rock Castle County, Kentucky.[94] He married Maud Pearch on 5 February 1917 in Summit County, Ohio. Maud was the daughter of Sylvester Pearch and Elsie Brooks.[95] In 1942 when he registered for the WWII Draft they were living in Akron, Ohio

and he was working for the Firestone Tire and Rubber
Company.

- o Jonathan Nichols – Born on 19 May 1890 in Boyle
  County and died on 26 September 1949 in Mercer
  County, Kentucky.[96] He registered for the WWI Draft
  on 20 July 1917 while working in Vernon Colorado as
  a Bank Bookkeeper. He was described as tall, medium
  build with blue eyes and light brown hair.[97] He was
  buried in Mercer County, Kentucky.
- o Irene Nichols – Born in July 1899 in Kentucky.[98] She
  was listed in the home of her father on the 1910 census
  in Boyle County as Jean, age 10.

- Richard G. Nichols – Born on 3 October 1851 in Boyle County,
  Kentucky and died on 4 March 1914 in Danville, Boyle
  County, Kentucky. He was buried in Bellevue Cemetery in
  Danville.[99] Richard's death certificate lists Emma Crawford
  as his mother which is an error on the part of the informant
  because Richard's father was still married to Agness Crutchfield at the time of Richard's birth. Richard was listed as
  divorced on his death certificate but was listed as single on the
  1910 census in Jefferson County, Kentucky.[100] No additional
  information is known about possible marriages or children.
- Reed S. Nichols – Born in 1853 in Danville, Boyle County,
  Kentucky and died in 1907 in Kentucky.[101] He was buried in
  Bellevue Cemetery in Danville.[102] He married Henrietta Dorothea Hommel, also known as Nettie Dorothea Hommel, on 30
  July 1876 in Danville.[103] Nettie was born in Lexington, Kentucky on 29 January 1854. She was the daughter of Henry
  Hommel, who was born in Germany, and Elizabeth Kennedy
  who was born in Scotland. In 1930 Nettie was listed on the
  census in Allegheny County, Pennsylvania in the household of
  her son-in-law George M. McLane, as Nettie Nichols, 76 and
  widowed.[104] Nettie died on 17 November 1935 in Mount Lebanon in Allegheny County, Pennsylvania. She was buried in
  Bellevue Cemetery in Danville, Kentucky.[105] Reed and Nettie
  had at least three children including[106]:
  - o Lowrie Nichols – Born on 28 June 1877 in Danville,
    and died on 29 March 1949 in Pittsburgh in Allegheny

County, Pennsylvania in the Hillsview Sanitarium. He apparently never married.[107]

o Reed Stoddard Nichols, Jr. – Born on 28 September 1878 in Danville and died on 9 August 1946 in North Franklin in Washington County, Pennsylvania in the Hillsview Sanitarium. He was listed as divorced on his death certificate. He was cremated on 12 August 1946.[108]

o Agnes Crutchfield Nichols – Born in September 1880 in Danville and died on 3 November 1955 in Mount Lebanon in Allegheny County, Pennsylvania.[109] She married George Mclure McLane on 21 April 1909 in Mulga in Jefferson County, Alabama.[110] They had at least one daughter who was named Dorothy. Funeral services were held for Agnes in Mount Lebanon, Pennsylvania before her body was shipped by train to Danville, for burial in Bellevue Cemetery. Active pallbearers were Henry L. Nichols, W. Barrett Nichols, John B. Nichols, Jr., John C. Nichols, John Nichols, III and Reed Nichols.[111]

Agness died on 17 April 1856 in Mercer County, Kentucky, at age 31. Her cause of death was apoplexy. She was buried in Bellevue Cemetery in Danville, Kentucky.[112]

Jonathan married Emma M. Crawford on 17 September 1866 in Boyle County.[113] Emma was born in November 1836 in Danville, Kentucky. She also went by the name of Emily.[114] Jonathan was listed on the 1870 census in Boyle County, Kentucky as Jna. B. Nichols, age 49 along with Emma C., age 33, William S., age 22, Richard C., age 19, Reed S., age 17, Fannie M., age 3, and Emma C., age 1. Real estate was valued at $2,500 and personal estate was listed as $1,750. Real estate value for Emma was listed as $2,500.

[115]Jonathan died on 25 April 1896 in Danville. He was buried in Bellevue Cemetery in Danville.[116] Emma died in 1909 in Boyle County. She was also buried in Bellevue Cemetery in Danville.[117]

Children of Jonathan B. Nichols and Emma M. Crawford:

▪ Fannie M. Nichols – Born in August 1867 in Boyle County, Kentucky and died on 16 June 1947 at her home in Danville,

Kentucky, at age 79 after having been an invalid for more than three years. She was buried in Bellevue Cemetery in Danville.[118] She never married.

- Emma Crawford Nichols – Born on 27 May 1869 in Boyle County and died on 1 August 1953 at McDowell Memorial Hospital in Danville, at age 84. Her funeral was held at 2:30 in the afternoon at the Stith Funeral Home in Danville with Dr. Jameson Jones, academic dean of Centre College, officiating.[119] She was buried in Bellevue Cemetery in Danville in Section 1, Lot 22.[120] Emma was a teacher in a school for the deaf in 1920 and 1930.[121] She never married.

- John B. Nichols – Born on 14 May 1870 in Danville, Boyle County, Kentucky and died on 10 July 1945 in Danville, at age 74. He was buried in Bellevue Cemetery in Danville.[122] He traveled to Haiti and Cuba in 1920.[123] He apparently never married.

- Mary Anne Nichols – Born on 1 December 1875 in Danville, Boyle County, Kentucky and died on 14 July 1954 in Ephraim MeDowell Memorial Hospital in Danville, Kentucky.[124] Funeral services were held at Stith Funeral Home with Dr. James M. Jones, academic dean of Centre College, and the Rev. Bruce Compton, pastor of the First Presbyterian Church officiating. She was buried in Cave Hill Cemetery in Louisville, Kentucky.[125] Mary married Harry Allan Shaw. Harry was born on 24 June 1881 in Louisville and died in 1921. He registered for the WWI Draft on 12 September 1918 and was described as medium height, medium build with dark gray eyes and black hair at the time. He was employed as a lawyer when he registered. He was also buried in Cave Hill Cemetery.[126] On the 1910 census they were listed without children. Number of children, if any, is unconfirmed.

- Samuel Harding Nichols – Born on 8 May 1878 in Boyle County and died 4 September 1948 in Sarasota, Florida. He was buried in Bellevue Cemetery in Danville, Kentucky.[127] He married Clarece McElroy after 1910. She was born on 2 August 1891 in Kentucky. Samuel was described as medium height with a medium build, light blue eyes and gray hair when he registered for the WWI Draft in 1918. He was living in

Danville at the time and employed as a cashier in the Boyle Bank and Trust Company of Danville. Clarece died on 21 April 1973 in Danville and was buried in Bellevue Cemetery.[128] Sam and Clarece had at least two children including:

o Samuel Harding Nichols, Jr. – Born on 1 May 1914 in Boyle County, Kentucky.[129] He married Margaret Howard on 24 September 1949. Samuel was employed as a professor of chemistry at the Alabama Polytechnic Institute at the time. In 1974 he retired after 30 years of work as a chemistry professor at Auburn University. Samuel and Margaret had at least two children, a daughter who graduated from Southwestern University at Memphis and a son who attended the U.S. Naval Academy with specialization in oceanography.[130]

o Clarece M. Nichols – Born on 11 December 1915 in Danville, Kentucky and died on 17 April 1950 in Danville. She was buried in Bellevue Cemetery in Danville. She graduated from the woman's department at Centre in 1936 and later took library work at Columbia University when she received the degree of bachelor of science in library science in 1937. In 1940 she was employed in the library at the University of Cincinnati.[131] Clarece married Jameson M. Jones who later served as academic dean of Centre College. Clarece and Jameson had at least two sons.[132]

Emmeline Crutchfield (1827-??)

Daughter of Richard D. Crutchfield and Anne Wheeler
Great-grandaunt of Taylor Cosby Cottrell, Jr.

Emmeline Crutchfield was born around 1827. She was the daughter of Richard D. Crutchfield and Anne Wheeler.[133] A bond for the marriage of Emmeline Crutchfield and Jonathan R. Nichols was signed on 16 November 1846 in Boyle County, Kentucky by Jonathan M. Nichols and Iona Nichols. She married Jonathan in November 1846.[134] Johnathan, also known as J.R. Nichols, was born around 1824 in Boyle County.

She was listed on the 1860 census in Boyle County in the household of Jonathan R. Nichols, as Emma, age 33. James, age 12, Jenny, age 8, Sally, age 7, Agnes, age 5, Walter, age 4, Alice, age 1, and Estelle, age 3/12.[135] Jonathan died in 1898, likely in Danville, Kentucky. He was buried in Bellevue Cemetery in Danville.[136] Emmeline likely died before 1900.

Variations in the spelling of the Nichols name, both in translation and even within individual documents, coupled with the large number of Nichols located in the Danville, and Boyle County area, have led to mistakes in both published works as well as the interpretation of original documents. In the case of the Crutchfield related Nichols lines this is compounded by the marriages of Emmeline to Jonathan R. Nichols and her sister Agness to Jonathan B. Nichols. Multiple sources were examined and used, rather than relying on individual sources, to determine the information that follows.

Children of Emmeline Crutchfield and Jonathan R. Nichols:

- James C. Nichols – Born in September 1848 in Danville in Boyle County, Kentucky and died on 19 May 1922 at Deacons Hospital in Louisville in Jefferson County, Kentucky, at age 73. He was buried on 21 May 1922 in Bellevue Cemetery in Danville in Section 1, Lot N1/2 25.[137] James married Catherine M. Farlee circa 1877. Catherine was also known as Katie. She was born in 1855 in Kentucky. Katie died on 13 September 1909 in Louisville. She was buried in Bellevue Cemetery in Danville, Kentucky.[138] James and Katie had at least one child including:
  o Ralph Hogan Nichols – Born on 3 November 1879 in Kentucky and died on 13 June 1880 in Kentucky. He was buried in Bellevue Cemetery in Danville.[139]
- Jennie Nichols – Born circa 1852 in Boyle County, Kentucky. She was listed on the 1860 census in Boyle County in the home of her father as Jenny, age 8 and attending school.[140] In 1870 she was found in the home of her father in Boyle County as Jennie, age 18.[141] No additional reliable information is known.
- Sallie M. Nichols – Born in 1853 in Danville, Kentucky and died on 25 February 1940 in San Antonio in Bexar County,

Texas. Her cause of death was cardiac failure following a ceberal hemorrhage.[142] She was buried in Bellevue Cemetery in Danville.[143] She married Louis H. Durham on 1 June 1875 in Boyle County, Kentucky.[144] Louis was born in 1851 in Boyle County and died on 4 March 1888 in Cincinnati, Kentucky. He was also buried in Bellevue Cemetery in Danville.[145] Sallie and Louis had at least three children including:

- o Martha M. Durham – Born on 10 March 1870 in Danville, Kentucky and died on 3 January 1957 in San Antonio in Bexar County, Texas. Her cause of death was a coronary occlusion. She was buried in Bellevue Cemetery in Danville, Kentucky.[146] Martha married Harold Powell Murray in 1879 in Brooklyn, New York. He was likely born on 8 November 1875 in Cincinnati, Ohio and registered for the WWI Draft while living in Cincinnati in 1918. He was described as tall with a stout build, gray eyes and gray hair at the time. In 1930 Martha and Harold were listed on the census in Hamilton County, Ohio with an adopted daughter named Edith Murray who was born about 1908.[147]
- o Emma J. Durham – Born in 1877 and died in 1887. She was buried in Bellevue Cemetery in Danville in Boyle County, Kentucky next to her brother Milton.[148]
- o Milton J. Durham – Born in 1879 and died in January 1880. He was buried in Bellevue Cemetery in Danville next to his sister Emma.[149]
- Agnes Nichols – Born in 1855 in Boyle County, Kentucky. She was listed on the 1860 census in Boyle County in the home of her father as Agnes, age 5.[150] It is likely she died before 1870 because she was not listed on the 1870 census.
- Walter B. Nichols – Born on 5 January 1857 in Kentucky and died on 29 July 1913 in Lexington in Fayette County, Kentucky at age 56 at his office. He was buried in Winchester Cemetery in Winchester, Clark County, Kentucky.[151] Walter was part owner of the Danville Tribune. Around 1892 he moved to Lexington and became associated with the Lexington Leader where he remained for about fifteen years before leaving the Leader to enter into the job printing business.[152] Walter

married Julia Bush circa 1882. Julia was born on 15 June 1863 also in Kentucky.[153] Julia Bush died on 10 February 1949 in Pulaski County, Arkansas. She was buried in Winchester Cemetery.[154] Walter and Julia had at least five children including[155]:

- o Tillie B. Nichols – Born in November 1884 in Kentucky. She married Leonidas Forister Barrier around 1910. Leonidas was born on 18 November 1884 and died on 9 January 1958. In 1910 Leonidas and Tillie were living in Little Rock in Pulaski County, Arkansas.[156] Leonidas was a military veteran and was buried in Rose Lawn Cemetery in Little Rock, Arkansas. Tillie was still living at the time of her husband's death.[157]

- o Julian Barrett Nichols – Born on 7 September 1886 in Danville, Kentucky and died on 28 November 1956 in Winchester in Clark County, Kentucky. He was buried in Winchester Cemetery in Clark County. He was described as tall with a slender build, blue eyes, and brown hair when he registered for the WWI Draft in 1917 while living in Lexington, Kentucky. He was working for the Chesapeake and Ohio Railroad at the time. Julian married Fannie Sue Bush prior to 1917. She was born in 1888 and died in 1963 in Clark County and was also buried in Winchester Cemetery next to her husband Julian.[158]

- o Janie June Nichols – Born in September 1885. She was a laboratory teacher at Hamilton College in Lexington, Kentucky and apparently living in a Boarding House at 603 North Broadway along with at 16 additional college employees.[159]

- o Margaret Nichols – Born in June 1890, likely on 21 June. She likely married Arthur Eddy Ferris who was born on 20 October 1893 in Decatur, New York and died on 30 July 1960. Margaret likely died on 21 January 1981 and was buried in Winchester Cemetery in Clark County, Kentucky Authur was also buried in Winchester Cemetery.[160]

○ Robert Lear Nichols – Born on 20 September 1893 in Kentucky and died on 9 April 1962.[161] He was described as medium height with a slender build, dark blue eyes and dark brown hair when he registered for the WWI Draft in 1917 while living in Lexington, Kentucky. Robert was married. His wife' name was Mabel. Robert was buried in White Chapel Memorial Park Cemetery in Troy in Oakland County, Michigan in the Temple of Memories Mausoleum, 2nnd floor, Section E.[162]

▪ Alice Nichols – Born on 21 October 1858 in Boyle County, Kentucky and died on 1 March 1940 in Wellington, Kansas.[163] She was listed on the 1860 census in Boyle County as Alice, age 1 and on the 1870 census of her father in Boyle County as Alice, age 11.[164] She was listed on the 1880 census of her father in Boyle County as Alice, age 21 and single.[165] Alice married George Ellis circa 1903 in Kansas. This was George's second marriage.[166] George and Alice apparently had no children. George died between the 1920 and 1930 census. Alice apparently died in her sleep and was found dead in bed the next morning. Funeral services were held for Alice on 5 March 1940 and she was buried in Prairie Lawn Cemetery in Wellington in Sumner County, Kansas.[167]

Alice Nichols

▪ Estelle Nichols – Born on 15 March 1860 in Danville, Boyle County, Kentucky and died on 15 January 1935 in Louisville, Jefferson County, Kentucky, at age 74. Her funeral was held at the residence of her brother John M. Nichols on South

Fourth Street in Danville. She was buried in Bellevue Cemetery in Danville.[168] She married W.G. Marks between 1880 and 1900. W.G. Marks died sometime before 1900.[169] They had at least two children including:

- o Lowrie Nicholas Marks – Born on 15 December 1887 in Danville and died on 15 January 1964 in Hardin County, Kentucky. He was described as tall with a slender build, blue eyes and light hair when he registered for the draft in 1917 while working as an electrician and living in Danville. He was buried in Bellevue Cemetery in Danville.[170]
- o Mary Dowling Marks – Born on 4 February 1886 in Danville and died on 22 August 1952 in the Wessinger Gaulbert Apartments in Louisville in Jefferson County, Kentucky. She was buried in Bellevue Cemetery in Danville.[171] She was also known as May Marks and never married.

- Jeremiah Boyle Nichols – Born on 1 March 1862 in Boyle County, Kentucky and died on 1 June 1944, likely in Aberdeen, Mississippi. He was buried in Bellevue Cemetery in Danville in Boyle County.[172] He was more commonly known as, and listed in records as J. Boyle Nichols or simply Boyle Nichols. However his full name was included in his obituary published in the Advocate-Messenger in Danville, Kentucky on 3 June 1944. He married

Jeremiah Boyle Nichols

twice, first to Cora VanPelt in 1891 in Boyle County and later to his second wife Edmonia who was from Aberdeen, Mississippi. She was the daughter of Danville's former postmaster

S.D. VanPelt and Florence VanPelt. Cora died on 2 December 1902 in Boyle County, at age 33 and was buried in Bellevue Cemetery.[173] Boyle and Edmonia has no children.[174] However, Boyle and Cora had at least four children including:

- o Harrod A. Nichols – Born in February 1893 in Kentucky, likely in Boyle County. He also went by the name of Henry and in 1944 was a Major in the Army stationed at Bowman Field near Louisville, Kentucky.[175] Harrod married and had at least two children with his wife Lilla.[176]

- o Alice L. Nichols – Born in February 1893 in Kentucky, likely in Boyle County and died before 1944.[177]

- o Leslie Nichols – Likely born in Danville before 1900 (not listed on 1900 census). Died before the obituary on J. Boyle was published in 1944. No additional information is known.[178]

- o Florence Elizabeth Nichols – Born on 19 February 1899 in Kentucky and died on 9 June 1987 in Stanislaus County, California. She was buried in Lakewood Memorial Park in Hughson in Stanislaus County. Florence married Henry Jesse Orr.[179] Henry was born on 28 January 1898 in Rice County, Minnesota and died on 27 August 1969 in Stanislaus County, California. He was also buried in Lakewood Memorial Park.[180]

- John Monroe Nichols – Born on 18 August 1864 in Danville, Kentucky and died on 9 January 1942 in Boyle County, at age 77. Funeral services were held in the Methodist Church with the pastor, Dr. Adolphus Gilliam, officiating. He was buried on 11 January in Bellevue Cemetery in Danville in Section AA, Lot 13.[181] John was a life-long member of the Methodist church, served as a member of the Board of Stewards, and was a past commander of Ryan Commandery No. 17, Knights Templar. He also held the highest office in each of the other Masonic bodies.[182] John married Boone Bush, the daughter of Tillie Clay Smith, in 1891. Boon Bush died on 29 May 1944 in Boyle County, Kentucky at age 76. Her cause of death was pulmonary tuberculosis. She was buried on 31 May 1944 in

Bellevue Cemetery in Danville in Section AA, Lot 13.[183] Pallbearers were Mayor Henry L. Bush, Barrett Nichols, John L. Durham, Lowrie Marks, Julian B. Nichols, Harrod Nichols and Lear Nichols, all sons and nephews of Boon Bush.[184] Following her death, the City Council of Danville offered resolutions honoring her for being a model wife, saintly mother, and

Walter Barrett Nichols

devoted member of her church.[185] John and Boone had at least three children including:[186]

- o Henry L. Nichols – Born on 4 August 1891 in Danville, Kentucky and died on 29 March 1971 in Boyle Country, Kentucky.[187] Henry married Jewel Beckham. He was described as tall with a slender build, blue eyes and light hair and employed by a Laundry when he registered for the WWI Draft in 1917. He was also serving as mayor of Danville when his mother died in 1944.
- o Walter Barrett Nichols – Born on 21 June 1894 in Kentucky, likely in Boyle County, and died on 17 October 1978. He was buried in Bellevue Cemetery in Danville, Kentucky.[188] Walter was described as tall with a slender build, blue eyes and light hair when he registered for the WWI Draft in 1917. He was working as a clerk for a laundry in Danville at the time.
- o Richard Bush Nichols – Born on 21 July 1894 in Danville, Kentucky and died on 21 July 1959 in Boyle County. He was described as medium height with a slender build, blue eyes, and brown hair when he registered for the WWI Draft in 1917 while living in Danville and working as the manager in a laundry. He married Hattie Arnold around 1915. She was born on

14 September 1893 in Washington, Kentucky and died on 4 July 1944 in Boyle County. They had at least two children including Mary B. Nichols and Robert A. Nichols. Richard and Hattie were both buried in Bellevue Cemetery in Danville.[189]

- Pattie Nichols – Born 6 August 1879 in Boyle County, Kentucky and died at 12:30 in the morning 14 May 1962 in Elmhurst Nursing Home in Harrodsburg. Funeral services were held at the Second Presbyterian Church with the Rev. Joseph O. Rand, pastor of the church, officiating. She was buried in Bellevue Cemetery in Danville in Boyle County.[190]

Rachel A. Crutchfield (1830-??)

Daughter of Richard D. Crutchfield and Anne Wheeler
Great-grandaunt of Taylor Cosby Cottrell, Jr.

Rachel A. Crutchfield was born in 1830 in Boyle County, Kentucky. She was the daughter of Richard D. Crutchfield and Anne Wheeler. She was listed on the 1850 census in the household of her mother Anne in Boyle County, Kentucky as Rachel A., age 20.[191] No additional information is known about Rachel.

Richard Ann Crutchfield (1831-1923)

Daughter of Richard D. Crutchfield and Anne Wheeler
Great-grandaunt of Taylor Cosby Cottrell, Jr.

Richard Ann Crutchfield was born on 26 August 1831 in Kentucky. She was the daughter of Richard D. Crutchfield and Anne Wheeler.[192] A bond for the marriage of Richard Ann Crutchfield and Ralph Georgi was signed on 5 June 1860 in Danville by Ralph Georgi and J.R. Nichols.[193] Ralph was born in 1833 in Germany. He was a professor of music by trade. Richard Ann was listed on the 1860 census in Boyle County in the home of her husband as

Ralph Georgi

Richard Ann, age 27. Real estate was valued at $500.[194] In 1870 she was listed on the census in Fayette County, Kentucky in the home of her husband as Richi. Ann, age 35. Annie, age 7 was also listed as was her sister Sarah Crutchfield, age 42.[195]

Children of Richard Ann Crutchfield and Ralph Georgi:

- Anna Georgi – Born circa 1861 in Kentucky and died on 2 October 1941 at Good Samaritan Hospital in Lexington in Fayette County, Kentucky. Her cause of death was complications from a fractured hip coupled with old age. She was buried on 17 October 1941 in Lexington Cemetery in Lexington, Kentucky.[196] She was also known as Anie W. and Hannah.

Anna Georgi

Ralph died on 2 November 1898 in Lexington, Kentucky at his home at 85 West 4th Street. His cause of death was cystitis. He was buried in Lexington Cemetery in Lexington, Kentucky.[197] Richard Ann died on 9 April 1923 in Lexington, at age 91 years, 7 months, and 14 days. Her cause of death was old age. She was buried on 12 April 1923 in Lexington Cemetery in Lexington, Kentucky in Section 10, Lot 98, Part SW1/2.[198]

Ann Crutchfield (1836-after 1850)

Daughter of Richard D. Crutchfield and Anne Wheeler
Great-grandaunt of Taylor Cosby Cottrell, Jr.

Ann Crutchfield was born in 1836 in Boyle County, Kentucky. She was the daughter of Richard D. Crutchfield and Anne Wheeler. She was listed on the 1850 census in Boyle County, Kentucky in the home of her mother as Ann, age 14. No additional information on Ann is known.[199]

Chapter 5 – John Sale Campbell Family

2nd Great-grandfather of Taylor Cosby Cottrell, Jr.

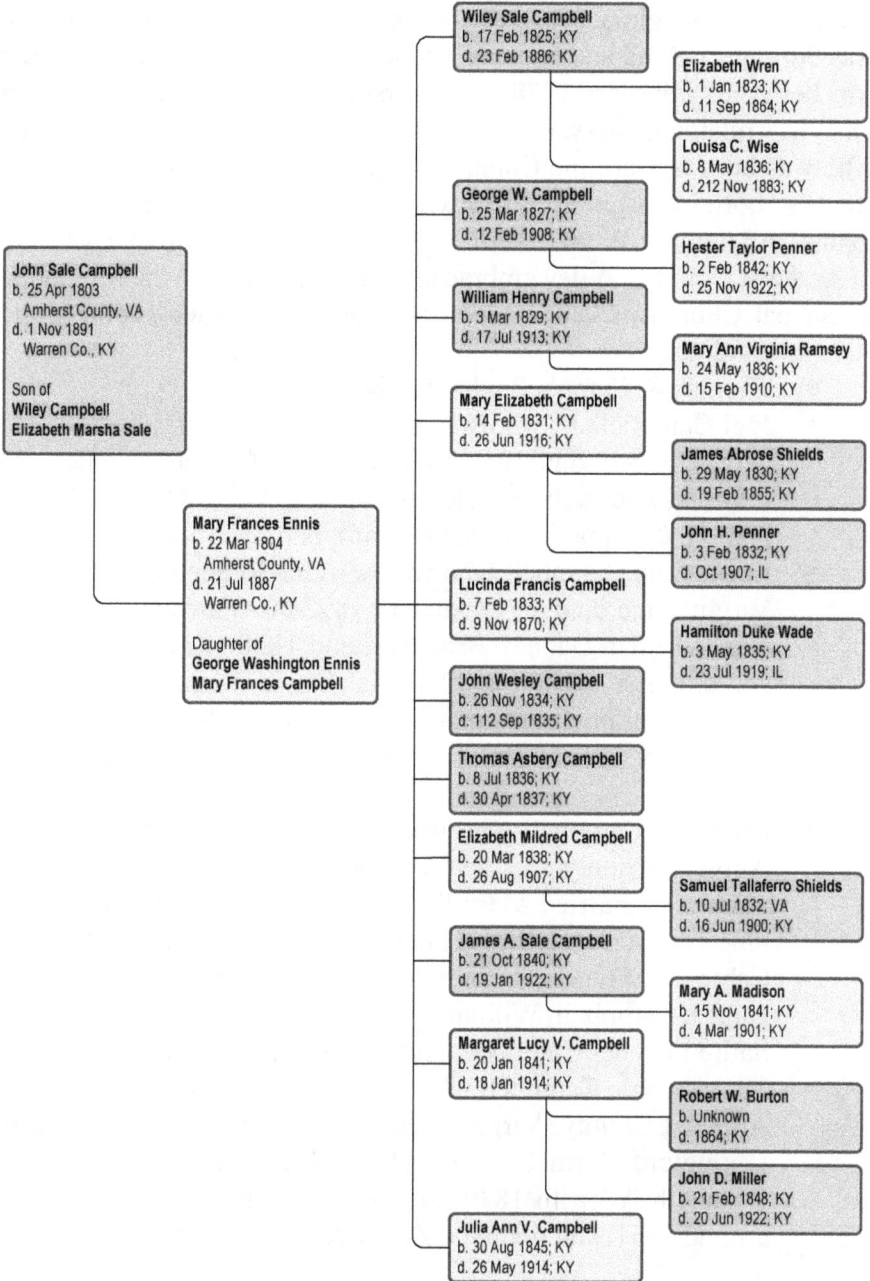

John Sale Campbell
b. 25 Apr 1803
 Amherst County, VA
d. 1 Nov 1891
 Warren Co., KY

Son of
Wiley Campbell
Elizabeth Marsha Sale

Mary Frances Ennis
b. 22 Mar 1804
 Amherst County, VA
d. 21 Jul 1887
 Warren Co., KY

Daughter of
George Washington Ennis
Mary Frances Campbell

Wiley Sale Campbell
b. 17 Feb 1825; KY
d. 23 Feb 1886; KY

Elizabeth Wren
b. 1 Jan 1823; KY
d. 11 Sep 1864; KY

Louisa C. Wise
b. 8 May 1836; KY
d. 212 Nov 1883; KY

George W. Campbell
b. 25 Mar 1827; KY
d. 12 Feb 1908; KY

Hester Taylor Penner
b. 2 Feb 1842; KY
d. 25 Nov 1922; KY

William Henry Campbell
b. 3 Mar 1829; KY
d. 17 Jul 1913; KY

Mary Ann Virginia Ramsey
b. 24 May 1836; KY
d. 15 Feb 1910; KY

Mary Elizabeth Campbell
b. 14 Feb 1831; KY
d. 26 Jun 1916; KY

James Abrose Shields
b. 29 May 1830; KY
d. 19 Feb 1855; KY

John H. Penner
b. 3 Feb 1832; KY
d. Oct 1907; IL

Lucinda Francis Campbell
b. 7 Feb 1833; KY
d. 9 Nov 1870; KY

Hamilton Duke Wade
b. 3 May 1835; KY
d. 23 Jul 1919; IL

John Wesley Campbell
b. 26 Nov 1834; KY
d. 112 Sep 1835; KY

Thomas Asbery Campbell
b. 8 Jul 1836; KY
d. 30 Apr 1837; KY

Elizabeth Mildred Campbell
b. 20 Mar 1838; KY
d. 26 Aug 1907; KY

Samuel Tallaferro Shields
b. 10 Jul 1832; VA
d. 16 Jun 1900; KY

James A. Sale Campbell
b. 21 Oct 1840; KY
d. 19 Jan 1922; KY

Mary A. Madison
b. 15 Nov 1841; KY
d. 4 Mar 1901; KY

Margaret Lucy V. Campbell
b. 20 Jan 1841; KY
d. 18 Jan 1914; KY

Robert W. Burton
b. Unknown
d. 1864; KY

John D. Miller
b. 21 Feb 1848; KY
d. 20 Jun 1922; KY

Julia Ann V. Campbell
b. 30 Aug 1845; KY
d. 26 May 1914; KY

John Sale Campbell was born on 25 April 1803 in Amherst County, Virginia near the Amherst Court House.[1] John was the son of Wiley Campbell and Elizabeth Marsha. His father Wiley was born on 8 July 1772 in Amherst County and died on 3 February 1842 in Amherst County, Virginia, at age 69. He was the son of Joel Campbell who was born in England and Nancy Elizabeth Mills. His mother Elizabeth was born on 7 February 1778 in Amherst County and died on 1 March 1843 in Amherst County, at age 65. She was the daughter of John Sale who was born in Caroline County, Virginia and Frances Sanders who was also born in Virginia. Wiley was also known as Wesley according to his son Thomas. Wiley and Elizabeth married on 18 November 1800 in Amherst County. Wiley embraced religion and joined the Methodist Episcopal Church in 1805.[2] John Sale had at least ten brothers and sisters including:

- Thomas S. Campbell who was born in 1801.[3]
- Joel Campbell Jr. who was born in 1802 in Virginia and died between 1841 and 1850. He married Elizabeth Fulcher and they had at least three children including Wiley Campbell, William H. Campbell, and James Campbell.[4]
- Lewis Sale Campbell who was born on 30 September 1804 in Virginia and died on 17 January 1892 in Amherst County. He married Eliza Dabney Brown around 1828. They had at least six children including Cornelia Lewis Campbell, Mildred Brown Campbell, Thomas Horace Campbell, Lucian Campbell, Lucy Ann Eliza Campbell, and Bernard Brightberry Campbell.[5]
- Gustavus Campbell who was born on 21 November 1808 in Amherst County and died on 7 May 1905 in Lynchburg, Virginia. He married Mary Elizabeth Horton. They had at least nine children including Thomas I. Campbell, Mary Elizabeth Campbell, Francis C. Campbell, James Wiley Campbell, Margaret J. Campbell, William A. Campbell, Mildred L. Campbell, Sallie Fletcher Campbell, and Lawrence Gary Campbell.[6]
- Thomas Sale Campbell who was born on 3 November 1810 in Amherst County, Virginia and died on 28 December 1888 in Lexington, North Carolina. He married three times, first to Elizabeth Allen in 1839, then to Mary (last name unknown) around 1851, and finally to Adelaide Lawrence Dupey in 1854.

He had at least three children with Elizabeth including Thomas Crawford Campbell, Catherine Campbell, and Elizabeth Campbell. He also had at least one child with his last wife Adelaide who was named Lizzie Campbell.[7]

- Mildred Campbell who was born in 1814 in Amherst County and died on 27 June 1884 in Amherst County. She married Joel Bethel. They had at least five children including Lelia Bethel, Robert M. Bethel, Thomas Howard Bethel, Cornelia Jane Bethel, and Carmelia J. Bethel.[8]
- Elizabeth Anne Campbell who was born in 1816 in Virginia. She married William P. Woodruff. They had at least nine children including William Alexander Woodruff, James Wiley Woodruff, Mildred E. Woodruff, Mary F. Woodruff, David E. Woodruff, Paulus P. Woodruff, Joel E. Woodruff, John T. Woodruff, and Thomas W. Woodruff.[9]
- Alexander Mills Campbell who was born on 11 August 1818 and died on 21 February 1870 in Virginia. He married Martha Ann Dinwiddie. They had at least ten children including Delia Allen Campbell, Ethelbert Bertram Campbell, Alexander Rufus Campbell, John Wiley Campbell, Robert Cornelius Campbell, Bettie Marshall Campbell, Cornelia Murrell Campbell, Joseph Dinwiddie Campbell, Mary Alexander Campbell, Willie Adelaide Campbell.[10]
- Elizabeth M. Campbell who was born in 1821 in Virginia and died before 1860 in Amherst County, Virginia. She married John Smith Tucker. They had at least five children including Sarah E. Tucker, Mildred A. Tucker, John Wilbur Tucker, Lewis C. Tucker, and Cornelius S. Tucker.[11]
- J. Wiley Campbell who was born in 1825 in Virginia and died on 18 August 1894 in Clarksville in Pike County, Missouri. He married Martha Ann Fox. They had at least nine children including Anna Cora Campbell, Ella Campbell, Mary Campbell, Mattie D. Campbell, Sudie Ledbetter Campbell, Bascom Campbell, Ivy Campbell, Thomas Bascom Campbell, and David Ivy Campbell.[12]

John Sale was a millwright and farmer. He immigrated to Kentucky in 1821 when he traveled from Virginia by horseback with his uncle Joel Allcock. The trip took several weeks and was over the mountains and through dense forests. He had inherited slaves and brought them on the trip. One Negro boy named Ellis Campbell rode behind him all the way to Bowling Green, Kentucky. John spent the first winter with his uncle and worked at his saw mill for twenty-five cents per day and board.[13]

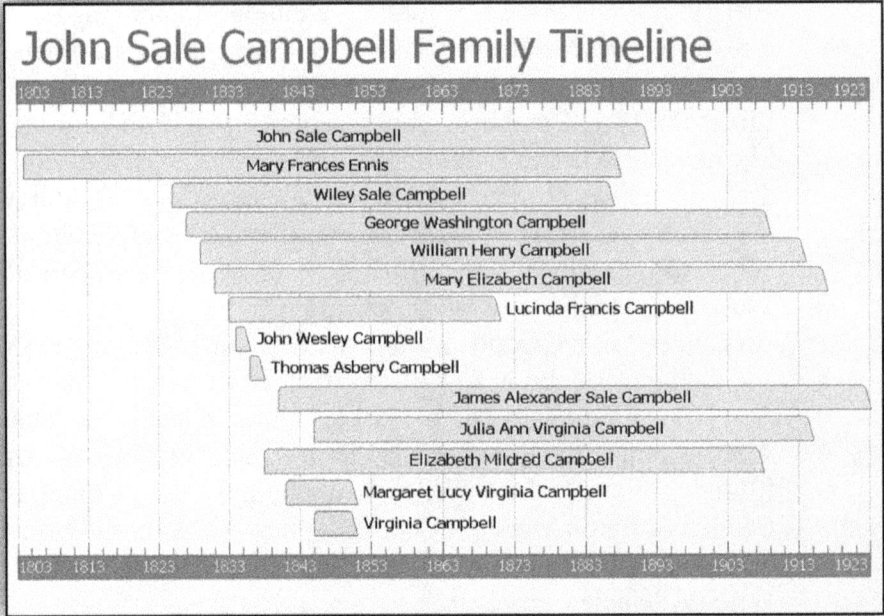

John Sale Campbell Family Timeline

John Sale Campbell
Mary Frances Ennis
Wiley Sale Campbell
George Washington Campbell
William Henry Campbell
Mary Elizabeth Campbell
Lucinda Francis Campbell
John Wesley Campbell
Thomas Asbery Campbell
James Alexander Sale Campbell
Julia Ann Virginia Campbell
Elizabeth Mildred Campbell
Margaret Lucy Virginia Campbell
Virginia Campbell

A bond for the marriage of John Sale Campbell was signed on 7 March 1824 in Bowling Green in Warren County in the sum of 50 pounds by John S. Campbell and George Ennis.[14] John married Mary Frances Ennis, the daughter of George Washington Ennis and Mary Frances Campbell on 11 March 1824 in Warren County near Rich Pond.[15] Mary Frances Ennis was born on 4 June 1804 in Nelson County, Virginia.[16] She and her parents had traveled in a caravan of wagons that left Amherst in 1805. The migration westward included the families of Ennis, Campbell, Page, Martin, Swinney, Allcock and others. According to family lore a trunk, which was later passed down to Zalame Cottrell and painted by her with original "Peter Hunt" designs, was brought from Virginia by Frances's parents on the wagon train and was then used by Frances to store her most prized possessions. The Ennis family settled south of Bowling Green, near Rich Pond

Grove.[17] Although not proven it is likely that John and Mary were part of the Ennis and Campbell families that joined the wagon caravan.

Mary's father George was born in 1770 in Amherst County, Virginia and died on 15 June 1835 in Rich Pond in Warren County.[18] Her mother Mary Frances was born on 12 September 1777 in Amherst County, Virginia and died on 16 September 1823 in Warren County. They were buried in the Ennis Cemetery in Rich Pond.[19]

Trunk belonging to Mary Frances Ennis

Mary had at least seven brothers and sisters by her father's first marriage to her mother Mary Frances including:

- Cornelius Ennis who was born in 1797 in Virginia and died before 1887. He married Mary Polly Johnson on 12 November 1817 in Warren County, Kentucky.[20]
- John Ennis who was born on 4 January 1800 in Amherst County and died on 9 August 1826 in Warren County. He married Nancy Butt. They had at least two children including James Rumsey Ennis and John W. Ennis.[21]
- Margaret Ennis who was born on 17 March 1801 in Amherst County, Virginia and died on 1 June 1888 in Warren County. She married James Dishman. They had at least six children including Ewing Dishman, Harvey Dishman, John Dishman, Sarah Dishman, Elizabeth Dishman, and Nancy Dishman.[22]
- Sarah Ennis who was born on 1 October 1810 in Warren County and died on 27 October 1887 in Warren County. She married William K. Phelps. They had at least thirteen children including James Riley Phelps, Mary F. Phelps, Wm. H. Phelps, John Wesley Phelps, Margaret E. Phelps, Louisa A. Phelps, Amanda W. Phelps, Joseph C. Phelps, Jane Ann Phelps, Georga Ann Phelps, Julia Ann Phelps, Thomas J. Phelps, and Millard Filmore Phelps.[23]

- Elizabeth Ennis who was born in 1813 in Kentucky and died after July 1887. She married Richard Breedlove. They had at least nine children including George Ann Breedlove, J.P. Breedlove, E.A. Breedlove, W. Henry Breedlove, Emiline E. Breedlove, Caroline E. Breedlove, J.T. Breedlove, Ewin Breedlove, and Jessie M. Breedlove.[24]
- Willis D. Ennis was born on 22 October 1816 in Warren County and died on 4 September 1898 in Carthage in Jasper County, Missouri. He married Caroline J. Hinds. They had at least ten children including James Richard Ennis, Mary Ellen Ennis, John Summerfield Ennis, Ann Elizabeth Ennis, Lucy Frances Ennis, Emoline Rebecca Ennis, George Kelly Ennis, William Payne Ennis, Edward Hines Ennis, and Augusta Caroline Ennis.[25]
- George Washington Ennis, Jr. who was born in 1819 and died before 1887.

Mary had at least two half-siblings from her father's second marriage to Matilda Allcock on 23 April 1824 including:

- Joseph Renolds Ennis who was born on 27 February 1825 in Warren County and died on 11 August 1848 in Warren County.[26]
- William Tennant Ennis who was born on 20 August 1826 in Warren County and died on 30 January 1862 in Warren County. He married Nancy Mandane Gatewood. They had at least six children including Victoria Josephine Ennis, Joseph Marshall Ennis, Mary Thomas Ennis, William Franklin Ennis, Emma Bell Ennis, and John Willis Ennis.[27]

John bought a farm of sixty acres near the John Butt's place and began housekeeping shortly after their marriage. The house consisted of two rooms with a stack chimney and was furnished with an old fashioned four poster cherry bed, a tripod, and a cherry bench. Hanks of spun cotton, wool, flax and tow were hung on wood pins. A box nailed to the wall that was fitted with shelves served as a kitchen cabinet. The dining table was a bail box that held the bride's table ware that consisted of pewter plates, a mug, one fork and two knives one of which was made of wood.[28]

John served an apprenticeship with Samuel Vontress in the Mill Wright's trade and later built his first mill for Peter Lawrence three miles from Woodburn, Kentucky on a big spring that emptied into Drake's Creek. He then built a horse mill for Hoe Skiles near Rich Pond. An interesting story about this mill surfaced in 1840 when a large poplar tree was cut and sawed and rafted to Bowling Green to be sawed into lumber at the mill. When they had sawed about half way through the log, they struck something much harder than wood. On splitting the log open an old-fashioned skillet was found near the center. Since the trees nearby where this log once stood were carved with Daniel Boone's name it was said that he stuck the handle of the skillet in the tree and left it and that the tree then grew around it.[29]

John was a Whig in his early life and held a "firm adherent to the Monroe Doctrine which stated that further efforts by European nations to colonize land in North or South America would be viewed as acts of aggression, and a staunch Democrat in later years". He cast his first vote for Henry Clay in the Presidential election in October 1824.[30]

In 1827 John visited Virginia and through the influence of a Christian women he heard preaching from the words, "For what is a man profited if he shall gain the whole world?" and he then came to Christ and joined the Methodist Church. He "became a very devout Christian and showed great devotion to the Church of his choice, and labored diligently for the peace and prosperity of the same."[31]

He was listed on the census of 1830 in Warren County, Kentucky as John Sale Campbell. White males in his household were; two males under age 5 (likely George Washington and William Henry), one male age 5 to 9 (likely Wiley Sale, and two males age 20 to 29 (likely included John Sale). White females in the household were; two females, age 15 to 19, and one female age 20 to 29 (likely Mary Frances). Also included in the household was one male slave, age 36 to 54.[32]

Mary was "born again" in 1833 and also joined the Methodist Church shortly afterward.[33] John was a well-known Mill Wright and one of the main builders of the Portage Railroad in 1932. This railroad ran from the river up Tenth Street to the Court House in Bowling Green.[34] He also built several mills in Warren County including the Massey Mill, The Dishman Mill, and the Cave Mill. In 1838 and 1839 John built a steam mill for J. Rumsey Skiles and Jacob Vanmeter near Bowling Green.[35]

He was listed on the 1840 census in Warren County as John Sale Campbell. White males included in his household were; one male age 5 to 9, two males age 10 to 14 (likely included Wiley Sale), one male age 20 go 29, and one male age 30 to 39 (likely included John Sale). White females in the household were; two females under age 5 (likely included Eliza Mildred), one female age 5 to 9 (likely Lucinda Francis), two females age 10 to 14 (likely included Mary Elizabeth), and one female age 20 to 29. Also included in the household were seven slaves; three males under age 10, one female under age 10, one female age 10 to 23, and two females age 24 to 35.[36]

In 1841 John built a threshing machine for Adam Britton near Mount Olivet Church. He improved on the patent by making a perforated floor when he crossed the slats to separate the wheat from the straw. He also bought property near Rich Pond in 1841 and built a family home which he occupied for the rest of his life. He sold a portion of his property to his son James just before his death. After his death, his daughter Elizabeth Shields bought the remaining property and thus the home became known as the Campbell-Shields home.[37]

In 1848 John built a mill with a treadwheel for a Mr. Holmanin in the eastern part of the county, a steam mill for John L. Rowe, and a water mill on Jenning's Creek. This was his last work as a mill wright.[38]

John was listed as John S. Campbell, age 47 on the 1850 census in Warren County, Kentucky as a farmer. Also listed in the household were Mary, age 46, Wiley S., age 25, George W., age 23, Wm. H., age 21, Lucinda F., age 17, Eliza. M., age 12, Alexr. J., age 10, Margaret, L.V., age 7, and Julia A., age 4. Real estate was valued at $4,020.[39]

In 1855 John build Locust Grove, a Southern Methodist Church, near his home. He was a member of the church at the time. He retired from his trade after finishing this church and devoted his time to farming, although he built a work-shop near his home and fitted it with a set of cabinet tools and a blacksmith's outfit where he continued to make items such as furniture.[40]

John was listed on the 1860 census in Warren County, Kentucky as John Campbell, age 57. Also listed were Mary, age 56, Frances, age 27, Alex, age 20, and Julia Ann, age 14. Real estate was valued at $13,575 and his personal estate was valued at $10,417. Although he still owned slaves in 1860 he was frank and sincere in his views and in defending his rights when the final crisis came between the states he "sacrificed his personal welfare and all partisan principles and voted for the Union."[41]

He appeared on the census of 1870 in Warren County, Kentucky as John S. Campbell, age 67. Mary, age 65 was listed as housekeeping with personal property valued at $2,000 and unable to read or write. John's estate was valued at $15,114 and his personal estate was listed as $10.250. Francis Cassaday, age 45 was listed as living as one of the family and unable to read or write and Joe Campbell, age 14 was listed as working on the farm and also unable to read or write. Joe's color was listed as black.[42]

In 1880 John was listed on the census in Warren County, Kentucky as John S. Campbell, age 77. His wife Mary, age 76 was listed as keeping house. A servant, Jane Casseda, age 50 was listed as cooking and single. Also listed was his daughter J.A. Suman, age 33 and her husband C.E. Suman, age 36. Both Mary and Jane were listed as unable to read or write.[43]

John left a will on 19 January 1888 in Warren County, Kentucky. He stated that it was his desire that his estate be dived equally between his children and that he had already advanced various sums of money to members of his family for which each must account for in the final settlement of his estate. The amounts already advanced included $1,1627.40 to Wiley S., $1,595.30 to George W., $1,567.52 to William H., $1,847.18 to Mary E. Penner, $1,819.13 to Eliza. M. Shields, $1,544.17 to James A., $2,227.10 to Lucy V. Miller, and $1,805.70 to Julia Suman. He also indicated that $1,000 of his estate was to be put out at interest for the benefit and support of Francis Casseda who had been a faithful servant in his family for a number of years and that if she was able to gain employment and the money was not needed for her support the interest

John Sale Campbell		
1830	Warren County, KY	N/A
1840	Warren County, KY	N/A
1850	Warren County, KY	Farmer
1860	Warren County, KY	Farmer
1870	Warren County, KY	Farmer
1880	Warren County, KY	Farmer

was to be kept with the principle and it was to be equally divided among his children after her death. He appointed his sons William H. Campbell, George W. Campbell, and James A. Campbell as executors.[44]

On 21 August 1888 John added a Codicil to his will that changed the amount of land that was to be reserved for the family grave yard from one third of an acre instead of the previous one half acre of land.[45]

He was a longtime member of the Methodist church. In April 1890 His residence, which was several miles in the country in the Three Springs neighborhood, was the scene of a large celebration honoring his 87th birthday. An article in a local newspaper related he had "lived a simple, unostentatious life and coming up with the old pioneer days of our country imbibed the frugal habits and honest impulses of that period, and has never outlived them." It also said "His life is an example worthy of emulation, and demonstrates what toil and application to business can accomplish. He has always been strictly temperate and never fell into the fast ways of the present fast age, and as a consequence is a comparatively hale old man at the age of 87 years."[46]

John Sale Campbell
Campbell-Shields Cemetery
Bowling Green, Kentucky

On 13 October 1890 John left a second Codicil to his will that indicated his daughter Julia A. Suman was to receive an additional $1,000 to her pro-rata as provided in the original will to compensate her for her services and attention to her parents in their helpless old age and afflictions.[47]

John and Mary had at least 15 children including Wiley Sale Campbell, George Washington Campbell, William Henry Campbell, Mary Elizabeth Campbell, Lucinda Francis Campbell, John Wesley Campbell, Thomas Asbery Campbell, Elizabeth Mildred Campbell, James Alexander Sale Campbell, Margaret Lucy Virginia Campbell, Virginia Campbell, and Julia Ann Campbell. According to Zalame

Cottrell, John and Mary had three additional children who "died when small."[48]

Mary Frances died on 21 July 1887 in Warren County, Kentucky at age 83 at her home in the Three Springs neighborhood. Funeral services were held on 22 July 1887 at her home by Rev. J.F. Redford of the Methodist church and F.T. Adair of the Cumberland Presbyterian church.[49] She was buried in the Campbell-Shields Graveyard, three miles south of Bowling Green, Kentucky.[50]

John died on 1 November 1891 in Warren County, Kentucky at age 88 at his home in the Three Springs neighborhood after having been in an unconscious condition for several days. His cause of death was a lingering illness of disease incident to old age. Funeral services were held in his residence by Rev. J.F. Redford. He was buried at the Campbell-Shields Graveyard, three miles South of Bowling Green by the side of his wife who preceded him to the grave four years earlier. "Like Jacob of old, he wanted his family buried on the

Mary Frances Ennis
Campbell-Shields
Cemetery
Bowling Green, Kentucky

ground he had purchased with his own money."[51] John's estate was probated on 23 November 1891 in Warren County, Kentucky.[52]

Wiley Sale Campbell (1825-1886)

Son of John Sale Campbell and Mary Frances Ennis
Great-granduncle of Taylor Cosby Cottrell, Jr.

Wiley Sale Campbell was born on 17 February 1825 in three Springs in Warren County, Kentucky. He was the son of John Sale

Campbell and Mary Frances Ennis.[53] He was likely listed on the census of 1830 in the household of his father John in Warren County, Kentucky, as a white male, age 5 to 9.[54] He also likely was listed on the 1840 census in Warren County, Kentucky as one of two white males, ages 15 to 19 living in his father's home.[55]

He was a Methodist and joined the church in 1846. In 1850 he was listed in the household of his father John on the census in Warren County as Wiley S., age 25.[56]

A bond for the marriage of Wiley Sale Campbell was signed on 5 August 1850 in Bowling Green, in the sum of 50 pounds by Wiley S. Campbell and Joseph Wren.[57] Wiley married Elizabeth J. Wren on 22 August 1850 in Warren County. Elizabeth was born on 1 January 1823 in Kentucky. She was the daughter of Joseph Wren and Elizabeth Jeane Evans and had five brothers and four sisters.[58]

Wiley was listed on the census of 1860 in Warren County as Wiley S., age 35 with real estate valued at $4,640 and a personal estate valued at $2,604. Eliz. J., age 37 and Mary J., age 8 were also listed in the household.[59]

Elizabeth died on 11 September 1864 in Warren County at age 41. She was buried in the Wren Campbell Graveyard in Warren County.[60]

Children of Wiley Sale Campbell and Elizabeth J. Wren:

- Mary Jane Campbell – Born circa 1852 in Kentucky and died on 9 June 1891 in Rich Pond, Warren County, Kentucky. Her cause of death was pneumonia following a prolonged illness of more than five weeks. Funeral Services were held on 10 June 1891 by Rev. R.F. Adair and Rev. M.M. Smith. She was buried in the Campbell-Shields Graveyard, also known as the John S. Campbell family burying ground, three miles south of Bowling Green.[61] She was a Presbyterian and a member of the Cumberland Presbyterian Church. She was noted throughout the area "for the sweetness of her disposition, her great kindness of heart, and her unselfishness and charity." Her gravestone indicated she was the wife of A.J. Kirby. No additional information on their marriage is known. However, the marriage would have occurred sometime after the 1880 census.[62]

- John William Campbell – Born on 19 May 1861 in Warren County, Kentucky and died on 5 March 1925 in Rockfield in Warren County, at age 63. His cause of death was angina pectoris. He was buried on 7 March 1925 in Trinity Presbyterian Church Cemetery in Three Springs in Warren County.[63] He married Della Mae Pruitt, the daughter of Sidney Walker Pruitt and Sarah Ann Sherry around 1887. Della was born on 3 May 1868 in Warren County.[64] Della Mae died on 17 August 1942 in Bowling Green, Kentucky, at age 74. She was also buried in Trinity Presbyterian Church Cemetery.[65] John and Della had at least three children including:
  - Ethel Correne Campbell – Born on 27 March 1888 in Bowling Green and died on 14 July 1953 in Tennessee. She was buried in Union Hill Cemetery in Gallatin in Sumner County, Tennessee. Ethel married Robert Homes Hicks who was born on 19 May 1889 in Sumner Tennessee and died on 25 November 1960 in Tennessee. Robert was also buried in Union Hill Cemetery.[66]
  - Bertice Campbell – Born in May 1890 in Kentucky and died on 22 July 1900 in Warren County. He was buried on 23 July 1900 at Trinity Presbyterian Church Cemetery in Warren County.[67]
  - Elizabeth Sarah Campbell – Born on 30 January 1901 in Warren County, Kentucky and died on 26 January 1974 in Warren County, at age 72. She was buried in Trinity Presbyterian Church Cemetery in Warren County.[68] She married Roscoe Edward Kennedy in 1922.[69] He was born on 15 November 1888 in Aurora, Missouri and died on 1 May 1950 in Bowling Green. He was also buried at Trinity Presbyterian Church Cemetery.[70]

A bond for the marriage of Wiley Sale Campbell and Louisa C. Wise was signed on 23 May 1865 in Warren County in the sum of $100 by W.S. Campbell and William A. Wise.[71] Wiley married Louisa on 24 May 1865 in Warren County, at the home of William A. Wise. Louisa was born on 8 May 1836 in Warren County.[72] She was the daughter of William and Marilla Wise.

Wiley appeared on the census of 1870 in Warren County as W.S. Campbell, age 45, with real estate value of $8,600 and a personal estate value of $2,000. His wife Louisa, age 32 and his daughter Mary J., age 18, along with his son John W., age 9 and Lenora, age 3 were also listed on the census.[73]

He was listed on the agricultural schedule of the 1880 census, of the Rich Pond District in Warren County, Kentucky; as the owner of a farm with 178 acres of improved land and 115 acres of unimproved land. The total value including land, buildings, machinery and livestock was $7,466. Eighty weeks of labor, costing $300 resulted in $962 of produce during 1879. Livestock included seven working cows and four milk cows which produced 200 pounds of butter the previous year. The farm included 8 additional cattle, one of which was purchased the previous year, and one which was slaughtered. The farm included 32 sheep and 10 lambs which produced 114 pounds of fleece, 35 swine, and 35 chickens which produced 200 eggs. During the previous year 37 acres of land were used to produce 935 bushels of Indian corn, and 36 acres produced 280 bushels of wheat. Additional crop produced included 25 bushels of potatoes and 1,900 pounds of tobacco. Eight acres of land held 400 apple trees and 20 peach trees which produced 400 bushels of apples. Twenty cords of lumber, valued at $40, were cut from the land in 1879.[74]

Wiley Sale Campbell

1830	Warren County, KY	N/A
1840	Warren County, KY	N/A
1850	Warren County, KY	A Laborer
1860	Warren County, KY	Farmer
1870	Warren County, KY	Farmer
1880	Warren County, KY	Farmer

Wiley appeared on the population schedule of the census of 1880 in Warren County as W. S. Campbell, age 55. His wife Louisa C., age 44 was listed as keeping house. His daughter Mary J., age 38, was listed as single and living at home. His son J. William, age 19 was listed as working on the farm and his daughter Nora, age 12 was listed at home. Also listed in the household was his son Elden, age 9 and daughter Nellie F., age 3.[75]

Children of Wiley Sale Campbell and Louisa C. Wise:

- Infant Daughter Campbell – Born and died January 1866 in Warren County, Kentucky. She was buried in the Campbell-Shields Graveyard, three miles south of Bowling Green.[76]

- Lenora S. Campbell – Born on 17 September 1867 in Warren County, Kentucky and died on 21 March 1887 in Rich Pond in Warren County, at age 19 at her father's old homestead. Funeral services were held on 23 March 1887 in Warren County at the residence of her grandfather, Squire John T. Campbell. She was buried in Campbell-Shields Graveyard, near Bowling Green. She was a member of the Methodist Episcopal Church.[77]

Lenora S Campbell
Campbell-Shields Cemetery
Bowling Green, Kentucky

- Eldon L. Campbell – Born on 16 January 1871 in Warren County, Kentucky and died on 25 April 1952 in Riverside Tuberculosis Hospital in Bowling Green, Kentucky. He was buried on 27 April 1952 in Fairview Cemetery in Bowling Green, in Cemetery 1, Section C, Site C-303.[78] He was a horse trader of show horses in 1952 and never married.

- Wiley Campbell – Born on 24 November 1874 in Warren County, Kentucky and died on 11 November 1878 in Warren County, at age 3. His cause of death was diphtheria. He was buried in the Campbell-Shields Graveyard, near Bowling Green.[79]

- Nellie Frances Campbell – Born on 28 January 1877 in Warren County, Kentucky and died on 21 November 1943 in Rich Pond, Warren County, at age 66.

Wiley Campbell
Campbell-Shields Cemetery
Bowling Green, Kentucky

Her cause of death was osteomyelitis since August which was due to acute arthritis for several years caused by an old hip fracture that occurred around 1940. She was buried on 23 November 1943 in Fairview Cemetery in Bowling Green in Cemetery 1, Section N, Site N-127w.[80] She married James Brown McLellan circa 1894.[81] James was born on 4 November 1874 in Bowling Green. He was the son of Robert McLellan and Lucinda McDonald. James died on 19 January 1953 at City-County Hospital in Bowling Green, at age 78. His cause of death was coronary thrombosis. He was buried in Fairview Cemetery in Bowling Green in Cemetery 1, Section N, Site N-127w.[82] James and Nellie had at least 12 children including:

- o Mary Lucille McLellan – Born in September 1895 in Kentucky, likely on 16 September.[83] She likely married Arril B. Bush around 1917 and died on 30 October 1963.
- o Julian Howard McLellan – Born on 22 December 1896 near Rich Pond in Warren County and died on 11 January 1936 at the T.J. Samson Community Hospital in Glasgow in Barren County, Kentucky. Julian married Ruth Geraldine Mason before 1918.[84] Ruth was born on 11 March 1893 in Warren County and died on 23 November 1892 in Warren County, at age 89. Julian and Ruth were buried in Fairview Cemetery in Bowling Green.[85]
- o Robert Campbell McLellan – Born on 15 December 1898 in Warren County and died on 24 September 1990 in Bowling Green. He was buried in Fairview Cemetery.[86] He occupation was listed as farmer and he was described as medium height and medium build with brown hair and brown eyes when he registered for the WWI draft in 1818.[87]
- o James Claborn McLellan – Born on 3 February 1901 in Warren County, Kentucky and died on 11 December 1962 in Warren County.[88] James married. His wife's name was Mattie. They had at least five children.

- o Nellie Rufine McLellan – Born on 13 February 1903 in Kentucky and died in November 1986 in Kentucky.[89] She married Caldwell Howlett on 10 August 1926 in Wilson County, Tennessee.[90]
- o Norman Gregory McLellan – Born on 26 August 1905 in Kentucky and died on 23 June 1976 in Warren County.[91]
- o Carrie Jean McLellan – Born circa 1908 in Kentucky.[92]
- o David Wiley McLellan – Born on 15 April 1910 in Kentucky and died on 6 May 1995 in Bowling Green, Kentucky.[93]
- o Joe Burns McLellan – Born on 25 December 1911 in Warren County and died on 29 December 1964 in Warren County.[94] He married Ruth Campbell Kellogg on 14 June 1938 in Mecklenburg, North Carolina. Ruth was the daughter of J.C. Schwingle and Irene Kellogg.[95]
- o George Leo McLellan – Born on 15 November 1914 in Warren County and died on 5 November 1977 in Warren County.[96] He was buried in Fairview Cemetery in Bowling Green. George was married. His wife's name was Hazel. She was born on 15 September 1915 in Warren County and died on 30 January 1997 in Bowling Green. She was buried next to George in Fairview Cemetery.[97] They had at least two children.
- o Sarah Virginia McLellan – Born on 4 May 1917 in Warren County, Kentucky and died on 30 August 2008 in Buncombe County, North Carolina. She was buried in The Christmount Columbarium in Black Mountain in Buncombe County, North Carolina with her husband Neal Wyndham in Section 1, C-1.[98] Neal was born on 10 April 1917 in South Carolina and died on 6 January 2011 in Buncombe County. He was a minister in the Disciples of Christ and served many congregations over several states including South Carolina, Tennessee, Kentucky, and North Carolina.[99]

o   William Harold McLellan – Born on 26 October 1919 in Warren County and died on 26 September 1997 in Bowling Green.[100]

Louisa died on 12 November 1883 in Rich Pond in Warren County, at age 47. Her Cause of death was pneumonia. She was buried in Pleasant Hill Cemetery in Warren County.[101]

Wiley left a will on 5 April 1885 in Warren County that stated it was his desire that his grave be enclosed with an iron fence and that the fence also enclose the graves of his children if he were buried by them. He left his household articles and furniture to be divided equally among his children and stated that Mary Jane, wife of A.J. Kirby, and his son J.W. Campbell, children of his first wife, were to receive the sum of Four Hundred and Twenty-Five Dollars to be divided equally between them because this was the amount he had received from his first wife's estate. He indicated that Eldon and Nellie were to receive the sum of One Hundred Dollars each to be used for the completion of their education and that Mary Jane was to receive fifty acres of land including his dwelling house, barns, and

Wiley Sale Campbell
Campbell-Shields Cemetery
Bowling Green, Kentucky

orchards but she was to pay each of the other four heirs the sum of Two Hundred Dollars each for improvements unless the dwelling and barn did not remain at the time of his death.[102]

Wiley also indicted in his will that J.W. Campbell was to receive fifty acres of land to be taken from the tract of land previously purchased from the Allender tract of land and that Elden was to receive the remaining fifty acres of land that had been purchased from the Allender tract of land. He stated that Lenora and Nellie were to receive the remainder of his lands, approximately 50 acres each and if they fell short of 50 acres each they were to be paid the difference at the rate of Fifteen Dollars per acre or if they are greater than 50 acres each they are to pay the estate the sum of Fifteen Dollars per acre above 50 acres. It was also his wish that his daughters Lenora and Nellie have a home with his daughter Mary Jane and her husband A.J. Kirby during their minority and that the remainder of his estate was to be divided equally between his five children. George Campbell, Wiley's brother, was listed in the will as the Executor.[103]

Wiley died on 23 February 1886 in Warren County, at age 61 at his home near Memphis Junction. His cause of death was complications of diseases for which he had been suffering for some time. He was buried in the Campbell Shields Graveyard, three miles south of Bowling Green.[104]

George Washington Campbell (1827-1908)

Son of John Sale Campbell and Mary Frances Ennis
Great-grandfather of Taylor Cosby Cottrell, Jr.

George Washington Campbell was born on 25 March 1827 in Warren County, Kentucky. He was the son of John Sale Campbell and Mary Frances Ennis.[105] Information on the George Washington Campbell Family, and George's life history, along with that for his wife Hester Taylor Penner and George and Hester's ten children is covered in detail in Section 2, Chapter 6, George Washington Campbell Family.

William Henry Campbell (1829-1913)

Son of John Sale Campbell and Mary Frances Ennis
Great-granduncle of Taylor Cosby Cottrell, Jr.

William Henry Campbell was born on 3 March 1829 near Three Springs in Warren County, Kentucky. He was the son of John Sale Campbell and Mary Frances Ennis.[106] William likely appeared on the census of 1830 in the household of his father John in Warren County, Kentucky as one of two white males, under age 5.[107] He was likely listed on the 1840 census in the household of his father John in Warren County, Kentucky as one of two white males, age 10 to 14.[108] In 1850 he was listed in the household of his father in Warren County, as Wm. H., age 21.[109]

A bond for the marriage of William Henry Campbell and Mary Ann Virginia Ramsey was signed on 29 January 1855 in Bowling Green, Kentucky in the sum of $100 by William H. Campbell and Booker Ramsey.[110] William married Mary Ann, who was the daughter of Rev. Booker Ramsey and Mahala Drake, on 1 February 1855 in Warren County. Mary was born on 24 May 1836 in Warren County. Her grandfather Tolton Drake was a decedent of Sir Francis Drake. She was 13 years old when her mother Mahala died around 1849, after which she was raised by her younger brothers.[111] After their marriage William and Mary located on 135 acres of land four miles north of Bowling Green where they built a family home.[112]

William Henry Campbell

William was listed on the census of 1860 in Warren County, as William Campbell, age 31 with real estate valued at $2,000 and a personal estate valued at $500. Also listed were Mary, age 24, Henry, age 6, Ready, a female, age 3, and James, age 1.[113] In 1870 he was listed on the Warren County census as W.H. Campbell, age 41 with real estate valued at $1,500 and a personal estate valued at $600. Mary V., age 35 was also listed along with Henry T., age 14, Ready A., age 12, James F., age 10, and John R., age 8, Willice B., age 6, and Walter E., age 4. Ellina, who was born in April 1870 was also listed in his household.[114]

In 1880 he appeared on the census in Warren County, Kentucky as William H. Campbell, age 51. His wife Margaret V., age 45, sons Henry T., age 24, James F., age 20, John R., age 18, and Willice B., age 16 were also living in his household.[115] By 1887 William owned 274 acres of land that was highly cultivated and was improved with a fine residence, out buildings, and an orchard of 1,000 trees.[116] He also owned 160 acres of land three miles from Wellington, Kansas and was, at one time, a member of the Grange. The Grange was an organization that was originally founded with the idea of educating and connecting farmers within America. At first granges were important because of the social outlet they provided rural farmers. They later made a move toward political involvement.

In 1888 William's father left a will stating that William was to receive an equal share of the estate except that he was responsible for accounting for an amount equal to $1,567.52 which had already been advanced to him by his father.[117] William and his family were guests at the 87th birthday celebration of his father on 25 April 1890. William was a member of the Cumberland Presbyterian Church and was a Democrat.[118]

In 1900 William was listed on the census in Warren County, as William H. Campbell, age 71 along with his wife Mary V., age 64 and sons James F., age 41 and Edward W., age 35. His grandson Hubert White, age 23 was also listed.[119]

In June 1909 Mary Ann was visited by her brother Thomas R. Ramsey of Claremore, Oklahoma. They had not seen each other in 15 years. She was a consistent member of the Cumberland Presbyterian Church in Mount Olivet, Kentucky. Her brother W.B. Ramsey of Denton, Texas planned to visit her in the spring of 1910. She had not heard from him in 45 years when she received a message that said, "Mary, I will see you in the by and by."[120]

Children of William Henry Campbell and Mary Ann Ramsey:

- Henry Thomas Campbell – Born on 20 December 1856 in Warren County, Kentucky and died on 12 January 1888 in Wellington in Sumner County, Kansas, at age 31. His remains were shipped by train and arrived in Bowling Green, Kentucky on the 5 o'clock train on the 16th of January 1888 and were then conveyed to the residence of Mr. William Temple, on Main Street. His cause of death was pneumonia. He was buried on 17 January 1888 in Fairview Cemetery in Bowling Green. Henry never married. His obituary indicated he "…was one of the most exemplary young men in Warren County. He was the pride of his family, and an honor to the community in which he lived...He generally attended public worship, at the church where he was converted, and where he was always welcome, and where he seemed to feel entirely at home."[121]

- James F. Campbell – Born on 6 January 1859 in Warren County, Kentucky and died on 24 June 1930 in Bowling Green, Kentucky, at age 73. His cause of death was chronic pulmonary tuberculosis. He was buried on 25 June 1930 in Fairview Cemetery in Bowling Green in Cemetery 1, Section C, Site C-190.[122] James likely married Mary Oliver around 1915. She was born circa 1874 in Kentucky and was the daughter of Thomas and Elmina Oliver. They apparently had no children.

- Margarett Reedy A. Campbell – Born on 27 September 1857 in Warren County, Kentucky and died on 19 April 1917 in Warren County, at age 59 at Watts Mill near Bowling Green. Her cause of death was cancer of the stomach. She was buried on 19 April 1917 in Fairview Cemetery in Bowling Green in Cemetery 1, Section F, Site F-94.[123] She married John Thomas White in 1875.[124] John Thomas was born on 8 September 1848 in Warren County and died on 8 June 1924 in Bowling Green, at age 75. His cause of death was a cerebral hemorrhage. He was buried on 9 June 1924 in Fairview Cemetery in Section F, Site F-94.[125] Margarett and John had at least 13 children including:

  o Warner Thomas White – Born on 2 October 1875 in Warren County and died on 13 April 1935 in Warren County. He was buried in Fairview Cemetery in Bowling Green in Section N, Site N-119e.[126] He married Betsey E. Jones, the daughter of Henry Clay Jones and Fanny E. Jenkins, after February 1918.[127] Betsey was born on 30 November 1877 in Kentucky and died on 14 February 1959 in Warren County. She was also buried in Fairview Cemetery next to her husband.[128]

  o William Hurbert White – Born on 7 December 1876 in Warren County and died on 31 January 1950 in Warren County. He was buried in Fairview Cemetery in Section N, Site N-110w.[129] He married Catherine Jones in

1906.[130] Catherine was born on 8 January 1876 in Kentucky and died on 8 August 1960 in Warren County. She was also buried in Fairview Cemetery next to her husband William.[131]

o   Ada White – Born on 14 February 1879 in Bowling Green and died on 5 March 1953 in the Gentry Nursing Home in Bowling Green. She was buried in Fairview Cemetery in Section F, Site F-94.[132] She married Jess J. Barbre who was born in 1878 and died on 4 May 1955 in Warren County.[133] He was buried next to Ada in Fairview Cemetery.[134]

o   Lena White – Born on 16 January 1881 in Warren County and died on 4 July 1977 in Warren County.[135] She was buried in Fairview Cemetery in Section N, Site N-350. She married Doctor James E. Lyle in 1915.[136] James was born on 8 September 1876 in Oakland in Warren County and died at the City Hospital in Bowling Green on 23 December 1944. He was buried next to his wife Lena in Fairview Cemetery.[137] They had at least one child, Allene P. Lyle.[138]

o   John White – Born on 11 December 1883 in Warren County, Kentucky.[139] He was living in Colorado when he registered for the WWI draft in 1918.

o   Eddie White – Born in December 1885 in Warren County, Kentucky.[140]

o   Charles Suman White – Born on 25 October 1887 in Warren County and died on 22 June 1950 in Northville in Wayne County, Michigan.[141] He was buried in Fairview Cemetery in Section F, Site F-95. He also was known as Charlie.[142]

o   James Campbell White – Born on 25 September 1890 in Warren County and died on 14 May 1958 at the City-County Hospital in Bowling Green. His death record indicated he was married, but seperated.[143] He was buried in Fairview Cemetery in Section F, Site F-94.[144]

o   Mary Reed White – Born on 23 October 1892 in Warren County and died on 18 October 1953 at the Rocky Mount Sanitarium in Rocky Mount in Edgecombe

County, North Carolina. She was buried in Pineview Cemetery in Rocky Mount.[145] She married William Earl Cade on 13 February 1912 in Clark County, Indiana.[146] William was born on 12 February 1891 in Kentucky and died on 29 July 1968 at Dorothea Dix Hospital in Raleigh in Wake County, North Carolina.[147] He was also buried in Pineview Cemetery. They had at least four children including Virginia White Cade, William Earl Cade, Earl Reed Cade, and Mary Reed Cade.[148]

o Willis A. White – Born on 30 August 1894 in Warren County and died on 19 July 1941 in Warren County. According to his death certificate he was divorced from his wife Marie at the time of his death. He was buried in Fairview Cemetery in Bowling Green in Section F, Site F-95.[149]

o Heriges White – Born in June 1896 in Warren County, Kentucky. It is likely that his full name was Briggs Heriges White and that he was born on 27 June 1896, died on 9 June 1971, and was buried in Fairview Cemetery.[150]

o Hines Mumford White – Born in February 1898 in Warren County and died on 23 October 1934. He was buried in Fairview Cemetery in Section F, Site F-05.[151] In 1930 he was listed on the census in Davidson County, Tennessee as an inmate in Nashville in the Davidson County Jail.

o Elizabeth White – Born around 1900 in Kentucky.[152]

▪ John R. Campbell – Born on 4 December 1860 in Warren County, Kentucky and died on 17 October 1938 in Bowling Green, Kentucky, at age 69. His cause of death was tuberculosis.[153] He was buried on 18 October 1939 in Fairview Cemetery in Section B, Site G-115.[154] He married Maggie A. Brown on 10 February 1897 in Warren County, with the ceremony performed by M.M. Smith at the residence of Maggie's father Jack Brown in the presence of Henry Lucas, Cooper Stone, and James Campbell.[155] Maggie was born on 10 October 1865 in Kentucky and died on 23 November 1958 in

Warren County, at age 93.[156] She was buried in Fairview Cemetery in Section B, Site G-115.[157] John and Maggie had at least one child:

- o Elvis Richard Campbell – Born on 23 February 1899 in Warren County and died on 3 February 1978 in the City Hospital in Bowling Green, Kentucky after a lengthy illness. He was buried in Fairview Cemetery in Section B, Site G-115. He married Lula J. Johnson around 1923. Lucy was born on 21 October 1900 in Kentucky and died on 6 July 1993 in Bowling Green. She was also buried in Fairview Cemetery next to her husband. They had at least two children including Dorothy V. Campbell and Mary L. Campbell.[158] Elvis served as mayor of Bowling Green from 1949 to 1953. His administration was responsible for nearly doubling the size of Bowling Green and for the initiative that resulted in Holly Carburator locating in Warren County.

- Willis B. Campbell – Born on 14 May 1862 in Kentucky and died on 13 November 1897 in Shelbyville, Shelby County, Kentucky, at age 35. He was buried in Fairview Cemetery in Section C, Site C-192.[159] According to research notes written by Zalame Brashear Cottrell, daughter of Della Campbell, Willis married Jimmie Bell sometime after 1880 and they had at least six children including Jennings Bell, Robert Bell, Shelley Bell, Frank Bell, Vincent Bell, and an unnamed daughter that died in infancy. No additional information is known.[160]

- Edward Walter Campbell – Born on 15 November 1864 in Warren County, Kentucky; Died on 24 October 1948 in Bowling Green, Kentucky, at age 83. His cause of death was viral pneumonia.[161] He was buried on 27 October 1948 in Fairview Cemetery in Bowling Green in Section C, Site C-192.[162] Edward married Ella Hill Kenn in 1912. She was born in July 1869 in Kentucky. Her first husband's last name was Kenn. She had at least one child with her first husband named Ruthie Henn.[163] Edward and Ella apparently had no children. Ella died on 7 January 1960 in Warren County. She was buried in Fairview Cemetery in Section C, Site C-192.[164]

- Lena Rivers Campbell – Born on 24 January 1870 in Bowling Green, Warren County, Kentucky and died on 29 August 1948 at Norton Infirmary in Louisville in Jefferson County, Kentucky at age 78. Her cause of death was general infection following a hip fracture the previous week.[165] She was buried on 2 September 1948 in Grove Hill Cemetery in Shelbyville, Shelby County, Kentucky. Lena married Robert Lee Bell on 22 September 1891 in Warren County, Kentucky at the home of her father William H. Campbell with Rev. M.M. Smith of the C.P. Church officiating.[166] Robert was born on 1 February 1863 in Shelby County, Kentucky and died on 18 November 1928 in Shelbyville, Kentucky. His cause of death was angina pectoris complicated by arterial sclerosis. He was also buried in Grove Hill Cemetery in Shelbyville.[167] Lena and Robert had at least five children including:
  - Robert James Bell – Born on 11 March 1899 in Shelby County, Kentucky and died on 10 December 1970 in Jefferson County, Kentucky. He was buried in Grove Hill Cemetery in Jefferson County.[168]
  - William Jennings Bryan Bell – Born on 21 September 1899 in Shelby County and died on 16 November 1918 in Shelbyville in Shelby County, Kentucky. He was listed as single on his death record. He was buried in Fern Hill Cemetery in Shelbyville.[169]
  - Shelby Bell – Born on 21 January 1902 in Kentucky and died on 28 June 19786 in Jefferson County.[170] He married Mildred Schlensker in 1926. Mildred was born around 1903 in Indiana.[171]
  - Frank Beard Bell – Born on 26 September 1904 in Shelby County and died on 2 January 1939 in Kings Daughters Hospital in Frankfort in Franklin County, Kentucky. He was buried in Grove Hill Cemetery in Shelbyville, Kentucky.[172]
  - Vinson C. Bell – Born on 10 January 1909 in Shelbyville and died on 13 April 2004 in Huntington in Cabell County, West Virginia.[173] He married Myrtle Marie Baldwin on 26 February 1929 in Kenova in Wayne County, West Virginia.[174] She was born in

1908 in Boyd County and died before 2004. They had at least one son William V. Bell.[175]

Mary Ann died on 15 February 1910 in Mount Olivet in Warren County Kentucky, at age 73. Funeral services were held on 17 February 1910 at their home in Warren County. Services were conducted by Rev. M.M. Smith and Rev. S.H. Eshman.[176] She was buried in Fairview Cemetery in Bowling Green in Section C, Site C-190.[177]

William moved into the home of his son John R. Campbell, likely after the death of his wife Mary. He left a will on 14 May 1918 in Warren County leaving his house on 11th Street in Bowling Green to his daughter, Reedy White and his house on Center Street in Bowling Green to his daughter Lena Bell. He left his livery stable on 11th Street to his son John R. Campbell and his house and lot on 10th street to his son James F. Campbell. He left his house and lot on 11th Street adjoining the property given to Reedy to his son W.E. Campbell. Any remaining proceeds after the sale of his assets were to be divided equally among his children. He appointed Potter-Matlock Trust Company of Bowling Green as executer of the will and directed that they employ and consult with C.U. McKlroy on all legal matters. William left Elina Simmons, who he stated had "lived with me for many years." the bed, bedding, and furniture she had used and directed his executor to turn over $500 to his son John R. Campbell to be held in trust for the use of Elina so long as she lives.[178]

William died on 17 July 1913 in Bowling Green at age 84 at the home of his son John R. Campbell on Center Street. His cause of death was heart disease following a ten-day illness. He was buried Fairview Cemetery in Bowling Green. Funeral services were held on 18 July 1913 at Cumberland Presbyterian Church in Bowling Green by Rev. S.H. Eshman.[179] His estate was probated on 25 July 1913 in Warren County, proved by the oaths of Robt. Rodes, Jr., and Wm. D. McElroy with E.C. Smith, Clerk of Warren County Court presiding.[180]

Mary Elizabeth Campbell (1831-1916)

Daughter of John Sale Campbell and Mary Frances Ennis
Great-grandaunt of Taylor Cosby Cottrell, Jr.

Mary Elizabeth Campbell was born on 14 February 1831 in Warren County, Kentucky.[181] She was the daughter of John Sale Campbell and Mary Frances Ennis. She likely appeared on the census of 1840 in the household of her father John Sale, age 10 to 14.[182] A bond for the marriage of Mary Elizabeth Campbell and James Ambrose Shields was signed on 27 May 1850 in Bowling Green, Warren County, Kentucky in the sum of 50 pounds by James Shields and John S. Campbell.[183] Mary Elizabeth married James on 29 May 1850 in Warren County. James was born on 29 May 1830 in Virginia. He was the son of John James Shields and Frances Ann Plunkett.[184]

Children of Mary Elizabeth Campbell and James Abrose Shields:

- John H. Shields – Born in 1851 in Kentucky and died on 7 April 1876, likely in Lawrence County, Illinois. John was buried in Pleasant Hill Cemetery in Lawrence County.[185] He was listed on the 1860 census in the household of John H. Penner in Warren County, Kentucky as John Shields, age 9.[186] He was listed on the 1870 census in Lawrence County, Illinois in the household of John H. Penner as John Shields, age 19 and working as a farmer.[187]
- Mary Francis Shields – Born on 22 February 1853 in Warren County, Kentucky.[188] She was listed on the 1860 census in Warren County in the home of John Penner as Frances Shields, age 7. Her brother John was also listed on the census.[189] No additional information is known.

James died on 19 February 1855 in Warren County at age 24. He was buried in the James Shields Graveyard in Warren County.[190] Mary Elizabeth then married John H. Penner, son of Peter Penner and Margaret Elizabeth Alford on 21 September 1857 in Warren County.[191] John was born on 3 February 1832 in Kentucky. Mary was listed on the 1860 census in the household of her husband John in Warren County as Mary, age 29 along with George Penner, age 1, John Shields, age 9, and Francis Shields, age 7. Real estate was valued at $500 and personal estate was valued at $600.[192]

John and Mary Penner and their children moved to Lawrence County, Illinois in late 1866 or early 1867.[193] Mary was listed on the 1870 census in the home of her husband in Lawrence County, Illinois as Mary, age 39. Also listed in the household were George, age 10, Sarah, age 7, James, age 3, and John Shields, age 19. Real estate was valued at $1,000 and personal estate was also valued at $1,000.[194] In

1880 John and Mary were listed on the census in Lawrence County as John H. Penner, age 48 along with his wife Mary E., age 49. Their daughter Sara E., age 16 and son James N., age 18 were also listed as attending school.[195]

Mary's father John Campbell left a will on 19 January 1888 stating that Mary was to receive an equal share of his estate except that she was responsible for accounting for an amount equal to $1567.52 which had already been advanced to her by her father. Each of her brothers and sisters had also received various amounts in advance and also had to account for these in the final settlement.[196]

Mary appeared on the 1900 census in Lawrence County in the home of her husband John as Mary E., age 69. Also listed was a servant Elizabeth Belcher and John's sister-in-law Julia A. Suman, age 54 and widowed. The census listed Mary as having had 10 children, seven of which were still living. Thus Mary likely had additional children not identified, either born with her first husband James Shields or her second husband, John Penner.[197]

Children of Mary Elizabeth Campbell and John H. Penner:

- George Franklin Penner – Born on 19 July 1858 in Warren County, Kentucky and died on 24 December 1873, likely in Lawrence County, Illinois.[198] He was buried in Pleasant Hill Cemetery in Lawrenceville in Lawrence County, Illinois.[199]
- Peter Wesley Penner – Born and died on 25 July 1860 in Warren County, Kentucky. He was buried in the Penner Cemetery in Warren County.[200]
- Eugene Penner – Born and died on 27 March 1862 in Warren County, Kentucky. He was buried in the Penner Cemetery.[201]
- Sarah Elizabeth Penner – Born on 13 June 1863 in Warren County, Kentucky and died on 28 January 1882 likely in Lawrence County, Illinois.[202] She was buried in Pleasant Hill Cemetery in Lawrenceville in Lawrence County, Illinois.[203]
- James Napoleon Penner – Born on 23 October 1866 in Warren County, Kentucky and died in 1951. He was buried in Lawrenceville City Cemetery in Lawrence County, Illinois.[204] James married Letha McCarroll on 23 October 1889 in Knox County, Indiana.[205] Letha, also known as Leathe, was the daughter of John McCarroll and Sophia Everetts. She was born

on 8 September 1867 in Viscennes, Indiana.[206] Letha died on 9 June 1947 and was buried in Lawrenceville, Illinois. According to her obituary she and her husband James had previously lived in Terre Haute, Indiana and been active members of the First United Brethren Church.[207]

- Bertha Penner – Born on 26 March 1869 in Warren County, Kentucky and died on 12 April 1869 in Warren County. She was buried in the Campbell-Shields Cemetery in Bowling Green.[208]

John died in October 1907 in Lawrenceville, Lawrence County, Illinois, at age 75. He was buried in Hollister Cemetery in Lawrence County, Illinois with the Rev. E.M. Pierson preaching the service.[209]

Mary was listed on the 1910 census in Vigo County, Indiana in the home of her son James N. Penner, as Mary E., age 79 and widowed. They were living at 100 18th Street in Harrison Township at the time.[210]

Mary died on 26 June 1916 at 75 South 18th Street in Terre Haute in Vigo County, Indiana, at age 85 in the home of her son James. Funeral services were held in her son's home on 27 June 1916. She was buried on 28 June in Hollister Cemetery in Lawrence, Illinois.[211]

Lucinda Francis Campbell (1833-1870)

Daughter of John Sale Campbell and Mary Frances Ennis
Great-grandaunt of Taylor Cosby Cottrell, Jr.

Lucinda Francis Campbell was born on 7 February 1833 in Warren County, Kentucky. She was the daughter of John Sale Campbell and Mary Frances Ennis.[212] Lucinda likely appeared on the census of 1840 in the household of John Sale Campbell in Warren County, as the white female, age 5 to 9.[213] She was listed on the 1850 census in the home of her father John in Warren County, as Lucinda F., age 17.[214]

Lucinda married Hamilton Duke Wade circa 1860 in Warren County. Hamilton was born on 3 May 1835 in Butlersville, Kentucky. He was the son of John Wade and Anna Benedict.[215] He had previously been married to Mary Carpenter with whom he had one child, Linsey A. Wade, born around 1860 in Kentucky.[216]

Lucinda was listed on the 1870 census in the home of her husband Hamilton in Warren County as Lucinda F., age 38. Also listed in the home were Linsey A., age 10, and Levi F., age 8.[217]

Children of Lucinda F. Campbell and Hamilton Duke Wade:

- Levi Franklin Wade – Born on 22 September 1861 in Allen County, Kentucky and died on 3 July 1913 in Bowling Green, Kentucky, at age 51. His cause of death was tuberculosis.[218] He was buried on 4 July 1913 in Fairview Cemetery in Bowling Green.[219] Levi married Permelia Belle Jones around 1880. She was born on 23 November 1858 in Tennessee and died on 20 January 1935 in Warren County.[220] Levi and Permelia had at least five children including:
  - o Dora Wade – Born on 13 February 1881 in Kentucky and died on 14 June 1919 in Warren County.[221] She was buried in Fairview Cemetery in Bowling Green.[222] Dora married Clarence William Runner on 31 December 1902 in Sumner County, Tennessee.[223] He was born in 1885 and died on 16 April 1951. He was also buried in Fairview Cemetery.[224] They had at least four children including Garland Runner, Alice Runner, Viola Runner, and Alma Runner.[225]
  - o Fanny Wade – Born 5 September 1882 in Kentucky and died 6 December 1955 in Warren County.[226] She was buried in Fairview Cemetery. Fanny married Ruben Lee Butts around 1901. Ruben was born 20 May 1872 and died 28 February 1951 in Bowling Green. He was the son of William Butts and Hester Jane Stanley.[227] He was also buried in Fairview Cemetery.[228] They had at least two children including Ely Wade and Mary Wade.[229]
  - o Frank Edward Wade – Born on 26 February 1887 in Bowling Green and died on 16 December 1963 in the Eastern State Hospital in Williamsburg, Virginia.[230] He was buried in Forest Lawn Cemetery and Mausoleum in Richmond, Virginia in Section 22.[231]. Frank married Geneva Long Freeman around 1908. She was the daughter of Arthur Mills Freeman and Mattie Lenora Long.[232] They had at least two children including Winfrey F. Wade and Aurtha W. Wade.[233]

o   Mary Wade – Born about 1891 in Kentucky.[234]   She was listed in the home of her father on the 1910 census in Warren County as Mary, age 19 and single.

o   Lottie Wade – Born about 1899 in Kentucky.[235] She was listed in the home of her father on the 1910 census in Warren County as Lottie, age 11.

- Infant Son – Born and died on 5 November 1870 in Warren County, Kentucky.   He was buried in the Campbell-Shields Graveyard, three miles south of Bowling Green, Kentucky.[236]

Lucinda died on 9 November 1870 in Warren County at age 37. She was buried in the Campbell-Shields Cemetery near Bowling Green.[237]

Hamilton married Amanda E Forth around 1873.   Amanda was born in 1852 in Kentucky. She was the daughter of E.D. and Mahala Forth. Hampton was listed as the head of household on the 1880 census in Warren County as H.D. Wade, age 45 along with his wife Amanda E., age 28. Also listed in the household were his sons Lyndsy, age 20, Levi F., age 18, Charles E., age 5,

Lucinda F Campbell
Campbell-Shields Cemetery
Bowling Green, Kentucky

Samuel K., age 3, and Finns, age 6m. His daughter-in-law Perniella B., age 22 and his daughter Fannie, age 6 were also listed.[238]

Children of Hamilton Duke Wade and Amanda E. Forth:

- Fannie Wade – Born circa 1874 in Kentucky. No additional information is known.[239]
- Charles Edgar Wade – Born on 23 May 1875 in Bowling Green, Kentucky and died on 20 November 1948, likely in

Madison County, Illinois. He was buried in Oakwood Cemetery in Upper Alton in Madison County, Illinois.[240] Charles married Cora Richmond on 28 November 1894 in Elkhart, Indiana.[241] Cora was born on 12 August 1878 and died on 18 January 1944, likely in Madison County, Illinois. She was also buried in Oakland Cemetery in Upper Alton. Charles and Cora had at least six children including:

- o Nina J. Wade – Born about 1901 in Illinois, likely on 23 January. She likely married Henry A Chism and had at least three children before her death on 20 December 1972. She was likely buried in Keller Cemetery in Chesterfield in Macoupin County, Illinois with her husband Henry.[242]
- o William H. Wade – Born in Illinois, likely on 10 October 1903 and likely died on 25 November 1973 in Los Angeles, California.[243] He was buried in Oakwood Cemetery in Upper Alton, Illinois.[244]
- o Ellis B. Wade – Born about 1909 in Illinois.[245]
- o Charles Wade – Born in Illinois in 1910, likely on 24 July 1910. [246] He likely died on 23 December 1988 and was buried in Oakwood Cemetery in Upper Alton, Illinois.[247] If these dates are correct he married and he and his wife Ethel had at least two children including Donivan Wade and Roger Wade.
- o Woodrow Wade – Born about 1914 in Illinois.[248]
- o Juanita M. Wade – Born in Illinois. She also went by the name of Waunita.[249] She was likely born in 1918, died in 1969, and was buried in Memorial Park Cemetery in Tulsa, Oklahoma. She likely married John Cochran who was born on 13 June 1919 and died on 10 November 1995.[250] John served in the U.S. Army from 19 August 1949 until 31 January 1963.

- Samuel Hendricks Wade – Born on 24 March 1877 in Kentucky. He was described as tall with a slender build, gray eyes and brown hair in 1918. His wife's name was Essie.[251] They had at least four children including Charles E. Wade, Cecil E.

Wade, Nema Wade, and Samuel A. Wade.[252] Samuel Hendricks died in 1955 and was buried in Charity Baptist Cemetery in Macoupin County, Illinois.[253]

- Finis Wade – Born on 17 December 1879 in Glasgow, Kentucky and died on 30 September 1952. He was buried in Chesterfield Cemetery in Macoupin County, Illinois.[254] Finns married Maud L. Starkweather around 1904.[255] They had at least two children including Marguratte Elizabeth Wade and Geneva M. Wade.[256]

Amanda died in 1898, likely in Macoupin Count, likely in Macoupin Count, Illinois. She was buried in Loomis Cemetery in Chesterfield in Macoupin County.[257]

Hamilton died on 23 July 1919 in Medora in Macoupin County, Illinois.[258] He was buried in Loomis Cemetery in Chesterfield in Macoupin County, Illinois with his wife Amanda.[259]

John Wesley Campbell (1834-1835)

Son of John Sale Campbell and Mary Frances Ennis
Great-granduncle of Taylor Cosby Cottrell, Jr.

John Wesley Campbell was born on 26 November 1834 in Warren County, Kentucky. He was the son of John Sale Campbell and Mary Frances Ennis. John died on 12 September 1835 in Warren County.[260]

Thomas Asbery Campbell (1836-1837)

Son of John Sale Campbell and Mary Frances Ennis
Great-granduncle of Taylor Cosby Cottrell, Jr.

Thomas Asbery Campbell was born on 8 July 1836 in Warren County, Kentucky. He was the son of John Sale Campbell and Mary Frances Ennis. Thomas died on 30 April 1837 in Warren County.[261]

Elizabeth Mildred Campbell (1838-1907)

Daughter of John Sale Campbell and Mary Frances Ennis
Great-grandaunt of Taylor Cosby Cottrell, Jr.

Elizabeth Mildred Campbell was born on 20 March 1838 in Warren County, Kentucky. She was the daughter of John Sale Campbell and Mary Frances Ennis.[262] She likely appeared on the census of 1840 in the household of her father John Sale in Warren County as one of the two white females under 5.[263] She was listed on the 1850 census of her father in Warren County as Eliza. M., age 12.[264]

Elizabeth married Samuel Taliaferro Shields, the son of John J. Shields and Francis A. Shields on 29 May 1855 in Warren County.[265] Samuel was born on 10 July 1832 in Virginia near Lynchburg.[266] Elizabeth was listed on the 1860 census in Warren County in the home of her husband as Eliza., age 22 along with Mary, age 5, Cornelia, age 3, and Bob, age 1/12. Samuel had a personal estate valued at $1,500 at that time.[267] In 1870 Elizabeth was found on the census in Warren County in the household of her husband Samuel as Eliza. M., age 30 along with Mary H., age 14, Cornelia T., age 12, and Samuel J., age 8. William A., age 1 and Eugenia V., age 1 were also listed in the household. Real estate was valued at $2,500.[268]

On the 1880 agricultural schedule of the Greencastle District in Warren County, the family farm had 115 acres of improved land and 225 acres of unimproved land. The total value including land, buildings, machinery and livestock was $1,795. Livestock included five horses, two mules, and four milk cows which produced 200 pounds of butter the previous year. The farm included 10 sheep, one of which was slaughtered, and 5 lambs birthed during 1879. The sheep produced 25 pounds of fleece. There were also 8 swine and 14 chickens which produced 75 eggs. During the previous year 35 acres of land were used to produce 1000 bushels of Indian corn, 20 acres produced 200 bushels of oats, and 14 acres produced 70 bushels of wheat. Additional crop produced included one bushel of dry beans, 14 bushels of potatoes, and 20 bushels of sweet potatoes. Two acres held 15 apple trees which produced 100 bushels of apples and forty cords of lumber, valued at $20, were cut from the land in 1879.[269]

Elizabeth was listed on the 1880 census in Warren County in the household of her husband Samuel as Eliza., age 42. Their daughters Mary H., age 24 and Virginia, age 12 were listed as single and attending school. Their sons Samuel J., age 17 and William A., age 14 were listed as laborers while their son John E., age 7 was listed as attending school.[270]

Elizabeth's father John Campbell left a will on 19 January 1888 stating that she was to receive an equal share of his estate except that she was responsible for accounting for an amount equal to $1,819.13 which had already been advanced to her by her father. Each of her brothers and sisters had also received various amounts in advance and also had to account for these in the final settlement. After her father's death in 1891 Elizabeth bought the remaining property and thus her father's home became known as the Campbell-Shields home.[271]

She was a Methodist and was described as "...a women of sterling character, solid worth, and deep piety...not a woman of many words and chaffy conversation, but sober, grave, and temperate. She was a foe of all vice, especially tobacco and whiskey."[272] She left a will on 13 July 1904 in Warren County that left tracts of land to her daughters Cornelia F. Maxey and Mary Ann Shields and the remainder of her land to her sons Samuel Shields and William Shields. The remainder of her estate, both personal and real, was to be divided between her five children. Her will also indicated that she was appointing her son Eddie (John Edward Shields) as the executor of her estate.[273]

Elizabeth Mildred Campbell
Campbell-Shields Cemetery
Bowling Green, Kentucky

In mid-July 1907, "Mrs. Shields was returning home from a visit to a neighbor and in going through a gate, the wind blew it against her with such force as to knock her to the ground, where she lay in a hard rain for some time before anyone knew what had happened. She was large and the injuries were so serious that she could not arise and it was said if she had not held her head up she would have drowned. When found she was in a helpless condition and was carried into the house, where medical aid was summoned." She never fully recovered from the injuries in this incident and they ultimately led to her death in August.[274]

Children of Elizabeth M. Campbell and Samuel T. Shields:

- Mary Ann Shields – Born on 29 July 1856 in Warren County, Kentucky and died on 11 January in Bowling Green, Kentucky, at age 87. Her cause of death was chronic bronchitis. She was buried on 12 January 1944 in the Campbell-Shields Cemetery in Bowling Green, Kentucky. Mary never married.[275]

- Cornelia Frances Shields – Born on 30 August 1858 in Warren County, Kentucky and died on 11 January 1924 in Warren County, at age 65. Her cause of death was vascular heart failure. She was buried on 15 January 1924 in Barren River Baptist Cemetery in Warren County.[276] She married Warren Woodson Maxey in 1877 in Warren County. Warren Maxey was born on 7 January 1857 in Warren County. He

Mary Ann Shields
Campbell-Shields Cemetery
Bowling Green, Kentucky

was the son of John Jackson Maxey and Elizabeth Hudnell.[277] Warren died on 15 April 1934. He was also buried on 17 April 1934 in Barren River Baptist Cemetery in Woodburn in Warren County.[278] Cornelia and Warren had at least ten children including:

  - Julia A. Maxey – Born on 27 April 1879 in Kentucky and died on 25 November 1966 in Hillsborough County, Florida. She was buried in Orange Hill Cemetery in Tampa in Hillsborough County.[279] She married John Henry Bradshaw on 22 November 1904 in Marion, Indiana.[280] John was born on 9 February 1882 and died on 16 May 1941. He was also buried in Orange Hill Cemetery.[281] They had at least three children including Alvin Bradshaw, William Bradshaw, and John H. Bradshaw.[282]

- o Boardly Evans Maxey – Born on 13 September 1880 in Warren County and died on 8 March 1912 in Warren County. He was buried in Highland Cemetery in Hadley in Warren County.[283] He married Eva Donnie Sprouse in 1903. They had at least three children including Lena Rivers Maxey, Floyd B. Maxey, and Lydia Maxey.[284]
- o Minnie Maxey – Born on 4 June 1883 in Warren County and died on 22 July 1911 in Warren County. She married John R. Sweeney and they had at least one child Homer H. Sweeney. John re-married after Minnie's death and had an additional five children. Minnie was buried in Highland Cemetery in Bowling Green.[285]
- o Laura Allie Maxey – Born on 10 March 1886 in Warren County and died on 4 May 1964 in Warren County. She was buried in Barren River Baptist Cemetery in Barren River, Kentucky.[286] She married James G. Vinson who was born on 17 October 1878 and died on 17 July 1937. He was also buried in Barren River Baptist Cemetery.[287] They apparently had no children.
- o Jesse Adalbert Maxey – Born on 11 November 1887 in Warren County and died on 15 October 1972 in Warren County. He was buried in Halls Chapel Cemetery in Bowling Green, Kentucky.[288] He married. His wife's name was Eula and her last name was likely Clair. They had at least four children including Yancee Maxey, Anna R. Maxey, Karl E. Maxey, and Ralena M. Maxey.[289]
- o Charlie Woodson Maxey – Born on 19 March 1890 and died on 17 July 1962 in Florida. He was buried in Fort Myers Cemetery in Lee County, Florida.[290] He married Lillie Lamons who was born on 28 April 1903 and died on 12 December 1987. She was also buried in Fort Myers Cemetery.[291] They had at least five children including Margie Maxey, Charles Maxey, Vernon Maxey, Mary Maxey, and Clarine Maxey.[292]
- o Mary E. Maxey – Born on 12 April 1892 in Warren County and died on 26 November 1988 in Bowling

Green, Kentucky. She was buried in Chapel Hill Memorial Gardens in Bowling Green.[293] She married Daniel Tims who was born on 20 May 1886 in Georgia and died on 15 September 1973 in Bowling Green. He was also buried in Chapel Hill Memorial Gardens.[294] They had at least two children including Mildred C. Tims, Mary C. Tims.[295]

o Willie Frank Maxey – Born on 25 January 1894 in Bowling Green, Kentucky and died in August 1974, likely in New Jersey. He was married. His wife's name was Edna and they had at least three children including Clarence Maxey, Floyd Maxey, and Frank Maxey.[296]

o Roy Irvin Maxey – Born 25 August 1898 in Warren County and died on 18 August 1969 in Warren County. He was buried in Barren River Baptist Cemetery in Warren County.[297] He Married Irene Atkinson. They had at least two children including Thelma Jane Maxey and Bettie Louise Maxey. Irene was also buried in Barren River Baptist Cemetery.[298]

o Corlis H. Maxey – Born in February 1900 and likely died before the 1910 census where he was not listed.[299]

▪ Lemeul Charles Shields – Born on 22 April 1860 in Hadley in Warren County, Kentucky and died on 1 September 1861 in Hadley. He was buried in the Campbell-Shields Cemetery, three miles south of Bowling Green, Kentucky.[300]

▪ Samuel James Shields – Born 25 July 1862 in Warren County, Kentucky and died 13 May 1946 in the Three Springs Community in Warren County. His cause of death was chronic nephritis. He was buried 14 May 1946 in the Campbell-Shields Cemetery south of Bowling Green.[301] He married Blanche Isabell Fordyce, the daughter of Mary J. Carter, around 1886.[302] Blanche was born 10 September 1861 in Lawrence County, Illinois and died 23 March 1923 on Watts Mill Road in Warren County. Her cause of death was labored pneumonia. She was buried on 26 March 1923 in the Campbell-Shields Cemetery.[303] Samuel and Blanche had at least six children including:

o Charlie E. Shields – Born on 19 April 1887 in Warren County and died on 23 June 1887 in Warren County.

He was buried in the Campbell-Shields Cemetery in Bowling Green.[304]

o   Bessie Fern Shields – Born on 31 July 1888 in Bowling Green and died on 18 February 1947 in Tacoma in Pierce County, Washington. She was buried in the New Tacoma Cemetery in University Place in Pierce County, Washington.[305] Bessie married Oswald Claude Cuthbert around 1911. He was born in September 1887 in Nashville, Tennessee and died on 7 November 1974 in Puyallup in Pierce County, Washington. He was also buried in New Tacoma Cemetery. They had at least two children including Elsie Cuthbert and Grene Cuthbert.[306]

o   Clarence Samuel Shields – Born on 27 November 1890 in Wellington in Sumner County, Kentucky and died on 16 March 1959 in Dade County, Florida. He was buried in Palms Woodlawn Cemetery in Naranja in Miami-Dade County.[307]

o   Mary B. Shields – Born in November 1893 in Warren County, Kentucky. In 1910 she was living with her father and was listed on the census as Mary B, age 27 and single.[308]

o   Harley B. Shields – Born on 20 September 1895 in Warren County.[309] He registered for the draft for World War II in 1942 while living in Dupont in Jefferson County, Indiana reporting. He was employed by the U.S. Government at the time.[310] He died in December 1975.[311]

o   Frederick Taleforo Shields – Born on 27 May 1898 in Warren County, Kentucky. He registered for the draft for World War II in 1942 while living in Warren County, Kentucky. He was working as a farmer at the time.[312] He died in December 1973 in Kentucky.[313]

- Unnamed Daughter – Stillborn on 10 January 1865 in Warren County, Kentucky. She was buried in the Campbell-Shields Cemetery south of Bowling Green, Kentucky.[314]
- William A. Shields – Born on 1 April 1866 in Kentucky and died on 11 March 1937, at age 70. He was buried in Fairview Cemetery in Bowling Green, Kentucky.[315] He married Vallie Atchison sometime after 1880.[316] Vallie was born on 14 June 1871 in Warren County. She was the daughter of Andrew J. Atchison and Margaret E. Price. William and Vallie had no children. Vallie died on 27 June 1946 at 640 East 11th Street in Bowling Green, at age 75. Her cause of death was cardiac failure. She was also buried on 29 July 1946 in Fairview Cemetery in Section B, Site B-30.[317]
- Eugenia Virginia Shields – Born on 1 February 1869 in Warren County, Kentucky and died on 7 March 1891 in Warren County. She was buried in the Campbell-Shields Cemetery three miles south of Bowling Green.[318]
- John Edward Shields – Born on 25 July 1873 in Bowling Green and died on 29 September 1909 in Warren County, at age 36. He was buried in the Campbell-

Eugenia Virginia Shields
Campbell-Shields Cemetery
Bowling Green, Kentucky

John Edward Shields
Campbell-Shields Cemetery
Bowling Green, Kentucky

Shields Cemetery south of Bowling Green. John never married.[319] He left a will on 6 January 1908 in Warren County leaving all property, of every kind, to his sister Mary Ann Shields. His estate was probated on 25 October 1909 in the Warren County Court in Bowling Green.[320]

Samuel died on 16 June 1900 in Warren County, at age 67. His cause of death was falling out of his loft. He was buried in the Campbell-Shields Cemetery, south of Bowling Green.[321]

Elizabeth died on 26 August 1907 in Warren County, at age 69 at her home near Greenwood. Her cause of death was from a combination of injuries sustained from the fall at the gate approximately six weeks earlier coupled with heart failure. Funeral services were held on 28 August 1907 in Warren County at her home by Bro. B.A. Cundiff, assisted by Bro. D.S. Bowles. She was buried in the Campbell-Shields Cemetery south of Bowling Green. Her estate was probated on 25 September 1907 at the Warren County Court in Bowling Green.[322]

James Alexander Sale Campbell (1840-1922)

Son of John Sale Campbell and Mary Frances Ennis
Great-granduncle of Taylor Cosby Cottrell, Jr.

James Alexander Sale Campbell was born on 21 October 1840 in Warren County, Kentucky. He was the son of John Sale Campbell and Mary Frances Ennis.[323] He appeared on the census of 1850 in the household of his father John Sale in Warren County as Alexr. D., age 10.[324] In 1860 he was listed on the Warren County census in the home of his father as Alex, age 20 and having attended school within the year. He was listed as a laborer on the census.[325]

A bond for the marriage of James Alexander Sale Campbell and Mary A. Madison was signed on 18 October 1865 in Bowling Green, Kentucky in the sum of $100 by James A. Campbell and J.R. Madison. James married Mary A. Madison, the daughter of Joel Richard Madison and Mary Jane Herrington, on 18 October 1865 in Warren County at the residence of J.R. Madison, Mary's father. Mary was born on 15 November 1841 in Kentucky.[326]

James was listed on the 1870 census in Warren County as Jas. A. Campbell, age 29 along with Mary, age 28 and Ready S., age 3. Real estate was valued at $2,500 and his personal estate was valued at $736. James was listed as a farmer on the census.[327]

The 1880 agricultural schedule of the Rich Pond District in Warren County listed James as the owner of a farm with 64 acres of improved land and 12 acres of unimproved land. Total value including land, buildings, machinery and livestock was listed as $4,350. Hired labor costs during 1879 for 61 weeks at a cost of $200 resulted in 650 pounds of butter the previous year. The farm included 3 additional cattle which were purchased the previous year, one which was sold, and one which was slaughtered. The farm also included 150 chickens which produced 365 eggs. During the previous year 18 acres of land were used to produce 750 bushels of Indian corn, 7 acres produced 100 bushels of oats, and 12 acres produced 100 bushels of wheat. Additional crop produced included 12 bushels of potatoes and 4,000 pounds of tobacco. One acre of land held 100 apple trees and 15 peach trees which produced 10 bushels of apples. Fifteen cords of lumber, valued at $30, were cut from the land in 1879.[328]

James built a family home around 1885 on a piece of land which adjoined his father's land and later bought the acreage from his father just before his father's death in 1891.[329] James's father left a will on 19 January 1888 stating that James was to receive an equal share of his estate except that he was responsible for accounting for an amount equal to $1805.70 which had already been advanced to him by his father. Each of his brothers and sisters had also received various amounts in advance and also had to account for these in the final settlement.[330]

James appeared on the census of 1900 in Warren County as James Campbell, age 59 along with his wife Mary, age 65, daughters Ready, age 33 and Florence, age 24, and his son Herbert, age 28. His farm, which he owned free of mortgage, was listed on farm schedule 221.[331]

Children of James Alexander Campbell and Mary A. Madison:

- Reedie Letitia Campbell – Born in December 1866 in Kentucky and died on 10 November 1938 in Dade County, Florida, at age 71. She was buried in Fairview Cemetery in Bowling Green in Section C, Site C-303.[332] Reedie married Henry Skiles Potter on 15 January 1908 in Warren County. Henry was born in 1867 in Kentucky.[333] They later moved to Florida where Henry was a caretaker of a grove in 1930. They had no children. After

Reedie died in 1938 Henry married Laura B. Bailey on 19 July 1944 in Miami in Dade County, Florida. Henry died on 22 January 1956 in Dade County. He was buried in Fairview Cemetery in Section C, Site C-303.[334]

- Herbert Willis Campbell – Born on 19 February 1871 in Warren County, Kentucky and died on 2 January 1951 in Bowling Green, at age 79. His cause of death was cerebral Apoplexy. He was buried on 4 January 1951 in Fairview Cemetery in Section 0, Site 10-54w.[335] Herbert married Virginia Blanch Isbell on 4 December 1901 in Warren County at the home of Virginia's father Walter Isbell. Virginia was born on 7 January 1877 in Kentucky. She was also known as Virginia Blanch Isbell. Herbert and Virginia had no children. Virginia died on 17 August 1951 in Bowling Green, at age 74. Her cause of death was diabetes. She was buried on 19 August 1951 in Fairview Cemetery in Bowling Green, in Section 0, Site 10-54w.[336]

- Florence Campbell – Born on 5 March 1877 in Warren County, Kentucky and died on 10 January 1949 in the Bowling Green Warren County Hospital, at age 71. Her cause of death was cardiac failure. She was buried on 13 January 1949 in Fairview Cemetery in Bowling Green, in Section C, Site C-303.[337] Florence married Leroy S. Thomas, the son of Sam Thomas and Fannie Lucas, around 1905.[338] Leroy was born on 27 November 1882 in Warren County, died on 3 April 1946 in Warren County, at age 63, and was also buried in Fairview Cemetery in Bowling Green, in Section C, site C-303.[339] They had at least one child including:
  - o Ulyes Thomas – Born on 24 September 1918 in Bowling Green, Kentucky and died on 16 October 1992 in Wyoming, likely in Cheyenne.[340]

Mary died on 4 March 1901 at her home in Three Springs in Warren County, at age 59. Funeral services were held in her home by the Rev. Johnson, pastor of Trinity Church, assisted by Rev. M.M. Smith. Her casket was covered with ferns and evergreens and rare flowers. She was buried in Fairview Cemetery in Bowling Green in Section C, Site C-303.[341]

A bond for the marriage of James Alexander Sale Campbell and Virginia Montagne Jenkins was signed on 4 January 1904 in Bowling

Green by James A. Campbell and E.C. Smith. James married Virginia the same day in Warren County. Virginia was born on 30 July 1852 in Campbellsville, Kentucky. She was the daughter of Robert Semper Montagne and Margaret Cox.[342]

James was listed on the 1910 Warren County census as J.A. Campbell, age 69 along with his wife Virgie, age 55. Virgie was listed as the mother of one child, with no children living.[343] It is assumed that this would have been a child from a previous marriage.

James left a will on 6 May 1913 in Warren County, witnessed by Whit Potter and S.M. Matlock, appointing his son Herbert as executor. The will cancelled a previously recorded contract with Virgie and stated that she was to receive his house which was situated on the Eastern side of Broadway in Bowling Green and all of the household and kitchen furniture. He further directed that following her death, the remainder of his estate was to be sold and equally divided between his children Rudie L. Potter, Herbert Campbell, and Florence Thomas.[344]

He was listed on the 1920 Warren County census as Jas. A. Campbell, age 79 along with his wife Virginia, age 65. He owned his home free of mortgage. They were listed as living at 846 Broadway in Bowling Green on the census.[345]

James died on 19 January 1922 in Bowling Green, at age 81 at 9:00 in the morning. His cause of death was pneumonia.[346] He was buried on 29 January 1922 in Fairview Cemetery in Section C, Site C-303.[347] His estate was probated on 23 January 1922 in Warren County, proved by the oaths of J. Whit Potter and S.M. Matlock with H. Lell Kelley, Clerk of Warren County presiding.[348]

Virginia died on 10 July 1926 in the Kings Daughters Home for Incurables in Louisville in Jefferson County, Kentucky, at age 73. Her cause of death was acute gastroenteritis. She was buried on 12 July 1926 in Fairview Cemetery in Section C, Site C-303.[349]

Margaret Lucy Virginia Campbell (1841-1850)

Daughter of John Sale Campbell and Mary Frances Ennis
Great-grandaunt of Taylor Cosby Cottrell, Jr.

Margaret Lucy Virginia Campbell was born on 20 January 1841 in Warren County, Kentucky. She was the daughter of John Sale Campbell and Mary Frances Ennis.[350] She was listed on the 1850 census in

Warren County in the household of her father John Sale as Margaret L.V., age 7.[351]

A bond for the marriage of Margaret Lucy Virginia Campbell and Robert W. Burton was signed on 22 November 1859 in Warren County. Margaret married Robert on 25 November 1859 in Warren County.[352] Robert Burton died in 1864 in Kentucky.[353]

Children of Margaret L.V. Campbell and Robert W. Burton:

- James R. Burton – Born in 1861 in Kentucky and died after June 1904.[354] A bond for the marriage of James R. Burton and Julia Richardson was signed on 4 December 1882 in Warren County, by James R. Burton and J.D. Miller. James married Julia on 7 December 1882.[355]

Margaret married John D. Miller on 16 September 1869 in Warren County at the home of George Campbell.[356] John was born on 21 February 1848 in Warren County. He was the son of Jacob G. Miller.[357] Margaret was listed on the 1870 census in Warren County in the home of her husband John as Margaret L.V., age 27 along with James Campbell, age 9.[358] It is assumed that James Campbell was actually James Burton, Margaret's son from her first marriage. In 1880 she was listed on the Warren County census with her husband John D. Miller as Margaret C., age 37 along with her daughter Minnie, age 9, and John's stepson James Burton, age 19.[359] Margaret also went by the name of Lucy.

Lucy's father John Campbell left a will on 19 January 1888 stating that Lucy was to receive an equal share of his estate except that she was responsible for accounting for an amount equal to $2,227.10 which had already been advanced to her by her father. Each of her brothers and sisters had also received various amounts in advance and also had to account for these in the final settlement.[360]

In 1900 she was listed on the census in Warren County in the home of her husband as Lucy V., age 57 along with their daughter Andrey B., age 14 and son Auther C., age 9.[361]

Children of Margaret L.V. Campbell and John D. Miller:

- Minnie W. Miller – Born on 26 October 1871 in Kentucky and died on 10 October 1922 in Bowling Green, at age 50. Her cause of death was cancer. She was buried on 12 October 1922 in Fairview Cemetery in Single Graves, Site 69-12.[362] Minnie married Joseph L. Erwin sometime after 1886. Joseph was born on 8 April 1859 in Kentucky. He was the son of David Erwin and Mary Moore.[363] In 1920 they were living in a boarding house in Warren County owned by Joseph. Seventeen boarders were living in the house at the time.[364] According to Minnie's will they had at one child including Andy Erwin whose married name was Hendricks. Joseph died on 31 December 1940 at 523 Maple Street in Bowling Green, at age 81. His cause of death was carcinoma of the stomach. Joseph was buried on 6 January 1941 in Fairview Cemetery in Single Graves, Site 69-13.[365]

Clarence W. Miller
Campbell-Shields Cemetery
Bowling Green, Kentucky

- Clarence W. Miller – Born on 19 February 1873 in Warren County, Kentucky and died on 8 May 1873 in Warren County. Clarence was buried in the Campbell-Shields Graveyard south of Bowling Green.[366]

- Audrey B. Miller – Born in October 1885 in Warren County, Kentucky.[367] She was living with her father on the 1900 census in Warren County and was listed as Audrey R., age 14 and single.

- Authur Clarence Miller – Born on 24 August 1890 in Warren County, Kentucky and died on 16 October 1943.[368] He was buried in Louisville Memorial Gardens in Jefferson County, Kentucky.[369] Authur married Kate Lewis around 1910. She was also known as Katie[370]. They had at least three children including:
    o Earl C. Miller – Born on 10 September 1913 in Warren County, Kentucky and died on 13 August 1974 in San Diego, California.[371]

o Robert R. Miller – Born on 2 November 1919 in War-ren County.[372] It is likely his full name was Robert Rhodes Miller as he was listed as Rhodes on the 1930 census. He was living with his father in 1940 in Jeffer-son County and was listed on the census as Robert, age 20 and single.

o Alleta C. Miller – Born on 4 June 1921 in Warren County.[373] She was living with her father and was listed on the Jefferson County census in 1930 as Alleta C., age 8.

Margaret Lucy died on 18 January 1914 in Richardsville in Warren County, Kentucky, at age 72. Her cause of death was a val-var heart lesion following an illness of several days. Funeral services were held in the Green River Union Church in Richards-ville by the Rev. Cassady. She was buried on 19 January 1914 in the Green River Union Church Cemetery.[374]

John died on 20 June 1922 in Richardsville, at age 74. He was listed as a farmer on his death cer-tificate. John was buried in the Green River Union Cemetery graveyard on 21 June 1922.[375]

Green River Union Cemetery
Richardsville, Kentucky

Virginia Campbell (1845-1850)

Daughter of John Sale Campbell and Mary Frances Ennis
Great-grandaunt of Taylor Cosby Cottrell, Jr.

Virginia Campbell was born circa 1844 in Kentucky. She was the daughter of John Sale Campbell and Mary Frances Ennis. Virginia died before 1850. No additional information is known.[376]

Julia Ann Virginia Campbell (1845-1914)

Daughter of John Sale Campbell and Mary Frances Ennis
Great-grandaunt of Taylor Cosby Cottrell, Jr.

Julia Ann Campbell was born on 30 August 1845 in Warren County, Kentucky. She was the daughter of John Sale Campbell and Mary Frances Ennis.[377] She was listed on the census of 1850 in Warren County, Kentucky in the household of her father John Sale as Julia A., age 4.[378] In 1860 she was found on the Warren County census in the home of her father as Julia Ann, age 14.[379]

She married Charles E. Suman, the son of Eli and Julia Suman, on 31 March 1869. Charles was born on 6 January 1844 in Louisville in Jefferson County, Kentucky.[380] Julia was listed on the 1870 census with her husband Charles in Warren County, Kentucky as Julia A., age 24. Real estate was valued at $800 and personal estate was listed as $150.[381]

Charles was a Yard Master on the railroad in 1870. After serving as Yard Master in Bowling Green, he was made conductor on the road running from Bowling Green to Nashville, Tennessee. Around 1874 he became an invalid from an illness and during the next 10 years he visited the Hot Springs twice and had the best medical assistance to be found in the state.[382]

In 1880 they were living in the home of Julia's father John Sale Campbell. Charles was listed as C.E. Suman, age 36 and Julia was listed as J.A. Suman, age 33.[383]

Charles died on 18 July 1884 in Warren County, at age 40. Funeral services were held on 19 July 1884 in Warren County. His cause of death was from a long time illness. He was buried in Louisville in Jefferson County, Kentucky in Cave Hill Cemetery in Louisville.[384]

Julia's father John Campbell left a will on 19 January 1888 stating that Julia was to receive an equal share of his estate except that she was responsible for accounting for an amount equal to $1,805.70 which had already been advanced to her by her father. Each of her brothers and sisters had also received various amounts in advance and also had to account for these in the final settlement. On 25 April 1890 she was the hostess for her father's 87th birthday celebration at his home near Bowling Green.[385]

In 1900 Julia was listed on the household of her brother-in-law John H. Penner in Lawrence County, Illinois as Julia A. Suman, age 54 and widowed.[386] According to an article published in a Warren County newspaper she had placed an order for a Wellington piano in golden oak from Mr. Lawson, assumed to be from Warren County, and paid for it by check. In 1910 she was listed on the census in the household of Herbert Willis Campbell in Warren County as Julia A. Suman, age 60 and widowed.[387]

Julia died on 26 May 1914 in Bowling Green, at age 68. Her cause of death was peritonitis with a contributory pelvic tumor. She was buried on 27 May 1914 in Fairview Cemetery in Bowling Green in Section G, Site G-104.[388]

Chapter 6 – George Washington Campbell Family

Great-grandfather of Taylor Cosby Cottrell, Jr.

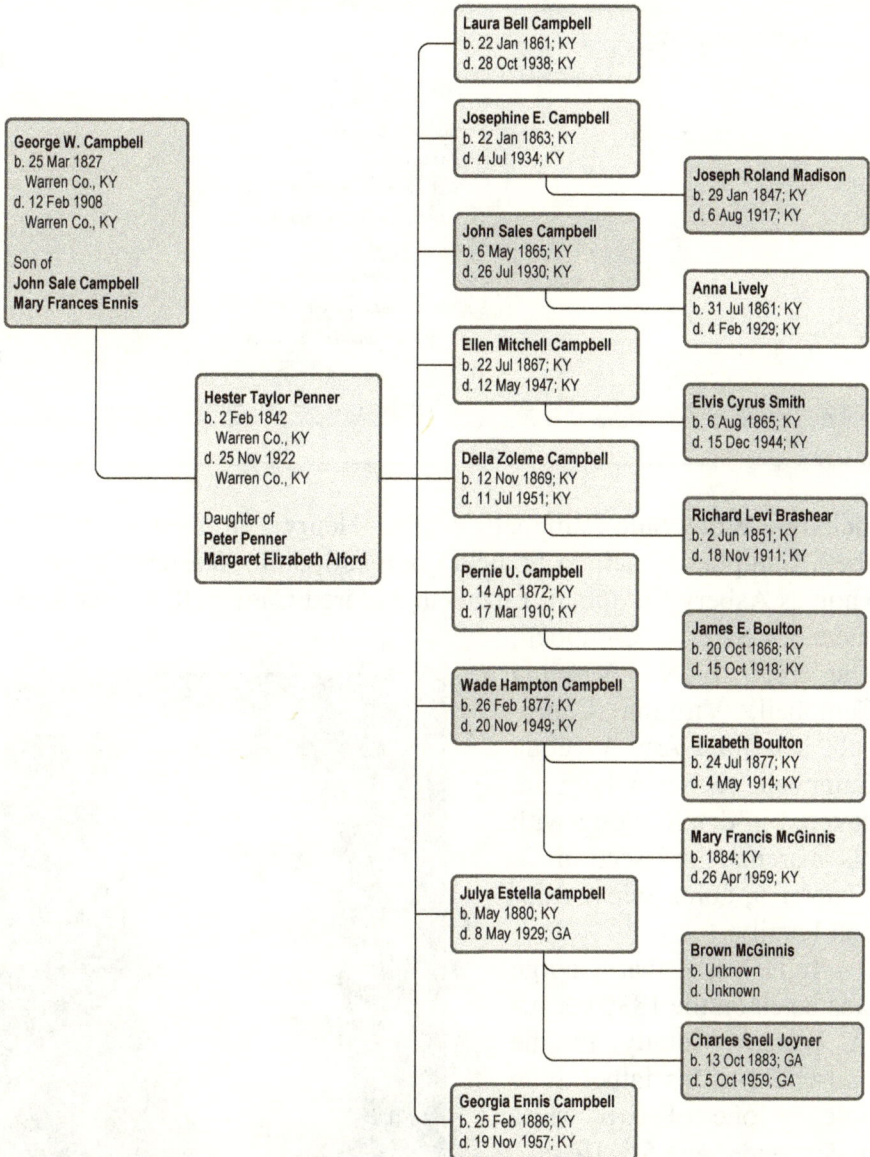

George W. Campbell
b. 25 Mar 1827
  Warren Co., KY
d. 12 Feb 1908
  Warren Co., KY

Son of
John Sale Campbell
Mary Frances Ennis

Hester Taylor Penner
b. 2 Feb 1842
  Warren Co., KY
d. 25 Nov 1922
  Warren Co., KY

Daughter of
Peter Penner
Margaret Elizabeth Alford

Laura Bell Campbell
b. 22 Jan 1861; KY
d. 28 Oct 1938; KY

Josephine E. Campbell
b. 22 Jan 1863; KY
d. 4 Jul 1934; KY

Joseph Roland Madison
b. 29 Jan 1847; KY
d. 6 Aug 1917; KY

John Sales Campbell
b. 6 May 1865; KY
d. 26 Jul 1930; KY

Anna Lively
b. 31 Jul 1861; KY
d. 4 Feb 1929; KY

Ellen Mitchell Campbell
b. 22 Jul 1867; KY
d. 12 May 1947; KY

Elvis Cyrus Smith
b. 6 Aug 1865; KY
d. 15 Dec 1944; KY

Della Zoleme Campbell
b. 12 Nov 1869; KY
d. 11 Jul 1951; KY

Richard Levi Brashear
b. 2 Jun 1851; KY
d. 18 Nov 1911; KY

Pernie U. Campbell
b. 14 Apr 1872; KY
d. 17 Mar 1910; KY

James E. Boulton
b. 20 Oct 1868; KY
d. 15 Oct 1918; KY

Wade Hampton Campbell
b. 26 Feb 1877; KY
d. 20 Nov 1949; KY

Elizabeth Boulton
b. 24 Jul 1877; KY
d. 4 May 1914; KY

Mary Francis McGinnis
b. 1884; KY
d.26 Apr 1959; KY

Julya Estella Campbell
b. May 1880; KY
d. 8 May 1929; GA

Brown McGinnis
b. Unknown
d. Unknown

Charles Snell Joyner
b. 13 Oct 1883; GA
d. 5 Oct 1959; GA

Georgia Ennis Campbell
b. 25 Feb 1886; KY
d. 19 Nov 1957; KY

George Washington Campbell was born on 25 March 1827 in Warren County, Kentucky. He was the son of John Sale Campbell and
Mary Frances Ennis.[1] George had at least eleven brothers and sisters

George W. Campbell Family Timeline

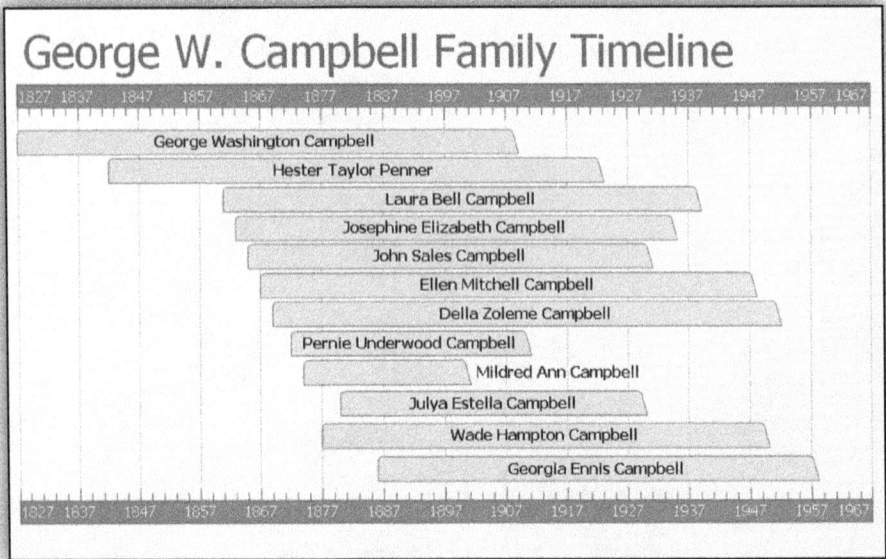

| 1827 | 1837 | 1847 | 1857 | 1867 | 1877 | 1887 | 1897 | 1907 | 1917 | 1927 | 1937 | 1947 | 1957 | 1967 |

George Washington Campbell
Hester Taylor Penner
Laura Bell Campbell
Josephine Elizabeth Campbell
John Sales Campbell
Ellen Mitchell Campbell
Della Zoleme Campbell
Pernie Underwood Campbell
Mildred Ann Campbell
Julya Estella Campbell
Wade Hampton Campbell
Georgia Ennis Campbell

including Wiley Sale Campbell, William Henry Campbell, Mary Elizabeth Campbell, Lucinda Francis Campbell, John Wesley Campbell, Thomas Asbery Campbell, Elizabeth Mildred Campbell, James Alexander Sale Campbell, Margaret Lucy Virginia Campbell, Virginia Campbell, and Julia Ann Virginia Campbell, each of whom are covered in detail, along with his parents, in Section 2, Chapter 5, John Sale Campbell Family.

It is likely that George was listed on the 1830 census in Warren County in the household of his father John Sale as one of two white males, under age 5.[2] He also likely appeared on the 1840 census of Warren County in the home of his father as one

George Washington Campbell

of two white males, ages 10 to 14.[3] In 1850 he was listed in the home of his father in Warren County as George W., age 23.[4]

A bond for the marriage of George Washington Campbell and Hester Taylor Penner was signed on 20 November 1858 in Bowling Green, Kentucky by George W. Campbell and John R. Penner.[5] George married Hester, the daughter of Peter Penner and Margaret Elizabeth Alford, on 25 November 1858 in Warren County. Hester was born on 2 February 1842 in Warren County.[6] She had at least eleven brothers and sisters including Margaret Polly Ann Penner,

Hester Taylor Penner

Louisa Penner, Martha Penner, Mary Malvina Penner, John H. Penner, William F. Penner, Peter W. Penner, Milburn Jay Penner, Elizabeth F. Penner, Josephene Penner, and Calvin B. Penner each of whom are covered in detail, along with her parents, in Section 2, Chapter 7, Peter Penner Family.

On the 1860 census in Warren County George was listed as George Campbell, age 32 with a real estate value of $2,600 and a personal estate valued at $2,000. His wife Hester, age 19 was also listed along with a farm laborer living in the home.[7]

In 1868 George built a home on a farm he bought from John Whalen. The residence was occupied in later years by his daughters Miss Georgia and Miss Laura Campbell. It was said that many members of the family and friends frequently gathered on happy occasions at the home.[8] He appeared on the 1870 census in Warren County as Geo. W. Campbell, age 44 with an estate valued at $5,000 and personal property valued at $2,000. His wife Hester T., age 29 was also listed along with Laura B., age 9 and Josephine, age 7 and attending school. John S., age 5, Mary E., age 3, and Della, age 6/12 were also listed. A farm laborer, age 17 was also living in the household.[9]

In 1880 George was listed on the Warren County census as George Campbell, age 53. His wife Hester, age 33 was listed as keeping house. Included in the household were 7 daughters; Laura, age 19, Josephine, age 17, Ellen, age 12, Della (name unreadable), age 10, Pernie (name unreadable), age 8, Mildred, age 5, and Julia, age one month. Also included in the household were 2 sons; John, age 15 and Wade H., age 3.[10]

George Washington Campbell Home

George was listed as owning a farm on the 1880 agricultural schedule of Gochean District in Warren County that included 41 acres of improved land and 15 acres of unimproved land. Total value including land, buildings, machinery and livestock was listed as $700. Livestock included one horse, two mules, and one milk cow which produced 75 pounds of butter the previous year. The farm included 18 swine and 12 chickens which produced 50 eggs during 1879. During the previous year 15 acres of land were used to produce 450 bushels of Indian corn, 5 acres produced 100 bushels of oats, and 7 acres produced 35 bushels of whey. Additional crop produced included one bushel of dry beans, 5 bushels of potatoes, and 2000 pounds of tobacco. Eighteen cords of lumber, valued at $18, were cut from the land in 1879.[11]

George's father John Sale left a will on 19 January 1888 stating that George was to receive an equal share of his estate except that he was responsible for accounting for an amount equal to $1595.30 which had already been advanced to him by his father. Each of his brothers and sisters had also received various amounts in advance and also had to account for these in the final settlement.[12]

George and his family were guests at the 87th birthday celebration of his father, John S. Campbell on 25 April 1890.[13] On 6 June 1892

George left a will in Warren County, Kentucky, witnessed by J.E. Potter and H.P. Potter. George appointed his son John S. Campbell as executor and directed that all of his estate and property, both real and personal including stocks, bonds, notes, accounts, and money was to go to his wife Hester except if she remarried in which case she was to take the estate and property according to the provisions of the laws of the State of Kentucky. In the following provisions of his will, George specifically left detailed instructions for the care of each of his daughters who were single on 6 June 1892. These provisions were to be in effect in the event his wife Hester remarried or died. George ultimately left his remaining estate, after all of the 14 elements of the will had been carried out, to be equally divided among his remaining children.[14]

On 10 January 1893 George signed the marriage bond for his daughter Della Zoleme Campbell to be married to Richard Levi Brashear. Richard also signed binding them to the Commonwealth of Kentucky in the sum of One Hundred Dollars in the event the marriage did not take place.[15]

George was listed on the 1900 census in Warren County as George W. Campbell, age 73. Also listed was his wife Hester T., age 58 and children Laura B., age 39, Elen M., age 32, Wade H., age 23, Julie E., age 20, and Georgia E., age 14. George and Hester were listed as having been married for 42 years and Hester was listed as the mother of 10 children, 9 of whom were living at the time of the census. Wade was working as a farm laborer and Georgia was in school.[16]

George died on 12 February 1908 in Warren County, at age 80. His cause of death was pneumonia. He

George Washington Campbell		
1830	Warren County, KY	N/A
1840	Warren County, KY	N/A
1850	Warren County, KY	A Laborer
1860	Warren County, KY	Farmer
1870	Warren County, KY	Farmer
1880	Warren County, KY	Farmer
1900	Warren County, KY	Farmer

was buried on 13 February 1908 in Fairview Cemetery in Bowling Green in Section A, Site A-86.[17] His estate was probated on 9 March 1908 in Warren County after having been initially offered to the court for probate on 24 February 1908, but delayed due to the death of one of the witnesses to the will, H.P. Potter. Final probate occurred after proof by the oath of Geor. Willis and the matter laid over and then being proved by the deposition of J.E. Potter.[18]

Hester appeared on the 1910 census in Warren County as Hester T. Campbell, age 49, widowed and mother of 10 children with 8 living. Her daughters Laura B., age 49, Julie E., age 29, and Georgia E., age 24, all single, were also listed. A 16-year-old child, Arthur Clark, was also listed as a "Boy to Raise."[19]

Hester left a will on 28 August 1912 in Warren County, witnessed by J.M. Taylor and Lillie Almond. She left her daughter Laura and son George her home and any other article of her household and kitchen furniture that either of them may want and then directed that the remaining of her estate be divided equally between all of her children. She appointed her sons John and Wade as executors.[20]

George W. Campbell & Hester Taylor Penner
Fairview Cemetery
Bowling Green, Kentucky

In 1920 she was listed on the census in Warren County as Hester Campbell, age 70. Her daughters Laura, age 57 and Georgia, age 33 were listed as single. Her granddaughter Clyde Boulton, age 24 and grandson Geo. Madison, age 30, both single, were also listed on the census.[21]

Hester died on 25 November 1922 in Warren County, at age 80. She was buried in Fairview Cemetery in Bowling Green in A, Site A-86.[22] Her estate was probated on 25 December 1922 in Warren County, proved by the oaths of J.M. Taylor and Lillie Almond.[23]

Laura Bell Campbell (1861-1938)

Daughter of George W. Campbell and Hester T. Penner
Grandaunt of Taylor Cosby Cottrell, Jr.

Laura Bell Campbell was born on 22 January 1861 in Warren County, Kentucky. She was the daughter of George Washington Campbell and Hester Taylor Penner.[24] She was listed on the 1870 census in the home of her father George as Laura B., age 9 and attending school.[25]

In 1880 she was listed in her father's household on the census in Warren County as Laura Bell, age 19 and single.[26] She was found on the 1900 census in Warren County in the home of her father as Laura B., age 39 and single.[27]

After her father's death in 1908 Laura and her sister Georgia occupied their father's home and they became known as "Miss Laura" and "Miss Georgia". The home was originally built in 1868. It was said that members of the family and friends gathered there on many happy occasions and that "the latch-string was always on the outside and many Bowling Green young people loved to go there for picnics and fun."[28]

Laura Bell Campbell

Laura was listed on the 1910 census in Warren County in the home of her mother as Laura B., age 49 and single.[29] She was named in her mother's will on 28 August 1912, witnessed by J.M. Taylor and Lillie Almond. The will left her home and any other article of her household and kitchen furniture to Laura and her brother George with the stipulation that they could have whatever they wanted and that the remaining of her estate was to be divided equally between all of her children.[30]

Laura was listed on the 1920 census in Warren County in the home of her mother as Laura, age 57 and single.[31] In 1930 she was listed as Laura Campbell, age 69 along with her sister Georgia, age 44. Also listed in the household was her adopted daughter Bertha Douglas, age 26. Her home, which was located in Richardsville, was valued at $8,000.[32]

Child of Laura Bell Campbell:

- Bertha Douglas – Born on 8 November 1902 in Warren County, Kentucky and died on 11 October 1985 in Warren County, at age 83.[33] Bertha was the adopted daughter of Laura

Bell Campbell. Information on birth parents is unknown. Bertha married Robert W. Moulder on 5 February 1944 in Warren County. Robert was born on 14 December 1911 in Fulton, Kentucky and died on 3 July 1989 in Bowling Green, at age 77.[34] The 1949 Bowling green City Directory listed Robert W. (Bertha) Sheet Metal Contractor, Heating and Ventilating and Furnace Repairs at 544 E. 10th. Street thus it appears they were owners of a contracting business located in their home.[35]

Bertha Douglas

Laura died 28 October 1938 in Warren County, at age 77 in her home in the Rays Branch neighborhood on the Richardsville Road following an illness of about six months. Her cause of death was arteriosclerosis. Funeral services were held at the Rays Branch Methodist Church with the Rev. J.L. McGee, pastor of the church conducting the service assisted by Rev. Dr. G.W. Hummell, presiding elder

Laura Bell Campbell
Fairview Cemetery
Bowling Green, Kentucky

of the district. Pallbearers were Dr. James W. Blackburn, Dr. John H. Blackburn, E.J. Miller, A.J. Miller, C.A. Smith, and A.Y. Patterson. She was buried in Fairview Cemetery in Bowling Green in Section A, Site A-86.[36]

Josephine Elizabeth Campbell (1863-1934)

Daughter of George W. Campbell and Hester T. Penner
Grandaunt of Taylor Cosby Cottrell, Jr.

Josephine Elizabeth Campbell was born on 22 January 1863 in Rays Branch in Warren County, Kentucky. She was the daughter of

George Washington Campbell and Hester Taylor Penner.[37] She was listed on the 1870 census in the home of her father George as Josephine, age 7 and attending school.[38] In 1880 she was listed on the Warren County census in the home of her father as Josephine, age 17 and single.[39]

She married Joseph Roland Madison, son of Joel Richard Madison and Mary Jane Herrington on 23 December 1884 in Warren County at the residence of J. Campbell in the presence of Bruce Madison and George Campbell.[40] Joseph was born on 29 January 1847 in Warren County, Kentucky.[41] Joseph was a graduate of the Transylvania University in Lexington, Kentucky with a degree in English Literature, Mathematics, and Civil Engi-

Josephine Elizabeth Campbell

neering. He was employed for a time as a Civil Engineer on the Chicago and North-Western Railroad which was engaged in bridge building for the King Bridge Company in Cleveland, Ohio. He taught school for a short time in Illinois before returning to Kentucky where he taught in both Logan and Warren Counties until he turned his attention to farming in 1883.[42]

She was listed on the 1910 census in Warren County in the home of her husband Joseph as Josephine, age 47 and the mother of 9 children with 8 living. Her sons Fonzo C., age 24, George W., age 20, and Joel R., age 10 along with daughters Betsey, age 22, Novio C., age 18, Mary H., age 16, Wilkins J., age 14, and Ruth, age 8 were also listed.[43]

Children of Josephine E. Campbell and Joseph R. Madison:

- Alphonso Campbell Madison – Born on 5 December 1885 in Warren County, Kentucky and died on 13 June 1932 in Bowling Green, Kentucky at age 46. His cause of death was from high blood pressure and a cardio hemorrhage. He was buried on 15 June 1932 in Fairview Cemetery in Section F, Site F-111.[44] He married Katie Berdean Howell in 1917. She was born on 20 January 1898 in Warren County. She was the daughter of Jame Howell and Madie Miller.[45] Katie died on 21 March 1925 in Warren County, at age 27. Her cause of death was typhoid fever. She was also buried in Fairview Cemetery.[46] Alphonso married Minnie McAlister in 1926. Minnie was born around 1895 in Kentucky.[47] No additional information is known.

- Betsy Madison – Born on 23 December 1887 in Warren County, Kentucky and died on 16 July 1941 in Bellefonte in Centre County, Pennsylvania at age 53. She was buried in Lexington Cemetery in Lexington, Fayette County, Kentucky.[48] Betsy In 1919 Betsy was a teacher in a commission school. She married Wayland Rhoads, the son of McHenry Rhoads and Ree Crawford around 1922. Wayland died on 6 July 1972 in Muhlenberg County, Kentucky at age 79. He was buried in Lexington Cemetery in Lexington, Kentucky.[49] Betsy and Wayland had two daughters born before 1930 at least one additional child including:
    o William McHenry Rhoads – Born on 28 August 1924 in Lexington in Fayette County, Kentucky and died on 23 August 1996 in Louisville in Jefferson County, Kentucky, at age 71.[50] He was buried in Lakeside Memorial Gardens in Somerset in Pulaski County, Kentucky.[51] William married Mary K. Floyd on 23 December 1988 in Jefferson County.[52]

- George Washington Madison – Born on 10 September 1889 in Warren County, Kentucky and died on 7 January 1967 in Warren County, at age 77. He was buried on 9 January 1967 in Chapel Hill Memorial Gardens in Bowling Green.[53] George was described as tall with a slender build, blue eyes and light hair when he registered for the WWI Draft in 1917 while living in Bowling Green. He married Elizabeth King between 1930 and 1938.[54] They had at least two children, a daughter born in 1939 and a daughter born in 1944. Elizabeth died on 26 January 1993 in Bowling Green, at age 81. She was buried in Chapel Hill Memorial Gardens in Bowling Green.[55]

- Novice C. Madison – Novice was born around 1892 in Warren County, Kentucky and died on 11 March 1984 in Warren County. She was buried in Fairview Cemetery in Bowling Green.[56] She married Lonnie Robert Robinson, the son of Rufas L. Robinson, around 1910.[57] Lonnie died on 26 May 1955 in Warren County, at age 64. He was also buried in Fairview Cemetery.[58] They had at least one child including:
    o William Gray Robinson – Born on 20 April 1916 in Warren County and died on 5 September 2003 in Warren County, at age 87. He was buried in Fairview Cemetery.[59] He was also known as Billy. He began military service on 17 January 1941 as a Sergeant in the National Guard. In 1941 he had finished four years of college, was still single, and was working as either an entertainer or in the motion picture industry.[60]

- Mary H. Madison – Mary was born on 29 May 1893 in Warren County, Kentucky and died on 13 December 1978 in Jefferson County, Kentucky.[61] Mary married Emil Gustav Pormann, son of Emil Gustav and Lydia Bertha Pormann in 1921.[62] Emil was born on 6 August 1893 in Sodz, Poland, Russia. He immigrated to Jefferson County, Kentucky in 1902 with his parents, brothers, and sisters.[63] Emil died on 5 June 1962 in Jefferson County, Kentucky at age 68.[64] They had at least one child including:
    o Marilyn M. Pormann – Born on 27 October 1922 in Jefferson County and died on 27 November 2011 in Louisville at the Twinbrook Nursing Home. She was buried in Evergreen Cemetery in Louisville, Kentucky. She married Frank H. Landers and they had at least one child.[65] Frank was likely born on 25 March 1919 and died in December 1981.[66]

- Wilkins J. Madison – Born on 11 June 1895 in Warren County, Kentucky and died on 5 January 1979 in Henderson County, Kentucky at age 83.[67] She married Collis Wilkerson Robinson on 21 September 1913 in Sumner County, Tennessee.[68] Collis was born on 6 May 1895 in Nashville, Tennessee.[69] Wilkins and Collis divorced in 1931.[70] Collis died on 3 March 1970 in

Warren County, at age 74. He was buried in Fairview Cemetery. [71] Wilkins then re-married around 1932.[72] Her second husband was William Allen Settle who was born on 23 January 1890 and died on 21 June 1957. He was also buried in Fairview Cemetery.[73] Wilkins and William apparently had no children, However Wilkins had at least three children with her first husband Collis including:

- o R.L. Robinson, Jr. – Born on 25 November 1914 in Warren County and died on 30 January 1917 at the age of 2 years, 2 months, and 5 days from chronic bronchitis in Bowling Green. He was buried in Fairview Cemetery in Site 38-28.[74]
- o Anna Josephine Robinson – Born on 15 April 1925 in Warren County and died on 22 February 1996 in Henderson County, Kentucky.[75] She married John H. Stocking.[76] He was born on 28 January 1923 and died on 24 March 2002 in Henderson County.[77]
- o Collis Robinson, Jr. – Born on 5 August 1926 in Bowling Green and died on 24 April 1957 in Covington in Kenton County, Kentucky, at age 30. He was buried in Floral Hills Cemetery in Kenton County, Kentucky. Collis was listed as married on his death record. The informant was listed as Mrs. Thelma Trosper Robinson, who was likely his wife.[78]

- Joel Roland Madison – Born on 12 October 1900 in Bowling Green, Kentucky. He married Doris Williams Williamson sometime after 1920. Doris was born on 22 September 1910 in Graham, Texas. Joel was described as tall with a medium build with gray eyes and brown hair when he registered for the WWI Draft in 1918 while living in Bowling Green. Joel and Doris apparently had no children. Joel died on 15 April 1975 in Graham in Young County, Texas, at age 75.[79] Doris died on 6 November 1977 in Graham, Texas. She was buried in Oak Grove Cemetery in Graham, Texas.[80]
- Ruth Madison – Born circa 1902 in Warren County, Kentucky. Listed on the 1910 census of her father as Ruth, age 8, living on the Richardsville Road, and attending school.[81] No additional information is known about Ruth.

- Jessie Brown Madison – Born in September 1904 in Warren County, Kentucky and died on 23 October 1905 in Warren County, Kentucky, at age 1. He was buried in Fairview Cemetery in Bowling Green in Section A, Site A-86.[82]

Joseph Madison died on 6 August 1917 in Bowling Green, at age 70. His cause of death was chronic intestinal nephritis. He was buried on 8 August 1917 in Fairview Cemetery in Section F, Site F-111.[83]

Josephine was listed on the 1920 census in Warren County as Josie D. Madison, age 57 and widowed. She owned her home free of mortgage. Alphonso C., age 34 was also listed as her married son along with Katie, age 21 who was listed as her daughter-in-law.[84] On the 1930 census she listed as Josie, age 67 and was living with her son George Washington Madison on Garvin Lane in Warren County.[85]

Josephine died on 4 July 1934 in Bowling Green, at age 71. Her cause of death was heart related disease suffered since 1930. She was buried in Fairview Cemetery in Section F, Site F-111.[86]

John Sales Campbell (1865-1930)

Son of George W. Campbell and Hester T. Penner
Granduncle of Taylor Cosby Cottrell, Jr.

John Sales Campbell was born on 6 May 1865 in Warren County, Kentucky. He was the son of George Washington Campbell and Hester Taylor Penner.[87] He was listed on the 1870 census in Warren County in the home of his father George as John S., age 5.[88] In 1880 he was found on the census in Warren County in the home of his father as John, age 15, and attending school.[89]

A bond for the marriage of John Sales Campbell and Anna Lively was sighed on 15 December 1891 in Warren County by John S. Campbell. John married Anna, who was the daughter of John Monroe Lively and Elizabeth O. Coleman, on 16 December 1891 in Bowling Green. The ceremony was performed by Ed. E. Joiner in the presence of Eugene H. Gerard.[90] Anna was born on 31 July 1861 in Warren County.[91]

John was named in the will of his father on 6 June 1892 in Warren County. His father appointed him as executor and directed that his estate be passed to John's mother Hester unless she remarried. The will left detailed instructions for caring for John's sisters who were unmarried at the time and for handling his remaining estate which was to be divided equally to his living brothers and sisters. These provisions were to be in effect in the event John's mother Hester remarried or died.[92]

John was listed on the 1910 census in Warren County as John S., age 44 along with his wife Anna L., age 46, his son Walton L., age 15, and daughter Francis E., age 12. His mother-in-law Lizzie O. Penner, age 70 and widowed was also listed in his household. They were living on a farm, free of mortgage, which was located on the Richardsville Road at the time.[93]

John Sales Campbell

John was named in the will of his mother Hester on 28 August 1912 in Warren County. She left her home to John's sister Laura and brother George and directed that any remaining estate be divided equally between her children. She appointed John's brothers John B. and Wade H. as executors.[94] John appeared on the 1920

John Sales Campbell		
1870	Warren County, KY	N/A
1880	Warren County, KY	N/A
1900	Warren County, KY	Unknown
1910	Warren County, KY	Farmer
1920	Warren County, KY	Farmer

census in Warren County as John S., age 54 along with his wife Anna E., age 58, son Walton L., age 25, and daughter Francis E., age 23.[95]

Children of John Sales Campbell and Anna Lively:

- Walton Lively Campbell – Born on 14 July 1894 in Bowling Green, Kentucky and died on 14 April 1949 in Jefferson County, Kentucky, at age 54 at his home in Louisville. His cause of death was cerebral Hemorrhage. He was buried on 16 April 1949 in the Zachary Taylor National Cemetery in Louisville, in Section C, Site 49.[96] Walton was described as short with gray eyes and black hair when he registered for the WWI Draft in 1917. He served in the military from 3 June 1918 until his discharge on 30 September 1921. He married Anna Katherine Ridsdale sometime before 1924.[97] She was born on 28 November 1904 in Jefferson County, Kentucky and was the daughter of Mary Breedlove and Roy Ridsdale. Anna died on 2 May 1975 in Jefferson County, at age 70. She was also buried on 6 May 1975 in Zachary Taylor National Cemetery in Louisville in Section C, Site 50.[98] In 1938 Walton was living on Route 3 in Warren County and in April 1940 he was working as an assistant meat packer foreman. Walton and Anna had a daughter born around 1937 and at least one additional child including:

- o John Sales Campbell - Born on 16 September 1924 in Lexington in Fayette County, Kentucky and died in February 1984, likely in Louisville. He was buried in Calvary Cemetery in Louisville.[99] John married Emma Frances Roberts who was born on 11 February 1929 in Louisville and died on 31 January 2007 in Louisville. She was also buried in Calvary Cemetery.[100] They had at least one daughter and two sons.[101]
- Francis E. Campbell – Born in 1903 in Kentucky.[102] Francis married Louis R. Currey in 1923. Louis was born on 14 September 1897 in Davidson County, Tennessee and was the son of Louis Robert Currey and Fannie Weaver Turbeville.[103] In 1930 they were living in Nashville, Tennessee at 2009 24th Avenue South. Louis died in April 1968 in Tennessee. Date and location of death of Francis is unknown.[104] They apparently had no children.

Anna died on 4 February 1929 in Warren County at the age of 67. Her cause of death was apoplexy and kidney trouble after a fall off of a veranda. She was buried on 5 February 1929 in Fairview Cemetery in Bowling Green in Section C, Site C-240 with Gerard Funeral Home handling the arrangements.[105]

John died on 26 July 1930 at his home on the Richardsville Road in Bowling Green, at age 65 at 7:45 in the evening. His cause of death was cardiac decompensation. He was buried in Fairview Cemetery on 28 July 1930 in Section D, Site C-240.[106]

Ellen Mitchell Campbell (1867-1947)

Daughter of George W. Campbell and Hester T. Penner
Grandaunt of Taylor Cosby Cottrell, Jr.

Ellen Mitchell Campbell was born on 22 July 1867 in Warren County, Kentucky. She was the daughter of George Washington Campbell and Hester Taylor Penner.[107] She was listed on the 1870 census in Warren County in the home of her father George as Mary E., age 3.[108] In 1880 she was found on the census of her father in Warren County as Ellen, age 12 and attending school.[109]

Ellen Mitchell Campbell

On 13 January 1900 Ellen and her sister Mildred, who was an invalid, boarded the southbound train out of Bowling Green to go south for Mildred's health. During the trip Mildred became rapidly worse and as Ellen "bent over the berth and caught the last whispered message for loved ones at home" Mildred died. The train reached Thomasville about 2:00 in the morning on Sunday the 14th of January where the body was taken charge of by an undertaker and prepared for shipment back to Kentucky. Later that afternoon Mildred's remains were taken to the railway station and she was taken back, accompanied by her sister Ellen, to her "old Kentucky home."[110]

Ellen was listed on the 1900 census in Warren County in the home of her father as Ellen M., age 32 and single.[111] Ellen married Elvis Cyrus Smith, the son of Herschel Porter Smith and Ellen E. Shobe, on 10 December 1902 in Rays Branch in Warren County.[112]

Elvis was born on 6 August 1865 in Oakland in Warren County. He had previously been married to Ada Garvin sometime before 1894.[113] Elvis and Ada had at least one child Virginia T. Smith, who was born in 1894 in Bowling Green, married John Brent Donaldson around 1911, died on 11 February 1968 in the City County Hospital in

Bowling Green, and was buried in Fairview Cemetery.[114] Ada was employed as the secretary-treasurer of Planter's Tobacco Warehouse in Warren County for 47 years and then at the Beech Bend Park Office for the last 15 years of her life.[115]

Ellen was listed on the 1910 census in Warren County in the home of her husband Elvis as Ellen C., age 42. Also listed in the household was Elvis's daughter from his first marriage Virginia T., age 18 as well as the three children of Elvis and Ellen including Sara B., age 6, Hester S., age 2, and George P, age 4. They were living on Beach Bend Road near Bowling Green at the time. Elvis was employed as the Warren County Court Clerk at the time.[116]

In 1920 Ellen was found on the census in Warren County in the home of her husband as Ellen C., age 52 along with her daughters Sarah, age 15, and Hester, age 12, and son George P, age 14.[117] She was listed on the 1930 census with her husband in Warren County as Ellen, age 60 along with her daughter Hester, age 32. They were living on Garvin Lane at the time.[118]

Children of Ellen Mitchell Campbell and Elvis Cyrus Smith:

- Sarah Beauchamp Smith – Born on 30 January 1904 in Bowling Green, Kentucky and died on 15 January 2005 in Louisville, at age 100. She was buried in Fairview Cemetery in Bowling Green.[119] Sarah married Allen Leroy Dodd around 1926. Allen was born on 13 July 1901 in Pennsylvania and died on 12 May 1988 in Bowling Green. He was buried in Fairview Cemetery.[120] Sarah and Allen had at least three children including a son and two daughters.[121]

- George Porter Smith – Born on 4 May 1906 in Warren County, Kentucky and died on 28 January 1924 in Delefield in Warren County at age 17. His cause of death was leukemia. He was buried on 6 February 1924 in Fairview Cemetery in Section G, Site G-106.[122]

- Hester Shobe Smith – Born on 23 July 1907 in Bowling Green, Kentucky and died on 25 December 2006 in St. Vincent Memorial Hospital in Taylorville in Christian County, Illinois at age 99. Memorial services were held on 30 December 2006 at the First Presbyterian Church in Taylorville. She was buried in Fairview Cemetery in Bowling Green, Kentucky.[123] Hester married Paul Gunther Gottschalk in 1934 in Bowling Green, Kentucky.[124] Paul was born on 25 October 1905 in Krefeid, Germany. He was listed on the "non-immigrant-manifest" of the S.S. Cleveland that departed Hamburg, Germany on 7 July 1927 and arrived in the port of New York on 21 July 1927. He was traveling under Immigration Visa Number 491 at the time.[125] Hester and Paul had at one child, a son who was born on 13 June 1935 in Portsmouth, Virginia. In 2005 they lived in Taylorsville, Illinois where Hester was a retired librarian from the Taylorville High School and a member and Elder of the First Presbyterian Church in Taylorville. She had served as president of the Taylorville Education Association and the school employee credit union and was the past Regent of Peter Meyer Charter DAR, past President of St. Vincent Hospital Auxiliary, and a member of Phi Chapter Delta Kappa Gamma and the retired teachers' association. She was also a Kentucky Colonel.[126] Paul Senior died on 7 September 1978. He was buried in Fairview Cemetery in Bowling Green.[127]

Ellen died on 12 May 1947 at her home on Beach Bend Road in Warren County, at age 79. Her cause of death was myocardial failure. She was buried on 18 May 1947 in Fairview Cemetery in Section G, Site G-106.[128]

Elvis died on 15 December 1944 at his home on Beach Bend Road, at age 79. His cause of death was uremia due to cardio vascular renal disease of more than 4 years. He was buried on 30 December 1944 in Fairview Cemetery in Section G, Site G-106.[129]

Della Zoleme Campbell (1869-1951)

Daughter of George W. Campbell and Hester T. Penner
Grandaunt of Taylor Cosby Cottrell, Jr.

Della Zoleme Campbell was born on 12 November 1869 in Bowling Green in Warren County, Kentucky. She was the daughter of George Washington Campbell and Hester Taylor Penner.[130] Information on Della and her husband Richard Levi Brashear and their four children is covered in detail in Section 2, Chapter 3, Richard Levi Brashear Family.

Pernie Underwood Campbell (1872-1910)

Daughter of George W. Campbell and Hester T. Penner
Grandaunt of Taylor Cosby Cottrell, Jr.

Pernie Underwood Campbell was born on 14 April 1872 in Rays Branch in Warren County, Kentucky. She was the daughter of George Washington Campbell and Hester Taylor Penner.[131] She was listed on the 1880 census in the household of her father George in Warren County, as what appears to be Pernie, age 8.[132]

A bond for the marriage of Pernie Underwood Campbell and James E. Boulton was signed on 29 November 1893 in Warren County, Kentucky.[133]

Purnie Underwood Campbell

James was born on 20 October 1868 in Warren County and was the son of William E. Boulton and Mary F. McGinnis.[134]

James was listed on the 1910 census in Warren County as James E. Boulton, age 41, head of household, and widowed. His daughters Clide O., age 15 and Mildred J., age 8 were also listed in his household.[135]

Pernie died on 17 March 1910 in Green Castle in Warren County, at age 37. Funeral services were held on 18 March 1910.[136] James died on 15 October 1918 in Warren County at age 49. They were both buried in Fairview Cemetery in Bowling Green.[137]

Children of Pernie Underwood Campbell and James E. Boulton:

- Clyde Aurelia Boulton – Born on 6 November 1894 in Warren County, Kentucky and died on 19 March 1984 in Bowling Green, Kentucky, at age 89. She was buried in Fairview Cemetery in Section H, Site H-127.[138] Clyde married John G. Cates, son of Samuel J. Cates and Minerva Thrailkill in 1927. John was born on 27 September 1896 in Muhlenberg County,

Kentucky.[139]   He was a veteran of WWI and in 1930 was a newspaper agent. Clyde was a high school teacher in 1930 and later became a professor at Western Kentucky University in Bowling Green. Clyde and John had no children. John died on 11 June 1973 in Bowling Green, at age 76. He was buried in Fairview Cemetery in Section H, Site H-127.[140]

- Mildred James Boulton – Born on 13 August 1902 in Kentucky and died on 18 July 1981 in Muhlenberg County, Kentucky. She was buried in Fairview Cemetery in Bowling Green. Mildred married Wayland Rhoads, the son of McHenry Rhoads and Ree Crawford, circa 1942.[141] Wayland was born on 30 September 1892 in Frankfort, Kentucky.[142] He was described as tall with a medium build, blue eyes and brown hair when he registered for the WWI draft in 1917 while living in Independence in Kenton County, Kentucky. He was a professor at a state university in 1920. Wayland was previously married to Betsy Madison, the daughter of Joseph Roland Madison and Josephine Elizabeth Campbell. Betsy and Wayland were listed on the 1940 census in Fayette County, Kentucky with a son and two daughters.[143] Betsy died on 16 July 1941 in Bellefonte in Centre County, Pennsylvania, at age 53 and was buried in the Lexington Cemetery in Kentucky.[144] Wayland died on 6 July 1972 and was also buried in Lexington Cemetery.[145]

Mildred Ann Campbell (1874-1900)

Daughter of George W. Campbell and Hester T. Penner
Grandaunt of Taylor Cosby Cottrell, Jr.

Mildred Ann Campbell was born on 2 December 1874 in Kentucky. She was the daughter of George Washington Campbell and Hester Taylor Penner.[146] She was listed on the 1880 census in the household of her father George in Warren County as Mildred, age 5, disabled and attending school.[147]

She was named in the will of her father on 6 June 1892 where he specifically detailed instructions for the care of each of his unmarried daughters including Mildred. These provisions were to be in effect in the event that his wife, Mildred's mother Hester, remarried or died.[148]

Mildred and her sister Ellen boarded the southbound train out of Bowling Green on Saturday morning, the 13th of January 1900. Mildred, who was an invalid, was going south for her health. During the trip Mildred became rapidly worse and as Ellen "bent over the berth and caught the last whispered message for loved ones at home" Mildred died. The train reached Thomasville about 2:00 on Sunday morning, the 14th of January where Mildred's body was taken charge of by an undertaker and prepared for shipment back to Kentucky. Later that afternoon Mildred's remains were taken to the railway station and she was taken back, accompanied by her sister Ellen, to her "old Kentucky home."[149]

Mildred Ann Campbell

Mildred's death occurred on 13 January 1900 in Alabama at the age of 25 while passing southbound through Alabama on the train.[150] She was buried in Fairview Cemetery in Bowling Green in Section A, Site A-86.[151]

Wade Hampton Campbell (1877-1949)

Son of George W. Campbell and Hester T. Penner
Granduncle of Taylor Cosby Cottrell, Jr.

Wade Hampton Campbell was born on 26 February 1877 in Warren County, Kentucky. He was the son of George Washington Campbell and Hester Taylor Penner.[152] Wade was listed on the 1880 census in the household of his father George in Warren County as Wade H., age 3.[153] He was named in the will of his father on 6 June 1892 which was filed in Warren County. His brother John S. Campbell was appointed as executor of the will.[154] In 1900 Wade was listed on the census in Warren County in the home of his father as Wade H., age 23 and single.[155]

A bond for the marriage of Wade Hampton Campbell and Elizabeth Boulton was signed on 26 March 1901 in Bowling Green, Kentucky. Wade married Elizabeth, who was the daughter of William E. Boulton and Mary F. McGinnis, on 27 March 1901 at the home of R.K. McGinnis located on the Louisville and Nashville Pike near Bowling Green.[156] Elizabeth was born on 24 July 1877 in Warren County.[157] Her father William was born on 4 July 1830 and died on 7 November

Wade Hampton Campbell

1910 in Warren County. Her mother Mary was born on 28 July 1844 and died on 21 April 1904. They were both buried in Halls Chapel Cemetery in Bowling Green.[158] Wade's wife Elizabeth was a devout Christian and a member of the Methodist Church.

Wade was listed on the 1910 census in Warren County as Wade H. Campbell, age 33 along with his wife Elizabeth, age 30 and their daughter Bessie May, age 2.[159] He was named in the will of his mother Hester on 28 August 1912 in Warren County where he was appointed as co-executor along with his brother John B. Campbell.[160]

Children of Wade Hampton Campbell and Elizabeth Boulton:

- Grace Mae Campbell – Born on in Kentucky, likely on 18 November 1907. She was also known as Bessie Mae and Bess.[161] She married James Monroe Ford sometime after 1930.[162] James was born on 10 January 1911 in Rockfield, Kentucky. He was also known as Jimmie. James died on 2 August 1947 at Thomas Landing on the Barren River Road in Warren County, at age 36. He was buried in Fairview Cemetery in Section N, Site N-132w.[163] Grace and James had at least three children including:
  - o Bettie Jean Ford - Born on 29 February 1936 in Warren County and died on 6 January 1937 at 29 Watts Mill

Road in Lost River in Warren County. She was buried in Fairview Cemetery in Bowling Green.[164]

o James Campbell Ford - Stillborn on 24 February 1938 in the City-County Hospital in Bowling Green. He was buried in Fairview Cemetery.[165]

o James Hampton Ford - Born 4 August 1939 in Bowling Green and died 28 October 1939 in the City-County Hospital in Bowling Green. He was buried in Fairview Cemetery.[166]

Elizabeth died on 4 May 1914 in Bowling Green, at age 36 at her home on the Nashville pike near Crump's Mill. Her cause of death was rheumatism of the heart following an eight-day illness. Funeral services were held on 5 May 1914 at her residence with the Rev. B.S. Harper conducting the services. She was buried on 5 May 1914 in Fairview Cemetery in Bowling Green.[167]

A bond for the marriage of Wade Hampton Campbell and Mary Francis McGinnis was signed on 1 February 1916 in Bowling Green. Wade married Mary Francis on 2 February 1916 in Bowling Green. Mary Francis was born in 1884 in Warren County to Jessie and Mildred Moorman.[168] According to the 1930 census Mary's marriage to Wade was her second marriage, the first having been around 1912.

Wade was listed on the 1920 census in Warren County as Wade Campbell, age 42 along with his wife Mary, age 38 and two daughters Bessie May, age 12 and Mildred, age 1 month. He owned his own farm which was listed on farm schedule 26.[169] In 1930 he was found on the census in Warren County as Wade H. Campbell, age 53, owning his own home valued at $3,000 and his farm which was listed on farm schedule 71. His wife Mary F., age 47 was also listed along with two daughters Bessie M., age 22 and Mildred E., age 11.[170] In 1938 he was found in the Bowling Green City Directory as living on Route 4 in Warren County with personal property valued at $1,735 and as owning 180 acres of land.[171]

Children of Wade Hampton Campbell and Mary F. McGinnis:

▪ James Campbell – Stillborn on 24 May 1917 in Warren County, Kentucky at the family home on the Nashville Pike near Bowling Green. He was buried on 25 May 1917 in Fairview Cemetery in Bowling Green in Section G, Site G-104.[172]

- Mildred E. Campbell – Born on 29 July 1918 in Kentucky and died on 6 October 1978 in Bowling Green, at age 60 while an inpatient of Colonial Manor Nursing Home. Her last address before being admitted to Colonial Manor was 1341 State Street in Bowling Green. Her cause of death was heart disease and arteriolosclerosis which had an onset about one year prior to her death. Funeral services were held on 9 October 1978 at the J.C. Kirby Funeral Home in Bowling Green. She was buried in Fairview Cemetery.[173] Mildred was a member of the First Baptist Church and a graduate of Bowling Green Business University. She married Alphonse J. Soriero sometime after 1942.[174] Alphonse was born on 22 April 1910 in New York and was the son of Angelo Soriero and Caroline Soriero both of whom were born in Italy.[175] His father Angelo immigrated to the United States from Italy in 1898. He was naturalized in the State of New York on 26 May 1902. Alphonse enlisted the Army as a Private on 2 May 1942 at Fort Jay Governors Island in New York. His enlistment record indicated he was a semi-skilled chauffeur and driver of busses, taxis, trucks, and tractors and that he was single at that time. He was described as 67 inches in height and weighing 164 pounds.[176] Alfonse died on 27 June in Warren County, Kentucky at age 61. He was buried in Fairview Cemetery.[177]

Wade died on 20 November 1949 in Warren County, at age 72 at his home on the Nashville Road just outside Bowling Green. His cause of death was Colon ailment coupled with hypertensive heart disease. He was buried on 22 November 1949 in Fairview Cemetery in Bowling Green in Section G, Site G-104.[178] Mary Francis died on 26 April 1959 in Warren County. She was also buried in Fairview Cemetery in Section G, Site G-104.[179]

Julya Estella Campbell (1880-1929)

Daughter of George W. Campbell and Hester T. Penner
Grandaunt of Taylor Cosby Cottrell, Jr.

Julia Estella Campbell was born in May 1880 in Kentucky. She was the daughter of George Washington Campbell and Hester Taylor

Penner. She was listed on the 1880 census in the household of her father George in Warren County as Julia, age 2 months.[180] She was named in her father's will on 6 June 1892 where her father detailed specific instructions for the care of each of his daughters who were single on the date of the will.[181] She was found on the 1900 census in the household of her father in Warren County as Julia E., age 20 and single.[182]

Julya Estella Campbell

Julia married Brown McGinnis, the son of T.J. McGinnis, on 31 October 1900 in Bowling Green. Doctor William Irvine, pastor of the First Presbyterian Church, performed the ceremony. Wedding attendants were Misses Jimmie and Eva Lively, Julia's Sister Miss Ellen Campbell, and Messrs. Ras. Donaldson, Sam McFarland and Wade Campbell. The bridesmaids were handsomely attired in white and each bore a huge bouquet of white chrysanthemums. Following the ceremony, the bridal party went to the home of T.J. McGinnis where they attended a reception. They took up housekeeping on the Tobe Rogers farm in the bend near Bowling Green.[183] No additional information is known about Brown McGinnis. However it is interesting to note that Julia was listed on the 1910 census of her mother Hester in Warren County as Julia E. Campbell, age 29 and single.[184]

Julia married Charles Snell Joyner, the son of Huel Benjamin Joyner and Marianna Floried Snell, sometime after the 1910 census.[185] Charles was born on 13 October 1883 in Macon in Bibb County, Georgia.[186]

Julia was found on the 1920 census in the home of her husband Charles in Bibb County, Georgia as Julia C., age 39 along with their daughters Charlote J., age 6 and Majoi, age 5. Marrieva Joyner,

Charles mother, age 60 and widowed was also living in the household. They were living at 101 Summett Avenue in Macon at the time.[187]

Children of Julia Estella Campbell and Charles Snell Joyner:

- Charlotte Josephine Joyner – Born on 2 January 1913 in Macon in Bibb County, Georgia and died on 8 May 2005. She married Haywood B. Ainsworth who was born on 25 October 1907 and died on 2 July 1978.[188]
- Marjorie Joyner – Born on 5 July 1914 in Bibb County, Georgia and died on 30 June 1959 in Bibb County, Georgia at a local hospital after an extended illness. She was buried on 1 July 1959 in Riverside Cemetery in Macon in Bibb County, Georgia in Hydrangea, Row C, Lot 5.[189] She married Herman Isaac Mueller, the son of Curt Mueller and Marie McCrary, likely on 2 September 19033 in Aiken, South Carolina.[190] Herman was born on 10 December 1914 and died on 26 December 1997. He was also buried in Riverside Cemetery.[191]
- Huel Campbell Joyner – Born on 3 September 1919 in Bibb County, Georgia and died on 19 September 1919 in Macon in Bibb County, at age 16 days. Funeral services were held on 20 September 1919 in Macon. He was buried on 20 September 1919 in Riverside Cemetery in in Macon in Honeysuckle, Row C18, Lot 1.[192]
- Charlie M. Joyner – Born circa 1923 in Bibb County, Georgia. No additional information is known about Charlie.[193]

Julia died on 8 May 1929 in Bibb County, Georgia. Funeral services were held on 10 May 1929 at her residence on Summit Avenue in Macon with the Dr. C.R. Jenkins, pastor of the Mulberry Street Methodist Church and Dr. E.C. Lacy, pastor of the First Christian Church in charge of the services. She was buried on 10 May 1929 in Riverside Cemetery in Macon in Honeysuckle, Row C18, Lot 1.[194]

Charles married Effie McCrary in 1932 in Bibb County, Georgia. She died two years later on 18 August 1934.[195]

Charles died on 5 October 1959 in Bibb County at a local hospital. Funeral services were held on 7 October 1959 in Macon at the First Christian Church with the Rev. Dr. Clyde S. Sherman officiating. He was buried on 7 October 1959 in Riverside Cemetery in Honeysuckle, Row C18, Lot 1.[196]

Georgia Ennis Campbell (1886-1957)

Daughter of George W. Campbell and Hester T. Penner
Grandaunt of Taylor Cosby Cottrell, Jr.

Georgia Ennis Campbell was born on 25 February 1886 in Rays Branch in Warren County, Kentucky. She was the daughter of George Washington Campbell and Hester Taylor Penner.[197] She was listed on the 1900 census in the household of her father George in Warren County as Georgia E., age 14 and single.[198]

After her father's death Georgia and her sister "Miss Laura" occupied their father's home, which was originally built in 1868. It

Georgia Ennis Campbell

was said that members of the family and friends gathered there on many happy occasions and that "the latch-string was always on the outside and many Bowling Green young people loved to go there for picnics and fun."[199] She appeared on the census of 1910 in the home of her mother, Hester, in Warren County as Georgia E., age 24 and single.[200]

In 1920 she was found in the home of her mother, Hester, in Warren County as Georgia Campbell, age 54 along with her cousin P.C. Penner, age 59 and Bertha Douglas, age 38 who was listed as a house keeper.[201] She was listed on the 1930 census in Warren County in the household of her sister Laura Bell Campbell as Georgia, age 44 and single.[202]

In 1938 she was listed in the Bowling Green City Directory as living on Route 6 in Warren County with personal property valued at $25.[203] She was listed on the 1940 Warren County census as Georgia Campbell, age 54 along with her cousin P.C. Penner, age 59 and Bertha

Douglas, age 38 who was listed as a house keeper. Georgia's occupation was listed as a farm laborer on the census.[204]   Around 1947 Georgia moved from the Rays Branch area to the home of Bertha and Robert Moulder at 805 E. 10th Street in Bowling Green where she remained until her death.[205] She was an organizer of the Rays Branch Methodist Church. She never married.

Georgia Ennis Campbell
Fairview Cemetery
Bowling Green, Kentucky

Georgia died on at 11:00 in the evening at the City-County Hospital in Bowling Green, at age 71 after an illness of 18 days. Funeral services were held on 21 November 1957 at the Gerard Bradley Chapel in Bowling Green with the Rev. Harold Sharber officiating and Dr. Walter L. Munday assisting. She was buried in Fairview Cemetery in Bowling Green.[206]

Chapter 7 – Peter Penner Family

2nd Great-grandfather of Taylor Cosby Cottrell, Jr.

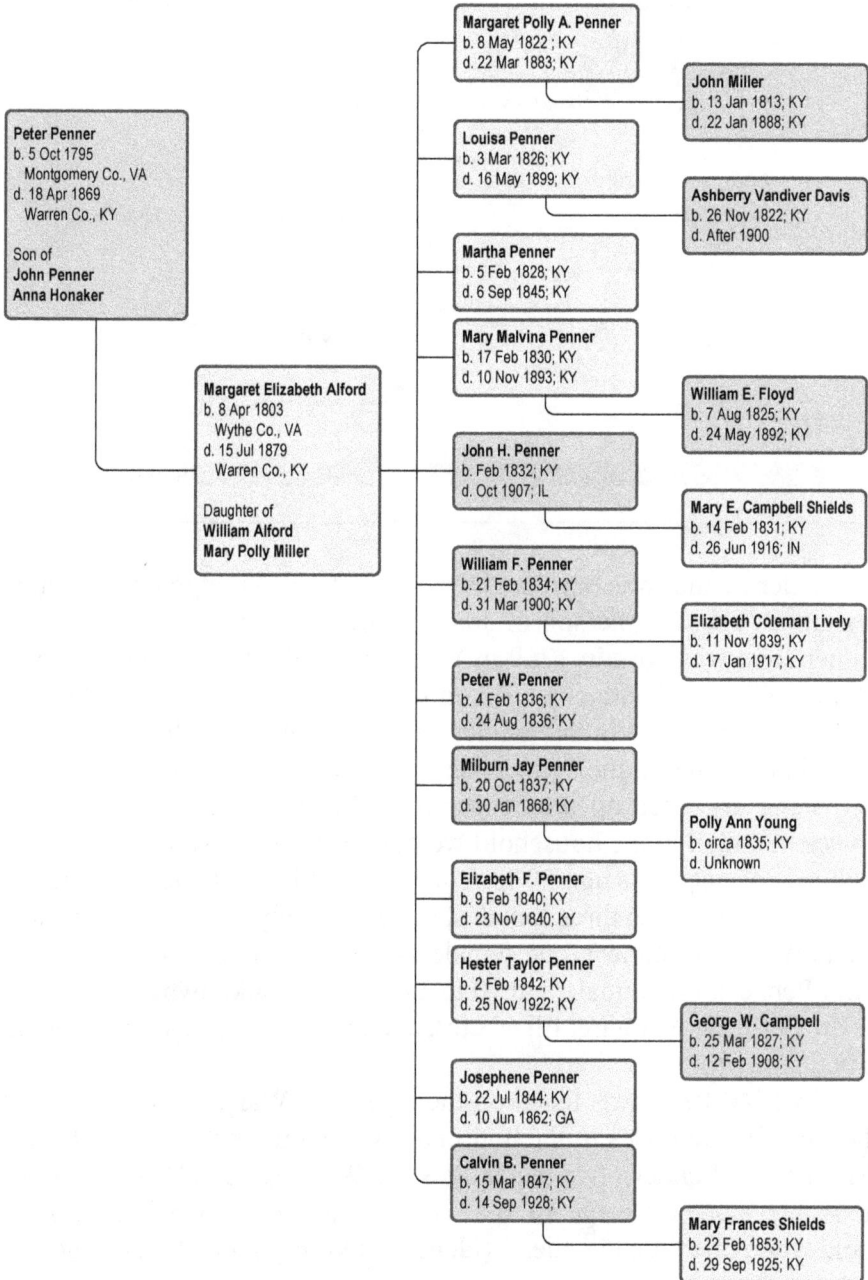

Peter Penner
b. 5 Oct 1795
    Montgomery Co., VA
d. 18 Apr 1869
    Warren Co., KY

Son of
John Penner
Anna Honaker

Margaret Elizabeth Alford
b. 8 Apr 1803
    Wythe Co., VA
d. 15 Jul 1879
    Warren Co., KY

Daughter of
William Alford
Mary Polly Miller

Margaret Polly A. Penner
b. 8 May 1822 ; KY
d. 22 Mar 1883; KY

John Miller
b. 13 Jan 1813; KY
d. 22 Jan 1888; KY

Louisa Penner
b. 3 Mar 1826; KY
d. 16 May 1899; KY

Ashberry Vandiver Davis
b. 26 Nov 1822; KY
d. After 1900

Martha Penner
b. 5 Feb 1828; KY
d. 6 Sep 1845; KY

Mary Malvina Penner
b. 17 Feb 1830; KY
d. 10 Nov 1893; KY

William E. Floyd
b. 7 Aug 1825; KY
d. 24 May 1892; KY

John H. Penner
b. Feb 1832; KY
d. Oct 1907; IL

Mary E. Campbell Shields
b. 14 Feb 1831; KY
d. 26 Jun 1916; IN

William F. Penner
b. 21 Feb 1834; KY
d. 31 Mar 1900; KY

Elizabeth Coleman Lively
b. 11 Nov 1839; KY
d. 17 Jan 1917; KY

Peter W. Penner
b. 4 Feb 1836; KY
d. 24 Aug 1836; KY

Milburn Jay Penner
b. 20 Oct 1837; KY
d. 30 Jan 1868; KY

Polly Ann Young
b. circa 1835; KY
d. Unknown

Elizabeth F. Penner
b. 9 Feb 1840; KY
d. 23 Nov 1840; KY

Hester Taylor Penner
b. 2 Feb 1842; KY
d. 25 Nov 1922; KY

George W. Campbell
b. 25 Mar 1827; KY
d. 12 Feb 1908; KY

Josephene Penner
b. 22 Jul 1844; KY
d. 10 Jun 1862; GA

Calvin B. Penner
b. 15 Mar 1847; KY
d. 14 Sep 1928; KY

Mary Frances Shields
b. 22 Feb 1853; KY
d. 29 Sep 1925; KY

Peter Penner Family Timeline

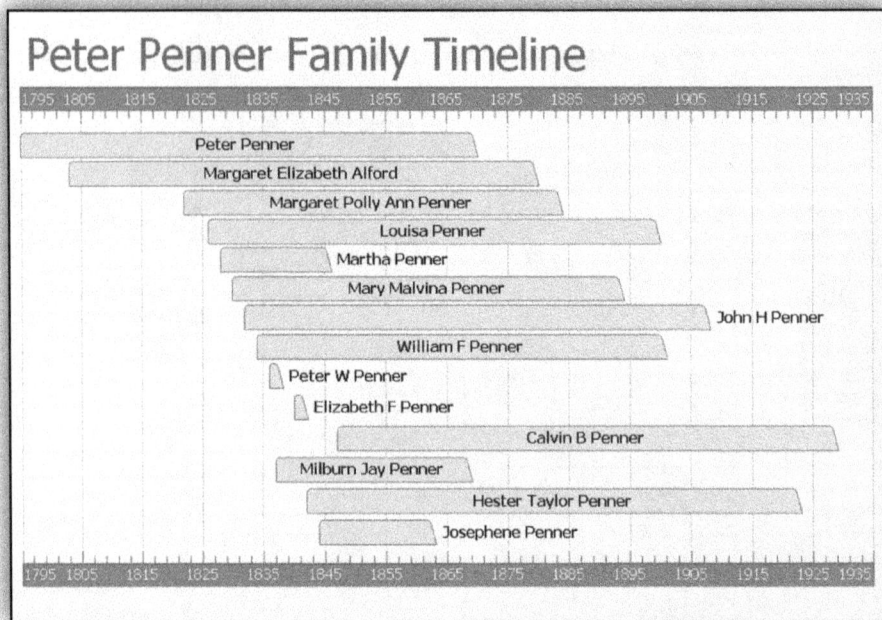

Peter Penner was born on 5 October 1795 in Montgomery County, Virginia. He was the son of John Penner and Anna Honaker.[1] His father John was born in 1769 in Virginia and died in October 1833 in Warren County, Kentucky.[2] His mother Anna was born in 1775, also in Virginia and died in September 1830 in Kentucky.[3] John and Anna were both buried in the Penner Cemetery in Warren County.

Peter appeared on the census of 1830 in Warren County; white males included in the household were; one male age 10 to 14 (identity unknown); one male age 30 to 39 (Peter). White females included in the household were; three females, under 5 (likely Louisa, Martha, and Mary Malvina Penner), one female age 5 to 9 (likely Margaret Polly Ann Penner), one female age 10 to 14 (identity unknown), one female 20 to 29 (likely Margaret Elizabeth), and one female age 40 to 49 (identity unknown).[4]

In 1840 Peter was listed on the census in Warren County as Peta Penner. White males in the household were; one male under 5 (likely Milburn Jay Penner); two males ages 5 to 9 (likely John H. and William F. Penner); one male age 40 to 49 (Peter). White females in the household were; one female under 5 (identity unknown); one female age 5 to

9 (identify unknown); two females ages 10 to 14 (likely Louisa and Martha Penner); one female age 15 to 19 (likely Margaret Polly Ann Penner); one white female age 30 to 39 (likely Margaret Elizabeth).[5]

A bond for the marriage of Peter Penner and Margaret Elizabeth Alford was signed on 31 December 1821 in Bowling Green in Warren County, Kentucky by Peter Penner and Benjamin Miller. Peter married Margaret Elizabeth, who was the daughter of William Alford and Mary Polly Miller, on 3 January 1822 in Warren County.[6]

Margaret was born on 8 April 1803 in Wythe County, Virginia.[7] Her father William Alford was born around 1775 in Wythe County, Virginia and died in 1821 in Warren County, Kentucky. He was the son of Thomas Alford and Elizabeth Field and married Margaret's mother Mary around 1800.[8] Margaret's mother Mary Polly Miller was born in 1780 in Wythe County, Virginia and died in 1830 in Kentucky. She remarried John Honaker after William's death. John was born in 1790 in Wythe County and died in 1845 in Warren County. Margaret was buried in Green River Union Cemetery. Her grave marker indicated she was the

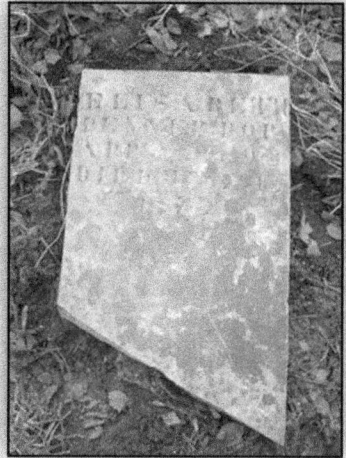

Margaret Elizabeth Alford Penner
Penner Cemetery
Courtesy of Faye Meredith

first woman buried in the cemetery after her body was brought from across Green Viber on sled drawn by 2 oxen.[9] Margaret had at least five brothers and sisters including:

- Moses Alford who was born in 1761 in Wythe County, Virginia, married Mary Polly Lavender in august 1821, and died on 6 September 1822 in Wythe County, Virginia.[10]
- John Alford who was born in 1763 in Wythe County, Virginia and died in 1851 in Montgomery County, Virginia.[11]
- James Alford who was born in 1766 in Wythe County, Virginia.[12]

- Elizabeth Alford who was born in 1775 in Wythe County, Virginia, married Joseph Baker on 28 February 1793, and died in 1870 in Wythe County.[13]
- Charles Alford who was born in 1779 in Wythe County, Virginia.[14]

Peter was listed on the 1850 census in Warren County as Peter Penner, age 52 with real estate valued at $2,250. Also listed in the household was Elizabeth, age 46, Louisa, age 22, Malvina, age 20, John H., age 18, William F., age 16, Milburn J., age 18, Hester G., age 10, Josephine, age 8, and Calvin B., age 3. In 1860 Peter was listed on the census in Warren County as Peter Penner, age 64 along with Elizabeth, age 57, William, age 23, Josephine, age 16, and Calvin, age 10. A farm laborer, Richard Flora was also listed in the household. Real estate was valued at $4,000 and his personal estate was valued at $6,000.[15]

Peter Penner
Penner Cemetery
Courtesy of Faye Meredith

Peter left a will on 1 July 1864 in Bowling Green, Kentucky which left the majority of his estate to his wife Elizabeth and specified that his sons William and Calvin were to receive his home property and then detailed various specific bequests to each of his children.[16]

Peter died on 18 April 1869 in Warren County, Kentucky, at age 73. He was buried in the Penner Cemetery in Warren County. His estate was probated in May 1869 in Bowling Green at the Warren County Courthouse.[17]

Margaret Elizabeth was listed on the 1870 census in

Peter Penner		
1850	Warren County, KY	Farmer
1860	Warren County, KY	Farmer

Warren County as Elizabeth Penner, age 67 along with William F., age 36, Polly A., age 36, Joseph W., age 11, Henry F., age 10, Puter M., age 8, John C., age 6, and James H., age 3. Real estate was valued at $1,800 and personal estate was valued at $500.[18] Margaret died on 15 July 1879 in Warren County, at age 76. She was buried in Warren County in the Penner Grave Yard located on the road between Anna Store and Richardsville near Bowling Green.[19]

Margaret Polly Ann Penner (1822-1883)

Daughter of Peter Penner and Margaret Elizabeth Alford
Great-Grandaunt of Taylor Cosby Cottrell, Jr.

Margaret Polly Ann Penner was born on 8 May 1822 in Warren County, Kentucky. She was the daughter of Peter Penner and Margaret Elizabeth Alford.[20]

She was likely listed on the 1830 census in Warren County in the home of her father as a female, age 5 to 9.[21]

Margaret married John Miller on 21 November 1838 in Warren County. John was born on 13 January 1813 in Warren County. He was the son of John Benjamin Miller and Mary Polly.[22]

Margaret was listed on the 1850 census in Warren County in the home of Jno. Miller, age 37 as M.A. Miller, age 27. Also listed was P.P. Miller, age 8, A.H. Miller, age 5, M.F. Miller, age 3, and J.W. Miller, age 8. John was listed as a farmer. She was listed on the 1860 census of John Miller in Warren County as Polly Ann, age 37.

John Miller
Green River Union Cemetery
Courtesy of Faye Meredith

Along with Peter, age 17, Albert, age 15, Martha, age 13, John, age 10, Anna, age 8, Henry, age 6, and Joseph, age 2.[23]

In 1870 she was listed as Mary A., age 47 on the census of John Miller, age 57. Peter P., age 28, John W., age 20, Anne E., age 18, Henry E., age 14, Joseph S., age 11, Mary A., age 8, Josephine, age 5, and C.D. age 16 were also listed in the household.[24] In 1880 Margaret was listed as Mary, age 56, wife of John Miller, age 66. Also listed were their sons Henry A., age 26 and Joseph S., age 21 along with their daughter Josephine, age 15. An adopted son by the name of Jessie C., age 7, whose last name was unreadable on the census, was also listed.[25]

Margaret died on 22 March 1883 in Warren County, Kentucky, at age 60.[26] John Died on 22 January 1888 in Warren County, Kentucky at age 75. They were both buried in Green River Union Cemetery.[27]

Margaret Polly Ann Penner
Green River Union Cemetery
Courtesy of Faye Meredith

Children of Margaret Polly Ann Penner and John Miller:

- Peter Penner Miller – Born on 4 May 1842 in Richardsville in Warren County, Kentucky and died on 8 May 1928 in Hopkinsville in Christian County, Kentucky at age 86. He was buried in Green River Union Cemetery in Richardsville.[28] Peter married Elecif Dee Thacker around 1870. She was born on 9 April 1854 in Richardsville. Elecif died on 6 June 1923 in Richardsville, at age 69. She was also buried in Green River Union Cemetery.[29] Peter and Elecif had at least seven children including:

Peter Penner Miller
Courtesy of Faye Merideth

  o George Henry Miller – Born on 2 March 1872 in Richardsville in Warren County, Kentucky and died on 2 July 1939 in Warren County, at age 67. He was buried in Mount Zion Church of Christ Cemetery in Bowling Green.[30] George married twice, first to Carrie D. Phillips Cohron and then to Della A. Keown. Carrie had at

least two children from a
previous marriage.[31]
George and Della had at
least one child, Cletis Ray
Miller who was born on 10
August 1896 in Warren
County and died on 12 Feb-
ruary 1987 in Bowling
Green. He was also buried
in Mount Zion Church of
Christ Cemetery.[32]

Elecif Dee Thacker
Courtesy of Fay Meredith

o Albert Arthur Miller – Born
on 31 January 1876 in Richardsville in Warren County
and died on 24 July 1898 in Warren County, at age 22.
He was buried in Green River Union Cemetery.[33]

o Clarence McElroy Miller – Born on 27 December 1877
in Richardsville and died on 25 November 1955 in
Warren County, at
age 77. He was
buried in Green
River Union Cem-
etery.[34] Clarence
married Ada Marie
Manning who was
born in 1882 and
died in 1940. Ada
was also buried in
Green River Union
Cemetery. They

Clarence Miller and Ada Manning
Green River Union Cemetery
Courtesy of Faye Meredith

had at least one child including Clarence Sledge Miller.[35]

o Charles E. Miller – Born on 23 September 1888 in Warren County, Kentucky and died on 29 March 1955 in
Bradenton in Manatee County, Florida.[36] Charles began military service on 30 April 1904 in Bowling
Green and ended service on 24 April 1907 at Fort Logan in Colorado. In 1908 he married Hester Morgan

who was born on 17 December 1889 and died on 8 February 1943. They were both buried in Fairview Cemetery.[37]

o Annie Belle Miller – Born on 8 November 1882 in Richardsville, Kentucky and died on 4 January 1921 in Bowling Green, at age 38.[38] She married Charles Oliver Beck on 25 March 1908 in Warren County.[39] Charles was born on 24 November 1876 and died on 10 July 1968 in Bowling Green, at age 91.[40] They had at least three children including Clarence Wilbur Beck[41], Lloyd Dauno Beck[42], and Elsie Geraldine Beck[43]. Both Annie and Charles were buried in Plumb Springs Cemetery in Plumb Springs in Warren County, Kentucky.[44]

Annie Belle Miller
Plum Springs Cemetery
Courtesy of Faye Meredith

o James Kelley Miller – Born on 23 April 1886 in Richardsville, Kentucky and died on 5 January 1898 in Warren County, at age 11. He was buried in Green River Union Cemetery in Richardsville.[45]

o Claude Lee Miller – Born on 12 January 1891 in Richardsville and died on 24 September 1974 in Bowling Green, at age 83. He married Erma Ethel Beck on 15 January 1913. She was born on 22 December 1892 in Kentucky.[46] They had at least three children including Margery Kathileen Miller who was born on 21 December 1913 and died on 29 April 2004[47], Roger Lee Miller who was born on 31 January 1915 and died on 29 January 1991[48], and Verta Louise Miller who was born on 21 October 1917 and died on 6 November 1991[49]. Erma died on 5 February 1919 in Richardsville. Claude married Blanche Ann Elder after Erma's death.

Blanche was born on 29 August 1894 in Reedyville in Butler County, Kentucky and died on 16 December 1943 in Richardsville. They had at least one child including Claudie Adel Miller who was born on 4 November 1920 and died on 25 April 1990. Claude married a third time

Claude Lee Miller
Courtesy of Fay Meredith

to Enuice (Baird) Brown on 18 May 1946.[50] Claude, Erma, and Blanche were all buried in Green River Union Cemetery in Richardsville. Enuice was buried in Mount Olivet Cumberland Presbyterian Cemetery in Warren County.

- Albert Henry Miller – Born on 16 October 1844 in Warren County, Kentucky and died on 23 August 1874 in Warren County, at age 29. He was buried in the Penner Cemetery.[51]
- Martha Frances Miller – Born on 30 January 1847 in Warren County, Kentucky and died on 7 July 1868 in Warren County. She was buried in the Penner Cemetery in Warren County.[52]
- John William Miller – Born on 17 October 1849 in Warren County, Kentucky and died on 22 January 1888 in Warren County. John was listed on the 1860 and 1870 census living with his father in Warren County. In 1870 he was working as a laborer. He married Emeline E. Breedlove around 1860.[53] They had at least three children including:
  o Anna Miller who was born circa 1869 in Kentucky and likely in Bowling Green.
  o Ada C. Miller who was born in August 1877 in Kentucky, likely in Bowling Green and died on 12 September 1908 in Warren County. She married John J. Basham on 29 January 1896 in Sumner County, Tennessee. John was born on n12 April 1875 in Edmonson

County, Kentucky and died on 10 October 1897 in Warren County. It is likely Ada re-married after John's death to George Washington Basham who was born on 14 April 1879 in Edmonson County and died on 28 May 1950 in Warren County. Ada likely had one child, Johnnie Ethel Basham with her first husband John and at least three children with her second husband George including Charles M. Basham, William Riley Basham, and Fannie Basham. Ada, John, and George were all buried in Green River Union Cemetery.[54]

- o Raleigh C. Miller who was born on 5 August 1879 in Kentucky, likely in Bowling Green and died on 21 May 1917 in Warren County. He married Birdie Ruth Evans on 24 December 1915 in Marion County, Indiana. She was the daughter of Roy L. Evans and Dovie Miller. Birdie was listed as divorced on the 1940 census. Raleigh was buried in Mount Olivet Cumberland Presbyterian Cemetery in Warren County.[55]

- Ann E. Miller – Born on 19 April 1852 in Warren County, Kentucky and died on 6 January 1929 in Warren County. She was listed on the 1860 and 1870 census living with her father in Warren County. Ann married Albert H. Miller on 7 December 1871.[56] Albert was born on 6 February 1847 and died on 4 February 1891. They were buried together in Fairview Cemetery.[57] They had at least two children including:

- o Laura J. Miller who was born on 8 August 1875 in Kentucky, married, husband's last name was Jones, likely Fred W. Jones, and died at 10:00 in the evening on 19 September 1913 in Warren County, Kentucky. She was buried in Fairview Cemetery in Bowling Green.[58]

- o Mary Miller who was born about 1878 in Kentucky, likely in Bowling Green.

- Henry Adison Miller – Born on 10 July 1855 in Warren County, Kentucky and died on 19 August 1905 in Warren County, at age 50. He was buried in the Green River Union Cemetery in Richardsville.[59] Henry married twice, first to Nettie Galloway on 14 January 1885 and then to Sallie Manning on 1 January 1891.[60] Henry and Sallie had at least six children including:

- o Hubert M. Miller who was born on 31 October 1891 in Warren County and died on 3 February 1963 in the City-County Hospital in Bowling Green. He was buried in Fairview Cemetery
- o Jonnie M. Miller who was born on 8 July 1893 and died on 2 February 1954.
- o Duggie Miller who was born on 8 March 1895 and died on 3 August 1953 at the City-County in Bowling Green. He was buried in Fairview Cemetery.
- o Mildred Miller who was born on 3 October 1898 and died on 27 September 1984.
- o Willie Miller who was born on 14 August 1906 and died on 17 March 1961.
- o John Miller who was born on 19 January 1902 and died on 24 February 1929.[61]

- Joseph S. Miller – Born on 21 June 1858 in Warren County, Kentucky and died on 1 January 1884 in Warren County, at age 25. He was buried in Green River Union Cemetery in Richardsville, in Warren County. He apparently never married.[62]
- Mary A. Miller – Born in 1862 in Warren County, Kentucky. She was listed in the home of her father in Warren County on the 1870 census. No additional information is known.
- Josephine Miller – Born on 30 June 1864 in Warren County, Kentucky and died on 29 June

Joseph S. Miller
Green River Union Cemetery
Courtesy of Faye Meredith

1897 in Warren County, Kentucky at age 32. She was buried in Green River Union Cemetery in Richardsville in Warren County.[63]

Louisa Penner (1826-1899)

Daughter of Peter Penner and Margaret Elizabeth Alford
Great-Grandaunt of Taylor Cosby Cottrell, Jr.

Louisa Penner was born on 3 March 1826 in Warren County, Kentucky. She was the daughter of Peter Penner and Margaret Elizabeth Alford.[64] She was listed on the 1850 census in the home of Peter Penner in Warren County as Louisa, age 22.[65] She married Ashberry Vandiver Davis, likely between 1850 and 1853. Ashberry was born on 26 November 1822 in Warren County.[66]

Children of Louisa Penner and Ashberry Vandiver Davis:

- Joseph Davis – Born on 21 January 1854 in Warren County, Kentucky and died on 10 September 1854 in Warren County. He was buried in the Penner Cemetery in Warren County.[67]
- Peter P. Davis – Born on 8 March 1858 in Warren County, Kentucky and died on 11 March 1858 in Warren County. He was buried in the Penner Cemetery in Warren County.[68]
- Drew C. Davis – Born on 10 January 1863 in Warren County, Kentucky and died on 9 October 1864 in Warren County. He was buried in the Penner Cemetery in Warren County.[69]

Louisa died on 16 March 1899 in Warren County, Kentucky at age 73. She was buried in the Penner Cemetery in Warren County, which is located on the road between Anna Store and Richardsville near Bowling Green.[70] The date of death of Ashberry is unknown but is likely after 1900 he appears to have been listed on the 1900 census in Green Castle in Warren County in the home of William O. Davis as Ashbury V. Davis, age 77 and widowed. Ashberry was also buried in the Penner Cemetery.[71]

Martha Penner (1828-1845)

Daughter of Peter Penner and Margaret Elizabeth Alford
Great-Grandaunt of Taylor Cosby Cottrell, Jr.

Martha Penner was born on 5 February 1828 in Warren County, Kentucky. She was the daughter of Peter Penner and Margaret Elizabeth Alford. Martha died on 6 September 1845 in Warren County, at age 17. She was buried in the Penner Cemetery in Warren County.[72]

Mary Malvina Penner (1830-1893)

Daughter of Peter Penner and Margaret Elizabeth Alford
Great-Grandaunt of Taylor Cosby Cottrell, Jr.

Mary Malvina Penner was born on 17 February 1830 in Warren County, Kentucky. She was the daughter of Peter Penner and Margaret Elizabeth Alford.[73] Mary was listed on the 1850 census in the household of Peter Penner in Warren County as Malvina, age 20.[74]

Mary married William E. Floyd likely sometime between 1850 and 1853. William was born on 7 August 1825 in Warren County.[75]

William died on 24 May 1892 in Warren County at age 66. He was buried on 26 May 1892 in Mount Pleasant Church of Christ Cemetery in Richardsville in Warren County.[76]

Mary died on 10 November 1893 in Warren County at age 63. She was also buried in Mount Pleasant Church of Christ Cemetery.[77]

Children of Mary Malvina Penner and William E. Floyd:

- John B. Floyd – Born on 7 June 1853 in Kentucky and died on 21 March 1933 in Anna in Warren County, Kentucky. He was buried in Mount Pleasant Church of Christ Cemetery in Richardsville in Warren County. John never married.[78]
- Ann E. Floyd – Born circa 1855 in Kentucky and died on 15 November 1932 in Bowling Green. She was buried in Mount Pleasant Church of Christ Cemetery in Richardsville. She married Faunt E. Willis. He preceded her in death.[79]
- Crittendon Floyd – Born on 2 December 1858 in Warren County, Kentucky and died on 18 October 1880 in Anna in Warren County. He was buried in Sand Hill Cemetery in Warren County. He never married.[80]
- Clinton Floyd – Born on 29 October 1861 in Kentucky and died on 13 December 1932 in Warren County, Kentucky. His cause of death was cerebral hemorrhage.[81] Clinton married Etta Runner on 30 April 1891 in Sumner County, Tennessee.[82] Etta was born on 15 February 1874 and died on 31 May 1955 at age 81. They were both buried in Mount Pleasant Church of Christ Cemetery in Richardsville. Clinton and Etta apparently had no children.[83]

- Douglas Floyd – Born circa 1865. He was listed on the 1870 and 1880 census in the home of his father William in Warren County, Kentucky.[84]
- America F. Floyd – Born on 8 July 1866 in Warren County, Kentucky and died on 9 March 1936 in Warren County. She was buried in Mount Pleasant Church of Christ Cemetery in Richardsville. She never married.[85]
- Nancy Floyd – Born on 29 March 1870 in Anna in Warren County, Kentucky and died on 8 July 1953 in Warren County. She was buried in Mount Pleasant Church of Christ Cemetery in Richardsville.[86] She likely married Charles M. Wilson around 1897. Charles was born on 21 October 1875.[87] Charles died on 25 December 1939 and was also buried in Mount Pleasant Church of Christ Cemetery.[88] Nancy and Charles had at least six children including:
  - Goldie Kate Wilson who was born on 24 August 1898 in Kentucky, Married Elwood Young and died on 28 March 1947 in Warren County. She was buried in Mount Pleasant Church of Christ Cemetery in Richardsville, Kentucky.
  - Hubert Wilson who was born on 3 August 1903 in Kentucky and died on 16 July 1961 in Bowling Green. His cause of death was heart disease. He was buried in Mount Pleasant Church of Christ Cemetery.
  - Claud C. Wilson who was born on 17 December 1904 in Warren County and died on 8 august 1957 at the Kentucky Baptist Hospital in Louisville, Kentucky. His cause of death was a cerebral hemorrhage. He was buried in Mount Pleasant Church of Christ Cemetery.
  - Maud Wilson who was born around 1906 in Kentucky.
  - Dillie Wilson who was born on 21 October 1908 in Kentucky and died on 24 June 1936 at the City Hospital in Bowling Green. Her cause of death was a gastric hemorrhage during childbirth. She married Paul Runner. Dillie was buried in Mount Pleasant Church of Christ Cemetery.

- o Novice Wilson who was born on 8 September 1911 and died on 16 May 2008. Novice married Beecham Wilson who was born on 31 August 1906 and died in 1 November 1957 at the City-County Hospital in Bowling Green. His cause of death was heart disease. Beecham was the son of Thomas Wilson and Candice Vincent. Novice and Beecham were both buried in Mount Pleasant Church of Christ Cemetery.[89]
- Lucy Lee Floyd – Born on 9 February 1874 in Kentucky; Died on 12 February 1946 in Warren County, Kentucky. Her cause of death was cerebral apoplexy. She was buried in Mount Pleasant Church of Christ Cemetery in Richardsville on 13 February 1946. Lucy never married.[90]

John H. Penner (1832-1907)

Son of Peter Penner and Margaret Elizabeth Alford
Great-Granduncle of Taylor Cosby Cottrell, Jr.

John H. Penner was born on 3 February 1832 in Kentucky. He was the son of Peter Penner and Margaret Elizabeth Alford. He was listed on the 1850 census in the household of Peter in Warren County as Hohn H., age 18 and attending school.[91]

A bond for the marriage of John H. Penner was signed on 21 September 1857 in Bowling Green in Warren County by John H. Penner and John S. Campbell. John married Mary Elizabeth (Campbell) Shields, the daughter of John Sale Campbell and Mary Frances Ennis, on 21 September 1857 in Warren County.[92] Mary Elizabeth was born on 14 February 1831 in Warren County and had been widowed when her first husband James Abrose Shields died.[93] She had at least two children from her marriage to James including John Shields and Mary Francis Shields. Additional information on James and Mary's first marriage and their children can be found in Section 1, Chapter 5, John Sale Campbell Family under Mary Elizabeth Campbell.

John was listed on the 1860 census in Warren County as John Penner, age 28 with real estate valued at $500 and a personal estate valued at $600. Mary, age 29 was also listed along with George, age 1, John Shields, age 9, and Francis Shields, age 7. John and Francis were children from Mary's first marriage.[94]

In late 1866 or early 1867 John and Mary and their children moved to Lawrence County, Illinois where they appeared on the 1870 census. John Penner, age 38 was listed as head of household with real estate valued at $1,000 and a personal estate valued at $1,000. Mary, age 39, George, age 10, Sara, age 7, James, age 3, and John Shields, age 19 were also listed in the household.[95]

John was found on the 1880 census in Lawrence County, Illinois as John H. Penner, age 48 along with his wife Mary E., age 49, daughter Sarah E., age 16, and son James N., age 18. Sarah and James attended school within the year.[96]

John was ordained around 1882 in the United Brethren Church and traveled for the Bible Society from time to time until his death.[97] In 1900 he was listed on the Lawrence County census as John H. Penner, age 68 along with his wife Mary E., age 69. Also listed in the home was a servant Elizabeth Belcher and John's sister-in-law Julia A. Suman, age 54 who was widowed.[98] According to his obituary he and Mary had eight children, thus two additional children remain unidentified and are not listed below.[99]

John H. Penner		
1850	Warren County, KY	Farmer
1860	Warren County, KY	Physician
1870	Lawrence County, IL	Farmer
1880	Lawrence County, IL	Farmer
1900	Lawrence County, IL	Minister

Children of John H. Penner and Mary Elizabeth Campbell:

- George Franklin Penner – Born on 19 July 1858 in Warren County, Kentucky and died on 24 December 1873 in Illinois at age 15. He was buried in Pleasant Hill Cemetery in Lawrence County, Illinois.[100]
- Peter Wesley Penner – Born and died on 25 July 1860 in Warren County, Kentucky. He was buried in the Penner Cemetery in Warren County.[101]
- Eugene Penner – Born and died on 27 March 1862 in Warren County, Kentucky. He was buried in the Penner Cemetery in Warren County.[102]
- Sarah Elizabeth Penner – Born on 13 June 1863 in Warren County, Kentucky and died on 28 January 1882 in Illinois, likely in Lawrence County, at age 18. She was buried in Pleasant Hill Cemetery in Lawrence County.[103]

- James Napoleon Penner – Born in October 1866 in Warren County, Kentucky and died in 1951 in Illinois, likely in Lawrence County. He was buried in the Lawrenceville City Cemetery in Lawrence County, Illinois in Addition 1905, Section 3.[104] James married Letha M. McCarroll on 23 October 1889 in Knox County, Indiana. Letha was born on 8 September 1867 in Vincennes in Knox County.[105] Letha died on 9 June 1947 in Lawrenceville at age 79. She was buried in the Lawrenceville City Cemetery.[106]
- Bertha Penner – Born on 26 March 1869 in Warren County, Kentucky and died on 12 April 1869 in Warren County. She was buried in the Campbell-Shields Cemetery near Bowling Green in Warren County.[107]

John died on 2 November 1907 in Lawrenceville in Lawrence County, Illinois at age 75. Funeral services were held in South Lawrence with the Rev. E.M. Pierson preaching the service. He was buried in Hollister Cemetery in South Lawrence.[108]

Mary was found on the 1910 census in the household of her son James N. Penner in Vigo County, Indiana as Mary E., age 79 and widowed. She was living with James and his wife Letha at 100 18th Street in Harrison Township at the time.[109]

Mary died on 26 June 1916 in her son's home at 75 South 18th Street in Terre Haute in Vigo County, Indiana at age 85. Her cause of death was apoplexy from mitral insufficiency. Funeral services were held at her son's home on 27 June 1916. She was buried on 28 June 1916 in Lawrenceville.[110]

William F. Penner (1834-1900)

Son of Peter Penner and Margaret Elizabeth Alford
Great-Granduncle of Taylor Cosby Cottrell, Jr.

William F. Penner was born on 21 February 1834 in Warren County, Kentucky.[111] He was the son of Peter Penner and Margaret Elizabeth Alford. He was listed on the 1850 census in Warren County in the household of his father Peter as William F., age 16 and attending school.[112] He was found in the home of his father on the 1860 Warren County census as William, age 23.[113]

William registered for the draft for the Civil War in February 1864 while living in Warren County. He was working as a farmer at the time.[114] In 1870 he was listed on the census in the household of his mother Elizabeth in Warren County as William F., age 36.[115]

William married Elizabeth O. Coleman Lively on 10 March 1880 in Bowling Green. Elizabeth was born on 11 November 1839 in Bowling Green. She was the daughter of Larkin Coleman and Jane J. Breedlove.[116] She was previously married to John Monroe Lively on 3 October 1860 in Warren County. John and Elizabeth had two children including Anna Lively who was born around 1863 in Missouri and Joanna Lively who was born around 1865 in Kentucky. John died sometime before the 1870 census when Elizabeth was listed as widowed along with Anna and Joanna.[117]

William was listed as William F. Penner, age 46 on the 1880 census in Warren County along with his wife Elizabeth O., age 38, step daughters Annie Lively, age 17 and J. Lively, age 15, and nephew Peter Penner, age 16. Annie J., and Peter were attending school. William was listed on the census as maimed, crippled, bedridden, or otherwise disabled.[118]

William left a will on 23 March 1900 in Warren County appointing his wife Elizabeth as Executor, witnessed by Will C. Strother, the Rev. R.B. Campbell, and G.E. Speck.[119] William died on 31 March 1900 in Warren County at age 66. He was buried in Fairview Cemetery in Bowling Green in Section C, Site C-0240.[120] His estate was probated on 23 April 1900 in Warren County, proved by the oath of Will C. Strother, one of the attesting witnesses to William's will, who also proved the signatures and attestation of the other witnesses, R. B. Campbell and G.E. Speck.[121]

Elizabeth was listed on the 1910 census of Warren County in the home of her son-in-law John Sales Campbell as Lizzie O. Penner, age 70 and widowed. She was listed as the mother of three children with only one child, Anna L. Lively, still living. Thus she likely had an unidentified child either with her first husband John Monroe Lively or with her second husband William Penner.[122] Elizabeth died on 17 January 1917 in Warren County at age 77 at the home of her daughter Anna on the Richardsville Road. Her cause of death was Bright's Disease. Funeral services were held on 19 January 1917 at Rays Branch Methodist Episcopal Church in Warren County with the Rev. B.S. Harper officiating and the Rev. B.F. Copas assisting. She was buried in Fair-view Cemetery in Section C, Site C-240.[123]

Peter W. Penner (1836-1836)

Son of Peter Penner and Margaret Elizabeth Alford
Great-Granduncle of Taylor Cosby Cottrell, Jr.

Peter W. Penner was born on 4 February 1836 in Warren County, Kentucky. He was the son of Peter Penner and Margaret Elizabeth Alford. Peter died on 24 August 1836 in Warren County. He was buried in the Penner Cemetery in Warren County.[124]

Milburn Jay Penner (1837-1868)

Son of Peter Penner and Margaret Elizabeth Alford
Great-Granduncle of Taylor Cosby Cottrell, Jr.

Milburn Jay Penner was born on 20 October 1837 in Kentucky. He was the son of Peter Penner and Margaret Elizabeth Alford.[125] Milburn was listed on the 1850 census in Warren County in the household of Peter Penner as Milburn J., age 13 and attending school.

Milburn married Polly Ann Young on 8 November in Sumner County, Tennessee. Polly was born in 1835 in Kentucky. Milburn was listed on the 1860 census in Warren County as Milburn Penner, age 22, along with Polly Ann, age 25, Joseph, age 1, and Henry, age 3/12.[126]

Children of Milburn Jay Penner and Polly Ann Young:

- Joseph W. Penner – Born on 17 October 1858 in Kentucky and died on 4 November 1935 in Edmondson County, Kentucky at age 77. He was buried in Kinser Cemetery in Edmondson County, Kentucky.[127] Joseph married Hadie Ann Cowles who was born on 19 December 1866, the daughter of Albert King Cowles and Ruthia Ann Wingfield. Hadie died on 11 May 1931 and was also buried in the Kinser Cemetery.[128] Joseph and Hadie had at least one child including:
    - Joseph Austin Penner who was born on 19 September 1898 and died on 30 January 1983. He was buried in Kinser Cemetery in Edmonson County, Kentucky.[129]
- Henry F. Penner – Born in April 1860 in Kentucky. He married Spicy A. Simmons before 1880. Henry was listed on the

1880 census in the home of Ama Simmons as Henry Penner, age 21, son-in-law, and married. His wife Spicy A. Penner, age 20 was also listed.[130] No additional information is known.

- Peter Monroe Penner – Born on 27 July 1862 in Bowling Green, Kentucky and died on 6 September 1925 in Waxahachie in Ellis County, Texas. He was buried in the Waxahachie City Cemetery in Ellis County, Texas.[131] Peter married Sarah J. Craighead around 1888. Sarah was born on 3 August 1865 in Kentucky. She was the daughter of William Craighead and Mary Jane Coffey. Sarah died on 13 May 1940 in Waxahachie, Texas. She was also buried in the Waxahachie City Cemetery.[132] Peter and Sarah had at least five children including:

  o Lillie Ann Penner who was born on 9 February 1890 in Nashville, Tennessee and died on 23 November 1941 in Waxahachie in Ellis County, Texas.[133] She married George W. Bevels around 1899.[134] George was born on 18 April 1888 and died on 6 July 1972. They were both buried in Waxahachie City Cemetery in Waxahachie, Texas.[135]

  o Albert Monroe Penner who was born on 23 October 1896 in Waxahachie, Texas and died in Ellis County, Texas. He was buried in Waxahachie City Cemetery. Albert married Maude Molee Mitchell. They had at least four children including Clara Jane Penner, Clinton Monroe Penner, Iva Claudine Penner, and Robert Edward Penner.[136]

  o Johnnie Mae Penner who was born on 2 August 1901 in Ellis County, Texas and died on 2 February 1950 in Miles in Runnels County, Texas. She was buried in Miles Cemetery in Runnels County, Texas. Johnnie married Richard Deering Coleman.[137]

  o Charlie Edwards Penner who was born on 4 December 1904 in Ellis County, Texas and died on 9 March 1917 in Waxahachie, Texas. He was buried in Waxahachie City Cemetery in Waxahachie, Texas.[138]

  o Hester B. Penner who was born on 3 August 1909 in Waxahachie, Texas and died on 23 August 1976 in Dallas, Texas. Hester married, her husband's last name was Johnson. She was buried in Laurel Land Memorial Park in Dallas County in Dallas, Texas.[139]

- John C. Penner – Born on 31 August 1865 in Edmonson County, Kentucky and died on 20 October 1942 in Denton County, Texas. He was buried in Belew Cemetery in Aubrey in Denton County in Block 5, Lot 11, Space 5.[140] John married Carrie Sabathna Jordan in 1893. Carrie was born on 1 October 1875. Carrie died on 2 September 1913. She was buried in Waxahachie City Cemetery in Ellis County, Texas.[141] John and Carrie had at least three children including:

  o John Taylor Penner who was born on 9 January 1894 in Edmondson County, Kentucky and died on 30 April 1982 in Denton, Texas. He was buried in Belew Cemetery in Aubrey in Denton County, Texas. John was described as tall with a slender build and blue eyes with brown hair when he registered for the WWI Draft in 1917. He was employed by his father as a farmer at the time. John married Jessie Stubblefield.[142]

  o Lester Arthur Penner who was born on 19 December 1896 in Kentucky and was pronounced dead on arrival at the Shannon Hospital on 21 June 1967 in San Angelo in Tom Green County, Texas. His cause of death was a coronary occlusion. Lester was living in San Angelo Texas when he registered for the WWII Draft in 1942. He indicated that his employment was odd jobs at the time. Lester was buried in Eola Cemetery in Concho County, Texas.[143]

  o Ulysses C. Penner who was born on 4 September 1899 in Kentucky and died on 30 July 1890 in Pilot Point in Denton County, Texas.[144] He was described as tall with a slender build, blue eyes and brown hair when he registered for the WWI Draft in 1918. He was living in Texas at the time and listed his occupation as the National Guard.[145] Ulysses was buried in Belew Cemetery in Aubrey in Denton County, Texas in Block D-4,Lot 1, Space 5. His gravestone read Pvt. U.S. Army, World War II.[146]

- James H. Penner – Born around 1868 in Warren County, Kentucky. James was listed on the 1870 census in Warren County in the home of his father as James H., age 3.[147] He was also listed in the 1880 census with his mother Polly as James, age 12.[148] No additional information is known.

Milburn died on 30 January 1868 in Warren County, Kentucky at age 30. He was buried in the Penner Cemetery in Warren County.[149]

Polly appeared on the census of 1870 in the household of her mother-in-law Elizabeth Penner in Warren County as Polly A., age 36. Also listed were Joseph W. Penner, age 11, Henry F. Penner, age 10, Puter M. Penner, age 8, John C. Penner, age 6, and James H. Penner, age 3.[150]

Polly married John Flora on 9 September 1877 in Warren County, Kentucky[151]. John had previously been married and had at least four children from his previous marriage who were listed on the 1880 census in Edmondson County, Kentucky along with Polly who was listed as Polly Ann Flora, age 45. Her sons John and James were also listed in the household.[152] It is likely Polly died before the 1900 census.

Elizabeth F. Penner (1840-1840)

Daughter of Peter Penner and Margaret Elizabeth Alford
Great-Grandaunt of Taylor Cosby Cottrell, Jr.

Elizabeth F. Penner was born on 9 February 1840 in Kentucky. She was the daughter of Peter Penner and Margaret Elizabeth Alford. She died on 23 November 1840 in Warren County and was buried in the Penner Cemetery in Warren County.[153]

Hester Taylor Penner (1842-1922)

Daughter of Peter Penner and Margaret Elizabeth Alford
Great-Grandmother of Taylor Cosby Cottrell, Jr.

Hester Taylor Penner was born on 2 February 1842 in Warren County, Kentucky. She was the daughter of Peter Penner and Margaret Elizabeth Alford.[154] Information on Hester and her husband George Washington Campbell and their ten children is covered in detail in Section 2, Chapter 6, George Washington Campbell Family.

Josephene Penner (1844-1862)

Daughter of Peter Penner and Margaret Elizabeth Alford
Great-Grandaunt of Taylor Cosby Cottrell, Jr.

Josephene Penner was born on 26 July 1844 in Warren County, Kentucky. She was the daughter of Peter Penner and Margaret Elizabeth Alford.[155] She appeared on the census of 1850 in the household of Peter Penner in Warren County as Josephine, age 8 and attending school.[156] She was found on the 1860 census in the home of her father Peter as Josephine, age 16 and attending school.[157]

Josephine apparently married twice. Her first husband was Isaac Newton Miller. Her second husband's last name was Evans. Josephine died on 10 June 1862 in Warren County at age 17. Her name on her gravestone was Josephene Evans. She was buried in the Penner Cemetery in Warren County.[158]

Calvin B. Penner (1847-1928)

Son of Peter Penner and Margaret Elizabeth Alford
Great-Granduncle of Taylor Cosby Cottrell, Jr.

Calvin B. Penner was born on 15 March 1847 in Warren County, Kentucky. He was the son of Peter Penner and Margaret Elizabeth Alford.[159] He appeared on the census of 1850 in the home of Peter Penner in Warren County as Calvin B., age 3.[160] In 1860 he was listed on the census in Warren County as Calvin, age 10 and attending school.[161]

Calvin married Mary Frances Shields, the daughter of James Abrose Shields and Mary Elizabeth Campbell on 21 December 1868 in Warren County.[162] Mary was born on 22 February 1853 in Warren County and likely died before 1876.[163]

Calvin married Frances Fannie Young on 22 October 1876 in Warren County at the residence of L.P. Arnold.[164] He was listed on the 1900 census in Warren County as Calvin B. Penner, age 53 along with his wife Francis, age 49, sons Peter C., age 19 and John W., age 14 and daughters Amanda L., age 16 and Elizabeth F., age 12. He owned his farm which was listed on farm schedule 52 free of mortgage.[165] In 1910 he was found on the census in Warren County as Calvin B. Penner, age 63 along with his wife Francis, age 59, son Peter C., age 30, and daughter Mandy L., age 27.[166]

In 1920 he was found on the Warren County census as Calvin Penner, age 60. His wife Fannie, age 58, son Peter, age 36 and daughter Mandy, age 31 were also listed in his household.[167]

Children of Calvin B. Penner and Frances Fannie Young:

- George W. Penner – Born on 5 April 1879 in Kentucky and died on 10 April 1879 in Warren County. He was buried in the Penner Cemetery in Warren County.[168]
- Peter Cunningham Penner – Born in July 1880 in Warren County and died on 1 January 1962 in Warren County at age 81.[169] He registered for the WWI Draft on 12 September 1918 while living in Warren County. He was described as medium height, medium to stout build with brown eyes and black hair. He was working as a farmer at the time. He never married. Peter was buried in Chapel Hill Memorial Gardens in Bowling Green.[170]
- Amanda L. Penner – Born on 6 August 1883 in Warren County, Kentucky and died on 29 April 1959 in Warren County at age 75. She was buried in the Green River Union Cemetery in Richardsville in Warren County, Kentucky. Amanda was also known as Mandy.[171] She married Francis C. Tatum sometime before 1926 in Warren County. Francis was born on 3 March 1875 in Kentucky. They apparently had no children. Francis died on 5 September 1957 in Warren County and was also buried in Green River Union Cemetery.
- John Wesley Penner – Born on 28 September 1885 in Warren County and died on 30 September 1966 in Bowling Green in Warren County at age 81. He was buried in Mount Olivet Cumberland Presbyterian Cemetery in Warren County.[172] His estate was probated on 10 October 1966 in Bowling Green at the Warren County Courthouse.[173] John married Maggie Holman, daughter of Robert Adam Holman, on 31 July 1906 in Warren County at the home of Maggie's father.[174] He registered for the WWI Draft on 12 September 1918 while living in Warren County. He was described as medium height, slender build with grey eyes and light brown hair and was working as a farmer at the time.[175] Maggie died on 27 May 1965 in Jefferson County, Kentucky at age 81. She was also buried in

Mount Olivet Cumberland Presbyterian Cemetery.[176] John and Maggie had at least five children including:

- o Elizabeth Penner who was born and died on 25 December 1906. She was buried in Mount Olivet Cumberland Presbyterian Cemetery in Warren County, Kentucky, in Plot 172.[177]
- o Robert Brown Penner who was born on 3 February 1908 in Warren County and died on 1 June 1945 in Warren County, at age 37. His cause of death was an acute cardiac attack. He was buried on 5 June 1945 in Mount Olivet Cumberland Presbyterian Cemetery, in Plot 566.[178]
- o Mary Frances Penner who was born on 7 December 1909 in Warren County and died on 31 December 1909 in Warren County. She was buried in Mount Olivet Cumberland Presbyterian Cemetery, in Plot 173.[179]
- o John Edward Penner who was born on 3 February 1911 in Warren County and died on 22 September 1926 in Warren County, at age 15. His cause of death was typhoid fever. His occupation on his death record was listed as day labor. He was buried in Mount Olivet Cemetery on 23 September 1926.[180]
- o William Hazel Penner who was born on 8 September 1914 in Warren County and died on 11 February 1990 in Kentucky, at age 75. He served in the U.S. Army from 30 September 1942 until he was separated on 24 December 1945. He married Mable Ellen on 29 November 1952. Mable died on 28 June 1992 in Bowling Green, at age 82. They were both buried in Fairview Cemetery in Bowling Green.[181]
- Elizabeth Frances Penner – Born on 2 September 1888 in Warren County, Kentucky and died on 16 August 1970 in Kentucky at age 81. She was buried in Green River Union Cemetery in Richardsville in Warren County.[182] Elizabeth married Edward Everett Flora on 28 December 1908 in Warren County, Kentucky. Edward was born on 22 January 1881 in Warren County and died on 12 December 1966 in Warren County at age 85. He was also buried in Green River Union

Cemetery in Warren County.[183] Elizabeth and Edward had at least one child including:

- o Clarence Edward Flora who was born on 26 May 1911 and died on 19 June 1973. He was an employee of WBKO-TV in Bowling Green. He married Nola Florence Richards on 14 November 1937. Clarence and Nola were buried in Green River Union Cemetery.[184]

Mary Frances died on 29 September 1925 in Warren County at age 75. She was buried in Mount Olivet Cumberland Presbyterian Cemetery in Warren County.[185]

Calvin died on 14 September 1928 in Bowling Green, at age 81. His cause of death was a fractured left hip. He was buried on 16 September 1928 in Mount Olivet Cumberland Presbyterian Cemetery in Warren County.[186]

Section 3 – Maps

The maps in this section plot the known geographical locations of the events surrounding the lives of people covered in this publication where the specific location is known. State maps are included where larger numbers of individual events took place.

Cottrell Surname Maps

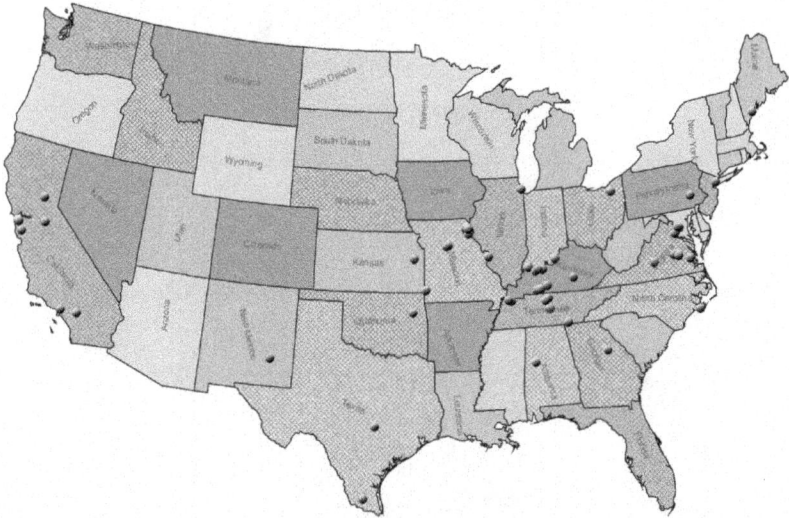

Cottrell in the Continental United States

Cottrell in California

Cottrell in Missouri

Cottrell in Kentucky

Cottrell in Virginia

Cottrell in Tennessee

Cosby Surname Maps

Cosby in the Continental United States

Cosby in Montana

Cosby in California

Cosby in Kentucky

Cosby in Virginia

Cosby in Tennessee

Lashbrook Surname Maps

Lashbrook in the Continental United States

Lashbrook in Kentucky

Lashbrook in Tennessee

Lashbrook in California

Lashbrook in Illinois

Lashbrook in Indiana

Taylor Surname Maps

Taylor in the Continental United States

Taylor in Kentucky

Taylor in Tennessee

Taylor in North Carolina

Taylor in Illinois

Taylor in Indiana

Section 4 – Photographs & Documents

The original photographs and documents in this section are either in the possession of the author or are in the public domain. The selection that follows was chosen by the author to graphically depict the lives and hardships that led to the events depicted in the life stories of the Paternal and Maternal ancestral lines in Section 1 and 2 of this publication. Dates and locations of the photographs, documents, and events are included if known or circa dates are estimated where the author believes reasonable accuracy is possible from clues in the photograph or location.

Family Photographs

Nellie Jane Cottrell
Taylor Cosby Cottrell, Sr.
Photograph taken in 1908

Taylor Cosby Cottrell, Sr.
Age 18 ½ months
Photograph taken in 1907

Taylor Cosby Cottrell, Sr.
Jo Ann Cottrell
20 July 1931 in Richmond, Virginia

Taylor Cosby Cottrell, Sr.
Jo Ann Cottrell
1929 in Kyrock, Kentucky

Peter Cottrell
Mary Magdalene (Rosa) Cosby
Photograph taken during the Civil War Era

Nellie Jane Lashbrook
Taylor Cosby Cottrell, Sr.
Estella Zalame Brashear
TC Cottrell (Author)
Photograph taken in July 1951

Cottrell-Brashear Family Linage

Minnie Jane Cottrell
Jo Ann Cottrell
Nellie Jane Lashbrook
Photograph taken around 1936

TC Cottrell, Sr.
Engine Instructor
10 October 1942

TC Cottrell (Author)
Kathleen Hope Brashear
Taylor Cosby Cottrell, Sr.
Evelyn Brashear
Estella Zalame Brashear
Photograph taken around 1960

Jo Ann Cottrell
16 July 1929

George Washington Campbell
Hester Penner
Photograph taken before 1908

Anne Wheeler
Photograph taken before 1860

Robert Lansdale Brashear
Kathleen Hope Brashear
Photograph taken around 1896

Martha Hope Crutchfield
Photograph taken around 1890

Cottrell-Brashear Family Linage

Camila Lansdale Brashear
Photograph taken around 1930

Walter Curran Brashear
Photograph taken around 1900

Melvin Cosby Cottrell
Photograph likely taken before 1910

James Dudley Lashbrook
Photograph likely taken around 1935

Bluegrass Airlines Staff
First meeting of the personnel of Bluegrass Airlines
Photograph Taken on 15 May 1945
Helm Hotel in Bowling Green, Kentucky

Second Left to Right:
TC Cottrell, Mechanic; **Dorothy A Patton,** Louisville Agent; **Shirley Payne,**
Paducah Agent
Mrs. C.G. Adams, Ashland Agent; **B.W. Stuart,** Owner

Standing Left to Right:
J.E. Stuart, Owner; **M.W. Stuart**, Owner; **Mary Elizabeth Tatum**, Bookkeeper
Vince O'Brien, Pilot; **Fred Rovner**, Pilot

Not Present
Eulus Morrison, Assistant Mechanic

Family Homes and Buildings

R. L. Brashear home –

Our home which burned to ground
when I was 5 yrs. old – 1913.

This picture was probably made when
Papa was a widower for 6 yrs & Uncle
Curran & family lived with him.

7- 23 - 31

Ocean View Va.

Front view of
our cottage show-
ing Mutt's truck
Dr's car & mine and

Family Documents

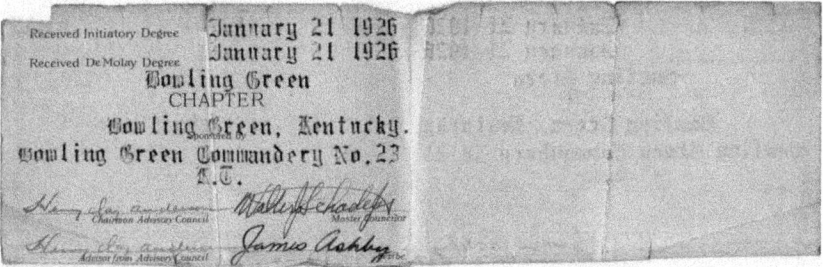

"QSL" Card used by the Author and his Father
to ac knowledge Amateur Radio contacts throughout the world

Free-Lance Copywriter   (212) 989-7280

JOANNA COTTRELL
Newspaper • Catalogues • Direct Mail

105 Bank Street, New York, N.Y. 10014

HOLLEY
Carburetor Co.
BOWLING GREEN, KY.

T. C. COTTRELL   RUSSELVILLE ROAD
QUALITY MANAGER   PHONE: A.C. 502-842-1681

SOCIAL SECURITY ACT
ACCOUNT NUMBER
403-07-9428
HAS BEEN   ESTABLISHED FOR
Taylor Cosby Cottrell
12/18/36.
DATE OF ISSUE   EMPLOYEE'S SIGNATURE

SOCIAL SECURITY ACT
ACCOUNT NUMBER
404-34-9424
HAS BEEN   ESTABLISHED FOR
JO ANNE COTTRELL

COMMONWEALTH OF KENTUCKY
OPERATOR'S LICENSE
For $1.00   No. 1361184
1937-38
NAME Mrs. Nellie Cottrell

THE AMERICAN NATIONAL RED CROSS

THIS CERTIFIES THAT
Mrs. Zalame Cottrell
HAS COMPLETED THE   Standard   COURSE
OF INSTRUCTION IN FIRST AID TO THE INJURED AT
Elkton, Ky.

August 12, 1942

9236
Kentucky Guild of Artists and Craftsmen
BEREA, KENTUCKY
Charter Membership Card

This is to certify that Zélême Cottrell

is a charter Craftsman member

President   Secretary

ZALAME'S ANTIQUES

CHINA
GLASSWARE
FURNITURE

ZALAME B. COTTRELL   ELKTON, KY.

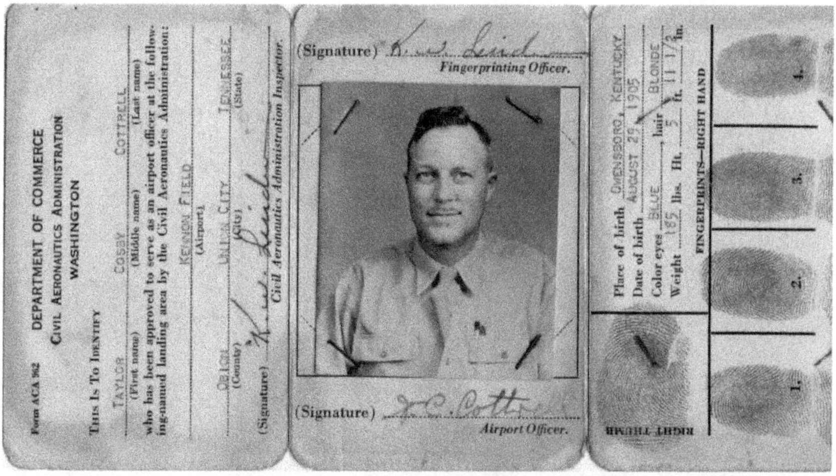
Form ACA 962
DEPARTMENT OF COMMERCE
CIVIL AERONAUTICS ADMINISTRATION
WASHINGTON
THIS IS TO IDENTIFY
TAYLOR COSBY COTTRELL
(First name) (Middle name) (Last name)
who has been approved to serve as an airport officer at the following-named landing area by the Civil Aeronautics Administration:
KENNON FIELD
(Airport)
OBION UNION CITY TENNESSEE
(County) (City) (State)
(Signature)
Civil Aeronautics Administration Inspector.
(Signature)
Fingerprinting Officer.
(Signature)
Airport Officer.
Place of birth OWENSBORO, KENTUCKY
Date of birth AUGUST 29, 1905
Color eyes BLUE hair BLONDE
Weight 185 lbs. Ht. 5 ft. 11 1/2 in.
FINGERPRINTS—RIGHT HAND
1. 2. 3. 4.
RIGHT THUMB

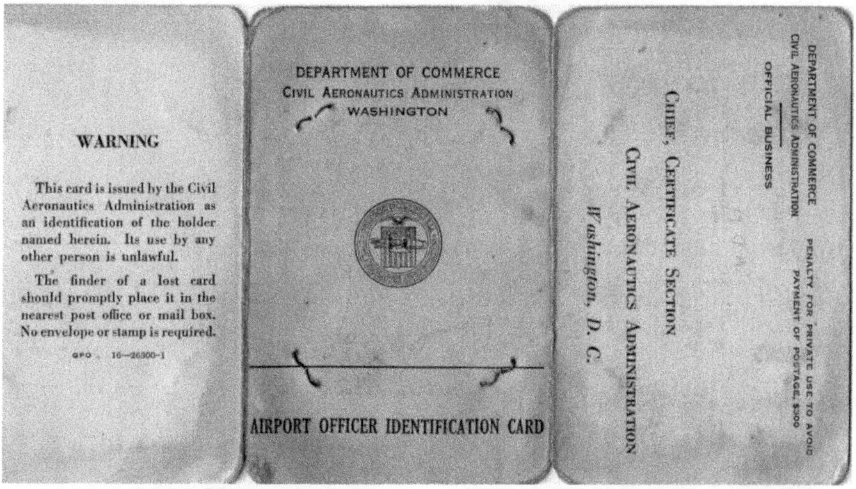
WARNING
This card is issued by the Civil Aeronautics Administration as an identification of the holder named herein. Its use by any other person is unlawful.
The finder of a lost card should promptly place it in the nearest post office or mail box. No envelope or stamp is required.
GPO 16—26300-1
DEPARTMENT OF COMMERCE
CIVIL AERONAUTICS ADMINISTRATION
WASHINGTON
AIRPORT OFFICER IDENTIFICATION CARD
DEPARTMENT OF COMMERCE
CIVIL AERONAUTICS ADMINISTRATION
OFFICIAL BUSINESS
PENALTY FOR PRIVATE USE TO AVOID PAYMENT OF POSTAGE, $300
CHIEF, CERTIFICATE SECTION
CIVIL AERONAUTICS ADMINISTRATION
Washington, D. C.

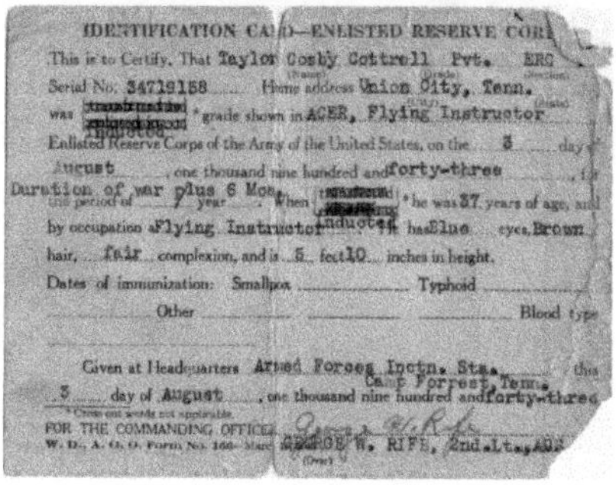
IDENTIFICATION CARD—ENLISTED RESERVE CORPS
This is to Certify, That Taylor Cosby Cottrell Pvt. ERC
Serial No. 34719158 Home address Union City, Tenn.
grade shown in ACER, Flying Instructor
Enlisted Reserve Corps of the Army of the United States, on the 3 day of August, one thousand nine hundred and forty-three
Duration of war plus 6 Mos.
he was 37 years of age, and by occupation a Flying Instructor he has Blue eyes, Brown hair, fair complexion, and is 5 feet 10 inches in height.
Dates of immunization: Smallpox Typhoid
Other Blood type
Given at Headquarters Armed Forces Inctn. Sta. Camp Forrest, Tenn. this 3 day of August, one thousand nine hundred and forty-three
FOR THE COMMANDING OFFICER
GEORGE W. RIFE, 2nd.Lt.,AGD
W. D., A. G. O. Form No. 166

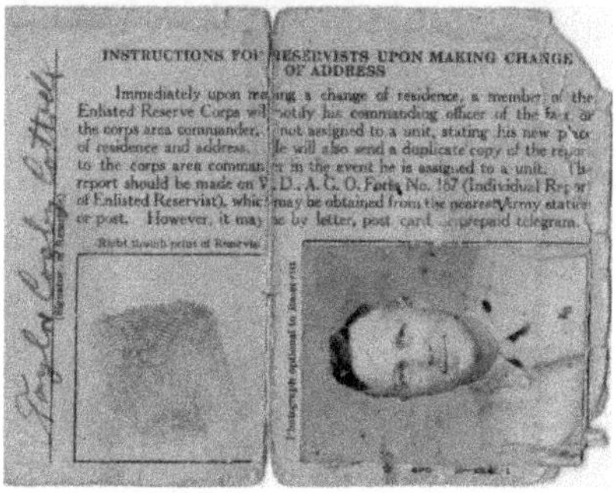
INSTRUCTIONS FOR RESERVISTS UPON MAKING CHANGE OF ADDRESS
Immediately upon making a change of residence, a member of the Enlisted Reserve Corps will notify his commanding officer of the fact, or the corps area commander, if not assigned to a unit, stating his new place of residence and address. He will also send a duplicate copy of the report to the corps area commander in the event he is assigned to a unit. The report should be made on W. D., A. G. O. Form No. 167 (Individual Report of Enlisted Reservist), which may be obtained from the nearest Army station or post. However, it may be by letter, post card, or prepaid telegram.
Right thumb print of Reservist
Taylor Cosby Cottrell

The Stamps contained in this Book are valid only after the lawful holder of this Book has signed the certificate below, and are void if detached contrary to the Regulations. (A father, mother, or guardian may sign the name of a person under 18.) In case of questions, difficulties, or complaints, consult your local Ration Board.

Certificate of Book Holder

I, the undersigned, do hereby certify that I have observed all the conditions and regulations governing the issuance of this War Ration Book; that the "Description of Book Holder" contained herein is correct; that an application for issuance of this book has been duly made by me or on my behalf; and that the statements contained in said application are true to the best of my knowledge and belief.

Della Zalame Brashear [Book Holder's Own Name]

Any person signing on behalf of Book Holder must sign his or her own name below

and indicate relationship to Book Holder

Kathleen Hohn Brashear or daughter (Father, Mother, or Guardian)

OPA Form No. R-302

UNITED STATES
OF AMERICA

War Ration Book One

WARNING

1 Punishments ranging as high as Ten Years' Imprisonment or $10,000 Fine, or Both, may be imposed under United States Statutes for violations thereof arising out of infractions of Rationing Orders and Regulations.

2 This book must not be transferred. It must be held and used only by or on behalf of the person to whom it has been issued, and anyone presenting it thereby represents to the Office of Price Administration, an agency of the United States Government, that it is being so held and so used. For any misuse of this book it may be taken from the holder by the Office of Price Administration.

3 In the event either of the departure from the United States of the person to whom this book is issued, or his or her death, the book must be surrendered in accordance with the Regulations.

4 Any person finding a lost book must deliver it promptly to the nearest Ration Board.

OFFICE OF PRICE ADMINISTRATION

Nº 240774 —51

Certificate of Registrar

This is to Certify that pursuant to the Rationing Orders and Regulations administered by the OFFICE OF PRICE ADMINISTRATION, an agency of the United States Government,

(Name, Address, and Description of person to whom the book is issued:)

Brashear Della Zalame
(Last name) (First name) (Middle name)
Louisville Road
(Street No. or P. O. Box No.) (Street or R. F. D.)
Bowling Green Warren Kentucky
(City or town) (County) (State)

Stamps must not be detached except in the presence of the retailer, his employee, or person authorized by him to make delivery.

5 ft 3 in. 113 lbs. Blue Grey 72 yrs. Sex { Male ☐ Female ☒
(Height) (Weight) (Color of eyes) (Color of hair) (Age)

has been issued the attached War Ration Stamps this 6th day of May 1942, upon the basis of an application signed by himself ☐, herself ☐, or on his or her behalf by his or her husband ☐, wife ☐, father ☐, mother ☐, exception ☒ (Check one.)

Gerold H. Miller (Signature) (Registrar)

Local Board No. 46 County Warren State Kentucky

WAR RATION STAMP 22	WAR RATION STAMP 20
WAR RATION STAMP 19	

30395DW UNITED STATES OF AMERICA
OFFICE OF PRICE ADMINISTRATION

WAR RATION BOOK TWO

IDENTIFICATION

Della Z. Brashear
(Name of person to whom book is issued)
Louisville Rd.
(Street number or rural route)
Bowling Green Ky 72 F
(City or post office) (State) (Age) (Sex)

ISSUED BY LOCAL BOARD No. 116 Warren Ky
(Local board number) (County) (State)
Bowling Green
(City)
By *Gerold Gossnort*
(Signature of issuing officer)

SIGNATURE *Della Z. Brashear*
(To be signed by the person to whom this book is issued. If such person is unable to sign because of age or incapacity, another may sign in his behalf)

OFFICE OF PRICE ADM.
30395—

WARNING

1 This book is the property of the United States Government. It is unlawful to sell or give it to any other person, or to use it or permit anyone else to use it, except to obtain rationed goods for the person to whom it was issued.

2 This book must be returned to the War Price and Rationing Board which issued it, if the person to whom it was issued is inducted into the armed services of the United States, or leaves the country for more than 30 days, or dies. The address of the Board appears above.

3 A person who finds a lost War Ration Book must return it to the War Price and Rationing Board which issued it.

PERSONS WHO VIOLATE RATIONING REGULATIONS ARE SUBJECT TO $10,000 FINE OR IMPRISONMENT, OR BOTH.

OPA Form No. R-121

30393DW UNITED STATES OF AMERICA
OFFICE OF PRICE ADMINISTRATION

WAR RATION BOOK TWO

IDENTIFICATION

Kathleen H. Brashear
(Name of person to whom book is issued)
Louisville Road
(Street number or rural route)
Bowling Green Ky 46 F
(City or post office) (State) (Age) (Sex)

ISSUED BY LOCAL BOARD No. 116 Warren Ky
(Local board number) (County) (State)
Bowling Green
(City)
By *Gerold Gossnort*
(Signature of issuing officer)

SIGNATURE *Kathleen H. Brashear*
(To be signed by the person to whom this book is issued. If such person is unable to sign because of age or incapacity, another may sign in his behalf)

OFFICE OF PRICE ADM.
30393—

WARNING

1 This book is the property of the United States Government. It is unlawful to sell or give it to any other person, or to use it or permit anyone else to use it, except to obtain rationed goods for the person to whom it was issued.

2 This book must be returned to the War Price and Rationing Board which issued it, if the person to whom it was issued is inducted into the armed services of the United States, or leaves the country for more than 30 days, or dies. The address of the Board appears above.

3 A person who finds a lost War Ration Book must return it to the War Price and Rationing Board which issued it.

PERSONS WHO VIOLATE RATIONING REGULATIONS ARE SUBJECT TO $10,000 FINE OR IMPRISONMENT, OR BOTH.

OPA Form No. R-121

Cottrell-Brashear Family Linage

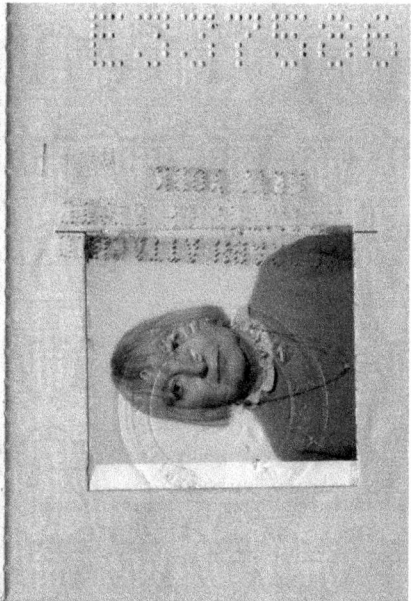

WARNING: ALTERATION, ADDITION OR MUTILATION OF ENTRIES IS PROHIBITED. ANY UNOFFICIAL CHANGE WILL RENDER THIS PASSPORT INVALID.

NAME—NOM
JOANNA COTTRELL

SEX—SEXE / BIRTHPLACE—LIEU DE NAISSANCE
F KENTUCKY, U.S.A.

BIRTH DATE—DATE DE NAISSANCE
JULY 16, 1928

NATIONALITY—NATIONALITÉ
UNITED STATES OF AMERICA

ISSUE DATE—DATE DE DÉLIVRANCE
FEB. 17, 1984

EXPIRES ON—EXPIRE LE
FEB. 16, 1994

SIGNATURE OF BEARER—SIGNATURE DU TITULAIRE
NOT VALID UNTIL SIGNED

PASSPORT NUMBER
NUMÉRO DU PASSEPORT   E 337586

PEN AND INK ENTRY OF THE PASSPORT NUMBER BY THE BEARER

FOR YOUR PROTECTION PLEASE FILL IN THE NAMES AND ADDRESSES BELOW.

BEARER'S ADDRESS IN THE UNITED STATES:
ADRESSE DU TITULAIRE AUX ETATS-UNIS:

BEARER'S FOREIGN ADDRESS:
ADRESSE DU TITULAIRE A L'ETRANGER:

IN CASE OF DEATH OR ACCIDENT NOTIFY THE NEAREST AMERICAN DIPLOMATIC OR CONSULAR OFFICE AND THE INDIVIDUAL NAMED BELOW.
EN CAS DE DECES OU D'ACCIDENT, PRIERE D'AVISER LE SERVICE DIPLOMATIQUE OU CONSULAIRE DES ETATS-UNIS LE PLUS PROCHE, AINSI QUE LA PERSONNE NOMMEE CI-DESSOUS.

Name
Nom   *Joanna Cottrell*

Address
Adresse   *105 Bank St. Apt 2R*
NYC NY 10014

The Secretary of State of the United States of America hereby requests all whom it may concern to permit the citizen/national of the United States named herein to pass without delay or hindrance and in case of need to give all lawful aid and protection.

Le Secrétaire d'Etat des Etats-Unis d'Amérique prie par les présentes toutes autorités compétentes de laisser passer le citoyen ou ressortissant des Etats-Unis titulaire du présent passeport, sans délai ni difficulté et, en cas de besoin, de lui accorder toute aide et protection légitimes.

POSTAL TELEGRAPH – COMMERCIAL CABLES

CLARENCE H. MACKAY, PRESIDENT

| TELEGRAMS TO ALL AMERICA | CABLEGRAMS TO ALL THE WORLD |

RECEIVED AT
TELEPHONES
JUST CALL "(POSTAL)
OFFICE NEXT KUDD HOTEL

Signal after the number of words—
"Blue" indicates (Day Letter) "N. L."
(Night Letter) or "Nite" (Night
Telegram)

DELIVERY NO.

STANDARD TIME INDICATED ON THIS MESSAGE

Form 16 Dbl

7VK 13 VIA LEITCHFIELD KY 843A

KYROCK KY JULY 16 1928

MRS NELLIE COTTRELL

511 SAINT ANN ST OWENSBORO KY

SEVEN POUND GIRL ARRIVED THIS MORNING BOTH DOING WELL SEND BED AT ONCE

T C

SPECIAL
RUSH
DELIVERY

BETTER STICK TO THE POSTAL
FASTEST ON EARTH

ordered 27 June 2001
postmarked 14 Aug 2001

| Form 508-5 TREASURY DEPARTMENT INTERNAL REVENUE SERVICE (Revised July 1937) | U. S. SOCIAL SECURITY ACT APPLICATION FOR ACCOUNT NUMBER | 405-16-3347 |

EACH ITEM SHOULD BE FILLED IN, IF ANY ITEM IS NOT KNOWN WRITE "UNKNOWN"

1. ZALAME (EMP OYEE'S FIRST NAME) BRASHEAR (MIDDLE NAME) COTTRELL (LAST NAME)
CARRIED WOMEN GIVE MAIDEN FIRST NAME, MAIDEN LAST NAME, AND HUSBAND'S LAST NAME

2. (STREET AND NUMBER) 3. Elkton (POST OFFICE) Ky (STATE)

4. Elkton Motor Co. (BUSINESS NAME OF PRESENT EMPLOYER) 5. Elkton Ky. (BUSINESS ADDRESS OF PRESENT EMPLOYER)

6. 30 (AGE AT LAST BIRTHDAY) 7. May 28 1908 (DATE OF BIRTH (MONTH) (DAY) (YEAR)) (SUBJECT TO LATER VERIFICATION) 8. Warren s Ky (PLACE OF BIRTH)

9. R.L. Brashear (FATHER'S FULL NAME, REGARDLESS OF WHETHER LIVING OR DEAD) 10. Della B. Campbell (MOTHER'S FULL MAIDEN NAME, REGARDLESS OF WHETHER LIVING OR DEAD)

11. SEX: MALE ___ FEMALE ✓ (CHECK (✓) WHICH) 12. COLOR: WHITE ✓ NEGRO ___ OTHER ___ (CHECK (✓) WHICH) (SPECIFY)

13. GIVE DATE YOU BECAME AN EMPLOYEE (IF YOU BEGAN EMPLOYMENT AFTER NOV. 24, 1936) Mar 1, '39

14. HAVE YOU FILLED OUT A CARD LIKE THIS BEFORE? no (IF ANSWER IS "YES" ENTER PLACE AND DATE OF ORIGINAL FILING AND REASONS FOR FILING AGAIN)

15. Nov. 25 1939 (DATE SIGNED) 16. Zalame B. Cottrell (EMPLOYEE'S SIGNATURE AS USUALLY WRITTEN—DO NOT PRINT)

DETACH ALONG THIS LINE

≈ 426 ≈

Cottrell-Brashear Family Linage

In the Name of the Father, and of the Son, and of the Holy Ghost. Amen.

We do Certify:

That, according to the ordinance of Christ Himself, we did administer to

JO ANNE COTTRELL

THE SACRAMENT OF

Holy Baptism

thereby making HER a member of Christ, the Child of God, and an Inheritor of the Kingdom of Heaven, on the 19TH day of FEBRUARY, in the Year of our Lord, One Thousand Nine Hundred AND 43 in ST. JAMES Church, UNION CITY, in the Diocese of TENNESSEE
(Signed) Rev. L. Q. Wilson

Parents MR. T.C. COTTRELL
MRS. T.C. COTTRELL

Sponsors or Witnesses MRS. W.D. McANULTY
MRS. G.G. LOBDELL

Date of Birth JULY 16, 1928
Place of Birth KYROCK, KY.

In the Name of The Father, And of The Son, and of The Holy Ghost. Amen.

We do Certify:

That, according to the ordinance of Christ Himself, we did administer to

Zelamo Brashear

THE SACRAMENT OF

Holy Baptism

thereby making her a Member of Christ, the Child of God, and an Inheritor of the Kingdom of Heaven; on the Nineteenth day of April, in the Year of our Lord, One Thousand Nine Hundred and Twenty four; the said administration being in Christ Church, Bowling Green, in the Diocese of Kentucky
(Signed) A.C. Clifton 16

Parents Richard Brashear
Sella Brashear

Sponsors or Witnesses Sella Brashear
Kathleen Brashear

Date of Birth May 28, 1908

Signature William B. Gray
Civil Aeronautics Representative

Signature William B. Gray
Fingerprinting Officer

This certificate is not valid after
May 12, 1948

Place of birth ____
Date of birth AUG. 29, 1908 hair GREY
Color eyes Blue Ht. 5 ft. 11 in.
Weight 185 lbs.

FINGERPRINTS—RIGHT HAND

RIGHT THUMB

Pet Talk

By Joanna Cottrell

Stolen pets don't usually make the big headlines, but the tearful loss cries out in the owner's heart. One Soho family had this experience recently and they offer some helpful tips.

Going out to a local cafe one evening they tied up Gus, their 12 year old 100 pound German Shepard near the door and went inside. It was still light and there was only one woman reading at an outside table. They ordered and decided to stay inside, but checked outside from time to time. Then the moment came when they noticed both the woman and dog were gone.

They immediately called the police who were quick to respond. They went around the neighborhood asking questions and a local bartender remembered he had served an erratic acting woman with a large dog. They called the A.S.P.C.A. Put up posters in this and surrounding areas.

Only Gus knows the true drama but he was finally located at the A.S.P.C.A. They strongly advise that you keep going back to the A.S.P.C.A. and look in the bins yourself. Unfortunately, stolen pets are not that uncommon, though it is hard for animal lovers to believe anyone could be so cruel.

NEUTERING ANY NON-BREDDING DOGS AND CATS HAS MANY ADVANTAGES...advises Dr. Charles Lumley, D.V.M. / PET POPULATION CONTROL. ELIMINATING NEGATIVE BEHAVIOR like urine spraying in cats, aggression and fighting in male dogs. IT ALSO REDUCES THE EVIDENCE OF BREAST CANCER IN FEMALE DOGS if sprayed on or before the first heat. NEUTERING SURGERY IS COMMONLY DONE AT SIX MONTHS OF AGE, BUT MAY BE PERFORMED SAFELY IN YOUNGER AND OLDER ANIMALS. Some neutered animals tend to gain weight, so be careful of overfeeding. Dr. Lumley practices at PETMENDERS ANIMAL HOSPITAL, 158 Duane Street. 212-406-0970.

LOOKING FOR AN URBAN DWELLER DOG?...The WELSH CORGI is just as happy in a city flat as a country estate. Both the Cardigan and Pembrooke breeds were once working animals used for rushing small game, guarding buildings, ratting and herding. Yet they make excellent house pets and are particularly affectionate with children. They love to join in on jogging, travel well and though low set are graceful in their movements. Approximately 12 inches in height, they are just the right size for most apartments. (And, yes, the Queen of England does raise Welsh Corgis!)

THE PET BAR AT 98 THOMPSON STREET WILL HAVE THE ANNUAL PET PSYCHIC ON SATURDAY, OCTOBER 29, BETWEEN 2:00 AND 7:00 P.M. COME IN TO GIVE YOUR PET A READING. This Halloween event has become a favorite in the neighborhood. Find out if your loved one has secret yearnings to be a circus star. Was your pet honored by kings and queens in a former life? Really doesn't like to be called Baby-sweetkins? For more information call 212-274-0485.

PET TRIVIA
Mahatma Gandhi said "The greatness of a nation and its moral progress can be measured by the way its animals are treated."

Joanna Cottrell Article
Joanna wrote a column titled "Pet Talk"
for The Villager, a local paper published weekly
in Greenwich Village in Manhattan

The article above appeared in the 12 October 1994 issue on page 36

General References

The material used by the author in the research and writing of this book came from libraries, archives, websites, books, manuscripts, documents passed down to the author by his family, and personal knowledge. Specific sources, organized by chapter, are contained in the Sources Section. What follows is a general list of where the author found the information.

Research Institutions Visited

- Claiborne County Courthouse, Port Gibson, MS
- Daughters of the American Revolutions Library, Washington, DC
- Family History Library, Salt Lake City, UT
- Mississippi State Archives, Jackson, MS
- National Archives, Washington, DC
- Owensboro Public Library, Owensboro, KY
- Franklin County Library, Russellville, KY
- The Kentucky Building, Bowling Green, KY
- Virginia State Archives, Richmond, VA
- Warren County Courthouse, Bowling Green, KY

Cemeteries Visited

- Bethabara Baptist Church Cemetery, Philpot, KY
- Campbell-Shields Cemetery, Bowling Green, KY
- Elmwood Cemetery, Owensboro, KY
- Fairview Cemetery, Bowling Green, KY
- Hollywood Cemetery, Richmond, VA
- Macedonia Baptist Church Cemetery, Philpot, KY
- Maple Grove Cemetery, Russellville, KY
- Maury Cemetery, Richmond, VA
- Mount Calvary Catholic Cemetery, Salt Lake City, UT
- Riverview Cemetery, Richmond, VA
- Rosehill Cemetery, Owensboro, KY
- Wintergreen Cemetery, Port Gibson, MS

Websites and Databases

- history.ky.gov
- kdia.ky.gov
- www.ancestry.com
- www.billiongraves.com
- www.familysearch.org
- www.findagrave.com
- www.fold3.com
- www.genealogybank.com

- www.godfrey.org
- www.mocavo.com
- www.newslibrary.com
- www.newspapers.com
- www.lva.virginia.gov
- www.sos.mo.gov/archives
- www.worldvitalrecords.com

Family Documents and Manuscripts

- Memoirs of Nellie Jane Lashbrook
- Memoirs of Estella Zalame Brashear
- Memoirs of Kathleen Hope Brashear
- Memoirs of Taylor Cosby Cottrell, Jr.
- Scrapbook kept by Kathleen Hope Brashear
- Family Bible Records

Principal Reference Books

- *Fairview Cemetery, Bowling Green, Kentucky*, Volumes I, II, & III, compiled by Patricia E Reid
- *Lashbrooke, Lashbrooks and Lashbrook (of the United States)*, compiled by Mary K Gritt Lashbrook
- *Duval Family of Virginia 1701 Descendants of Daniel Duval, Huguenot and Allied Families*, compiled by Bessie Berry Grabowskii
- *Daviess County, Kentucky Marriage Records*, Volumes I, & II, Harold Bishop Morgan
- *The Life Beautiful, Being Extracts from the Diary of W.H. Dawson*, written by W.H. Dawson
- *A Brashear(s) Family History,* Volumes 1-9, Charles Brashear
- *My Wife's Family,* Noah H. Bradly

Bibliography

Adjutant General's Office, letter. 9 May 1932, from War Department, Washington DC, to Unknown Recipient.

Amateur Radio QSL Card for T.C. Cottrell Jr. and T.C. Cottrell Sr., Undated.

American Red Cross First Aid Certificate for Zalame Brashear, 12 Aug 1942.

Amherst County Virginia marriage bonds 1753-1853. 1936. FHL US/CAN Book 975.5496 V2a, Family History Library, Salt Lake City, Utah.

Andrew G. Mischel, letter. 2 oct 1973, from 412-414 East Main, Owensboro Kentucky 42301, to Mrs. T.C. Cottrell.

Archbold, Annie. The Traditional Arts and Crafts of Warren County, Kentucky. Bowling Green, Kentucky: Bowling Green-Warren County Arts Commission.

Baily, Davis Fulton and Arleta Wolfe. The Wills of Amherst County Virginia 1761-1865. Easley, South Carolina: Southern Historical Press, Inc.

Bain, Donald W. Journal of the North Carolina Annual Conference of the Methodist Episcopal Church, South, Fifty-Third Seccion at Greensboro, N.C.. Raleigh, N.C.: E.M. Uzzell, Steam Printer and Binder.

Bellevue Cemetery. Database. Find A Grave. http://www.findagrave.com.

Bible Records, 1830-1909. Database. Virginia Historical Society. http://www.vahistorical.org.

Bischoff, Pamela. "Membership Question Dealing with Zalame Cottrell." E-mail from <info@kyguild.org> at P.O. Box 291, Berea, Kentucky.

Booth, A.J., letter. 14 Jan 1971, from Holley Inc., Carburetor Division, Warren, Michigan, to T.C. Cottrell.

Bowling Green High School Attendance Report for Zalame Brashear.

Bowling Green High School Diploma for Zalame Cottrell, given on 1 June 1927, at Bowling Green, Kentucky.

Bowling Green Kentucky. Cottrell Family Papers. Rotary Hobby Fair Participation Award.

Bowling Green Mfg. Co. News and Report.

Brashear, Charles. A Brashear(s) Family History, Descendants of Robert and Benois Brasseur, Volume 4, Brashear(s) Families of the Ohio Valley. Clearlake Oaks, California: Charles Brashear Books, Etc., 2002.

Brashear, Kathleen Hope. Remembrances of Bowling Green.

Brashear, Walter Curren, letter to Martha Crutchfield.

Bullitt County Genealogical Society. History-Families Bullitt County, Kentucky. Paducha, Kentucky: Turner Publishing Company, 1996, FHL US/CAN 976.9453 H2b.

Business Card for Zalame's Antiques, circa 1950.

Business Card for Zeleme Cottrell's Handicraft Shop, circa 1950.

Business Travel for TC Cottrell from October 1998 to June 2003, 29 May 2003, list was compiled from actual travel expense reports on 29 May 2003.

Business Writing Certificate for Zalame Brashear, 3 May 1923.

Byrd, Ken, letter. 27 Feb 1990, from 1213 High Street, Bowling Green, KY 42101, to T.C. Cottrell, Jr.

Campbell History. 1960.

Campbell-Shields Cemetery (Warren County, Kentucky; approximately three miles south of Bowling Green on the Calvary Baptist Church property near the intersection of Elrod Road and William H. Natcher Green River Parkway). Grave markers.

Certificate of Appointment as Lay Reader for Taylor C. Cottrell.

Certificate of Baptism for Taylor C. Cottrell, Jr.

Certificate of Baptism for Zalame Brashear.

Certificate of Commemoration for Mrs. T.C. Cottrell from the Governor of Kentucky, 3 Jun 1977.

Certificate of Completion of Modern Business Practice Course for Taylor C Cottrell, 12 Dec 1961.

Certificate of Confirmation for Taylor Cosby Cottrell.

Certificate of Confirmation for Zalame Brashear.

Certificate of Ownership to Mrs. T.C. Cottrell for Lot 16, Section R, Plat 1, Fairview Cemetery, 19 May 1971.

Children of Alexander Cosby and Dorcas Sidney, downloaded from Ancestry.com family tree 56260584 on 17 May 2015 by TC Cottrell.

City of Danville, Kentucky, Bellevue Cemetery Interments, Alphabetical. Database. Danville Kentucky. www.danvilleky.org.

Civil Aeronautics Authority Airman Certificate for Taylor Cosby Cottrell, 23 Dec 1941.

Civil Aeronautics Authority Airman Rating for Taylor Cosby Cottrell, 23 Dec 1941.

Civil Aeronautics Authority Ground Instructor Certificate for Taylor Cosby Cottrell, 27 Aug 1942.

Civil Aeronautics Authority Ground Instructor Rating for Taylor Cosby Cottrell, 27 Aug 1942.

Collins, Lewis. Warren County, Kentucky History & Biographies. P.O. Box 400; Signal Mountain, Tennessee 37377-0400: Signal Mountain Press, 2002, FHL US/CAN 976.974 D3w.

Compiled Service Records of Confederate Soldiers Who Served in Organizations from the State of Virginia. Subscription database. Footnote.com. http://www.footnote.com.

Contract of Sale for property at 868 Nutwood, Warren County, Bowling Green, Kentucky, 7 May 1973.

Cottrell-Brashear Family Linage

Copy of Last Will and Testament, 25 May 1971. Zalame Cottrell.

Cottrell Burials in Elmwood Cemetery According to the Kentucky Historical Society Cemetery Database.

Cottrell Family Bible Record, 1733 - 1882, accessed on Library of Virginia on-line, 13 July 2002; files A21023 and A20137.

Cottrell Family Bible Record, 1837 - 1961, accessed on Library of Virginia on-line, 13 July 2002; files 25994.

Cottrell Family Papers. Marriage Records.

Cottrell Jr, Taylor C, personal knowledge.

Cottrell, Joseph Frey, family data. The Holman New Self-Pronouncing Sunday-School Teachers Bible, Baptist Book Concern Edition. Louisville, Kentucky: A.J. Holman & Co., Ltd, 1894. Present owner Taylor C Cottrell Jr.

Cottrell, Minnie Jane (Hooker). Cottrell Family Information.

Cottrell, Nellie J. (Lashbrook). Childhood and Youth.

Cottrell, Nellie J. (Lashbrook). Earliest Memories.

Cottrell, Nellie J. (Lashbrook). Family Lore of Uncle Sariah.

Cottrell, Nellie J. (Lashbrook). Lashbrook Data.

Cottrell, Nellie J. (Lashbrook). Memories of a Pet Lamb. Undated.

Cottrell, Nellie J. (Lashbrook). Memories of Childhood.

Cottrell, Nellie Lashbrook, family data. Holy Bible, King James Version. Cleveland and New York: The World Publishing Company, Present owner Taylor C Cottrell Jr.

Cottrell, Nellie Lashbrook, family data. The Holy Bible, Self-Pronouncing Edition. Akron, Ohio: The Saalfield Publishing Co. Present owner Taylor C Cottrell Jr.

Cottrell, Taylor C. "Campbell-Brashear Cemetery Lot Photo Survey, Fairview Cemetery, Bowling Green, Kentucky." Privately held by Taylor C Cottrell.

Cottrell, Taylor C. "Joseph F Cottrell Cemetery Lot Photo Survey, Hollywood Cemetery, Richmond, Virginia." Privately held by Taylor C Cottrell.

Cottrell, Zalame (Brashear). Beech Bend Brashears.

Cottrell, Zalame (Brashear). Brashear and Baker Family Data.

Cottrell, Zalame (Brashear). Brashear and Campbell Family Data.

Cottrell, Zalame (Brashear). Brashear Research Notes.

Cottrell, Zalame Brashear, letter. 2 Jul 1983, from 868 Nutwood Avenue, Bowling Green Kentucky, to T.C. Cottrell, Jr.

Dawson, W.H.. The Life Beautiful, Being Extracts from the Diary of W.H. Dawson. Hartford, Kentucky: McDowell Publications.

Deposit receipt for Zalame Cottrell's 1/2 share of Georgia Campbell's estate, 17 Feb 1959.

Diefenderfer, Beverly Scrutchfield. "Re: Elizabeth Jane Crutchfield - KY/TN." Crutchfield Family Forum, discussion list, 16 November 2001. http://genforum.genealogy.com.

Disponett, Roberta S. "Jefferson County, Kentucky, Research Report One" to Lena Taylor Heltsley; 221 East 23rd Street, Owensboro, Kentucky. 27 September 1977.

Dodd, Jordan, compiler. "Kentucky Marriages, 1802-1850." Subscription database. Ancestry.com. www.ancestry.com.

Duke, Walter Garland. Henry Duke, Councilor His Descendants and Connections. Richmond Virginia: The Dietz Press, Incorporated, 1949, FHL 929.273, D885.

Early American Marriages: Virginia to 1850. Online Ancestry.com, accessed on 21 August 2004.

Early Price List for Cottrell Limited Editions, Undated.

Economic Highways of Warren County and Bowling Green. Online http://www.wku.edu/Library/mused/rrr3/ech.html.

Ed Phelps. "DESTINY - DEATH - DOOMED." Ancestry Message Boards, discussion list, 8 July 2002. http://boards.ancestry.com/localities.northam.usa.states.kentucky.counties.warren : 25 February 2014.

Edgeworth, Michael J.. Daviess County, Kentucky Order Book "D," 1837-1846. P.O. Box 1932, Owensboro, Kentucky, 42302: West Central Kentucky Family Research Association, 1977, FHL US/CAN 976.9864 P28e.

Edmund West. "Family Data Collection - Births." Subscription database. Ancestry.com.

Edmund West. "Family Data Collection - Individual Records Database." Subscription database. Ancestry.com.

Edmund West. "Family Data Collection - Marriages" Subscription database. Ancestry.com.

Elmwood Cemetery. Elmwood Cemetery Early Records and History, Register of Interments, Elmwood Cemetery, 1877-1885 & 1900-1902. n.p.: n.pub.

Elmwood Cemetery. Marker Transcriptions and Cottrell Family Area Drawing. Cottrell Family Papers. 867 Jamestown Drive, Rockledge, Florida 32955.

Elmwood Cemetery. Marker Transcriptions and Lashbrook Family Area Drawing.

Elmwood Cemetery. Plot Map.

Enlisted Reserve Corp Identification Card for Taylor C. Cottrell, 3 Aug 1943.

Ennis Cemetery. Database. Find A Grave. http://www.findagrave.com.

Ennis Family History. Online <http://archiver.rootsweb.com/th/read/ENNIS/2000-12/0976595810> accessed on 2 June 2005.

Estate Settlement Checks written to Brashear Heirs of the William H Brashear Estate, 6 January 1944.

Fackler, Calvin Morgan. Early Days in Danville. 1941. Reprint Utica, Kentucky: McDowell Publications, 2002.

Fairview Cemetery. Cemetery marker data.

Cottrell-Brashear Family Linage

FamilySearch. "Virginia Select Marriages, 1785-1940." Subscription database. Ancestry.com.

Florida. Jacksonville. State Department of Health and Rehabilitative Services. Death Registration. Estella Zalame Brashear Cottrell certificate.

Francis Cosby (1510-80), Stradbally, Queen's County and the Tutor conquest of Leinster, Francis Cosby (1510-80), Stradbally, Queen's County, History Ireland, Ireland's History Magazine, Volume 15, Issue 5, Features Section (Sep/Oct 2006).

Genealogical Abstracts from Reported Deaths The Nashville Christian Advocate 1890-1893. Online <www.tngenweb.org> accessed on 29 December 2004.

Georgia Ennis Campbell. Campbell History by Georgia Ennis Campbell. 1944.

Gottschalk Family Tree. Subscription database. Ancestry.com. http://www.ancestry.com.

Gottschalk, Paul. "Re: Greetings [Henry Campbell Information]." E-mail from <pggott@yahoo.com> at Hayward, Wisconsin. 8 June 2008.

Gottschalk, Paul. "Re: Henry Campbell Marriages." E-mail from <pggott@yahoo.com> at Hayward, Wisconsin. 8 June 2008.

Guardianship Designation of Joanna Cottrell, 23 October 1997, prepared by Paul Jeselsohn, Attorney, New York, New York.

Hansen, Michael. "Campbell Shields Cemetery - Smallhouse Pike Area." E-mail from <toymart@wavecable.com> at Bremerton, Washington. 11 September 2004.

Harris, Malcolm H.. History of Louisa County, Virginia. Richmond, Virginia: TheDietz Press, 1936.

Hatcher, Patricia Law. "Abstract of Graves of Revolutionary Patriots." Subscription database. Ancestry.com. http://www.ancestry.com : 2007.

Health Care Proxy for Joanna Cottrell, 23 October 1997.

Heltsley, Lena Taylor. "Four Generation Taylor Family Pedigree Chart".

Henley Index, The Library of Virginia Digital Image Database, Film 144. Online <ajax.lva.lib.va.us> accessed on 30 September 2006.

High School Graduation Booklet for Zalame Brashear.

History of the DuPont William Spruance Cellophane Plant. Online http://heritage.dupont.com/floater/fl_spruance/floater.shtml.

Hollywood Cemetery. Database. Find A Grave. http://www.findagrave.com.

Honorable Discharge from the Army of the United States for Taylor C. Cottrell, Sr., 19 Apr 1944.

IGI Individual Record. Database. FamilySearch. http://www.familysearch.org.

Illinois Depratment of Financial and Professional Regulation, Division of Insurance, Slave Registry Detail for death payment for a slave death to Jefferson Cosby. Online <www.idfpr.com> accessed on 3 January 2005.

Inter-State Publishing Co.. History of Daviess County, Kentucky. 1883. Reprint Utica, KY: McDowel Publications, 1980.

Jacobs, Philip P. The Campaign Against Tuberculosis in the United States. Philadelphia, Pennsylvania: Wm. F. Fell Company, 1908. Digital images. Google Books. http://www.google.com/books : 2010.

JanVieira. Ancestry.com. http://trees.ancestry.com/tree/2808/family/familyview: 2009.

Johnson, J. Stoddard. Memorial History of Louisville From Its First Settlement to the Year 1896. Chicago and New York: American Biographical Publishing Company, 1896, FHL US/CAN Film 1000051, Item 1.

Jordan Dodd. "Kentucky Marriages to 1850." Subscription database. Ancestry.com. http://www.ancestry.com : 2004.

Kansas. Allen County. 1855 State Census, population schedule. Digital image. Ancestry.com (http://www.ancestry.com : 2008).

Kentucky Department for Libraries and Archives. "Kentucky Death Records, 1852-1953." Subscription database. Ancestry.com. http://www.ancestry.com.

Kentucky Division of Epidemiology and Health Planning. "Kentucky Death Index, 1911-2000." Subscription database. Ancestry.com. http://www.ancestry.com : 2004.

Kentucky Guild of Artists and Craftsmen Membership Card for Zalame Cottrell, Undated, as a charter Craftsman member, Cottrell Family Papers, 867 Jamestown Drive, Rockledge, Florida 32955.

Kentucky Marriages to 1850. Online Ancestry.com.

Kentucky Probate Records, 1727-1990. Digital images. Ancestry.com. www.ancestry.com.

Kentucky Vocational School News, Volume one, Number two, Sumerset, Kentucky, Spring 1949.

Kentucky. Boyle County. Marriage records; 1842-1955. Boyle County (Kentucky) Clerk of the County Court. FHL microfilm 191806, bk1, p135. Family History Library, Salt Lake City, Utah.

Kentucky. Daviess County. Vital records, 1852-1953; indexes, 1815-1967. Clerk of the County Court. Book 13, p. 457, FHL microfilm 1759323. Family History Library, Salt Lake City, Utah.

Kentucky. Daviess County. Vital records, 1852-1953; indexes, 1815-1967. Clerk of the County Court. Book O, p. 651, FHL microfilm 582238. Family History Library, Salt Lake City, Utah.

Kentucky. Elkton. Social Security Administration. Social Security Form SSA-9638.

Kentucky. Frankfort. Department of Health Bureau of Vital Statistics. Brashear, Estella Zalame special certificate of birth.

Kentucky. Frankfort. Department of Health Bureau of Vital Statistics. Brashear, Robert L special certificate of birth.

Kentucky. Frankfort. Department of Health Bureau of Vital Statistics. Cottrell, Taylor Cosby special certificate of birth.

Kentucky. Frankfort. Department of Health Bureau of Vital Statistics. Death Registration. Kathleen Hope Brashear certificate.

Cottrell-Brashear Family Linage

Kentucky. Frankfort. Department of Health Bureau of Vital Statistics. Death Registration. Nellie Jane Cottrell certificate.

Kentucky. Frankfort. Department of Health Bureau of Vital Statistics. Death Registration. Sarah M. Lashbrook certificate.

Kentucky. Frankfort. Department of Health Bureau of Vital Statistics. Death Registration. Taylor Cosby Cottrell certificate.

Kentucky. Frankfort. Department of Health Bureau of Vital Statistics. Death Registration. William H Brashear certificate.

Kentucky. Harrodsburg. Marriage Bond of William Barnett and Tabitha Paddox. unknown author. unknown volume. Mercer County Courthouse, Office of County Clerk, Harrodsburg, Kentucky.

Kentucky. Jefferson County. Marriage Records, 1781-1951. Clerk of the County Court. FHL microfilm 817866. Family History Library, Salt Lake City, Utah.

Kentucky. Jefferson County. Marriage Records, 1781-1951. Clerk of the County Court. FHL microfilm 819589. Family History Library, Salt Lake City, Utah.

Kentucky. Louisville Jefferson County Courthouse Marriage Records.

Kentucky. Mercer County. Mercer County Kentucky Will Book 7. Menaugh, Marie. FHL microfilm 855032, item7, p26. Family History Library, Salt Lake City, Utah.

Kentucky. Nelson County. 1850 US Census, population schedule. Digital image. Ancestry.com (http://www.ancestry.com : 2005).

Kentucky. Owensboro. Elmwood Cemetery. Cemetery marker data.

Kentucky. Todd County. 1940 US Census, population schedule. Digital image. Ancestry.com (http://www.ancestry.com).

Kentucky. Warren County Courthouse. Deed of Conveyance from Mrs. W.A. Lee to Mrs. Nellie Cottrell, 12 Dec 1936.

Kentucky. Warren County. Marriage Book A. Warren County Courthouse, Clerk Warren County Court.

Kentucky. Warren County. Marriage Book B. Warren County Courthouse, Clerk Warren County Court.

Kentucky. Warren County. Marriage Book E. Warren County Courthouse, Clerk Warren County Court.

Kentucky. Warren County. Marriage Book ML61. Warren County Courthouse, Clerk Warren County Court.

Kentucky. Warren County. Marriage Book S. Warren County Courthouse, Clerk Warren County Court.

Kentucky. Warren County. Marriage Records, 1797-1965, Vols. Q-T 1877-1888, bonds & certificates only. Clerk of the County Court. FHL microfilm 1944289, book W, p. 200. Family History Library, Salt Lake City, Utah.

Kentucky. Warren County. Probate Records, 1797-1985, Vols. D, 4-6 1827-1927 - v. D. Clerk of the County Court. FHL microfilm 1904209, v5. Family History Library, Salt Lake City, Utah.

Kentucky. Warren County. Probate Records, 1797-1985, Vols. D, 4-6 1827-1927 - v. D. Clerk of the County Court. FHL microfilm 1904209, v6. Family History Library, Salt Lake City, Utah.

Kentucky. Warren County. Will Book W15. Warren County Courthouse, Clerk Warren County Court.

Kentucky. Warren County. Will Book W4. Warren County Courthouse, Clerk Warren County Court.

Lashbrook Family Cemetery. Database. Find A Grave. http://www.findagrave.com.

Lashbrook, James B. Journal. late 1800s.

Lashbrook, Mary K (Gritt). Lashbrooke, Lashbrooks and Lashbrook (of the United States). 11129 Pleasant Ridge Road; Utica, Kentucky 42376: McDowell Publications, 1986.

Lashbrook, Mary K. "Family Group Sheet for Worden Graham Lashbrook". Compiled 25 February 1984. P.O. Box 238, Slack Creek, WI 45106.

Lashbrook, Quinton, compiler. "Our Lashbrook Family Connections." Database. RootsWeb's WorldConnect Project. http://wc.rootsweb.ancestry.com/cgi-bin/igm.cgi?db=lashbrook.

Last Will and Testament, 1 Nov 1988. Zalame Cottrell.

Last Will and Testament, 12 Nov 1954. Zalame Cottrell.

Last Will and Testament, 15 July 1982. Kathleen H. Brashear.

Last Will and Testament, 23 Oct 1997. Joanna Cottrell.

Last Will and Testament, 24 December 1900. Walter C Brashear.

Last Will and Testament, 9 Nov 1992. Jo Anne Cottrell.

Leslie Method of Writing Certificate for Zalame Brashear, 20 Feb 1925.

Macedonia Baptist Church Cemetery (Daviess County, Kentucky). Grave markers.

Macedonia Baptist Church Cemetery. Database. Find A Grave. http://www.findagrave.com.

Manuscripts and Folklife Archives, Department of Library Special Collections. MSS 230 Warren County, Kentucky - Marriage Bonds. 31 December 1821. Kentucky Library and Museum, Western Kentucky University, Bowling Green, Kentucky.

Manuscripts and Folklife Archives, Department of Library Special Collections. MSS 230 Warren County, Kentucky - Marriage Bonds. 8 March 1824. Kentucky Library and Museum, Western Kentucky University, Bowling Green, Kentucky.

Marriage Bonds of Henrico County, Virginia, 1782-1853. Online, Ancestry.com.

Marshall Family Tree. Ancestry.com.

Master Mason Membership Card for Taylor C. Cottrell, 6 Mar 1970.

Meade, Bishop. Old Churches, Ministers and Families of Virginia. volume II. Philadelphia, Pennsylvania: J.B. Lippincott & Co., 1857).

Cottrell-Brashear Family Linage

Messenger Inquirer, Owensboro. Kentucky.

Miller, Roy D., letter. 11 Aug 1955, from Children's United World Art Foundation, 132 S. 18th St., Philadelphia 3, PA, to Mrs. T.C. Cottrell.

Morgan, Harold Bishop. Daviess County, Kentucky Marriage Records Volume 1, 1780 through 1914. 11129 Pleasant Ridge Road, Utica, Kentucky: McDowell Publications, 2004.

Nacy Brashear's Bible, accessed on Family Tree of Levi L Brashear, maintained by slbrinton on Ancestry.com.

National Society of the Colonial Dames of America in the Commonwealth of Virginia. "Christ Church Parish, Virginia Records, 1615-1812."

National Society of the Colonial Dames of America. "Christ Church Parish, Virginia Records, 1653-1812." Subscription database. Ancestry.com.

Nellie J. Cottrell, letter. 13 May 1971, from Nursing Home, Bowling Green Kentucky.

Nellie J. Cottrell, letter. 18 Jan 1970, from 1530 State Street, Bowling Green Kentucky.

Nellie J. Cottrell. Funeral Book.

Nellie J. Cottrell. Kentucky Operator License.

Netolicka, Robert, letter. 2 October 2001, from Johnson Controls Headquarters, Milwaukee, Wisconson, to T. C. Cottrell, Jr.

New York, New York. Department of Health Vital Records. Death Registration. Joanna Cottrell certificate.

Noah H Bradley. My Wife's Family. Pawhatan, Virginia: H. Bradley, 1922.

NY Surrogate's Court Letters Testamentary appointing Taylor Cosby Cottrell as executor for Joanna Cottrell's estate, 29 October 1998.

Office of County Clerk, Louisville, Kentucky. Jefferson County Courthouse, Jefferson County Wills, 22 July 1846.

Order Approving Final Settlement and Discharge of Co-Executors - Estate of Kathleen H Brashear, 16 June 1987.

Order of DeMolay Membership Card for Taylor C. Cottrell, 21 Jan 1926.

Owensboro Messenger Inquirer, Owensboro Kentucky.

Owensboro Messenger, Daviess County, Kentucky.

Parish Records, 1861-1919, Christ Episcopal Church, Bowling Green, KY, Baptisms, Confirmations, Marriages, Burials, 1942.

Parish Records, 1861-1919, Christ Episcopal Church, Bowling Green, KY, Includes some records of Glasgow and Russellville Missions.

Park City Daily News, Bowling Green, Kentucky.

Parsons, Major, letter. 1 Oct 1943, from 67th AAF Flying Training Detachment, Union City, Tennessee, to T.C. Cottrell.

Pastor, Joan, letter. 14 Dec 1970, from Colt Industries, 430 Park Avenue, New York, New York, to T.C. Cottrell.

Patricia E Reid and Barbara O Ford compilers. Fairveiw Cemetery, Bowling Green, Kentucky, Cemetery 1. Volume 1. Kentucky: unknown publisher, 1989.

Penmanship Certificate for Zalame Brashear, 15 Aug 1926.

Penner Cemetery. Database. Find A Grave. http://www.findagrave.com.

Perrin, W H, J H Battle and G C Kniffin. History of Kentucky Illustrated, Edition 3. 1887. Reprint Greenville, South Carolina: Southern Historical Press, Inc., 1999.

Peter Cottrell Will, Henrico County Court, 17 April 1816. Online <www.cottrellweb.com/docs.htm>.

Pollock, Michael E.. Marriage Bonds of Henrico County, Virginia 1782-1853. Baltimore, Maryland: Genealogical Publishing Co., Inc., 1984, FHL US/CAN 975.5453 V2p.

Postcard Of The Antilla Hotel in Coral Gables Florida, Undated, documenting the temporary residence of TC and Zalame Cottrell during April and May of 1944.

Power of Attorney of Kathleen Brashear Appointing Zalame Cottrell, 18 October 1974.

Power of Attorney of Richard H Brashear Appointing Della Z Brashear, 8 July 1942.

Power of Attorney of Zalame Brashear Appointing Della Brashear, 9 April 1943, executed in Union City, Tennessee.

Provost Marshall General's Bureau. "U.S., Civil War Draft Registrations Records, 1863-1865." Subscription database. Ancestry.com. http://www.ancestry.com : 2012.

Record of Baptisms for Richard Levi Brashear Family, providence unknown, likely prepared by Christ Episcopal Church at the request of a member of the Brashear family.

Release From From Duties as Director of Ground School for Taylor Cosby Cottrell, 19 Apr 1944.

Retainer agreement between Taylor Cosby Cottrell, Jr. and Paul Jeselsohn, Attorney at Law.

Richard Cottrell Will, Henrico County Court, 6 February 1792. Online <www.cottrellweb.com/rico/docs.htm>.

Ricks, Joel. Goochland County, Virginia Marriage Bonds, 1730-1854. Salt Lake City, Utah: Genealogical Society of Utah, 1936.

Rosehill Elmwood Cemetery. Database. Find A Grave. http://www.findagrave.com.

Sacramento, California. Department of Health Bureau of Vital Statistics. Death Registration. Joseph Frey Cottrell certificate.

Sale of Brashear Lands - Curren Walter Brashear Estate, undated.

Scifres, David. "Re: Quick Question." E-mail from <david@scifres.com> at Bowling Green Kentucky. 8 November 2009.

Silent Keys, QST Amateur Radio, Number 8, Volume LV (August 1971).

Social Security Administration. "Social Security Death Index." Database. Ancestry.com. http://www.ancestry.com.

Cottrell-Brashear Family Linage

Sumpter, Irene Moss. Our Heritage An Album of Early Warren County Kentucky Land Marks. Clarksville, Tennessee: Jostens Publications, 1976.

T.C. Cottrell, Sr., Telegram. 16 July 1928, from Kyrock, Kentucky, to Mrs. Nellie Cottrell.

Taylor C Cottrell, Jr.. Commercial Pilot License. Cottrell Family Papers. 867 Jamestown Drive, Rockledge, Florida 32955.

Taylor C. Cottrell. Funeral Book.

Tennessee. Gallatin. Sumner County Office of Court Clerk Marriage Records.

The American Home - Pattern No. 1316 - Glasses and Pitcher - by Zeleme, Copyrighted September 1950, Cottrell Family Papers, 867 Jamestown Drive, Rockledge, Florida 32955.

The Filson Club. Jefferson County Virginia Kentucky Early Marriages Book 1. 719 E. 6th Street; Owensboro, Kentucky 42301: Cook & McDowell Publications.

The Library of Virginia. "Family Data Collection - Births." Subscription database. Ancestry.com. http://www.ancestry.com.

The Library of Virginia. "Family Data Collection - Individual Records." Subscription database. Ancestry.com. http://www.ancestry.com.

The Virginia Genealogy Society. Death Notices from Richmond, Virginia Newspapers 1821-1840. Richmond, Virginia: Virginia Genealogical Society.

Thirtieth High School Reunion Program for Zalame Cottrell, 15 May 1957.

Thomas L Aud. "Thomas L. Aud also commented on his status." E-mail.

Thomas, O.L.. Ancestral Graves in Warren County, Kentucky, Volume 1. Warren County, Kentucky: Warren County Historical Society, c1980, FHL US/CAN 976.974 V3t.

Thomas, O.L.. Ancestral Graves in Warren County, Kentucky, Volume 2. 205 Clements Avenue; Glasgow, Kentucky 42141-3409: Gorin Genealogical Publishing, c1980, FHL US/CAN 976.974 V3t V.2.

Transcription of Family Data from Bible Concordance owned by Mrs. Howard Daniel.

Transcription of Family Data from Louisa Taylor's Bible

Transcription of Family Data from Mrs. Catherine Foreman Lashbrook's Bible

Tyler, Lyon Gardiner. Encyclopedia of Virginia Biography. Volume I. Maryland: Genealogical Publishing Company, Inc.

U.S. and International Marriage Records, 1560-1900. Subscription database. Ancestry.com. http://www.ancestry.com.

U.S. City Directories - 1937/38-1949. Database. Ancestry.com. http://www.ancestry.com.

U.S. City Directories, 1822-1989. Database. Ancestry.com. http://www.ancestry.com.

US Census, 1820 population schedule. Digital image. Ancestry.com (http://www.ancestry.com).

US Census, 1830 population schedule. Digital image. Ancestry.com (http://www.ancestry.com).

US Census, 1840 population schedule. Digital image. Ancestry.com (http://www.ancestry.com).

US Census, 1850 population schedule. Digital image. Ancestry.com (http://www.ancestry.com).

US Census, 1860 population schedule. Digital image. Ancestry.com (http://www.ancestry.com).

US Census, 1870 population schedule. Digital image. Ancestry.com (http://www.ancestry.com).

US Census, 1880 agricultural schedule, Digital image, Ancestry.com (http://www.ancestry.com)

US Census, 1880 population schedule. Digital image. Ancestry.com (http://www.ancestry.com)

US Census, 1900 population schedule. Digital image. Ancestry.com (http://www.ancestry.com).

US Census, 1910 population schedule. Digital image. Ancestry.com (http://www.ancestry.com).

US Census, 1920 population schedule. Digital image. Ancestry.com (http://www.ancestry.com).

US Census, 1930 population schedule. Digital image. Ancestry.com (http://www.ancestry.com).

US Census, 1940 population schedule. Digital image. Ancestry.com (http://www.ancestry.com).

Vale, John, letter. 9 May 1944, from Embry-Riddle Company, to Ration Board.

Virginia Marriages to 1800. Online Ancestry.com.

Virginia Marriages, 1740-1850. Online Ancestry.com.

Virginia, Death Records, 1912-2014. Subscription database. Ancestry.com. http://www.ancestry.com.

War Ration Book One for Della Zalame Brashear, 6 May 1942.

West-Central Kentucky Family Research Association. Daviess County, Kentucky Cemeteries Volume 1. Hartford, Kentucky: McDowell Publications, 1977.

Westerfield, Thomas W. Kentucky Genealogy and Biography Volume II (Extract). P.O. Box 1554; Owensboro, Kentucky: Genealogical Reference Company, 1971, FHL US/CAN 976.9 D3wt Vol.2.

Zalame Brashear Cottrell's Campbell Family Data. Circa 1958.

Sources

Section 1 – Chapter 1 – William Cottrell Family

[1] Cottrell Family Bible Record, 1733 - 1882, *Library of Virginia* (http://www.la.virginia.gov: accessed on 13 July 2002).

[2] Ibid.

[3] Mrs Charles A Wahking, "Cottrell Bible Records," *Kentucky Historical Society Register*, Volume 28, Number 84 (July 1930).

[4] Cottrell Family Bible Record, 1733 - 1882, *Library of Virginia*.

[5] Ibid.

[6] "Virginia Vital Records #1, 1600s-1800s," Genealogy.com (http://www.genealogy.com: accessed 10 September 2005), entry for William Hutchinson and Elizabeth Cottrell.

[7] 1850 US Census, Henrico County, Virginia, population schedule, Western Division, page 537B, dwelling 490, family 517, William Hutchinson; *Ancestry.com* (http://www.ancestry.com: accessed 8 September 2005); citing National Archives microfilm M432, roll 951.

[8] Jordan Dodd, compiler, "Kentucky Marriages, 1802-1850," subscription database, *Ancestry.com* (http://www.ancestry.com: accessed 8 August 2008), for Abel Cottrell and Rosa Thornton (27 April 1810).

[9] "Cottrell Cemetery," database, *Find A Grave* (http://www.findagrave.com: accessed 19 April 2013), entry for Rose Thornton Cottrell, 6 September 1857; citing memorial # 87634636.

[10] "Cottrell Cemetery," database, *Find A Grave* (http://www.findagrave.com: accessed 19 April 2013), entry for Peter Cottrell, 8 Oct 1855; citing memorial # 7861218.

[11] "Cottrell Cemetery," database, *Find A Grave* (http://www.findagrave.com: accessed 19 April 2013), entry for James P Cottrell, 26 July 1890; citing memorial # 7861213.

[12] Macedonia Baptist Church Cemetery (Daviess County, Kentucky), Multiple Grave Marker, photographed by T.C. Cottrell, 27 March 2011.

[13] Michael E. Pollock, compiler, *Marriage Bonds of Henrico County, Virginia 1782-1853* (Baltimore, Maryland: Genealogical Publishing Co., Inc., 1984), FHL US/CAN 975.5453 V2p.

[14] "Reuben Cottrell Bible Record Transcript," copied on 8 April, 1960 from the original record, by M.J. Edgeworth for the Gen. Evan Shelby Chapter of the DAR in Owensboro, Kentucky, Richard Cottrell, *The Cottrell Web* (http://www.cottrellweb.com: accessed 6 July 2007).

[15] Jordan Dodd, "Kentucky Marriages, 1802-1850", for Joseph Cottrell and Lucy Bryant (5 January 1815), Individual transcription of marriage records held by the individual counties in Kentucky.

[16] Cottrell Family Bible Record, 1733 - 1882, *Library of Virginia*.

[17] Jordan R Dodd, compiler, "Virginia Marriages, 1740-1850," subscription database, *Ancestry.com* (http://www.ancestry.com: accessed 8 August 2008), for Jefferson Wilkerson and Susan Cottrell (29 April 1823).

[18] Cottrell Family Bible Record, 1733 - 1882, *Library of Virginia*.

[19] Virginia Marriages, 1740-1850, *Ancestry.com*, (www.ancestry.com; accessed on 30 July 2006), entry for William Cottrell and Sally Duval.

[20] Bessie Berry Grabowskii, *The DuVal Family of Virginia, 1701, Descendants of Daniel DuVal, Huguenot and Allied Families* (Richmond, Virginia: Press of the Dietz Printing Company, 1931), pages 95-98.

[21] *Peter Cottrell Will*, Henrico County Court, 17 April 1816, (http://www.cottrellweb.com.il).

[22] Bessie Berry Grabowskii, *The DuVal Family of Virginia, 1701*, page 97.

[23] Early American Marriages: Virginia to 1850, *Ancestry.com* (http://www.ancestry.com: accessed on 21 August 2004), entry for William Cottrell and Susan Halsey.

[24] Taylor C Cottrell, "Joseph F Cottrell Cemetery Lot Photo Survey, Hollywood Cemetery, Richmond, Virginia," privately held by Taylor C Cottrell, Rockledge, Florida; Markers and plot information photographed and recorded on 23 February 2011, by Taylor C Cottrell.

[25] The Virginia Genealogy Society, Death Notices from Richmond, Virginia Newspapers 1821-1840 (Richmond, Virginia: Virginia Genealogical Society, 1987).

[26] *Henley Index*, The Library of Virginia Digital Image Database, (http://www.ajax.lva.lib.va.us: accessed on 30 September 2006), Stephen Duval to Susan Cottrell.

[27] *Cottrell Family Bible Record, 1837 - 1961*, Library of Virginia (http://www.lva.virginia.gov: accessed on 13 July 2002.

[28] 1850 US Census, Chesterfield County, Virginia, population schedule, The Upper District, page 106, dwelling 782, family 818, Steven Duvall; digital images, *Ancestry.com*, (http://www.ancestry.com: accessed 20 March 2005); citing National Archives microfilm M432, roll 940.

[29] Bessie Berry Grabowskii, *The DuVal Family of Virginia, 1701, page 95.*

[30] Virginia Marriages, 1785-1940, *Ancestry.com* (http://www.ancestry.com: accessed on 8 October 2015) entry for William Frith and Susan Duval.

[31] "Hollywood Cemetery," *Find A Grave,* (http://www.findagrave.com: accessed 9 October 2015), entry for William F Frith, October 1887; citing memorial # 93141214.

[32] 1860 US Census, Goochland County, Virginia, population schedule, Dover Mills, page 935, dwelling 697, family 665, William Frith; *Ancestry.com* (http://www.ancestry.com: accessed 10 October 2015); citing National Archives microfilm M653, roll 1347.

[33] "Hollywood Cemetery" database, *Find A Grave*, entry for William F Frith, 5 October 1887.

[34] Taylor C Cottrell, "Joseph F Cottrell Cemetery Lot Photo Survey,"

[35] Bessie Berry Grabowskii, *The DuVal Family of Virginia, 1701, page 98.*

[36] Michael E. Pollock, compiler, *Marriage Bonds of Henrico County, Virginia 1782-1853* (Baltimore, Maryland: Genealogical Publishing Co., Inc., 1984), FHL US/CAN 975.5433 V2p.

[37] 1840 US Census, Henrico County, Virginia, population schedule, page 244, Richard Dabney, *Ancestry.com* (http://www.ancestry.com: accessed 12 January 2016); citing National Archives microfilm M704, roll 561.

[38] Ibid.

[39] Pollock, *Marriage Bonds of Henrico County, Virginia 1782-1833.*

[40] "Snead Cemetery," database, Find A Grave (http://www.findagrave.com: accessed 12 March 2016), entry for Sarah Elizabeth Harkrider Snead, 3 August 1881; citing memorial #20682517.

[41] "Snead Cemetery," database, Find A Grave (http://www.findagrave.com: accessed 12 March 2016), entry for John Snead, 10 February 1885; citing memorial #20682435.

[42] 1850 US Census, Hanover County, Virginia, population schedule, West District, page 378B, dwelling 601, family 601, John Srear (Snead); *Ancestry.com* (http://www.ancestry.com: accessed 15 March 2016); citing National Archives microfilm M653, roll 949.

[43] "Berea Baptist Church Cemetery," database, *Find A Grave* (http://www.findagrave.com: accessed 1 March 2016), entry for Alonzo Boardman Snead, 1912; citing memorial #9775672.

[44] "Virginia Select Marriages, 1785-1940," *Ancestry.com* (http://www.ancestry.com: accessed 1 March 2016), entry for Alonza B. Snead and Louisa W. George; 2 December 1860, FHL Film No. 31689.

[45] "Deep Run Baptist Church Cemetery," database, *Find A Grave* (http://www.findagrave.com: accessed 1 March 2016), entry for Anna Boardman Snead Bowles, 15 April 1946; citing memorial #127138299.

[46] "Berea Baptist Church Cemetery," database, *Find A Grave* (http://www.findagrave.com: accessed 1 March 2016), entry for Joseph Malcom Snead, 27 June 1954; citing memorial #73466018.

[47] "Berea Baptist Church Cemetery," database, *Find A Grave* (http://www.findagrave.com: accessed 1 March 2016), entry for Otie Lee Scott, 26 April 1949; citing memorial #14654343.

[48] "Virginia Select Marriages, 1785-1940," *Ancestry.com* (http://www.ancestry.com: accessed 1 March 2016), entry for Lemuel A. Snead and Lizzie E. Wood; 31 January 1900, FHL Film No. 2048451.

[49] "U.S. Civil War Soldier Records and Profiles, 1861-1865," *Ancestry.com* (http://www.ancestry.com: accessed 1 March 2016), entry for Robert J. Snead; original data compiled by Historical Data Systems of Kingston, MA.

[50] 1850 US Census, Hanover County, Virginia, population schedule, West District, page 378B, dwelling 601, family 601, John Srear (Snead).

[51] "Berea Baptist Church Cemetery," database, *Find A Grave* (http://www.findagrave.com: accessed 1 March 2016), entry for Edwin Shook Snead, 1 November 1932; citing memorial #20682551.

[52] "Virginia Select Marriages, 1785-1940," *Ancestry.com* (http://www.ancestry.com: accessed 1 March 2016), entry for Edwin Shook Snead and Rosaline Victoria Johnson; 1 January 1868, FHL Film No. 2048451.

[53] "Berea Baptist Church Cemetery," database. Find A Grave (http://www.findagrave.com: accessed 12 March 2016, entry for Rosalin V. Johnson Snead, 20 June 1923; citing memorial #20682572.

[54] "Berea Baptist Church Cemetery," database, *Find A Grave* (http://www.findagrave.com: accessed 12 March 2016), entry for Robert William Snead, 21 November 1968; citing memorial #73463739.

[55] "Berea Baptist Church Cemetery," database, *Find A Grave* (http://www.findagrave.com: accessed 12 March 2016), entry for Lillie Snead Tinsley, 3 October 1969; citing memorial #14081892.

[56] "Berea Baptist Church Cemetery," database. Find A Grave (http://www.findagrave.com: accessed 12 March 2016, entry for Daisy Snead Johnson, 30 January 1975; citing memorial #32175064.

[57] Minnie Jane (Hooker) Cottrell, Cottrell Family Data, memo without sources attributed to Minnie Jane (Hooker) Cottrell, in the private collection of Taylor Cosby Cottrell, Jr.

[58] Ibid.

[59] Joel Ricks, compiler, *Goochland County, Virginia Marriage Bonds, 1730-1854,* (Salt Lake City, Utah: Genealogical Society of Utah, 1936).

[60] Minnie Jane (Hooker) Cottrell, Cottrell Family Data.

[61] 1850 US Census, Hanover County, Virginia, population schedule, page 378B, dwelling 56, family 56, John W Cottrell; *Ancestry.com* (www.ancestry.com: accessed 31 December 2004); citing National Archives microfilm M432, roll 946.

[62] 1860 US Census, Goochland County, Virginia, population schedule, Post Office Dover Mills, page 70, dwelling 540, family 521, Jno W Cottrell; *Ancestry.com* (www.ancestry.com: accessed 4 September 2005); citing National Archives microfilm M653, roll 1347.

[63] 1870 US Census, Goochland County, Virginia, population schedule, Dover Mines Post Office, page 78, dwelling 539, family 539, John W Cottrell; *Ancestry.com* (Virginia. Goochland County: accessed 4 September 2005); citing National Archives microfilm M593, roll 1649.

[64] 1880 US Census, Goochland County, Virginia, population schedule, Dover District, Enumeration District (ED) 55, page 31C, dwelling 249, family 279, J.W. Cottrell; *Ancestry.com* (http://www.ancestry.com: accessed 4 September 2005); citing National Archives microfilm T9, roll 1367.

[65] Cottrell Family Information, original memos and documents held in the private collection of Taylor C. Cottrell, Jr.

[66] 1900 US Census, Goochland County, Virginia, population schedule, Dover Magisterial District, Enumeration District (ED) 13, page 13A, dwelling 243, family 246, John W Cottrell; *Ancestry.com* (www.ancestry.com: accessed 4 September 2005); citing National Archives microfilm T623, roll 1710.

[67] Cottrell Family Information.

[68] Minnie Jane (Hooker) Cottrell, Cottrell Family Data.

[69] Cottrell Family Information.

[70] "Virginia Death Records, 1912-2014," *Ancestry.com* (http://www.ancestry.com: accessed 16 July 2015), for Henry Leon Cottrell (8 February 1923), Certificate No. 7245.

[71] "Virginia Death Records, 1912-2014," *Ancestry.com* (http://www.ancestry.com: accessed 16 July 2015), for Rosa Belle Cottrell (23 November 1935), Certificate No. 26347.

[72] "Virginia Death Records, 1912-2014," *Ancestry.com* (http:www.ancestry.com: accessed 1 March 2016), entry for Edna Withers Tilman (26 October 1977), Certificate No. 77031565.

[73] "Bethel United Methodist Church Cemetery," database, *Find A Grave* (http://www.findagrave.com: accessed 1 March 2016), entry for Ira Baughan Cottrell, 11 April 1947; citing memorial #59747925.

[74] "Bowles Cemetery," database, *Find A Grave* (http://www.findagrave.com: accessed 1 March 2016), entry for Stuart C. Cottrell, 21 April 1935; citing memorial #24984017.

[75] "Virginia Death Records, 1912-2014," *Ancestry.com* (http:www.ancestry.com: accessed 1 March 2016), entry for Sadie Cottrell Alvis (15 May 1970), Certificate No. 70014621.

[76] "U.S. Veterans Gravesites, ca.1775-2006," *Ancestry.com* (http://www.ancestry.com: accessed 1 March 2016), entry for Anna C. Lange, 17 April 1966.

[77] "Virginia Death Records, 1912-2014," *Ancestry.com* (http://www.ancestry.com: accessed 16 July 2015), for Stewart Holland Cottrell (28 January 1930), Certificate No. 849.

[78] Cottrell Family Information.

[79] "Virginia Death Records, 1912-2014," *Ancestry.com* (http://www.ancestry.com: accessed 16 July 2015), for Susie R Cottrell (29 March 1914), Certificate No.5827.

[80] Minnie Jane (Hooker) Cottrell, Cottrell Family Data.

[81] Taylor C Cottrell, "Joseph F Cottrell Cemetery Lot Photo Survey, Hollywood Cemetery, Richmond, Virginia," privately held by Taylor C Cottrell; Markers and plot information photographed and recorded on 23 February 2011, by Taylor C Cottrell.

[82] "U.S. Civil War Soldier Records and Profiles,"*Ancestry.com* (www.ancestry.com: accessed 18 April 2010), for Joseph F Cottrell (20 August 1864).

[83] Taylor C Cottrell, "Joseph F Cottrell Cemetery Lot Photo Survey."

[84] 1870 US Census, Henrico County, Virginia, population schedule, Richmond, Enumeration District (ED) 76, page 64D, dwelling 488, family 579, Joseph F Cottrell; digital images, *Ancestry.com* (http://www.ancestry.com: accessed 18 March 2010); citing National Archives microfilm T9, roll 1371.

[85] 1880 US Census, Henrico County, Virginia, population schedule, Richmond, page 355A, dwelling 1732, family 2051, Joseph Catrell; *Ancestry.com* (http://www.ancestry.com: accessed 21 March 2010); citing National Archives microfilm publication M593, roll 1654.

[86] Taylor C Cottrell, "Joseph F Cottrell Cemetery Lot Photo Survey,"

[87] 1870 US Census, Henrico County, Virginia, population schedule, population schedule, Enumeration District (ED) 76, page 64D, dwelling 488, family 579, Joseph F Cottrell.

[88] Taylor C Cottrell, "Joseph F Cottrell Cemetery Lot Photo Survey."

[89] "Virginia Death Records, 1912-2014," *Ancestry.com* (www.ancestry.com: accessed 16 July 2015), for Emma Jane Cottrell (23 April 1952), Certificate No.8828.

[90] "Bible Records, 1830-1909," database, Virginia Historical Society (http://www.vahistorical.org: accessed 25 July 2009), entry for Peter and Rosa (Cosby) Cottrell.

[91] "Virginia Select Marriages, 1785-1940," *Ancestry.com* (http://www.ancestry.com: accessed 9 October 2015), for Richard H Cottrell and Mary R Laughton (25 May 1853), FHL Film 31650.

[92] 1860 US Census, Chesterfield County, Virginia, population schedule, Manchester Northern District, Manchester, page 441, dwelling 952, family 965, Rich H Cottrell; *Ancestry.com* (http://www.ancestry.com: accessed 3 September 2005); citing National Archives microfilm M653, roll 1340.

[93] *Cottrell Family Bible Record, 1837 - 1961*, Library of Virginia (http://www.lva.virginia.gov: accessed on 13 July 2002); files 25994.

[94] "District of Columbia, Select Deaths and Burials, 1840-1964," *Ancestry.com* (http://www.ancestry.com: accessed 9 October 2015), for Clara Cottrell-Baird (23 August 1929).

[95] "Virginia Death Records, 1912-2014," *Ancestry.com* (http://www.ancestry.com: accessed 9 October 2015), for Nora A Diuguid (17 October 1944), Certificate 5924.

[96] "Spring Hill Cemetery," database, *Find A Grave* (http://www.findagrave.com: accessed 1 March 2016), entry for Laughton D. Diuguid, 31 May 1905; citing memorial #99224547.

[97] "Spring Hill Cemetery," database, *Find A Grave* (http://www.findagrave.com: accessed 1 March 2016), entry for Mary Sampson Diuguid, 25 August 1968; citing memorial #102374473.

[98] Ibid

[99] "Virginia Genealogical Society Quarterly, Abstracts from the John K. Martin Papers," subscription database, *Ancestry.com* (http://www.ancestry.com: accessed 27 May 2005), for William Cottrell (October 1974), volume XII, number 4.

[100] 1850 US Census, Chesterfield County, Virginia, population schedule, The Upper District, page 106, dwelling 782, family 818, Steven Duvall; *Ancestry.com* (http://www.ancestry.com: accessed 20 March 2005); citing National Archives microfilm M432, roll 940.

[101] Daviess County, Kentucky, Vital records, 1852-1953; indexes, 1815-1967, marriage bond for Luther Cottrell and Sarah Kirk, Book C, page 87, FHL microfilm 582231, Family History Library, Salt Lake City, Utah.

[102] Elmwood Cemetery Marker Transcriptions and Cottrell Family Area Drawing; Created by Taylor Cosby Cottrell, Jr.

[103] "Virginia Genealogical Society Quarterly, Abstracts from the John K. Martin Papers".

[104] 1870 US Census, Daviess County, Kentucky, population schedule, Upper Town Precinct, Owensboro City, page 325A, dwelling 3, family 3, Luther J Cottrell; *Ancestry.com* (http://www.ancestry.com: accessed 21 March 2003); citing National Archives microfilm M593, roll 458.

[105] 1880 US Census, Daviess County, Kentucky, population schedule, Owensboro, Enumeration District (ED) 166, page 16D, dwelling 134, family 164, Luther J Cottrell; *Ancestry.com* (http://www.ancestry.com: accessed 3 September 2005); citing National Archives microfilm T9, roll 444.

[106] Louisville - Kentucky Directories - 1890 - Luther Cottrell, Cottrell Family Papers.

[107] 1900 US Census, Chesterfield County, Virginia, population schedule, Manchester District, Enumeration District (ED) 6, page 107B, dwelling 233, family 251, E.G. Hooker; *Ancestry*.com (http://www.ancestry.com: accessed 20 April 2006); citing National Archives microfilm T624, roll 1705.

[108] 1900 US Census, Toulumne County, California, population schedule, Third Township, Enumeration District (ED) 126, page 6b, dwelling 145, family 146, Carlon; *Ancestry.com* (http://www.ancestry.com: accessed 28 May 2006); citing National Archives microfilm T623, roll 116.

[109] Funeral of Mrs. Sarah Jane Cottrell, The Owensboro Messenger, Daviess County, Kentucky, 2 February 1916, page 2.

[110] 1920 US Census, Daviess County, Kentucky, population schedule, Owensboro, Ward 1, Enumeration District (ED) 31, page 1A, dwelling 8, family 9, L.J. Cottrell; *Ancestry.com* (http://www.ancestry.com: accessed 30 September 2006); citing National Archives microfilm T625, roll 567.

[111] West Central Kentucky Family Research Association, Elmwood Cemetery - A Partial List (Utica, Kentucky: McDowell Publications, 2008), FHL US/CAN 976.9864/01 V32.

[112] Elmwood Cemetery Marker Transcriptions and Cottrell Family Area Drawing.

[113] "Kentucky Death Records, 1852-1953," *Ancestry.com* (http://www.ancestry.com: accessed 26 November 2007), for J.W. Cottrell (30 May 1921).

[114] West Central Kentucky Family Research Association, Elmwood Cemetery.

[115] 1850 US Census, Chesterfield County, Virginia, population schedule, The Upper District, page 106, dwelling 782, family 818, Steven Duvall; *Ancestry.com* (http://www.ancestry.com: accessed 20 March 2005); citing National Archives microfilm publication M432, roll 940

[116] *Cottrell Family Bible Record, 1837 - 1961*, Digital image. *Library of Virginia* (http://www.la.virginia.gov: accessed on 13 July 2002); files 25994, all handwriting appears the same, obit for Benjamin Cottrell.

[117] "Virginia Genealogical Society Quarterly, Abstracts from the John K. Martin Papers".

[118] 1860 US Census, Henrico County, Virginia, population schedule, Western Subdivision, Richmond Post Office, page 980, dwelling 733, family 764, Elizabeth Pilcher; *Ancestry.com* (http://www.ancestry.com: accessed 3 September 2005); citing National Archives microfilm M653, roll 1353.

Cottrell-Brashear Family Linage

[119] *Cottrell Family Bible Record, 1837 - 1961*, Digital image. *Library of Virginia.*
[120] Ibid.
[121] 1870 US Census, Richmond County, Virginia, population schedule, Richmond Clay Ward, Richmond, page 385 & 386, dwelling 831, family 1095, Benjamin Cottrell; *Ancestry.com* (http://www.ancestry.com: accessed 3 September 2005); citing National Archives microfilm M593, roll 1653.
[122] 1880 US Census, Daviess County, Kentucky, population schedule, Owensboro, Enumeration District (ED) 166, page 16D, dwelling 134, family 164, Luther J Cottrell; *Ancestry.com* (http://www.ancestry.com: accessed 3 September 2005); citing National Archives microfilm T9, roll 444.
[123] 1900 US Census, Henrico County, Virginia, population schedule, Richmond City, Enumeration District (ED) 68, page 16A, dwelling 235, family 310, Benjamin Cottrell; *Ancestry.com* (http://www.ancestry.com: accessed 26 May 2010); citing National Archives microfilm T623, roll 1738.
[124] "Obituary Benjamin Cottrell," *Richmond Times Dispatch*, 28 February 1906, page 2, Obituary, *Genealogy Bank* (www.genealogybank.com: accessed 18 September 2015).
[125] *Cottrell Family Bible Record, 1837 - 1961*, Digital image. *Library of Virginia.*
[126] "Mrs. Ernest Cornell," *Richmond Times Dispatch*, 1 March 1946, page 26, Obituary, *Genealogy Bank* (www.genealogybank.com: accessed 18 September 2015).
[127] "Virginia Death Records, 1912-2014," *Ancestry.com* (http://www.ancestry.com: accessed 10 March 2016), for Douglas E. Wilhoyte (1 April 1929), Certificate No.10983.
[128] "Virginia Death Records, 1912-2014," *Ancestry.com* (http://www.ancestry.com: accessed 16 July 2015), for Virginia Lee Cottrell (8 July 1949), Certificate No.14961.
[129] "Virginia Death Records, 1912-2014," *Ancestry.com* (http://www.ancestry.com: accessed 16 July 2015), for Olive Cottrell (28 September 1951), Certificate No. 20063.
[130] "Virginia, Deaths and Burials Index, 1853-1917," *Ancestry.com* (http://www.ancestry.com: accessed 9 October 2015), for Bernice Cottrell (11 August 1869), FHL Film Number 2048591.
[131] "Virginia Death Records, 1912-2014," *Ancestry.com* (http://www.ancestry.com: accessed 16 July 2015), for Lelia Dowell Cottrell (22 September 1937), Certificate No. 3609324.
[132] Taylor C Cottrell, "Benjamin Cottrell Cemetery Lot Photo Survey, Hollywood Cemetery, Richmond, Virginia," privately held by Taylor C Cottrell, Rockledge, Florida; Markers and plot information photographed and recorded on 23 February 2011, by Taylor C Cottrell.
[133] Taylor C Cottrell, "Benjamin Cottrell Cemetery Lot Photo Survey, Hollywood Cemetery, Richmond, Virginia," privately held by Taylor C Cottrell, Rockledge, Florida; Markers and plot information photographed and recorded on 23 February 2011, by Taylor C Cottrell.
[134] "Florida Death Index, 1877-1998 Record," *Ancestry.com* (http://www.ancestry.com : accessed 6 August 2006), for Philip Rutherford Cottrell (18 April 1978).
[135] Taylor C Cottrell, "Henry Messerschmitt Cemetery Lot Photo Survey, Hollywood Cemetery, Richmond, Virginia," privately held by Taylor C Cottrell, Rockledge, Florida; Markers and plot information photographed and recorded on 23 February 2011, by Taylor C Cottrell.
[136] Ibid.
[137] Social Security Administration, "Social Security Death Index," database, *Ancestry.com* (http://www.ancestry.com : accessed 12 February 2010), entry for Margaret C Phillips, 1994, SS no. 231-62-5111.

[138] "R.W. Phillips Sr. Succumbs at 68," *Richmond Times Dispatch* (Richmond, Virginia), 8 February 1968, p. 14, col. 5, Obituary for R.W. Phillips, Sr., *Genealogy Bank* (www.genealogybank.com: accessed 27 January 2013).

[139] "Hollywood Cemetery," database, Find A Grave (http://www.findagrave.com: accessed 7 April 2016), entry for Robert Wellford Phillips, Jr., 14 July 2009; citing memorial #93513897.

[140] "Hollywood Cemetery," database, Find A Grave (http://www.findagrave.com: accessed 7 April 2016), entry for Lelia Dowell Toone, 3 December 2005; citing memorial #155378540.

[141] "Virginia Birth Records, 1864-2014," database, *Ancestry.com* (http://www.ancestry.com: accessed 7 April 2016), entry for Howard Cottrell Phillips, 10 March 1931.

[142] "Forest Lawn Cemetery," database, *Find A Grave* (http://www.findagrave.com: accessed 27 January 2013), entry for James Dowell Cottrell, 30 August 1989; citing memorial# 58208022.

[143] "Forest Lawn Cemetery," database, *Find A Grave* (http://www.findagrave.com: accessed 27 January 2013), entry for James Dowell Cottrell, 30 August 1989; citing memorial# 58208022.

[144] Cottrell Family Bible Record, 1837 - 1961, *Library of Virginia*, (www.lva.virginia.gov: accessed 13 July 2002); files 25994, all handwriting appears the same, obit for Benjamin Cottrell included.

[145] Ibid.

[146] 1920 US Census, Henrico County, Kentucky, population schedule, Richmond City, Enumeration District (ED) 78, page 22B, dwelling 391, family 496, B. Howard Cottrell; *Ancestry.com* (http://www.ancestry.com : accessed 6 September 2006); citing National Archives microfilm T625, roll 1909.

[147] Hollywood Cemetery (Richmond City, Virginia), Joseph Howard & Marie L Walz Cottrell marker, Section 18, Lot 18-57, photographed by T.C. Cottrell, 21 February 2011.

[148] Hollywood Cemetery (Richmond City, Virginia), Joseph Howard & Marie L Walz Cottrell marker, Section 18, Lot 18-57, photographed by T.C. Cottrell, 21 February 2011.

[149] "Virginia Death Records, 1912-2014," *Ancestry.com* (http://www.ancestry.com: accessed 16 July 2015), for Benjamin Howard Cottrell (30 May 1961), Certificate No. 12383.

[150] "Virginia Death Records, 1912-2014," *Ancestry.com* (http://www.ancestry.com: accessed 16 July 2015), for Estelle Cottrell Hening (27 February 1946), Certificate No. 3943.

[151] *Cottrell Family Bible Record, 1837 - 1961*, Digital image. *Library of Virginia*.

[152] Ibid

[153] 1850 US Census, Chesterfield County, Virginia, population schedule, The Upper District, page 106, dwelling 782, family 818, Steven Duvall; *Ancestry.com* (http://www.ancestry.com: accessed 20 March 2005); citing National Archives microfilm M432, roll 940.

[154] 1860 US Census, Goochland County, Virginia, population schedule, Dover Mills, page 89, dwelling 697, family 665, William Frith; *Ancestry.com* (http://www.ancestry.com: accessed 6 September 2015); citing National Archives microfilm M653, roll 135.

[155] Inter-State Publishing Co., *History of Daviess County, Kentucky* (1883; reprint Utica, KY: McDowell Publications, 1980), pages 675-676.

[156] Bessie Berry Grabowskii, *The DuVal Family of Virginia, 1701, page 102*.

[157] Inter-State Publishing Co., *History of Daviess County, Kentucky*.

[158] 1870 US Census, Daviess County, Kentucky, population schedule, Masonville, page 214, dwelling 43, family 43, Seth Duvall; *Ancestry.com* (http://www.ancestry.com: accessed 14 June 2009); citing National Archives microfilm M593, roll 458.

[159] 1880 US Census, Daviess County, Kentucky, agricultural schedule, page 4, Seth A Duvall; NARA microfilm publication M1528, roll 20

[160] 1880 US Census, Daviess County, Kentucky, population schedule, Masonville, Enumeration District (ED) 173, page 6B, dwelling 41, family 43, Seth A Duvall; *Ancestry.com* (http://www.ancestry.com: accessed 14 June 2009); citing National Archives microfilm T9, roll 411

[161] Bessie Berry Grabowskii, *The DuVal Family of Virginia, 1701.*

[162] "Elm Grove Cemetery," database, *Find A Grave* (http://www.findagrave.com: accessed 1 September 2014), entry for Mary A Duval, 5 July 1909; citing memorial # 76406658.

[163] 1910 US Census, Labette County, Kansas, population schedule, Elm Grove, Enumeration District (ED) 129, page 7A, dwelling 2, family 2, Samuel S Duval; *Ancestry.com* (http://www.ancestry.com: accessed 6 September 2009); citing National Archives microfilm T624, roll 444

[164] Bessie Berry Grabowskii, *The DuVal Family of Virginia, 1701, page 102.*

[165] 1930 US Census, Okmulgee County, Oklahoma, population schedule, Hamilton Township, Enumeration District (ED) 56-09, page 6B, dwelling 123, family 128, E.D. Glass; *Ancestry.com* (http://www.ancestry.com: accessed 6 September 2009); citing National Archives microfilm T626, roll 1921

[166] "Elm Grove Cemetery," database, *Find A Grave* (http://www.findagrave.com: accessed 1 September 2014), entry for Mary A Duval, 5 July 1909; citing memorial # 76406658.

[167] Bessie Berry Grabowskii, *The DuVal Family of Virginia, 1701, page 96-07.*

[168] 1930 US Census, Okmulgee County, Oklahoma, population schedule, Hamilton Township, Enumeration District (ED) 56-09, page 6B, dwelling 123, family 128, E.D. Glass; *Ancestry.com* (http://www.ancestry.com: accessed 6 September 2009); citing National Archives microfilm T626, roll 1921.

[169] Ibid.

[170] "Newton School Cemetery," database, *Find A Grave* (http://www.findagrave.com: accessed 1 September 2014), entry for Garna E Newton Duval, 26 November 1981; citing memorial # 26944247.

[171] Bessie Berry Grabowskii, *The DuVal Family of Virginia, 1701, page 96-97.*

[172] Ibid.

[173] "La Harpe Cemetery," database, *Find A Grave* (http://www.findagrave.com: accessed 15 May 2013), entry for Benjamin A DuVal, 5 January 1913; citing memorial #39811930.

[174] "La Harpe Cemetery," database, *Find A Grave* (http://www.findagrave.com: accessed (10 March 2016), entry for Theodore A. DuVal, 3 February 1905; citing memorial #38711841.

[175] "Eldorado Cemetery," database, *Find A Grave* (http://www.findagrave.com: accessed 10 March 2016), entry for Thelma Duval Basham, 3 May 1985; citing memorial #29693719.

[176] Ibid.

[177] "Arapaho Cemetery," database, Find A Grave (http://www.findagrave.com: accessed 10 March 2016), entry for China Ann Gifford, 1972; citing memorial #79466362.

Section 1 – Chapter 2 Sources – Peter Cottrell Family

[1] "Bible Records, 1830-1909," database, Virginia Historical Society (http://www.vahistorical.org: accessed 25 July 2009), entry for Peter and Rosa (Cosby) Cottrell

[2] Noah H Bradley, *My Wife's Family* (Pawhatan, Virginia: H. Bradley, 1922).

[3] "Compiled Service Records of Confederate Soldiers Who Served in Organizations from the State of Virginia," subscription database, *Footnote.com* (http://www.footnote.com: accessed 16 October 2008), for Peter Cottrell, National Archives and Records Administration, microfilm publication M324.

[4] Letter from Adjutant General's Office (War Department, Washington DC) to Unknown Recipient, 9 May 1932.

[5] 1870 US Census, Daviess County, Kentucky, population schedule, Owensboro, page 325A, dwelling 2, family 2, Peter Cottrell; *Ancestry.com* (http://www.ancestry.com: accessed 21 March 2003); citing National Archives microfilm M593, roll 458.

[6] Elmwood Cemetery, Elmwood Cemetery Early Records and History, Register of Interments, Elmwood Cemetery, 1877-1885 & 1900-1902.

[7] Elmwood Cemetery Marker Transcriptions and Cottrell Family Area Drawing.

[8] Noah H Bradley, *My Wife's Family*.

[9] "Bible Records, 1830-1909," database, *Virginia Historical Society* (http://www.vahistorical.org/: accessed 25 July 2009), entry for Peter and Rosa (Cosby) Cottrell

[10] Noah H Bradley, *My Wife's Family,* page 232.

[11] 1850 US Census, Chesterfield County, Virginia, population schedule, The Upper District, page 105B, dwelling 765, family 801, Jefferson Cosby; *Ancestry.com* (http://www.ancestry.com: accessed 1 January 2005); citing National Archives microfilm M432, roll 940.

[12] Noah H Bradley *My Wife's Family* (Pawhatan, Virginia: H. Bradley, 1922).

[13] Ibid.

[14] "Chesterfield County, Virginia Deaths, 1882-88," subscription database, *Ancestry.com* (http://www.ancestry.com: accessed 27 January 2005), for T.J. Cosby (14 November 1887).

[15] "Virginia, Death Records, 1912-2014," subscription database, *Ancestry.com* (http://www.ancestry.com: accessed 14 June 2015), for Ira Lafayette Cosby, Richmond, Virginia Department of Health, Certificate No 1934008692.

[16] "Pawhatan County, Virginia Births, 1853-96," subscription database, *Ancestry.com* (http://www.ancestry.com: accessed 27 January 2005), for No Name Cosby (26 Apr 1866), page 75.

[17] Noah H Bradley *My Wife's Family*.

[18] Ibid.

[19] "Pawhatan County, Virginia Births, 1853-96," subscription database, *Ancestry.com* (http://www.ancestry.com: accessed 27 January 2005), for Philip Cosby (16 Jun 1864), page 71.

[20] "Pawhatan County, Virginia Births, 1853-96," subscription database, *Ancestry.com* (http://www.ancestry.com: accessed 27 January 2005), for No Name Cosby (26 Apr 1866), page 75.

[21] 1850 US Census, Chesterfield County, Virginia, population schedule, The Upper District, page 105B, dwelling 765, family 801, Jefferson Cosby; *Ancestry.com* (http://www.ancestry.com: accessed 1 January 2005); citing National Archives microfilm M432, roll 940.

[22] Noah H Bradley *My Wife's Family.*

[23] "Virginia, Death Records, 1912-2014," subscription database, *Ancestry.com* (http://www.ancestry.com: accessed 14 June 2015), for Florence Cosby Hughes, Richmond, Virginia Department of Health, Certificate No 1935027882.

[24] "Maury Cemetery," database, *Find A Grave* (http://www.findagrave.com: accessed 28 February 2014), entry for Howell Hunter Cosby, 20 December 1897; citing memorial # 22208757.

[25] 1880 US Census, Spencer County, Indiana, population schedule, The Town of Grandview, Enumeration District (ED) 45, page 68A, dwelling 77, family 85, Branch E Cosby; *Ancestry.com* (http://www.ancestry.com: accessed 1 January 2005); citing National Archives microfilm T9, roll 311.

[26] Noah H Bradley *My Wife's Family.*

[27] "California Death Index, 1940-1997," subscription database, *Ancestry.com* (http://www.ancestry.com: accessed 10 January 2010), for Rosa R Cottrell (30 January 1963).

[28] "Grand View Memorial Park," database, Find A Grave (http://www.findagrave.com: accessed 8 April 2016), entry for Maude Champe Howard, 21 May 1958; citing memorial #47535699.

[29] Noah H Bradley *My Wife's Family.*

[30] "Kentucky Death Records, 1852-1953," subscription database, *Ancestry.com* (http://www.ancestry.com: accessed 28 April 2009), for Mrs Addie Cosby (28 March 1914).

[31] "John S. Cosby," *Richmond Times Dispatch* (Richmond, Virginia), 7 April 1940, page 18, column 4, Death Notice, subscription database, *GenealogyBank* (http://www.genealogybank.com: accessed 25 August 2012).

[32] Noah H Bradley *My Wife's Family.*

[33] "Dover Baptist Church Cemetery," database, *Find A Grave* (http://www.findagrave.com: accessed 16 May 2013), entry for Lorenza Dow Stratton, 1928; citing memorial # 17877215.

[34] "Virginia Select Marriages, 1785-1940," database, Ancestry.com (http://www.ancestry.com: accessed 7 April 2016), entry for Lewis Stratton and Martha Ninaver Stratton, 22 March 1883, FHL Film #2048452.

[35] "Dover Baptist Church Cemetery," database, *Find A Grave* (http://www.findagrave.com: accessed 16 May 2013), entry for James Moseley Stratton, 1903; citing memorial # 11123186.

[36] 1860 US Census, Chesterfield County, Virginia, population schedule, Northern District, Manchester Post Office, page 24, dwelling 185, family 191, Jeff Cosby; *Ancestry.com* (http://www.ancestry.com: accessed 1 January 2005); citing National Archives microfilm M653, roll 1340.

[37] 1880 US Census, Chesterfield County, Virginia, population schedule, Midlothian, Enumeration District (ED) 74, page 228B, dwelling 11, family 12, Jefferson Cosby; *Ancestry.com* (http://www.ancestry.com: accessed 1 January 2005); citing National Archives microfilm T9, roll 1361.

[38] 1880 US Census, Chesterfield County, Virginia, population schedule, Midlothian, Enumeration District (ED) 74, page 228B, dwelling 11, family 12, Jefferson Cosby; *Ancestry.com* (http://www.ancestry.com: accessed 1 January 2005); citing National Archives microfilm T9, roll 1361.

[39] Taylor C Cottrell, "W. Upshure Bass Cemetery Lot Photo Survey, Hollywood Cemetery, Richmond, Virginia," privately held by Taylor C Cottrell, Rockledge, Florida; Markers and plot information photographed and recorded on 23 February 2011, by Taylor C Cottrell.

[40] "Virginia, Death Records, 1912-2014," subscription database, *Ancestry.com* (http://www.ancestry.com: accessed 14 June 2015), for Nettie Lou Bass, Richmond, Virginia Department of Health, Certificate No 1961015638.

[41] Joel Ricks, compiler, *Goochland County, Virginia Marriage Bonds, 1730-1854* (Salt Lake City, Utah: Genealogical Society of Utah, 1936), FHL US/CAN 975.5455 V2r.

[42] "Green Hill Cemetery," database, *Find A Grave* (http://www.findagrave.com: accessed 24 April 2015), entry for Monterey C Morrissett, 2 May 1907; citing memorial # 65836110.

[43] Noah H Bradley *My Wife's Family.*

[44] "North Carolina Death Certificates, 1909-1975," subscription database, *Ancestry.com* (http://www.ancestry.com: accessed 29 March 2009), for Allen Lynnwood Morrissett (23 March 1960), certificate 8719.

[45] "Green Hill Cemetery," database, *Find A Grave* (http://www.findagrave.com: accessed 24 April 2015), entry for Irvin Morrissett, 2 May 1907; citing memorial # 65836175.

[46] "Green Hill Cemetery," database, *Find A Grave* (http://www.findagrave.com: accessed 24 April 2015), entry for Wellington Morrissett, 6 June 1919; citing memorial # 65836157.

[47] "Green Hill Cemetery," database, *Find A Grave* (http://www.findagrave.com: accessed 24 April 2015), entry for Vivian Morrissett, 11 November 1961; citing memorial # 65836140.

[48] "Green Hill Cemetery," database, *Find A Grave* (http://www.findagrave.com: accessed 24 April 2015), entry for Pearl Morrissett, 2 May 1907; citing memorial # 65836125.

[49] "Maury Cemetery," database, *Green Hill Cemetery* (http://www.findagrave.com: accessed 7 June 2015), entry for Sgt. Beverly Farrar Morrissett, 5 July 1922; citing memorial #14305299.

[50] "L.C. Cosby, 90, Dies at His Home," *Richmond Times Dispatch* (Richmond, Virginia), 13 March 1941, p. 12, Col. 4, Obit for Luther Calvin Cosby, subscription database, *GenealogyBank* (www.genealogybank.com: accessed 26 August 2012).

[51] Noah H Bradley *My Wife's Family.*

[52] "Mount Pisgah Methodist Church Cemetery," database, *Find A Grave* (http://www.findagrave.com: accessed 2 September 2012), entry for Calvin Watkins Cosby, 20 January 1948; citing memorial# 24869053.

[53] "Mount Pisgah Methodist Church," database, *Find A Grave* (http://www.findagrave.com: accessed 2 September 2012), entry for Irving Hancock Cosby, 1971; citing memorial# 24869111.

[54] 1930 US Census, Chesterfield County, Virginia, population schedule, Midlothian, Enumeration District (ED) 21-16, page 9A, dwelling 177, family 179, Irvin H Cosby; *Ancestry.com* (http://www.ancestry.com: accessed 1 August 2006); citing National Archives microfilm T626, roll 2440.

[55] "Hollywood Cemetery," database, *Find A Grave* (http://www.findagrave.com: accessed 7 June 2015), entry for Richard H Cosby, 12 May 1926; citing memorial #92988343.

[56] Noah H Bradley *My Wife's Family.*

[57] "Bethel Baptist Church Cemetery," database, *Find A Grave* (http://www.findagrave.com: accessed 2 September 2012), entry for Charles M Cosby, 1940; citing memorial# 15067329.

[58] Noah H Bradley *My Wife's Family.*

[59] "Virginia Death Records, 1912-2014," subscription database, *Ancestry.com* (http://www.ancestry.com: accessed 16 July 2015), for Jefferson Judson Cosby (24 November 1957), Certificate No. 28332.

[60] "American Soldiers of World War I," subscription database, *Ancestry.com* (http://www.ancestry.com: accessed 20 August 2006), for Bernard J Cosby.

[61] Noah H Bradley *My Wife's Family.*

[62] "Bethel Baptist Church," database, *Find A Grave* (http://www.findagrave.com: accessed 2 September 2012), entry for Maggie F Cosby, 1950; citing memorial# 15054545.

[63] Noah H Bradley *My Wife's Family.*

[64] "Virginia Death Records, 1912-2014," database, Ancestry.com (http://www.ancestry.com: accessed 7 April 2016), entry for Elma P. Haithcock, 22 February 1984, certificate #84005436.

[65] "Myrtle Hill Cemetery," database, Find A Grave (http://www.findagrave.com: accessed 7 April 2016), entry for Samuel Sumpter Puryear, 5 July 1981; citing memorial #113410619.

[66] "Mrs. C.E. Harris," *Richmond Times Dispatch* (Richmond, Virginia), 16 February 1934, p. 4, col. 4, Funeral Notice for Nannie Lee Harris, subscription database, *GenealogyBank* (www.genealogybank.com: accessed 25 August 2012).

[67] Social Security Administration, "Social Security Death Index," database, *Ancestry.com* (http://www.ancestry.com: accessed 21 Apr 2009), entry for Edgar Harris, 1975, SS no. 227-16-8335.

[68] Noah H Bradley, *My Wife's Family.*

[69] "John S. Cosby," *Richmond Times Dispatch* (Richmond, Virginia), 7 April 1940, page 18, column 4, Death Notice, subscription database, *GenealogyBank* (www.genealogybank.com: accessed 25 August 2012).

[70] "Mount Pisgah Methodist Church," database, *Find A Grave* (http://www.findagrave.com: accessed 2 September 2012), entry for Stuart Shelby Cosby, 15 July 1981; citing memorial# 24869067.

[71] "Mount Pisgah Methodist Church Cemetery," database, *Find A Grave* (http://www.findagrave.com: accessed 2 September 2012), entry for Jannett Jewett Cosby, 5 February 1941; citing memorial# 24879326.

[72] Noah H Bradley, *My Wife's Family.*

[73] "Funeral of Mrs. Cosby," *Richmond Times Dispatch* (Richmond, Virginia), 12 March 1905, p. 13, col. 5, Funeral Notice for Nancy Cosby, subscription database, *GenealogyBank* (www.genealogybank.com: accessed 25 August 2012).

[74] "Bible Records, 1830-1909," database, *Virginia Historical Society* (http://www.vahistorical.org: accessed 25 July 2009), entry for Peter and Rosa (Cosby) Cottrell; Original Bible in possession of Paul Frank Meyers, Phoenix, Arizona in 1983, photocopied by James H. Harding, Richmond, Virginia. In 1985 Mr. Harding presented photocopies to the Virginia Historical Society. They are currently on file in the manuscript collection, call number, Mss6:4 C8295:1. Copies were secured by TC Cottrell by mail on 27 July 2009 from the Virginia Historical Society.

[75] 1870 US Census, Daviess County, Kentucky, population schedule, Upper Town Precinct, Owensboro City, page 325A, dwelling 2, family 2, Peter Cottrell; digital images, *Ancestry.com* (http://www.ancestry.com: accessed 21 March 2003); citing National Archives microfilm publication M593, roll 458.

[76] West Central Kentucky Family Research Association, Elmwood Cemetery - A Partial List (Utica, Kentucky: McDowell Publications, 2008), FHL US/CAN 976.9864/01 V32.

[77] Elmwood Cemetery Marker Transcriptions and Cottrell Family Area Drawing.

[78] Noah H Bradley, *My Wife's Family*, page 233-237.

[79] "Bible Records, 1830-1909," *Virginia Historical Society* (http://www.vahistorical.org: accessed 25 July 2009), entry for Peter and Rosa (Cosby) Cottrell.

[80] Minnie Jane (Hooker) Cottrell, Cottrell Family Data.

[81] "Bible Records, 1830-1909," database, *Virginia Historical Society* (http://www.vahistorical.org: accessed 25 July 2009), entry for Peter and Rosa (Cosby) Cottrell.

[82] 1870 US Census, Daviess County, Kentucky, population schedule, Upper Town Precinct, Owensboro City, page 325A, dwelling 2, family 2, Peter Cotterell; *Ancestry.com* (http://www.ancestry.com: accessed 21 March 2003); citing National Archives microfilm M593, roll 458.

[83] 1880 US Census, Daviess County, Kentucky, population schedule, Masonville, Enumeration District (ED) 173, page 6B, dwelling 41, family 43, Seth A Duvall; *Ancestry.com* (http://www.ancestry.com: accessed 14 June 2009); citing National Archives microfilm T9, roll 411.

[84] 1900 US Census, Tuolumne County, California, population schedule, Enumeration District (ED) 126, page 6b, dwelling 145, family 146, Carlon; *Ancestry.com* (http://www.ancestry.com: accessed 28 May 2006); citing National Archives microfilm T623, roll 116.

[85] "California Voter Registrations, 1900-1968," *Ancestry.com* (https://www.ancestry.com: accessed 29 April 2008), for Charles Ashby Cottrell, California State Library.

[86] "Joe Cottrell Dies in California", *Owensboro Messenger*, Daviess County, Kentucky, 31 October 1908, page 3.

[87] 1910 US Census, Calaveras County, California, population schedule, Angels Twp., Enumeration District (ED) 14, page 11B, dwelling 251, family 259, Janetta M Crooks; *Ancestry.com* (http://www.ancestry.com: accessed 28 May 2006); citing National Archives microfilm T624, roll 73.

[88] 1920 US Census, Calaveras County, California, population schedule, Enumeration District (ED) 15, page 6B, dwelling 125, family 126, Janetta M Crooks; *Ancestry.com* (http://www.ancestry.com: accessed 17 August 2007); citing National Archives microfilm T625, roll 94.

[89] "Honolulu, Hawaii, Passenger and Crew Lists, 1900-1959," digital images, *Ancestry.com* (http://www.ancestry.com: accessed 9 September 2012), List of United States Citizens, Sonoma, San Francisco to Honolulu, Hawaii, arriving 6 June 1921, page 188, Charles A Cosby; citing National Archives, microfilm publication A3422, roll 65.

[90] Noah H Bradley, *My Wife's Family*, page 233-237.

[91] "Bible Records, 1830-1909," database, *Virginia Historical Society*.

[92] 1870 US Census, Daviess County, Kentucky, population schedule, Upper Town Precinct, Owensboro City, page 325A, dwelling 2, family 2, Peter Cotterell; *Ancestry.com* (http://www.ancestry.com: accessed 21 March 2003); citing National Archives microfilm publication M593, roll 458.

[93] 1880 US Census, Daviess County, Kentucky, population schedule, Owensboro, Enumeration District (ED) 166, page 251D, dwelling 1127, family 495, Jno R Chapman; *Ancestry.com* (http://www.ancestry.com: accessed 15 January 2005); citing National Archives microfilm T9, roll 411.

[94] Noah H Bradley, *My Wife's Family*, page 233-237.

[95] 1900 US Census, Chesterfield County, Virginia, population schedule, Manchester District, Enumeration District (ED) 6, page 13B, dwelling 232, family 250, William H Harrison; *Ancestry.com* (http://www.ancestry.com: accessed 17 August 2007); citing National Archives microfilm T623, roll 623.

[96] 1910 US Census, Chesterfield County, Virginia, population schedule, Manchester District, Enumeration District (ED) 7, page 20B, dwelling 373, family 407, William H Harrison; *Ancestry.com* (http://www.ancestry.com: accessed 17 August 2007); citing National Archives microfilm T624, roll 1625.

[97] "Virginia, Death Records, 1912-2014," *Ancestry.com* (http://www.ancestry.com: accessed 14 June 2015), for Lillie Verina Harrison, Richmond, Virginia Department of Health, Certificate No 1916029800.

[98] 1930 US Census, Chesterfield County, Virginia, population schedule, Richmond City, Enumeration District (ED) 116-128, page 4B, dwelling 33, family 37, William L Harrison; *Ancestry.com* (http://www.ancestry.com: accessed 17 August 2007); citing National Archives microfilm T626, roll 2478.

[99] Noah H Bradley, *My Wife's Family,* page 233-237.

[100] Ibid

[101] "Bible Records, 1830-1909," database, *Virginia Historical Society.*

[102] "Virginia, Death Records, 1912-2014," *Ancestry.com* (http://www.ancestry.com: accessed 14 June 2015), for James Ashby Harrison, Richmond, Virginia Department of Health, Certificate No 1917009530.

[103] Beth Fridley, compiler, "Chesterfield County, Virginia Deaths, 1889-96," *Ancestry.com* (http://www.ancestry.com: accessed 17 August 2007), for L.V. Harrison (23 December 1895).

[104] "Virginia, Death Records, 1912-2014," *Ancestry.com* (http://www.ancestry.com: accessed 14 June 2015), for Mary Harrison Cosby, Richmond, Virginia Department of Health, Certificate No 1923011558.

[105] Noah H Bradley, *My Wife's Family*

[106] Ibid

[107] Ibid

[108] "Florida Death Index, 1877-1998," subscription database, *Ancestry.com* (http://www.ancestry.com: accessed 17 August 2007), for Linda H Meyers (8 November 1975).

[109] Noah H Bradley, *My Wife's Family,* page 233-237.

[110] Ibid

[111] 1930 US Census, Roanoke County, Virginia, population schedule, Catawba Sanitarium, Enumeration District (ED) 81-6, page 2B, Catawba Sanatorium (Elizabeth and Virginia Harrison patients); *Ancestry.com* (http://www.ancestry.com: accessed 17 August 2007); citing National Archives microfilm T626, roll 883.

[112] Taylor C Cottrell, "William H Harrison Cemetery Lot Photo Survey, Hollywood Cemetery, Richmond, Virginia," privately held by Taylor C Cottrell, Rockledge, Florida; Markers and plot information photographed and recorded on 23 February 2011, by Taylor C Cottrell.

[113] Noah H Bradley, *My Wife's Family,* page 233-237.

[114] "Maury Cemetery," database, *Find A Grave* (http://www.findagrave.com: accessed 26 October 2015), entry Lillian Hall Harrison, 22 August 1992; citing memorial # 51758930.

[115] Hollywood Cemetery (Richmond City, Virginia), William Henry Harrison Jr and Martha Dyson Harrison marker, Pavilion Section, Lot PAV-112, photographed by T.C. Cottrell, 21 February 2011.

[116] "Miss Elizabeth C. Harrison," *Richmond Times Dispatch* (Richmond, Virginia), 21 December 2934, page 14, Obituary, subscription database, *Genealogy Bank* (http://www.genealogybank.com: accessed 9 June 2013).

[117] 1930 US Census, Roanoke County, Virginia, population schedule, Catawba Sanatorium, Enumeration District (ED) 81-6, page 2B, Catawba Sanatorium (Elizabeth and Virginia Harrison patients).

[118] "Bible Records, 1830-1909," database, Virginia Historical Society (http://www.vahistorical.org: accessed 25 July 2009), entry for Peter and Rosa (Cosby) Cottrell; Original Bible in possession of Paul Frank Meyers, Phoenix, Arizona in 1983, photocopied by James H. Harding, Richmond, Virginia.

[119] Noah H Bradley, *My Wife's Family*, page 233-237.

[120] "Bible Records, 1830-1909," database, Virginia Historical Society (http://www.vahistorical.org: accessed 25 July 2009), entry for Peter and Rosa (Cosby) Cottrell; Original Bible in possession of Paul Frank Meyers, Phoenix, Arizona in 1983, photocopied by James H. Harding, Richmond, Virginia.

[121] 1870 US Census, Daviess County, Kentucky, population schedule, Upper Town Precinct, Owensboro City, page 325A, dwelling 2, family 2, Peter Cotterell; *Ancestry.com* (http://www.ancestry.com: accessed 21 March 2003); citing National Archives microfilm M593, roll 458.

[122] 1880 US Census, Spencer County, Indiana, population schedule, The Town of Grandview, Enumeration District (ED) 45, page 68A, dwelling 77, family 85, Branch E Cosby; *Ancestry.com* (http://www.ancestry.com: accessed 1 January 2005); citing National Archives microfilm T9, roll 311.

[123] 1910 US Census, Elkhart County, Indiana, population schedule, Elkhart City, Enumeration District (ED) 13, page 147B, dwelling 25, family 25, Melvin Cottrell; *Ancestry.com* (http://www.ancestry.com: accessed 8 September 2004); citing National Archives microfilm T624, roll 347.

[124] "California Death Index, 1940-1997," subscription database, Ancestry.com (http://www.ancestry.com: accessed 22 March 2009), for Jessie Cottrell (12 November 1949).

[125] Joe Cottrell Dies in California, Owensboro Messenger, Daviess County, Kentucky, 31 October 1908, page 3.

[126] 1910 US Census, Elkhart County, Indiana, population schedule, Enumeration District (ED) 13, page 147B, dwelling 25, family 25, Melvin Cottrell.

[127] "California Voter Registrations, 1900-1968," subscription database, Ancestry.com (http://www.ancestry.com: accessed 8 November 2008), for Melvin Cottrell (1916).

[128] "California Voter Registrations, 1900-1968," subscription database, Ancestry.com (http://www.ancestry.com: accessed 8 November 2008), for Melvin Cottrell (1918).

[129] 1920 US Census, San Francisco County, California, population schedule, District 37, Enumeration District (ED) 139, page 8B, dwelling 184, family 184, Melvin Cottrell; *Ancestry.com* (http://www.ancestry.com: accessed 1 August 2004); citing National Archives microfilm T625, roll 136.

[130] Cottrell, Oakland Tribune, Oakland, California, 17 March 1957, p 49.

[131] "California Voter Registrations, 1900-1968," subscription database, Ancestry.com (http://www.ancestry.com: accessed 8 November 2008), for Melvin Cottrell (1926).

[132] 1930 US Census, San Francisco County, California, population schedule, San Francisco, Enumeration District (ED) 38-67, page 15A, dwelling 642, family 294, Melvin Cottrell; *Ancestry.com* (http://www.ancestry.com: accessed 20 March 2005); citing National Archives microfilm T626, roll 197.

[133] "Mr. and Mrs. Cottrell Visiting Mrs. Hooker," Richmond Times Dispatch (Richmond, Virginia), 11 June 1935, page 4, col. 11, Newspaper Article, subscription database, Genealogy Bank (www.genealogybank.com: accessed 25 August 2012).

[134] 1940 US Census, Alameda County, California, population schedule, Oakland City, Enumeration District (ED) 61-82, page 13A, dwelling 206, Melvin Cottrell; *Ancestry.com* (http://www.ancestry.com: accessed 9 September 2012); citing National Archives microfilm T6267, roll 442.

[135] "California Death Index, 1940-1997," *Ancestry.com* (http://www.ancestry.com: accessed 14 September 2004), for Melvin Cottrell (14 March 1870).

[136] "Bible Records, 1830-1909," database, Virginia Historical Society (http://www.vahistorical.org: accessed 25 July 2009), entry for Peter and Rosa (Cosby) Cottrell.

[137] 1880 US Census, Daviess County, Kentucky, population schedule, Masonville Precinct, Enumeration District (ED) 173, page 393A, dwelling 65, family 68, John L Kirk; *Ancestry.com* (http://www.ancestry.com: accessed 25 April 2004); citing National Archives microfilm publication T9, roll 411.

[138] "Mrs. Hooker Dies at Home; Rites Today," *Richmond Times Dispatch* (Richmond, Virginia), 26 February 1945, page 9, Col. 3, Obit for Minnie J. Cottrell Hooker, *Genealogy Bank* (www.genealogybank.com: accessed 26 August 2012).

[139] Noah H Bradley, *My Wife's Family*, page 233-237.

[140] 1900 US Census, Chesterfield County, Virginia, population schedule, Manchester District, Enumeration District (ED) 6, page 107B, dwelling 233, family 251, E.G. Hooker; *Ancestry.com* (http://www.ancestry.com: accessed 20 April 2006); citing National Archives microfilm T624, roll 1705.

[141] 1910 US Census, Chesterfield County, Virginia, population schedule, Manchester District, Enumeration District (ED) 6, page 17B, dwelling 219, family 230, Edmond Hooker; *Ancestry.com* (http://www.ancestry.com: accessed 20 April 2006); citing National Archives microfilm T624, roll 1625.

[142] 1920 US Census, Chesterfield County, Kentucky, population schedule, Richmond, Enumeration District (ED) 161, page 14A, dwelling 218, family 292, Edmond G Hooker; *Ancestry.com* (http://www.ancestry.com: accessed 20 April 2006); citing National Archives microfilm T624, roll 1625.

[143] "Virginia, Death Records, 1912-2014," *Ancestry.com* (http://www.ancestry.com: accessed 14 June 2015), for Edmond Goodman Hooker, Richmond, Virginia Department of Health, Certificate No 1921003348.

[144] 1930 US Census, Chesterfield County, Virginia, population schedule, Richmond, Enumeration District (ED) 116-7, page 20A, dwelling 180, family 206, Minnie J Hooker; *Ancestry.com* (http://www.ancestry.com: accessed 20 April 2006); citing National Archives microfilm T626, roll 2479.

[145] "U.D.C. Entertainment," *Richmond Times Dispatch* (Richmond, Virginia), 5 April 1933, page 9, col. 4 & 5, Newspaper Article, *Genealogy Bank* (www.genealogybank.com: accessed 25 August 2012).

[146] "Mrs. Hooker Heads W.C.T.U. Unit Here," *Richmond Times Dispatch* (Richmond, Virginia), 15 September 1938, page 8, col. 4, Newspaper Article, *Genealogy Bank* (www.genealogybank.com: accessed 25 August 2012).

[147] "Hooker - Fell asleep Sunday," *Richmond Times Dispatch* (Richmond, Virginia), 26 February 1945, page 13, col. 7, Death Notice, *Genealogy Bank* (www.genealogybank.com: accessed 25 August 2012).

[148] Taylor C Cottrell, "E C Hooker Cemetery Lot Photo Survey, Maury Cemetery, Richmond, Virginia," privately held by Taylor C Cottrell, Rockledge, Florida; Markers and plot information photographed and recorded on 20 February, 2011, by Taylor C Cottrell.

[149] "Virginia Death Records 1912-2014," *Ancestry.com* (http://www.ancestry.com: accessed 14 June 2015), for Raymond Cottrell Hooker, Richmond, Virginia Department of Health, Certificate No 1970017847.

[150] "News of South Richmond," *Richmond Times Dispatch* (Richmond, Virginia), 5 June 1912, page 7, col. 6, Newspaper Article, *Genealogy Bank* (www.genealogybank.com: accessed 25 August 2012).

[151] "Wedding of Interest To-Day," *Richmond Times Dispatch* (Richmond, Virginia), 12 June 1918, page 7, col. 1, Marriage Record for First Lieutenant Raymond Cottrell Hooker and Miss Esther Maude Cheatham, *Genealogy Bank* (www.genealogybank.com: accessed 2 September 2012).

[152] 1930 US Census, Chesterfield County, Virginia, population schedule, Richmond, Enumeration District (ED) 116-69, page 21A, dwelling 136, family 154, Raymond C Hooker; *Ancestry.com* (http://www.ancestry.com: accessed 29 May 2006); citing National Archives microfilm T626, roll 2479

[153] House Joint Resolution No. 697, On the death of Dr. Raymond Cottrell Hooker, Jr., 3 February 1995.

[154] "College Set Is Returning for Holidays," *Richmond Times Dispatch* (Richmond, Virginia), 21 December 1943, page 12, column 6, Newspaper Article, subscription database, *GenealogyBank* (www.genealogybank.com: accessed 25 August 2012).

[155] "Maury Cemetery," database, *Find A Grave* (http://www.findagrave.com: accessed 25 April 2009), entry Esther Cheatham Hooker, 16 June 1936; citing memorial # 23947633.

[156] "Dr. Hooker and Mrs. Beal Are Wed Here," *Richmond Times Dispatch* (Richmond, Virginia), 11 August 1938, page 31, col. 1, Wedding announcement for Dr. Raymond C. Hooker and Mrs. Edna Nesbit Beal, subscription database, *Genealogy Bank* (www.genealogybank.com: accessed 25 August 2012).

[157] "Bethlehem United Methodist Church Cemetery," database, *Find A Grave* (http://www.findagrave.com: accessed 7 October 2012), entry for Edna Nesbit Hooker, 1993; citing memorial# 22322246.

[158] Noah H Bradley, *My Wife's Family*, page 233-237.

[159] Ibid.

[160] "Services Slated Friday for Dr. John Slaughter," *Spartanburg Herald* (Spartanburg, South Carolina), 31 May 1979, D2, Obituary, *Google* (www.google.com: accessed 9 September 2012).

[161] 1940 US Census, Jefferson County, Alabama, population schedule, Homewood City, Enumeration District (ED) 37-88, page 61A, dwelling 120, John L Slaughter; *Ancestry.com* (http://www.ancestry.com : accessed 8 September 2012); citing National Archives microfilm publication T6267, roll 42.

[162] "Alabama National Cemetery," database, *Find A Grave* (http://www.findagrave.com: accessed 30 May 2016), entry for Jane A La Rogue Slaughter Hardenbergh, 14 September 2009; citing memorial #43779127.

[163] "Maury Cemetery," database, *Find A Grave* (http://www.findagrave.com: accessed 25 April 2009), entry Edmond Anderson Hooker, 27 April 1989; citing memorial # 22213689.

[164] Noah H Bradley, *My Wife's Family*, page 233-237.

[165] "Maury Cemetery," database, *Find A Grave* (http://www.findagrave.com: accessed 26 October 2015), entry Ernestine Hatcher Hooker, 6 April 1997; citing memorial # 2213519.

[166] "Funerals To-Day, the funeral of Peter Cosby Hooker," *Richmond Times Dispatch* (Richmond, Virginia), 13 April 1904, page 2, col. 4, Funeral Notice, *Genealogy Bank* (www.genealogybank.com: accessed 25 August 2012).

[167] "Funeral Services for infant child of Mr. and Mrs. E.G. Hooker," *Richmond Times Dispatch* (Richmond, Virginia), 26 February 1907, page 3, col. 6, Funeral Notice, , *Genealogy Bank* (www.genealogybank.com : accessed 25 August 2012).

[168] Noah H Bradley, *My Wife's Family.*

[169] "Miss Hooker, Mr. Herthel Are Married," *Richmond Times Dispatch* (Richmond, Virginia), 9 November 1947, page 51, col. 6, Wedding announcement for Albert William Herthel and Dorcas Goodman Hooker, *Genealogy Bank* (www.genealogybank.com: accessed 25 August 2012).

[170] Ibid.

[171] Noah H Bradley, *My Wife's Family.*

[172] Family data, Nellie Lashbrook Cottrell, Holy Bible, King James Version (Cleveland and New York: The World Publishing Company, unknown publish date); present owner Taylor C Cottrell Jr., Rockledge, Florida.

Section 1 – Chapter 3 Sources – Joseph Frey Cottrell Family

[1] Joseph Frey Cottrell, Death Registration 205403 (1908), Department of Health Bureau of Vital Statistics, Sacramento, California.

[2] "Joe Cottrell Dies in California", *Owensboro Messenger*, Daviess County, Kentucky, 31 October 1908, page 3.

[3] 1880 US Census, Daviess County, Kentucky, population schedule, Boston Precinct, Enumeration District (ED) 172, page 382D, dwelling 165, family 166, John T Harrison; *Ancestry.com* (http://www.ancestry.com: accessed 25 April 2004); citing National Archives microfilm T9, roll 411.

[4] Nellie J. (Lashbrook) Cottrell, Childhood and Youth, handwritten memories without sources, original in the possession of the author.

[5] Joseph Frey Cottrell cemetery marker, Elmwood Cemetery, Owensboro, Kentucky; photographed by T.C. Cottrell, 9 Jun 2002.

[6] "Joe Cottrell Dies in California", *Owensboro Messenger.*

[7] Family data, Nellie Lashbrook Cottrell, *Holy Bible*, King James Version (Cleveland and New York: The World Publishing Company, unknown publish date); present owner Taylor C Cottrell Jr., Rockledge, Florida.

[8] Letter from Nellie J. Cottrell (1530 State Street, Bowling Green Kentucky) to Mrs. Betty White, 18 Jan 1970.

[9] Family data, Joseph Frey Cottrell, *The Holman New Self-Pronouncing Sunday-School Teachers Bible*, Baptist Book Concern Edition (Louisville, Kentucky: A.J. Holman & Co., Ltd, 1894); present owner Taylor C Cottrell Jr., Rockledge, Florida.

[10] Resolutions Adopted upon Death of Joe F Cottrell, *unknown newspaper title*, Owensboro, Kentucky.

[11] Council Elects Martin Yewell as City Prosecutor to Succeed Joe Cottrell, *Owensboro Messenger*, Daviess County, Kentucky, 3 November 1908, page 7.

[12] "Joe Cottrell Dies in California", *Owensboro Messenger,*

[13] West Central Kentucky Family Research Association, *Elmwood Cemetery - A Partial List* (Utica, Kentucky: McDowell Publications, 2008), FHL US/CAN 976.9864/01 V32.

[14] Nellie Jane Cottrell, Death Registration 7227460 (1972), Department of Health Bureau of Vital Statistics, Frankfort, Kentucky.

[15] Nellie J. (Lashbrook) Cottrell, Earliest Memories, memories handwritten by Nellie Lashbrook.

[16] Ibid.

[17] Ibid.

[18] Nellie J. (Lashbrook) Cottrell, Memories of a Pet Lamb, Undated, handwritten notes, written by Nellie Lashbrook at the request of her grandson Taylor Cosby Cottrell, Jr.

[19] Nellie J. (Lashbrook) Cottrell, Earliest Memories.

[20] Ibid.

[21] Ibid.

[22] Ibid.

[23] Nellie J. (Lashbrook) Cottrell, Childhood and Youth Memories, Undated, handwritten notes, written by Nellie Lashbrook at the request of her grandson Taylor Cosby Cottrell, Jr.

[24] Ibid.

[25] Ibid.

[26] 1900 US Census, Daviess County, Kentucky, population schedule, Magisterial District No. 8, Enumeration District (ED) 39, page 2A, dwelling 26, family 26, James B Lashbrook; *Ancestry.com* (http://www.ancestry.com: accessed 11 March 2003); citing National Archives microfilm T623, roll 518.

[27] Daviess County, Kentucky, Vital records, Vols. 11-13 1902-1904, marriage bond for Joe F. Cottrell and Nellie J. Lashbrook, Book 13, page 457, FHL microfilm 1759323.

[28] Letter from Nellie J. Cottrell (1530 State Street, Bowling Green Kentucky) to Mrs. Betty White, 18 Jan 1970.

[29] Joseph Frey Cottrell, Death Registration 205403 (1908), Department of Health Bureau of Vital Statistics, Sacramento, California.

[30] 1910 US Census, Daviess County, Kentucky, population schedule, Magisterial District 5, Enumeration District (ED) 52, page 6B, dwelling 123, family 124, Sarah M Lashbrook; *Ancestry.com* (http://www.ancestry.com: accessed 10 March 2003); citing National Archives microfilm T624, roll 473.

[31] 1920 US Census, Daviess County, Kentucky, population schedule, Owensboro, precinct 5, Enumeration District (ED) 29, page 6A, dwelling 94, family 122, Nellie J. Cottrell; *Ancestry.com* (http://www.ancestry.com: accessed 6 March 2003); citing National Archives microfilm T625, roll 567.

[32] Telegram from T.C. Cottrell (Kyrock, Kentucky) to Mrs. Nellie Cottrell, 16 July 1928; Cottrell Family Papers (867 Jamestown Drive, Rockledge, Florida). Announced birth of Jo Anne Cottrell.

[33] 1930 US Census, Daviess County, Kentucky, population schedule, Owensboro, Enumeration District (ED) 30-15, page 3A, dwelling 49, family 31, Sarah Lashbrook; *Ancestry.com* (http://www.ancestry.com: accessed 9 March 2003); citing National Archives microfilm T626, roll 741.

[34] Letter from Zalame Brashear Cottrell (Bowling Green Kentucky) to T.C. Cottrell, Jr., 2 Jul 1983 detailing her life during 44 years of marriage.

[35] Deed of Conveyance from Mrs. W.A. Lee to Mrs. Nellie Cottrell, Book 179:543, Warren County Courthouse, Bowling Green, Kentucky.

[36] Nellie J. Cottrell Kentucky Operator License; Issued 24 July 1937, expired 31 July 1938.

[37] 80-Year-Old Doll Collector Is Champion Woman Whittler, *Park City Daily News*, Bowling Green, Kentucky, 27 Aug 1961.

[38] Ibid.

[39] Transfer of Ownership to Mrs. Nelly Cottrell for the East 3-4 by 10-0 of the South East 16-8 by 10-0 of Lot 16, Section I.

[40] Nellie Jane Cottrell, Death Registration 7227460 (1972), Department of Health Bureau of Vital Statistics, Frankfort, Kentucky.

[41] Mrs. Nellie Cottrell, *Park City Daily News*, Bowling Green, Kentucky.

[42] Letter from Andrew G. Mitchel (412-414 East Main, Owensboro Kentucky 42301) to Mrs. T.C. Cottrell, 2 October 1973

[43] Taylor Cosby Cottrell, special certificate of birth 20816 (1905), Department of Health Bureau of Vital Statistics, Frankfort, Kentucky.

Section 1 – Chapter 4 Sources – Taylor Cosby Cottrell, Sr. Family

[1] Taylor Cosby Cottrell, special certificate of birth 20816 (1905), Department of Health Bureau of Vital Statistics, Frankfort, Kentucky.

[2] Personal knowledge of Taylor C Cottrell Jr.

[3] Taylor Cosby Cottrell, special certificate of birth.

[4] Letter from Nellie J. Cottrell (1530 State Street, Bowling Green Kentucky) to Mrs. Betty White, 18 Jan 1970.

[5] 1910 US Census, Daviess County, Kentucky, population schedule, Magisterial District 5, Enumeration District (ED) 52, page 6B, dwelling 123, family 124, Sarah M Lashbrook; *Ancestry.com* (http://www.ancestry.com: accessed 10 March 2003); citing National Archives microfilm T624, roll 473.

[6] 1920 US Census, Daviess County, Kentucky, population schedule, Owensboro, precinct 5, Enumeration District (ED) 29, page 6A, dwelling 94, family 122, Nellie J. Cottrell; *Ancestry.com* (http://www.ancestry.com: accessed 6 March 2003); citing National Archives microfilm T625, roll 567.

[7] The way it was [Ogden College Football Team between 1920 and 1928], *Park City Daily News*, Bowling Green, Kentucky, 8-A.

[8] Did You Know?, *Bowling Green Mfg. Co. News and Report, Vol. 7 No. 2*, Bowling Green, Kentucky, May 1964, Page 2.

[9] The way it was [Ogden College Football Team between 1920 and 1928].

[10] Western's Cottrell Has Fine Record, *Kentucky Vocational School News, Volume one, Number two*, Somerset, Kentucky, Spring 1949, Page 4.

[11] Order of DeMolay Membership Card for Taylor C. Cottrell, 21 Jan 1926.

[12] Marriage Record of T.C. Cottrell and Zalame Brashear, Sumner County Office of Court Clerk, Gallatin, Tennessee.

[13] Did You Know?, *Bowling Green Mfg. Co. News and Report, Vol. 1, No. 10*, Bowling Green, Kentucky, February 1957, Page 3.

[14] Economic Highways of Warren County and Bowling Green, *Western Kentucky University*, (http://www.wku.edu: accessed 10 March 2003).

[15] Women in Business, *The Park City Daily News*, Bowling Green Kentucky, 10 Sep 1950.

[16] Telegram from T.C. Cottrell (Kyrock, Kentucky) to Mrs. Nellie Cottrell, 16 July 1928; Cottrell Family Papers (867 Jamestown Drive, Rockledge, Florida).

[17] Letter from Zalame Brashear Cottrell (Bowling Green Kentucky) to Jr. T.C. Cottrell, 2 Jul 1983.

[18] Ibid.

[19] 1930 US Census, Davidson County, Tennessee, population schedule, Old Hickory, Enumeration District (ED) 19-244, page 30A, dwelling 470, family 604, Taylor C Cottrell; *Ancestry.com* (http://www.ancestry.com: accessed 9 March 2003); citing National Archives microfilm T626, roll 2243.

[20] Letter, Zalame Brashear Cottrell to T.C. Cottrell, 2 July 1983.

[21] Ibid.

[22] Did You Know?, *Bowling Green Mfg. Co. News and Report.*

[23] Taylor Cosby Cottrell, Social Security Form SSA-9638 (Baltimore, Maryland: Social Security Administration, 18 Dec 1936).

[24] Letter, Zalame Brashear Cottrell to T.C. Cottrell, 2 July 1983.

[25] Ibid.

[26] Ibid.

[27] 1940 US Census, Todd County, Kentucky, population schedule, Elkton, Enumeration District (ED) 110-6, page 62B, dwelling 334, J T Lashbrook; *Ancestry.com* (http://www.ancestry.com: accessed 28 July 2012); citing National Archives microfilm T6267, roll 1358.

[28] Western's Cottrell Has Fine Record, *Kentucky Vocational School News, Volume one, Number two*, Summerset, Kentucky, Spring 1949, Page 4.

[29] Civil Aeronautics Authority Airman Certificate for Taylor Cosby Cottrell, 23 Dec 1941.

[30] Civil Aeronautics Authority Airman Rating for Taylor Cosby Cottrell, 23 Dec 1941.

[31] *Vocational School News*, Spring 1949, Page 4.

[32] Letter, Zalame Brashear Cottrell to T.C. Cottrell, 2 July 1983.

[33] Civil Aeronautics Authority Ground Instructor Certificate for Taylor Cosby Cottrell, 27 Aug 1942.

[34] Honorable Discharge from the Army of the United States for Taylor C. Cottrell, Sr., 19 Apr 1944.

[35] Enlisted Reserve Corp Identification Card for Taylor C. Cottrell, 3 Aug 1943.

[36] Letter from Major Parsons (67th AAF Flying Training Detachment, Union City, Tennessee) to T.C. Cottrell, 1 Oct 1943.

[37] Release from Duties as Director of Ground School for Taylor Cosby Cottrell, 19 Apr 1944.

[38] Postcard of the Antilla Hotel in Coral Gables Florida.

[39] Letter from John Vale (Embry-Riddle Company) to Ration Board, 9 May 1944.

[40] *Vocational School News*, Spring 1949, Page 4.

[41] Certificate of Confirmation for Taylor Cosby Cottrell, (8 Apr 1945), in Christ Episcopal Church, Bowling Green, Warren County, Kentucky, presented by A.L Kirshaw, confirmed by Bishop Clingman

[42] *Vocational School News*, Spring 1949, Page 4.

[43] *Daily News*, 10 Sep 1950.

[44] The American Home - Pattern No. 1316 - Glasses and Pitcher - by Zeleme, Copyrighted September 1950.

[45] Did You Know?, *Bowling Green Mfg. Co. News and Report.*

[46] Certificate of Appointment as Lay Reader for Taylor C. Cottrell, (12 Nov 1952), in Christ Church, Bowling Green, Kentucky.

[47] Warren County, Kentucky, Will Book W15, P 123 (12 November 1954), Taylor Cosby Cottrell, Sr.; Warren County Courthouse, Clerk Warren County Court. Copied at County Courthouse in Bowling Green, Kentucky on 11 September 2014 by TC Cottrell.

[48] Zalame Cottrell will (12 Nov 1954), Last Will and Testament.

[49] Certificate of Completion of Modern Business Practice Course for Taylor C Cottrell, 12 Dec 1961.

[50] Personal knowledge of Taylor C Cottrell, Jr.

[51] Did You Know?, *Bowling Green Mfg. Co. News and Report.*

[52] Master Mason Membership Card for Taylor C. Cottrell, 6 Mar 1970.

[53] Letter from Joan Pastor (Colt Industries, 430 Park Avenue, New York, New York) to T.C. Cottrell, 14 Dec 1970.

[54] Letter from Nellie J. Cottrell to Mrs. Betty White.

[55] Personal knowledge of Taylor C Cottrell, Jr.

[56] Taylor Cosby Cottrell, Death Registration 711978 (1971), Department of Health Bureau of Vital Statistics, Frankfort, Kentucky.

[57] B.G. Man Dies of Heart Attack at Louisville, *Park City Daily News*, Bowling Green. Kentucky, 17 May 1971.

[58] Personal knowledge of Taylor C Cottrell, Jr.

[59] Thomas L Aud, "Thomas L. Aud also commented on his status," e-mail from e-mail address (Facebook) to TC Cottrell, 9 June 2013.

[60] T.C. Cottrell, *Messenger Inquirer*, Owensboro. Kentucky, 19 May 1971.

[61] Unknown Author, "Silent Keys," *QST Amateur Radio*, Number 8, Volume LV (August 1971).

[62] Estella Zalame Brashear, special certificate of birth (1908), Department of Health Bureau of Vital Statistics, Frankfort, Kentucky.

[63] 1910 US Census, Warren County, Kentucky, population schedule, Magisterial District 3, Enumeration District (ED) 116, page 10B, dwelling 180, family 180, Richard L Brashear; *Ancestry.com* (http://www.ancestry.com: accessed 10 March 2003); citing National Archives microfilm T624, roll 504.

[64] 1920 US Census, Warren County, Kentucky, population schedule, Bristow district, Enumeration District (ED) 130, page 1A, dwelling 8, family 9, Della Brashear; *Ancestry.com* (http://www.ancestry.com: accessed 9 March 2003); citing National Archives microfilm T625, roll 600.

[65] Business Writing Certificate for Zalame Brashear, 3 May 1923.

[66] Certificate of Baptism for Zalame Brashear, (19 Apr 1924), in Christ Episcopal Church, Bowling Green, Warren County, Kentucky, sponsors were Della Brashear, Kathleen Lashbrook.

[67] Bowling Green High School Attendance Report for Zalame Brashear at age 15, Circa May 1924.

[68] Certificate of Confirmation for Zalame Brashear, (26 Oct 1924), in Christ Episcopal Church, Bowling Green, Warren County, Kentucky, presented by Rev W. Elliston, confirmed by Bishop Charles E. Woodcock

[69] Leslie Method of Writing Certificate for Zalame Brashear, 20 Feb 1925.

[70] Bowling Green High School Attendance Report for Zalame Brashear at age 17, Circa May 1926.

[71] Marriage Record of T.C. Cottrell and Zalame Brashear, Sumner County Office of Court Clerk, Gallatin, Tennessee.

[72] High School Graduation Booklet for Zalame Brashear.

[73] Women in Business, *The Park City Daily News*, Bowling Green Kentucky, 10 Sep 1950.

[74] Letter from Zalame Brashear Cottrell to Jr. T.C. Cottrell, Jr. 2 Jul 1983.

[75] 1930 US Census, Davidson County, Tennessee, population schedule, Old Hickory, Enumeration District (ED) 19-244, page 30A, dwelling 470, family 604, Taylor C Cottrell; *Ancestry.com* (http://www.ancestry.com: accessed 9 March 2003); citing National Archives microfilm T626, roll 2243.

[76] Ibid.

[77] Letter from Zalame Brashear Cottrell to Jr. T.C. Cottrell, Jr. 2 Jul 1983.

[78] Ibid.

[79] "U.S. City Directories - 1937/38-1949," database, *Ancestry.com* (http://www.ancestry.com: accessed 20 March 2009); citing "*Caron's Bowling Green Warren County Kentucky City Directory 1949 Including Rural Routes* (Bowling Green, Kentucky: Caron Directory Company)".

[80] Letter from Zalame Brashear Cottrell to Jr. T.C. Cottrell, Jr. 2 Jul 1983.

[81] Ibid.

[82] Business Card for Zalame's Antiques, circa 1950.

[83] 1940 US Census, Todd County, Kentucky, population schedule, Elkton, Enumeration District (ED) 110-6, page 62B, dwelling 334, J T Lashbrook; digital images, National Archives microfilm T6267, roll 1358.

[84] Letter from Zalame Brashear Cottrell to Jr. T.C. Cottrell, Jr. 2 Jul 1983.

[85] Power of Attorney of Zalame Brashear Appointing Della Brashear, 9 April 1943, executed in Union City, Tennessee.

[86] Estate Settlement Checks written to Brashear Heirs of the William H Brashear Estate, 6 January 1944.

[87] Postcard of the Antilla Hotel in Coral Gables Florida, Undated, documenting the temporary residence of TC and Zalame Cottrell during April and May of 1944.

[88] Women in Business, *The Park City Daily News*,

[89] Business Card for Zalame's Antiques.

[90] Personal knowledge of Taylor C Cottrell, Jr.

[91] The American Home - Pattern No. 1316 - Glasses and Pitcher - by Zeleme, Copyrighted September 1950.

[92] Warren County, Kentucky, Will Book W15, P 123 (12 November 1954), Taylor Cosby Cottrell, Sr.; Warren County Courthouse, Clerk Warren County Court. Copied at County Courthouse in Bowling Green, Kentucky on 11 September 2014 by TC Cottrell.

[93] Zalame Cottrell will (12 Nov 1954), Last Will and Testament.

[94] 30th High School Reunion Program for Zalame Cottrell, 15 May 1957.

[95] Brashear Property On Louisville Road, *Park City Daily News*, Bowling Green, Kentucky.

[96] Meteor Shower to Reach Peak Early This Week, *The Park City Daily News*, Bowling Green Kentucky.

[97] Personal knowledge of Taylor C Cottrell, Jr.

[98] Zalame Cottrell will (25 May 1971), Copy of Last Will and Testament.

[99] Clever Weaver, *The Park City Daily News*, Bowling Green Kentucky, 14 Apr 1972.

[100] Unique calendars will be sold, *The Park City Daily News*, Bowling Green Kentucky, 12 Sep 1974.

[101] Power of Attorney of Kathleen Brashear Appointing Zalame Cottrell, 18 October 1974, executed in Warren County, Kentucky.

[102] Sales and Purchasing Contract for Lots 34 and 35 near Port Oliver, Allen County, Kentucky, 29 October 1974.

[103] AYE for Art, *The Park City Daily News*, Bowling Green Kentucky, 27 Feb 1977.

[104] Certificate of Commemoration for Mrs. T.C. Cottrell from the Governor of Kentucky, 3 Jun 1977.

[105] Early Price List for Cottrell Limited Editions.

[106] Kathleen H. Brashear will (15 July 1982), Last Will and Testament.

[107] Antique valentine shows customs of another age, *The Park City Daily News*, Bowling Green Kentucky, 14 Feb 1986.

[108] Kathleen Hope Brashear, Death Registration 1168621874 (1986), Department of Health Bureau of Vital Statistics, Frankfort, Kentucky.

[109] Letter from William J. Parker (519 E. Tenth Street, Bowling Green, Kentucky 42102) to Mrs. Zalame Cottrell, 30 April 1987.

[110] Zalame Cottrell will (1 Nov 1988), Last Will and Testament.

[111] Personal knowledge of Taylor C Cottrell, Jr.

[112] Ibid.

[113] Ibid.

[114] Estella Zalame Brashear Cottrell, Death Registration 96-2950 (1996), State Department of Health and Rehabilitative Services, Jacksonville, Florida.

[115] Estella Zalame Cottrell, *Park City Daily News*, Bowling Green. Kentucky, 10 September 1996.

[116] Floral Tribute list for Zalame Cottrell's Funeral, 11 Sep 1996.

[117] Personal knowledge of Taylor C Cottrell, Jr.

[118] Joanna Cottrell, birth certificate 31651 (1928), Department of Health Bureau of Vital Statistics, Frankfort, Kentucky.

[119] 1930 US Census, Davidson County, Tennessee, population schedule, ED 19-244, page 30A, dwelling 470, family 604, Taylor C Cottrell.

[120] Postcard from Zalame B. Cottrell to Jo Anne Cottrell, 8 Mar 1938.

[121] "U.S. City Directories - 1937/38-1949," database, *Ancestry.com* (http://www.ancestry.com: accessed 20 March 2009); citing "*Caron's Bowling Green Warren County Kentucky City Directory 1949 Including Rural Routes* (Bowling Green, Kentucky: Caron Directory Company)".

[122] 1940 US Census, Todd County, Kentucky, population schedule, ED 110-6, page 62B, dwelling 334, J T Lashbrook.

[123] "Queen of All Lands", *Unidentified Todd County Kentucky Newspaper*, Todd County Kentucky, circa 1940.

[124] Certificate of Baptism for Jo Anne Cottrell, (19 Feb 1943), in Saint James Episcopal Church, Union City, Obion County, Tennessee.

[125] Certificate of Confirmation for Jo Anne Cottrell, (21 Feb 1943), in St. Jame's Episcopal Church, Union City, Tennessee.

[126] Miss Cottrell Entertains in Honor Of Her Guest, *Park City Daily News*, Bowling Green, Kentucky, Unidentified Date in 1944.

[127] Western Teachers College High School Diploma for Joanna Cottrell, given on 13 May 1946, at Bowling Green, Kentucky.

[128] Letter from Sally Edwards Reuter (27 Mt. Vernon Street, Charleston, Massachusetts) to Jr. T.C. Cottrell, 23 Jan 1999.

[129] Women in Business, *The Park City Daily News*.

[130] Ibid.

[131] Zalame Cottrell will, 1954 Will of Zalame Cottrell.

[132] Marriage Announcement for Jo Anne Cottrell and Lawrence A. Sloan.

[133] *Jo Anne Sloan* v. *Larry Sloan*, Divorce Case Number 2673, Winston County Circuit Court Clerk's Office, Double Springs, Winston County, Alabama.

[134] Personal knowledge of Taylor C Cottrell, Jr.

[135] Ibid.

[136] Ibid.

[137] Business Card for Joanna Cottrell as a Free-Lance Copywriter.

[138] United States Passport Number E337586, issued for Joanna Cottrell, 17 Feb 1984, expired on 16 Feb 1994.

[139] Tori Kieser, "Joanna Cottrell," e-mail to TC Cottrell, 1 September 2010.

[140] Passport, Joanna Cottrell.

[141] Jo Anne Cottrell will (9 Nov 1992), Last Will and Testament.

[142] Supreme Court of New York Juror Service Record for Joanna Cottrell, 29 Mar 1993.

[143] Personal knowledge of Taylor C Cottrell, Jr.

[144] Health Care Proxy for Joanna Cottrell, 23 October 1997.

[145] New York Living Will of Joanna Cottrell, 23 October 1997.

[146] T.C. Cottrell, Remembrances of the death of Joanna Cottrell.

[147] Joanna Cottrell, Death Registration 156-98-048197 (1998), Department of Health Vital Records, New York, New York.

[148] Bill for final care for Joanna's cat Clementine including cremation charge, 22 Oct 1998.

[149] Remembrances of Joanna Cottrell's death.

[150] Ibid

[151] State of New York Notice of Probate Form P-1 for Joanna Cottrell, 22 October 1998.

[152] Joanna Cottrell is dead; pet columnist was 70, *The Villager*, Manhattan, New York, 21 Oct 1998, Page 4.

[153] Redden's Funeral Home contract for arrangements for Joanna Cottrell, 22 Oct 1998.

[154] NY Surrogate's Court Letters Testamentary appointing Taylor Cosby Cottrell as executor for Joanna Cottrell's estate, 29 October 1998

[155] Remembrances of Joanna Cottrell's death.

Section 1 – Chapter 5 Sources – Jefferson M. Cosby Family

[1] "Family Data Collection - Individual Records Database," subscription database, *Ancestry.com* (http://www.ancestry.com: accessed 20 March 2005), for Jefferson M Cosby.

[2] Noah H Bradley *My Wife's Family.*

[3] Virginia Marriages, 1740-1850, Ancestry.com (http://www.ancestry.com: accessed on 1 January 2005), for Jefferson Cosby and Ann Wilson.

[4] Noah H Bradley *My Wife's Family* (Pawhatan, Virginia: H. Bradley, 1922), page 232-240.

[5] Ibid.

[6] Virginia Marriages, 1740-1850.

[7] Noah H Bradley, *My Wife's Family*, page 232-240.

[8] Ibid.

[9] Illinois Department of Financial and Professional Regulation, Division of Insurance, Slave Registry Detail for death payment for a slave death to Jefferson Cosby, IDFPR (http://www.idfpr.com).

[10] 1850 US Census, Chesterfield County, Virginia, population schedule, The Upper District, page 105B, dwelling 765, family 801, Jefferson Cosby, *Ancestry.com* (http://www.ancestry.com: accessed 1 January 2005); citing National Archives microfilm M432, roll 940.

[11] 1860 US Census, Chesterfield County, Virginia, population schedule, Northern District, Manchester Post Office, page 24, dwelling 185, family 191, Jeff Cosby, *Ancestry.com* (http://www.ancestry.com: accessed 1 January 2005); citing National Archives microfilm M653, roll 1340.

[12] 1870 US Census, Chesterfield County, Virginia, population schedule, Chester Post Office, page 306a, dwelling 1150, family 1173, Jefferson Cosby, *Ancestry.com*

(http://www.ancestry.com: accessed 1 January 2005); citing National Archives microfilm M593, roll 1640.

[13] 1880 US Census, Chesterfield County, Virginia, population schedule, Midlothian, Enumeration District (ED) 74, page 228B, dwelling 11, family 12, Jefferson Cosby, *Ancestry.com* (http://www.ancestry.com: accessed 1 January 2005); citing National Archives microfilm T9, roll 1361.

[14] Noah H Bradley *My Wife's Family,* page 232-240.

[15] 1900 US Census, Chesterfield County, Virginia, population schedule, Midlothian, Enumeration District (ED) 9, page 12A, dwelling 216, family 203, Charles M Cosby; *Ancestry.com* (http://www.ancestry.com: accessed 2 January 2005); citing National Archives microfilm T623, roll 1705.

[16] "Funeral of Mrs. Cosby," *Richmond Times Dispatch* (Richmond, Virginia), 12 March 1905, page 13, col. 5, Funeral Notice for Nancy Cosby, *Genealogy Bank* (www.genealogybank.com: accessed 25 August 2012).

[17] Noah H Bradley *My Wife's Family,* page 232-240.

[18] 1850 US Census, Chesterfield County, Virginia, population schedule, The Upper District, page 105B, dwelling 765, family 801, Jefferson Cosby; *Ancestry.com* (http://www.ancestry.com: accessed 1 January 2005); citing National Archives microfilm M432, roll 940.

[19] Noah H Bradley *My Wife's Family,* page 232-240.

[20] 1860 US Census, Chesterfield County, Virginia, population schedule, Northern District, Manchester Post Office, page 21, dwelling 165, family 174, Phillip Cosby; *Ancestry.com* (http://www.ancestry.com: accessed 26 January 2005); citing National Archives microfilm M653, roll 1340.

[21] "Chesterfield County, Virginia Deaths, 1882-88," *Ancestry.com* (http://www.ancestry.com: accessed 27 January 2005), for T.J. Cosby (14 November 1887).

[22] "Virginia, Death Records, 1912-2014," *Ancestry.com* (http://www.ancestry.com: accessed 14 June 2015), for Ira Lafayette Cosby, Virginia Department of Health, Certificate No 1934008692.

[23] "Bethel Baptist Church," database, *Find A Grave* (http://www.findagrave.com: accessed 2 September 2012), entry for Line E Duncan Cosby, 5 January 1944; citing memorial #7688541.

[24] "Bethel Baptist Church," database, *Find A Grave* (http://www.findagrave.com: accessed 2 September 2012), entry for Line E. Duncan Cosby.

[25] "Virginia Death Records 1912-2014," *Ancestry.com* (http://www.ancestry.com: accessed 10 March 2016), for Philip Ransome Cosby, Richmond, Virginia Department of Health, Certificate No 69-028704.

[26] "Edgewood Cemetery," database, *Find A Grave* (http://www.findagrave.com: accessed 28 February 2014), entry for William Wilson Bud Cosby, 23 July 2008; citing memorial # 79307403.

[27] "Port Republic Cemetery," database, Find A Grave (http://www.findagrave.com: accessed 10 March 2016), entry for R. Duncan Cosby, 1 August 1991; citing memorial #23860247.

[28] Social Security Administration, "Social Security Death Index," database, *Ancestry.com* (http://www.ancestry.com: accessed 10 March 2016), entry for Ira Cosby, 1984, SS no. 226-44-1503.

[29] Social Security Administration, "Social Security Death Index," database, *Ancestry.com* (http://www.ancestry.com: accessed 10 March 2016), entry for Elizabeth Carver, 1978, SS no. 258-72-3539.

[30] 1900 US Census, Craven County, North Carolina, population schedule, Newbern, Enumeration District (ED) 54, page 10B, dwelling 213, family 272, Ira Cosby; *Ancestry.com* (http://www.ancestry.com: accessed 21 May 2013); citing National Archives microfilm T623, roll 1190.

[31] "Chesterfield County, Virginia Births", for No Name Cosby (Oct 1860), page 69, listed as No Name, born dead in October 1860 in Chesterfield County, Virginia.

[32] Noah H Bradley *My Wife's Family,* page 232-240.

[33] 1870 US Census, Chesterfield County, Virginia, population schedule, Huguenot Township, Jefferson Post Office, page 26, dwelling 195, family 198, P L Cosby; *Ancestry.com* (http://www.ancestry.com: accessed 27 January 2005); citing National Archives microfilm M593, roll 1672.

[34] 1860 US Census, Pawhatan County, Virginia, population schedule, Pawhatan Post Office, page 65, dwelling 430, family 430, Virginia A Howard; *Ancestry.com* (http://www.ancestry.com: accessed 28 January 2005); citing National Archives microfilm M653, roll 1371.

[35] 1870 US Census, Chesterfield County, Virginia.

[36] 1880 US Census, Pawhatan County, Virginia, population schedule, Huguenot District, Enumeration District (ED) 183, page 137B, dwelling 88, family 88, Philip L Cosby; *Ancestry.com* (http://www.ancestry.com: accessed 27 January 2005); citing National Archives microfilm T9, roll 1383.

[37] "Pawhatan County, Virginia Births, 1853-96," *Ancestry.com* (http://www.ancestry.com: accessed 27 January 2005), for Philip Cosby (16 Jun 1864), page 71.

[38] 1900 US Census, Nottoway County, Virginia, population schedule, Haytokah District, Enumeration District (ED) 63, page 4A, dwelling 72, family 72, Philip Cosby; *Ancestry.com* (http://www.ancestry.com: accessed 21 May 2013); citing National Archives microfilm T623, roll 1721.

[39] Noah H Bradley *My Wife's Family.*

[40] "Virginia Death Records 1912-2014," *Ancestry.com* (http://www.ancestry.com: accessed 10 March 2016), for Lulu Mae Gunn, Richmond, Virginia Department of Health, Certificate No 80-005186.

[41] "Virginia Select Marriages, 185-1940," *Ancestry.com* (http://www.ancestry.com: accessed 10 March 2016) for Hattie F. Cosby and C.H. Hines, 16 December 1913; citing FHL Film No. 2048467.

[42] "Maury Cemetery," database, *Find A Grave* (http://www.findagrave.com: accessed 10 March 2016), entry for Bessie Cosby Bass, 28 January 1966; citing memorial #35755690.

[43] "Sunset Hill Cemetery," database, *Find A Grave* (http://www.findagrave.com: accessed 10 March 2016), entry for Phyllis V. Cosby, 25 April 1981; citing memorial #75598196.

[44] "Sunset Hill Cemetery," database, *Find A Grave* (http://www.findagrave.com: accessed 10 March 2016), entry for Ralph Leroy Cosby, 17 February 1998; citing memorial #75598198.

[45] "Pawhatan County, Virginia Births, 1853-96," *Ancestry.com* (http://www.ancestry.com: accessed 27 January 2005), for No Name Cosby (26 Apr 1866), page 75.

[46] 1850 US Census, Chesterfield County, Virginia, population schedule, The Upper District, page 105B, dwelling 765, family 801, Jefferson Cosby; *Ancestry.com* (http://www.ancestry.com: accessed 1 January 2005); citing National Archives microfilm p M432, roll 940.

[47] Ibid.

[48] Noah H Bradley *My Wife's Family.*

[49] 1860 US Census, Chesterfield County, Virginia, population schedule, Manchester Northern District, page 129, dwelling 367, family 380, B.E. Cosby; *Ancestry.com* (http://www.ancestry.com: accessed 29 January 2005); citing National Archives microfilm M653, roll 1340.

[50] "Virginia, Death Records, 1912-2014," *Ancestry.com* (http://www.ancestry.com: accessed 14 June 2015), for Florence Cosby Hughes, Virginia Department of Health, Certificate No 1935027882.

[51] "Maury Cemetery," database, *Find A Grave* (http://www.findagrave.com: accessed 28 February 2014), entry for Howell Hunter Cosby, 20 December 1897; citing memorial #22208757.

[52] 1880 US Census, Spencer County, Indiana, population schedule, The Town of Grandview, Enumeration District (ED) 45, page 68A, dwelling 77, family 85, Branch E Cosby; *Ancestry.com* (http://www.ancestry.com: accessed 1 January 2005); citing National Archives microfilm T9, roll 311.

[53] 1870 US Census, Chesterfield County, Virginia, population schedule, Manchester Post Office, page 346A, dwelling 385, family 419, John Walker; digital images, *Ancestry.com* (http://www.ancestry.com: accessed 29 January 2005); citing National Archives microfilm M593, roll 1640.

[54] Ibid.

[55] Noah H Bradley *My Wife's Family,* page 232-240.

[56] 1880 US Census, Spencer County, Indiana, population schedule, ED 45, page 68A, dwelling 77, family 85, Branch E Cosby.

[57] "Rose Hills Memorial Park," database, *Find A Grave* (http://www.findagrave.com: accessed 19 April 2013), entry for Rosa Russell Cottrell, 30 January 1963; citing memorial # 93421428.

[58] "Rose Hills Memorial Park," database, *Find A Grave* (http://www.findagrave.com: accessed 10 March 2016), entry for Cosby Monon Cottrell, 19 December 1968; citing memorial #93421300.

[59] "Rose Hills Memorial Park," database, *Find A Grave* (http://www.findagrave.com: accessed 10 March 2016), entry for Betty C. Wagner, 1 February 1988; citing memorial #93959887.

[60] 1880 US Census, Spencer County, Indiana, population schedule, ED 45, page 68A, dwelling 77, family 85, Branch E Cosby.

[61] "Lexington Cemetery," database, *Find A Grave* (http://www.findagrave.com: accessed on 10 March 2016), entry for Carlton Jay Curtis, 1960; citing memorial #36591102.

[62] "Lexington Cemetery," database, *Find A Grave* (http://www.findagrave.com: accessed on 10 March 2016), entry for Ramer Beatty Curtis, 21 January 1965; citing memorial #37659023

[63] "Hancock Chapel United Methodist Cemetery." Database, *Find A Grave* (http://www.findagrave.com: accessed on 10 March 2016), entry for Edward H. Curtis, 28 September 1978; citing memorial #28902523.

[64] "Grand View Memorial Park," database, *Find A Grave* (http://www.findagrave.com: accessed 19 April 2013), entry for Rosa Russell Cottrell, 30 January 1963; citing memorial #93421428.

[65] "U.S., School Yearbooks, 1880-2012," *Ancestry.com* (http://www.ancestry.com: accessed 1 June 2016), entry for Adeline Howard, 1932, Los Angeles High School.

[66] Harold Bishop Morgan, compiler, *Daviess County, Kentucky Marriage Records Volume 1, 1780 through 1914* (11129 Pleasant Ridge Road, Utica, Kentucky: McDowell Publications, 2004).

[67] Social Security Administration, "Social Security Death Index," database, *Ancestry.com* (http://www.ancestry.com: accessed 10 March 2016), entry for Florence Davis, 1907, SS no. 253-74-0498.

[68] 1900 US Census, Daviess County, Kentucky, population schedule, Vanover, Enumeration District (ED) 34, page 25a, dwelling 474, family 477, John Howard; *Ancestry.com* (http://www.ancestry.com: accessed 5 August 2007); citing National Archives microfilm T623, roll 623.

[69] 1910 US Census, Daviess County, Kentucky, population schedule, District 5, Enumeration District (ED) 44, page 3B, dwelling 44, family 44, Addie Cosby; *Ancestry.com* (http://www.ancestry.com: accessed 20 November 2015); citing National Archives microfilm T624, roll 473.

[70] "Kentucky Death Records, 1852-1953," *Ancestry.com* (http://www.ancestry.com: accessed 28 April 2009), for Mrs. Addie Cosby (28 March 1914).

[71] 1850 US Census, Chesterfield County, Virginia, population schedule, page 105B, dwelling 765, family 801, Jefferson Cosby.

[72] Noah H Bradley *My Wife's Family,* page 232-240.

[73] 1870 US Census, Chesterfield County, Virginia, population schedule, First Revenue Division, page 143, dwelling 1151, family 1174, Sarah Stratton; *Ancestry.com* (http://www.ancestry.com: accessed 6 August 2007); citing National Archives microfilm M593, roll 1640.

[74] 1880 US Census, Goochland County, Virginia, population schedule, Dover District, Enumeration District (ED) 173, page 16d, dwelling 134, family 152, Moses Stratton; *Ancestry.com* (http://www.ancestry.com: accessed 6 August 2007); citing National Archives microfilm T9, roll 1367

[75] 1900 US Census, Goochland County, Virginia, population schedule, Dover District, Enumeration District (ED) 34, page 9a & 9b, dwelling 169, family 167, James M Stratton; *Ancestry.com* (http://www.ancestry.com: accessed 5 August 2007); citing National Archives microfilm T623, roll 623

[76] "Dover Baptist Church Cemetery," database, *Find A Grave* (http://www.findagrave.com: accessed 16 May 2013), entry for Judith Stratton; citing memorial # 60997146.

[77] "Dover Baptist Church Cemetery," database, *Find A Grave* (http://www.findagrave.com: accessed 16 May 2013), entry for Lorenza Dow Stratton, 1928; citing memorial #17877215.

[78] "Dover Baptist Church Cemetery," database, *Find A Grave* (http://www.findagrave.com: accessed 10 March 2016), entry for Norman Stratton, 10 July 1915; citing memorial #60951002.

[79] "Dover Baptist Church Cemetery," database, *Find A Grave* (http://www.findagrave.com: accessed 10 March 2016), entry for William Moseley Stratton, 20 February 1909; citing memorial #19818945.

[80] "Spring Hill Cemetery," database, *Find A Grave* (http://www.findagrave.com: accessed 10 March 2016), entry for Ninna Stratton Ripley, 27 April 1960; citing memorial #114897183.

[81] 1880 US Census, Goochland County, Virginia, population schedule, ED 173, page 16d, dwelling 134, family 152, Moses Stratton, listed as age 19 and born in Virginia.

[82] "Bible Records, 1830-1909," database, *Virginia Historical Society* (http://www.vahistorical.org: accessed 25 July 2009), entry for Peter and Rosa (Cosby) Cottrell; Copies were secured by TC Cottrell by mail on 27 July 2009 from the Virginia Historical Society.

[83] "John S. Cosby," *Richmond Times Dispatch* (Richmond, Virginia), 7 April 1940, page 18, col. 4, Death Notice, *Genealogy Bank* (www.genealogybank.com: accessed 25 August 2012).

[84] 1850 US Census, Chesterfield County, Virginia, population schedule, page 105B, dwelling 765, family 801, Jefferson Cosby, listed as Sarah, age 10.

[85] 1880 US Census, Chesterfield County, Virginia, population schedule, ED 74, page 228B, dwelling 11, family 12, Jefferson Cosby, listed as Sarah J Stratton.

[86] Ibid.

[87] Ibid.

[88] Taylor C Cottrell, "W. Upshure Bass Cemetery Lot Photo Survey, Hollywood Cemetery, Richmond, Virginia," privately held by Taylor C Cottrell, Rockledge, Florida; Markers and plot information photographed and recorded on 23 February 2011, by Taylor C Cottrell.

[89] "Virginia, Death Records, 1912-2014," *Ancestry.com* (http://www.ancestry.com: accessed 14 June 2015), for Nettie Lou Bass, Virginia Department of Health, Certificate #1961015638.

[90] 1880 US Census, Goochland County, Virginia.

[91] 1910 US Census, Chesterfield County, Virginia, population schedule, Midlothian, Enumeration District (ED) 11, page 2B, dwelling 40, family 49, L. Shelby Bass; *Ancestry.com* (http://www.ancestry.com: accessed 21 May 2013); citing National Archives microfilm T624, roll 1625.

[92] 1920 US Census, Chesterfield County, Virginia, population schedule, Midlothian, Enumeration District (ED) 16, page 9A, dwelling 159, family 160, Shelwin T. Bass; *Ancestry.com* (http://www.ancestry.com: accessed 21 May 2013); citing National Archives microfilm T625, roll 1885.

[93] "Hollywood Cemetery," database, *Find A Grave* (http://www.findagrave.com: accessed 19 November 2015), entry for Sallie S. Stratton, September 1922; citing memorial #93890720.

[94] 1850 US Census, Chesterfield County, Virginia.

[95] 1860 US Census, Chesterfield County, Virginia, population schedule, Manchester Post Office, page 24, dwelling 185, family 191, Jeff Cosby; *Ancestry.com* (http://www.ancestry.com: accessed 1 January 2005); citing National Archives microfilm M653, roll 1340

[96] Noah H Bradley *My Wife's Family,* page 232-240.

[97] 1870 US Census, Chesterfield County, Virginia, population schedule, First Revenue Division, Chester Post Office, page 306a, dwelling 1150, family 1173, Jefferson Cosby; *Ancestry.com* (http://www.ancestry.com: accessed 1 January 2005); citing National Archives microfilm publication M593, roll 1640.

[98] 1880 US Census, Pittsylvania County, Virginia, population schedule, First Ward, Danville, Enumeration District (ED) 179, page 23, dwelling 166, family 267, Beverly F Morrissett; *Ancestry.com* (http://www.ancestry.com: accessed 29 March 2009); citing National Archives microfilm T9, roll 1385.

[99] 1900 US Census, Danville Independent City, Virginia, population schedule, Danville City, Enumeration District (ED) 100, page 2A, dwelling 18, family 20, Beverly Morrissett; *Ancestry.com* (http://www.ancestry.com: accessed 29 March 2009); citing National Archives microfilm T623, roll 1733.

[100] 1910 US Census, Danville Independent City, Virginia, population schedule, Danville Ward 3, Enumeration District (ED) 21, page 3A, dwelling 40, family 41, Beverly F Morrissett; *Ancestry.com* (http://www.ancestry.com: accessed 29 March 2009); citing National Archives microfilm T624, roll 1626.

[101] "Family Data for Beverly F Morrissett" Obituary, originally published on 7 July 1922 in Danville, Virginia, bettykwood_1, *Ancestry.com* (http://trees.ancestry.com: accessed 25 May 2015).

[102] "North Carolina Death Certificates, 1909-1975," *Ancestry.com* (http://www.ancestry.com: accessed 29 March 2009), for Allen Lynnwood Morrissett (23 March 1960), certificate 8719.

[103] 1930 US Census, Guilford County, North Carolina, population schedule, Greensboro, Enumeration District (ED) 292, page 17A, dwelling 292, family 326, Allen L Morrissett; *Ancestry.com* (http://www.ancestry.com: accessed 12 April 2009); citing National Archives microfilm T625, roll 1695.

[104] "North Carolina Death Certificates, 1909-1975," *Ancestry.com* (http://www.ancestry.com: accessed 12 April 2009), for Janie Morrissett (4 August 1961), certificate 22682.

[105] "Pine Hill Cemetery,", database, *Find A Grave* (http://www.findagrave.com: accessed 13 March 2016), entry for Cosby L. Morrissett, 6 November 1983; citing memorial #51947936.

[106] "Green Hill Cemetery," database, *Find A Grave* (http://www.findagrave.com: accessed 13 March 2016), entry for Hilda V. Linehan, 18 July 1993; citing memorial #65836549.

[107] "Guilford Memorial Park," database, *Find A Grave* (http://www.findagrave.com: accessed 13 March 2016), entry for Charlotte R. Morrissett Darnell, 17 December 1990; citing memorial #85156905.

[108] "Green Hill Cemetery," database, *Find A Grave* (http://www.findagrave.com: accessed 24 April 2015), entry for Irvin Morrissett, 2 May 1907; citing memorial #65836175.

[109] Ibid.

[110] Ibid.

[111] Ibid.

[112] "Family Data for Beverly F Morrissett.

[113] 1860 US Census, Chesterfield County, Virginia, population schedule, page 24, dwelling 185, family 191, Jeff Cosby, listed as Monterey, age 12.

[114] 1870 US Census, Chesterfield County, Virginia, population schedule, page 306a, dwelling 1150, family 1173, Jefferson Cosby.

[115] 1860 US Census, Chesterfield County, Virginia, population schedule, page 24, dwelling 185, family 191, Jeff Cosby, listed as Monterey, age 12.

[116] Noah H Bradley *My Wife's Family,* page 232-240.

[117] 1900 US Census, Chesterfield County, Virginia, population schedule, Midlothian District, Enumeration District (ED) 9, page 6A, dwelling 104, family 110, Luther C Cosby; *Ancestry.com* (http://www.ancestry.com: accessed 2 August 2006); citing National Archives microfilm T623, roll 1705.

[118] 1910 US Census, Chesterfield County, Virginia, population schedule, Midlothian, Enumeration District (ED) 11, page 10B, dwelling 184, family 184, Luther C Cosby; *Ancestry.com* (http://www.ancestry.com: accessed 2 August 2006); citing National Archives microfilm T624, roll 1625.

[119] 1920 US Census, Chesterfield County, Virginia, population schedule, Midlothian, Enumeration District (ED) 16, page 11B, dwelling 212, family 213, Luther C Cosby; *Ancestry.com* (http://www.ancestry.com: accessed 2 January 2005); citing National Archives microfilm T625, roll 1885.

[120] 1930 US Census, Chesterfield County, Virginia, population schedule, Midlothian District, Enumeration District (ED) 21-16, page 9A, dwelling 177, family 179, Irvin H

Cosby; *Ancestry.com* (http://www.ancestry.com: accessed 1 August 2006); citing National Archives microfilm T626, roll 2440.

[121] "Virginia, Death Records, 1912-2014," *Ancestry.com* (http://www.ancestry.com: accessed 13 March 2016), for Calvin Watkins Cosby, Virginia Department of Health, Certificate No. 1434.

[122] "Virginia Select Marriages, 1785-1940," *Ancestry.com* (http://www.ancestry.com: accessed 13 March 2016) for Calvin W. Cosby and Phyllis V. Cosby, 26 July 1917; citing FHL Film No. 2048457.

[123] "Virginia, Death Records, 1912-2014," *Ancestry.com* (http://www.ancestry.com: accessed 13 March 2016), for Phyllis Virginius Cosby, Virginia Department of Health, Certificate No 81-013641.

[124] "Virginia Divorce Records, 1918-2015," *Ancestry.com* (http://www.ancestry.com: accessed 13 March 2016) for Calvin W. Cosby and Phyllis U. Cosby, 25 June 1928; citing certificate 28-001101.

[125] "Mount Pisgah Methodist Church Cemetery," database, *Find A Grave* (http://www.findagrave.com: accessed 2 September 2012), entry for Calvin Watkins Cosby, 20 January 1948; citing memorial# 24869053.

[126] "Virginia, Death Records, 1912-2014," *Ancestry.com* (http://www.ancestry.com: accessed 13 March 2016), for Phyllis Virginius Cosby.

[127] 1920 US Census, Richmond (Independent City), Virginia, population schedule, Madison, Enumeration District (ED) 164, page 6A, dwelling 94, family 106, Calvin W. Cosby; *Ancestry.com* (http://www.ancestry.com: accessed 13 March 2016); citing National Archives microfilm T625, roll 1911.

[128] "Virginia Marriage Records, 1936-2014," *Ancestry.com* (http://www.ancestry.com: accessed 13 March 2016) for Fay Cosby and Charles S. Scott, 30 March 1942; citing certificate 6637.

[129] "Mount Pisgah Methodist Church," database, *Find A Grave* (http://www.findagrave.com: accessed 2 September 2012), entry for Irving Hancock Cosby, 1971; citing memorial# 24869111.

[130] "Dale Memorial Park," database, *Find A Grave* (http://www.findagrave.com: accessed 13 March 2016), for Irving H. Cosby, Jr., 20- May 1994; citing memorial #44638452.

[131] "U.S. World War II Draft Registration Cards, 1942," *Ancestry.com* (http://www.ancestry.com: accessed 1 August 2006), for Irving H Cosby Sr., National Archives and Records Administration, Roll WW2_2369902; Local board: Chesterfield, Virginia.

[132] "Mount Pisgah Methodist Church," database, *Find A Grave* (http://www.findagrave.com: accessed 20 November 2015), entry for Anna Watkins Cosby, 1928; citing memorial #24869008.

[133] "Providence United Methodist Church Cemetery," database, *Find A Grave* (http://www.findagrave.com: accessed 13 March 2016), for Thomas W. Cosby, 5 November 1986; citing memorial #23185336.

[134] "Mount Pisgah Methodist Church Cemetery," database, *Find A Grave* (http://www.findagrave.com: accessed 2 September 2012), entry for Calvin Watkins Cosby, 20 January 1948; citing memorial# 24869053.

[135] "L.C. Cosby, 90, Dies at His Home," *Richmond Times Dispatch* (Richmond, Virginia), 13 March 1941, page 12, Col. 4, Obit for Luther Calvin Cosby, *Genealogy Bank* (www.genealogybank.com: accessed 26 August 2012).

[136] "Virginia, Death Records, 1912-2014," *Ancestry.com* (http://www.ancestry.com: accessed 13 March 2016), for Richard Hamilton Cosby, Virginia Department of Health, Certificate No. 11693.

[137] 1860 US Census, Chesterfield County, Virginia, population schedule, page 24, dwelling 185, family 191, Jeff Cosby, listed as Luther, age 7.

[138] 1870 US Census, Chesterfield County, Virginia, population schedule, page 306a, dwelling 1150, family 1173, Jefferson Cosby, listed as Luther C.

[139] 1880 US Census, Chesterfield County, Virginia, population schedule, ED 74, page 228B, dwelling 11, family 12, Jefferson Cosby, listed as son.

[140] Noah H Bradley *My Wife's Family.*

[141] 1900 US Census, Chesterfield County, Virginia, population schedule, Manchester, Enumeration District (ED) 6, page 13B, dwelling 229, family 246, Richard H Cosby; *Ancestry.com* (http://www.ancestry.com: accessed 2 January 2005); citing National Archives microfilm T623, roll 1705.

[142] 1920 US Census, Chesterfield County, Virginia, population schedule, Midlothian, Enumeration District (ED) 16, page 9a, dwelling 159, family 160, Sherwin T Bass; *Ancestry.com* (http://www.ancestry.com: accessed 26 January 2005); citing National Archives microfilm T625, roll 1885.

[143] "Hollywood Cemetery," database, *Find A Grave* (http://www.findagrave.com: accessed 7 June 2015), entry for Richard H Cosby, 12 May 1926; citing memorial #92988343.

[144] "Virginia, Death Records, 1912-2014," *Ancestry.com* (http://www.ancestry.com: accessed 13 March 2016), for Charles Monroe Cosby, Virginia Department of Health, Certificate No. 25671.

[145] 1860 US Census, Chesterfield County, Virginia, population schedule, page 24, dwelling 185, family 191, Jeff Cosby, listed as R H, age 6.

[146] 1870 US Census, Chesterfield County, Virginia, population schedule, page 306a, dwelling 1150, family 1173, Jefferson Cosby, listed as Richard.

[147] 1880 US Census, Chesterfield County, Virginia, population schedule, ED 74, page 228B, dwelling 11, family 12, Jefferson Cosby, listed as son.

[148] Noah H Bradley *My Wife's Family,* page 232-240.

[149] 1900 US Census, Chesterfield County, Virginia, population schedule, Midlothian, Enumeration District (ED) 9, page 12A, dwelling 216, family 203, Charles M Cosby; *Ancestry.com* (http://www.ancestry.com: accessed 2 January 2005); citing National Archives microfilm T623, roll 1705.

[150] 1910 US Census, Chesterfield County, Virginia, population schedule, Midlothian, Enumeration District (ED) 12, page 6B, dwelling 131, family 131, Charles M Cosby; *Ancestry.com* (http://www.ancestry.com: accessed 26 January 2005); citing National Archives microfilm T624, roll 1625.

[151] 1920 US Census, Chesterfield County, Virginia, population schedule, Midlothian, Enumeration District (ED) 17, page 259B, dwelling 174, family 178, Charles M Cosby; *Ancestry.com* (http://www.ancestry.com: accessed 28 January 2005); citing National Archives microfilm T625, roll 1885.

[152] 1930 US Census, Chesterfield County, Virginia, population schedule, Midlothian, Enumeration District (ED) 21-18, page 10A, dwelling 139, family 139, Charles M Cosby; *Ancestry.com* (http://www.ancestry.com: accessed 26 January 2005); citing National Archives microfilm T626, roll 2440.

[153] "Virginia Death Records, 1912-2014," *Ancestry.com* (http://www.ancestry.com: accessed 16 July 2015), for Jefferson Judson Cosby (24 November 1957), Virginia Department of Health, Richmond, Virginia, certificate 28332.

[154] "Marriage Announced," *Richmond Times Dispatch* (Richmond, Virginia), 16 Oct 1921, page 32, col. 1, Wedding announcement for Jefferson Judson Cosby and Daisy Dell, *Genealogy Bank* (www.genealogybank.com: accessed 25 August 2012).

[155] Noah H Bradley *My Wife's Family,* page 232-240.

[156] "Sea Lawn Memorial Park," database, *Find A Grave* (http://www.findagrave.com: accessed 13 March 2016), entry for Bernard Jackson Cosby, 24 October 1985; citing memorial #26592401.

[157] "American Soldiers of World War I," *Ancestry.com* (http://www.ancestry.com: accessed 20 August 2006), for Bernard J Cosby.

[158] Noah H Bradley *My Wife's Family,* page 232-240.

[159] "Global, Find A Grave Index for Burials at Sea and other Select Burial Locations," database, *Find A Grave* (http://www.findagrave.com: accessed 13 March 2016), entry for Emmett Donald Farmer, Jr., 14 April 2010; citing memorial #76433894.

[160] "Eastern Shore Chapel Cemetery," database, *Find A Grave* (http://www.findagrave.com: accessed 13 March 2016), entry for Monroe N. Farmer, 3 December 1992; citing memorial #75561544.

[161] "Rites to Be Held for C.M. Cosby," *Richmond Times Dispatch,* 15 November 1940, page 30, col. 6, Funeral Notice for Charles Monroe Cosby, *Genealogy Bank* (www.genealogybank.com: accessed 25 August 2012).

[162] "Bethel Baptist Church," *Find A Grave* (http://www.findagrave.com: accessed 2 September 2012), entry for Maggie F Cosby, 1950; citing memorial #15054545.

[163] 1860 US Census, Chesterfield County, Virginia, population schedule, page 24, dwelling 185, family 191, Jeff Cosby, listed as Lilia, age 1.

[164] 1870 US Census, Chesterfield County, Virginia, population schedule, page 306a, dwelling 1150, family 1173, Jefferson Cosby, listed as Lillie.

[165] Noah H Bradley *My Wife's Family,* page 232-240.

[166] 1900 US Census, Pittsylvania County, Virginia, population schedule, Danville, Enumeration District (ED) 98, page 5A, dwelling 106, family 119, Joseph G Puryear; *Ancestry.com* (http://www.ancestry.com: accessed 21 April 2009); citing National Archives microfilm T623, roll 1733.

[167] 1920 US Census, Campbell County, Virginia, population schedule, Falling River, Enumeration District (ED) 74, page 16A, dwelling 165, family 77, Richard Puryear; *Ancestry.com* (http://www.ancestry.com: accessed 20 November 2015); citing National Archives microfilm T625, roll 1884.

[168] Noah H Bradley *My Wife's Family,* page 232-240.

[169] Ibid.

[170] "Virginia, Select Marriages, 1785-1940," Ancestry.com (http://www.ancestry.com: accessed 20 November 2015), for Elma W. Puryear (30 June 1908).

[171] "Virginia Divorce Records, 1918-2014," Ancestry.com (http://www.ancestry.com: accessed 20 November 2015), for Samuel Spencer Haithcock (20 April 1931).

[172] "Saint Alban's Memorial Grove," database, *Find A Grave* (http://www.findagrave.com: accessed 13 March 2016), entry for Howard Spencer Haithcock, 19 September 2002; citing memorial #144344511.

[173] 1920 US Census, Richmond (Independent City), Virginia, population schedule, Enumeration District (ED) 118, page 19B, dwelling 350, family 336, Samuel Hathcock; *Ancestry.com* (http://www.ancestry.com: accessed 13 March 2016); citing National Archives microfilm T625, roll 1911.

[174] 1900 US Census, Pittsylvania County, Virginia, population schedule, Danville, Enumeration District (ED) 98, page 5A, dwelling 106, family 119, Joseph G Puryear; *Ancestry.com* (http://www.ancestry.com: accessed 21 April 2009); citing National Archives microfilm T623, roll 1733.

[175] Noah H Bradley *My Wife's Family,* page 232-240.

[176] 1900 US Census, Pittsylvania County, Virginia, population schedule, ED 98, page 5A, dwelling 106, family 119, Joseph G Puryear.

[177] "U.S. Department of Veterans Affairs BIRLS Death File, 1850-2010," *Ancestry.com* (http://www.ancestry.com: accessed 20 November 2015), for Sumpter Puryear (5 July 1981).

[178] "Georgia Death Index," *Ancestry.com* (http://www.ancestry.com: accessed 20 November 2015), for Sumpter S. Puryear (5 July 1981).

[179] "Virginia Death Records, 1912-2014," *Ancestry.com* (http://www.ancestry.com: accessed 20 November 2015), for Joseph G. Puryear (21 June 1920), Virginia Department of Health, Richmond, Virginia.

[180] "Virginia Death Records, 1912-2014," *Ancestry.com* (http://www.ancestry.com: accessed 20 November 2015), for Mrs. Lelia Cosby Puryear (29 October 1930), Virginia Department of Health, Richmond, Virginia.

[181] 1870 US Census, Chesterfield County, Virginia, population schedule, page 306a, dwelling 1150, family 1173, Jefferson Cosby, listed as Nannie, age 7.

[182] Ibid.

[183] 1880 US Census, Chesterfield County, Virginia, population schedule, ED 74, page 228B, dwelling 11, family 12, Jefferson Cosby, listed as Nannie L.

[184] Noah H Bradley *My Wife's Family*, page 232-240.

[185] 1910 US Census, Pittsylvania County, Virginia, population schedule, Danville, Enumeration District (ED) 16, page 8A, dwelling 141, family 170, Chas E Harris; *Ancestry.com* (http://www.ancestry.com: accessed 21 April 2009); citing National Archives microfilm T624, roll 1626

[186] 1920 US Census, Pittsylvania County, Virginia, population schedule, Danville City, Enumeration District (ED) 31, page 5A, dwelling 79, family 94, Chas E Harris; *Ancestry.com* (http://www.ancestry.com: accessed 21 April 2009); citing National Archives microfilm publication T625, roll 1886.

[187] Noah H Bradley *My Wife's Family,* page 232-240.

[188] Noah H Bradley *My Wife's Family,* page 232-240.

[189] "Mountain View Cemetery," database, *Find A Grave* (http://www.findagrave.com: accessed 13 March 2016), entry for Edgar Randolph Harris, 27 January 1996; citing memorial #126213170.

[190] "Green Hill Cemetery," database, *Find A Grave* (http://www.findagrave.com: accessed 13 March 2016), entry for Georgia Winifred Harris, 15 October 1936; citing memorial #142587869.

[191] "Mountain View Cemetery," database, *Find A Grave* (http://www.findagrave.com: accessed 13 March 2016), entry for Estelle Harris Womack, 19 January 1994; citing memorial #126024241.

[192] "North Carolina Marriage Records, 1741-02011," *Ancestry.com* (http://www.ancestry.com: accessed 13 March 2016), entry for Edgar Starr Harris, Jr. and Ethel Lucy Fowlkes (8 June 1946).

[193] "U.S. Social Security Applications and Claims Index, 1936-2007," *Ancestry.com* (http://www.ancestry.com: accessed 13 March 2016), for Ethel Fowlkes Harris (September 1993).

[194] "Reports of Deaths of American Citizens Abroad, 1835-1974," Ancestry.com (http://www.ancestry.com: accessed 20 November 2015), for Randolph Cosby Harris (28 July 1957).

[195] "Forest Hill Cemetery," *Find A Grave* (http://www.findagrave.com: accessed 20 November 2015), entry for Randolph Charles Harris, Sr., 1957; citing memorial #14931343.

Cottrell-Brashear Family Linage

[196] "Reports of Deaths of American Citizens Abroad, 1835-1974," Ancestry.com (http://www.ancestry.com: accessed 20 November 2015),

[197] "Abraham Lincoln National Cemetery," database, *Find A Grave* (http://www.findagrave.com: accessed 13 March 2016), entry for Randolph C. Harris, Jr., 10 September 2011; citing memorial #77742191.

[198] "World War II and Korean Conflict Veterans Interred Overseas," *Ancestry.com* (http://www.ancestry.com: accessed 13 March 2016), entry for George P. Harris, 12 December 1944.

[199] Noah H Bradley My Wife's Family, page 232-240.

[200] "Forest Hill Cemetery," *Find A Grave* (http://www.findagrave.com: accessed 20 November 2015), entry for Nannie Lee Harris, Sr., 1934; citing memorial #142587893.

[201] "Forest Hill Cemetery," *Find A Grave* (http://www.findagrave.com: accessed 20 November 2015), entry for Charles E. Harris, 1945; citing memorial #1423587885.

[202] "Virginia Death Records, 1912-2014," *Ancestry.com* (http://www.ancestry.com: accessed 13 March 2016), for John Stuart Cosby (6 April 1940), Virginia Department of Health, Richmond, Virginia, certificate 9798.

[203] 1870 US Census, Chesterfield County, Virginia, population schedule, page 306a, dwelling 1150, family 1173, Jefferson Cosby; *Ancestry.com* (http://www.ancestry.com: accessed 21 April 2009); citing National Archives microfilm publication.

[204] 1880 US Census, Chesterfield County, Virginia, population schedule, ED 74, page 228B, dwelling 11, family 12, Jefferson Cosby; *Ancestry.com* (http://www.ancestry.com: accessed 21 April 2009); citing National Archives microfilm publication.

[205] Noah H Bradley My Wife's Family, page 232-240.

[206] 1910 US Census, Chesterfield County, Virginia, population schedule, Midlothian, Enumeration District (ED) 21-25, page 11A, dwelling 154, family 154, Janette Cosby; *Ancestry.com* (http://www.ancestry.com: accessed 16 June 2016); citing National Archives microfilm T627, roll 4255.

[207] 1920 US Census, Chesterfield County, Virginia, population schedule, Midlothian, Enumeration District (ED) 16, page 8B, dwelling 154, family 155, John S Cosby; *Ancestry.com* (Virginia. Chesterfield County: accessed 26 January 2005); citing National Archives microfilm T625, roll 1885.

[208] 1930 US Census, Chesterfield County, Virginia, population schedule, Midlothian, Enumeration District (ED) 21-16, page 8B, dwelling 161, family 163, John S Cosby; *Ancestry.com* (http://www.ancestry.com: accessed 26 January 2005); citing National Archives microfilm T626, roll 2440.

[209] 1940 US Census, Chesterfield County, Virginia, population schedule, Midlothian, Enumeration District (ED) 21-16, page 8B, dwelling 193, John S Cosby; *Ancestry.com* (http://www.ancestry.com: accessed 26 January 2005); citing National Archives microfilm T626, roll 2440.

[210] "Mount Pisgah Methodist Church," database, *Find A Grave* (http://www.findagrave.com: accessed 2 September 2012), entry for Stuart Shelby Cosby, 15 July 1981; citing memorial# 24869067

[211] "Virginia, Marriage Records, 1936-2014," *Ancestry.com* (http://www.ancestry.com: accessed 20 November 2015), Stuart Shelby Cosby and Eron M. Fore (19 November 1942).

[212] "Mount Pisgah Methodist Church," *Find A Grave* (http://www.findagrave.com: accessed 20 November 2015), entry for Eron Fore Cosby, 1999; citing memorial #24869087.

[213] "Mount Pisgah Methodist Church Cemetery," *Find A Grave* (http://www.findagrave.com: accessed 2 September 2012), entry for John Stuart Cosby, 6 April 1940; citing memorial# 24879330.

[214] "Mount Pisgah Methodist Church Cemetery," *Find A Grave* (http://www.findagrave.com: accessed 2 September 2012), entry for Jannett Jewett Cosby, 5 February 1941; citing memorial# 24879326.

Section 1 – Chapter 6 Sources – Norris L. Lashbrook Family

[1] Nellie J. (Lashbrook) Cottrell, Lashbrook Family Data, handwritten memories without sources.

[2] Ibid.

[3] Transcription of Family Data from Mrs. Catherine Foreman Lashbrook's Bible owned by Mrs. Howard Daniel, Owensboro Kentucky, published date 1875, transcribed by Thana White Cottrell sometime during the 1970s at the home of Mrs. Howard Daniel, the granddaughter of Catherine Foreman Lashbrook, Cottrell Family Papers, 867 Jamestown Drive, Rockledge, Florida.

[4] Mary K (Gritt) Lashbrook, compiler, *Lashbrooke, Lashbrooks and Lashbrook (of the United States)* (11129 Pleasant Ridge Road; Utica, Kentucky 42376: McDowell Publications, 1986).

[5] Transcription of Family Data from Mrs. Catherine Foreman Lashbrook's Bible owned by Mrs. Howard Daniel, Owensboro Kentucky, published date 1875, transcribed the 1970s at the home of Mrs. Howard Daniel, the granddaughter of Catherine Foreman Lashbrook.

[6] Quinton Lashbrook, compiler, "Our Lashbrook Family Connections," database, *RootsWeb's WorldConnect Project* (http://wc.rootsweb.ancestry.com: accessed 27 July 2008), database entries for Lashbrook family.

[7] Inter-State Publishing Co., *History of Daviess County, Kentucky* (1883; reprint Utica, KY: McDowel Publications, 1980), page 692.

[8] Michael J. Edgeworth, compiler, *Daviess County, Kentucky Order Book "D", 1837-1846* (P.O. Box 1932, Owensboro, Kentucky, 42302: West Central Kentucky Family Research Association, 1977), FHL US/CAN 976.9864 P28e.

[9] Inter-State Publishing Co., *History of Daviess County, Kentucky.*

[10] "Lashbrook Family Cemetery," database, *Find A Grave* (http://www.findagrave.com: accessed 11 October 2014), entry for Norris L Lashbrook, 6 October 1846; citing memorial #134128635.

[11] Nellie J. (Lashbrook) Cottrell, Lashbrook Family Data.

[12] Harold Bishop Morgan, compiler, *Daviess County, Kentucky Marriage Records Volume 1, 1780 through 1914* (11129 Pleasant Ridge Road, Utica, Kentucky: McDowell Publications, 2004), page 671.

[13] Mary K (Gritt) Lashbrook, compiler, *Lashbrooke, Lashbrooks and Lashbrook (of the United States)* (11129 Pleasant Ridge Road; Utica, Kentucky 42376: McDowell Publications, 1986), page 28.

[14] 1850 US Census, Daviess County, Kentucky, population schedule, District 1, page 358B, dwelling 185, family 189, George AR Wilhite; *Ancestry.com* (http://www.ancestry.com: accessed 2 February 2005); citing National Archives microfilm M432, roll 198.

[15] 1860 US Census, Daviess County, Kentucky, population schedule, Owensboro Post Office, page 128, dwelling 1001, family 1001, AR Wilhite; *Ancestry.com* (http://www.ancestry.com: accessed 2 February 2005); citing National Archives microfilm M653, roll 364.

[16] Nellie J. (Lashbrook) Cottrell, Family Lore of Uncle Sariah, handwritten notes without sources.

[17] Lists of Prisoners Register of Deaths and Morning Reports of Prisoners 1862-65, micro publication 598, volumes 328-331; Selected Records of the War Department Relating to

Confederate Prisoners of War 1861-1865; *Camp Morton, Indiana, Military* (Washington, DC: National Archives and Records Administration), roll 102.

[18] 1870 US Census, Daviess County, Kentucky, population schedule, Masonville Precinct, Post Office: Masonville, page 216A, dwelling 59, family 59, Jas B Lashbrook; *Ancestry.com* (http://www.ancestry.com: accessed 19 May 2004); citing National Archives microfilm M593, roll 458.

[19] Macedonia Baptist Church Cemetery (Daviess County, Kentucky), Catherine Wilhoyte marker, photographed by T.C. Cottrell, 27 March 2011.

[20] "Owensboro Area Obituary Index, 1842-1919," *Daviess County Public Library* (http://obits.dcplibrary.org: accessed 25 November 2015), entry for G.A.R. Wilhite, 31 January 1888.

[21] Nellie J. (Lashbrook) Cottrell, Lashbrook Family Data.

[22] 1850 US Census, Daviess County, Kentucky, population schedule, page 358B, dwelling 185, family 189, George AR Wilhite.

[23] Quinton Lashbrook, compiler, "Our Lashbrook Family Connections," database, *Roots Web's World Connect Project* (http://wc.rootsweb.ancestry.com: accessed 27 July 2008), database entries for Lashbrook family.

[24] 1860 US Census, Campbell County, Kentucky, population schedule, Post Office: California, page 170, dwelling 1173, family 1173, W.T. Dotson; *Ancestry.com* (http://www.ancestry.com: accessed 4 July 2004); citing National Archives microfilm M653, roll 360.

[25] 1870 US Census, McCracken County, Kentucky, population schedule, Division No 111 Paducah, Post Office: Paducah, page 34, dwelling 258, family 238, William Dotson; *Ancestry.com* (http://www.ancestry.com: accessed 4 July 2004); citing National Archives microfilm M593, roll 487.

[26] 1885 Kansas State Census, Harvey County, Kansas, population schedule, Newton, line 5, for M.Y. Dotson household; "Kansas State Census Collection, 1855-1925," *Ancestry.com* (http://www.ancestry.com: accessed 30 May 2009); citing National Archives microfilm KS1885_55.

[27] "Greenwood Cemetery," database, *Find A Grave* (http://www.findagrave.com: accessed 2 January 2013), entry for William A Dotson, 1879; citing memorial# 35129937.

[28] 1870 US Census, McCracken County, Kentucky, population schedule, page 34, dwelling 258, family 238, William Dotson, listed as age 13.

[29] "Greenwood Cemetery," database, *Find A Grave* (http://www.findagrave.com: accessed 2 January 2013), entry for William S Dotson, 7 March 1923; citing memorial# 100410582.

[30] 1880 US Census, Harvey County, Kansas, population schedule, The West Half of Newton, Enumeration District (ED) 2, page 445A, dwelling 39, family 41, Martha Dotson; *Ancestry.com* (Kansas. Harvey County: accessed 4 July 2004); citing National Archives microfilm T9, roll 382.

[31] 1910 US Census, Henry County, Kansas, population schedule, Newton Ward 1, Enumeration District (ED) 41, page 8B, dwelling 190, family 196, William S Dotson; *Ancestry.com* (http://www.ancestry.com: accessed 17 May 2009); citing National Archives microfilm T624, roll 441.

[32] "Greenwood Cemetery," database, *Find A Grave* (http://www.findagrave.com: accessed 2 January 2013), entry for Mary E. Dotson, 3 June 1954; citing memorial #24800344.

[33] "Mission Burial Park South," database, *Find A Grave* (http://www.findagrave.com: accessed 13 March 2016), entry for William Harrison Dotson, 5 July 1969; citing memorial #134731986.

[34] "Texas Death Certificates, 1903-1982," *Ancestry.com* (http://www.ancestry.com: accessed 13 March 2016), entry for Katheryn Dotson Murray (6 October 1975), certificate 75385.

[35] 1910 US Census, Henry County, Kansas, population schedule, Newton Ward 1, Enumeration District (ED) 41, page 8B, dwelling 190, family 196, William S Dotson.

[36] "Greenwood Cemetery," database, *Find A Grave* (http://www.findagrave.com: accessed 2 January 2013), entry for Edward T Dotson, 1887; citing memorial #35129978.

[37] 1910 US Census, Harvey County, Kansas, population schedule, Newton, Enumeration District (ED) 47, page 11B, dwelling 253, family 269, Walter L Hulick; *Ancestry.com* (http://www.ancestry.com: accessed 8 May 2013); citing National Archives microfilm publication T624, roll 441.

[38] "California Death Index 1940-1997," *Ancestry.com* (http://www.ancestry.com: accessed 20 November 2015), for Walter Lytle Hulick (31 May 1955).

[39] "California Death Index 1940-1997," *Ancestry.com*, for Walter Lytle Hulick.

[40] "Cypress View Mausoleum and Crematory," database, *Find A Grave* (http://www.findagrave.com: accessed 13 March 2016), entry for Alice Lavallee, 1984; citing memorial #122235148.

[41] 1910 US Census, Harvey County, Kansas, population schedule, Newton, Enumeration District (ED) 47, page 11B, dwelling 253, family 269, Walter L Hulick.

[42] "Cypress View Mausoleum and Crematory," database, *Find A Grave* (http://www.findagrave.com: accessed 13 March 2016), entry for Ernest O. Hulick, 1975; citing memorial #122235146.

[43] 1880 US Census, Harvey County, Kansas, population schedule, The West Half of Newton, Enumeration District (ED) 2, page 445A, dwelling 39, family 41, Martha Dotson.

[44] 1885 Kansas State Census, Harvey County, Kansas, population schedule, Newton, line 5, for M.Y. Dotson household; "Kansas State Census Collection, 1855-1925," *Ancestry.com* (http://www.ancestry.com: accessed 30 May 2009); citing National Archives microfilm KS1885_55.

[45] 1895 Kansas State Census, Harvey County, Kansas, population schedule, Newton, line 4, for Martha Y Dotson household; "Kansas State Census Collection, 1855-1925," *Ancestry.com* (http://www.ancestry.com: accessed 30 May 2009); citing National Archives microfilm V115_58.

[46] "Greenwood Cemetery," database, *Find A Grave* (http://www.findagrave.com: accessed 2 January 2013), entry for Martha Yewell Dotson, 9 February 1899; citing memorial #35130011.

[47] Nellie J. (Lashbrook) Cottrell, Lashbrook Family Data.

[48] 1850 US Census, Daviess County, Kentucky, population schedule, page 358B, dwelling 185, family 189, George AR Wilhite.

[49] Mary K (Gritt) Lashbrook, *Lashbrooke, Lashbrooks and Lashbrook*, page 52.

[50] 1860 US Census, Ohio County, Kentucky, population schedule, Caney District, Post Office: Briggs Mills, page 143, dwelling 999, family 999, Gabriel Acton; *Ancestry.com* (http://www.ancestry.com: accessed 4 July 2004); citing National Archives microfilm M653, roll 390.

[51] Ibid.

[52] 1870 US Census, Ohio County, Kentucky, population schedule, Sulphur Springs Precinct, Post Office Hartford, page 512B, dwelling 27, family 27, Gabriel Acton; *Ancestry.com* (http://www.ancestry.com: accessed 4 July 2004); citing National Archives microfilm M593, roll 492.

[53] "Kentucky Death Records, 1852-1953," *Ancestry.com* (http://www.ancestry.com: accessed 25 December 2007), for Sarah C Duke (20 July 1919), certificate 22021.

[54] Mary K (Gritt) Lashbrook, *Lashbrooke, Lashbrooks and Lashbrook*, page 52.

[55] Mary K (Gritt) Lashbrook, *Lashbrooke, Lashbrooks and Lashbrook*, page 53.

[56] "Sunnydale Cemetery," database, *Find-A-Grave* (http://www.findagrave.com: accessed 16 June 2016), entry for Fannie M. Berry Duke, 10 March 1964; citing memorial #37476222.

[57] 1900 US Census, Ohio County, Kentucky, population schedule, Hartford Magisterial District, Enumeration District (ED) 100, page 13A, dwelling 230, family 235, Robert N Duke; *Ancestry.com* (http://www.ancestry.com: accessed 24 February 2007); citing National Archives microfilm T623, roll 546.

[58] 1860 US Census, Ohio County, Kentucky, population schedule, page 143, dwelling 999, family 999, Gabriel Acton.

[59] Ibid.

[60] "Kentucky Death Records, 1852-1953," *Ancestry.com* (http://www.ancestry.com: accessed 25 December 2007), for William Lee Acton (5 July 1931), certificate 16444.

[61] W.L. Acton, *Owensboro Messenger*, Daviess County, Kentucky, 7 July 1931, page unknown. secured by T.C. Cottrell on 10 June 2009 by mail request to the Daviess County Public Library, Owensboro, Kentucky.

[62] 1930 US Census, Daviess County, Kentucky, population schedule, Owensboro, Enumeration District (ED) 30-21, page 1A, dwelling 9, family 11, William B Acton; *Ancestry.com* (http://www.ancestry.com: accessed 1 June 2009); citing National Archives microfilm T626, roll 741

[63] 1880 US Census, Daviess County, Kentucky, population schedule, Masonville, Enumeration District (ED) 173, page 395A, dwelling 64, family 64, George Wilhoyte; *Ancestry.com* (http://www.ancestry.com: accessed 4 July 2004); citing National Archives microfilm T9, roll 411

[64] Inter-State Publishing Co., *History of Daviess County*, page 692.

[65] Ohio County, *Owensboro Messenger*, Daviess County, Kentucky, 13 August 1903, page unknown. secured by T.C. Cottrell on 10 June 2009 by mail request to the Daviess County Public Library, Owensboro, Kentucky.

[66] Nellie J. (Lashbrook) Cottrell, Lashbrook Family Data.

[67] 1850 US Census, Daviess County, Kentucky, population schedule, page 358B, dwelling 185, family 189, George AR Wilhite.

[68] Mary K (Gritt) Lashbrook, *Lashbrooke, Lashbrooks and Lashbrook*, page 53.

[69] 1860 US Census, Daviess County, Kentucky, population schedule, Owensboro Post Office, page 888, dwelling 467, family 467, Jno. B. Barton; Ancestry.com (http://www.ancestry.com: accessed 20 November 2015), citing National Archives microfilm M 653, roll 364.

[70] 1870 US Census, Daviess County, Kentucky, population schedule, Masonville Precinct, Post Office: Masonville, page 1, dwelling 4, family 4, John B Burton; *Ancestry.com* (http://www.ancestry.com: accessed 4 July 2004); citing National Archives microfilm M593, roll 458.

[71] Mary K (Gritt) Lashbrook, *Lashbrooke, Lashbrooks and Lashbrook*, page 53.

[72] Ibid.

[73] Ibid.

[74] Ibid.

[75] Ibid.

[76] Ibid.

[77] Daviess County, Kentucky, Vital records, 1852-1953; indexes, 1815-1967, marriage bond for Samuel E Burton and Ella Ellis, Book 2, page 403, FHL microfilm 583177, Family History Library, Salt Lake City, Utah.

[78] "Kentucky Death Records, 1852-1953," *Ancestry.com* (http://www.ancestry.com: accessed 7 June 2009), for Ella Burton (28 May 1923), citing Kentucky Birth, Marriage and Death Records from the Kentucky Department for Libraries and Archives, Frankfort, Kentucky.

[79] 1940 US Census, Daviess County, Kentucky, population schedule, Upper Town, Enumeration District (ED) 30-42, page 12A, dwelling 69, Paul Kirk; *Ancestry.com* (http://www.ancestry.com: accessed 31 May 2016); citing National Archives microfilm publication T627, roll 1299.

[80] 1910 US Census, Daviess County, Kentucky, population schedule, Magisterial District 6, Enumeration District (ED) 47, page 12B, dwelling 263, family 272, S.E. Burton; *Ancestry.com* (http://www.ancestry.com: accessed 7 June 2009); citing National Archives microfilm T624, roll 473.

[81] "Kentucky Birth Index, 1911-1999," *Ancestry.com* (http://www.ancestry.com: accessed 31 May 2016), for Grace C. Burton, citing Kentucky Birth, Marriage and Death Records from the Kentucky Department for Libraries and Archives, Frankfort, Kentucky.

[82] "Owensboro Area Obituary Index (1842-1919: Detailed abstracts of obituaries)," database, *Kentucky Room Daviess County Public Library* (http://obits.dcplibrary.org: accessed 1 January 2010), entry for Mrs. John B. Burton, 15 April 1875; citing record 32 of 41.

[83] 1880 US Census, Daviess County, Kentucky, population schedule, Masonville Precinct, Enumeration District (ED) 173, page 391A, dwelling 4, family 4, John B Burton; *Ancestry.com* (http://www.ancestry.com: accessed 15 November 2004); citing National Archives microfilm T9, roll 411.

[84] Harold Bishop Morgan, compiler, *Daviess County, Kentucky Marriage Records Volume 1,* page 90.

[85] "Kentucky Death Records, 1852-1963," *Ancestry.com* (http://www.ancestry.com: accessed 20 November 2015), for Emma Q Burton, citing Kentucky Birth, Marriage and Death Records from the Kentucky Department for Libraries and Archives, Frankfort, Kentucky.

[86] 1900 US Census, Warren County, Kentucky, population schedule, Magisterial District #6, Enumeration District (ED) 97, page 4B, dwelling 75, family 75, Jack A Burton; *Ancestry.com* (http://www.ancestry.com: accessed 30 September 2007); citing National Archives microfilm T623, roll 518.

[87] 1910 US Census, Warren County, Kentucky, population schedule, Magisterial District #6, Enumeration District (ED) 97, page 11B, dwelling 243, family 250, J.B. Burton; *Ancestry.com* (http://www.ancestry.com: accessed 30 September 2007); citing National Archives microfilm T624, roll 473.

[88] John B Burton, *Owensboro Messenger*, Daviess County, Kentucky, 3 October 1911, page 6.

[89] West-Central Kentucky Family Research Association *Daviess County, Kentucky Cemeteries*, Volume 2 (P.O. Box 1465, Owensboro, Kentucky: West-Central Kentucky Family Research Association, 1977).

[90] John B Burton, *Owensboro Messenger*, page 6.

[91] "World War I Draft Registration Cards, 1917-1918," *Ancestry.com* (http://www.ancestry.com: accessed 6 June 2009), for Ludwell Hunter Burton, citing United States, Selective Service System. World War I Selective Service System Draft Registration Cards, 1917-1918. Washington, D.C.: National Archives and Records Administration. Microfilm publication M1509, Daviess County, Kentucky; Roll: 1653352; Draft Board: 0.

Cottrell-Brashear Family Linage

[92] *Owensboro Messenger*, 3 October 1911, page 6.

[93] 1920 US Census, Daviess County, Kentucky, population schedule, Whitesville, Enumeration District (ED) 53, page 7B, dwelling 156, family 156, Hunter L Burton; *Ancestry.com* (http://www.ancestry.com: accessed 6 June 2009); citing National Archives microfilm T625, roll 567.

[94] "Kentucky Death Records, 1852-1963," *Ancestry.com,* for Emma Q Burton.

[95] Nellie J. (Lashbrook) Cottrell, Lashbrook Family Data.

[96] 1850 US Census, Daviess County, Kentucky, population schedule, page 358B, dwelling 185, family 189, George A.R. Wilhite.

[97] 1860 US Census, Daviess County, Kentucky, population schedule, page 128, dwelling 1001, family 1001, A.R. Wilhite.

[98] Inter-State Publishing Co., *History of Daviess County*, page 692.

[99] Daviess County, Kentucky, Vital records, 1852-1953; indexes, 1815-1967, marriage bond for William Lashbrook and Lucy Bean, Book J, page 137, FHL microfilm 582235, Family History Library, Salt Lake City, Utah.

[100] Inter-State Publishing Co., *History of Daviess County*, page 692.

[101] 1870 US Census, Daviess County, Kentucky, population schedule, Masonville, Post Office Masonville, page 216B, dwelling 62, family 62, William M Lashbrook; *Ancestry.com* (http://www.ancestry.com: accessed 19 May 2004); citing National Archives microfilm M593, roll 458.

[102] 1880 US Census, Daviess County, Kentucky, population schedule, Masonville Precinct, Enumeration District (ED) 173, page 393B, dwelling 42, family 44, William M Lashbrook; *Ancestry.com* (http://www.ancestry.com: accessed 18 May 2004); citing National Archives microfilm T9, roll 411.

[103] 1880 US Census, Daviess County, Kentucky, agricultural schedule, page 4, William M Lashbrook; NARA microfilm publication M1528, roll 20.

[104] 1900 US Census, Daviess County, Kentucky, population schedule, Magisterial District No. 6, Enumeration District (ED) 35, page 1B, dwelling 17, family 17, William M Lashbrook; *Ancestry.com* (http://www.ancestry.com: accessed 18 May 2004); citing National Archives microfilm T623, roll 518.

[105] 1910 US Census, Daviess County, Kentucky, population schedule, Magisterial District 6, Enumeration District (ED) 47, page 11b, dwelling 236, family 243, W M Lashbrook; *Ancestry.com* (http://www.ancestry.com: accessed 30 January 2005); citing National Archives microfilm T624, roll 473.

[106] Daviess County, Kentucky, Wills, 1812-1936, Vols. E-H 1896-1936 - v. G, will of William Martin Lashbrook, FHL microfilm 1913778, p154, Family History Library, Salt Lake City, Utah.

[107] 1920 US Census, Daviess County, Kentucky, population schedule, Magisterial District #6, Enumeration District (ED) 53, page 6A, dwelling 124, family 124, William M Lashbrook; *Ancestry.com* (http://www.ancestry.com: accessed 18 May 2004); citing National Archives microfilm T625, roll 567.

[108] "Kentucky Death Records, 1852-1953," *Ancestry.com* (http://www.ancestry.com: accessed 20 November 2007), for Norris Lashbrook (26 November 1935), certificate 26706.

[109] Daviess County, Kentucky, Vital records, 1852-1953; indexes, 1815-1967, marriage bond for Norris Lashbrook and Leorna Williams, Book 1, page 399 FHL microfilm 583177, Family History Library, Salt Lake City, Utah.

[110] Death Comes to Rev. Lashbrook, *Owensboro Messenger*, Daviess County, Kentucky, 27 November 1935.

[111] "Kentucky Death Records, 1852-1953," *Ancestry.com* (http://www.ancestry.com: accessed 27 January 2008), for Emma Lorena Lashbrook (12 August 1943), certificate 19698.

[112] Lawrence C Lashbrook Dead, *Owensboro Messenger-Inquirer*, Owensboro, Kentucky, 9 July 1989. Hereinafter cited as Owensboro Messenger-Inquirer.

[113] "Rosehill Elmwood Cemetery," database, *Find A Grave* (http://www.findagrave.com: accessed 8 March 2011), entry for George W Lashbrook, 1956; citing memorial# 61575463.

[114] Quinton Lashbrook, "Our Lashbrook Family Connections", database entries for Lashbrook family.

[115] 1920 US Census, Daviess County, Kentucky, population schedule, Owensboro, Enumeration District (ED) 34, page 3a, dwelling 53, family 56, George Lashbrook; *Ancestry.com* (http://www.ancestry.com: accessed 24 February 2007); citing National Archives microfilm T625, roll 625.

[116] 1930 US Census, Daviess County, Kentucky, population schedule, Owensboro City, Enumeration District (ED) 30-25, page 3b, dwelling 60, family 67, George Lashbrook; *Ancestry.com* (http://www.ancestry.com: accessed 24 February 2007); citing National Archives microfilm T626, roll 741.

[117] Mary K (Gritt) Lashbrook, *Lashbrooke, Lashbrooks and Lashbrook*, page 103.

[118] 1920 US Census, Daviess County, Kentucky, population schedule, ED 34, page 3a, dwelling 53, family 56, George Lashbrook.

[119] "Kentucky Death Index, 1911-2000," *Ancestry.com* (http://www.ancestry.com: accessed 29 August 2004), for Thomas J Lashbrook (13 August 1965), volume 35, certificate 17355.

[120] Mary K (Gritt) Lashbrook, *Lashbrooke, Lashbrooks and Lashbrook*, page 103.

[121] Mary K (Gritt) Lashbrook, *Lashbrooke, Lashbrooks and Lashbrook*, page 103.

[122] "Rosehill Elmwood Cemetery," database, *Find A Grave* (http://www.findagrave.com: accessed 13 March 2016), entry for Harry Eugene Lashbrook, Sr., 14 February 1972; citing memorial #55558251.

[123] "Rosehill Elmwood Cemetery," database, *Find A Grave* (http://www.findagrave.com: accessed 13 March 2016), entry for Walter H. Lashbrook, Sr., 17 January 1919; citing memorial #66668282.

[124] Social Security Administration, "Social Security Death Index," *Ancestry.com* (http://www.ancestry.com: accessed on 13 March 2016), entry for Robert Lashbrook, 1984, SS no. 310-01-5384.

[125] "Rosehill Elmwood Cemetery," database, *Find A Grave* (http://www.findagrave.com: accessed 13 March 2016), entry for Frank Ford Lashbrook, 15 November 1969; citing memorial #66879780.

[126] "Rosehill Elmwood Cemetery," database, *Find A Grave* (http://www.findagrave.com: accessed 8 March 2011), entry for George W Lashbrook, 1956; citing memorial # 61575463.

[127] "Rosehill Elmwood Cemetery," database, *Find A Grave* (http://www.findagrave.com: accessed 8 March 2011), entry for Henry Lashbrook, 1955; citing memorial # 61585305.

[128] Mary K (Gritt) Lashbrook, *Lashbrooke, Lashbrooks and Lashbrook*, page 103.

[129] "Kentucky Death Records, 1852-1953," *Ancestry.com* (http://www.ancestry.com: accessed 28 January 2008), for Carrie Elnora Lashbrook (22 October 1950), certificate 5019347.

[130] "Rosehill Elmwood Cemetery," database, *Find A Grave* (http://www.findagrave.com: accessed 13 March 2016), entry for Leadrew Bruner Lashbrook, 11 March 1937; citing memorial #636090840.

[131] Mary K (Gritt) Lashbrook, *Lashbrooke, Lashbrooks and Lashbrook*, page 104.

[132] Social Security Administration, "Social Security Death Index," *Ancestry.com* (http://www.ancestry.com: accessed on 13 March 2016), entry for Martin Lashbrook, 1968, SS no. 404-03-4333.

[133] "Chapel Hill Memorial Gardens Cemetery," database, *Find A Grave* (http://www.findagrave.com: accessed 13 March 2016), entry for Roy Bean Lashbrook, 1994; citing memorial #86348996.

[134] "Rosehill Elmwood Cemetery," database, *Find A Grave* (http://www.ancestry.com: accessed 13 March 2016), entry for Ernest Gardner Lashbrook, 24 August 2000; citing memorial #105394681.

[135] Yeiser Lashbrook, *Messenger Inquirer*, Daviess County, Kentucky, 19 December 1967, page 10A, column 1 and 2.

[136] Timothy D Cox, compiler, *Ohio County Marriage Index Volume 2, 1906-1993* (Publisher Address Unknown: Publisher Unknown, 1996), FHL US/CAN 976.9835 V2ct V.2.

[137] Elmwood Cemetery Office, *Elmwood & Rose Hill Cemetery Burials: G-M (circa 1914-1999)* (2020 Frederica Street, Owensboro, Kentucky: Daviess County Public Library).

[138] "U.S. Veterans Cemeteries, ca.1800-2006," *Ancestry.com* (http://www.ancestry.com: accessed 16 November 2006), for Lodford Freeman Lashbrook (31 October 2000), volume 44, certificate 21949.

[139] Social Security Administration, "Social Security Death Index," *Ancestry.com* (http://www.ancestry.com: accessed 6 September 2009), entry for Austin Lashbrook, 1919, SS no. 269-14-1916.

[140] Perry T Ryan, *The Last Public Execution in America* (www.geocities.com/Lastpublichang: downloaded 7 September 2004), originally published 1992).

[141] Mary K (Gritt) Lashbrook, *Lashbrooke, Lashbrooks and Lashbrook*, page 53.
[142] Ibid.
[143] Mary K (Gritt) Lashbrook, *Lashbrooke, Lashbrooks and Lashbrook*, page 105.

[144] Daviess County, Kentucky, Vital records, 1852-1953; indexes, 1815-1967, marriage bond for Walter Burton and Katie B Lashbrook, Book 19, page 132, FHL microfilm 1759326, Family History Library, Salt Lake City, Utah.
[145] Ibid.
[146] Mary K (Gritt) Lashbrook, *Lashbrooke, Lashbrooks and Lashbrook*, page 105.
[147] Mary K (Gritt) Lashbrook, *Lashbrooke, Lashbrooks and Lashbrook*, page 54.
[148] Ibid.

[149] "Rosehill Elmwood Cemetery," database, *Find A Grave* (http://www.findagrave.com: accessed 8 March 2011), entry for William Martin Lashbrook, 1920; citing memorial # 61585754.

[150] Daviess County, Kentucky, Wills, 1812-1936, Vols. E-H 1896-1936 - v. G, will of William Martin Lashbrook, FHL microfilm 1913778, vG, p154, Family History Library, Salt Lake City, Utah.

[151] 1930 US Census, Daviess County, Kentucky, population schedule, magisterial district six, Enumeration District (ED) 30-44, page 12B, dwelling 258, family 258, Lucy Lashbrook; *Ancestry.com* (Kentucky. Daviess County: accessed 19 May 2004); citing National Archives microfilm T626, roll 742.

[152]"Rosehill Elmwood Cemetery," database, *Find A Grave* (http://www.findagrave.com: accessed 8 March 2011), entry for Lucy J Bean Lashbrook, 1940; citing memorial# 61585771.

[153] Nellie J. (Lashbrook) Cottrell, Lashbrook Family Data.

[154] 1850 US Census, Daviess County, Kentucky, population schedule, page 358B, dwelling 185, family 189, George AR Wilhite.

[155] 1860 US Census, Daviess County, Kentucky, population schedule, page 128, dwelling 1001, family 1001, AR Wilhite.

[156] "Compiled Service Records of Confederate Soldiers Who Served in Organizations from the State of Kentucky," *Footnote.com* (http://www.footnote.com: accessed 15 October 2008), for S.D. Lashbrook, National Archives and Records Administration, Microfilm M319, First (Butler's) Calvary.

[157] Ibid.

[158] Ibid.

[159] Prison Ledgers of Prisoners' Accounts and Cash Books 1864-65, micro publication 498, volumes 332-334; Selected Records of the War Department Relating to Confederate Prisoners of War 1861-1865; *Camp Morton, Indiana, Military* (Washington, DC: National Archives and Records Administration), roll 103.

[160] Nellie J. (Lashbrook) Cottrell, Family Lore of Uncle Sariah.

[161] Lists of Prisoners Register of Deaths and Morning Reports of Prisoners 1862-65, micro publication 598, volumes 328-331; Selected Records of the War Department Relating to Confederate Prisoners of War 1861-1865; *Camp Morton, Indiana, Military* (Washington, DC: National Archives and Records Administration), roll 102.

[162] Nellie J. (Lashbrook) Cottrell, Family Lore of Uncle Sariah.

[163] Macedonia Baptist Church Cemetery (Daviess County, Kentucky), Seariah D Lashbrook marker, photographed by T.C. Cottrell, 27 March 2011.

[164] Nellie J. (Lashbrook) Cottrell, Lashbrook Family Data.

[165] Ibid.

[166] "Lashbrook Family Cemetery," database, *Find A Grave* (http://www.findagrave.com: accessed 11 October 2014), entry for Mildred Rebecca Lashbrook, 19 May 1846; citing memorial # 134128757.

Section 1 – Chapter 7 Sources – James B. Lashbrook Family

[1] Transcription of Family Data from Bible Concordance owned by Mrs. Howard Daniel, Owensboro Kentucky, undated, transcription by Nellie J. Cottrell.

[2] 1850 US Census, Daviess County, Kentucky, population schedule, District 1, page 358B, dwelling 185, family 189, George AR Wilhite; *Ancestry.com* (http://www.ancestry.com: accessed 2 February 2005); citing National Archives microfilm M432, roll 198.

[3] 1860 US Census, Daviess County, Kentucky, population schedule, Owensboro Post Office, page 128, dwelling 1001, family 1001, AR Wilhite; *Ancestry.com* (http://www.ancestry.com: accessed 2 February 2005); citing National Archives microfilm M653, roll 364.

[4] 1870 US Census, Daviess County, Kentucky, population schedule, Masonville Precinct, Post Office: Masonville, page 216A, dwelling 59, family 59, Jas B Lashbrook; *Ancestry.com* (http://www.ancestry.com: accessed 19 May 2004); citing National Archives microfilm M593, roll 458.

[5] James B Lashbrook Journal, late 1800s, Cottrell Family Papers.

[6] Ibid.

[7] Ibid.

Cottrell-Brashear Family Linage

[8] Daviess County, Kentucky, Vital records, 1852-1953; indexes, 1815-1967, marriage bond for J.B. Lashbrook and S.M. Taylor, Book O, page 651, FHL microfilm 582238, Family History Library, Salt Lake City, Utah.

[9] 1860 US Census, Daviess County, Kentucky, population schedule, District No. 1, Post Office Owensboro, page 789, dwelling 998, family 798, J M Taylor; *Ancestry.com* (http://www.ancestry.com: accessed 2 May 2004); citing National Archives microfilm M653, roll 364.

[10] 1870 US Census, Daviess County, Kentucky, population schedule, Masonville Precinct, Post Office: Masonville, page 215B, dwelling 54, family 54, Jefferson M Taylor; *Ancestry.com* (http://www.ancestry.com: accessed 1 May 2004); citing National Archives microfilm M593, roll 458.

[11] James B Lashbrook Journal, late 1800s, Cottrell Family Papers.

[12] 1880 US Census, Daviess County, Kentucky, population schedule, Masonville Precinct, Enumeration District (ED) 173, page 396C, dwelling 87, family 92, James Lashbrook; *Ancestry.com* (http://www.ancestry.com: accessed 25 April 2004); citing National Archives microfilm T9, roll 411.

[13] James B Lashbrook Journal, late 1800s, Cottrell Family Papers.

[14] 1900 US Census, Daviess County, Kentucky, population schedule, Magisterial District No. 8, Enumeration District (ED) 39, page 2A, dwelling 26, family 26, James B Lashbrook; *Ancestry.com* (http://www.ancestry.com: accessed 11 March 2003); citing National Archives microfilm T623, roll 518.

[15] Nellie J. (Lashbrook) Cottrell, Lashbrook Family Data.

[16] Mr. J.B. Lashbrook Dead, *Owensboro Messenger*, Daviess County, Kentucky, 8 November 1904, page 1.

[17] Elmwood Cemetery Marker Transcriptions and Lashbrook Family Area Drawing; Cottrell Family Papers.

[18] 1910 US Census, Daviess County, Kentucky, population schedule, Magisterial District 5, Enumeration District (ED) 52, page 6B, dwelling 123, family 124, Sarah M Lashbrook; *Ancestry.com* (http://www.ancestry.com: accessed 10 March 2003); citing National Archives microfilm T624, roll 473.

[19] 1920 US Census, Daviess County, Kentucky, population schedule, Upper Town, Enumeration District (ED) 58, page 7B, dwelling 138, family 148, Sarah M Lashbrook; *Ancestry.com* (http://www.ancestry.com: accessed 13 March 2003); citing National Archives microfilm T625, roll 567.

[20] 1930 US Census, Daviess County, Kentucky, population schedule, Precinct 15, Owensboro, Enumeration District (ED) 30-15, page 3A, dwelling 49, family 31, Sarah Lashbrook; *Ancestry.com* (http://www.ancestry.com: accessed 9 March 2003); citing National Archives microfilm T626, roll 741.

[21] Sarah M. Lashbrook, Death Registration 040814 (1935), Department of Health Bureau of Vital Statistics, Frankfort, Kentucky. Hereinafter cited as death certificate no. 040814.

[22] Nellie J. (Lashbrook) Cottrell, Lashbrook Family Data.

[23] 1880 US Census, Daviess County, Kentucky, population schedule, ED 173, page 396C, dwelling 87, family 92, James Lashbrook, listed as age 36.

[24] 1910 US Census, Daviess County, Kentucky, population schedule, ED 52, page 6B, dwelling 123, family 124, Sarah M Lashbrook.

[25] Transcription from Mrs. Catherine Foreman Lashbrook's Bible.

[26] "Kentucky Death Records, 1852-1953," *Ancestry.com* (http://www.ancestry.com: accessed 26 November 2007), for Hellen Hall Lashbrook (20 April 1934), certificate 10526.

[27] "World War I Draft Registration Cards, 1917-1918," *Ancestry.com* (http://www.ancestry.com: accessed 1 July 2006), for Jefferson Taylor Lashbrook, citing United States, Selective Service System. World War I Selective Service System Draft Registration Cards, 1917-1918. Washington, D.C.: National Archives and Records Administration. Microfilm M1509, Daviess County, Kentucky; Roll 1653352; Draft Board: 0.

[28] 1920 US Census, Daviess County, Kentucky, population schedule, Owensboro, Enumeration District (ED) 29, page 5A, dwelling 72, family 97, Jefferson T Lashbrook; *Ancestry.com* (http://www.ancestry.com: accessed 17 May 2004); citing National Archives microfilm T625, roll 567.

[29] J. Taylor Lashbrook, *Owensboro Messenger*, Daviess County, Kentucky, 25 October 1955, page unknown. secured by T.C. Cottrell on 10 June 2009 by mail request to the Daviess County Public Library, Owensboro, Kentucky.

[30] 1930 US Census, Todd County, Kentucky, population schedule, Eklton City, Enumeration District (ED) 110-7, page 3A, dwelling 64, family 74, Taylor Lashbrook; *Ancestry.com* (Kentucky. Todd County: accessed 20 November 2004); citing National Archives microfilm T626, roll 778.

[31] "Kentucky Death Records, 1852-1953," *Ancestry.com* (http://www.ancestry.com: accessed 26 November 2007), for Hellen Hall Lashbrook (20 April 1934), certificate 10526.

[32] 1940 US Census, Todd County, Kentucky, population schedule, Elkton, Enumeration District (ED) 110-6, page 62B, dwelling 334, J T Lashbrook; *Ancestry.com* (http://www.ancestry.com: accessed 28 July 2012); citing National Archives microfilm T6267, roll 1358.

[33] Lenda Anderson, "James Taylor Lashbrook," e-mail (privately held by author) to T.C. Cottrell; email (privately held by author), 27 October 2009.

[34] "Kentucky Death Records, 1852-1953," *Ancestry.com* (http://www.ancestry.com: accessed 20 November 2007), for Jefferson Taylor Lashbrook (24 October 1944), certificate 21949.

[35] Nellie J. (Lashbrook) Cottrell, Lashbrook Family Data.

[36] Ibid.

[37] 1900 US Census, Daviess County, Kentucky, population schedule, ED 39, page 2A, dwelling 26, family 26, James B Lashbrook.

[38] 1910 US Census, Crittenden County, Arkansas, population schedule, Tyronza Township, Enumeration District (ED) 40, page 10A, dwelling 225, family 225, Foreman Lashbrook; *Ancestry.com* (http://www.ancestry.com: accessed 17 September 2005); citing National Archives microfilm T624, roll 48.

[39] Daviess County, Kentucky, Vital records, 1852-1953; indexes, 1815-1967, marriage bond for F.K. Lashbrook and Jessie Small, Book 19, page 596, FHL microfilm 1759326, Family History Library, Salt Lake City, Utah.

[40] "Kentucky Death Records, 1852-1953," *Ancestry.com* (http://www.ancestry.com: accessed 20 November 2007), for Claire L Lashbrook (9 July 1920).

[41] 1920 US Census, Shelby County, Tennessee, population schedule, Memphis City, Enumeration District (ED) 218, page 7B, dwelling 132, family 155, Foreman K Lashbrook; *Ancestry.com* (http://www.ancestry.com: accessed 6 March 2003); citing National Archives microfilm T625, roll 1765.

[42] 1930 US Census, Shelby County, Tennessee, population schedule, Memphis City, Enumeration District (ED) 9, page 20A, family 1, Foreman K. Lashbrook; digital images, *Ancestry.com* (http://www.ancestry.com: accessed 8 March 2003); citing National Archives microfilm T626, roll 2278.

[43] "U.S. City Directories, 1822-1995," *Ancestry.com* (http://www.ancestry.com: accessed 1 June 2016), entry for Forman K. Lashbrook, Memphis, Tennessee, City Directory, 1933.

[44] "U.S. City Directories, 1822-1995," *Ancestry.com* (http://www.ancestry.com: accessed 1 June 2016), entry for Forman K. Lashbrook, Memphis, Tennessee, City Directory, 1954.

[45] 1940 US Census, Shelby County, Tennessee, population schedule, Memphis City, Enumeration District (ED) 19-24, page 13B, dwelling 276, F. K. Lashbrook; *Ancestry.com* (http://www.ancestry.com: accessed 28 July 2012); citing National Archives microfilm T6267, roll 2967.

[46] Wayne, "Obituary for Frances Lashbrook Felix," *Desoto County Obits - 5.16.6*, discussion list, 16 May 2006 (http://genforum.genealogy.com: accessed 9 June 2013).

[47] Note from Frances L. Felix (Lashbrook) (8841 Cypress Cove, Southaven, Mississippi 38671) to TC Cottrell, Dec 1998

[48] "U.S. Department of Veterans Affairs BIRLS Death File, 1850-2010," *Ancestry.com* (http://www.ancestry.com: accessed 11 January 2014), entry for Robert Felix, 14 May 1923; citing Beneficiary Identification Records Locator Subsystem (BIRLS) Death File. Washington, D.C.: U.S. Department of Veterans Affairs.

[49] "Robert Edward Felix: Newspaper Obituary and Death Notice," *The Commercial Appeal* (Memphis, Tennessee), 6 September 1993, page A10, Obituary, *Genealogy Bank* (www.genealogybank.com: accessed 5 January 2014).

[50] "Kentucky Death Records, 1852-1953," *Ancestry.com* (http://www.ancestry.com: accessed 20 November 2007), for Claire L Lashbrook (9 July 1920).

[51] Transcription from Mrs. Catherine Foreman Lashbrook's Bible.

[52] 1930 US Census, Shelby County, Tennessee, population schedule, ED 9, page 20A, family 1, Foreman K Lashbrook.

[53] "U.S. World War II Army Enlistment Records, 1938-1946," *Ancestry.com* (http://www.ancestry.com: accessed 20 September 2009), for James S Lashbrook, National Archives and Records Administration, Record Group 64.

[54] "Forest Hill Cemetery Midtown," database, *Find A Grave* (http://www.findagrave.com: accessed 15 December 2015), entry for Margaret Rice Lashbrook, 5 July 1985; citing memorial #153940629.

[55] Foreman K Lashbrook, *Messenger Inquirer*, Daviess County, Kentucky, 2 March 1969, page 8D, column 4

[56] Social Security Administration, "Social Security Death Index," database, *Ancestry.com* (http://www.ancestry.com: accessed 23 November 2007), entry for Jessie S. Lashbrook, 1988, SS no. 410-12-5103.

[57] "Forest Hill Cemetery Midtown," database, *Find A Grave* (http://www.findagrave.com: accessed 9 December 2015), entry for Jessie Small Lashbrook, 18 May 1988; citing memorial #153940603.

[58] Nellie J. (Lashbrook) Cottrell, Lashbrook Family Data.

[59] Nellie J. (Lashbrook) Cottrell, Memories of Childhood

[60] Transcription from Mrs. Catherine Foreman Lashbrook's Bible.

[61] Nellie J. (Lashbrook) Cottrell, Lashbrook Family Data.

[62] Ibid.

[63] 1900 US Census, Daviess County, Kentucky, population schedule, ED 39, page 2A, dwelling 26, family 26, James B Lashbrook.

[64] J.D. Lashbrook, Civic Leader, Dies Here, *The News-Democrat*, Russellville, Kentucky, front page.

[65] 1910 US Census, Daviess County, Kentucky, population schedule, ED 52, page 6B, dwelling 123, family 124, Sarah M Lashbrook.

[66] "World War I Draft Registration Cards", for James Dudley Lashbrook, citing United States, Selective Service System. World War I Selective Service System Draft Registration Cards, 1917-1918. Washington, D.C.: National Archives and Records Administration. Microfilm M1509, Daviess County, Kentucky; Roll 1653352; Draft Board: 0.

[67] *The News-Democrat Obituary for J.D. Lashbrook*, front page.

[68] 1920 US Census, Logan County, Kentucky, population schedule, Russellville, Enumeration District (ED) 57, page 14A, dwelling 314, family 361, James D Lashbrook; *Ancestry.com* (http://www.ancestry.com: accessed 5 March 2003); citing National Archives microfilm T625, roll 588.

[69] Logan County Genealogical Society, *Logan County Kentucky Funeral Home Records* (Russellville, Kentucky: Logan County Genealogical Society, 1996), FHL US/CAN 976.976 V38.

[70] 1930 US Census, Logan County, Kentucky, population schedule, Russellville, Enumeration District (ED) 71-3, page 6B, dwelling 104, family 114, James D Lashbrook; *Ancestry.com* (http://www.ancestry.com: accessed 8 March 2003); citing National Archives microfilm T626, roll 767

[71] Family data, Nellie Lashbrook Cottrell, *The Holy Bible*, Self-Pronouncing Edition (Akron, Ohio: The Saalfield Publishing Co., unknown publish date).

[72] *The News-Democrat Obituary for J.D. Lashbrook*, front page.

[73] Services held today for Mrs. J.D. Lashbrook, *The News-Democrat*, 24 September 1973.

[74] 1940 US Census, Logan County, Kentucky, population schedule, Russellville, Enumeration District (ED) 70-3, page 8B, dwelling 298, J D Lashbrook; *Ancestry.com* (http://www.ancestry.com: accessed 28 July 2012); citing National Archives microfilm T6267, roll 1333

[75] "World War II Draft Registration Cards, 1942," *Ancestry.com* (http://www.ancestry.com: accessed 1 June 2016), for James Dudley Lashbrook, citing National Archives and Records Administration. Record Group Number: 147.

[76] *The News-Democrat Obituary for J.D. Lashbrook*, front page.

[77] James Dudley Lashbrook, Death Registration 19198 (15 September 1949), Department of Health Bureau of Vital Statistics, Frankfort, Kentucky.

[78] Unfinished Purposes, *The News-Democrat*, Russellville, Kentucky, page 2.

[79] *The News-Democrat Obituary for J.D. Lashbrook*, front page.

[80] "Kentucky Death Index, 1911-2000," *Ancestry.com* (http://www.ancestry.com: accessed 1 March 2005), for Sophie H Lashbrook (22 September 1973), volume 54, certificate 26535.

[81] Transcription from Mrs. Catherine Foreman Lashbrook's Bible.

[82] 1900 US Census, Daviess County, Kentucky, population schedule, ED 39, page 2A, dwelling 26, family 26, James B Lashbrook.

[83] Harold Bishop Morgan, compiler, *Daviess County, Kentucky Marriage Records Volume 2, 1915 through 1950* (11129 Pleasant Ridge Road, Utica, Kentucky: McDowell Publications, 2004).

[84] "Rosehill Elmwood Cemetery," database, *Find A Grave* (http://www.findagrave.com: accessed 1 June 2016), entry for Stonewall Jackson Daniel, 30 July 1941; citing memorial #135025402.

[85] "Rosehill Elmwood Cemetery," database, *Find A Grave* (http://www.findagrave.com: accessed 1 June 2016), entry for Gertrude Howard Daniel, 9 May 1954; citing memorial #135025446.

[86] Transcription from Mrs. Catherine Foreman Lashbrook's Bible.

[87] 1930 US Census, Daviess County, Kentucky, population schedule, Magisterial District 77-8, Enumeration District (ED) 30-49, page 13A, dwelling 268, family 274, Howard W Daniels; *Ancestry.com* (http://www.ancestry.com: accessed 9 March 2003); citing National Archives microfilm T626, roll 742.

[88] 1940 US Census, Daviess County, Kentucky, population schedule, Enumeration District (ED) 20-418, page 8A, dwelling 165, Howard W Daniel; *Ancestry.com* (http://www.ancestry.com: accessed 28 July 2012); citing National Archives microfilm T6267, roll 1299.

[89] Lenda Anderson, "James Taylor Lashbrook," e-mail, 27 October 2009.

[90] "Owensboro Memorial Gardens," database, *Find A Grave* (http://www.findagrave.com: accessed 8 March 2011), entry for Lenore Daniel Smeathers, 31 January 2011; citing memorial# 65049113.

[91] Daniel-Smeathers Wedding Takes Place, *Unidentified Owensboro Newspaper*, Owensboro, Kentucky, page 6.

[92] Untitled Obituary on Marvin J Smeathers, *Messenger Inquirer*, Owensboro. Kentucky, 20 November 1990. secured from Owensboro Messenger Inquirer web site on 16 August 2004 by TC Cottrell. Hereinafter cited as Messenger Inquirer Obituary for Marvin J Smeathers.

[93] Ibid.

[94] Transcription from Mrs. Catherine Foreman Lashbrook's Bible.

[95] Howard W Daniels Funeral Card, originally owned by Nellie Lashbrook Cottrell. At her death this card passed to her daughter-in-law, Zalame Brashear Cottrell. Upon the death of Zalame Cottrell this card passed to her son Taylor C Cottrell.

[96] Untitled Obituary on Louise Lashbrook Daniel, *Messenger Inquirer*, Owensboro. Kentucky, 23 September 1993. secured from Owensboro Messenger Inquirer web site on 16 August 2004 by TC Cottrell.

[97] Ibid.

Section 1 – Chapter 8 Sources – Jefferson Mandred Taylor Family

[1] Transcription of Family Data from Louisa Taylor's Bible owned by Nellie Lashbrook Cottrell, Bowling Green Kentucky, published 1849.

[2] Nellie J. (Lashbrook) Cottrell, Memories of Early Childhood, handwritten memories without sources.

[3] 1830 US Census, Jefferson County, Kentucky, population schedule, Louisville, page 101, John Taylor; *Ancestry.com* (http://www.ancestry.com: accessed 17 Oct 2013); citing Cottrell Family Papers microfilm publication M19, roll 38.

[4] 1840 US Census, Jefferson County, Kentucky, population schedule, page 151, dwelling 258, Mary M Taylor; *Ancestry.com* (http://www.ancestry.com: accessed 12 September 2013); citing National Archives microfilm M704, roll 115.

[5] Ibid.

[6] Nellie J. (Lashbrook) Cottrell, Childhood and Youth, handwritten memories without sources.

[7] Jefferson County, Kentucky, Marriage Records, 1781-1951, marriage bond and marriage record for Jefferson M Tailor and Louisa Jane Kerlin, FHL microfilm 819589, Family History Library, Salt Lake City, Utah.

[8] Nellie J. (Lashbrook) Cottrell, Childhood and Youth.

[9] 1850 US Census, Nelson County, Kentucky, population schedule, District 1, page 310A, dwelling 495, family 405, Jefferson Taylor; *Ancestry.com* (http://www.ancestry.com: accessed 17 September 2005); citing National Archives microfilm M432, roll 215.

[10] 1860 US Census, Daviess County, Kentucky, population schedule, District No. 1, Post Office Owensboro, page 789, dwelling 998, family 798, J M Taylor; *Ancestry.com* (http://www.ancestry.com: accessed 2 May 2004); citing National Archives microfilm publication M653, roll 364.

[11] Nellie J. (Lashbrook) Cottrell, Childhood and Youth.

[12] Ibid.

[13] 1870 US Census, Daviess County, Kentucky, population schedule, Masonville Precinct, Post Office: Masonville, page 215B, dwelling 54, family 54, Jefferson M Taylor; *Ancestry.com* (http://www.ancestry.com: accessed 1 May 2004); citing National Archives microfilm M593, roll 458.

[14] 1880 US Census, Daviess County, Kentucky, population schedule, Masonville Precinct, Enumeration District (ED) 173, page 395A, dwelling 64, family 67, Jefferson Taylor; *Ancestry.com* (http://www.ancestry.com: accessed 3 May 2004); citing National Archives microfilm T9, roll 411.

[15] Transcription of Family Data from Louisa Taylor's Bible.

[16] West-Central Kentucky Family Research Association, compiler, *Daviess County, Kentucky Cemeteries Volume 1* (Hartford, Kentucky: McDowell Publications, 1977).

[17] Rest On, Gallant Warriors, *Owensboro Messenger Inquirer*, Owensboro Kentucky, 16 September 1996.

[18] 1900 US Census, Daviess County, Kentucky, population schedule, Magisterial District 8, Enumeration District (ED) 39, page 2A, dwelling 25, family 25, Louisa J Taylor; *Ancestry.com* (http://www.ancestry.com: accessed 11 March 2003); citing National Archives microfilm T623, roll 518.

[19] "Kentucky Death Records, 1852-1953," subscription database, *Ancestry.com* (http://www.ancestry.com: accessed 20 November 2007), for Louisa J Taylor (2 November 1911), certificate 28013.

[20] Macedonia Baptist Church Cemetery (Daviess County, Kentucky), Jefferson Mandred and Louisa Jane Taylor marker, photographed by T.C. Cottrell, 27 March 2011.

[21] Transcription of Family Data from Louisa Taylor's Bible owned by Nellie Lashbrook Cottrell, Bowling Green Kentucky, published 1849.

[22] Transcription of Family Data from Louisa Taylor's Bible.

[23] 1860 US Census, Daviess County, Kentucky, population schedule, page 789, dwelling 998, family 798, J M Taylor.

[24] 1870 US Census, Daviess County, Kentucky, population schedule, page 215B, dwelling 54, family 54, Jefferson M Taylor.

[25] Daviess County, Kentucky, Vital records, 1852-1953; indexes, 1815-1967, marriage bond for C.E. Taylor and Martha Cooper, Book O, page 75, FHL microfilm 582238, Family History Library, Salt Lake City, Utah.

[26] Ancestor Chart for Wanda Jean Heltsley, copied 28 March 2011, Taylor vertical file, Daviess County Public Library, Owensboro, Kentucky.

[27] 1880 US Census, Daviess County, Kentucky, population schedule, Masonville, Enumeration District (ED) 173, page 396B, dwelling 79, family 84, Charles E Taylor; digital

images, *Ancestry.com* (Kentucky. Daviess County: accessed 3 May 2004); citing National Archives microfilm T9, roll 411.

[28] 1900 US Census, Daviess County, Kentucky, population schedule, Magisterial District 8, Enumeration District (ED) 39, page 383B, dwelling 19, family 19, C.E. Taylor; *Ancestry.com* (http://www.ancestry.com: accessed 3 May 2004); citing National Archives microfilm T623, roll 518.

[29] Lena Taylor Heltsley, "Four Generation Taylor Family Pedigree Chart", 5 January 1977 (221 E. 23rd Street, Owensboro, Kentucky). This sheet offers no documentation.

[30] Wanda Jean Heltsley Ancestor Chart.

[31] Lena Taylor Heltsley, "Taylor Family Pedigree Chart".

[32] Macedonia Baptist Church Cemetery (Daviess County, Kentucky), Ora H Taylor marker, photographed by T.C. Cottrell, 27 March 2011.

[33] "Rosehill Elmwood Cemetery," database, *Find A Grave* (http://www.findagrave.com: accessed 15 May 2013), entry for Lena Taylor Heltsley, 28 January 1994; citing memorial # 109098837.

[34] "Rosehill Elmwood Cemetery," database, *Find A Grave* (http://www.findagrave.com: accessed 15 May 2013), entry for John Truman Heltsley, 5 August 1967; citing memorial # 106129183.

[35] Ambrose Taylor, *Messenger & Inquirer*, Daviess County, Kentucky, 20 February 1968, page 8A, column 3.

[36] "Kentucky Marriages, 1785-1979," database, *FamilySearch* (https://familysearch.org: accessed 27 October 2013), entry for Ambros Taylor and Katheryne Moreland, 11 January 1905; citing GS Film # 1759324.

[37] 1930 US Census, Daviess County, Kentucky, population schedule, District 8, Enumeration District (ED) 30-50, page 9B, dwelling 207, family 212, Ambrose M Taylor; *Ancestry.com* (http://www.ancestry.com: accessed 20 August 2006); citing National Archives microfilm T626, roll 742.

[38] Macedonia Baptist Church Cemetery (Daviess County, Kentucky), Ambrose M and Katheryn M. Taylor marker, photographed by T.C. Cottrell, 27 March2011.

[39] Mrs. Mercedes Robinson, *Messenger Inquirer*, Daviess County, Kentucky, 1 August 1967, page 8A, column 4.

[40] Lenda Anderson, "Re: 1000 apologies," e-mail (2521 River Run Cove; Owensboro, Kentucky) to TC Cottrell, 5 August 2009.

[41] Robert M. Robinson, *Messenger Inquirer*, Daviess County, Kentucky, 6 January 1967, page 6A, column 7.

[42] "Kentucky Birth Index, 1911 - 1999," subscription database, *Ancestry.com* (www.ancestry.com: accessed 16 August 2009), for W H Robinson (2009), volume 115, certificate 57427.

[43] "Rosehill Elmwood Cemetery," database, *Find A Grave* (http://www.findagrave.com: accessed 18 March 2016), entry for Evelyn Robinson Craig, 20 October 2001; citing memorial #106185291.

[44] "Rosehill Elmwood Cemetery," database, *Find A Grave* (http://www.findagrave.com: accessed 18 March 2016), entry for Herschel Curtis Craig, 20 October 2002; citing memorial #1061852901.

[45] "Rosehill Elmwood Cemetery," database, *Find A Grave* (http://www.findagrave.com: accessed 18 March 2016), entry for Bobbie Robinson Burdette, 14 March 2002; citing memorial #106190450.

[46] "Rosehill Elmwood Cemetery," database, *Find A Grave* (http://www.findagrave.com: accessed 18 March 2016), entry for Raymond Russell Burdette, 23 January 1989; citing memorial #106190447.

[47] "Fairmont Cemetery," database, *Find A Grave* (http://www.findagrave.com: accessed 18 March 2016), entry for Frank E. Robinson, 25 August 2007; citing memorial #21179773.

[48] 1900 US Census, Daviess County, Kentucky, population schedule, District 8, Enumeration District (ED) 38, page 359B, dwelling 13, family 13, William Nelson; digital images, *Ancestry.com* (http://www.ancestry.com: accessed 4 May 2004); citing National Archives microfilm T623, roll 518.

[49] "Rosehill Elmwood Cemetery," database, *Find A Grave* (http://www.findagrave.com: accessed 6 July 2014), entry for Celeste P Taylor Norris, 9 August 1973; citing memorial #108000636.

[50] Harold Bishop Morgan, compiler, *Daviess County, Kentucky Marriage Records Volume 1, 1780 through 1914* (11129 Pleasant Ridge Road, Utica, Kentucky: McDowell Publications, 2004).

[51] "Kentucky Death Records, 1852-1953," subscription database, *Ancestry.com* (http://www.ancestry.com: accessed 21 August 2009), for Isaac Newton Norris (19 December 1945), certificate 25234.

[52] Man Drops Dead in Local Restaurant, *Owensboro Messenger*, Daviess County, Kentucky, 20 December 1945, page 10, column 7.

[53] 1940 US Census, Daviess County, Kentucky, population schedule, Owensboro, Enumeration District (ED) 30-16, page 9B, dwelling 185, Isaac N Norris; *Ancestry.com* (http://www.ancestry.com: accessed 22 May 2013); citing National Archives microfilm T627, roll 1298.

[54] "Kentucky Birth Index, 1911-1999," *Ancestry.com* (http://www.ancestry.com: accessed 18 March 2016), entry for Dixie M. Norris, 24 October 1915; citing Certificate 51428.

[55] "Kentucky Death Index," *Ancestry.com* (http://www.ancestry.com: accessed 18 March 2016), entry for Dixie N. Bruner, 23 January 1978; citing Certificate 2441.

[56] "Owensboro Memorial Gardens," database, *Find A Grave* (http://www.findagrave.com: accessed 18 March 2016), entry for Samuel Newton Norris, 19 November 2002; citing memorial #108001406.

[57] "North Carolina Death Collection, 1908-1996 Record," subscription database, *Ancestry.com* (http://www.ancestry.com: accessed 30 July 2006), for Arnold Crisman Taylor (August 1981).

[58] The Brevard Station Museum Web Site, Citizens, Arnold C Taylor, Sr., (www.brevardstation.com/taylor.html: Accessed on 9 September 2006).

[59] 1910 US Census, Gaston County, North Carolina, population schedule, River Bend, Enumeration District (ED) 61, page 7B, dwelling 126, family 129, Arnold C Taylor; *Ancestry.com* (http://www.ancestry.com: accessed 20 August 2006); citing National Archives microfilm T624, roll 1112.

[60] "Family View Chart for Ada Elnora (Ensley) Taylor" Family View Chart, Burke Family Tree-1, *Ancestry.com* (http://http://trees.ancestry.com/tree/52477197: accessed 22 April 2013).

[61] 1910 US Census, Gaston County, North Carolina, population schedule, River Bend Township, Enumeration District (ED) 61, page 7B, dwelling 126, family 129, Arnold C Taylor; *Ancestry.com* (http://www.ancestry.com: accessed 20 August 2006); citing National Archives microfilm T624, roll 1112.

[62] "North Carolina Death Certificates, 1909-1975," subscription database, *Ancestry.com* (http://www.ancestry.com: accessed 28 September 2013), for Mrs. Ada Elnora Taylor (21 September 1935), certificate 206.

[63] The Brevard Station Museum Web Site, Arnold C Taylor, Sr.

[64] 1930 US Census, Gaston County, North Carolina, population schedule, Stanley, Enumeration District (ED) 36-35, page 10A, dwelling 185, family 188, Arnold C Taylor; *Ancestry.com* (North Carolina. Gaston County: accessed 29 July 2006); citing National Archives microfilm T626, roll 1692

[65] "North Carolina Death Indexes, 1908-2004," *Ancestry.com* (http://www.ancestry.com: accessed 18 March 2016), for Arnold Chrisman Taylor, Jr. (31 December 1997).

[66] "Raleigh Memorial Park," database, *Find A Grave* (http://www.findagrave.com: accessed 18 March 2016), entry for Margaret Fay Lyles, 19 January 2006; citing memorial #89967927.

[67] "Raleigh Memorial Park," database, *Find A Grave* (http://www.findagrave.com: accessed 18 March 2016), entry for Flay Morrison Taylor, 21 December 1911; citing memorial #899676271.

[68] "North Carolina Birth Indexes, 1800-2000," *Ancestry.com* (http://www.ancestry.com: accessed 18 March 2016), for Merle Virginia Taylor (30 January 1915); citing Roll NCVR_B_C040_68001, Vol. 12, Page 810.

[69] "North Carolina Birth Indexes, 1800-2000," *Ancestry.com* (http://www.ancestry.com: accessed 18 March 2016), for Mildred Elnora Taylor (15 June 1919); citing Roll NCVR_B_C0-50_68001, Vol. 2, Page 292.

[70] "Bethabara Baptist Church Cemetery," database, *Find A Grave* (http://www.findagrave.com: accessed 9 March 2011), entry for Louise Taylor, 4 December 1971; citing memorial# 60843674.

[71] "Union Cemetery," database, *Find A Grave* (http://www.findagrave.com: accessed 23 December 2013), entry for William D Taylor, 1979; citing memorial # 90627618.

[72] 1940 US Census, Delaware County, Indiana, population schedule, Muncie, Enumeration District (ED) 18-24, page 7A, family 222, W.D. Taylor; *Ancestry.com* (http://www.ancestry.com: accessed 27 October 2013); citing National Archives microfilm T627, roll 1038.

[73] "Union Cemetery," database, *Find A Grave* (http://www.findagrave.com: accessed 25 December 2013), entry for Mildred Abbott Taylor, 1974; citing memorial # 90627475.

[74] "North Carolina Death Collection, 1908-1996 Record," subscription database, *Ancestry.com* (http://www.ancestry.com: accessed 3 September 2006), for Cooper Ellis Taylor (27 June 1986).

[75] "North Carolina, Marriage Records, 1741-2011," subscription database, *Ancestry.com* (www.ancestry.com: accessed 3 April 2015), for Cooper E Taylor and Catharine E Carroll (21 December 1929).

[76] 1930 US Census, Pitt County, North Carolina, population schedule, Greenville Town, Enumeration District (ED) 74-28, page 9A, dwelling 157, family 207, Cooper E Taylor; *Ancestry.com* (http://www.ancestry.com: accessed 3 September 2006); citing National Archives microfilm T626, roll 1741.

[77] 1940 US Census, Daviess County, Kentucky, population schedule, Upper Town, Enumeration District (ED) 30-43, page 8A, dwelling 137, Ambrose Taylor; *Ancestry.com* (http://www.ancestry.com: accessed 22 May 2013); citing National Archives microfilm T627, roll 1299.

[78] Personal knowledge of Taylor C Cottrell Jr.

[79] "Macedonia Baptist Church Cemetery," database, *Find A Grave* (http://www.findagrave.com: accessed 9 March 2011), entry for Martha Miranda Cooper Taylor, 4 March 1909; citing memorial # 60842939.

[80] 1910 US Census, Daviess County, Kentucky, population schedule, District 8, Enumeration District (ED) 52, page 228A, dwelling 7, family 7, Charles E Taylor; *Ancestry.com* (Kentucky. Daviess County: accessed 6 May 2004); citing National Archives microfilm T624, roll 473.

[81] Daviess County, Kentucky, Wills, 1812-1936; Indexes, 1815-1868, will of C.E. Taylor, FHL microfilm 1913778, vG, page 228-231, Family History Library, Salt Lake City, Utah.

[82] 1920 US Census, Daviess County, Kentucky, population schedule, District 8, Enumeration District (ED) 58, page 1A, dwelling 5, family 5, Charles E Taylor; *Ancestry.com* (http://www.ancestry.com: accessed 17 September 2005); citing National Archives microfilm T625, roll 567.

[83] "Macedonia Baptist Church Cemetery," database, *Find A Grave* (http://www.findagrave.com: accessed 9 March 2011), entry for Charles Edmundson Taylor, 12 September 1921; citing memorial # 60842913.

[84] Suit Filed to Stop Cemetery Location, *Owensboro Messenger Inquirer*, Owensboro Kentucky, 22 September 1995.

[85] Transcription of Family Data from Louisa Taylor's Bible.

[86] 1860 US Census, Daviess County, Kentucky, population schedule, page 789, dwelling 998, family 798, J M Taylor.

[87] 1870 US Census, Daviess County, Kentucky, population schedule, page 215B, dwelling 54, family 54, Jefferson M Taylor.

[88] Harold Bishop Morgan, compiler, *Daviess County, Kentucky Marriage Records Volume 1, 1780 through 1914* (11129 Pleasant Ridge Road, Utica, Kentucky: McDowell Publications, 2004).

[89] "Kentucky Birth Records, 1852-1910," subscription database, *Ancestry.com* (http://www.ancestry.com: accessed 16 August 2009), for Ira W Dawson (8 October 1853).

[90] 1880 US Census, Daviess County, Kentucky, population schedule, Masonville, Enumeration District (ED) 173, page 8D, dwelling 57, family 59, Ira W Dawson; *Ancestry.com* (http://www.ancestry.com: accessed 16 August 2009); citing National Archives microfilm T9, roll 411.

[91] "Family Data for Ira Weldon Dawson" Genealogy Database, David Scifres, *Ancestry.com* (http://trees.ancestry.com/tree/11639419: accessed 22 August 2009).

[92] Daviess County, Kentucky, Vital records, 1852-1953; indexes, 1815-1967, marriage bond for Eula J Brooks and Elizabeth E Dawson, Book 10, page 225, FHL microfilm 1759322, Family History Library, Salt Lake City, Utah.

[93] Eula J Brooks, *Owensboro Messenger*, Daviess County, Kentucky, 12 November 1946, page 10, column 5.

[94] "Family Data for Ira Weldon Dawson," David Scifres, *Ancestry.com*.

[95] "Rosehill Elmwood Cemetery," database, *Find A Grave* (http://www.findagrave.com: accessed 15 May 2013), entry for Nancy Virginia Dawson Emrich, 16 March 1972; citing memorial # 63739617.

[96] "Family Data for Ira Weldon Dawson," David Scifres, *Ancestry.com*.

[97] "Rosehill Elmwood Cemetery," database, *Find A Grave* (http://www.findagrave.com: accessed 15 May 2013), entry for Ira Otto Emrich, 6 February 1978; citing memorial #63739611.

[98] "Rosehill Elmwood Cemetery," database, *Find A Grave* (http://www.findagrave.com: accessed 15 May 2013), entry for Rae Vivian Emrich Taylor, 16 March 2016; citing memorial #63362583.

[99] "Rosehill Elmwood Cemetery," database, *Find A Grave* (http://www.findagrave.com: accessed 15 May 2013), entry for Donald Miller Taylor, 16 March 2016; citing memorial #63363387.

[100] "Pinecrest Cemetery," database, *Find A Grave* (http://www.findagrave.com: accessed 18 March 2016), entry for Charles Weldon Emrich; citing memorial #144501601.

[101] "Florida Marriages Indexes, 1822-1875 and 1927-2001," *Ancestry.com* (www.ancestry.com: accessed on 18 March 2016), entry for Charles Weldon Emrich and Lydia Margaretta Eurich (10 January 1986); citing Certificate 004559.

[102] Carmie Dawson, *Messenger Inquirer*, Daviess County, Kentucky, 18 October 1967, page 5A, column 2.

[103] "Highland Lawn Cemetery," database, *Find A Grave* (http://www.findagrave.com: accessed 30 May 2013), entry for Adah C Dawson, 1981; citing memorial # 25759419.

[104] 1940 US Census, Vigo County, Indiana, population schedule, Terre Haute, Enumeration District (ED) 84-17, page 9A, dwelling 201, William Dawson; *Ancestry.com* (http://www.ancestry.com: accessed 22 May 2013); citing National Archives microfilm T627, roll 1103.

[105] "Highland Lawn Cemetery," database, *Find A Grave* (http://www.findagrave.com: accessed 30 May 2013), entry for William R. Dawson, 19 February 1999; citing memorial #156604562.

[106] "Rosehill Elmwood Cemetery," database, *Find A Grave* (http://www.findagrave.com: accessed 30 May 2013), entry for Felix Ira Dawson, 8 April 1962; citing memorial # 63786849.

[107] "Rosehill Elmwood Cemetery," database, *Find A Grave* (http://www.findagrave.com: accessed 30 May 2013), entry for Auro Irene Martin Dawson, 17 December 1968; citing memorial #63787516.

[108] "Family Data for Ira Weldon Dawson," David Scifres, *Ancestry.com.*

[109] "Rosehill Elmwood Cemetery," database, *Find A Grave* (http://www.findagrave.com: accessed 18 March 2016), entry for Arnold Marion Dawson, 26 June 1969; citing memorial #106357110.

[110] "Maplewood Cemetery," database, *Find A Grave* (http://www.findagrave.com: accessed 18 March 2016), entry for Carlin F. Dawson, 8 January 1976; citing memorial #97950861.

[111] "Owensboro Memorial Gardens," database, *Find A Grave* (http://www.fndagrave.com: accessed 18 March 2016), entry for Minnie Lou Dawson Belford, 30 September 1985' citing memorial #81936829.

[112] "Kentucky Birth Index, 1911-1999," *Ancestry.com* (http://www.ancestry.com: accessed on 18 March 2016), entry for Virginia M. Dawson (25 November 1920).

[113] "U.S. Social Security Death Index, 1935-2014," *Ancestry.com* (http://www.ancestry.com: accessed 18 March 2016), entry for Elisabeth Meserve (21 July 2011).

[114] "Rosehill Elmwood Cemetery," database, *Find A Grave* (http://www.findagrave.com: accessed 30 May 2013), entry for Mary Helen Taylor, 10 November 2007; citing memorial #65988190.

[115] "Kentucky Death Records, 1852-1953," subscription database, *Ancestry.com* (http://www.ancestry.com: accessed 22 August 2009), for Miller K Dawson (9 December 1948), certificate 24760.

[116] Harold Bishop Morgan, *Daviess County, Kentucky Marriage Records Volume 1.*

[117] "Family Data for Ira Weldon Dawson," David Scifres, *Ancestry.com.*

[118] "U.S. Social Security Applications and Claims Index, 1936-2007," *Ancestry.com* (http://www.ancestry.com: accessed 18 March 2016), entry for Kathryn Elisabeth Long (1 December 1999).

[119] "Michigan Marriage Records, 1867-1952," *Ancestry.com* (http://www.ancestry.com: accessed 18 March 2016), entry for Kathryn Dawson and Clifton Long (10 August 1936).

[120] "Rosehill Elmwood Cemetery," database, *Find A Grave* (http://www.findagrave.com: accessed 16 March 2016), entry for Roy Jones Dawson, 26 July 1959; citing memorial #106265401.

[121] "Rosehill Elmwood Cemetery," database, *Find A Grave* (http://www.findagrave.com: accessed 16 March 2016), entry for Bonnie A. Trail Dawson, 20 June 1978; citing memorial #106265406.

[122] "U.S. Social Security Applications and Claims Index, 1936-2007," *Ancestry.com* (http://www.ancestry.com: accessed 18 March 2016), entry for Thurman Miller Dawson (29 May 1993).

[123] John M Dawson, *Messenger Inquirer*, Daviess County, Kentucky, 22 November 1985, page 2C, column 1.

[124] Harold Bishop Morgan, *Daviess County, Kentucky Marriage Records Volume 2.*

[125] "Global Find a Grave Index for Burials at Sea and Other Select Burial Locations, 1300s-Current," database, *Find A Grave* (http://www.findagrave.com: accessed 18 March 2016), entry for Dr. Royce Edmund Dawson, 2 December 2012.

[126] "Rosehill Elmwood Cemetery," database, *Find A Grave* (http://www.findagrave.com: accessed 16 March 2016), entry for Morris Elton Dawson, 24 August 2007; citing memorial #21170072.

[127] "Rosehill Elmwood Cemetery," database, *Find A Grave* (http://www.findagrave.com: accessed 16 March 2016), entry for Lillian Morgan Dawson, 17 August 2014; citing memorial #134535053.

[128] Mrs. John Dawson, *Owensboro Messenger*, Daviess County, Kentucky, 24 April 1927, page 12, column 3.

[129] Harold Bishop Morgan, *Daviess County, Kentucky Marriage Records Volume 2.*

[130] "Family Data for Ira Weldon Dawson," David Scifres, *Ancestry.com.*

[131] Death Comes to Mrs. J. Dawson, *Owensboro Messenger*, Daviess County, Kentucky, 3 September 1936, page 5, column 6.

[132] Ex-Daviess School Board Chief Dies, *Messenger Inquirer*, Daviess County, Kentucky, 22 November 1985, page 2C, column 1.

[133] "Rosehill Elmwood Cemetery," database, *Find A Grave* (http://www.findagrave.com: accessed 9 March 2011), entry for Marie D Dawson, 1957; citing memorial# 64186809.

[134] *Messenger Inquirer*, 22 November 1985, page 2C, column 1.

[135] Mrs. Ira W. Dawson, *Owensboro Messenger*, Daviess County, Kentucky, 28 August 1897, page 5, column 2.

[136] 1900 US Census, Daviess County, Kentucky, population schedule, Upper Town, Enumeration District (ED) 39, page 384A, dwelling 24, family 24, Ira Dawson; *Ancestry.com* (http://www.ancestry.com: accessed 16 August 2009); citing National Archives microfilm T623, roll 518.

[137] 1910 US Census, Daviess County, Kentucky, population schedule, Magisterial District 6, Enumeration District (ED) 47, page 3A, dwelling 49, family 50, Ira Dawson; *Ancestry.com* (http://www.ancestry.com: accessed 16 August 2009); citing National Archives microfilm T624, roll 473.

[138] Burial of Ira W Dawson, *Owensboro Messenger*, Daviess County, Kentucky, 10 May 1918, page 6, column 3.

[139] "Kentucky Death Records, 1852-1953," subscription database, *Ancestry.com* (http://www.ancestry.com: accessed 27 September 2009), for Mary C Dawson (15 August 1951), certificate 5115825.

[140] Transcription of Family Data from Louisa Taylor's Bible.

[141] 1860 US Census, Daviess County, Kentucky, population schedule, page 789, dwelling 998, family 798, J M Taylor.

[142] 1870 US Census, Daviess County, Kentucky, population schedule, page 215B, dwelling 54, family 54, Jefferson M Taylor.

[143] The Late Thomas Taylor, *undocumented Daviess County newspaper*, Owensboro, Kentucky.

[144] Ibid.

[145] Transcription of Family Data from Louisa Taylor's Bible.

[146] 1860 US Census, Daviess County, Kentucky, population schedule, page 789, dwelling 998, family 798, J. M. Taylor.

[147] 1870 US Census, Daviess County, Kentucky, population schedule, page 215B, dwelling 54, family 54, Jefferson M. Taylor.

[148] 1880 US Census, Daviess County, Kentucky, population schedule, ED 173, page 395A, dwelling 64, family 67, Jefferson Taylor.

[149] "Kentucky Death Records, 1852-1953," subscription database, *Ancestry.com* (http://www.ancestry.com: accessed 20 November 2007), for W R Taylor (10 July 1921), certificate 14434.

[150] Transcription of Family Data from Louisa Taylor's Bible.

[151] 1870 US Census, Daviess County, Kentucky, population schedule, page 215B, dwelling 54, family 54, Jefferson M. Taylor.

[152] 1880 US Census, Daviess County, Kentucky, population schedule, ED 173, page 395A, dwelling 64, family 67, Jefferson Taylor.

[153] Daviess County, Kentucky, Vital records, 1852-1953; indexes, 1815-1967, marriage bond for Raleigh Bryant and Emma Taylor, Book R1, page 503, FHL microfilm 582241, Family History Library, Salt Lake City, Utah.

[154] "Kentucky Death Records, 1852-1953," subscription database, *Ancestry.com* (http://www.ancestry.com: accessed 6 August 2008), for Raleigh Bryant (12 December 1934), certificate 29970.

[155] 1900 US Census, Warren County, Kentucky, population schedule, Upper Town, Enumeration District (ED) 38, page 8B, dwelling 162, family 162, Rolla D Bryant; *Ancestry.com* (http://www.ancestry.com: accessed 24 November 2007); citing National Archives microfilm T623, roll 518.

[156] 1910 US Census, Daviess County, Kentucky, population schedule, Magisterial District 8, Enumeration District (ED) 53, page 1A, dwelling 1, family 1, Raleigh D Bryant; *Ancestry.com* (http://www.ancestry.com: accessed 6 August 2008); citing National Archives microfilm T624, roll 473.

[157] 1920 US Census, Daviess County, Kentucky, population schedule, Upper Town, Enumeration District (ED) 59, page 4B, dwelling 77, family 78, R.D. Bryant; *Ancestry.com* (http://www.ancestry.com: accessed 6 August 2008); citing National Archives microfilm T625, roll 567.

[158] "Rosehill Elmwood Cemetery," database, *Find A Grave* (http://www.findagrave.com: accessed 15 May 2013), entry for Hortense Bryant Kirk, 19 January 1949; citing memorial # 64552734.

[159] Daviess County, Kentucky, Vital records, 1852-1953; indexes, 1815-1967, marriage bond for James A Kirk and Hortense S Bryant, Book 14, page 31, FHL microfilm 1759324, Family History Library, Salt Lake City, Utah.

[160] "Rosehill Elmwood Cemetery," database, *Find A Grave* (http://www.findagrave.com: accessed 15 May 2013), entry for James Arthur Kirk, 3 September 1934; citing memorial # 64552719.

[161] 1930 US Census, Jackson County, Missouri, population schedule, Kansas City, Enumeration District (ED) 81, page 13A, dwelling 177, family 182, James A. Kirk; *Ancestry.com* (http://www.ancestry.com: accessed 18 March 2016); citing National Archives microfilm T626,roll 1195.

[162] "Kentucky Death Records, 1852-1953," subscription database, *Ancestry.com* (http://www.ancestry.com: accessed 6 August 2008), for Hue Mandrid Bryant (1 December 1916), certificate 29837.

[163] "Kentucky Death Records, 1852-1953," subscription database, *Ancestry.com* (http://www.ancestry.com: accessed 6 August 2008), for William Ellis Bryant (24 June 1947), certificate 13243.

[164] 1930 US Census, McCracken County, Kentucky, population schedule, Paducah, Enumeration District (ED) 73-12, page 11A, dwelling 249, family 270, William E Bryant; *Ancestry.com* (http://www.ancestry.com: accessed 28 March 2010); citing National Archives microfilm T626, roll 768.

[165] "Kentucky Death Records, 1852-1953," subscription database, *Ancestry.com* (http://www.ancestry.com: accessed 28 March 2010), for Emma Mae Bryant (14 May 1952).

[166] 1940 US Census, McCracken County, Kentucky, population schedule, Paducah, Enumeration District (ED) 73-22, page 9B, dwelling 361, family 198, William E. Bryan; *Ancestry.com* (http://www.ancestry.com: accessed 19 March 2016); citing National Archives microfilm T627, roll 1334.

[167] "Rosehill Elmwood Cemetery," database, *Find A Grave* (http://www.findagrave.com: accessed 15 May 2013), entry for Harriett Bryant Lewis for Charles Cadwallader Lewis, 17 December 1986; citing memorial # 73832104.

[168] "Rosehill Elmwood Cemetery," database, *Find A Grave* (http://www.findagrave.com: accessed 15 May 2013), entry for Charles Cadwallader Lewis, 3 March 1948; citing memorial #73832077.

[169] "Rosehill Elmwood Cemetery," database, *Find A Grave* (http://www.findagrave.com: accessed 16 May 2013), entry for Samuel Jefferson Bryant, 17 January 1958; citing memorial #71184596.

[170] "Rosehill Elmwood Cemetery," database, *Find A Grave* (http://www.findagrave.com: accessed 16 May 2013), entry for Martine M. Norton Bryant, 10 December 1988; citing memorial #136918110.

[171] 1930 US Census, Daviess County, Kentucky, population schedule, Owensboro, Enumeration District (ED) 30-9, page 1B, dwelling 21, family 24, Samuel J Bryant; *Ancestry.com* (http://www.ancestry.com: accessed 23 November 2013); citing National Archives microfilm T626, roll 741.

[172] "Rosehill Elmwood Cemetery," database, *Find A Grave* (http://www.findagrave.com: accessed 16 May 2013), entry for Elizabeth L. Bryant Kerrick, 19 February 2011; citing memorial #65911408.

[173] "Rosehill Elmwood Cemetery," database, *Find A Grave* (http://www.findagrave.com: accessed 16 May 2013), entry for Estel Kerrick, 24 July 1994; citing memorial #23572367.

[174] "Cave Hill Cemetery," database, *Find A Grave* (http://www.findagrave.com: accessed 16 May 2013), entry for Dorothy Bryant Muir, 10 December 2002; citing memorial #139917633.

[175] 1910 US Census, Daviess County, Kentucky, population schedule, Magisterial District 8, Enumeration District (ED) 53, page 1A, dwelling 1, family 1, Raleigh D Bryant; *Ancestry.com* (http://www.ancestry.com: accessed 6 August 2008); citing National Archives microfilm T624, roll 473.

[176] 1920 US Census, Daviess County, Kentucky, population schedule, Upper Town, Enumeration District (ED) 59, page 4B, dwelling 77, family 78, R.D. Bryant; *Ancestry.com* (http://www.ancestry.com: accessed 6 August 2008); citing National Archives microfilm T625, roll 567.

[177] "World War I Draft Registration Cards, 1917-1918," *Ancestry.com* (http://www.ancestry.com: accessed 28 March 2010), for James Raleigh Bryant, citing United States, Selective Service System. World War I Selective Service System Draft Registration Cards, 1917-1918. Washington, D.C.: National Archives and Records Administration. Microfilm publication M1509, Daviess County, Kentucky; Roll 1653352; Draft Board: 0.

[178] "Kentucky Death Records, 1852-1953," subscription database, *Ancestry.com* (http://www.ancestry.com: accessed 6 August 2008), for Raleigh Bryant (12 December 1934), certificate 29970.

[179] "Kentucky Death Records, 1852-1953," subscription database, *Ancestry.com* (http://www.ancestry.com: accessed 20 November 2007), for Emma Bryant (9 August 1950), certificate 5015732.

[180] Transcription and original pages from Louisa Taylor's Bible.

[181] 1860 US Census, Daviess County, Kentucky, population schedule, page 789, dwelling 998, family 798, J. M. Taylor.

[182] 1880 US Census, Daviess County, Kentucky, population schedule, ED 173, page 395A, dwelling 64, family 67, Jefferson Taylor.

[183] "Kentucky Marriages, 1852-1914," subscription database, *Ancestry.com* (http://www.ancestry.com: accessed 6 August 2008), for C.M. Maple and Zeralda Taylor (15 August 1894).

[184] "Kentucky Death Records, 1852-1953," subscription database, *Ancestry.com* (http://www.ancestry.com: accessed 6 August 2008), for Charles N Maple (3 May 1952), certificate 5214993.

[185] 1900 US Census, Jefferson County, Kentucky, population schedule, Cross Roads, Enumeration District (ED) 152, page 5B, dwelling 93, family 94, Charles Maple; *Ancestry.com* (http://www.ancestry.com: accessed 6 August 2008); citing National Archives microfilm publication T623, roll 553.

[186] 1910 US Census, Jefferson County, Kentucky, population schedule, Cross Roads, Enumeration District (ED) 19, page 3A, dwelling 52, family 52, Charles M Maple; *Ancestry.com* (http://www.ancestry.com: accessed 6 August 2008); citing National Archives microfilm publication T624, roll 483.

[187] 1920 US Census, Jefferson County, Kentucky, population schedule, Louisville, Enumeration District (ED) 20, page 3B, dwelling 55, family 56, Charles N Maple; *Ancestry.com* (http://www.ancestry.com: accessed 6 August 2008); citing National Archives microfilm publication T625, roll 568.

[188] 1930 US Census, Jefferson County, Kentucky, population schedule, District 3, Enumeration District (ED) 56-201, page 2B, dwelling 37, family 38, Charles N Maple; *Ancestry.com* (http://www.ancestry.com: accessed 6 August 2008); citing National Archives microfilm publication T626, roll 752.

[189] 1940 US Census, Jefferson County, Kentucky, population schedule, 2nd Magisterial District, Enumeration District (ED) 56-35, page 10B, dwelling 182, Charles Maple; *Ancestry.com* (http://www.ancestry.com: accessed 22 May 2013); citing National Archives microfilm publication T627, roll 1321.

[190] "Pennsylvania Run Cemetery," database, *Find A Grave* (http://www.findagrave.com: accessed 10 December 2015), entry for William Mandred Maple, 16 June 1984; citing memorial # 131224772.

[191] 1940 US Census, Jefferson County, Kentucky, population schedule, 2nd Magisterial District, Enumeration District (ED) 56-35, page 10B, dwelling 183, Mandred Maple; *Ancestry.com* (http://www.ancestry.com: accessed 22 May 2013); citing National Archives microfilm publication T627, roll 1321.

[192] "Pennsylvania Run Cemetery," database, *Find A Grave* (http://www.findagrave.com: accessed 10 December 2015), entry for Evelyn Coe Maple, 17 December 1987; citing memorial # 131224822.

[193] "Kentucky Death Records, 1852-1953," subscription database, *Ancestry.com* (http://www.ancestry.com: accessed 6 August 2008), for Mrs. Zerelda Maple (26 February 1948), certificate 5738.

[194] "Kentucky Death Records, 1852-1953," subscription database, *Ancestry.com* (http://www.ancestry.com: accessed 6 August 2008), for Charles N Maple (3 May 1952), certificate 5214993.

[195] Transcription and original pages from Louisa Taylor's Bible.

[196] 1870 US Census, Daviess County, Kentucky, population schedule, page 215B, dwelling 54, family 54, Jefferson M. Taylor.

[197] 1880 US Census, Daviess County, Kentucky, population schedule, ED 173, page 395A, dwelling 64, family 67, Jefferson Taylor.

[198] Daviess County, Kentucky, Vital records, 1852-1953; indexes, 1815-1967, marriage bond for John M Taylor and Henrietta Birkhead, Book V, p. 241, FHL microfilm 582244, Family History Library, Salt Lake City, Utah.

[199] "Kentucky Death Records, 1852-1953," subscription database, *Ancestry.com* (http://www.ancestry.com: accessed 24 November 2007), for Mrs. John Morgan Henrietta Taylor (Birkhead) (10 May 1938), certificate 13786.

[200] 1900 US Census, Daviess County, Kentucky, population schedule, Magisterial District 8, Enumeration District (ED) 39, page 393A, dwelling 212, family 214, John M Taylor; *Ancestry.com* (http://www.ancestry.com: accessed 19 May 2004); citing National Archives microfilm T623, roll 518.

[201] 1910 US Census, Daviess County, Kentucky, population schedule, Magisterial District 8, Enumeration District (ED) 52, page 4B, dwelling 80, family 81, John M Taylor; *Ancestry.com* (http://www.ancestry.com: accessed 29 May 2004); citing National Archives microfilm publication T624, roll 473.

[202] 1920 US Census, Daviess County, Kentucky, population schedule, Upper 8th District, Enumeration District (ED) 58, page 1A, dwelling 13, family 14, Morgan J Taylor; *Ancestry.com* (http://www.ancestry.com: accessed 16 October 2005); citing National Archives microfilm T625, roll 567.

[203] 1930 US Census, Daviess County, Kentucky, population schedule, District 8, Enumeration District (ED) 30-50, page 10A, dwelling 217, family 223, John M Taylor; *Ancestry.com* (http://www.ancestry.com: accessed unknown accessed date); citing National Archives microfilm T626, roll 472.

[204] 1910 US Census, Daviess County, Kentucky, population schedule, ED 52, page 4B, dwelling 80, family 81, John M Taylor.

[205] "Kentucky Death Index, 1911-2000," subscription database, *Ancestry.com* (http://www.ancestry.com: accessed 25 August 2009), for Roy B Taylor (17 February 1960), volume 5, certificate 2307.

[206] "World War I Draft Registration Cards, 1917-1918," subscription database, *Ancestry.com* (http://www.ancestry.com: accessed 29 July 2006), for Roy Birkhead Taylor, citing United States, Selective Service System. World War I Selective Service System Draft Registration Cards, 1917-1918. Washington, D.C.: National Archives and Records Administration. Microfilm publication M1509, Daviess County, Kentucky; Roll 1653353; Draft Board: 0.

[207] "Rosehill Elmwood Cemetery," database, *Find A Grave* (http://www.findagrave.com: accessed 10 December 2015), entry for Frances Taylor, 10 December 1988; citing memorial # 104395767.

[208] 1930 US Census, Daviess County, Kentucky, population schedule, District 8, Enumeration District (ED) 30-50, page 10A, dwelling 217, family 224, Roy B Taylor; *Ancestry.com* (http://www.ancestry.com: accessed 3 September 2006); citing National Archives microfilm T626, roll 472.

[209] "Kentucky Death Records, 1852-1953," subscription database, *Ancestry.com* (http://www.ancestry.com: accessed 24 November 2007), for Mrs. John Morgan Henrietta Taylor (Birkhead) (10 May 1938), certificate 13786.

[210] 1940 US Census, Daviess County, Kentucky, population schedule, Upper Town, Enumeration District (ED) 40-42, page 1B, dwelling 14, J Morgan Taylor; *Ancestry.com* (http://www.ancestry.com: accessed 22 May 2013); citing National Archives microfilm T627, roll 1299.

[211] "Kentucky Death Records, 1852-1953," subscription database, *Ancestry.com* (http://www.ancestry.com: accessed 20 November 2007), for John M Taylor (22 February 1945), certificate 2887.

[212] Transcription and original pages from Louisa Taylor's Bible.

[213] Ibid.

[214] Ibid.

[215] Ibid.

[216] 1870 US Census, Daviess County, Kentucky, population schedule, page 215B, dwelling 54, family 54, Jefferson M. Taylor.

[217] 1880 US Census, Daviess County, Kentucky, population schedule, ED 173, page 395A, dwelling 64, family 67, Jefferson Taylor.

[218] "Indiana Index to Select Marriages 1780-1992," Ancestry.com (www.ancestry.com: accessed 10 December 2015), entry for Joseph B. Hite and Susie H. Taylor.

[219] "Macedonia Baptist Church Cemetery," database, *Find A Grave* (http://www.findagrave.com: accessed 10 December 2015), entry for Joseph Butler Hite, 1 June 1938; citing memorial # 60553622.

[220] 1900 US Census, Daviess County, Kentucky, population schedule, Whitesville, Enumeration District (ED) 35, page 11A, dwelling 211, family 212, Joseph B. Hite; *Ancestry.com* (http://www.ancestry.com: accessed 19 May 2004); citing National Archives microfilm T623, roll 518.

[221] 1910 US Census, Daviess County, Kentucky, population schedule, Magisterial District 6, Enumeration District (ED) 47, page 5B, dwelling 120, family 113, J.B. Hite; *Ancestry.com* (http://www.ancestry.com: accessed 10 December 2015); citing National Archives microfilm T624, roll 473.

[222] 1920 US Census, Daviess County, Kentucky, population schedule, Upper 8th District, Enumeration District (ED) 48, page 7B, dwelling 126, family 143, Joseph B. Hite;

Ancestry.com (http://www.ancestry.com: accessed 16 October 2005); citing National Archives publication T625, roll 567.

[223] 1930 US Census, Daviess County, Kentucky, population schedule, Magisterial District #6, Enumeration District (ED) 44, page 9A, dwelling 184, family 184, Joe Hite; *Ancestry.com* (http://www.ancestry.com: accessed unknown accessed date); citing National Archives microfilm T626, roll 742.

[224] "California Death Index, 1940-1997," *Ancestry.com* (www.ancestry.com: accessed 16 March 2016), entry for Joseph William Hite (20 August 1985).

[225] "Mount Hope Cemetery," database, *Find A Grave* (http://www.findagrave.com: accessed 19 March 2016), entry for Orion Maxwell Hite, 5 April 1986; citing memorial # 34776725.

[226] "Mount Hope Cemetery," database, *Find A Grave* (http://www.findagrave.com: accessed 19 March 2016), entry for Ruth Hope Ford Hite, 18 July 1951; citing memorial #34776729.

[227] "Memorial Gardens Cemetery," database, *Find A Grave* (http://www.findagrave.com: accessed 19 March 2016), entry for Donald L. Hite, 23 October 1991; citing memorial #18881444.

[228] "Florida Death Index 1877-1998," database, *Ancestry.com* (www.ancestry.com: accessed on 10 December 2015), Joseph Douglas Hite, July 1969.

[229] "U.S. Social Security Applications and Claims Index, 1936-2007," *Ancestry.com* (www.ancestry.com: accessed on 19 March 2016), Anna Sue Hite (16 January 1989).

[230] "Rosehill Elmwood Cemetery," database, *Find A Grave* (http://www.findagrave.com: accessed 10 December 2015), entry for Leslie Ward Hite, 2 July 1963; citing memorial # 65202701.

[231] "Macedonia Baptist Church Cemetery," database, *Find A Grave* (http://www.findagrave.com: accessed 10 December 2015), entry for Joseph Butler Hite.

[232] 1940 US Census, Jefferson County, Kentucky, population schedule, Owensboro, Enumeration District (ED) 30-15, page 1B, dwelling 15, Joseph Hite; *Ancestry.com* (http://www.ancestry.com: accessed 10 December 2015); citing National Archives microfilm T627, roll 1298.

[233] "Macedonia Baptist Church Cemetery," database, *Find A Grave* (http://www.findagrave.com: accessed 10 December 2015), entry for Susan Haney Taylor Hite, 29 August 1956; citing memorial # 60553267.

[234] Transcription and original pages from Louisa Taylor's Bible.

[235] Ibid.

[236] 1880 US Census, Daviess County, Kentucky, population schedule, ED 173, page 395A, dwelling 64, family 67, Jefferson Taylor.

[237] 1900 US Census, Daviess County, Kentucky, population schedule, Upper Town, Enumeration District (ED) 39, page 2A, dwelling 28, family 28, C. Daniel; *Ancestry.com* (http://www.ancestry.com: accessed 14 December 2015); citing National Archives microfilm T623, roll 1854.

[238] "Macedonia Baptist Church Cemetery," database, *Find A Grave* (http://www.findagrave.com: accessed 10 December 2015), Charles Todd Daniel, Sr., 16 May 1929; citing memorial # 135020505.

[239] 1900 US Census, Daviess County, Kentucky, population schedule, Upper Town, Enumeration District (ED) 39, page 2A, dwelling 28, family 28, C. Daniel.

[240] 1910 US Census, Daviess County, Kentucky, population schedule, Magisterial District 8, Enumeration District (ED) 52, page 1B, dwelling 17, family 17, Charles T. Daniel;

Ancestry.com (http://www.ancestry.com: accessed 14 December 2015); citing National Archives microfilm T624, roll 473.

[241] 1920 US Census, Daviess County, Kentucky, population schedule, Upper 8th District, Enumeration District (ED) 58, page 3A, dwelling 62, family 66, Charles T. Daniel; *Ancestry.com* (http://www.ancestry.com: accessed 14 December 2015); citing National Archives microfilm T625, roll 567.

[242] "Macedonia Baptist Church Cemetery," database, *Find A Grave* (http://www.findagrave.com: accessed 10 December 2015), Charles Todd Daniel.

[243] 1930 US Census, Daviess County, Kentucky, population schedule, Owensboro, Enumeration District (ED) 29, page 10B, dwelling 259, family 278, Louise Daniel; *Ancestry.com* (http://www.ancestry.com: accessed unknown accessed date); citing National Archives microfilm T626, roll 742.

[244] 1940 US Census, Jefferson County, Kentucky, population schedule, Louisville, Enumeration District (ED) 121-174, page 6A, dwelling 198, Louise Daniel; *Ancestry.com* (http://www.ancestry.com: accessed 14 December 2015); citing National Archives microfilm publication T627, roll 1299.

[245] 1940 US Census, Jefferson County, Kentucky, population schedule, Louisville, Enumeration District (ED) 121-174, page 6A, dwelling 198, Louise Daniel.

[246] "Forest Hill Cemetery Midtown," database, *Find A Grave* (http://www.findagrave.com: accessed 10 December 2015), Mildred Emma Daniel McCall, 25 May 1983; citing memorial # 77026158.

[247] "Memphis Funeral Home and Memorial Gardens," database, *Find A Grave* (http://www.findagrave.com: accessed 19 March 2016), entry for William Karlin Robinson, 21 September 1998; citing memorial #77205829.

[248] "Forest Hill Cemetery-South," database, *Find A Grave* (http://www.findagrave.com: accessed 19 March 2016), entry for Elizabeth Ann Robinson Sipes, 11 September 2012; citing memorial #96879401.

[249] "Forest Hill Cemetery-South," database, *Find A Grave* (http://www.findagrave.com: accessed 19 March 2016), entry for Roy William Sipes, 10 March 2012; citing memorial #86691050.

[250] "Macedonia Baptist Church Cemetery," database, *Find A Grave* (http://www.findagrave.com: accessed 10 December 2015), entry for Louise Taylor Daniel, 28 January 1949; citing memorial #135025517.

[251] "Rosehill-Elmwood Cemetery," database, *Find A Grave* (http://www.findagrave.com: accessed 19 March 2016), entry for George Clayton Daniel, 28 January 1964; citing memorial #110003788.

[252] "Rosehill-Elmwood Cemetery," database, *Find A Grave* (http://www.findagrave.com: accessed 19 March 2016), entry for Anna Lee King Williams, 1 August 1998; citing memorial #110003787.

[253] 1930 US Census, Daviess County, Kentucky, population schedule, Owensboro, Enumeration District (ED) 29, page 10B, dwelling 259, family 278, Louise Daniel.

[254] 1940 US Census, Jefferson County, Kentucky, population schedule, Louisville, Enumeration District (ED) 121-174, page 6A, dwelling 198, Louise Daniel.

[255] "Macedonia Baptist Church Cemetery," database, *Find A Grave* (http://www.findagrave.com: accessed 10 December 2015), entry for Louise Taylor Daniel, 28 January 1949; citing memorial # 135025517.

[256] Transcription and original pages from Louisa Taylor's Bible.

Section 2 – Chapter 1 Sources – Levi Brashear Family

[1] Nacy Brashear's Bible, accessed on Family Tree of Levi L Brashear, *Ancestry.com* (htttp://www.ancestry.com: accessed 26 July 2012), information was copied from The Writings in A Brashear Family Bible; Bible printed by Alexander Kincaid His Majesty's Printer, MDCCLXIX 1769.

[2] Charles Brashear *A Brashear(s) Family History, Descendants of Robert and Benois Brasseur, Volume 4, Brashear(s) Families of the Ohio Valley* (Clearlake Oaks, California: Charles Brashear Books, Etc., 2002), page 8.

[3] W H Perrin, J H Battle and G C Kniffin, *History of Kentucky Illustrated, Edition 3* (1887; reprint Greenville, South Carolina: Southern Historical Press, Inc., 1999), page 873

[4] Charles Brashear *A Brashear(s) Family History, Descendants of Robert and Benois Brasseur, Volume 4, Brashear(s) Families of the Ohio Valley* (Clearlake Oaks, California: Charles Brashear Books, Etc., 2002).

[5] Ibid.

[6] Nacy Brashear's Bible, accessed on Family Tree of Levi L Brashear, maintained by slbrinton on Ancestry.com, information was copied from The Writings in A Brashear Family Bible; Bible printed by Alexander Kincaid His Majesty's Printer, MDCCLXIX 1769.

[7] Charles Brashear *A Brashear(s) Family History, Descendants of Robert and Benois Brasseur, Volume 4, Brashear(s) Families of the Ohio Valley.*

[8] Ibid.

[9] Nacy Brashear's Bible

[10] Charles Brashear *A Brashear(s) Family History, Descendants of Robert and Benois Brasseur, Volume 4, Brashear(s) Families of the Ohio Valley.*

[11] Kentucky Marriages to 1850, *Ancestry.com* (http://www.ancestry.com: accessed 20 June 2004), Levi Brashear and Camilla Landsdale.

[12] W H Perrin, J H Battle and G C Kniffin, *History of Kentucky Illustrated*, page 873.

[13] Zalame (Brashear) Cottrell, Brashear Family Notes, handwritten notes citing *The Brashear - Brashears Family 1449 – 1929.*

[14] W H Perrin, J H Battle and G C Kniffin, *History of Kentucky Illustrated*, page 873.

[15] Charles Brashear *Brashear(s) Family History, Volume 4*, page 389.

[16] Zalame (Brashear) Cottrell, Brashear Family Notes.

[17] "Students at Science Hill School in Shelbyville in 1825" Genealogy History Database, Donald Murphy, *Shelby County Kentucky GenWeb* (http://www.rootsweb.ancestry.com: accessed 12 January 2009).

[18] Brashear Family Papers, Letter written by Camilla L. Brashear, 1930, Copied by TC Cottrell from Folklife Archives, Brashear Family Papers (SC 91)", located in the Kentucky Library, Western Kentucky University, Kentucky Library and Museum, Western Kentucky University, Bowling Green, Kentucky.

[19] Department of Library Special Collections Manuscripts and Folklife Archives, MSS 230 Warren County, Kentucky - Marriage Bonds, 1 September 1831, Marriage record for AWP Parker and Camilla S Brashear, Box 9, Folder 8, 1831, Kentucky Library and Museum, Western Kentucky University, Bowling Green, Kentucky.

[20] "Andrew William Parker Family Information" Genealogy Database, Paul Cox Ostrander, *The Ostrander's of Florence New Jersey* (http://familytreemaker.genealogy.com: accessed 31 January 2009).

[21] "Kentucky Death Records, 1852-1953," *Ancestry.com* (http://www.ancestry.com: accessed 14 April 2008), for Corilla P Irvine (28 December 1913), certificate 31380.

[22] Charles Brashear *Brashear(s) Family History, Volume 4*, p. 390.

[23] Ibid.

[24] Boyle County Genealogical Association, compiler, *Boyle County, Kentucky, Cemetery Records, 1792-1992* (Utica, Kentucky: McDowell Publications, 1992), FHL US/CAN 976.9523 V38b.

[25] "Bellevue Cemetery," database, *Find A Grave* (http://www.findagrave.com: accessed 15 May 2013), entry for William Porter Irvin, 1 November 1938; citing memorial # 43702392

[26]Margaret Logan Morris, *The Irvins, Doaks, Logans and McCampbells of Virginia and Kentucky* (22 Delta Drive, Pawtucket, Road Island: Quintin Publications, unknown publish date).

[27] "Bellevue Cemetery," database, *Find A Grave* (http://www.findagrave.com : accessed 15 May 2013), entry for Camilla Irvin Young, 1 December 1922; citing memorial # 43725897

[28] "Kentucky Death Records, 1852-1953," subscription database, *Ancestry.com* (http://www.ancestry.com: accessed 25 February 2014), for Melancthon Young (9 February 1924).

[29] Kentucky Wills and Probate Records, 1774-1989, *Ancestry.com* (http://www.ancestry.com: accessed 16 June 2016), entry for Melancthon Young, 18 September 1923, Probate Records, Volume K-M, 1865-1927.

[30] 'Irvin,' *The Advocate-Messenger*, Danville, Kentucky, April 8, 1930, Page 4, *Newspapers.com*, (https://www.newspapers.com: accessed 9 February 1016); image 143094689.

[31] "Bellevue Cemetery," database, *Find A Grave* (http://www.findagrave.com: accessed 15 May 2013), entry for Alexander Macy Irvine, 24 October 1895; citing memorial #43702530.

[32] Ibid.

[33] Charles Brashear *A Brashear(s) Family History, Descendants of Robert and Benois Brasseur, Volume 4, Brashear(s) Families of the Ohio Valley* (Clearlake Oaks, California: Charles Brashear Books, Etc., 2002).

[34] Boyle County Genealogical Association, *Boyle County, Kentucky Cemetery Records*, FHL US/CAN 976.9523 V38b.

[35] "Kentucky Death Records, 1852-1953," subscription database, *Ancestry.com* (http://www.ancestry.com: accessed 24 January 2014), for Charles H Irvin (transcribed as Tovine) (28 December 1944), certificate 26003.

[36] "Kentucky Death Records, 1852-1953," subscription database, *Ancestry.com* (http://www.ancestry.com: accessed 24 January 2014), for Hannah Simmons Irvine (11 May 1952), certificate 528912.

[37] "Bellevue Cemetery," database, *Find A Grave* (http://www.findagrave.com: accessed 24 January 2014), entry for Lela B Irvin, 1960; citing memorial # 43702162. Cottrell Digital Image Cd05302.

[38] "Bellevue Cemetery," database, *Find A Grave* (http://www.findagrave.com: accessed 15 May 2013), entry for Harry Irvin, 24 October 1895; citing memorial #43702530.

[39] Margaret Logan Morris, *The Irvins, Doaks, Logans and McCampbells.*

[40] Boyle County Genealogical Association, *Boyle County, Kentucky Cemetery Records*, FHL US/CAN 976.9523 V38b.

[41] "U.S. World War I Draft Registration Cards, 1917-1918," *Ancestry.com* (http://www.ancestry.com: accessed 16 March 2016), entry for Andrew Todd Irvin.

[42] 1920 US Census, Fayette County, Kentucky, population schedule, Lexington Ward, page 3B, Andrew T. Irvin, *Ancestry.com* (http://www.ancestry.com: accessed 16 March 2016); citing National Archives microfilm T625, roll 568.

[43] "Parker Family Information," Paul Cox Ostrander, *The Ostrander's of Florence New Jersey.*

[44] "Claiborne County Chancery Court Case Files 1803-1891 no M19-P1," digital images, *FamilySearch.org* (www.familysearch.org: accessed 17 January 2014), entry for Andrew A.W.P. Parker; citing Mississippi, Probate Records, 1781-1930, Claiborne Chancery Court Case Files 1803-1891 no M19-P1, Image 1803-1881, FHL # 43391101, Filmed 9 December 1992.

[45] "Parker Family Information," Paul Cox Ostrander, *The Ostrander's of Florence New Jersey.*

[46] "Claiborne County Chancery Court Case Files 1803-1891 no M19-P1," *FamilySearch.org*, entry for Andrew A.W.P. Parker.

[47] "Wintergreen Cemetery," database, *Find A Grave* (http://www.findagrave.com: accessed 17 January 2014), entry for Andrew William P. Parker, 22 November 1837; citing memorial # 56946156.

[48] "Claiborne County Chancery Court Case Files 1803-1891 no M19-P1," *FamilySearch.org*, entry for Andrew A.W.P. Parker.

[49] Ibid.

[50] Ibid.

[51] Charles Brashear *Brashear(s) Family History, Volume 4*, p. 389.

[52] Lillian Ockerman, compiler, *Nelson County Kentucky Marriages Bonds, Consents and Ministers Returns, 1833-1848* (P.O. Box 409, Bardstown, KY 40004: Nelson County Genealogical Society), FHL US/CAN 976.9495, V2o, V4.

[53] "U.S. Federal Census Mortality Schedules, 1850-1885," *Ancestry.com* (http://www.ancestry.com: accessed 20 December 2015), entry for Sarah F. Temple, December 1949; citing National Archives microfilm publication T655, roll 13.

[54] 1850 US Census, Warren County, Kentucky, population schedule, page 93B, dwelling 387, family 387, J.C. Temple.

[55] 1850 US Census, Warren County, Kentucky, population schedule, District 2, page 93B, dwelling 387, family 387, J.C. Temple, *Ancestry.com* (http://www.ancestry.com: accessed 20 December 2015); citing National Archives microfilm publication M432, roll 220.

[56] "Indiana Marriage Index 1800-1941," *Ancestry.com* (http://www.ancestry.com: accessed 20 December 2015), James R. Temple and Mary McCoy), 24 April 1867.

[57] 1880 US Census, Warrick County, Indiana, population schedule, Anderson, Enumeration District (ED) 59, page 232A, family 9, James R. Temple; *Ancestry.com* (http://www.ancestry.com: accessed 20 December 2015); citing National Archives microfilm T9, roll 320.

[58] 1885 Florida State Census, Hernando County, Florida, population schedule, page 112, J.R. Temple, *Ancestry.com* (http://www.ancestry.com: accessed 20 December 2015): citing National Archives microfilm M845, roll 4.

[59] "Fairview Cemetery (South Section)," database, *Find A Grave* (http://www.findagrave.com: accessed 20 December 2015), entry for Dr. James R. Temple, 2 August 1906; citing memorial #46534800.

[60] 1880 US Census, Warrick County, Indiana, population schedule, Anderson, page 232A, family 9, James R. Temple; *Ancestry.com* (http://www.ancestry.com: accessed 16 March 2016); citing National Archives microfilm T9, roll 320

[61] "Tucker Hill Cemetery," database. *Find A Grave* (http://www.findagrave.com: accessed 16 March 2016), entry for Warner R. Temple, 1 October 1887; citing memorial #86605279.

[62] 1880 US Census, Warrick County, Indiana, population schedule, Anderson, page 232A, family 9, James R. Temple; *Ancestry.com* (http://www.ancestry.com: accessed 16 March 2016).

[63] "Fairview Cemetery (South Section)," database, *Find A Grave* (http://www.findagrave.com: accessed 19 March 2016), entry for Charlie Brashear Temple, 15 October 1910; citing memorial #46534799.

[64] "Fairview Cemetery (South Section)," database, *Find A Grave* (http://www.findagrave.com: accessed 19 March 2016), entry for Willie Temple, 16 June 1893; citing memorial #47150937.

[65] "U.S. World War I Draft Registration Cards, 1917-1918," *Ancestry.com* (http://www.ancestry.com: accessed 16 March 2016), entry for William James Temple.

[66] "California Death Index, 1940-1997," *Ancestry.com* (http://www.ancestry.com: accessed 16 March 2016), entry for Max G. Temple, 1 September 1941.

[67] "Melrose Abbey Memorial Park," database, *Find A Grave* (http://www.findagrave.com: accessed 19 March 2016), entry for Max G. Temple, 1941; citing memorial #131315003.

[68] "Melrose Abbey Memorial Park," database, *Find A Grave* (http://www.findagrave.com: accessed 19 March 2016), entry for Myrtle M. Temple, 1939; citing memorial #131315002.

[69] 1920 US Census, Hall County, Texas, population schedule, Memphis, page 10A, Max G. Temple, *Ancestry.com* (http://www.ancestry.com: accessed 10 April 2016); citing National Archives microfilm T625, roll 1808.

[70] "Texas Birth Certificates, 1903-1932," database, Ancestry.com (http://www.ancestry.com: accessed 10 April 2016), entry for Maxine Temple, 28 January 1904.

[71] "Fairhaven Memorial Park," database, *Find A Grave* (http://www.findagrave.com: accessed 19 March 2016), entry for Blanche Temple Palmer, 13 October 1976; citing memorial #32869274.

[72] 1850 US Census, Warren County, Kentucky, population schedule, page 93B, dwelling 387, family 387, J.C. Temple.

[73] "U.S. National Homes for Disabled Volunteer Soldiers 1866-1938," *Ancestry.com* (http://www.ancestry.com: accessed 20 December 2015), entry for Walter R. Temple.

[74] "Kentucky Marriages 1851-1900," Ancestry.com (http://www.ancestry.com: accessed 20 December 2015), Jonathan Clark temple and Eliz W. Allen Page, 13 November 1851.

[75] 1870 US Census, Livingston County, Missouri, population schedule, Chillicothe, page 477B, dwelling 226, family 227, Charles Williams; *Ancestry.com* (http://www.ancestry.com: accessed 20 December 2015); citing National Archives microfilm publication M593, roll 789.

[76] Charles Brashear *Brashear(s) Family History, Volume 4*, page 390.

[77] Charles Brashear *Brashear(s) Family History, Volume 4*, page 392.

[78] "Presidio la Bahia," database, *Find A Grave* (http://www.findagrave.com: accessed 7 May 2013), entry for Richard G Brashear, 27 March 1836; citing memorial # 8017273.

[79] Zalame (Brashear) Cottrell, Brashear Family Notes.

[80] Charles Brashear *Brashear(s) Family History, Volume 4*, page 394.

[81] Ibid.

[82] Ibid.

[83] W H Perrin, J H Battle and G C Kniffin, *History of Kentucky Illustrated*, page 873.

Section 2 – Chapter 2 Sources – Walter Curran Brashear Family

[1] William H Brashear, Death Registration 12615 (1942), Department of Health Bureau of Vital Statistics, Frankfort, Kentucky.

[2] Zalame (Brashear) Cottrell, Brashear and Baker Family Data, handwritten notes.

[3] W H Perrin, J H Battle and G C Kniffin, *History of Kentucky Illustrated, Edition 3* (1887; reprint Greenville, South Carolina: Southern Historical Press, Inc., 1999), page 873.

[4] Letter from Walter Curren Brashear (Bowling Green Kentucky) to Ben C Grinder, 19 November 1846; Cottrell Family Papers (867 Jamestown Drive, Rockledge, Florida). Discussing his gloomy feelings.

[5] Ibid.

[6] Letter from Walter Curren Brashear (Near Bowling Green Kentucky) to Martha Crutchfield, 27 December 1846; Cottrell Family Papers (867 Jamestown Drive, Rockledge, Florida). Discussing the hardships Martha will encounter on the frontier if she accepts his marriage proposal.

[7] Letter from Walter Curren Brashear (Near Bowling Green Kentucky) to Martha Crutchfield, 26 January 1847; Cottrell Family Papers (867 Jamestown Drive, Rockledge, Florida). Proposing a time frame for Walter to go to Danville to marry Martha.

[8] Letter from Walter Curren Brashear (Bowling Green Kentucky) to Martha Crutchfield, 4 March 1847; Cottrell Family Papers (867 Jamestown Drive, Rockledge, Florida). Confirming date of arrival in Danville of the 19th of April.

[9] Letter from Walter Curren Brashear (Bowling Green Kentucky) to Martha Crutchfield, 15 April 1947; Cottrell Family Papers (867 Jamestown Drive, Rockledge, Florida). Detailing illness but confirming plans to arrive by Monday evening.

[10] Boyle County, Kentucky, Marriage records; 1842-1955, marriage bond for Walter C Brashear and Martha Crutchfield, FHL microfilm 191806, bk1, p135, Family History Library, Salt Lake City, Utah.

[11] "Kentucky Probate Records, 1727-1990," digital images, *Ancestry.com* (www.ancestry.com: accessed 17 October 2013), entry for James P Crutchfield, 12 June 1843; citing Boyle County Administrator Bonds, 1842-1852, Image 32.

[12] Calvin Morgan Fackler, *Early Days in Danville* (1941; reprint Utica, Kentucky: McDowell Publications, 2002), FHL US/CAN 976.9523/D1 H2f.

[13] "City of Danville, Kentucky, Bellevue Cemetery Interments, Alphabetical," database, *Danville Kentucky* (www.danvilleky.org: accessed 24 January 2014).

[14] Descendants of Charles McKinney, (http://www.geocities.com/bertdooley/McKinney_Line.html: Accessed on 15 December 2007).

[15] Calvin Morgan Fackler, *Early Days in Danville*.

[16] 1870 US Census, Fayette County, Kentucky, population schedule, Lexington Ward 2, page 33, dwelling 204, family 236, Ralph Georgi; *Ancestry.com* (http://www.ancestry.com: accessed 21 December 2007); citing Family History Library microfilm M593, roll 593.

[17] Calvin Morgan Fackler, *Early Days in Danville*.

[18] 1850 US Census, Boyle County, Kentucky, population schedule, District 2, page 331, dwelling 174, family 198, Ann Crutchfield; *Ancestry.com* (http://www.ancestry.com: accessed 15 December 2007); citing Family History Library microfilm M432, roll 493.

[19] "Kentucky Death Records, 1852-1953," subscription database, *Ancestry.com* (http://www.ancestry.com: accessed 11 December 2007), for Rich Ann Georgi (9 April 1923), certificate 10579.

Cottrell-Brashear Family Linage

[20] "Kentucky Death Records, 1852-1953," subscription database, *Ancestry.com* (http://www.ancestry.com: accessed 21 December 2007), for Prof Ralph Georgi (2 November 1898), certificate 3166.

[21] "Kentucky Death Records, 1852-1953," subscription database, *Ancestry.com* (http://www.ancestry.com: accessed 21 December 2007), for Miss Anna Georgi (22 October 1941), certificate 23841.

[22] W H Perrin, J H Battle and G C Kniffin, *History of Kentucky Illustrated*, page 873.

[23] 1860 US Census, Warren County, Kentucky, population schedule, Post Office Bowling Green, page 841B, dwelling 1239, family 1239, Wm. C. Brashears; *Ancestry.com* (http://www.ancestry.com: accessed 28 April 2004); citing National Archives microfilm publication M653, roll 398.

[24] "U.S., Civil War Draft Registrations Records, 1863-1865," subscription database, *Ancestry.com* (http://www.ancestry.com: accessed 26 July 2012), for Walter C Brashear (February 1864), ARC Identifier: 4213514.

[25] Parish Records, 1861-1919, Christ Episcopal Church, Bowling Green, KY, Baptisms, Confirmations, Marriages, Burials, 1942, Copied by TC Cottrell from Folklife Archives, Manuscripts &; "Christ Episcopal Church - Bowling Green, Kentucky (SC 2219)", located in the Kentucky Library, Western Kentucky University, Kentucky Library and Museum, Western Kentucky University, Bowling Green, Kentucky.

[26] Parish Records, 1861-1919, Christ Episcopal Church, Bowling Green, KY, includes some records of Glasgow and Russellville Missions, 1942, Copied by TC Cottrell from Folklife Archives, Manuscripts &; "Christ Episcopal Church - Bowling Green, Kentucky (SC 2219)", located in the Kentucky Library, Western Kentucky University, Kentucky Library and Museum, Western Kentucky University, Bowling Green, Kentucky.

[27] 1870 US Census, Warren County, Kentucky, population schedule, Bowling Green Precinct, Post Office Bowling Green, page 8B, dwelling 112, family 112, Walter Brashear; *Ancestry.com* (http://www.ancestry.com: accessed 7 August 2004); citing National Archives microfilm M593, roll 502.

[28] Parish Records, 1861-1919, Christ Episcopal Church, Bowling Green, KY, Includes some records of Glasgow and Russellville Missions, 1942.

[29] 1880 US Census, Warren County, Kentucky, population schedule, Subdivision No 228, Enumeration District (ED) 228, page 67D, family 135, Walter C Brashear; *Ancestry.com* (http://www.ancestry.com: accessed 8 August 2004); citing National Archives microfilm T9, roll 444.

[30] 1880 US Census, Warren County, Kentucky, agricultural schedule, page 11A, Walter C Brashear; NARA microfilm publication M1528, roll 31.

[31] Parish Records, 1861-1919, Christ Episcopal Church, Bowling Green, KY, Includes some records of Glasgow and Russellville Missions, 1942.

[32] Walter C Brashear will (24 December 1900), Last Will and Testament, Cottrell Family Papers, 867 Jamestown Drive, Rockledge, Florida.

[33] Zalame (Brashear) Cottrell, Brashear and Baker Family Data, handwritten notes.

[34] Patricia E Reid and Barbara O Ford compilers *Fairview Cemetery, Bowling Green, Kentucky, Cemetery 1*, Volume 1 (Kentucky: unknown publisher, 1989), page 69.

[35] Parish Records, 1861-1919, Christ Episcopal Church, Bowling Green, KY, Includes some records of Glasgow and Russellville Missions, 1942.

[36] 1900 US Census, Warren County, Kentucky, population schedule, Bowling Green, Enumeration District (ED) 99, page 15, dwelling 26, family 26, Walter C Brashear; *Ancestry.com* (http://www.ancestry.com: accessed 7 August 2004); citing National Archives microfilm T623, roll 553.

[37] Walter C Brashear will (24 December 1900), Last Will and Testament, Cottrell Family Papers, 867 Jamestown Drive, Rockledge, Florida.

[38] Warren County, Kentucky, Probate Records, 1797-1985, Vols. D, 4-6 1827-1927 - v. D, will of Walter C Brashear, FHL microfilm 1904209, volume 5, page 386, Family History Library, Salt Lake City, Utah.

[39] Walter Brashear Dead, *Owensboro Messenger*, Daviess County, Kentucky, 11 June 1902.

[40] Patricia E Reid and Barbara O Ford compilers *Fairview Cemetery, Bowling Green, Kentucky, Cemetery 1*, page 69.

[41] *Owensboro Messenger*, 11 June 1902, page 7.

[42] Warren County, Kentucky, Probate Records, 1797-1985, Vols. D, 4-6 1827-1927 - v. D, will of Walter C Brashear, FHL microfilm 1904209, volume 5, page 386, Family History Library, Salt Lake City, Utah.

[43] Zalame (Brashear) Cottrell, Brashear and Baker Family Data.

[44] 1860 US Census, Warren County, Kentucky, population schedule, page 841B, dwelling 1239, family 1239, Wm C Brashears.

[45] 1870 US Census, Warren County, Kentucky, population schedule, page 8B, dwelling 112, family 112, Walter Brashear.

[46] "Kentucky Marriage Records, 1852-1914," subscription database, *Ancestry.com* (http://www.ancestry.com: accessed 19 November 2007), for R.K. McGinnis and Estella Brashear (11 December 1878).

[47] "Kentucky Death Records, 1852-1953," subscription database, *Ancestry.com* (http://www.ancestry.com: accessed 19 April 2008), for R.K. McGinnis (28 December 1921), certificate 28402.

[48] 1870 US Census, Warren County, Kentucky, population schedule, Post Office: Bowling Green, page 91A, dwelling 161, family 161, DB Campbell; *Ancestry.com* (http://www.ancestry.com: accessed 16 October 2004); citing National Archives microfilm M593, roll 502.

[49] 1880 US Census, Warren County, Kentucky, population schedule, Subdivision 225, Enumeration District (ED) 116, page 64A, dwelling 169, Robert McGinnis; *Ancestry.com* (http://www.ancestry.com: accessed 16 October 2004); citing National Archives microfilm T9, roll 444.

[50] 1900 US Census, Warren County, Kentucky, population schedule, Bristow, Enumeration District (ED) 97, page 9A, dwelling 163, family 163, Robert R McGinnis; *Ancestry.com* (http://www.ancestry.com: accessed 16 October 2004); citing National Archives microfilm T623, roll 553.

[51] 1910 US Census, Warren County, Kentucky, population schedule, District 4, Enumeration District (ED) 119, page 20B, dwelling 382, family 423, Robert McGinnis; *Ancestry.com* (http://www.ancestry.com: accessed 16 October 2004); citing National Archives microfilm T624, roll 505.

[52] "Kentucky Death Records, 1852-1953," subscription database, *Ancestry.com* (http://www.ancestry.com: accessed 20 November 2007), for Walter B McGinnis (1 September 1943), certificate 21258.

[53] Funeral is Held for "Mac" McGinnis, *Unidentified Warren County Kentucky Newspaper*, Warren County. Kentucky.

[54] "Missouri Marriage Records, 1805-2002," subscription database, *Ancestry.com* (http://www.ancestry.com: accessed 12 April 2008), for Walter B McGinnis and Minnie Myers (1 January 1902).

[55] 1910 US Census, Livingston County, Missouri, population schedule, Chillicothe, Ward 4, Enumeration District (ED) 101, page 3A, dwelling 60, family 60, Walter B McGinnis; *Ancestry.com* (http://www.ancestry.com: accessed 21 January 2008); citing National Archives microfilm T624, roll 796.

[56] 1920 US Census, Livingston County, Missouri, population schedule, Chillicothe, Ward 4, Enumeration District (ED) 102, page 1A, dwelling 8, family 8, Wm E Myers; *Ancestry.com* (http://www.ancestry.com: accessed 21 January 2008); citing National Archives microfilm T625, roll 918.

[57] 1940 US Census, Warren County, Kentucky, population schedule, Bowling Green, Enumeration District (ED) 114-14, page 24B, family 506, William H Brashear; *Ancestry.com* (http://www.ancestry.com: accessed 16 February 2014); citing National Archives microfilm T627, roll 1360.

[58] "Kentucky Death Records, 1852-1953," subscription database, *Ancestry.com* (http://www.ancestry.com: accessed 19 November 2007), for Mrs. Stella McGinnis (3 November 1912), certificate 29125.

[59] Patricia E Reid and Barbara O Ford compilers *Fairview Cemetery, Bowling Green, Kentucky, Cemetery 1*, page 69.

[60] 1920 US Census, Warren County, Kentucky, population schedule, Magisterial District #4, Enumeration District (ED) 133, page 1B, dwelling 21, family 22, Robert K McGinnis; *Ancestry.com* (http://www.ancestry.com: accessed 16 October 2004); citing National Archives microfilm T625, roll 600.

[61] 1920 US Census, Warren County, Kentucky, population schedule, Magisterial District #4, Enumeration District (ED) 133, page 1B, dwelling 21, family 22, Robert K McGinnis; *Ancestry.com* (http://www.ancestry.com: accessed 16 October 2004); citing National Archives publication T625, roll 600.

[62] "Kentucky Death Records", for R.K. McGinnis (28 December 1921), certificate 28402.

[63] Patricia E Reid and Barbara O Ford compilers *Fairview Cemetery, Bowling Green, Kentucky, Cemetery 1*, page 69.

[64] Warren County, Kentucky, Kentucky Probate Records, 1727-1990, will of R.K. McGinnis, FHL microfilm 1904209, Will Book 6, page 405, Family History Library, Salt Lake City, Utah.

[65] "Kentucky Death Records, 1852-1953," subscription database, *Ancestry.com* (http://www.ancestry.com: accessed 27 November 2009), for Sallie McGinnis (12 June 1952), certificate 5213291.

[66] Patricia E Reid and Barbara O Ford compilers *Fairview Cemetery, Bowling Green, Kentucky, Cemetery 1*, page 69.

[67] "Kentucky Death Records, 1852-1953," subscription database, *Ancestry.com* (http://www.ancestry.com: accessed 11 November 2007), for Richard L Brashear (18 November 1911), certificate 29883.

[68] Zalame (Brashear) Cottrell, Brashear and Baker Family Data.

[69] 1860 US Census, Warren County, Kentucky, population schedule, page 841B, dwelling 1239, family 1239, Wm. C. Brashears, listed as age 35.

[70] Parish Records, 1861-1919, Christ Episcopal Church.

[71] Ibid.

[72] 1870 US Census, Warren County, Kentucky, population schedule, page 8B, dwelling 112, family 112, Walter Brashear.

[73] 1880 US Census, Warren County, Kentucky, agricultural schedule, page 11A, Walter C Brashear; NARA microfilm M1528, roll 31.

[74] 1900 US Census, Warren County, Kentucky, population schedule, Bristow Magisterial District, Enumeration District (ED) 97, page 74a, dwelling 164, family 164, Archie W Baker; *Ancestry.com* (http://www.ancestry.com: accessed 21 August 2004); citing National Archives microfilm T623, roll 553.

[75] "Kentucky Death Records, 1852-1953," subscription database, *Ancestry.com* (http://www.ancestry.com: accessed 20 November 2007), for Arch W. Baker (7 November 1933), certificate 27585.

[76] Parish Records, 1861-1919, Christ Episcopal Church.

[77] 1900 US Census, Warren County, Kentucky, population schedule, Bristow Magisterial District, Enumeration District (ED) 97, page 74a, dwelling 164, family 164, Archie W Baker; *Ancestry.com* (http://www.ancestry.com: accessed 21 August 2004); citing National Archives microfilm T623, roll 553.

[78] 1910 US Census, Warren County, Kentucky, population schedule, District No 3, Enumeration District (ED) 116, page 10b, dwelling 174, family 174, Arch W Baker; *Ancestry.com* (http://www.ancestry.com: accessed 13 August 2004); citing National Archives microfilm publication T624, roll 504.

[79] 1920 US Census, Warren County, Kentucky, population schedule, Bristow, Enumeration District (ED) 130, page 1A, dwelling 2, family 2, Arch W Baker; *Ancestry.com* (http://www.ancestry.com: accessed 21 January 2008); citing National Archives microfilm T625, roll 690.

[80] 1930 US Census, Warren County, Kentucky, population schedule, Bristow, Enumeration District (ED) 114-29, page 11A, dwelling 258, family 259, Arch W Baker; *Ancestry.com* (http://www.ancestry.com: accessed 21 January 2008); citing National Archives microfilm T626, roll 780.

[81] "Kentucky Death Records, 1852-1953," subscription database, *Ancestry.com* (http://www.ancestry.com: accessed 20 November 2007), for Mrs. Arch W. Baker (2 August 1933), certificate 20069.

[82] Patricia E Reid and Barbara O Ford compilers *Fairview Cemetery, Bowling Green, Kentucky, Cemetery 1*, page 69.

[83] "Kentucky Death Records", for Arch W. Baker (7 November 1933), certificate 27585.

[84] Patricia E Reid and Barbara O Ford compilers *Fairview Cemetery, Bowling Green, Kentucky, Cemetery 1*, page 69.

[85] William H Brashear, Death Registration 12615 (1942), Department of Health Bureau of Vital Statistics, Frankfort, Kentucky, certificate # 12615.

[86] 1860 US Census, Warren County, Kentucky, population schedule, page 841B, dwelling 1239, family 1239, Wm. C. Brashears, listed as age 35.

[87] 1870 US Census, Warren County, Kentucky, population schedule, page 8B, dwelling 112, family 112, Walter Brashear.

[88] 1880 US Census, Warren County, Kentucky, agricultural schedule, page 11A, Walter C Brashear; NARA microfilm M1528, roll 31.

[89] 1900 US Census, Warren County, Kentucky, population schedule, ED 99, page 15, dwelling 26, family 26, Walter C Brashear.

[90] W.H. Brashear Taken by Death, *Daily News*, Bowling Green, Kentucky.

[91] Beech Bend Park, *The Times Journal*, Bowling Green Kentucky, 14 May 1908.

[92] 1910 US Census, Warren County, Kentucky, population schedule, Magisterial District No 5, Enumeration District (ED) 122, page 1B, dwelling 22, family 22, William H Brashear; *Ancestry.com* (http://www.ancestry.com: accessed 8 August 2004); citing National Archives microfilm T624, roll 505.

Cottrell-Brashear Family Linage

[93] Unidentified Agency, *The Electric Railway Journal, Index to Volume XLII* (New York, New York: McGraw Publishing Company, Inc., 1913).

[94] 1920 US Census, Warren County, Kentucky, population schedule, Bowling Green, Enumeration District (ED) 139, page 14B, dwelling 317, family 329, William H Brashear; *Ancestry.com* (http://www.ancestry.com: accessed 8 August 2004); citing National Archives microfilm T625, roll 600.

[95] 1930 US Census, Warren County, Kentucky, population schedule, Bowling Green, Enumeration District (ED) 114-11, page 2A, dwelling 29, family 29, William Brashear; *Ancestry.com* (http://www.ancestry.com: accessed 8 August 2004); citing National Archives microfilm T626, roll 779.

[96] Associated Gas and Electric Company, State of New York, Seven Percent Convertible Obligation Issued to William H Brashear, 4 September 1934.

[97] "U.S. City Directories - 1937/38-1949," database, *Ancestry.com* (http://www.ancestry.com: accessed 20 March 2009); citing *"Caron's Bowling Green Kentucky City Directory for 1937-1938 - Warren County Section* (Bowling Green, Kentucky: Caron Directory Company)".

[98] 1940 US Census, Warren County, Kentucky, population schedule, Bowling Green, Enumeration District (ED) 114-14, page 24B, family 506, William H Brashear;*Ancestry.com* (http://www.ancestry.com: accessed 16 February 2014); citing National Archives microfilm T627, roll 1360.

[99] William H Brashear, death certificate no. 12615, listed as single.

[100] W.H. Brashear Taken by Death, *Daily News*, Bowling Green, Kentucky.

[101] Final Report for the Estate of W.H. Brashear, 22 May 1944.

[102] "Beech Bend Park," *Wikipedia: The Free Encyclopedia*, Wikimedia Foundation, Inc., (http://www.wikipedia.org: accessed 17 June 2016), date site last updated (15 June 2016).

[103] Zalame (Brashear) Cottrell, Brashear and Baker Family Data.

[104] 1860 US Census, Warren County, Kentucky, population schedule, page 841B, dwelling 1239, family 1239, Wm. C. Brashears, listed as age 35.

[105] 1870 US Census, Warren County, Kentucky, population schedule, page 8B, dwelling 112, family 112, Walter Brashear.

[106] Parish Records, 1861-1919, Christ Episcopal Church.

[107] 1880 US Census, Warren County, Kentucky, agricultural schedule, page 11A, Walter C. Brashear; NARA microfilm publication M1528, roll 31.

[108] Warren County, Kentucky Burial Permits, 1877-1913, Transcripts made from the Original Permits in the Kentucky Library, Western Kentucky University, selected entries A-K, Kentucky Library and Museum, Western Kentucky University, Bowling Green, Kentucky.

[109] Zalame (Brashear) Cottrell, Brashear and Baker Family Data.

[110] 1860 US Census, Warren County, Kentucky, population schedule, page 841B, dwelling 1239, family 1239, Wm. C. Brashears, listed as age 35.

[111] Parish Records, 1861-1919, Christ Episcopal Church.

[112] 1870 US Census, Warren County, Kentucky, population schedule, page 8B, dwelling 112, family 112, Walter Brashear.

[113] 1880 US Census, Warren County, Kentucky, population schedule, Smiths Grove, Enumeration District (ED) 239, page 261A, dwelling 1, family 1, L A Hasdell; *Ancestry.com* (http://www.ancestry.com: accessed 8 August 2004); citing National Archives microfilm publication T9, roll 445.

[114] Warren County, Kentucky, Marriage Record Book S, P 51 (17 October 1883), Curran W Brashear and Mattie Arl; Warren County Courthouse, Clerk Warren County Court.

Copied at County Courthouse in Bowling Green, Kentucky on 11 September 2014 by TC Cottrell.

[115] "Kentucky Death Records, 1852-1953," subscription database, *Ancestry.com* (http://www.ancestry.com: accessed 20 November 2007), for Mattie Arl Brashear (6 September 1945), certificate 20154.

[116] 1900 US Census, Warren County, Kentucky, population schedule, Bowling, Enumeration District (ED) 102, page 8A, dwelling 141, family 165, Curren W Brashear; digital images, *Ancestry.com* (http://www.ancestry.com: accessed 28 April 2004); citing National Archives microfilm T623, roll 553

[117] Walter C Brashear will (24 December 1900), Last Will and Testament

[118] 1910 US Census, Warren County, Kentucky, population schedule, District No 4, Enumeration District (ED) 119, page 12B, dwelling 217, family 246, Curren W Brashear; *Ancestry.com* (http://www.ancestry.com: accessed 8 August 2004); citing National Archives microfilm T624, roll 505.

[119] 1920 US Census, Warren County, Kentucky, population schedule, Bowling Green, Enumeration District (ED) 133, page 3A, dwelling 64, family 70, Curren W Brashear; *Ancestry.com* (http://www.ancestry.com: accessed 9 August 2004); citing National Archives microfilm T625, roll 600.

[120] "Kentucky Death Index, 1911-2000," subscription database, *Ancestry.com* (http://www.ancestry.com: accessed 14 November 2004), for Corinne Brashear (11 January 1968), volume 5, certificate 2121.

[121] "Businesses in Warren County Kentucky - Dressmaking," *Western Kentucky University* (www.wku.edu: accessed on 31 December 2004).

[122] Walter C Brashear, Death Registration 558384 (1955), Department of Health Bureau of Vital Statistics, Frankfort, Kentucky.

[123] Warren County, Kentucky, Marriage Bond Book 1, P 131 (19 February 1951), Walter C Brashear and Mary D Burton; Warren County Courthouse, Clerk Warren County Court. Copied at County Courthouse in Bowling Green, Kentucky on 11 September 2014 by TC Cottrell.

[124] "Fairview Cemetery," database, *Find A Grave* (http://www.findagrave.com: accessed 11 October 2014), entry for Mary D Burton Brashear, 25 July 1968; citing memorial # 126568840.

[125] "U.S. City Directories - 1937/38-1949," database, *Ancestry.com* (http://www.ancestry.com: accessed 20 March 2009); citing "*Caron's Bowling Green Kentucky City Directory for the Years 1937-1938* (Bowling Green, Kentucky: Caron Directory Company)".

[126] "Fairview Cemetery," database, *Find A Grave* (http://www.findagrave.com: accessed 11 October 2014), entry for Mary D Burton Brashear.

[127] 1920 US Census, Warren County, Kentucky, population schedule, Magisterial District 4, Enumeration District (ED) 133, page 1B, dwelling 3, family 3, Della Brashear; *Ancestyry.com* (http://www.ancestry.com: accessed 10 August 2004); citing National Archives microfilm T625, roll 600.

[128] "U.S. Social Security Death Index, 1935-2014," *Ancestry.com* (http://www.ancestry.com: accessed 209 March 2016), entry for Camilla B. Shellman.

[129] "Kentucky Marriage Index, 1973-1999," *Ancestry.com* (http://www.ancestry.com: accessed 24 March 2016), for Camilla B. Hougland and Joseph M. Shellman (29 June 1974), certificate 14983.

[130] "Mount Kenton Cemetery," database, *Find A Grave* (http://www.findagrave.com: accessed 20 March 2016), entry for Joseph M Shellman, 26 February 2009; citing memorial #114123444.

Cottrell-Brashear Family Linage

[131] "Kentucky Death Records, 1852-1953," *Ancestry.com* (http://www.ancestry.com: accessed 19 November 2007), for Mildred B Gilmore (9 April 1920), certificate 12782.

[132] Patricia E Reid and Barbara O Ford compilers *Fairview Cemetery, Bowling Green, Kentucky, Cemetery 1*, Volume 1 (Kentucky: unknown publisher, 1989).

[133] Parish Records, 1861-1919, Christ Episcopal Church.

[134] Ibid.

[135] 1910 US Census, Warren County, Kentucky, population schedule, enumeration district 119, page 12B, dwelling 217, family 246, Curren W Brashear.

[136] "Kentucky Death Records", for Mildred B Gilmore (9 April 1920), certificate 12782.

[137] "World War I Draft Registration Cards", for Nathaniel M Gilmore, citing United States, Selective Service System. World War I Selective Service System Draft Registration Cards, 1917-1918. Washington, D.C.: National Archives and Records Administration. Microfilm publication M1509, Warren County, Kentucky; Roll 1653845; Draft Board: 0.

[138] "Kentucky Death Index, 1911-2000," subscription database, *Ancestry.com* (http://www.ancestry.com: accessed 13 April 2008), for Nathaniel M Gilmore (27 April 1966), volume 19, certificate 9740.

[139] "Texas Death Index, 1903-2000," subscription database, *Ancestry.com* (http://www.ancestry.com: accessed 28 September 2013), for Curran Arl Brashear (7 January 1955), certificate 2307

[140] "U.S. Headstone Applications for Military Veterans, 1925-1963," *Ancestry.com* (www.ancestry.com: accessed 2 June 2013), entry for Curran Arl Brashear, 7 January 1955; citing Records of the Office of the Quartermaster General, 1774-1985, Record Group 92, The National Archives at College Park, College Park, Maryland.

[141] 1910 US Census, Warren County, Kentucky, population schedule, enumeration district 119, page 12B, dwelling 217, family 246, Curren W Brashear.

[142] "World War I Draft Registration Cards", for Curren Arl Brashear, citing United States, Selective Service System. World War I Selective Service System Draft Registration Cards, 1917-1918. Washington, D.C.: National Archives and Records Administration. Microfilm publication M1509, Warren County, Kentucky; Roll 1653844; Draft Board: 0.

[143] "U.S. Headstone Applications for Military Veterans, 1925-1963" *Ancestry.com*, entry for Curran Arl Brashear, 7 January 1955.

[144] 1920 US Census, Warren County, Kentucky, population schedule, enumeration schedule 133, page 3A, dwelling 64, family 70, Curren W Brashear.

[145] "Texas, Death Certificates, 1903-1982," subscription database, *Ancestry.com* (http://www.ancestry.com: accessed 16 July 2015), for Helen Cummings Brashear (12 February 1979), Certificate No. 11175.

[146] Ibid.

[147] Claude Lane Brashear, *The Greenwood Commonwealth*, Greenwood, Mississippi, 22 January 1988, page 2, column 5 and 6.

[148] "World War I Draft Registration Cards, 1917-1918," subscription database, *Ancestry.com* (http://www.ancestry.com: accessed 1 July 2006), for Claude L Brashear, citing United States, Selective Service System. World War I Selective Service System Draft Registration Cards, 1917-1918. Washington, D.C.: National Archives and Records Administration. Microfilm publication M1509, Warren County, Kentucky; Roll 1653844; Draft Board: 0.

[149] Warren County, Kentucky, Marriage Record Book 11, P 110 (15 June 1921), Claude L Brashear and Katie T Murphy; Warren County Courthouse, Clerk Warren County Court. Copied at County Courthouse in Bowling Green, Kentucky on 11 September 2014 by TC Cottrell.

[150] Social Security Administration, "Social Security Death Index," *Ancestry.com* (http://www.ancestry.com: accessed 2 June 2013), entry for Katie Brashear, 1985, SS no. 405-14-5998.

[151] Mrs. Katie Brashear, *Daily News*, Bowling Green, Kentucky, 30 January 1985.

[152] 1940 US Census, Warren County, Kentucky, population schedule, Bowling Green, Enumeration District (ED) 114-5, page 24A, dwelling 592, Claud Brashear; *Ancestry.com* (http://www.ancestry.com: accessed 22 May 2013); citing National Archives microfilm T627, roll 1360

[153] "Odd Fellows Cemetery," database, *Find A Grave* (http://www.findagrave.com: accessed 21 March 2016), entry for Corrine Hope Brashear, 18 September 2014; citing Memorial #136129191.

[154] "U.S. Social Security Applications and Claims Index, 1935-2007," Ancestry.com (http://www.ancestry.com: accessed 21 March 2016), for Harold Lane Brashear (14 October 1994).

[155] "U.S. Department of Veterans Affairs BIRLS Death File, 1850-2010," digital images, *Ancestry.com* (www.ancestry.com: accessed 25 December 2013), entry for Harold Brashear, 14 October 1994; citing Beneficiary Identification Records Locator Subsystem (BIRLS) Death File. Washington, D.C.: U.S. Department of Veterans Affairs.

[156] "Kentucky Birth Index, 1911-1999," Ancestry.com (http://www.ancestry.com: accessed 21 March 2016), entry for David A. Brashear (1 December 1932).

[157] William B Brashear, Death Registration 6519091 (1965), Department of Health Bureau of Vital Statistics, Frankfort, Kentucky.

[158] Ibid.

[159] "World War I Draft Registration Cards, 1917-1918," subscription database, *Ancestry.com* (http://www.ancestry.com: accessed 1 July 2006), for William Bottom Brashear, citing United States, Selective Service System. World War I Selective Service System Draft Registration Cards, 1917-1918. Washington, D.C.: National Archives and Records Administration. Microfilm M1509, Warren County, Kentucky; Roll 1653844; Draft Board: 0.

[160] 1930 US Census, Warren County, Kentucky, population schedule, Bowling Green, Enumeration District (ED) 114-4, page 3B, dwelling 63, family 82, William B Brashear; *Ancestry.com* (http://www.ancestry.com: accessed 11 August 2004); citing National Archives microfilm T626, roll 779.

[161] "Kentucky Death Records, 1852-1953," subscription database, *Ancestry.com* (http://www.ancestry.com: accessed 20 November 2007), for Curren W Brashear (2 November 1931), certificate 28066.

[162] 1940 US Census, Warren County, Kentucky, population schedule, Bowling Green, Enumeration District (ED) 114-5, page 15A, dwelling 627, Mattie A. Brashear; *Ancestry.com* (http://www.ancestry.com: accessed 6 January 2016); citing National Archives microfilm publication T627, roll 1360.

[163] "Kentucky Death Records, 1852-1953," subscription database, *Ancestry.com* (http://www.ancestry.com: accessed 20 November 2007), for Mattie Arl Brashear (6 September 1945), certificate 20154.

[164] Brashear and Baker Family Data.

[165] 1860 US Census, Warren County, Kentucky, population schedule, page 841B, dwelling 1239, family 1239, Wm. C. Brashears, listed as age 35.

[166] Parish Records, 1861-1919, Christ Episcopal Church.

[167] 1870 US Census, Warren County, Kentucky, population schedule, page 8B, dwelling 112, family 112, Walter Brashear.

[168] 1880 US Census, Warren County, Kentucky, agricultural schedule, page 11A, Walter C. Brashear; NARA microfilm M1528, roll 31.

[169] Patricia E Reid and Barbara O Ford compilers *Fairview Cemetery, Bowling Green, Kentucky, Cemetery 1.*

[170] Brashear and Baker Family Data.

[171] Parish Records, 1861-1919, Christ Episcopal Church.

[172] 1870 US Census, Warren County, Kentucky, population schedule, page 8B, dwelling 112, family 112, Walter Brashear.

[173] Parish Records, 1861-1919, Christ Episcopal Church.

[174] 1880 US Census, Warren County, Kentucky, agricultural schedule, page 11A, Walter C. Brashear; NARA microfilm publication M1528, roll 31.

[175] 1900 US Census, Warren County, Kentucky, population schedule, enumeration district 99, page 15, dwelling 26, family 26, Walter C Brashear.

[176] W.H. Brashear Taken by Death, *Daily News*, Bowling Green, Kentucky.

[177] 1910 US Census, Warren County, Kentucky, population schedule, page 1B, dwelling 22, family 22, William H Brashear.

[178] 1920 US Census, Warren County, Kentucky, population schedule, page 14B, dwelling 317, family 329, William H Brashear.

[179] 1930 US Census, Warren County, Kentucky, population schedule, page 2A, dwelling. 29, family 29, William Brashear.

[180] "Kentucky Death Records, 1852-1953," subscription database, *Ancestry.com* (http://www.ancestry.com: accessed 20 November 2007), for Dora Brashear (16 July 1938), certificate 18661.

[181] Brashear and Baker Family Data.

[182] Parish Records, 1861-1919, Christ Episcopal Church.

[183] 1870 US Census, Warren County, Kentucky, population schedule, page 8B, dwelling 112, family 112, Walter Brashear.

[184] Parish Records, 1861-1919, Christ Episcopal Church.

[185] 1880 US Census, Warren County, Kentucky, agricultural schedule, page 11A, Walter C. Brashear; NARA microfilm publication M1528, roll 31.

[186] 1900 US Census, Warren County, Kentucky, population schedule, page 15, dwelling 26, family 26, Walter C Brashear.

[187] W.H. Brashear Taken by Death, *Daily News*, Bowling Green, Kentucky.

[188] 1910 US Census, Warren County, Kentucky, population schedule, page 1B, dwelling 22, family 22, William H Brashear.

[189] 1920 US Census, Warren County, Kentucky, population schedule, page 14B, dwelling 317, family 329, William H Brashear.

[190] 1930 US Census, Warren County, Kentucky, population schedule, page 2A, dwelling. 29, family 29, William Brashear.

[191] "Kentucky Death Records, 1852-1953," subscription database, *Ancestry.com* (http://www.ancestry.com: accessed 19 November 2007), for Miss Virginia Light Brashear (6 May 1936), certificate 14968.

Section 2 – Chapter 3 Sources – Richard Levi Brashear Family

[1] "Kentucky Death Records, 1852-1953," subscription database, *Ancestry.com* (http://www.ancestry.com: accessed 11 November 2007), for Richard L Brashear (18 November 1911), certificate 29883.

[2] 1860 US Census, Warren County, Kentucky, population schedule, Post Office Bowling Green, page 841B, dwelling 1239, family 1239, Wm C Brashears; *Ancestry.com* (http://www.ancestry.com: accessed 28 April 2004); citing National Archives microfilm M653, roll 398.

[3] 1870 US Census, Daviess County, Kentucky, population schedule, Upper Town Precinct, Owensboro City, page 325A, dwelling 2, family 2, Peter Cotterell; *Ancestry.com* (http://www.ancestry.com: accessed 21 March 2003); citing National Archives microfilm M593, roll 458.

[4] W H Perrin, J H Battle and G C Kniffin, *History of Kentucky Illustrated, Edition 3* (1887; reprint Greenville, South Carolina: Southern Historical Press, Inc., 1999), page 873, Richard L Brashear.

[5] 1880 US Census, Warren County, Kentucky, population schedule, Subdivision No 228, Enumeration District (ED) 228, page 67D, family 135, Walter C Brashear; *Ancestry.com* (http://www.ancestry.com: accessed 8 August 2004); citing National Archives microfilm T9, roll 444.

[6] W H Perrin, J H Battle and G C Kniffin, *History of Kentucky Illustrated*, page 873, Richard L Brashear.

[7] Warren County, Kentucky, Marriage Record Book S, P 170 (25 September 1885), RL Brashear and AW Baker; Warren County Courthouse, Clerk Warren County Court. Copied at County Courthouse in Bowling Green, Kentucky on 11 September 2014 by TC Cottrell.

[8] "Kentucky Death Records, 1852-1953," subscription database, *Ancestry.com* (http://www.ancestry.com: accessed 25 December 2007), for Mrs Margaret A. Shaffer (19 July 1918), certificate 16105.

[9] Zalame (Brashear) Cottrell, Brashear and Baker Family Data, handwritten notes without sources, Cottrell Family Papers, 867 Jamestown Drive, Rockledge, Florida.

[10] Ibid.

[11] 1850 US Census, Warren County, Kentucky, population schedule, District 1, page 3, dwelling 36, family 36, L.F. Baker; *Ancestry.com* (http://www.ancestry.com: accessed 21 May 2009); citing National Archives microfilm M432, roll 220.

[12] "Kentucky Death Records, 1852-1953," subscription database, *Ancestry.com* (http://www.ancestry.com: accessed 20 November 2007), for Arch W. Baker (7 November 1933), certificate 27585.

[13] Brashear and Baker Family Data.

[14] Ibid.

[15] Ibid.

[16] "Kentucky Birth Records, 1852-1910," subscription database, *Ancestry.com* (http://www.ancestry.com: accessed 3 July 2009), for Fanny Baker (1856), citing Kentucky Birth, Marriage and Death Records – Microfilm (1852-1910). Microfilm rolls #994027-994058. Kentucky Department for Libraries and Archives, Frankfort, Kentucky.

[17] "Kentucky Birth Records, 1852-1910," subscription database, *Ancestry.com* (http://www.ancestry.com: accessed 3 July 2009), for Henry Baker (7 April 1859), citing Kentucky Birth, Marriage and Death Records – Microfilm (1852-1910). Microfilm rolls #994027-994058. Kentucky Department for Libraries and Archives, Frankfort, Kentucky.

[18] "Kentucky Birth Records, 1852-1910," subscription database, *Ancestry.com* (http://www.ancestry.com: accessed 3 July 2009), for Bunch (10 November 1859), citing Kentucky Birth, Marriage and Death Records – Microfilm (1852-1910). Microfilm rolls #994027-994058. Kentucky Department for Libraries and Archives, Frankfort, Kentucky.

[19] Kathleen Hope Brashear, Remembrances of Bowling Green, 27 March 1985, handwritten memories without sources.

[20] Patricia E Reid and Barbara O Ford compilers *Fairview Cemetery, Bowling Green, Kentucky, Cemetery 1*, Volume 1 (Kentucky: unknown publisher, 1989).

[21] Warren County, Kentucky, Marriage Records, 1797-1965, Vols. Q-T 1877-1888, bonds & certificates only, FHL microfilm 1944289, book W, p. 200, Family History Library, Salt Lake City, Utah.

[22] Kathleen Hope Brashear, Remembrances of Bowling Green, 27 March 1985.

[23] 1900 US Census, Warren County, Kentucky, population schedule, Bristow, Enumeration District (ED) 97, page 9, dwelling 168, family 169, Richard L Brashear; *Ancestry.com* (http://www.ancestry.com: accessed 10 March 2003); citing National Archives microfilm T623, roll 553.

[24] Record of Baptisms for Richard Levi Brashear Family, providence unknown, likely prepared by Christ Episcopal Church at the request of a member of the Brashear family, passed from Zalame Brashear Cottrell to her son Taylor C Cottrell, Jr. after her death.

[25] Kathleen Hope Brashear, Remembrances of Bowling Green, 27 March 1985.

[26] 1910 US Census, Warren County, Kentucky, population schedule, District No 3, Enumeration District (ED) 116, page 10B, dwelling 180, family 180, Richard L Brashear; *Ancestry.com* (http://www.ancestry.com: accessed 10 March 2003); citing National Archives microfilm T624, roll 504.

[27] Ibid.

[28] Funeral of R.L. Brashear, *unidentified Warren County, Kentucky newspaper*, Kentucky. Original clipping found in loose scrapbook belonging to Kathleen Brashear, which passed to her daughter, Zalame Brashear Cottrell and then to Mrs. Cottrell's son, Taylor C Cottrell, Jr. Original pages in the possession of Mr. Cottrell, June 2004.

[29] 1920 US Census, Warren County, Kentucky, population schedule, Bristow district, Enumeration District (ED) 130, page 1A, dwelling 8, family 9, Della Brashear; *Ancestry.com* (Kentucky. Warren County: accessed 9 March 2003); citing National Archives microfilm publication T625, roll 600.

[30] 1930 US Census, Warren County, Kentucky, population schedule, Bristow, enumeration district (ED) 114-29, page 11B, dwelling 266, family 267, Della Brashear; *Ancestry.com* (http://www.ancestry.com: accessed 9 March 2003); citing National Archives microfilm publication T626, roll 780.

[31] Park Row Paragraphs by Jane Morningstar, *Park City Daily News*, Bowling Green, Kentucky. Original clipping found in loose scrapbook belonging to Kathleen Brashear, which passed to her daughter, Zalame Brashear Cottrell and then to Mrs. Cottrell's son, Taylor C Cottrell, Jr. Original pages in the possession of Mr. Cottrell, June 2004.

[32] "U.S. City Directories - 1937/38-1949," database, *Ancestry.com* (http://www.ancestry.com: accessed 20 March 2009); citing "*Caron's Bowling Green Kentucky City Directory for 1937-1938 - Warren County Section* (Bowling Green, Kentucky: Caron Directory Company)".

[33] 1940 US Census, Warren County, Kentucky, population schedule, Bristow, Enumeration District (ED) 114-30, page 19A, dwelling 407, Mrs Della Brashear; *Ancestry.com* (http://www.ancestry.com: accessed 15 April 2012); citing National Archives microfilm T6267, roll 1360.

[34] War Ration Book One for Della Zalame Brashear, 6 May 1942.

[35] "Kentucky Death Records, 1852-1953," subscription database, *Ancestry.com* (http://www.ancestry.com: accessed 20 November 2007), for Della C Brashear (11 July 1951), certificate 5115181.

[36] Fairview Cemetery (Bowling Green, Warren County, Kentucky), Della C Brashear marker, Campbell-Brashear Plot, photographed by T.C. Cottrell, 1 April 2011.

[37] Robert L Brashear, Engineer, dies: Rites Will Be Tomorrow, *unidentified Warren County, Kentucky newspaper*, Kentucky, 24 August 1954. Original clipping found in loose scrapbook belonging to Kathleen Brashear, which passed to her daughter, Zalame Brashear Cottrell and then to Mrs. Cottrell's son, Taylor C Cottrell, Jr. Original pages in the possession of Mr. Cottrell, June 2004.
[38] Brashear Family Record of Baptisms.
[39] 1900 US Census, Warren County, Kentucky, population schedule, enumeration district 97, page 9, dwelling 168, family 169, Richard L Brashear, age listed as 48, born in Kentucky.
[40] Kathleen Hope Brashear, Remembrances of Bowling Green, 27 March 1985.
[41] Ibid.
[42] Robert L Brashear, Engineer, dies: Rites Will Be Tomorrow, *unidentified Warren County, Kentucky newspaper*, Kentucky, 24 August 1954.
[43] 1910 US Census, Warren County, Kentucky, population schedule, enumeration district 116, page 10B, dwelling 180, family 180, Richard L Brashear, age listed as 58, born in Kentucky.
[44] "World War I Draft Registration Cards, 1917-1918," subscription database, *Ancestry.com* (http://www.ancestry.com: accessed 1 July 2006), for Robert L Brashear, citing United States, Selective Service System. World War I Selective Service System Draft Registration Cards, 1917-1918. Washington, D.C.: National Archives and Records Administration. Microfilm publication M1509, Warren County, Kentucky; Roll 1653844; Draft Board: 0.
[45] 1920 US Census, Warren County, Kentucky, population schedule, enumeration district 130, page 1A, dwelling 8, family 9, Della Brashear.
[46] Author Unknown, "Complete List of Winners in August Picture Contest," *Popular Science*, vol. 110, no. 1 (January 1927).
[47] Robert L Brashear, Engineer, dies: Rites Will Be Tomorrow, *unidentified Warren County, Kentucky newspaper*, Kentucky, 24 August 1954.
[48] 1940 US Census, Warren County, Kentucky, population schedule, enumeration district 114-30, page 19A, dwelling 407, Mrs Della Brashear.
[49] Sale of Brashear Lands - Curren Walter Brashear Estate, undated, Cottrell Family Papers.
[50] Postcard from Walter B McGinnis (address unknown) to Robert L Brashear.
[51] Final Settlement of Robert L Brashear as Administrator of the Estate of Della Z Brashear, July 1952.
[52] Robert L Brashear will (7 August 1951), Last Will and Testament, Cottrell Family Papers.
[53] Ibid.
[54] Certificate of Confirmation for Robert L Brashear, (21 June 1953), in Christ Episcopal Church, Bowling Green, Warren County, Kentucky, presented by Rev Leighton Arsuault, confirmed by Bishop Charles Clingman.
[55] Robert L Brashear, Death Registration 5416810 (1954), Department of Health Bureau of Vital Statistics, Frankfort, Kentucky.
[56] Robert L Brashear, Engineer, dies: Rites Will Be Tomorrow, *unidentified Warren County, Kentucky newspaper*, Kentucky, 24 August 1954.
[57] Flower List and Related Funeral Information for Robert L Brashear, 25 August 1954.
[58] Robert L Brashear, Engineer, dies: Rites Will Be Tomorrow, *unidentified Warren County, Kentucky newspaper*, Kentucky, 24 August 1954.
[59] Fairview Cemetery (Bowling Green, Warren County, Kentucky), Robert L Brashear marker, Campbell-Brashear Plot, photographed by T.C. Cottrell, 1 April 2011.

[60] Kathleen Hope Brashear, Form 3227, Application for Social Security Number (Baltimore, Maryland: Social Security Administration, 10 May 1962).

[61] Brashear Family Record of Baptisms.

[62] 1900 US Census, Warren County, Kentucky, population schedule, page 9, dwelling 168, family 169, Richard L Brashear, age listed as 48.

[63] Letter from W.R. McNeill (Bowling Green City Schools) To Whom It May Concern, 14 March 1966; Cottrell Family Papers (867 Jamestown Drive, Rockledge, Florida). confirming that Kathleen H Brashear was enrolled in College Street School in 1902.

[64] Kathleen Hope Brashear, Remembrances of Bowling Green, 27 March 1985.

[65] The Way It Was, *Park City Daily News*, Bowling Green, Kentucky, 25 August 1985.

[66] Brashear Family Record of Baptisms.

[67] 1910 US Census, Warren County, Kentucky, population schedule, page 10B, dwelling 180, family 180, Richard L Brashear, age listed as 58.

[68] Advanced Certificate for Teaching Presented to Kathleen Hope Brashear by Western Kentucky State Normal School, 27 July 1917.

[69] 1920 US Census, Warren County, Kentucky, population schedule, enumeration district 130, page 1A, dwelling 8, family 9, Della Brashear.

[70] Teachers Contract Between Kathleen Brashear and the Board of Education of Bowling Green, Kentucky, 11 May 1923.

[71] Teachers Contract Between Kathleen Brashear and the Board of Education of Bowling Green, Kentucky, 30 May 1925.

[72] Teachers Contract Between Kathleen Brashear and the Board of Education of Bowling Green, Kentucky, 12 may 1926.

[73] 1930 US Census, Warren County, Kentucky, population schedule, page 11B, dwelling 266, family 267, Della Brashear.

[74] Teachers Contract Between Kathleen Brashear and the Board of Education of Bowling Green, Kentucky, 24 May 1935.

[75] Luncheon Is Given for Miss Brashear, *Park City Daily News*, Bowling Green, Kentucky.

[76] 1940 US Census, Warren County, Kentucky, population schedule, enumeration district 114-30, page 19A, dwelling 407, Mrs Della Brashear.

[77] War Ration Book One for Kathleen Hope Brashear, 6 May 1942.

[78] 1963-1964 Program - Delta Chapter of Kentucky Delta Kappa Gamma Society.

[79] Miss Brashear Enjoys Fancy Cooking Hobby, *Park City Daily News*, Bowling Green, Kentucky. taken from a 1963 newspaper.

[80] Park Row Paragraphs by Jane Morningstar, *Park City Daily News*, Bowling Green, Kentucky. Original clipping found in loose scrapbook belonging to Kathleen Brashear, which passed to her daughter, Zalame Brashear Cottrell and then to Mrs. Cottrell's son, Taylor C Cottrell, Jr.

[81] Notice to Take Depositions - Board of Education of Bowling Green, Kentucky Plaintiff, 23 March 1965.

[82] Kathleen H. Brashear will (15 July 1982), Last Will and Testament.

[83] Happy Birthday, Miss Brashear (Christ Episcopal Church Bulletin), 22 September 1985.

[84] Kathleen Hope Brashear, Death Registration 1168621874 (1986), Department of Health Bureau of Vital Statistics, Frankfort, Kentucky.

[85] Miss Cathleen Brashear, *unidentified Kentucky newspaper*, Kentucky, 6 August 1986. most likely from the Louisville, Kentucky Courier Journal.

[86] Fairview Cemetery (Bowling Green, Warren County, Kentucky), Kathleen H Brashear marker, Campbell-Brashear Plot, photographed by T.C. Cottrell, 1 April 2011.

[87] Order Approving Final Settlement and Discharge of Co-Executors - Estate of Kathleen H Brashear, 16 June 1987.

[88] Richard Herschel Brashear, Form SS-5, Application for Social Security Number (Baltimore, Maryland: Social Security Administration, 24 November 1936).

[89] Brashear Family Record of Baptisms.

[90] 1910 US Census, Warren County, Kentucky, population schedule, page 10B, dwelling 180, family 180, Richard L Brashear, age listed as 58.

[91] 1920 US Census, Warren County, Kentucky, population schedule, enumeration district 130, page 1A, dwelling 8, family 9, Della Brashear.

[92] Letter from Lynn Brashear (183 Cottage field Way, Draper, Utah) to Jr. T.C. Cottrell, 22 October 2004.

[93] Social Security Administration, "Social Security Death Index," database, *Ancestry.com* (http://www.ancestry.com: accessed 18 November 2006), entry for Evelyn Brashear, 1973, SS no. 528-02-1837.

[94] "U.S. Social Security Death Index, 1935-2014," *Ancestry.com* (http://www.ancestry.com: accessed 11 April 2016), entry for John Burritt, December 1965.

[95] "Parma Union Cemetery," database, *Find A Grave* (http://www.findagrave.com: accessed 11 April 2016), entry for John W. Burritt, 1965; citing memorial #137293597.

[96] "California Death Index, 1940-1997," *Ancestry.com* (http://www.ancestry.com: accessed 11 April 2016), entry for Ruth Beatrice Edic), 12 January 1997.

[97] "Alpine Cemetery," database, *Find A Grave* (http://www.findagrave.com: accessed 11 April 2016), entry for Ruth Beatrice Edic, 12 January 1997; citing memorial #55064195.

[98] "U.S. Social Security Applications and Claims Index, 1936-2007," *Ancestry.com* (http:www.ancestry.com: accessed 11 April 2016), entry for John Burton Burritt, 31 January 1989.

[99] Richard H Brashear "Dick", *The Salt Lake Tribune*, Salt Lake City, Utah, 27 February 2002, page D6. The Salt Lake Tribune, online <www.sltrib.com>, accessed 7 July 2002.

[100] "New Orleans Passenger Lists, 1820-1945 Record," *Ancestry.com* (http://www.ancestry.com: accessed 29 September 2006), List of United States Citizens, *Cartago*, Cristobal, Canal Zone to New Orleans, arriving 21 December 1926, Richard H Brashear; citing National Archives, microfilm publication T905, roll 114.

[101] 1930 US Census, Erie County, New York, population schedule, Kenmore Village, Enumeration District (ED) 15-459, page 1A, dwelling 8, family 18, Richard Brashear; digital images, *Ancestry.com* (http://www.ancestry.com: accessed 28 July 2012); citing National Archives microfilm T626, roll 1437.

[102] Richard Herschel Brashear, Form SS-5.

[103] 1940 US Census, Albany County, New York, population schedule, Albany, Enumeration District (ED) 63-1, page 12B, dwelling 299, Richard H Brashear; *Ancestry.com* (http://www.ancestry.com: accessed 28 July 2012); citing National Archives microfilm T6267, roll 2818.

[104] Letter from Richard H Brashear (Albany, New York) to Della Z Brashear, 9 July 1942.

[105] Richard H Brashear "Dick", *The Salt Lake Tribune*, Salt Lake City, Utah, 27 February 2002, page D6. The Salt Lake Tribune, online <www.sltrib.com>, accessed 7 July 2002.

[106] Burial Card for Richard H Brashear, Jr., from Mount Calvary Cemetery Office, Salt Lake City, Utah, secured by his late father's nephew TC Cottrell on 18 October 2006 at the cemetery during a research trip.

[107] Ibid.

[108] Miss Evelyn M Fiore Wed to New Scotland Physicist, *Unidentified Newspaper*, Kentucky. Original clipping found in loose scrapbook pages of Della Z Campbell Brashear, which passed to her daughter, Zalame Brashear Cottrell and then to Mrs. Cottrell's son, Taylor C Cottrell, Jr. Original pages in the possession of Mr. Cottrell, June 2004.

[109] Miss Evelyn M Fiore Wed to New Scotland Physicist, *Unidentified Newspaper*, Kentucky. Original clipping found in loose scrapbook pages of Della Z Campbell Brashear, which passed to her daughter, Zalame Brashear Cottrell and then to Mrs. Cottrell's son, Taylor C Cottrell, Jr. Original pages in the possession of Mr. Cottrell, June 2004.

[110] Social Security Administration, "Social Security Death Index," database, *Ancestry.com* entry for Evelyn Brashear.

[111] Burial Card for Evelyn M Brashear., from Mount Calvary Cemetery Office, Salt Lake City, Utah, secured by her late husband's nephew TC Cottrell on 18 October 2006 at the cemetery during a research trip.

[112] Marriage Announcement for Richard H Brashear and Grace M Cummings.

[113] Grace "Pat" Brashear - "The Angel Lady", *The Salt Lake Tribune*, Salt Lake City, Utah, 15 September 2005, page B6. The Salt Lake Tribune, online <www.sltrib.com>, accessed 13 October 2005.

[114] Richard Brashear, *Bowling Green Daily News*, Bowling Green. Kentucky, 18 February 1982.

[115] Burial Card for Richard Brashear Sr., from Mount Calvary Cemetery Office, Salt Lake City, Utah, secured by his nephew TC Cottrell on 18 October 2006 at the cemetery during a research trip,

[116] *The Salt Lake Tribune Obituary for Grace "Pat" Brashear*, 15 September 2005, page B6.

[117] Estella Zalame Brashear, special certificate of birth (1908), Department of Health Bureau of Vital Statistics, Frankfort, Kentucky.

Section 2 – Chapter 4 Sources – Richard D. Crutchfield Family

[1] Mercer County, Kentucky, Mercer County Kentucky Will Book 7, will of William Crutchfield, FHL microfilm 855032, item7, page 26, Family History Library, Salt Lake City, Utah.

[2] Calvin Morgan Fackler, *Early Days in Danville* (1941; reprint Utica, Kentucky: McDowell Publications, 2002), FHL US/CAN 976.9523/D1 H2f.

[3] "Bellevue Cemetery," database, *Find A Grave* (http://www.findagrave.com: accessed 11 September 2010), entry for Agnes D Sevier Crutchfield, 11 June 1831; citing memorial # 11622952.

[4] Beverly Scrutchfield Diefenderfer, "Re: Elizabeth Jane Crutchfield - KY/TN," *Crutchfield Family Forum*, discussion list, 16 November 2001 (http://genforum.genealogy.com: accessed 3 January 2010).

[5] Elizabeth Prather, compiler, "Mercer County, Kentucky: Marriages (1786-1800) & Wills (1786-1801)," subscription database, *Ancestry.com* (http://www.ancestry.com: accessed 9 January 2010), for Thos Kenton and Kezia Crutchfield (25 April 1794).

[6] Beverly Scrutchfield Diefenderfer. "Re: Elizabeth Jane Crutchfield - KY/TN." *Crutchfield Family Forum.*

[7] Ibid.

[8] Ibid.

[9] 1850 US Census, Boyle County, Kentucky, population schedule, District 2, page 363A, dwelling 195, family 221, William Crutchfield; *Ancestry.com* (http://www.ancestry.com: accessed 9 January 2010); citing National Archives microfilm publication M432, roll 192.

[10] "Perryville Cemetery," database, *Find A Grave* (http://www.findagrave.com: accessed 16 May 2013), entry for Agnes D Crutchfield Sevier, 15 March 1814; citing memorial # 16366546.

[11] Beverly Scrutchfield Diefenderfer, "Re: Elizabeth Jane Crutchfield - KY/TN," *Crutchfield Family Forum.*

[12] Ibid.

[13] Calvin Morgan Fackler, *Early Days in Danville.*

[14] Ibid.

[15] Calvin Morgan Fackler, *Early Days in Danville.*

[16] 1820 US Census, Mercer County, Kentucky, page 91, Richard Crutchfield; *Ancestry.com* (http://www.ancestry.com: accessed 9 January 2016); citing National Archives microfilm M33, roll 26.

[17] 1830 US Census, Mercer County, Kentucky, Shaker, page 311, Rich Crutchfield; *Ancestry.com* (http://www.ancestry.com: accessed 9 January 2016); citing National Archives microfilm M19, roll 39.

[18] 1840 US Census, Mercer County, Kentucky, population schedule, Danville, page 156, Richard D. Crutchfield; *Ancestry.com* (http://www.ancestry.com: accessed 9 January 2016); citing National Archives microfilm M704, roll 119.

[19] "City of Danville, Kentucky, Bellevue Cemetery Interments, Alphabetical," database, *Danville Kentucky* (www.danvilleky.org: accessed 24 January 2014).

[20] "Kentucky Probate Records, 1727-1990," *Ancestry.com* (www.ancestry.com: accessed 17 October 2013), entry for James P Crutchfield, 12 June 1843; citing Boyle County Administrator Bonds, 1842-1852, Image 32.

[21] 1850 US Census, Boyle County, Kentucky, population schedule, District 2, page 331, dwelling 174, family 198, Ann Crutchfield; *Ancestry.com* (http://www.ancestry.com: accessed 15 December 2007); citing Family History Library microfilm M432, roll 493.

[22] 1860 US Census, Boyle County, Kentucky, Slave schedule, page 150, Ann Crutchfield, owner or manager, *Ancestry.com* (http://www.ancestry.com: accessed 9 January 2016); citing Family History Library microfilm M653.

[23] 1860 US Census, Boyle County, Kentucky, population schedule, Danville, page 907, dwelling 406, family 407, Ann Crutchfield; *Ancestry.com* (http://www.ancestry.com: accessed 9 January 2016); citing Family History Library microfilm M654, roll 356.

[24] Descendants of Charles McKinney, online family database, *Geocities.com* (http://www.geocities.com/bertdooley/McKinney_Line; accessed on 15 December 2007).

[25] Ibid.

[26] 1850 US Census, Lincoln County, Tennessee, population schedule, District 2, page 209, dwelling 32, family 32, Robert McKinney; *Ancestry.com* (http://www.ancestry.com: accessed 21 December 2007); citing Family History Library microfilm M432, roll 299.

[27] 1860 US Census, Lincoln County, Tennessee, population schedule, Fayetteville, page 79, dwelling 1619, family 1550, R.R. McKinney; *Ancestry.com* (http://www.ancestry.com: accessed 9 January 2016), citing Family History Library microfilm M653, roll 1261.

[28] Descendants of Charles McKinney.

[29] "Tennessee State Marriages, 1780-2002," *Ancestry.com* (www.ancestry.com: accessed 7 January 2016), for Joel McKinney and Nancy A. Thompson, citing Tennessee State Library and Archives; Nashville, Tennessee.

[30] 1870 US Census, Jefferson County, Tennessee, population schedule, Jefferson, page 24, dwelling 185, family 185, Joel McKinny; *Ancestry.com* (http://www.ancestry.com: accessed 9 January 2016), citing Family History Library microfilm M593, roll 1540.

[31] "Tennessee Deaths and Burials Index, 1874-1955," *Ancestry.com* (http://www.ancestry.com: accessed 24 March 2016), entry for Benjamin Edward McKinney, 31 May 1914, FHL Film No. 1299622.

[32] 1870 US Census, Jefferson County, Tennessee, population schedule, Jefferson, page 24, dwelling 185, family 185, Joel McKinny.

[33] Ibid.

[34] Ibid.

[35] "Mount Airy United Methodist Church Cemetery, "database, *Find A Grave* (http://www.findagrave.com), entry for Rachel Day; citing Memorial #66505491.

[36] "Tennessee Death Records, 1908-1958," *Ancestry.com* (www.ancestry.com: accessed 24 March 2016) for Joel Elisha McKinney, citing Tennessee State Library and Archives; Nashville, Tennessee, certificate 58-007501.

[37] Edmund West, compiler, "Family Data Collection - Births," *Ancestry.com* (http://www.ancestry.com: accessed 22 December 2007), for Martha Cordelia McKinney (1839).

[38] 1850 US Census, Lincoln County, Tennessee, population schedule, page 209, dwelling 32, family 32, Robert McKinney.

[39] "Tennessee Death Records, 1908-1958," *Ancestry.com* (www.ancestry.com: accessed 7 January 2016) for John V. McKinney, citing Tennessee State Library and Archives; Nashville, Tennessee, roll 154.

[40] "Tennessee Death Records, 1872-1923," *Ancestry.com* (http://www.ancestry.com: accessed 7 January 2016), for Mrs. Dana McKinney, citing Tennessee State Library and Archives; Nashville, Tennessee, roll M-21.

[41] 1880 US Census, Lincoln County, Tennessee, population schedule, enumeration district 123, page 116A, dwelling 415, family 427, J.V. McKinney; *Anncestry.com* (www.ancestry.com: accessed 7 January 2016), citing Family History Library microfilm T9, roll 1267.

[42] "West View Cemetery," database, *Find A Grave* (http://www.findagrave.com: accessed 14 June 2016),entry for Robert Jefferson McKinney; citing Memorial #35215457.

[43] "Alabama Deaths and Burials Index, 1881-1974," *Ancestry.com* (www.ancestry.com: accessed 14 June 2016), entry for Reuben D. McKinney, reference FHL Film Number 1908280.

[44] "Tennessee Death and Burials Index, 1874-1955," *Ancestry.com* (www.ancestry.com: accessed 24 March 2016), for Henry T. McKinney, Tennessee State Library and Archives; Nashville, Tennessee, FHL Film #18776847.

[45] "Tennessee Deaths and Burials Index, 1874-1955," *Ancestry.com* (www.ancestry.com: accessed 24 March 2016) entry for James Kelso McKinney (11 September 1945), FHL Film No #2137362.

[46] "Tennessee Death Records, 1908-1958," *Ancestry.com* (www.ancestry.com: accessed 24 March 2016), entry for John Vardaman McKinney, 4 January 1939, certificate #686.

[47] "U.S. City Directories, 1822-1955," *Ancestry.com* (www.ancestry.com: accessed 24 March 2016), entry for C. Dana McKinney; citing Chattanooga, Tennessee, City Directory, 1933.

[48] "Forest Hills Cemetery," database, *Find A Grave* (http://www.findagrave.com: accessed 24 March 2016), entry for Kathryn Simmons McKinney; citing Memorial #75110931.

[49] "Tennessee Delayed Birth Records, 1869-1909," *Ancestry.com* (http://www.ancestry.com: accessed 24 March 2016), Entry for Marion Odell McKinney, 24 November 1887.

[50] "Forest Hills Cemetery," database, *Find A Grave* (http://www.findagrave.com: accessed 24 March 2016), entry for Marion Odell McKinney; citing Memorial #143477594.

[51] Descendants of Charles McKinney.

[52] 1860 US Census, Lincoln County, Tennessee, population schedule, Fayetteville, page 79, dwelling 1619, family 1550, R.R. McKinney.

[53] Descendants of Charles McKinney.

[54] 1850 US Census, Lincoln County, Tennessee, population schedule, page 209, dwelling 32, family 32, Robert McKinney.

[55] 1860 US Census, Lincoln County, Tennessee, population schedule, Fayetteville, page 79, dwelling 1619, family 1550, R.R. McKinney.

[56] Descendants of Charles McKinney.

[57] 1860 US Census, Lincoln County, Tennessee, population schedule, Fayetteville, page 79, dwelling 1619, family 1550, R.R. McKinney.

[58] 1880 US Census, Navarro County, Texas, population schedule, enumeration district 130, page 370C, dwelling 289, family 297, Henry C. McKinney; *Ancestry.com* (www.ancestry.com: accessed 10 January 2016), citing Family History Library microfilm publication T9, roll 1321.

[59] Ibid.

[60] Ibid.

[61] "Oakwood Cemetery," database, *Find A Grave* (http://www.findagrave.com: accessed 24 March 2016), entry for Arthur D. McKinney, Sr., 1937; citing Memorial #134863582.

[62] 1880 US Census, Navarro County, Texas, population schedule, enumeration district 130, page 370C, dwelling 289, family 297, Henry C. McKinney.

[63] Ibid.

[64] 1900 US Census, Navarro County, Texas, population schedule, Kerens, enumeration district 102, page 14A, dwelling 103, family 103, Hal McKinney; *Ancestry.com* (www.ancestry.com: accessed 10 January 2016), citing Family History Library microfilm T623, roll 1662.

[65] Descendants of Charles McKinney.

[66] 1850 US Census, Lincoln County, Tennessee, population schedule, page 209, dwelling 32, family 32, Robert McKinney.

[67] 1860 US Census, Lincoln County, Tennessee, population schedule, Fayetteville, page 79, dwelling 1619, family 1550, R.R. McKinney.

[68] Edmund West, compiler, "Family Data Collection - Births," subscription database, *Ancestry.com* (http://www.ancestry.com: accessed 22 December 2007), for Jennie F McKinney (1852).

[69] "Tennessee Death Records, 1908-1958," *Ancestry.com* (http://www.ancestry.com: accessed on 7 February 2016), entry for Mrs. Jennie Thomas, 2 September 1914. citing Tennessee State Library and Archives; Nashville, Tennessee.

[70] "Tennessee State Marriages, 1780-2002," *Ancestry.com* (http://www.ancestry.com: accessed on 7 February 2016), entry for Miss Jennie F. McKinnie and A.S. Thomas, 7 November 1871, citing Tennessee State Library and Archives; Nashville, Tennessee.

[71] "Rose Hill Cemetery," database, *Find A Grave* (http://www.findagrave.com: accessed 7 February 2016), entry for Abednego S. Thomas, 1903; citing memorial #118484483.

Cottrell-Brashear Family Linage

[72] "Tennessee Deaths and Burials Index, 1874-1955," *Ancestry.com* (http://www.ancestry.com: accessed on 7 February 2016), entry for Mary Crutchfield Williams, 25 August 1940, citing FHL 1876890.

[73] "Tennessee State Marriages, 1780-2002," *Ancestry.com* (http://www.ancestry.com: accessed on 7 February 2016), entry for John Knight Williams and Mary Kercheval McKinney, 7 November 1882, citing Tennessee State Library and Archives; Nashville, Tennessee.

[74] "Rose Hill Cemetery," database, *Find A Grave* (http://www.findagrave.com: accessed 7 February 2016), entry for John Knight Williams, 6 November 1926; citing memorial #121991483.

[75] "Rose Hill Cemetery," database, *Find A Grave* (http://www.findagrave.com: accessed 24 March 2016), entry for Abednego Thomas Williams, 27 November 1970; citing memorial #1133179034.

[76] "Tennessee State Marriages, 1780-2002," *Ancestry.com* (http://www.ancestry.com: accessed 24 March 2016), entry for Abednego Thomas Williams and Margaret Carter (22 November 1911).

[77] "Rose Hill Cemetery," database, *Find A Grave* (http://www.findagrave.com: accessed 24 March 2016), entry for Margaret Carter Williams, 4 June 1948; citing memorial #103525248.

[78] "Mount Hope Cemetery," database, *Find A Grave* (http://www.findagrave.com: accessed 14 June 2016), entry for Orra Williams Pitner, 1 January 1989; citing memorial #156926823.

[79] "Old Fayetteville City Cemetery," database, *Find A Grave* (http://www.findagrave.com: accessed 7 February 2016), entry for Elizabeth McKinney, 26 February 1875; citing memorial #45047533.

[80] Descendants of Charles McKinney.

[81] Charles Brashear *A Brashear(s) Family History, Descendants of Robert and Benois Brasseur, Volume 4, Brashear(s) Families of the Ohio Valley* (Clearlake Oaks, California: Charles Brashear Books, Etc., 2002).

[82] 1850 US Census, Boyle County, Kentucky, population schedule, District 2, page 331, dwelling 174, family 198, Ann Crutchfield; *Ancestry.com* (http://www.ancestry.com: accessed 15 December 2007); citing Family History Library microfilm publication M432, roll 493.

[83] 1870 US Census, Fayette County, Kentucky, population schedule, Lexington Ward 2, page 33, dwelling 204, family 236, Ralph Georgi; *Ancestry.com* (http://www.ancestry.com: accessed 21 December 2007); citing Family History Library microfilm publication M593, roll 593.

[84] "Kentucky Death Records, 1852-1953," *Ancestry.com* (http://www.ancestry.com: accessed 21 December 2007), for Agnes C Nichols (17 April 1856).

[85] Boyle County, Kentucky, Marriage records; 1842-1955, marriage bond for Jonathan Nichols and Agnes C Crutchfield, FHL microfilm 191806, bk1, page 101, Family History Library, Salt Lake City, Utah.

[86] 1850 US Census, Boyle County, Kentucky, population schedule, District 2, page 358, dwelling 148, family 169, Jonathan Nichols; *Ancestry.com* (http://www.ancestry.com: accessed 22 December 2007); citing Family History Library microfilm publication M432, roll 488.

[87] "Kentucky Death Records, 1852-1953," *Ancestry.com* (http://www.ancestry.com: accessed 21 December 2007), for William S Nichols (3 February 1912), certificate 3280.

[88] "City of Danville, Kentucky, Bellevue Cemetery Interments, Alphabetical," database, *Danville Kentucky* (www.danvilleky.org: accessed 24 January 2014).

[89] "Kentucky Death Records, 1852-1963," *Ancestry.com* (http://www.ancestry.com: accessed 7 February 2016), for Margaret Moore Nichols (3 September 1938), certificate 23500.

[90] "Kentucky Death Records", for William S Nichols (3 February 1912).

[91] 1900 US Census, Boyle County, Kentucky, population schedule, Perryville, Enumeration District (ED) 9, page 2A, dwelling 22, family 22, W.S. Nickels; *Ancestry.com* (http://www.ancestry.com: accessed 7 February 2016); citing National Archives microfilm publication T623, roll 509.

[92] Ibid.

[93] Ibid.

[94] "U.S. World War II Draft Registration Cards, 1942," *Ancestry.com* (http://www.ancestry.com: accessed 24 March 2016), entry for Daniel Moore Nichols (4 September 1887).

[95] "Summit County Ohio Marriages Records, 1840-1980," *Ancestry.com* (http://www.ancestry.com: accessed 24 March 2016), entry for Daniel M. Nichols and Maud Pearch (5 February 1917).

[96] "Kentucky Death Records, 1852-1963," *Ancestry.com* (http://www.ancestry.com: accessed 24 March 2016), entry for John C. Nichols, 26 September 1959, certificate #59-20137.

[97] "U.S. World War I Draft Registration Cards, ,1917-1918," *Ancestry.com* (http://www.ancestry.com: accessed 24 March 2016), entry for John C. Nichols.

[98] 1900 US Census, Boyle County, Kentucky, population schedule, page 2A, dwelling 22, family 22, W.S. Nickels.

[99] "Bellevue Cemetery," database, *Find A Grave* (http://www.findagrave.com: accessed 11 September 2010), entry for Richard G Nichols, 4 March 1914; citing memorial # 41375338.

[100] Ibid.

[101] "Kentucky Birth Records, 1852-1910," *Ancestry.com* (http://www.ancestry.com: accessed 10 March 2009), for Reed J Nichols Jr. (28 September 1878).

[102] Boyle County Genealogical Association, compiler, *Boyle County, Kentucky, Cemetery Records, 1792-1992* (Utica, Kentucky: McDowell Publications, 1992), FHL US/CAN 976.9523 V38b.

[103] "Kentucky Marriage Records, 1852-1914," *Ancestry.com* (http://www.ancestry.com: accessed 25 April 2008), for Reed S Nichols and Nettie D Hommel (30 July 1876).

[104] 1930 US Census, Allegheny County, Pennsylvania, population schedule, Mount Lebanon, Enumeration District (ED) 905, page 11A, dwelling 247, family 270, George M. Mclane; *Ancestry.com* (http://www.ancestry.com: accessed 7 February 2016); citing National Archives microfilm T626, roll 1968.

[105] "Pennsylvania Death Certificates, 1906-1963," Ancestry.com (http://www.ancestry.com: accessed 7 February 2016), entry Henrietta Dorothea Nichols (17 November 1935).

[106] 1900 US Census, Boyle County, Kentucky, population schedule, District 4, Enumeration District (ED) 12, page 20B, dwelling 392, family 403, RS Nicholes; digital images, *Ancestry.com* (http://www.ancestry.com: accessed 16 May 2009); citing National Archives microfilm T623, roll 509.

[107] "Pennsylvania Death Certificates, 1906-1963," *Ancestry.com* (http://www.ancestry.com: accessed 24 March 2016), entry for Lowrie Nichols (20 March 1949), certificate 19280.

[108] "Pennsylvania Death Certificates, 1906-1963," *Ancestry.com* (http://www.ancestry.com: accessed 24 March 2016), entry for Reed S. Nichols (9 August 1946), certificate 17903.

[109] "Pennsylvania Death Certificates, 1906-1963," *Ancestry.com* (http://www.ancestry.com: accessed 24 March 2016), entry for Agnes N. McLane (3 November 1955), certificate 93971.

[110] "Alabama Select Marriages, 1816-1942," *Ancestry.com* (http://www.ancestry.com: accessed 24 March 2016), entry for George Mclure Mclane and Agnes Crutchfield Nichols (21 April 1909), FHL Film #1064429, Item 1, page 133.

[111] Mrs. McLane's Burial Rites Set Here Monday, *The Advocate-Messenger*, Danville, Kentucky, 6 November 1955, page 1, *Newspapers.com* (http://www.newspapers.com: accessed 11 February 2016).

[112] Boyle County Genealogical Association, *Boyle County, Kentucky Cemetery Records*, FHL US/CAN 976.9523 V38b.

[113] "Kentucky Marriages, 1851-1900," subscription database, *Ancestry.com* (http://www.ancestry.com: accessed 22 December 2008), for Jonathan B Nichols and Emma M Crawford (17 September 1866).

[114] "Bellevue Cemetery," database, *Find A Grave* (http://www.findagrave.com: accessed 11 September 2010), entry for Emily "Emma" Crawford Nichols, 1909; citing memorial # 41374963.

[115] 1870 US Census, Boyle County, Kentucky, population schedule, Precinct 1, page 18, dwelling 120, family 119, Jna B Nichols; *Ancestry.com* (http://www.ancestry.com: accessed 22 December 2007); citing Family History Library microfilm M593, roll 448

[116] Boyle County Genealogical Association, *Boyle County, Kentucky Cemetery Records*, FHL US/CAN 976.9523 V38b.

[117] "Bellevue Cemetery," database, *Find A Grave* (http://www.findagrave.com: accessed 11 September 2010), entry for Emily "Emma" Crawford Nichols, 1909; citing memorial # 41374963.

[118] "Kentucky Death Records, 1852-1953," subscription database, *Ancestry.com* (http://www.ancestry.com: accessed 22 December 2007), for Fannie M Nichols (16 June 1947), certificate 14828.

[119] Miss Nichols, 84, Claimed by Death, *The Advocate-Messenger*, Danville, Kentucky, 1 August 1853, *Newspapers.com* (http://www.newspapers.com: accessed 9 February 2016).

[120] "Kentucky Death Records, 1852-1953," subscription database, *Ancestry.com* (http://www.ancestry.com: accessed 22 December 2007), for Emma Crawford Nichols (1 August 1953), certificate 5315775.

[121] 1930 US Census, Boyle County, Kentucky, population schedule, Danville, Enumeration District (ED) 15, page 3B, dwelling 59, family 64, Fannie M Nichols; *Ancestry.com* (http://www.ancestry.com: accessed 28 March 2009); citing National Archives microfilm T626, roll 735.

[122] "Kentucky Death Records, 1852-1953," subscription database, *Ancestry.com* (http://www.ancestry.com: accessed 22 December 2007), for John B Nichols (10 July 1945), certificate 13933.

[123] "U.S. Passport Applications, 1795-1925," *Ancestry.com* (http://www.ancestry.com: accessed 22 December 2007), for J.B. Nichols, National Archives and Records Administration, certificate 57382.

[124] "Kentucky Birth Records, 1852-1910," *Ancestry.com* (http://www.ancestry.com: accessed 10 March 2009), for Mary A. Nichols (1 December 1875).

[125] Mrs. H.A. Shaw Dies at Hospital, *The Advocate-Messenger*, Danville, Kentucky, 15 July 1954, page 1, column 4, *Newspapers.com* (http://www.newspapers.com: accessed 9 February 2016).

[126] "Cave Hill Cemetery," database, *Find A Grave* (http://www.findagrave.com: accessed 9 February 2016), entry for Harry A. Shaw, 1921; citing memorial #128120726.

[127] "Bellevue Cemetery," database, *Find A Grave* (http://www.findagrave.com: accessed 9 February 2016), entry for Samuel H. Nichols, 4 September 1948, citing memorial #59732719.

[128] "Bellevue Cemetery," database, *Find A Grave* (http://www.findagrave.com: accessed 9 February 2016), entry for Clarece McElroy Nichols, 21 August 1973, citing memorial #59733004.

[129] "Kentucky Birth Index, 1911-1999," *Ancestry.com* (http://www.ancestry.com: accessed 24 March 2016), entry for Sam. H. Nichols, 1 May 1914, reference certification#22923, volume 1914.

[130] McGregor-Nichols Engagement Announced, *The Advocate-Messenger* (Danville, Kentucky), 17 July 1949, page 2, *Newspapers.com* (http://www.newspapers.com: accessed 12 June 2016).

[131] Mrs.Jack Bosley Resigns At Center, Miss Clarece Nichols is New Librarian, *The Advocate-Messenger* (Danville, Kentucky), August 16, 1940, page 1, *Newspapers.com* (http://www.newspapers.com: accessed 11 February 2016).

[132] "Bellevue Cemetery," database, *Find A Grave* (http://www.findagrave.com: accessed 24 March 2016), entry for Clarece Nichols Jones; citing memorial #59735515.

[133] Calvin Morgan Fackler, *Early Days in Danville* (1941; reprint Utica, Kentucky: McDowell Publications, 2002), FHL US/CAN 976.9523/D1 H2f.

[134] Boyle County, Kentucky, Marriage records; 1842-1955, marriage bond for Jonathon M Nichols and Emmeline Crutchfield, FHL microfilm 191806, bk1, p123, Family History Library, Salt Lake City, Utah.

[135] 1860 US Census, Boyle County, Kentucky, population schedule, Danville Post Office, page 54, dwelling 338, family 378, J R Nichols; *Ancestry.com* (http://www.ancestry.com: accessed 27 November 2009); citing National Archives microfilm M653, roll 356.

[136] "Bellevue Cemetery," database, *Find A Grave* (http://www.findagrave.com: accessed 7 February 2016), entry for J.R. Nichols, 1898; citing memorial #82181589.

[137] "Kentucky Death Records, 1852-1953," *Ancestry.com* (http://www.ancestry.com: accessed 2 March 2009), for James C Nichols (19 May 1922), certificate 11414.

[138] "Bellevue Cemetery," database, *Find A Grave* (http://www.findagrave.com: accessed 7 February 2016), entry for Katie M. Farlee, 13 September 1909; citing memorial #61557675.

[139] "Bellevue Cemetery," database, *Find A Grave* (http://www.findagrave.com: accessed on 25 March 2016), entry for Ralph Hogan Nichols; citing memorial #61557964.

[140] 1860 US Census, Boyle County, Kentucky, population schedule, page 54, dwelling 338, family 378, J R Nichols.

[141] 1870 US Census, Boyle County, Kentucky, population schedule, Danville, page 169, dwelling 217, family 232, John R. Nichols; *Ancestry.com* (http://www.ancestry.com: accessed 7 March 2009); citing National Archives microfilm M593, roll 448.

[142] "Texas Death Certificates, 1903-1982," *Ancestry.com* (http://www.ancestry.com: accessed 25 March 2016), entry for Sallie Nichols Durham (25 February 1940), certificate #6665.

[143] "Bellevue Cemetery," database, *Find A Grave* (http://www.findagrave.com: accessed 7 February 2016), entry for Sallie M. Durham, 28 February 1940, citing memorial #40667982.

[144] Jordon Dodd, compiler, "Kentucky Marriage Records, 1851-1900," *Ancestry.com* (http://www.ancestry.com: accessed 10 March 2009), for L H Durham and Sallie M Nichols (1 June 1875).

[145] "Bellevue Cemetery," database, *Find A Grave* (http://www.findagrave.com: accessed 7 February 2016), entry for Louis H. Durham, 4 March 1888, citing memorial #40668800.

[146] "Texas Death Certificates, 103-1982," *Ancestry.com* (http://www.ancestry.com: accessed 25 March 2016), entry for Martha Durham Murray (3 January 1957), certificate #36669082.

[147] "New York City Marriages, 1600s-1800s," *Ancestry.com* (http://www.ancestry.com: accessed 25 March 2016), entry for Harold P. Murray and Martha M. Durham (1897); Marriage ID: 2220681916, certificate #2925.

[148] "Bellevue Cemetery," database, *Ancestry.com* (http://www.ancestry.com: accessed 25 March 2016), entry for Emma J. Durham, 1887; citing memorial #40669013.

[149] "Bellevue Cemetery," database, *Ancestry.com* (http://www.ancestry.com: accessed 25 March 2016), entry for Milton J. Durham, January 1889; citing memorial #40672378.

[150] 1860 US Census, Boyle County, Kentucky, population schedule, page 54, dwelling 338, family 378, J R Nichols.

[151] "Kentucky Death Records, 1852-1953," *Ancestry.com* (http://www.ancestry.com: accessed 2 March 2009), for Walter B Nichols (29 July 1913), certificate 18403.

[152] Walter B. Nichols Died in Office at Lexington, *The Courier-Journal*, Louisville, Kentucky, Page 2, 30 July 1913, *Newspapers.com* (http://www.newspapers.com: accessed 25 March 2016).

[153] Winchester Cemetery," database, *Find A Grave* (http://www.findagrave.com: accessed 7 February 2016), entry for Julia Bush Nichols, 10 February 1949; citing memorial #25035806.

[154] "Winchester Cemetery," database, *Find A Grave* (http://www.findagrave.com: accessed 7 February 2016), entry for Julia Bush Nichols.

[155] 1910 US Census, Fayette County, Kentucky, population schedule, Lexington, Enumeration District (ED) 18, page 10B, dwelling 11, family 11, Walter B. Nichols; *Ancestry.com* (http://www.ancestry.com: accessed 7 February 2016); citing National Archives microfilm T624, roll 474.

[156] 1930 US Census, Pulaski County, Arkansas, population schedule, Little Rock, Enumeration District (ED) 41, page 2A, dwelling 36, family 39, Leonidas F. Barrier; *Ancestry.com* (http://www.ancestry.com: accessed 25 March 2016), citing National Archives microfilm T626, roll 92.

[157] "U.S. Headstone Applications for Military Veterans, 1925-1963," *Ancestry.com* (http://www.ancestry.com: accessed on 25 March 2016), entry for Leonidas Forister Barrier, 9 January 1958.

[158] "Winchester Cemetery," database, *Find A Grave* (http://www.findagrave.com: accessed on 25 March 2016), entry for Julian B. Nichols, 28 November 1956; citing memorial #25035807.

[159] 1930 US Census, Fayette County, Kentucky, population schedule, Lexington, Enumeration District (ED) 54, page 18B, John Barclay; *Ancestry.com* (http://www.ancestry.com: accessed 25 March 2016), citing National Archives microfilm T625, roll 568.

[160] "Winchester Cemetery," database, *Find A Grave* (http://www.findagrave.com: accessed on 25 March 2016), entry for Margaret R. Nichols Ferris, 21 January 1981; citing memorial #25030078.

[161] "U.S. Social Security Applications and Claims Index, 1936-2007," *Ancestry.com*, (http://www.ancestry.com: accessed 25 March 2016), entry for Robert L. Nichols, March 1962.

[162] "White Chapel Memorial Park Cemetery," database, *Find A Grave* (http://www.findagrave.com: accessed 25 March 2016), entry for Robert L. Nichols, 1962; citing memorial #142818590.

[163] "Prairie Lawn Cemetery," database, *Find A Grave* (http://www.findagrave.com: accessed on 9 February 2016), entry for Alice Ellis.

[164] 1870 US Census, Boyle County, Kentucky, population schedule, page 169, dwelling 217, family 232, John R Nichols.

[165] 1880 US Census, Boyle County, Kentucky, population schedule, Danville Post Office, Enumeration District (ED) 13, page 399C, dwelling 67, family 73, J R Nichols; *Ancestry.com* (http://www.ancestry.com: accessed 27 November 2009); citing National Archives microfilm T9, roll 404.

[166] 1910 US Census, Sumner County, Kansas, population schedule, Wellington, Enumeration District (ED) 173, page 3A, dwelling 59, family 61, Geo. Ellis; *Ancestry.com* (http://www.ancestry.com: accessed 9 February 2016), citing National Archives microfilm publication T624, roll 459.

[167] Death Comes to Mrs. Alice Ellis, *The Advocate-Messenger*, Danville, Kentucky, 4 March 1940, page 1. *Newspapers.com* (http://www.newspapers.com: accessed 9 February 2016).

[168] "Kentucky Death Records, 1852-1953," *Ancestry.com* (http://www.ancestry.com: accessed 2 March 2009), for Mrs. Estelle Nichols Marks (15 January 1935), certificate 1765.

[169] 1900 US Census, Boyle County, Kentucky, population schedule, Danville, Enumeration District (ED) 14, page 21A, dwelling 385, family 504, Estelle Marks; *Ancestry.com* (http://www.ancestry.com: accessed 7 February 2016); citing National Archives microfilm T623, roll 509.

[170] "Bellevue Cemetery," database, *Find A Grave* (http://www.findagrave.com: accessed 14 May 2016), entry for Lowrie Marks, 15 January 1964; citing memorial #42973692.

[171] "Bellevue Cemetery," database, *Find A Grave* (http://www.findagrave.com: accessed 14 May 2016), entry for Mary Dowling Marks, 22 August 1952; citing memorial #42973313.

[172] "Bellevue Cemetery," database, *Find A Grave* (http://www.findagrave.com: accessed 11 September 2010), entry for J Boyle Nichols, 1 June 1944; citing memorial # 44338336.

[173] "Bellevue Cemetery," database, *Find A Grave* (http://www.findagrave.com: accessed 11 September 2010), entry for Cora VanPelt Nichols, 2 December 1902; citing memorial # 44338361.

[174] J.B. Nichols Dies At Home in South, *The Advocate-Messenger* (Danville, Kentucky), 3 June 1944, page 1, *Newspapers.com* (http://www.newspapers.com: accessed 10 June 2016).

[175] 1940 US Census, Hinds County, Mississippi, population schedule, Jackson, Enumeration District (ED) 25-33A, page 6A, family 121, Harrod A. Nichols; *Ancestry.com* (http://www.ancestry.com: accessed 10 June 2016); citing National Archives microfilm publication T627, roll 2026.

[176] 1900 US Census, Boyle County, Kentucky, population schedule, Danville City, Enumeration District (ED) 14, page 118A, dwelling 325, family 427, Boyle Nichols; *Ancestry.com* (http://www.ancestry.com: accessed 9 January 2010); citing National Archives microfilm T623, roll 509.

Cottrell-Brashear Family Linage

[177] Ibid.

[178] J.B. Nichols Dies At Home in South, *The Advocate-Messenger* (Danville, Kentucky), 3 June 1944.

[179] "Lakewood Memorial Park," *Find A Grave* (http://www.findagrave.com: accessed 25 March 2016), entry for Florence Elizabeth Nichols Orr, 9 June 1987; citing memorial #61513722.

[180] "Lakewood Memorial Park," *Find A Grave* (http://www.findagrave.com: accessed 25 March 2016), entry for Henry Jesse Orr, 27 August 1969; citing memorial #61513684.

[181] "Kentucky Death Records, 1852-1953," subscription database, *Ancestry.com* (http://www.ancestry.com: accessed 22 December 2007), for John M Nichols (9 January 1942), certificate 238.

[182] John M. Nichols Dies at Home This Morning; Was Business Leader Here, *The Advocate-Messenger* (Danville, Kentucky), 9 January 1942, page 1, *Newspapers.com* (http://www.newspapers.com: accessed 9 February 2016).

[183] "Kentucky Death Records, 1852-1953," subscription database, *Ancestry.com* (http://www.ancestry.com: accessed 2 March 2009), for Mrs. Boone Bush Nichols (29 May 1944), certificate 15244.

[184] Mrs. J.M. Nichols Dies at Home on Monday Afternoon, *The Advocate-Messenger* (Danville, Kentucky), 30 May 1944, page 1, *Newspapers.com* (http://www.newspapers.com: accessed 11 February 2016).

[185] City Council Offers Resolutions Upon Death of Mrs. Boone B. Nichols, *The Advocate-Messenger* (Danville, Kentucky), 13 July 1944, page 5, *Newspapers.com* (http://www.newspapers.com: accessed 9 February 2016).

[186] 1910 US Census, Boyle County, Kentucky, population schedule, Precinct 13, Enumeration District (ED) 26, page 24A, dwelling 46, family 58, John M Nichols; digital images, *Ancestry.com* (http://www.ancestry.com: accessed 5 March 2009); citing National Archives microfilm T624, roll 465.

[187] "U.S. Social Security Death Index, 1935-2014," *Ancestry.com* (http://www.ancestry.com: accessed 25 March 2016), entry for Henry Nichols, March 1971.

[188] "Bellevue Cemetery," database, *Find A Grave*, (http://www.findagrave.com: accessed 25 March 2016), entry for Walter B. Nichols, 17 October 1978; citing memorial #82181607.

[189] "Bellevue Cemetery," database, *Find A Grave*, (http://www.findagrave.com: accessed 25 March 2016), entry for R.B. Nichols, 21 July 1959; citing memorial #82181603.

[190] Boyle County Genealogical Association, compiler, *Boyle County, Kentucky, Cemetery Records, 1792-1992* (Utica, Kentucky: McDowell Publications, 1992), FHL US/CAN 976.9523 V38b.

[191] 1850 US Census, Boyle County, Kentucky, population schedule, District 2, page 331, dwelling 174, family 198, Ann Crutchfield; *Ancestry.com* (http://www.ancestry.com: accessed 15 December 2007); citing Family History Library microfilm M432, roll 493.

[192] "Kentucky Death Records, 1852-1953," subscription database, *Ancestry.com* (http://www.ancestry.com: accessed 11 December 2007), for Rich Ann Georgi (9 April 1923), certificate 10579.

[193] Boyle County, Kentucky, Marriage records; 1842-1955, marriage bond for Ralph Georgi and Richard Ann Crutchfield, FHL microfilm 191807, bk4, p61, Family History Library, Salt Lake City, Utah.

[194] 1860 US Census, Boyle County, Kentucky, population schedule, Danville Post Office, page 39, dwelling 254, family 277, Ralph Georgi; *Ancestry.com*

(http://www.ancestry.com: accessed 25 December 2007); citing Family History Library microfilm M653, roll 356

[195] 1870 US Census, Fayette County, Kentucky, population schedule, Lexington Ward 2, page 33, dwelling 204, family 236, Ralph Georgi; *Ancestry.com* (http://www.ancestry.com: accessed 21 December 2007); citing Family History Library microfilm M593, roll 593

[196] "Kentucky Death Records, 1852-1953," subscription database, *Ancestry.com* (http://www.ancestry.com: accessed 21 December 2007), for Miss Anna Georgi (22 October 1941), certificate 23841.

[197] "Kentucky Death Records, 1852-1953," subscription database, *Ancestry.com* (http://www.ancestry.com: accessed 21 December 2007), for Prof Ralph Georgi (2 November 1898), certificate 3166.

[198] "Kentucky Death Records, 1852-1953," subscription database, *Ancestry.com* (http://www.ancestry.com: accessed 11 December 2007), for Rich Ann Georgi (9 April 1923), certificate 10579.

[199] 1850 US Census, Boyle County, Kentucky, population schedule, page 331, dwelling 174, family 198, Ann Crutchfield, listed as age 14 and born in Kentucky.

Section 2 – Chapter 5 Sources – John Sale Campbell Family

[1] O.L. Thomas, compiler, *Ancestral Graves in Warren County, Kentucky, Volume 1* (Warren County, Kentucky: Warren County Historical Society, c1980), FHL US/CAN 976.974 V3t.

[2] Lewis Collins, compiler, *Warren County, Kentucky History & Biographies* (P.O. Box 400; Signal Mountain, Tennessee 37377-0400: Signal Mountain Press, 2002), FHL US/CAN 976.974 D3w.

[3] John S Campbell, *Unidentified Bowling Green newspaper*, Warren County, Kentucky. Original clipping found in loose scrapbook pages of Della Z Campbell Brashear, which passed to her daughter, Zalame Brashear Cottrell and then to Mrs. Cottrell's son, Taylor C Cottrell, Jr. Original pages in the possession of Mr. Cottrell, June 2004.

[4] Zalame Brashear Cottrell's Campbell Family Data, Descendent File, Circa 1958, Cottrell Family Papers, 867 Jamestown Drive, Rockledge, Florida.

[5] Georgia Ennis Campbell, Campbell History by Georgia Ennis Campbell, 1944, original sent to Mandane Ennis's Aunt by Georgia Ennis Campbell in 1944 then passed on to TC Cottrell by Mandane on 23 August 2014, Cottrell Family Papers, 867 Jamestown Drive, Rockledge, Florida.

[6] Death of One Almost a Genterarian, *Unidentified Virginia newspaper*, Unidentified Virginia location, May 1905. Original clipping found in loose scrapbook pages of Della Z Campbell Brashear, which passed to her daughter, Zalame Brashear Cottrell and then to Mrs. Cottrell's son, Taylor C Cottrell, Jr. Original pages in the possession of Mr. Cottrell, June 2004.

[7] Zalame Brashear Cottrell's Campbell Family Data, Descendent File, Circa 1958.

[8] Ibid.

[9] 1860 US Census, Nelson County, Virginia, population schedule, Variety Mills, page 797, dwelling 779, family 799, Wm. P. Woodruff; *Ancestry.com* (http://www.ancestry.com: accessed 27 December 2014); citing National Archives microfilm M653, roll 1365.

[10] Bible of Alexander Mills Campbell and Martha Ann Dinwiddie Campbell, published date, 1 July 1980, accessed on Rootsweb 3 July 2005, from a transcription of the Alexander Mills Campbell Bible Record found in the family bible and posted by Melissa Baskette.

[11] Zalame Brashear Cottrell's Campbell Family Data, Descendent File, Circa 1958

[12] Ibid.

[13] Campbell History, typescript of Campbell Family history by Paul Gottschalk with cover letter from Hester Gottschalk, 1960.

[14] Warren County, Kentucky, Marriage Register Book A, P 38 (11 March 1824), John S. Campbell and Polly Ennis; Warren County Courthouse, Clerk Warren County Court. Copied at County Courthouse in Bowling Green, Kentucky on 11 September 2014 by TC Cottrell.

[15] W H Perrin, J H Battle and G C Griffin, *History of Kentucky Illustrated, Edition 3* (1887; reprint Greenville, South Carolina: Southern Historical Press, Inc., 1999), page 875, William H Campbell.

[16] Ibid.

[17] Irene Moss Sumpter, *Our Heritage an Album of Early Warren County Kentucky Land Marks,* (Clarksville, Tennessee: Jostens Publications, 1976).

[18] "Ennis Cemetery," database, *Find A Grave* (http://www.findagrave.com: accessed 1 September 2014), entry for George W Ennis, 15 June 1835; citing memorial # 82505586.

[19] "Ennis Cemetery," database, *Find A Grave* (http://www.findagrave.com: accessed 1 September 2014), entry for Mary Frances Campbell Ennis, 16 September 1823; citing memorial # 84973726.

[20] Death of Mrs. John S. Campbell, *Unidentified Bowling Green newspaper*, Warren County, Kentucky, November 1891. Original clipping found in loose scrapbook pages of Della Z Campbell Brashear, which passed to her daughter, Zalame Brashear Cottrell and then to Mrs. Cottrell's son, Taylor C Cottrell, Jr. Original pages in the possession of Mr. Cottrell, June 2004.

[21] "Butt-Hill Cemetery," database, *Find A Grave* (http://www.findagrave.com: accessed 11 October 2014), entry for John Ennis, 9 August 1826; citing memorial # 118744281.

[22] Lewis Collins, *Warren County, Kentucky History & Biographies.*

[23] *Unidentified Bowling Green newspaper*, November 1891.

[24] Death of Mrs. John S. Campbell, *Unidentified Bowling Green newspaper*, Warren County, Kentucky, November 1891.

[25] Tillie Smith O'Kelley, "ENNIS," *Warren County Kentucky*, discussion list, 19 August 1998 (http://boards.rootsweb.com: accessed 9 October 2007).

[26] Taylor C Cottrell, "Campbell-Shields Cemetery Lot Photo Survey, Campbell-Shields Cemetery, near Bowling Green, Kentucky," privately held by Taylor C Cottrell, Rockledge, Florida; Markers and plot information photographed and recorded on 31 March, 2011, by Taylor C Cottrell.

[27] Mandane Ennis, "Children of William Tennant Ennis and Nancy Mandane Gatewood update," e-mail TC Cottrell, 1 November 2014. Hereinafter cited as "Children of William Tennant and Nancy Mandane Ennis".

[28] Georgia Ennis Campbell, Campbell History by Georgia Ennis Campbell, 1944, original sent to Mandane Ennis's Aunt by Georgia Ennis Campbell in 1944 then passed on to TC Cottrell by Mandane on 23 August 2014.

[29] Campbell History, typescript of Campbell Family history by Paul Gottschalk.

[30] Ibid.

[31] John S Campbell, *Unidentified Bowling Green newspaper*, Warren County, Kentucky.

[32] 1830 US Census, Warren County, Kentucky, seventh district, page 66, John S Campbell; *Ancestry.com* (http://www.ancestry.com: accessed 23 October 2004); citing National Archives microfilm M19, roll 42.

[33] Mrs. Mary Campbell, wife of John S. Campbell, *Unidentified Bowling Green newspaper*, Warren County, Kentucky, November 1891. Original clipping found in loose scrapbook pages of Della Z Campbell Brashear, which passed to her daughter, Zalame Brashear Cottrell and then to Mrs. Cottrell's son, Taylor C Cottrell, Jr. Original pages in the possession of Mr. Cottrell, June 2004.

[34] Kathleen Hope Brashear, Remembrances of Bowling Green, undated but written prior to 1985, handwritten memories without sources.

[35] Campbell History, typescript of Campbell Family history by Paul Gottschalk.

[36] 1840 US Census, Warren County, Kentucky, population schedule, warren county, page 39, John S Campbell; digital images, *Ancestry.com* (http://www.ancestry.com: accessed 23 October 2004); citing National Archives microfilm M704, roll 125.

[37] Irene Moss Sumpter, *Early Warren County Kentucky Land Marks.*

[38] Campbell History, typescript of Campbell Family history by Paul Gottschalk.

[39] 1850 US Census, Warren County, Kentucky, population schedule, The Second District, page 72A, dwelling 90, family 90, John S Campbell; digital images, *Ancestry.com* (http://www.ancestry.com: accessed 31 May 2004); citing National Archives microfilm M432, roll 220

[40] Campbell History, typescript of Campbell Family history by Paul Gottschalk.

[41] 1860 US Census, Warren County, Kentucky, population schedule, District No 1, Post Office: Bowling Green, page 33, dwelling 331, family 331, John Campbell; *Ancestry.com* (http://www.ancestry.com: accessed 12 September 2004); citing National Archives microfilm M653, roll 398.

[42] 1870 US Census, Warren County, Kentucky, population schedule, Patter Precinct, Post Office: Rich Pond, page 21, dwelling 1115, family 204, John S Campbell; digital images, *Ancestry.com* (http://www.ancestry.com: accessed 31 May 2004); citing National Archives microfilm M593, roll 502.

[43] 1880 US Census, Warren County, Kentucky, population schedule, Rich Pond District, Enumeration District (ED) 232, page 133A, dwelling 199, family 204, John S Campbell; *Ancestry.com* (http://www.ancestry.com: accessed 31 May 2004); citing National Archives microfilm T9, roll 444.

[44] Warren County, Kentucky, Probate Records, 1797-1985, Vols. D, 4-6 1827-1927 - v. D, will of John S Campbell, FHL microfilm 1904209, volume 5, page 53, Family History Library, Salt Lake City, Utah.

[45] Ibid.

[46] Eighty-Seven Years - John S. Campbell Celebrates The Anniversary Of His Birth, *Unidentified Bowling Green newspaper*, Warren County, Kentucky, circa April 1890. Original clipping found in loose scrapbook pages of Della Z Campbell Brashear, which passed to her daughter, Zalame Brashear Cottrell and then to Mrs. Cottrell's son, Taylor C Cottrell, Jr. Original pages in the possession of Mr. Cottrell, June 2004.

[47] Warren County, Kentucky, Probate Records, 1797-1985, will of John S Campbell, FHL microfilm 1904209, v5, p53.

[48] Zalame Brashear Cottrell's Campbell Family Data, Descendent File, Circa 1958.

[49] Death of Mrs. John S. Campbell, *Unidentified Bowling Green newspaper*, Warren County, Kentucky, November 1891. Original clipping found in loose scrapbook pages of Della Z Campbell Brashear, which passed to her daughter, Zalame Brashear Cottrell and then to Mrs. Cottrell's son, Taylor C Cottrell, Jr. Original pages in the possession of Mr. Cottrell, June 2004

Cottrell-Brashear Family Linage

[50] Campbell-Shields Cemetery (Warren County, Kentucky; approximately three miles south of Bowling Green on the Calvary Baptist Church property near the intersection of El-rod Road and William H. Natcher Green River Parkway), Mary E Campbell marker, photographed by T.C. Cottrell, 1 April 2011.

[51] John S Campbell Dead, *Unidentified Bowling Green newspaper*, Warren County, Kentucky. Original clipping found in loose scrapbook pages of Della Z Campbell Brashear, which passed to her daughter, Zalame Brashear Cottrell and then to Mrs. Cottrell's son, Taylor C Cottrell, Jr. Original pages in the possession of Mr. Cottrell, June 2004.

[52] Warren County, Kentucky, Probate Records, 1797-1985, Vols. D, 4-6 1827-1927 - v. D, will of John S Campbell, FHL microfilm 1904209, volume 5, page 53, Family History Library, Salt Lake City, Utah.

[53] Tribute of Respect, *Unidentified Bowling Green newspaper*, Warren County, Kentucky, 23 Feb 1886. Original clipping found in loose scrapbook pages of Della Z Campbell Brashear, which passed to her daughter, Zalame Brashear Cottrell and then to Mrs. Cottrell's son, Taylor C Cottrell, Jr. Original pages in the possession of Mr. Cottrell, June 2004.

[54] 1830 US Census, Warren County, Kentucky, seventh district, page 66, John S. Campbell.

[55] 1840 US Census, Warren County, Kentucky, population schedule, page 39, John S. Campbell.

[56] 1850 US Census, Warren County, Kentucky, population schedule, page 72A, dwelling 90, family 90, John S. Campbell.

[57] Warren County, Kentucky, Marriage Bond Book H, P 121 (25 May 1865), W.S. Campbell and Louisa Wise; Warren County Courthouse, Clerk Warren County Court. Copied at County Courthouse in Bowling Green, Kentucky on 11 September 2014 by TC Cottrell.

[58] Ibid.

[59] 1860 US Census, Warren County, Kentucky, population schedule, Bowling Green, District No. 1, page 13, dwelling 126, family 126, Wiley S. Campbell; *Ancestry.com* (http://www.ancestry.com: accessed 21 June 2004); citing National Archives microfilm M653, roll 398.

[60] O.L. Thomas, compiler, *Ancestral Graves in Warren County, Kentucky, Volume 1* (Warren County, Kentucky: Warren County Historical Society, c1980), FHL US/CAN 976.974 V3t.

[61] Mrs Mary Kirby Dead, *Unidentified Bowling Green newspaper*, Warren County, Kentucky, 8 June 1891. Original clipping found in loose scrapbook pages of Della Z Campbell Brashear, which passed to her daughter, Zalame Brashear Cottrell and then to Mrs. Cottrell's son, Taylor C Cottrell, Jr. Original pages in the possession of Mr. Cottrell, June 2004.

[62] Ibid.

[63]"Kentucky Death Records, 1852-1953," subscription database, *Ancestry.com* (http://www.ancestry.com: accessed 4 April 2008), for J William Campbell (5 March 1925), certificate 8077.

[64] Zalame Brashear Cottrell's Campbell Family Data, Descendent File, Circa 1958.

[65] "Kentucky Death Records, 1852-1953," subscription database, *Ancestry.com* (http://www.ancestry.com: accessed 19 January 2008), for Della Mae Campbell (17 August 1942), certificate 19235.

[66] "Union Hill Cemetery," database, *Find A Grave*, (http://www.findagrave.com: accessed 25 March 2016), entry for Ethel Correne Campbell Hicks, 14 July 1953; citing memorial #44250285.

[67] Bertice Campbell, *Unidentified Bowling Green newspaper*, Warren County, Kentucky. Original clipping found in loose scrapbook pages of Della Z Campbell Brashear, which passed to her daughter, Zalame Brashear Cottrell and then to Mrs. Cottrell's son, Taylor C Cottrell, Jr. Original pages in the possession of Mr. Cottrell, June 2004.

[68] Zalame Brashear Cottrell's Campbell Family Data, Descendent File, Circa 1958.

[69] 1930 US Census, Warren County, Kentucky, population schedule, District 5, Enumeration District (ED) 114-32, page 8A, dwelling 167, family 176 and 177, Ross Kennedy; *Ancestry.com* (http://www.ancestry.com: accessed 1 November 2004); citing National Archives microfilm T626, roll 779.

[70] "Kentucky Death Records, 1852-1953," subscription database, *Ancestry.com* (http://www.ancestry.com: accessed 6 September 2009), for Roscoe Elwood Kennedy (1 May 1950), certificate 50-11092.

[71] Warren County, Kentucky, Marriage Register Book B, P 97 (24 May 1865), Wiley S. Campbell and Louisa C. Wise; Warren County Courthouse, Clerk Warren County Court. Copied at County Courthouse in Bowling Green, Kentucky on 11 September 2014 by TC Cottrell.

[72] Ibid.

[73] 1870 US Census, Warren County, Kentucky, population schedule, Covington Precinct, page 93A, dwelling 3, family 3, W.S. Campbell; digital images, *Ancestry.com* (http://www.ancestry.com: accessed 21 June 2004); citing National Archives microfilm M593, roll 502.

[74] 1880 US Census, Warren County, Kentucky, agricultural schedule, page 5, Wiley S. Campbell; NARA microfilm M1528, roll 31.

[75] 1880 US Census, Warren County, Kentucky, population schedule, Rich Pond District, Enumeration District (ED) 2, page 126B, dwelling 88, family 92, Wiley S. Campbell; *Ancestry.com* (http://www.ancestry.com: accessed 21 June 2004); citing National Archives microfilm T9, roll 444.

[76] Campbell-Shields Cemetery (Warren County, Kentucky; approximately three miles south of Bowling Green on the Calvary Baptist Church property near the intersection of Elrod Road and William H. Natcher Green River Parkway), Infant Daughter of Wiley Sale & Louisa C Campbell marker, photographed by T.C. Cottrell, 1 April 2011.

[77] An Untimely Death, *Unidentified Bowling Green newspaper*, Warren County, Kentucky. Original clipping found in loose scrapbook pages of Della Z Campbell Brashear, which passed to her daughter, Zalame Brashear Cottrell and then to Mrs. Cottrell's son, Taylor C Cottrell, Jr. Original pages in the possession of Mr. Cottrell, June 2004.

[78] "Kentucky Death Records, 1852-1953," subscription database, *Ancestry.com* (http://www.ancestry.com: accessed 19 January 2008), for Eldon Campbell (25 April 1952), certificate 528674.

[79] "Kentucky Death Records, 1852-1953," subscription database, *Ancestry.com* (http://www.ancestry.com: accessed 19 January 2008), for Wiley Campbell (11 November 1878).

[80] "Kentucky Death Records, 1852-1953," subscription database, *Ancestry.com* (http://www.ancestry.com: accessed 20 November 2007), for Nellie Frances McLellan (21 November 1943), certificate 25628.

[81] 1900 US Census, Warren County, Kentucky, population schedule, Hickory Flat No 6, Enumeration District (ED) 105, page 1A/2B, dwelling 19, family 19, J B McLellan, *Ancestry.com,* (http://www.ancestry.com: accessed 1 November 2004); citing National Archives microfilm T623, roll 553.

Cottrell-Brashear Family Linage

[82] "Kentucky Death Records, 1852-1953," subscription database, *Ancestry.com* (http://www.ancestry.com: accessed 20 November 2007), for James B McLellan (19 January 1953), certificate 531730.

[83] 1900 US Census, Warren County, Kentucky, population schedule, Hickory Flat No 6, Enumeration District (ED) 105, page 1A/2B, dwelling 19, family 19, J B McLellan

[84] "Fairview Cemetery," database, Find A Grave (http://www.findagrave.com: accessed on 25 March 2016), entry for Julian Harold McLellan; citing memorial #155346604.

[85] "Fairview Cemetery," database, Find A Grave (http://www.findagrave.com: accessed on 25 March 2016), entry for Ruth McLellan; citing memorial #146507651.

[86] "Kentucky Death Index, 1911-2000," subscription database, *Ancestry.com* (http://www.ancestry.com: accessed 5 November 2004), for Robert C McLellan (24 September 1990), volume 50, certificate 24730.

[87] "U.S. World War I Draft Registration Cards, 1917-1918," Ancestry.com (http://www.ancestry.com: accessed 28 March 2016), entry for Robert Campbell McLellan.

[88] "Kentucky Death Index, 1911-2000," subscription database, *Ancestry.com* (http://www.ancestry.com: accessed 30 August 2009), for James C McClellan (11 December 1962), volume 59, certificate 29045.

[89] "U.S. Social Security Death Index, 1935-2014," Ancestry.com (http://www.ancestry.com: accessed 25 March 2016), entry for Rufine Howlett, November 19086.

[90] "Tennessee State Marriages, 1780-2002," subscription database, *Ancestry.com* (http://www.ancestry.com: accessed 10 August 2014), for Caldwell Howlett and Rufue McClellan (10 August 1926).

[91] "Kentucky Death Index, 1911-2000," subscription database, *Ancestry.com* (http://www.ancestry.com: accessed 5 November 2004), for Norman G McLellan (23 June 1976), volume 31, certificate 15069.

[92] 1910 US Census, Warren County, Kentucky, population schedule, Rich Pond, Enumeration District (ED) 124, page 13A/B, dwelling 175, family 177, James B McLellan; *Ancestry.com* (http://www.ancestry.com: accessed 1 November 2004); citing National Archives microfilm T624, roll 505.

[93] Social Security Administration, "Social Security Death Index," database, *Ancestry.com* (http://www.ancestry.com: accessed 5 November 2004), entry for David W McLellan, 1995, SS no. 405-03-5624.

[94] "Kentucky Death Index, 1911-2000," subscription database, *Ancestry.com* (http://www.ancestry.com: accessed 5 November 2004), for Jo B McLellan (29 December 1964), volume 61, certificate 30194.

[95] "North Carolina Marriage Records, 1741-2011," Ancestry.com (http://www.ancestry.com: accessed 25 March 2016), entry for Jo Burns McLellan and Ruth Campbell Kellogg, 14 June 1938, certificate #221.

[96] "Kentucky Death Index, 1911-2000," subscription database, *Ancestry.com* (http://www.ancestry.com: accessed 5 November 2004), for George L McLellan (5 November 1977), volume 58, certificate 28866.

[97] "Fairview Cemetery," database, *Find A Grave* (http://www.findagrave.com: accessed 25 March 2016), for Hazel K. McLellan, 30 January 1997; citing memorial #121605713.

[98] "Christmount Columbarium," database, *Find A Grave* (http://www.findagrave.com: accessed 25 March 2016), for Sarah Virginia McLellan Wyndham, 30 August 2008; citing memorial #136798171.

[99] "Christmount Columbarium," database, *Find A Grave* (http://www.findagrave.com: accessed 25 March 2016), for Neal McLellan Wyndham, 6 January 2011; citing memorial #136798208.

[100] "Kentucky Death Index, 1911-2000," subscription database, *Ancestry.com* (http://www.ancestry.com: accessed 5 November 2004), for William H McLellan (26 September 1997), volume 54, certificate 26856.

[101] Wife of Mr. Wiley Campbell died, *Unidentified Bowling Green newspaper*, Warren County, Kentucky, November 1883. Original clipping found in loose scrapbook pages of Della Z Campbell Brashear, which passed to her daughter, Zalame Brashear Cottrell and then to Mrs. Cottrell's son, Taylor C Cottrell, Jr. Original pages in the possession of Mr. Cottrell, June 2004.

[102] Warren County, Kentucky, Probate Records, 1797-1985, Vols. D, 4-6 1827-1927 - v. D, will of Wiley S Campbell, FHL microfilm 1904209, volume 4, page 454-457, Family History Library, Salt Lake City, Utah.

[103] Ibid.

[104] Campbell-Shields Cemetery (Warren County, Kentucky), Wiley S Campbell marker.

[105] Zalame Brashear Cottrell's Campbell Family Data, Descendent File, Circa 1958.

[106] W. H. Perrin, J H Battle and G C Kniffin, *History of Kentucky Illustrated*, page 875, William H Campbell.

[107] 1830 US Census, Warren County, Kentucky, seventh district, page 66, John S Campbell.

[108] 1840 US Census, Warren County, Kentucky, population schedule, page 39, John S Campbell.

[109] 1850 US Census, Warren County, Kentucky, population schedule, page 72A, dwelling 90, family 90, John S Campbell.

[110] Warren County, Kentucky, Marriage Bond Book C, P 212 (29 January 1855), William H Campbell and Miss Mary Ann Virginia Ramsey; Warren County Courthouse, Clerk Warren County Court. Copied at County Courthouse in Bowling Green, Kentucky on 11 September 2014 by TC Cottrell.

[111] A Friend Pays Tribute to Mrs. Mary Campbell, *Unidentified Bowling Green newspaper*, Warren County, Kentucky, 10 February 1910. Original clipping found in loose scrapbook pages of Della Z Campbell Brashear, which passed to her daughter, Zalame Brashear Cottrell and then to Mrs. Cottrell's son, Taylor C Cottrell, Jr. Original pages in the possession of Mr. Cottrell, June 2004.

[112] Irene Moss Sumpter, *Our Heritage an Album of Early Warren County Kentucky Land Marks* (Clarksville, Tennessee: Jostens Publications, 1976).

[113] 1860 US Census, Warren County, Kentucky, population schedule, Bowling Green Ky, page 74, dwelling 510, family 510, William Campbell; *Ancestry.com* (http://www.ancestry.com: accessed 12 June 2004); citing National Archives microfilm M653, roll 398.

[114] 1870 US Census, Warren County, Kentucky, population schedule, Bowling Green Precinct, page 25, dwelling 161, family 161, W.H. Campbell; *Ancestry.com* (http://www.ancestry.com: accessed 12 June 2004); citing National Archives microfilm M593, roll 502.

[115] 1880 US Census, Warren County, Kentucky, population schedule, Enumeration District (ED) 36, page 71D, family 277, William H Campbell; *Ancestry.com* (http://www.ancestry.com: accessed 12 June 2004); citing National Archives microfilm T9, roll 444.

[116] Irene Moss Sumpter, *Early Warren County Kentucky Land Marks*.

[117] Warren County, Kentucky, Probate Records, 1797-1985, Vols. D, 4-6 1827-1927 - v. D, will of John S Campbell, FHL microfilm #1904209, volume 5, page 53, Family History Library, Salt Lake City, Utah.

[118] Eighty-Seven Years - John S. Campbell Celebrates the Anniversary Of His Birth, *Unidentified Bowling Green newspaper*, Warren County, Kentucky, circa April 1890. Original clipping found in loose scrapbook pages of Della Z Campbell Brashear, which passed to her daughter, Zalame Brashear Cottrell and then to Mrs. Cottrell's son, Taylor C Cottrell, Jr. Original pages in the possession of Mr. Cottrell, June 2004.

[119] 1900 US Census, Warren County, Kentucky, population schedule, Bristow, Enumeration District (ED) 97, page 14B, dwelling 272, family 275, William H Campbell; *Ancestry.com* (http://www.ancestry.com: accessed 29 September 2004); citing National Archives microfilm T623, roll 553.

[120] Eighty-Seven Years - John S. Campbell Celebrates the Anniversary Of His Birth, *Unidentified Bowling Green newspaper*, Warren County, Kentucky, circa April 1890.

[121] Henry T Campbell's Burial, *Unidentified Bowling Green newspaper*, Warren County, Kentucky. Original clipping found in loose scrapbook pages of Della Z Campbell Brashear, which passed to her daughter, Zalame Brashear Cottrell and then to Mrs. Cottrell's son, Taylor C Cottrell, Jr. Original pages in the possession of Mr. Cottrell, June 2004.

[122] "Kentucky Death Records, 1852-1963," Ancestry.com (http://www.ancestry.com: accessed 25 March 2016), entry for J.F. Campbell, 24 June 1930, certificate #15533.

[123] "Kentucky Death Records, 1852-1953," subscription database, *Ancestry.com* (http://www.ancestry.com: accessed 19 January 2008), for Margrett Read Campbell White (19 April 1917), certificate 12625.

[124] Zalame Brashear Cottrell's Campbell Family Data, Descendent File, Circa 1958.

[125] "Kentucky Death Records, 1852-1953," subscription database, *Ancestry.com* (http://www.ancestry.com: accessed 18 June 2008), for John Thomas White (8 June 1924), certificate 15042.

[126] Patricia E. Reid and Barbara O Ford compilers *Fairview Cemetery, Bowling Green, Kentucky, Cemetery 1*, Volume 1 (Kentucky: unknown publisher, 1989).

[127] Zalame Brashear Cottrell's Campbell Family Data, Descendent File, Circa 1958.

[128] Patricia E. Reid and Barbara O Ford compilers *Fairview Cemetery.*

[129] "Kentucky Death Records, 1852-1953," subscription database, *Ancestry.com* (http://www.ancestry.com: accessed 17 June 2008), for William Hubert White (31 January 1950), certificate 503751.

[130] Zalame Brashear Cottrell's Campbell Family Data, Descendent File, Circa 1958.

[131] Patricia E. Reid and Barbara O Ford compilers *Fairview Cemetery.*

[132] "Kentucky Death Records, 1852-1953," subscription database, *Ancestry.com* (http://www.ancestry.com: accessed 17 June 2008), for Ada White Barbre (5 March 1953), certificate 539058.

[133] Zalame Brashear Cottrell's Campbell Family Data, Descendent File, Circa 1958.

[134] Patricia E. Reid and Barbara O Ford compilers *Fairview Cemetery.*

[135] Social Security Administration, "Social Security Death Index," database, *Ancestry.com* (http://www.ancestry.com: accessed 17 June 2008), entry for Lena Lyle, 1992, SS no. 404-92-2918.

[136] Zalame Brashear Cottrell's Campbell Family Data, Descendent File, Circa 1958.

[137] "Kentucky Death Records, 1852-1953," subscription database, *Ancestry.com* (http://www.ancestry.com: accessed 17 June 2008), for J.E. Lyle (23 December 1044), certificate 68108.

[138] "Kentucky Birth Index, 1911-1999," subscription database, *Ancestry.com* (http://www.ancestry.com: accessed 17 June 2008), for Allene P Lyle (7 September 1919), volume 108, certificate 53789.

[139] Zalame Brashear Cottrell's Campbell Family Data, Descendent File, Circa 1958.

[140] Ibid.

[141] "Michigan Death Records, 1867-1950," Ancestry.com (http://www.ancestry.com: accessed 25 March 2016), entry for Charles S. White, 22 June 1950, File #82181236.

[142] Patricia E. Reid and Barbara O Ford compilers *Fairview Cemetery.*

[143] "Kentucky Death Records, 1852-1953," subscription database, *Ancestry.com* (http://www.ancestry.com: accessed 25 March 2016), for James Campbell White (14 May 1958), certificate 5811815.

[144] Patricia E. Reid and Barbara O Ford compilers *Fairview Cemetery.*

[145] "North Carolina Death Collection, 1908-1996," subscription database, *Ancestry.com* (http://www.ancestry.com: accessed 22 September 2007), for Mary Reed Cade (18 October 1953).

[146] "Indiana Marriage Collection, 1800-1841," subscription database, *Ancestry.com* (http://www.ancestry.com: accessed 22 September 2007), for William E Cade and Mary Reed White (13 February 1912), book 23 October 1892, OS page 15.

[147] "North Carolina Death Certificates, 1909-1975," subscription database, *Ancestry.com* (http://www.ancestry.com: accessed 18 June 2008), for William Earl Cade (29 July 1968), certificate 25427.

[148] 1930 US Census, Edgecomb County, North Carolina, population schedule, Rocky Mount City, Enumeration District (ED) 33-28, page 1A, dwelling 2, family 2, William E Cade;.*com* (http://www.ancestry.com: accessed 15 September 2007); citing National Archives microfilm publication T626, roll 1688.

[149] "Kentucky Death Records, 1852-1953," subscription database, *Ancestry.com* (http://www.ancestry.com: accessed 18 June 2008), for Willis White (19 July 1941), certificate 18664.

[150] "Fairview Cemetery," database, *Find A Grave* (http://www.findagrave.com: accessed 25 March 2016), for Briggs Heriges White, 9 June 1971; citing memorial #119215122.

[151] "Fairview Cemetery," database, *Find A Grave* (http://www.findagrave.com: accessed 25 March 2016), for Hines Mumford White, 23 October 1934; citing memorial #120841188.

[152] 1910 US Census, Warren County, Kentucky, population schedule, Bowling Green, Enumeration District (ED) 118, page 6A, dwelling 105, family 109, J. T. White; *Ancestry.com* (http://www.ancestry.com: accessed 15 September 2007); citing National Archives microfilm publication T624, roll 505.

[153] "Kentucky Death Records, 1852-1953," subscription database, *Ancestry.com* (http://www.ancestry.com: accessed 19 January 2008), for John R Campbell (9 January 1942), certificate 26188.

[154] Patricia E. Reid and Barbara O Ford compilers *Fairview Cemetery.*

[155] Warren County, Kentucky, Marriage Bond Book Y, P 299 (9 February 1897), J.R. Campbell and Maggie Brown; Warren County Courthouse, Clerk Warren County Court. Copied at County Courthouse in Bowling Green, Kentucky on 11 September 2014 by TC Cottrell.

[156] "Kentucky Death Index, 1911-2000," subscription database, *Ancestry.com* (http://www.ancestry.com: accessed 8 October 2006), for Maggie B Campbell (23 November 1958), volume 56, certificate 27705.

[157] Patricia E. Reid and Barbara O Ford compilers *Fairview Cemetery.*

[158] Elvis Campbell, former mayor of BG, dies, *Unidentified Bowling Green newspaper,* Warren County, Kentucky. Original clipping found in loose scrapbook pages of Della Z Campbell Brashear, which passed to her daughter, Zalame Brashear Cottrell and then to Mrs.

Cottrell's son, Taylor C Cottrell, Jr. Original pages in the possession of Mr. Cottrell, June 2004.

[159] Patricia E. Reid and Barbara O Ford compilers *Fairview Cemetery.*

[160] Zalame Brashear Cottrell's Campbell Family Data, Descendent File, Circa 1958.

[161] "Kentucky Death Records, 1852-1953," subscription database, *Ancestry.com* (http://www.ancestry.com: accessed 19 January 2008), for Edward W Campbell (24 October 1948), certificate 21890.

[162] Patricia E. Reid and Barbara O Ford compilers *Fairview Cemetery.*

[163] 1900 US Census, Grayson County, Kentucky, population schedule, Shrewsbury Precinct, Enumeration District (ED) 25, page 10B, dwelling 161, family 164, Ella Keen; digital images, *Ancestry.com* (http://www.ancestry.com: accessed 19 June 2008); citing National Archives microfilm publication T623, roll 523.

[164] Patricia E. Reid and Barbara O Ford compilers *Fairview Cemetery.*

[165] "Kentucky Death Records, 1852-1953," subscription database, *Ancestry.com* (http://www.ancestry.com: accessed 15 June 2008), for Lena Rivers Campbell Bell (29 August 1948), certificate 18594.

[166] Warren County, Kentucky, Marriage Record Book V, P 312 (22 September 1891), RL Bell and Lena Rivers Campbell; Warren County Courthouse, Clerk Warren County Court. Copied at County Courthouse in Bowling Green, Kentucky on 11 September 2014 by TC Cottrell.

[167] "Kentucky Death Records, 1852-1953," subscription database, *Ancestry.com* (http://www.ancestry.com: accessed 25 December 2007), for Robert Lee Bell (18 November 1928), certificate 288791.

[168] "Kentucky Death Index, 1911-2000," subscription database, *Ancestry.com* (http://www.ancestry.com: accessed 13 June 2008), for Robert J Bell (10 December 1970), volume 61, certificate 30415.

[169] "Kentucky Death Records, 1852-1953," subscription database, *Ancestry.com* (http://www.ancestry.com: accessed 20 November 2007), for Wm Jennings Bryan Bell (16 November 1918), certificate 36836.

[170] "Kentucky Death Index, 1911-2000," subscription database, *Ancestry.com* (http://www.ancestry.com: accessed 15 June 2008), for Shelby Bell (28 June 1986), volume 36, certificate 17888.

[171] 1930 US Census, Jefferson County, Kentucky, population schedule, Louisville, Enumeration District (ED) 56-100, page 18B, dwelling 215, family 349, Shelby Bell; *Ancestry.com* (http://www.ancestry.com: accessed 17 June 2008); citing National Archives microfilm T626, roll 756.

[172] "Kentucky Death Records, 1852-1953," subscription database, *Ancestry.com* (http://www.ancestry.com: accessed 14 June 2008), for Frank Beard Bell (2 January 1939), certificate 6576.

[173] "United States Obituary Collection," subscription database, *Ancestry.com* (http://www.ancestry.com: accessed 13 June 2008), for Vinson C Bell (13 April 2004). Taken from The Herald-Dispatch, 16 April 2004; Huntington, West Virginia.

[174] "West Virginia, Marriages Index, 1785-1971," subscription database, *Ancestry.com* (http://www.ancestry.com: accessed 21 February 2014), for Vinson C Bell and Myrtle M Baldwin.

[175] 1930 US Census, Cabell County, West Virginia, population schedule, Huntington City, Enumeration District (ED) 65, page 12B, dwelling 263, family 301, Vinson Bell; *Ancestry.com* (http://www.ancestry.com: accessed 17 June 2008); citing National Archives microfilm T626, roll 1228.

[176] A Friend Pays Tribute to Mrs. Mary Campbell, *Unidentified Bowling Green newspaper*, Warren County, Kentucky, 10 February 1910.

[177] Patricia E. Reid and Barbara O Ford compilers *Fairview Cemetery*

[178] Warren County, Kentucky, Probate Records, 1797-1985, Vols. D, 4-6 1827-1927 - volume D, will of W.H. Campbell, FHL microfilm #1904209, volume 6, page 178, Family History Library, Salt Lake City, Utah.

[179] Wm. H. Campbell Pioneer of Warren County Passed Away this Afternoon - Burial, *Unidentified Bowling Green newspaper*, Warren County, Kentucky, 17 July 1913. Original clipping found in loose scrapbook pages of Della Z Campbell Brashear, which passed to her daughter, Zalame Brashear Cottrell and then to Mrs. Cottrell's son, Taylor C Cottrell, Jr. Original pages in the possession of Mr. Cottrell, June 2004.

[180] Warren County, Kentucky, Probate Records, 1797-1985, Vols. D, 4-6 1827-1927 - volume D, will of W.H. Campbell.

[181] Mary E Penner, Death Registration 18864 (1917), Department of Health Bureau of Vital Statistics, Indianapolis, Indiana. Hereinafter cited as death certificate no. 18864.

[182] 1840 US Census, Warren County, Kentucky, population schedule, page 39, John S Campbell.

[183] Department of Library Special Collections Manuscripts and Folklife Archives, MSS 230 Warren County, Kentucky - Marriage Bonds, 16 September 1869, Marriage record for James A. Shields and Mary E. Campbell Box 16, Folder 2, 1850, Kentucky Library and Museum, Western Kentucky University, Bowling Green, Kentucky.

[184] Michael Hansen, (Bremerton, Washington) "RE: John S. Campbell Obituary - Kentucky," e-mail to Thana White Cottrell, 10 September 2004.

[185] "Pleasant Hill Cemetery," database, *Find A Grave* (http://www.findagrave.com: accessed 25 March 2016), for John H. Shields, 7 April 1876; citing memorial #32809150.

[186] 1860 US Census, Warren County, Kentucky, population schedule, Bowling Green, page 607, dwelling 268, family 268, John Penner; *Ancestry.com* (http://www.ancestry.com: accessed 27 March 2016); citing National Archives microfilm M653, roll 398.

[187] 1870 US Census, Lawrence County, Illinois, population schedule, Petty, page 133A, dwelling 60, family 60, John Penner; *Ancestry.com* (http://www.ancestry.com: accessed 27 March 2016); citing National Archives microfilm M593, roll 245.

[188] "Kentucky Birth Records, 1847-1911," *Ancestry.com* (http://www.ancestry.com: accessed 26 March 2016), entry for Mary F. Shields, 22 February 1853.

[189] 1860 US Census, Warren County, Kentucky, population schedule, Bowling Green, page 607, dwelling 268, family 268, John Penner.

[190] Campbell-Shields Cemetery (Warren County, Kentucky), James A Shields marker.

[191] Warren County, Kentucky, Marriage Bond Book D, P 429 (21 September 1857), John H. Penner and Mary E. Shields; Warren County Courthouse, Clerk Warren County Court. Copied at County Courthouse in Bowling Green, Kentucky on 11 September 2014 by TC Cottrell.

[192] 1860 US Census, Warren County, Kentucky, population schedule, Bowling Green, page 607, dwelling 268, family 268, John Penner.

[193] Dr. Penner - Former Citizen of This County, Dies at Lawrenceville, Ind., *Unidentified Warren County newspaper*, Warren County, Kentucky. Original clipping found in loose scrapbook pages of Della Z Campbell Brashear, which passed to her daughter, Zalame Brashear Cottrell and then to Mrs. Cottrell's son, Taylor C Cottrell, Jr. Original pages in the possession of Mr. Cottrell, June 2004.

[194] 1870 US Census, Lawrence County, Illinois, population schedule, Petty, page 133A, dwelling 60, family 60, John Penner.

Cottrell-Brashear Family Linage

[195] 1880 US Census, Lawrence County, Illinois, population schedule, Lawrence Township, Enumeration District (ED) 189, page 1A, dwelling 7, family 7, John H Penner; *Ancestry.com* (http://www.ancestry.com: accessed 16 September 2004); citing National Archives microfilm T9, roll 224.

[196] Warren County, Kentucky, Probate Records, 1797-1985, will of John S Campbell, FHL microfilm 1904209, volume 5, page 53.

[197] 1900 US Census, Lawrence County, Illinois, population schedule, Lawrence Township, Enumeration District (ED) 114, page 10B, dwelling 218, family 225, John H Penner; *Ancestry.com* (http://www.ancestry.com: accessed 16 September 2004); citing National Archives microfilm T623, roll 317.

[198] "Kentucky Birth Records, 1852-1910," subscription database, *Ancestry.com* (http://www.ancestry.com: accessed 15 May 2013), for George F Penner (19 July 1858).

[199] "Pleasant Hill Cemetery," database, *Find A Grave* (http://www.findagrave.com: accessed 22 March 2015), entry for George Franklin Penner, 24 December 1873; citing memorial #32800613.

[200] "Penner Cemetery," database, *Find A Grave* (http://www.findagrave.com: accessed 15 July 2014), entry for Peter Wesley Penner, 25 July 1860; citing memorial # 34013225.

[201] "Penner Cemetery," database, *Find A Grave* (http://www.findagrave.com: accessed 15 July 2014), entry for Eugene Penner, 27 March 1862; citing memorial # 33998602.

[202] Obituary - Died - Sarah Elizabeth, *Unidentified Bowling Green newspaper*, Warren County, Kentucky. Original clipping found in loose scrapbook pages of Della Z Campbell Brashear, which passed to her daughter, Zalame Brashear Cottrell and then to Mrs. Cottrell's son, Taylor C Cottrell, Jr. Original pages in the possession of Mr. Cottrell, June 2004.

[203] "Pleasant Hill Cemetery," database, *Find A Grave* (http://www.findagrave.com: accessed 22 March 2015), entry for Sarah Elizabeth Penner, 28 January 1882; citing memorial #32800673.

[204] "Lawrenceville City Cemetery," database, *Find A Grave* (http://www.findagrave.com: accessed 11 May 2013), entry for James N Penner, 1951; citing memorial # 16756379.

[205] "Indiana Marriages, 1845-1920," *Ancestry.com* (http://www.ancestry.com: accessed 20 October 2004), entry for J.N. Penner and L.M. McCorroll, 23 October 1889.

[206] "Illinois Deaths and Stillbirths Index, 1916-1947," subscription database, *Ancestry.com* (http://www.ancestry.com: accessed 15 May 2013), for Letha Penner (9 June 1947), FHL Film No. 1991775.

[207] Mrs James N Penner, *Terre Haute Star*, Terre Haute, Indiana, 10 June 1947, page 2.

[208] Taylor C Cottrell, "Campbell-Shields Cemetery Lot Photo Survey, Campbell-Shields Cemetery, near Bowling Green, Kentucky," privately held by Taylor C Cottrell, Rockledge, Florida; Markers and plot information photographed and recorded on 31 March, 2011, by Taylor C Cottrell.

[209] Death of Dr. J.J. Penner, *Unidentified Lawrence County newspaper*, Lawrence County, Illinois. Original clipping found in loose scrapbook pages of Della Z Campbell Brashear, which passed to her daughter, Zalame Brashear Cottrell and then to Mrs. Cottrell's son, Taylor C Cottrell, Jr. Original pages in the possession of Mr. Cottrell, June 2004.

[210] 1910 US Census, Vigo County, Indiana, population schedule, Harrison Township, Enumeration District (ED) 155, page 3A, dwelling 54, family 62, James N Penner; *Ancestry.com* (http://www.ancestry.com: accessed 16 October 2004); citing National Archives microfilm publication T624, roll 385.

[211] Mary E Penner, *Terre Haute Tribune*, Terre Haute, Indiana, 27 June 1916, page 2.

[212] Campbell-Shields Cemetery (Warren County, Kentucky), Lucinda Francis Campbell marker.

[213] 1840 US Census, Warren County, Kentucky, population schedule, page 39, John S Campbell.

[214] 1850 US Census, Warren County, Kentucky, population schedule, page 72A, dwelling 90, family 90, John S Campbell.

[215] "Illinois Deaths and Stillbirths Index, 1916-1947," *Ancestry.com* (http://www.ancestry.com: accessed 27 March 2016), entry for Hamilton Duke Wade, 25 July 1919, reference FHL Film #1562100.

[216] "Kentucky Marriage Records, 1852-1914," *Ancestry.com* (http://www.ancestry.com: accessed 27 March 2016), entry for Harrison D. Wade and Mary E. Carpenter, 15 October 1859.

[217]1870 US Census, Warren County, Kentucky, population schedule, Patter Precinct, page 21, dwelling 113, family 143, H D Wade; *Ancestry.com* (http://www.ancestry.com: accessed 31 May 2004); citing National Archives microfilm publication M593, roll 502.

[218] "Kentucky Death Records, 1852-1953," subscription database, *Ancestry.com* (http://www.ancestry.com: accessed 6 September 2009), for Lee F Wade (3 July 1913), certificate 20212.

[219] Patricia E Reid and Barbara O Ford compilers *Fairview Cemetery, Bowling Green, Kentucky, Cemetery 1.*

[220] "Fairview Cemetery," database, *Find A Grave* (www.findagrave.com: accessed 27 March 2016), entry for Permelia Belle Jones Wade, 20 January 1935; citing memorial #12335914.

[221] "Kentucky Death Records, 1852-1963," subscription database, *Ancestry.com* (http://www.ancestry.com: accessed 27 March 2016), for Mrs. Dora Runner (14 June 1919), certificate 19854.

[222] "Fairview Cemetery," database, Find A Grave (http://www.findagrave.com: accessed 27 March 2016), entry for Dora Wade Runner, 14 June 1919; citing memorial #12335972.

[223] "Tennessee State Marriages, 1780-2002," Ancestry.com (http://www.ancestry.com: accessed 27 March 2016), entry for Dora Wade, page 34.

[224] "Fairview Cemetery," database, Find A Grave (http://www.findagrave.com: accessed 27 March 2016), entry for Clarence William Runner, 16 April 1951; citing memorial #12335976.

[225] 1920 US Census, Warren County, Kentucky, population schedule, Bowling Green, Enumeration District (ED) 134, page 16B, dwelling 334, family 378, Clarence Runner; *Ancestry.com* (http://www.ancestry.com: accessed 27 March 2016); citing National Archives microfilm T625, roll 600.

[226] "Kentucky Death Records, 1852-1963," subscription database, *Ancestry.com* (http://www.ancestry.com: accessed 27 March 2016), for Fannie Wade Butts (6 December 1955), certificate 5526162.

[227] "Kentucky Death Records, 1852-1963," subscription database, *Ancestry.com* (http://www.ancestry.com: accessed 27 March 2016), for Rubin Lee Butts (28 February 1951), certificate 516221.

[228] "Fairview Cemetery," database, *Find A Grave* (http://www.findagrave.com: accessed 27 March 2016), entry for Lee Butts, 1951; citing memorial #121709847.

229 1930 US Census, Warren County, Kentucky, population schedule, Stallard Springs, Enumeration District (ED) 22, page 8B, dwelling 183, family 153, R. Lee Butts; *Ancestry.com* (http://www.ancestry.com: accessed 27 March 2016); citing National Archives microfilm publication T626, roll 779.

230 "Virginia Death Records, 1912-2014," *Ancestry.com* (http://www.ancestry.com: accessed 26 March 2016) entry for Frank Edward Wade, 16 December 1963, certificate #34506.

231 "Forest Lawn Cemetery and Mausoleum," database, *Find A Grave* (http://www.findagrave.com: accessed 26 March 2016), entry for Frank E. Wade; citing memorial #137068022.

232 "Virginia Death Records, 1912-2014," subscription database, *Ancestry.com* (http://www.ancestry.com: accessed 27 March 2016), entry for Geneva Long Freeman Wade, 4 June 1974, reference certificate #74018935.

233 1920 US Census, Jefferson County, Kentucky, population schedule, Louisville, Enumeration District (ED) 145, page 5B, dwelling 334, family 378, Edward F. Wade; *Ancestry.com* (http://www.ancestry.com: accessed 27 March 2016); citing National Archives microfilm T625, roll 581.

234 1910 US Census, Warren County, Kentucky, population schedule, Bowling Green, Enumeration District (ED) 118, page 16A, dwelling 319, family 344, L.F. Wade; *Ancestry.com* (http://www.ancestry.com: accessed 27 March 2016); citing National Archives microfilm T624, roll 505.

235 Ibid.

236 Campbell-Shields Cemetery, Infant Son of Hampton D & Lucinda Francis Wade marker, photographed by T.C. Cottrell, 1 April 2011.

237 Taylor C Cottrell, "Campbell-Shields Cemetery Lot Photo Survey," Markers and plot information photographed and recorded on 31 March, 2011, by Taylor C Cottrell.

238 1880 US Federal Census, Warren County, Kentucky, population schedule, Rich Pond District, Enumeration District (ED) 232, page 26B, dwelling 222, family 227, H D Wade; *Ancestry.com* (http://www.ancestry.com: accessed 1 December 2004); citing National Archives microfilm T9, roll 444.

239 Ibid.

240 "Oakwood Cemetery," database, *Find A Grave* (http://www.findagrave.com: accessed 27 March 2016), entry for Charles E. Wade, 20 November 1948; citing memorial #125999476.

241 "Indiana Marriage Index, 1800-1941," subscription database, *Ancestry.com* (http://www.ancestry.com: accessed 27 March 2016), entry for Charles Wade and Cora Richmond, 28 November 1894.

242 1910 US Census, Macoupin County, Illinois, population schedule, Chesterfield, Enumeration District (ED) 47, page 1A, dwelling 2, family 2, Charles E. Wade; *Ancestry.com* (http://www.ancestry.com: accessed 27 March 2016); citing National Archives microfilm publication T624, roll 308.

243 "California Death Index, 1940-1997," subscription database, *Ancestry.com* (http://www.ancestry.com: accessed 26 March 2016), entry for William H. Wade, 25 November 1973.

244 "Oakwood Cemetery," database, *Find A Grave* (http://www.findagrave.com: accessed on 26 March 2016), entry for William H. Wade, 1973; citing memorial #129527219.

245 1910 US Census, Macoupin County, Illinois, population schedule, Chesterfield, Enumeration District (ED) 47, page 1A, dwelling 2, family 2, Charles E. Wade.

[246] 1930 US Census, Madison County, Illinois, population schedule, Hartford, Enumeration District (ED) 97, page 13A, dwelling 5, family 5, Charles E. Wade; *Ancestry.com* (http://www.ancestry.com: accessed 27 March 2016); citing National Archives microfilm T626, roll 543.

[247] "Oakwood Cemetery," database, *Find A Grave* (http://www.findagrave.com: accessed on 26 March 2016), entry for Charles D. Wade, 23 December 1988; citing memorial #125989708.

[248] 1930 US Census, Madison County, Illinois, population schedule, Hartford, Enumeration District (ED) 97, page 13A, dwelling 5, family 5, Charles E. Wade.

[249] Ibid.

[250] "Memorial Park Cemetery," database, *Find A Grave* (http://www.findagrave.com: accessed 26 March 2016), entry for Juanita M. Cochran; citing memorial #69429287.

[251] "U.S. World War I Draft Registration Cards, 1917-1918," *Ancestry.com* (http://www.ancestry.com: accessed 25 March 2016), Samuel Hendricks Wade.

[252] 1930 US Census, Macoupin County, Illinois, population schedule, Bird, Enumeration District (ED) 35, page 4B, dwelling 82, family 82, Samuel H. Wade; *Ancestry.com* (http://www.ancestry.com: accessed 27 March 2016); citing National Archives microfilm T626, roll 388.

[253] "Charity Baptist Cemetery," database, *Find A Grave* (http://www.findagrave.com: accessed 25 March 2016), Samuel H. Wade, 1955; citing memorial #52668944.

[254] "Chesterfield Cemetery," database, *Find A Grave* (http://www.findagrave.com: accessed 25 March 2016), Finis Wade, 30 September 1952; citing memorial #91712094.

[255] "Chesterfield Cemetery," database, *Find A Grave* (http://www.findagrave.com: accessed 25 March 2016), Maude Wade, 14 March 1957; citing memorial #91712126.

[256] 1910 US Census, Macoupin County, Illinois, population schedule, Sooth Palmyra, Enumeration District (ED) 68, page 6B, dwelling 167, family 168, Finis Wade; *Ancestry.com* (http://www.ancestry.com: accessed 27 March 2016); citing National Archives microfilm T624, roll 309.

[257] "Loomis Cemetery," database, *Ancestry.com* (http://www.ancestry.com: accessed on 26 March 2016), entry for A.E. Forth Wade, 1898; citing memorial #91613398.

[258] "Loomis Cemetery," database, *Ancestry.com* (http://www.ancestry.com: accessed on 26 March 2016), entry for Hame D. Wade, 23 July 1919; citing memorial #91613408.

[259] "Illinois Deaths and Stillbirths Index, 1916-1947," *Ancestry.com* (http://www.ancestry.com: accessed 27 March 2016), entry for Hamilton Duke Wade.

[260] Zalame Brashear Cottrell's Campbell Family Data, Descendent File, Circa 1958.

[261] Ibid.

[262] Ibid.

[263] 1840 US Census, Warren County, Kentucky, population schedule, page 39, John S Campbell.

[264] 1850 US Census, Warren County, Kentucky, population schedule, page 72A, dwelling 90, family 90, John S Campbell.

[265] Genealogical Records Committee, *Marriage Register of Warren County, Kentucky (June 14, 1851 to December 30, 1869)* (Washington, DC: Daughters of the American Revolution, 1944-1945), FHL US/CAN 976.974 V2m.

[266] Michael Hansen, "Campbell Shields Cemetery," e-mail to TC Cottrell, 11 September 2004.

[267] 1860 US Census, Warren County, Kentucky, population schedule, District 2, Post Office Bowling Green, page 111, dwelling 770, family 770, Samuel Shields; *Ancestry.com*

(http://www.ancestry.com: accessed 13 September 2004); citing National Archives microfilm M653, roll 398.

[268] 1870 US Census, Warren County, Kentucky, population schedule, Hadley Precinct, Post Office Hadley, page 9, dwelling 56, family 56, Samuel T Shields; *Ancestry.com* (http://www.ancestry.com: accessed 13 September 2004); citing National Archives microfilm M593, roll 502.

[269] 1880 US Census, Warren County, Kentucky, agricultural schedule, page 31, Samuel Shields; NARA microfilm M1528, roll 31.

[270] 1880 US Census, Warren County, Kentucky, population schedule, Green Castle District, Enumeration District (ED) 235, page 198D, dwelling 368, family 367, Samuel Shields; *Ancestry.com* (http://www.ancestry.com: accessed 14 September 2004); citing National Archives microfilm T9, roll 444.

[271] Warren County, Kentucky, Probate Records, 1797-1985, will of John S. Campbell, FHL microfilm 1904209, volume 5, page 53.

[272] Mrs. Eliza M. Shields, *Unidentified Bowling Green newspaper*, Warren County, Kentucky, August 1907. Original clipping found in loose scrapbook pages of Della Z Campbell Brashear, which passed to her daughter, Zalame Brashear Cottrell and then to Mrs. Cottrell's son, Taylor C Cottrell, Jr. Original pages in the possession of Mr. Cottrell, June 2004.

[273] Warren County, Kentucky, Kentucky Probate Records, 1727-1990, will of Elizabeth M. Shields, FHL microfilm 1904209, Will Book 6, page 19, page 20, and page 21, Family History Library, Salt Lake City, Utah.

[274] Mrs. Shields Dies of Injuries, *Unidentified Bowling Green newspaper*, Warren County, Kentucky, 26 August 1907. Original clipping found in loose scrapbook pages of Della Z Campbell Brashear, which passed to her daughter, Zalame Brashear Cottrell and then to Mrs. Cottrell's son, Taylor C Cottrell, Jr. Original pages in the possession of Mr. Cottrell, June 2004.

[275] "Kentucky Death Records, 1852-1953," subscription database, *Ancestry.com* (http://www.ancestry.com: accessed 20 November 2007), for Mary Ann Shields (11 January 1944), certificate 3116.

[276] "Kentucky Death Records, 1852-1953," subscription database, *Ancestry.com* (http://www.ancestry.com: accessed 20 November 2007), for Mrs. Cornelia S. Maxey (11 January 1924), certificate 2526.

[277] Mrs. Shields Dies of Injuries, *Unidentified Bowling Green newspaper*, Warren County, Kentucky, 26 August 1907.

[278] "Kentucky Death Records, 1852-1953," subscription database, *Ancestry.com* (http://www.ancestry.com: accessed 20 November 2007), for Warren W. Maxey (15 April 1934), certificate 10582.

[279] "Orange Hill Cemetery," database, *Find A Grave* (http://www.findagrave.com: accessed 26 March 2016), entry for Julia A. Bradshaw, 25 November 1966; citing memorial #12087123.

[280] "Indiana Select Marriages Index, 1748-1993," subscription database, *Ancestry.com* (http://www.ancestry.com: accessed 26 March 2016), for Henry Bradshaw and Julia Maxey (22 November 1904), reference FHL Film #41352, page 204.

[281] "Orange Hill Cemetery," database, *Find A Grave* (http://www.findagrave.com: accessed 26 March 2016), entry for Julia A. Bradshaw.

[282] 1920 US Census, Polk County, Florida, population schedule, Lakeland, Enumeration District (ED) 165, page 19A, dwelling 431, family 469, John H. Bradshaw; *Ancestry.com*

(http://www.ancestry.com: accessed 27 March 2016); citing National Archives microfilm T625, roll 227.

[283] "Kentucky Death Records, 1852-1953," subscription database, *Ancestry.com* (http://www.ancestry.com: accessed 3 July 2008), for Boardly Maxey (8 March 1912), certificate 8627.

[284] 1900 US Census, Warren County, Kentucky, population schedule, Stallard Springs, Enumeration District (ED) 109, page 3B, dwelling 53, family 53, Warren W Maxey; *Ancestry.com* (http://www.ancestry.com: accessed 24 November 2007); citing National Archives microfilm T623, roll 553.

[285] "Kentucky Death Records, 1852-1953," subscription database, *Ancestry.com* (http://www.ancestry.com: accessed 5 July 2008), for Minnie Sweeney (22 July 1911), certificate 19612.

[286] "Barren River Baptist Cemetery," database, *Find A Grave* (http://www.findagrave.com: accessed 26 March 2016), entry for Laura A. Vinson, 4 May 1964; citing memorial #89105238.

[287] "Barren River Baptist Cemetery," database, *Find A Grave* (http://www.findagrave.com: accessed 26 March 2016), entry for James G. Vinson, 17 July 1937; citing memorial #89105156.

[288] "Halls Chapel Cemetery," database, *Find A Grave* (http://www.findagrave.com: accessed 26 March 2016), entry for Jesse Adalbert Maxey, 17 July 1937; citing memorial #39418719.

[289] 1930 US Census, Warren County, Kentucky, population schedule, Stallard Springs, Enumeration District (ED) 20, page 1A, dwelling 9, family 9, Jessie A. Maxey; *Ancestry.com* (http://www.ancestry.com: accessed 27 March 2016); citing National Archives microfilm publication T626, roll 779.

[290] "Fort Myers Cemetery," database, *Find A Grave* (http://www.findagrave.com: accessed 31 March 2016), for Charles Woodson Maxey, 17 July 1962; citing memorial #39584494.

[291] "Fort Myers Cemetery," database, *Find A Grave* (http://www.findagrave.com: accessed 31 March 2016), for Lillie Lamons Maxey, 12 December 1987; citing memorial #39584927.

[292] 1930 US Census, Lee County, Florida, population schedule, Tice, Enumeration District (ED) 06, page 4A, dwelling 81, family 80, Charles Maxey; *Ancestry.com* (http://www.ancestry.com: accessed 31 March 2016); citing National Archives microfilm T626, roll 323.

[293] "Chapel Hill Memorial Gardens," database, *Find A Grave* (http://www.findagrave.com: accessed 31 March 2016), for Mary Eliza Maxey Tims, 26 November 1988; citing memorial #145115148.

[294] "Chapel Hill Memorial Gardens," database, *Find A Grave* (http://www.findagrave.com: accessed 31 March 2016), for Daniel Dan Tims, 15 September 1973; citing memorial #145115097.

[295] 1930 US Census, Warren County, Kentucky, population schedule, Bristow, Enumeration District (ED) 28, page 1A, dwelling 3, family 3, Dan Tims; *Ancestry.com* (http://www.ancestry.com: accessed 31 March 2016); citing National Archives microfilm T626, roll 780.

[296] 1940 US Census, Morris County, New Jersey, population schedule, Rockaway, Enumeration District (ED) 14-100, page 63A, dwelling 198, Frank Maxey; *Ancestry.com* (http://www.ancestry.com: accessed 31 March 2016); citing National Archives microfilm T627, roll 2373.

[297] "Barren River Baptist Cemetery," database, *Find A Grave* (http://www.findagrave.com: accessed 31 March 2016), for Roy Irvin Maxey; citing memorial #148517548.

[298] "Barren River Baptist Cemetery," database, *Find A Grave* (http://www.findagrave.com: accessed 31 March 2016), for Irene Atkinson Maxey; citing memorial #148517538.

[299] 1900 US Census, Warren County, Kentucky, population schedule, Stallard Springs, Enumeration District (ED) 109, page 3B, dwelling 53, family 53, Warren W Maxey.

[300] Michael Hansen, "Campbell Shields Cemetery," e-mail to TC Cottrell, 11 September 2004.

[301] "Kentucky Death Records, 1852-1953," subscription database, *Ancestry.com* (http://www.ancestry.com: accessed 20 November 2007), for Sam J Shields (13 May 1946), certificate 12245.

[302] Michael Hansen, "Campbell Shields Cemetery," e-mail to TC Cottrell, 11 September 2004.

[303] "Kentucky Death Records, 1852-1953," subscription database, *Ancestry.com* (http://www.ancestry.com: accessed 20 November 2007), for Mrs. Blanch Isabell Shields (23 March 1923), certificate 9754.

[304] Campbell-Shields Cemetery (Warren County, Kentucky), Charlie E Shields marker.

[305] "New Tacoma Cemetery," database, *Find A Grave* (http://www.findagrave.com: accessed 31 March 2016), for Fern B. Cuthbert, 18 February 1974; citing memorial #153813341.

[306] "New Tacoma Cemetery," database, *Find A Grave* (http://www.findagrave.com: accessed 31 March 2016), for Oswald C. Cuthbert, 1974; citing memorial #153813342.

[307] "Palms Woodlawn Cemetery," database, *Find A Grave* (http://www.findagrave.com: accessed 31 March 2016), for Clarence S. Shields, 16 March 1959; citing memorial #71470904.

[308] 1910 US Census, Warren County, Kentucky, population schedule, Magisterial District 4, Enumeration District (ED) 119, page 7A, dwelling 5, family 5, S J Shields; digital images, *Ancestry.com* (http://www.ancestry.com: accessed 29 July 2006); citing National Archives microfilm publication T624, roll 505.

[309] "U.S. Social Security Death Index, 1935-2014," subscription database, Ancestry.com (http://www.ancestry.com: accessed 1 April 2016), entry for Harley Shields, Dec 1975.

[310] "U.S. World War II Draft Registration Cards, 1942," *Ancestry.com* (http://www.ancestry.com: accessed 24 December 2014), for Harley B Shields, National Archives and Records Administration.

[311] "U.S. Social Security Death Index, 1935-2014," *Ancestry.com* (http://www.ancestry.com: accessed 1 April 2016), entry for Harley Shields.

[312] "U.S. World War I Draft Registration Cards, 1917-1918," *Ancestry.com* (http://www.ancestry.com: accessed 1 April 2016), entry for Frederick Talefaro Shields, National Archives and Records Administration.

[313] "U.S. Social Security Death Index, 1935-2014," *Ancestry.com* (http://www.ancestry.com: accessed 1 April 2016), entry for Fred Shields, December 1973.

[314] "Campbell-Shields Cemetery" database, *Find A Grave*, entry for Infant Shields, 10 January 1865.

[315] Patricia E Reid and Barbara O Ford compilers *Fairview Cemetery, Bowling Green, Kentucky, Cemetery 1.*

[316] Zalame Brashear Cottrell's Campbell Family Data, Descendent File, Circa 1958.

[317] "Kentucky Death Records, 1852-1953," subscription database, *Ancestry.com* (http://www.ancestry.com: accessed 20 November 2007), for Vallie Atchison Shields (27 July 1946), certificate 16488.

[318] "Campbell-Shields Cemetery" database, *Find A Grave*, entry for Eugenia V Shields, 7 March 1909.

[319] Taylor C Cottrell, "Campbell-Shields Cemetery Lot Photo Survey," Markers and plot information photographed and recorded on 31 March, 2011, by Taylor C Cottrell.

[320] Warren County, Kentucky, Kentucky Probate Records, 1727-1990, will of J.E. Shields, FHL microfilm 1904209, Will Book 6, page 76, Family History Library, Salt Lake City, Utah.

[321] Campbell-Shields Cemetery (Warren County, Kentucky), Samuel T. Shields marker.

[322] Mrs. Eliza M. Shields, *Unidentified Bowling Green newspaper*, Warren County, Kentucky, August 1907. Original clipping found in loose scrapbook pages of Della Z Campbell Brashear, which passed to her daughter, Zalame Brashear Cottrell and then to Mrs. Cottrell's son, Taylor C Cottrell, Jr. Original pages in the possession of Mr. Cottrell, June 2004.

[323] Zalame Brashear Cottrell's Campbell Family Data, Descendent File, Circa 1958.

[324] 1850 US Census, Warren County, Kentucky, population schedule, page 72A, dwelling 90, family 90, John S Campbell.

[325] 1860 US Census, Warren County, Kentucky, population schedule, District No 1, Post Office: Bowling Green, page 33, dwelling 331, family 331, John Campbell; *Ancestry.com* (http://www.ancestry.com: accessed 12 September 2004); citing National Archives microfilm M653, roll 398.

[326] Warren County, Kentucky, Marriage Register Book B, P 102 (18 October 1865), James A Campbell and Mary A. Madison; Warren County Courthouse, Clerk Warren County Court. Copied at County Courthouse in Bowling Green, Kentucky on 11 September 2014 by TC Cottrell.

[327] 1870 US Census, Warren County, Kentucky, population schedule, Patter Precinct, page 21, dwelling 1116, family 146, James A. Campbell; *Ancestry.com* (http://www.ancestry.com: accessed 31 May 2004); citing National Archives microfilm M593, roll 502.

[328] 1880 US Census, Warren County, Kentucky, agricultural schedule, page 12, James A. Campbell; NARA microfilm publication M1528, roll 31.

[329] Irene Moss Sumpter, *Our Heritage an Album of Early Warren County Kentucky Land Marks* (Clarksville, Tennessee: Jostens Publications, 1976). Hereinafter cited as *Early Warren County Kentucky Land Marks*.

[330] Warren County, Kentucky, Probate Records, 1797-1985, will of John S. Campbell, FHL microfilm 1904209, volume 5, page 53.

[331] 1900 US Census, Warren County, Kentucky, population schedule, District No 4, Enumeration District (ED) 104, page 15A, dwelling 271, family 277, James Campbell; *Ancestry.com* (Kentucky. Warren County: accessed 7 November 2004); citing National Archives microfilm T623, roll 553.

[332] "Florida Death Index, 1877-1998," subscription database, *Ancestry.com* (http://www.ancestry.com: accessed 20 October 2007), for Reedie Letitia Potter (1938). Cottrell Digital Image Cd01624.

[333] "Kentucky Marriage Records, 1852-1914," subscription database, *Ancestry.com* (http://www.ancestry.com: accessed 20 October 2007), for H.S. Potter and Reedie Campbell (15 January 1908).

[334] "Florida Death Index, 1877-1998," subscription database, *Ancestry.com* (http://www.ancestry.com: accessed 20 October 2007), for Henry Skiles Potter (January 1956).

[335] "Fairview Cemetery," Find A Grave (http://www.findagrave.com: accessed 4 April 2016), entry for Herbert Willie Campbell, 2 January 1951; citing memorial #120753710.

[336] Ibid.

[337] "Kentucky Death Index, 1911-2000," subscription database, *Ancestry.com* (http://www.ancestry.com: accessed 25 November 2004), for Roy Thomas (3 April 1946), volume 21, certificate 10103.

[338] Zalame Brashear Cottrell's Campbell Family Data, Descendent File, Circa 1958.

[339] Patricia E Reid and Barbara O Ford compilers *Fairview Cemetery, Bowling Green, Kentucky, Cemetery 1.*

[340] Social Security Administration, "Social Security Death Index," database, *Ancestry.com* (http://www.ancestry.com: accessed 26 November 2004), entry for Ulyes Thomas, 1992, SS no. 405-18-7720.

[341] In Memoriam of Mrs. Mary Madison Campbell, Who Died March 4th, 1901, *Unidentified Bowling Green newspaper*, Warren County, Kentucky, 20 March 1901. Original clipping found in loose scrapbook pages of Della Z Campbell Brashear, which passed to her daughter, Zalame Brashear Cottrell and then to Mrs. Cottrell's son, Taylor C Cottrell, Jr. Original pages in the possession of Mr. Cottrell, June 2004.

[342] Warren County, Kentucky, Marriage Bond Book CC, P 118 (4 January 1904), James A Campbell and Mrs. Virgil M Jenkins; Warren County Courthouse, Clerk Warren County Court. Copied at County Courthouse in Bowling Green, Kentucky on 11 September 2014 by TC Cottrell.

[343] 1910 US Census, Warren County, Kentucky, population schedule, Magisterial District No 4, Enumeration District (ED) 118, page 18A, dwelling 360, family 387, J.A. Campbell; *Ancestry.com* (http://www.ancestry.com: accessed 7 November 2004); citing National Archives microfilm T624, roll 505.

[344] Warren County, Kentucky, Probate Records, 1797-1985, Vols. D, 4-6 1827-1927 - v. D, will of J.A. Campbell, FHL microfilm 1904209, volume 6, page 404, Family History Library, Salt Lake City, Utah.

[345] 1920 US Census, Warren County, Kentucky, population schedule, Bowling Green, Enumeration District (ED) 132, page 6A, dwelling 115, family 117, Jas A. Campbell; *Ancestry.com* (http://www.ancestry.com: accessed 23 December 2004); citing National Archives microfilm T625, roll 600.

[346] "Kentucky Death Records, 1852-1953," subscription database, *Ancestry.com* (http://www.ancestry.com: accessed 19 June 2008), for Jas A. Campbell (19 January 1922), certificate 2597.

[347] Patricia E Reid and Barbara O Ford compilers *Fairview Cemetery, Bowling Green, Kentucky, Cemetery 1.*

[348] Warren County, Kentucky, Probate Records, 1797-1985, Vols. D, 4-6 1827-1927 - v. D, will of J.A. Campbell, FHL microfilm 1904209, volume 6, page 404, Family History Library, Salt Lake City, Utah.

[349] "Kentucky Death Records, 1852-1953," subscription database, *Ancestry.com* (http://www.ancestry.com: accessed 29 March 2008), for Virgie M Campbell (10 July 1926), certificate 18098.

[350] Zalame Brashear Cottrell's Campbell Family Data, Descendent File, Circa 1958.

[351] 1850 US Census, Warren County, Kentucky, population schedule, page 72A, dwelling 90, family 90, John S Campbell.

[352] Warren County, Kentucky, Marriage Bond Book E, P 439 (22 November 1859), Robert W Burton and Margaret LV Campbell; Warren County Courthouse, Clerk Warren County Court. Copied at County Courthouse in Bowling Green, Kentucky on 11 September 2014 by TC Cottrell.

[353] Prominent Women Goes to Her Reward, *Unidentified Bowling Green newspaper*, Warren County, Kentucky, 18 June 1904. Original clipping found in loose scrapbook pages of Della Z Campbell Brashear, which passed to her daughter, Zalame Brashear Cottrell and then to Mrs. Cottrell's son, Taylor C Cottrell, Jr. Original pages in the possession of Mr. Cottrell, June 2004. Hereinafter cited as Unidentified Bowling Green newspaper.

[354] Ibid.

[355] Warren County, Kentucky, Marriage Bond Book R, P 389 (4 December 1883), James R Burton and Julia Richardson; Warren County Courthouse, Clerk Warren County Court. Copied at County Courthouse in Bowling Green, Kentucky on 11 September 2014 by TC Cottrell.

[356] Genealogical Records Committee, *Marriage Register of Warren County, Kentucky (June 14, 1851 to December 30, 1869)* (Washington, DC: Daughters of the American Revolution, 1944-1945), FHL US/CAN 976.974 V2m.

[357] "Kentucky Death Records, 1852-1953," subscription database, *Ancestry.com* (http://www.ancestry.com: accessed 21 March 2008), for John D Miller (20 June 1922), certificate 23276.

[358] 1870 US Census, Warren County, Kentucky, population schedule, Patter Precinct, page 21, dwelling 1114, family 144, John D Miller; *Ancestry.com* (http://www.ancestry.com: accessed 31 May 2004); citing National Archives microfilm M593, roll 502.

[359] 1880 US Census, Warren County, Kentucky, population schedule, Green Castle, Enumeration District (ED) 258, page 34B, dwelling 284, family 285, John Miller; *Ancestry.com* (http://www.ancestry.com: accessed 27 January 2008); citing National Archives microfilm T9, roll 444.

[360] Warren County, Kentucky, Probate Records, 1797-1985, will of John S. Campbell, FHL microfilm 1904209, volume 5, page 53.

[361] 1900 US Census, Warren County, Kentucky, population schedule, Green Castle, Enumeration District (ED) 94, page 7B, dwelling 131, family 131, John D Miller; *Ancestry.com* (http://www.ancestry.com: accessed 27 January 2008); citing National Archives microfilm T623, roll 553.

[362] "Kentucky Death Records, 1852-1953," subscription database, *Ancestry.com* (http://www.ancestry.com: accessed 20 November 2007), for Mrs Minnie Miller Erwin (10 October 1922), certificate 23273.

[363] Prominent Women Goes to Her Reward.

[364] 1920 US Census, Warren County, Kentucky, population schedule, Bowling Green, Enumeration District (ED) 135, page 2A, dwelling 25, family 33, Joe L. Erwin; *Ancestry.com* (http://www.ancestry.com: accessed 27 January 2008); citing National Archives microfilm T625, roll 600.

[365] "Kentucky Death Records, 1852-1953," subscription database, *Ancestry.com* (http://www.ancestry.com: accessed 27 January 2008), for Joseph Erwin (31 December 1940), certificate 30062.

[366] Campbell-Shields Cemetery (Warren County, Kentucky), Clarence W Miller marker.

[367] 1900 US Census, Warren County, Kentucky, population schedule, ED 94, page 7B, dwelling 131, family 131, John D Miller.

Cottrell-Brashear Family Linage

[368] "Kentucky Death Records, 1852-1953," subscription database, *Ancestry.com* (http://www.ancestry.com: accessed 2 April 2016), for Authur Clarence Miller (16 October 1943), certificate 22308.

[369] "Louisville Memorial Gardens," *Find A Grave* (http://www.findagrave.com: accessed 2 April 2016), entry for Arthur C. Miller, 1943; citing memorial #135997882.

[370] 1930 US Census, Jefferson County, Kentucky, population schedule, Louisville, Enumeration District (ED) 93, page 5A, dwelling 73, family 99, Arthur C. Miller; *Ancestry.com* (http://www.ancestry.com: accessed 2 April 2016); citing National Archives microfilm T626, roll 756.

[371] "California Death Index, 1940-1997," subscription database, *Ancestry.com* (http://www.ancestry.com: accessed 2 April 2016), for Earle C. Miller (13 August 1974).

[372] "Kentucky Birth Index, 1911-1999," subscription database, *Ancestry.com* (http://www.ancestry.com: accessed 2 April 2016), for Robert R. Miller (2 November 1919), certificate #5224, volume #11.

[373] "Kentucky Birth Index, 1911-1999," subscription database, *Ancestry.com* (http://www.ancestry.com: accessed 2 April 2016), for Aleta Miller (4 June 1921), certificate #38889, volume #78.

[374] "Kentucky Death Records, 1852-1953," subscription database, *Ancestry.com* (http://www.ancestry.com: accessed 20 November 2007), for Mrs. Lucy Miller (18 January 1914), certificate 2945.

[375] "Kentucky Death Records, 1852-1953," subscription database, *Ancestry.com* (http://www.ancestry.com: accessed 21 March 2008), for John D. Miller (20 June 1922), certificate 23276.

[376] 1860 US Census, Warren County, Kentucky, population schedule, District No 1, Post Office: Bowling Green, page 33, dwelling 331, family 331, John Campbell.

[377] Zalame Brashear Cottrell's Campbell Family Data, Descendent File, Circa 1958.

[378] 1850 US Census, Warren County, Kentucky, population schedule, page 72A, dwelling 90, family 90, John S Campbell.

[379] 1860 US Census, Warren County, Kentucky, population schedule, District No 1, Post Office: Bowling Green, page 33, dwelling 331, family 331, John Campbell.

[380] In Memory of Chas. E. Suman, *Unidentified Bowling Green newspaper*, Warren County, Kentucky. Original clipping found in loose scrapbook pages of Della Z Campbell Brashear, which passed to her daughter, Zalame Brashear Cottrell and then to Mrs. Cottrell's son, Taylor C Cottrell, Jr. Original pages in the possession of Mr. Cottrell, June 2004.

[381] 1870 US Census, Warren County, Kentucky, population schedule, Bowling Green Precinct, Post Office: Bowling Green, page 80, dwelling 532, family 533, C.E. Suman; *Ancestry.com* (http://www.ancestry.com: accessed 11 July 2004); citing National Archives microfilm M593, roll 502.

[382] In Memory of Chas. E. Suman, *Unidentified Bowling Green newspaper*, Warren County, Kentucky.

[383] 1880 US Census, Warren County, Kentucky, population schedule, Rich Pond District, Enumeration District (ED) 232, page 133A, dwelling 199, family 204, John S Campbell; *Ancestry.com* (http://www.ancestry.com: accessed 31 May 2004); citing National Archives microfilm publication T9, roll 444.

[384] In Memory of Chas. E. Suman, *Unidentified Bowling Green newspaper*, Warren County, Kentucky.

[385] Warren County, Kentucky, Probate Records, 1797-1985, Vols. D, 4-6 1827-1927 - v. D, will of John S Campbell, FHL microfilm 1904209, volume 5, page 53, Family History Library, Salt Lake City, Utah.

[386] 1900 US Census, Lawrence County, Illinois, population schedule, Lawrence Township, Enumeration District (ED) 114, page 10B, dwelling 218, family 225, John H Penner; *Ancestry.com* (http://www.ancestry.com: accessed 16 September 2004); citing National Archives microfilm T623, roll 317

[387] 1910 US Census, Warren County, Kentucky, population schedule, District No 4, Enumeration District (ED) 108, page 10A, dwelling 181, family 145, Herbert Campbell; *Ancestry.com* (http://www.ancestry.com: accessed 7 November 2004); citing National Archives microfilm T624, roll 553.

[388] "Kentucky Death Records, 1852-1953," subscription database, *Ancestry.com* (http://www.ancestry.com: accessed 20 November 2007), for Julia A. Suman (26 May 1914), certificate 14242.

Section 2 – Chapter 6 Sources – George W. Campbell Family

[1] "Kentucky Death Records, 1852-1953," subscription database, *Ancestry.com* (http://www.ancestry.com: accessed 19 January 2008), for Geo W Campbell (12 February 1908).

[2] 1830 US Census, Warren County, Kentucky, seventh district, page 66, John S Campbell; *Ancestry.com* (http://www.ancestry.com: accessed 23 October 2004); citing National Archives microfilm M19, roll 42.

[3] 1840 US Census, Warren County, Kentucky, population schedule, warren county, page 39, John S Campbell; *Ancestry.com* (http://www.ancestry.com: accessed 23 October 2004); citing National Archives microfilm M704, roll 125.

[4] 1850 US Census, Warren County, Kentucky, population schedule, The Second District, page 72A, dwelling 90, family 90, John S Campbell; *Ancestry.com* (http://www.ancestry.com: accessed 31 May 2004); citing National Archives microfilm M432, roll 220.

[5] Warren County, Kentucky, Marriage Bond Book E, P 219 (20 November 1858), George W Campbell and Hester T Penner; Warren County Courthouse, Clerk Warren County Court. Copied at County Courthouse in Bowling Green, Kentucky on 11 September 2014 by TC Cottrell.

[6] Warren County, Kentucky, Marriage Register Book B, P 53 (25 November 1858), George W Campbell and Hester T Penner; Warren County Courthouse, Clerk Warren County Court. Copied at County Courthouse in Bowling Green, Kentucky on 11 September 2014 by TC Cottrell.

[7] 1860 US Census, Warren County, Kentucky, population schedule, Bowling Green, page 86, dwelling 591, family 591, George Campbell; dig*iAncestry.com* (http://www.ancestry.com: accessed 25 June 2004); citing National Archives microfilm M653, roll 398.

[8] Irene Moss Sumpter, *Our Heritage an Album of Early Warren County Kentucky Land Marks* (Clarksville, Tennessee: Jostens Publications, 1976). Hereinafter cited as *Early Warren County Kentucky Land Marks*.

[9] 1870 US Census, Warren County, Kentucky, population schedule, Greencastle Post Office, page 200B, dwelling 231, family 231, Geo W Campbell; *Ancestry.com* (http://www.ancestry.com: accessed 25 June 2004); citing National Archives microfilm M593, roll 502.

[10] 1880 US Census, Warren County, Kentucky, population schedule, Green Castle District, Enumeration District (ED) 2, page 181A, dwelling 76, family 76, George Campbell; *Ancestry.com* (http://www.ancestry.com: accessed 25 April 2004); citing National Archives microfilm T9, roll 444.

[11] 1880 US Census, Warren County, Kentucky, agricultural schedule, page 19, George W Campbell; NARA microfilm M1528, roll 31.

[12] Warren County, Kentucky, Probate Records, 1797-1985, Vols. D, 4-6 1827-1927 - v. D, will of John S Campbell, FHL microfilm 1904209, volume 5, page 53, Family History Library, Salt Lake City, Utah.

[13] Eighty-Seven Years - John S. Campbell Celebrates the Anniversary of His Birth, *Unidentified Bowling Green newspaper*, Warren County, Kentucky, circa April 1890. Original clipping found in loose scrapbook pages of Della Z Campbell Brashear, which passed to her daughter, Zalame Brashear Cottrell and then to Mrs. Cottrell's son, Taylor C Cottrell, Jr. Original pages in the possession of Mr. Cottrell, June 2004.

[14] Warren County, Kentucky, Probate Records, 1797-1985, Vols. D, 4-6 1827-1927 - v. D, will of G.W. Campbell.

[15] Warren County, Kentucky, Marriage Records, 1797-1965, Vols. Q-T 1877-1888, bonds & certificates only, FHL microfilm 1944289, book W, page 200, Family History Library, Salt Lake City, Utah.

[16] 1900 US Census, Warren County, Kentucky, population schedule, Bowling Green, Enumeration District (ED) 3, page 7B, dwelling 123, family 123, George W Campbell; *Ancestry.com* (http://www.ancestry.com: accessed 24 September 2004); citing National Archives microfilm T623, roll 553.

[17] "Kentucky Death Records, 1852-1953," subscription database, *Ancestry.com* (http://www.ancestry.com: accessed 19 January 2008), for Geo W Campbell (12 February 1908).

[18] Warren County, Kentucky, Probate Records, 1797-1985, Vols. D, 4-6 1827-1927 - v. D, will of John S Campbell.

[19] 1910 US Census, Warren County, Kentucky, population schedule, District No 1, Enumeration District (ED) 112, page 10A, dwelling 106, family 106, Hester T Campbell; *Ancestry.com* (http://www.ancestry.com: accessed 24 September 2004); citing National Archives microfilm T624, roll 504.

[20] Warren County, Kentucky, Probate Records, 1797-1985, Vols. D, 4-6 1827-1927 - v. D, will of Hester T Campbell, FHL microfilm 1904209, volume 6, page 431, Family History Library, Salt Lake City, Utah.

[21] 1920 US Census, Warren County, Kentucky, population schedule, District 1, Enumeration District (ED) 126, page 9A, dwelling 184, family 184, Hester Campbell; *Ancestry.com* (http://www.ancestry.com: accessed 29 September 2004); citing National Archives microfilm T625, roll 600.

[22] Zalame Brashear Cottrell's Campbell Family Data, Descendent File, Circa 1958, Cottrell Family Papers, 867 Jamestown Drive, Rockledge, Florida.

[23] Warren County, Kentucky, Probate Records, 1797-1985, Vols. D, 4-6 1827-1927 - v. D, will of Hester T Campbell.

[24] "Kentucky Death Records, 1852-1953," subscription database, *Ancestry.com* (http://www.ancestry.com: accessed 19 January 2008), for Laura B Campbell (28 October 1938), certificate 25970.

[25] 1870 US Census, Warren County, Kentucky, population schedule, Greencastle Post Office, page 200B, dwelling 231, family 231, Geo W Campbell.

[26] 1880 US Census, Warren County, Kentucky, population schedule, Green Castle District, Enumeration District (ED) 2, page 181A, dwelling 76, family 76, George Campbell.

[27] 1900 US Census, Warren County, Kentucky, population schedule, Bowling Green, Enumeration District (ED) 3, page 7B, dwelling 123, family 123, George W Campbell.

[28] Irene Moss Sumpter, *Early Warren County Kentucky Land Marks*.

[29] 1910 US Census, Warren County, Kentucky, population schedule, Magisterial District No 1, Enumeration District (ED) 112, page 10A, dwelling 106, family 106, Hester T Campbell.

[30] Warren County, Kentucky, Probate Records, 1797-1985, Vols. D, 4-6 1827-1927 - v. D, will of Hester T Campbell.

[31] 1920 US Census, Warren County, Kentucky, population schedule, Greencastle District 1, Enumeration District (ED) 126, page 9A, dwelling 184, family 184, Hester Campbell.

[32] 1930 US Census, Warren County, Kentucky, population schedule, Green Castle, Enumeration District (ED) 114-30, page 2a, dwelling 30, family 31, Lara Campbell; *Ancestry.com* (http://www.ancestry.com: accessed 5 March 2007); citing National Archives microfilm T626, roll 780.

[33] "Kentucky Death Index, 1911-2000," digital images, *Ancestry.com* (www.ancestry.com: accessed 21 January 2014), entry for Bertha D Moulder, 11 October 1985; citing Volume 55, Certificate 27226.

[34] "Kentucky Death Index, 1911-2000," digital images, *Ancestry.com* (www.ancestry.com: accessed 21 January 2014), entry for Robert W Moulder, 3 July 1989; citing Volume 39, Certificate 19441.

[35] "U.S. City Directories, 1822-1995," Ancestry.com (http://www.ancestry.com: accessed 4 April 2016), entry for Bertha Moulder; citing Bowling Green, Kentucky, City Directory, 1949.

[36] Laura B Campbell, *Unidentified Bowling Green newspaper*, Warren County, Kentucky. Original clipping found in loose scrapbook belonging to Kathleen Brashear, which passed to her daughter, Zalame Brashear Cottrell and then to Mrs. Cottrell's son, Taylor C Cottrell, Jr. Original pages in the possession of Mr. Cottrell, June 2004.

[37] Zalame Brashear Cottrell's Campbell Family Data, Descendent File, Circa 1958.

[38] 1870 US Census, Warren County, Kentucky, population schedule, Greencastle Post Office, page 200B, dwelling 231, family 231, Geo W Campbell.

[39] 1880 US Census, Warren County, Kentucky, population schedule, Green Castle District, Enumeration District (ED) 2, page 181A, dwelling 76, family 76, George Campbell.

[40] Department of Library Special Collections Manuscripts and Folklife Archives, MSS 230 Warren County, Kentucky - Marriage Bonds, 23 December 1884, Marriage record for J. Roland Madison and Miss Jessie Campbell, Box 24, Folder 1, 1884, Kentucky Library and Museum, Western Kentucky University, Bowling Green, Kentucky.

[41] Lewis Collins, compiler, *Warren County, Kentucky History & Biographies* (P.O. Box 400; Signal Mountain, Tennessee 37377-0400: Signal Mountain Press, 2002), FHL US/CAN 976.974 D3w.

[42] Ibid.

[43] 1910 US Census, Warren County, Kentucky, population schedule, Magisterial District 5, Enumeration District (ED) 123, page 7A, dwelling 106, family 107, Roland Madison; *Ancestry.com* (http://www.ancestry.com: accessed 3 October 2004); citing National Archives microfilm T624, roll 505.

[44] "Kentucky Death Records, 1852-1953," subscription database, *Ancestry.com* (http://www.ancestry.com: accessed 20 November 2007), for A.C. Madison (13 June 1932), certificate 15168.

[45] Zalame Brashear Cottrell's Campbell Family Data, Descendent File, Circa 1958.

[46] "Kentucky Death Records, 1852-1953," subscription database, *Ancestry.com* (http://www.ancestry.com: accessed 31 August 2014), for Katie Berdean Madison (21 March 1925), certificate 8082.

[47] Zalame Brashear Cottrell's Campbell Family Data, Descendent File, Circa 1958.

[48] "Lexington Cemetery," database, *Find A Grave* (http://www.findagrave.com: accessed 20 February 2014), entry for Betsey Madison Rhoads, 16 July 1941; citing memorial # 42550574.

[49] "Lexington Cemetery," database, *Find A Grave* (http://www.findagrave.com: accessed 20 February 2014), entry for Wayland Rhoads, 6 July 1972; citing memorial # 42550518.

[50] "U.S. Social Security Application and Claims Index, 1956-2007," Ancestry.com (http://www.ancestry.com: accessed 4 April 2016), entry for William McHenry Rhoads, 23 August 1996.

[51] "Lakeside Memorial Gardens," database, *Find A Grave* (http://www.findagrave.com: accessed 4 April 2016), entry for William M. Rhoads, 23 August 1996; citing memorial #100995516.

[52] "Kentucky Marriage Index, 1973-1999," *Ancestry.com* (http://www.ancestry.com: accessed 4 April 2016), entry for William M. Rhoads and Mary K. Floyd (23 December 1988); citing certificate #44833, volume 90.

[53] "Kentucky Death Index, 1911-2000," subscription database, *Ancestry.com* (http://www.ancestry.com: accessed 27 November 2004), for George W Madison (7 January 1967), volume 4, certificate 1783.

[54] 1940 US Census, Warren County, Kentucky, population schedule, Bowling Green, Enumeration District (ED) 114-14, page 24A, dwelling 499, George W Madison; *Ancestry.com* (http://www.ancestry.com: accessed 6 September 2014); citing National Archives microfilm T6267, roll 1360

[55] "Chapel Hill Memorial Gardens," database, *Find A Grave* (http://www.findagrave.com: accessed 1 September 2014), entry for Elizabeth Mae King Madison, 26 January 1993; citing memorial # 18868919.

[56] "Kentucky Death Index, 1911-2000," subscription database, *Ancestry.com* (http://www.ancestry.com: accessed 3 October 2004), for Novice C Robinson (11 March 1984), volume 15, certificate 7115.

[57] Zalame Brashear Cottrell's Campbell Family Data, Descendent File, Circa 1958.

[58] "Kentucky Death Index, 1911-2000," subscription database, *Ancestry.com* (http://www.ancestry.com: accessed 25 September 2007), for Lonnie R Robinson (26 May 1955), volume 26, certificate 12733.

[59] "U.S. Veterans Gravesites, ca.1775-2006," subscription database, *Ancestry.com* (http://www.ancestry.com: accessed 4 February 2007), for Billy G RS Robinson (5 September 2003).

[60] "U.S. World War II Army Enlistment Records, 1938-1946," subscription database, *Ancestry.com* (http://www.ancestry.com: accessed 4 February 2007), for Billy G Robinson, National Archives and Records Administration, Record Group 64.

[61] "Kentucky Death Index, 1911-2000," subscription database, *Ancestry.com* (http://www.ancestry.com: accessed 29 May 2008), for Mary H Pormann (13 December 1978), volume 61, certificate 30276.

[62] Zalame Brashear Cottrell's Campbell Family Data, Descendent File, Circa 1958.

[63] "New York Passenger Lists, 1820-1957," subscription database, *Ancestry.com* (http://www.ancestry.com: accessed 4 February 2007), for Emil Poremann (22 August 1902), microfilm serial 15, roll T715_296.

[64] "Kentucky Death Index, 1911-2000," subscription database, *Ancestry.com* (http://www.ancestry.com: accessed 29 May 2008), for Emil G Pormann (5 June 1962), volume 27, certificate 13271.

[65] "Evergreen Cemetery," database, *Find A Grave* (http://www.findagrave.com: accessed 5 April 2016), entry for Marilyn P. Pormann Landers, 27 November 2011; citing memorial #82060003.

[66] "U.S. Social Security Death Index, 1935-2014," subscription database. *Ancestry.com* (http://www.ancestry.com: accessed 5 April 2016), for Frank Landers, December 1981.

[67] "Kentucky Death Index, 1911-2000," subscription database, *Ancestry.com* (http://www.ancestry.com: accessed 22 December 2004), for Wilkins M Settle (5 January 1979), volume 2, certificate 668.

[68] "Tennessee State Marriages, 1780-2002," subscription database, Ancestry.com (http://www.ancestry.com: accessed 4 April 2016), entry for Collis Robinson and Wilkins Madison (21 September 1913).

[69] "World War I Draft Registration Cards, 1917-1918," subscription database, *Ancestry.com* (http://www.ancestry.com: accessed 1 July 2006), for Collis Wilkerson Robinson, citing United States, Selective Service System. World War I Selective Service System Draft Registration Cards, 1917-1918. Washington, D.C.: National Archives and Records Administration. Microfilm publication M1509, Warren County, Kentucky; Roll 1653845.

[70] Zalame Brashear Cottrell's Campbell Family Data, Descendent File, Circa 1958.

[71] "Kentucky Death Index, 1911-2000," subscription database, *Ancestry.com* (http://www.ancestry.com: accessed 27 November 2004), for Collis W Robinson (3 March 1970), volume 16, certificate 7748.

[72] Zalame Brashear Cottrell's Campbell Family Data, Descendent File, Circa 1958.

[73] Patricia E Reid and Barbara O Ford compilers *Fairview Cemetery, Bowling Green, Kentucky, Cemetery 1.*

[74] "Kentucky Death Records, 1852-1953," subscription database, *Ancestry.com* (http://www.ancestry.com: accessed 29 May 2008), for R.L. Robinson Jr. (30 January 1917), certificate 2916.

[75] Social Security Administration, "Social Security Death Index," database, *Ancestry.com* (http://www.ancestry.com: accessed 29 May 2008), entry for Anna J Stocking, 1996, SS no. 403-22-1575.

[76] Zalame Brashear Cottrell's Campbell Family Data, Descendent File, Circa 1958.

[77] Social Security Administration, "Social Security Death Index," database, *Ancestry.com* (http://www.ancestry.com: accessed 29 May 2008), entry for John H Stocking, 2002, SS no. 401-28-6869.

[78] "Kentucky Death Records, 1852-1963," subscription database, *Ancestry.com* (http://www.ancestry.com: accessed 6 June 2016), for Collis W Robinson Jr. (24 April 1957), certificate 10355.

[79] "Oak Grove Cemetery," database, *Find A Grave* (http://www.findagrave.com: accessed 5 April 2016), entry for Joel R. Madison, 15 April 1975; citing memorial #54889716.

[80] "Oak Grove Cemetery," database, *Find A Grave* (http://www.findagrave.com: accessed 5 April 2016), entry for Doris W. Williamson Madison, 6 November 1977; citing memorial #54889833.

[81] 1910 US Census, Warren County, Kentucky, population schedule, Magisterial District 5, Enumeration District (ED) 123, page 7A, dwelling 106, family 107, Roland Madison; *Ancestry.com* (http://www.ancestry.com: accessed 3 October 2004); citing National Archives microfilm publication T624, roll 505

[82] Taylor C Cottrell, "Campbell-Brashear Cemetery Lot Photo Survey, Fairview Cemetery, Bowling Green, Kentucky," privately held by Taylor C Cottrell, Rockledge, Florida; Markers and plot information photographed and recorded on 1 April, 2011, by Taylor C Cottrell.

[83] "Kentucky Death Records, 1852-1953," subscription database, *Ancestry.com* (http://www.ancestry.com: accessed 12 May 2008), for Joseph Rollin Madison (6 August 1917), certificate 26513.

[84] 1920 US Census, Warren County, Kentucky, population schedule, Bristow District #3, Enumeration District (ED) 129, page 10B, dwelling 324, family 333, Josie D Madison; *Ancestry.com* (http://www.ancestry.com: accessed 1 July 2006); citing National Archives microfilm T625, roll 600.

[85] 1930 US Census, Warren County, Kentucky, population schedule, Bowling Green, Enumeration District (ED) 114-11, page 2B, dwelling 45, family 45, George Madison; *Ancestry.com* (http://www.ancestry.com: accessed 26 November 2004); citing National Archives microfilm T626, roll 779.

[86] "Kentucky Death Records, 1852-1953," subscription database, *Ancestry.com* (http://www.ancestry.com: accessed 20 November 2007), for Josephine Campbell Madison (4 July 1934), certificate 18617.

[87] "Kentucky Death Records, 1852-1953," subscription database, *Ancestry.com* (http://www.ancestry.com: accessed 24 November 2007), for John Sale Campbell (26 July 1930), certificate 18461.

[88] 1870 US Census, Warren County, Kentucky, population schedule, Greencastle Post Office, page 200B, dwelling 231, family 231, Geo W Campbell.

[89] 1880 US Census, Warren County, Kentucky, population schedule, Green Castle District, Enumeration District (ED) 2, page 181A, dwelling 76, family 76, George Campbell.

[90] Warren County, Kentucky, Marriage Bond Book V, P 346 (15 December 1891), John S Campbell and Annie M Lively; Warren County Courthouse, Clerk Warren County Court. Copied at County Courthouse in Bowling Green, Kentucky on 11 September 2014 by TC Cottrell.

[91] "Kentucky Death Records, 1852-1953," subscription database, *Ancestry.com* (http://www.ancestry.com: accessed 24 November 2007), for Anna Lively Campbell (4 February 1929), certificate 7854.

[92] Warren County, Kentucky, Probate Records, 1797-1985, Vols. D, 4-6 1827-1927 - v. D, will of G.W. Campbell, FHL microfilm 1904209, volume 6, page 33, Family History Library, Salt Lake City, Utah.

[93] 1910 US Census, Warren County, Kentucky, population schedule, District No 5, Enumeration District (ED) 123, page 6B, dwelling 103, family 104, John S. Campbell; *Ancestry.com* (http://www.ancestry.com: accessed 29 November 2004); citing National Archives microfilm T624, roll 505.

[94] Warren County, Kentucky, Probate Records, 1797-1985, Vols. D, 4-6 1827-1927 - v. D, will of Hester T. Campbell, FHL microfilm 1904209, volume 6, page 431, Family History Library, Salt Lake City, Utah.

[95] 1920 US Census, Warren County, Kentucky, population schedule, Bristow, Enumeration District (ED) 128, page 15b, dwelling 319, family 328, John B. Lashbrook; *Ancestry.com* (http://www.ancestry.com: accessed 5 March 2007); citing National Archives microfilm T625, roll 625.

[96] "U.S. Veterans Gravesites, ca.1775-2006," subscription database, *Ancestry.com* (http://www.ancestry.com: accessed 4 March 2007), for Walton Lively Campbell (16 April 1949).

[97] Zalame Brashear Cottrell's Campbell Family Data, Descendent File, Circa 1958.

[98] "U.S. Veterans Gravesites, ca.1775-2006," subscription database, *Ancestry.com* (http://www.ancestry.com: accessed 1 June 2008), for Anna K Campbell (6 May 1975).

[99] "Calvary Cemetery," database, *Find A Grave* (http://www.findagrave.com: accessed 5 April 2016), entry for John Sales Campbell; citing memorial #114799577.

[100] "Calvary Cemetery," database, *Find A Grave* (http://www.findagrave.com: accessed 5 April 2016), entry for Emma Frances Roberts Campbell; citing memorial #114799280.

[101] Ibid.

[102] 1910 US Census, Warren County, Kentucky, population schedule, Magisterial District No 5, Enumeration District (ED) 123, page 6B, dwelling 103, family 104, John S. Campbell.

[103] Zalame Brashear Cottrell's Campbell Family Data, Descendent File, Circa 1958.

[104] Social Security Administration, "Social Security Death Index," database, *Ancestry.com* (http://www.ancestry.com: accessed 26 July 2014), entry for Louis Currey, 1968, SS no. 409-62-6037.

[105] "Kentucky Death Records, 1852-1953," subscription database, *Ancestry.com* (http://www.ancestry.com: accessed 24 November 2007), for Anna Lively Campbell (4 February 1929), certificate 7854.

[106] "Kentucky Death Records, 1852-1953," subscription database, *Ancestry.com* (http://www.ancestry.com: accessed 24 November 2007), for John Sale Campbell (26 July 1930), certificate 18461.

[107] "Kentucky Death Records, 1852-1953," subscription database, *Ancestry.com* (http://www.ancestry.com: accessed 19 January 2008), for Ellen Campbell Smith (12 May 1947), certificate 12150.

[108] 1870 US Census, Warren County, Kentucky, population schedule, Greencastle Post Office, page 200B, dwelling 231, family 231, Geo W Campbell.

[109] 1880 US Census, Warren County, Kentucky, population schedule, Green Castle District, Enumeration District (ED) 2, page 181A, dwelling 76, family 76, George Campbell.

[110] Editor Triplett of the Times-Enterprise Writes of Miss Campbell's Death, *Unidentified Bowling Green newspaper*, Warren County, Kentucky, 17 January 1900. Original clipping found in loose scrapbook pages of Della Z Campbell Brashear, which passed to her daughter, Zalame Brashear Cottrell and then to Mrs. Cottrell's son, Taylor C Cottrell, Jr. Original pages in the possession of Mr. Cottrell, June 2004.

[111] 1900 US Census, Warren County, Kentucky, population schedule, Bowling Green, Enumeration District (ED) 3, page 7B, dwelling 123, family 123, George W Campbell.

[112] "Gottschalk Family Tree," subscription database, *Ancestry.com* (http://www.ancestry.com: accessed 7 June 2008), Paul G. Gottschalk.

[113] Ibid.

[114] Mrs. Donaldson Dies Sunday; Services Tuesday, *Unidentified Bowling Green newspaper*, Warren County, Kentucky. Original clipping found in loose scrapbook pages of Della Z Campbell Brashear, which passed to her daughter, Zalame Brashear Cottrell and then to Mrs. Cottrell's son, Taylor C Cottrell, Jr. Original pages in the possession of Mr. Cottrell, June 2004. Hereinafter cited as Unidentified Bowling Green newspaper.

[115] Mrs. Donaldson Dies Sunday; Services Tuesday, *Unidentified Bowling Green newspaper*, Warren County, Kentucky. Original clipping found in loose scrapbook pages of Della Z Campbell Brashear, which passed to her daughter, Zalame Brashear Cottrell and then to Mrs. Cottrell's son, Taylor C Cottrell, Jr. Original pages in the possession of Mr. Cottrell, June 2004.

[116] 1910 US Census, Warren County, Kentucky, population schedule, Enumeration District (ED) 3, page 2A, dwelling 29, family 29, Elvis C Smith; *Ancestry.com* (http://www.ancestry.com: accessed 19 September 2004); citing National Archives microfilm T624, roll 505.

[117] 1920 US Census, Warren County, Kentucky, population schedule, Bowling Green, Enumeration District (ED) 139, page 14B, dwelling 323, family 335, Elvis C Smith; *Ancestry.com* (http://www.ancestry.com: accessed 24 September 2004); citing National Archives microfilm T625, roll 600.

[118] 1930 US Census, Warren County, Kentucky, population schedule, Bowling Green, Enumeration District (ED) 114-11, page 2B, dwelling 45, family 45, Elvis Smith; *Ancestry.com* (http://www.ancestry.com: accessed 24 September 2004); citing National Archives microfilm T626, roll 779.

[119] Sarah S Dodd dies at age 100, *Bowling Green Daily News*, Bowling Green. Kentucky, 18 January 2005. secured from Owensboro Messenger Inquirer web site on 16 August 2004 by TC Cottrell.

[120] Zalame Brashear Cottrell's Campbell Family Data, Descendent File, Circa 1958, Cottrell Family Papers, 867 Jamestown Drive, Rockledge, Florida.

[121] 1940 US Census, Warren County, Kentucky, population schedule, Enumeration District (ED) 114-14, page 25A, family 621, Allen L. Dodd; Ancestry.com (http://www.ancestry.com: accessed 6 April 2016); citing National Archives microfilm T627, roll 1360.

[122] "Kentucky Death Records, 1852-1953," subscription database, *Ancestry.com* (http://www.ancestry.com: accessed 19 January 2008), for George Porter Smith (28 January 1924), certificate 2522.

[123] "Hester S. Gottschalk, 99, of Taylorville Died," *Breeze Courier (Taylorville, Illinois)*, 27 December 2006, Obituary Archives, Record Number 1164BE5DE260D3B8, ObitsArchive.com (http://oa.newsbank.com: accessed 25 February 2008).

[124] Zalame Brashear Cottrell's Campbell Family Data, Descendent File, Circa 1958.

[125] "New York, Passenger Lists, 1820-1957," subscription database, *Ancestry.com* (http://www.ancestry.com: accessed 14 June 2015), for Paul Guenther Gottschalk (21 July 1927), National Archives Record Group 36, Microfilm Roll 4093; Line 5; Page 90.

[126] "Hester S. Gottschalk," *Breeze Courier (Taylorville, Illinois)*, 27 December 2006.

[127] "Fairview Cemetery," database, *Find A Grave* (http://www.findagrave.com: accessed 6 April 2016), entry for Paul Gunther Gottschalk; citing memorial #120340061.

[128] "Kentucky Death Records", for Ellen Campbell Smith (12 May 1947), certificate 12150.

[129] "Kentucky Death Records, 1852-1953," subscription database, *Ancestry.com* (http://www.ancestry.com: accessed 19 January 2008), for Elvis C Smith (15 December 1944), certificate 28387.

[130] "Kentucky Death Records, 1852-1953," subscription database, *Ancestry.com* (http://www.ancestry.com: accessed 20 November 2007), for Della C Brashear (11 July 1951), certificate 5115181.

[131] Mrs J.E. Boulton Dies Early Today, *Unidentified Bowling Green newspaper*, Warren County, Kentucky, 17 March 1910. Original clipping found in loose scrapbook pages of Della Z Campbell Brashear, which passed to her daughter, Zalame Brashear Cottrell and then to Mrs. Cottrell's son, Taylor C Cottrell, Jr. Original pages in the possession of Mr. Cottrell, June 2004.

[132] 1880 US Census, Warren County, Kentucky, population schedule, Green Castle District, Enumeration District (ED) 2, page 181A, dwelling 76, family 76, George Campbell.

[133] Warren County, Kentucky, Marriage Record Book W, P 443 (29 November 1893), James E Boulton and Pernie Campbell; Warren County Courthouse, Clerk Warren County Court. Copied at County Courthouse in Bowling Green, Kentucky on 11 September 2014 by TC Cottrell.

T.C. Cottrell

[134] "Kentucky Death Records, 1852-1953," subscription database, *Ancestry.com* (http://www.ancestry.com: accessed 20 November 2007), for James E Boulton (15 October 1918), certificate 31306.

[135] 1910 US Census, Warren County, Kentucky, population schedule, Green Castle, Enumeration District (ED) 111, page 3A, dwelling 43, family 44, James E Boulton; *Ancestry.com* (http://www.ancestry.com: accessed 29 September 2004); citing National Archives microfilm T624, roll 504.

[136] Mrs J.E. Boulton Dies Early Today, *Unidentified Bowling Green newspaper*, Warren County, Kentucky, 17 March 1910.

[137] Kentucky Death Records, 1852-1953," subscription database, *Ancestry.com* (http://www.ancestry.com: accessed 20 November 2007), for James E Boulton (15 October 1918), certificate 31306.

[138] "Kentucky Death Index, 1911-2000," subscription database, *Ancestry.com* (http://www.ancestry.com: accessed 17 September 2006), for Clyde B Cates (10 March 1984), volume 15, certificate 7141.

[139] Zalame Brashear Cottrell's Campbell Family Data, Descendent File, Circa 1958.

[140] Patricia E Reid and Barbara O Ford compilers *Fairview Cemetery, Bowling Green, Kentucky, Cemetery 1.*

[141] Zalame Brashear Cottrell's Campbell Family Data, Descendent File, Circa 1958.

[142] "Lexington Cemetery," database, *Find A Grave* (http://www.findagrave.com: accessed 20 February 2014), entry for Wayland Rhoads, 6 July 1972; citing memorial #42550518.

[143] 1940 US Census, Warren County, Kentucky, population schedule, Enumeration District (ED) 34-45, page 11B, family 246, Wayland Rhoads; Ancestry.com (http://www.ancestry.com: accessed 6 April 2016); citing National Archives microfilm publication T627, roll 1303.

[144] "Lexington Cemetery," database, *Find A Grave* (http://www.findagrave.com: accessed 5 April 2016), entry for Betsey Madison Rhoads, 16 July 1941; citing memorial #42550574.

[145] "Lexington Cemetery," database, *Find A Grave* (http://www.findagrave.com: accessed 20 February 2014), entry for Wayland Rhoads.

[146] Zalame Brashear Cottrell's Campbell Family Data, Descendent File, Circa 1958.

[147] 1880 US Census, Warren County, Kentucky, population schedule, Green Castle District, Enumeration District (ED) 2, page 181A, dwelling 76, family 76, George Campbell.

[148] Warren County, Kentucky, Probate Records, 1797-1985, Vols. D, 4-6 1827-1927 - v. D, will of G.W. Campbell.

[149] Editor Triplett of the Times-Enterprise Writes of Miss Campbell's Death, *Unidentified Bowling Green newspaper*, Warren County, Kentucky, 17 January 1900.

[150] Ibid.

[151] Fairview Cemetery (Bowling Green, Warren County, Kentucky), Mildred A Campbell marker, Campbell-Brashear Plot, photographed by T.C. Cottrell, 1 April 2011.

[152] "Kentucky Death Records, 1852-1953," subscription database, *Ancestry.com* (http://www.ancestry.com: accessed 19 January 2008), for Wade H Campbell (20 November 1949), certificate 24080.

[153] 1880 US Census, Warren County, Kentucky, population schedule, Green Castle District, Enumeration District (ED) 2, page 181A, dwelling 76, family 76, George Campbell.

[154] Warren County, Kentucky, Probate Records, 1797-1985, Vols. D, 4-6 1827-1927 - v. D, will of G.W. Campbell.

[155] 1900 US Census, Warren County, Kentucky, population schedule, Bowling Green, Enumeration District (ED) 3, page 7B, dwelling 123, family 123, George W Campbell.

[156] Warren County, Kentucky, Marriage Bond Book AA, P 56 (26 March 1901), Wade H Campbell and Elizabeth Boulton; Warren County Courthouse, Clerk Warren County Court. Copied at County Courthouse in Bowling Green, Kentucky on 11 September 2014 by TC Cottrell.

[157] "Kentucky Death Records, 1852-1953," subscription database, *Ancestry.com* (http://www.ancestry.com: accessed 20 November 2007), for Elizabeth Campbell (4 May 1914), certificate 14236.

[158] "Halls Chapel Cemetery," database, *Find A Grave* (http://www.findagrave.com: accessed 6 June 2016), entry for Mary F. McGinnis Boulton, 6 July 1972; citing memorial #89229967.

[159] 1910 US Census, Warren County, Kentucky, population schedule, District No 6, Enumeration District (ED) 117, page 45B, dwelling 18, family 19, Wade H Campbell; *Ancestry.com* (http://www.ancestry.com: accessed 17 July 2004); citing National Archives microfilm T624, roll 505.

[160] Warren County, Kentucky, Probate Records, 1797-1985, Vols. D, 4-6 1827-1927 - v. D, will of Hester T Campbell, FHL microfilm 1904209, v6, p431, Family History Library, Salt Lake City, Utah.

[161] "Kentucky Death Records, 1852-1953," subscription database, *Ancestry.com* (http://www.ancestry.com: accessed 20 November 2007), for James Hampton Ford (29 October 1939), certificate 26251.

[162] Zalame Brashear Cottrell's Campbell Family Data, Descendent File, Circa 1958.

[163] "Kentucky Death Records, 1852-1953," subscription database, *Ancestry.com* (http://www.ancestry.com: accessed 24 November 2007), for James Monroe Ford (21 August 1947), certificate 18967.

[164] "Kentucky Death Records, 1852-1953," subscription database, *Ancestry.com* (http://www.ancestry.com: accessed 20 November 2007), for Bettie Jean Ford (6 January 1937), certificate 2786.

[165] "Kentucky Death Records, 1852-1953," subscription database, *Ancestry.com* (http://www.ancestry.com: accessed 20 November 2007), for James Campbell Ford (20 February 1938), certificate 5340.

[166] "Kentucky Death Records, 1852-1953," subscription database, *Ancestry.com* (http://www.ancestry.com: accessed 20 November 2007), for James Hampton Ford (29 October 1939), certificate 26251.

[167] Good Woman Passes Away, *Unidentified Bowling Green newspaper*, Warren County, Kentucky, 4 February 1914. Original clipping found in loose scrapbook pages of Della Z Campbell Brashear, which passed to her daughter, Zalame Brashear Cottrell and then to Mrs. Cottrell's son, Taylor C Cottrell, Jr. Original pages in the possession of Mr. Cottrell, June 2004.

[168] Warren County, Kentucky, Marriage Bond Book 2, P 82 (1 February 1916), Wade H Campbell and Mary McGinnis; Warren County Courthouse, Clerk Warren County Court. Copied at County Courthouse in Bowling Green, Kentucky on 11 September 2014 by TC Cottrell.

[169] 1920 US Census, Warren County, Kentucky, population schedule, Bowling Green, Enumeration District (ED) 181, page 5A, dwelling 45, family 50, Wade Campbell; *Ancestry.com* (http://www.ancestry.com: accessed 17 July 2004); citing National Archives microfilm T625, roll 600

[170] 1930 US Census, Warren County, Kentucky, population schedule, Bowling Green, Enumeration District (ED) 114-10, page 5A, dwelling 95, family 101, Wade H Campbell; *Ancestry.com* (http://www.ancestry.com: accessed 17 July 2004); citing National Archives microfilm T626, roll 779.

[171] "U.S. City Directories - 1937/38-1949," database, *Ancestry.com* (http://www.ancestry.com: accessed 20 March 2009); citing "*Caron's Bowling Green Kentucky City Directory for 1937-1938 - Warren County Section* (Bowling Green, Kentucky: Caron Directory Company)".

[172] "Kentucky Death Records, 1852-1953," subscription database, *Ancestry.com* (http://www.ancestry.com: accessed 24 November 2007), for James Campbell (24 May 1917), certificate 15725.

[173] Mildred Campbell Soriero, Death Registration 7826111 (1978), Department of Health Bureau of Vital Statistics, Frankfort, Kentucky. Hereinafter cited as death certificate no. 7826111.

[174] Personal knowledge of Taylor C Cottrell Jr.

[175] "Fairview Cemetery," database, *Find A Grave* (http://www.findagrave.com: accessed 5 April 2016), entry for Alphonse J. Soriero, 27 June 1971; citing memorial #120941146.

[176] "U.S. World War II Army Enlistment Records, 1938-1946," subscription database, *Ancestry.com* (http://www.ancestry.com: accessed 6 September 2014), for Alphonse J Soriero, National Archives and Records Administration, Record Group 64.

[177] "Fairview Cemetery," database, *Find A Grave* (http://www.findagrave.com: accessed 5 April 2016), entry for Alphonse J. Soriero.

[178] "Kentucky Death Records, 1852-1953," subscription database, *Ancestry.com* (http://www.ancestry.com: accessed 19 January 2008), for Wade H Campbell (20 November 1949), certificate 24080.

[179] Patricia E Reid and Barbara O Ford compilers *Fairview Cemetery, Bowling Green, Kentucky, Cemetery 1.*

[180] 1880 US Census, Warren County, Kentucky, population schedule, Green Castle District, Enumeration District (ED) 2, page 181A, dwelling 76, family 76, George Campbell.

[181] Warren County, Kentucky, Probate Records, 1797-1985, Vols. D, 4-6 1827-1927 - v. D, will of G.W. Campbell.

[182] 1900 US Census, Warren County, Kentucky, population schedule, Bowling Green, Enumeration District (ED) 3, page 7B, dwelling 123, family 123, George W Campbell.

[183] Pretty Wedding of Mr. Brown McGinnis and Miss Julya Campbell, *Unknown Kentucky Newspaper*, Kentucky.

[184] 1910 US Census, Warren County, Kentucky, population schedule, District No 1, Enumeration District (ED) 112, page 10A, dwelling 106, family 106, Hester T. Campbell; *Ancestry.com* (http://www.ancestry.com: accessed 24 September 2004); citing National Archives microfilm T624, roll 504.

[185] Zalame Brashear Cottrell's Campbell Family Data, Descendent File, Circa 1958.

[186] "Riverside Cemetery," database, *Find A Grave* (http://www.findagrave.com: accessed 11 September 2010), entry for Charles Snell Joyner, 5 October 1959; citing memorial # 56199275.

[187] 1920 US Census, Bibb County, population schedule, Macon Ward 1, Enumeration District (ED) 16, page 3A, dwelling 52, family 52, Charles S Joyner; *Ancestry.com* (http://www.ancestry.com: accessed 31 December 2012); citing National Archives microfilm publication T625, roll 235.

Cottrell-Brashear Family Linage

[188] "U.S. Social Security Applications and Claims Index, 1936-2007," *Ancestry.com* (http://www.ancestry.com: accessed 5 April 2016), entry for Charlotte Josephine Ainsworth, 8 May 2005.

[189] "Riverside Cemetery," database, *Find A Grave* (http://www.findagrave.com: accessed 11 September 2010), entry for Marjorie J Mueller, 30 June 1959; citing memorial # 56196727.

[190] Zalame Brashear Cottrell's Campbell Family Data, Descendent File, Circa 1958.

[191] "Riverside Cemetery," database, *Riverside Cemetery* (http://www.riversidecemetery.com: accessed 18 June 2016), entry for Herman I. Mueller, 26 December 1997; citing memorial #56196014.

[192] "Riverside Cemetery," database, *Riverside Cemetery* (http://www.riversidecemetery.com: accessed 17 November 2010), entry for Juel (Huel) Campbell Joyner, 19 September 1919.

[193] 1930 US Census, Greene County, North Carolina, population schedule, Carrs, District #1, Enumeration District (ED) 02, page 3B, dwelling 41, family 41, Charlie E. Joyner; *Ancestry.com* (http://www.ancestry.com: accessed 5 April 2016); citing National Archives microfilm T626, roll 1693.

[194] "Riverside Cemetery," database, *Riverside Cemetery* (http://www.riversidecemetery.com: accessed 17 November 2010), entry for Julya Campbell Joyner, 10 May 1929.

[195] Last Rites Today for Mrs. Joyner, *Unidentified newspaper*, Georgia, 19 August 1934.

[196] "Riverside Cemetery," database, *Find A Grave* (http://www.findagrave.com: accessed 11 September 2010), entry for Charles Snell Joyner, 5 October 1959; citing memorial # 56199275.

[197] Zalame Brashear Cottrell's Campbell Family Data, Descendent File, Circa 1958.

[198] 1900 US Census, Warren County, Kentucky, population schedule, Bowling Green, Enumeration District (ED) 3, page 7B, dwelling 123, family 123, George W Campbell.

[199] Irene Moss Sumpter, *Early Warren County Kentucky Land Marks.*

[200] 1910 US Census, Warren County, Kentucky, population schedule, District No 1, Enumeration District (ED) 112, page 10A, dwelling 106, family 106, Hester T Campbell; *Ancestry.com* (http://www.ancestry.com: accessed 24 September 2004); citing National Archives microfilm T624, roll 504.

[201] 1920 US Census, Bibb County, population schedule, Macon Ward 1, Enumeration District (ED) 16, page 3A, dwelling 52, family 52, Charles S Joyner; *Ancestry.com* (http://www.ancestry.com: accessed 31 December 2012); citing National Archives microfilm T625, roll 235.

[202] 1930 US Census, Warren County, Kentucky, population schedule, Green Castle, Enumeration District (ED) 114-30, page 2a, dwelling 30, family 31, Lara Campbell; *Ancestry.com* (http://www.ancestry.com: accessed 5 March 2007); citing National Archives microfilm T626, roll 780.

[203] "U.S. City Directories - 1937/38-1949," database, *Ancestry.com* (http://www.ancestry.com: accessed 20 March 2009); citing *"Caron's Bowling Green Kentucky City Directory for 1937-1938 - Warren County Section* (Bowling Green, Kentucky: Caron Directory Company)", entry for Georgia Campbell.

[204] 1940 US Census, Warren County, Kentucky, population schedule, Green Castle, Enumeration District (ED) 114-81, page 9A, dwelling 157, Georgia Campbell; digital images, *Ancestry.com* (http://www.ancestry.com: accessed 22 May 2013); citing National Archives microfilm publication T627, roll 1360.

[205] "U.S. City Directories - 1937/38-1949," database, *Ancestry.com* (http://www.ancestry.com: accessed 20 March 2009); citing "*Caron's Bowling Green Warren County Kentucky City Directory 1949 Including Rural Routes* (Bowling Green, Kentucky: Caron Directory Company)".

[206] Miss Georgia Campbell Dies Last Night at Local Hospital, *unidentified Kentucky newspaper*, Kentucky, 20 November 1957. given to TC Cottrell by Mandane Ennis on 20 February 2014, most likely originally published in the Bowling Green Park City Daily News.

Section 2 – Chapter 7 Sources – Peter Penner Family

[1] "Penner Cemetery," database, *Find A Grave* (http://www.findagrave.com: accessed 8 March 2011), entry for Anna Honaker Penner, 2 September 1830; citing memorial# 23970412.

[2] "Penner Cemetery," database, *Find A Grave* (http://www.findagrave.com: accessed 9 March 2011), entry for John Penner, 1 October 1833; citing memorial# 23970480. Cottrell Digital Image Cd04329.

[3] "Penner Cemetery," database, *Find A Grave* (http://www.findagrave.com: accessed 8 March 2011), entry for Anna Honaker Penner, 2 September 1830; citing memorial# 23970412.

[4] 1830 U.S. Census, Warren County, Kentucky, page 98, Peter Penner; *Ancestry.com* (http://www.ancestry.com: accessed 4 February 2016); citing National Archives microfilm publications M19, roll 42.

[5] 1840 U.S. Census, Warren County, Kentucky, page 72, Peter Penner; *Ancestry.com* (http://www.ancestry.com: accessed 4 February 2016); citing National Archives microfilm publications M704, Roll 125.

[6] "Kentucky Marriages to 1850," online database, Ancestry.com (http://www.ancestry.com: accessed 28 May 2006), entry for Peter Penner and Elizabeth Alford.

[7] "Kentucky Marriages to 1850," *Ancestry.com* (http://www.ancestry.com: accessed 28 May 2006), entry for Peter Penner and Elizabeth Alford.

[8] "Smith-Milam Family Tree" Genealogy Database, Mark Smith, *Ancestry.com* (http://www.ancestry.com: accessed 13 April 2016), entry for William Alford Sr.

[9] "Green River Union Cemetery," database, *Find A Grave* (http://www.findagrave.com: accessed 13 April 2016), entry for Mary Miller Honaker, 1830; citing memorial #8969156.

[10] Edmund West, compiler, "Family Data Collection – Individual Records," subscription database, *Ancestry.com* (http://www.ancestry.com: accessed 16 April 2016), entry for John Alford (1763).

[11] Edmund West, compiler, "Family Data Collection – Individual Records," subscription database, *Ancestry.com* (http://www.ancestry.com: accessed 16 April 2016), entry for Moses Alford (1761).

[12] Edmund West, compiler, "Family Data Collection – Births," subscription database, *Ancestry.com* (http://www.ancestry.com: accessed 16 April 2016), entry for James Alford (1766).

[13] Edmund West, compiler, "Family Data Collection – Individual Records," subscription database, *Ancestry.com* (http://www.ancestry.com: accessed 16 April 2016), entry for Elizabeth Alford (1775).

[14] Edmund West, compiler, "Family Data Collection – Births," subscription database, *Ancestry.com* (http://www.ancestry.com: accessed 16 April 2016), entry for Charles Alford (1779).

[15] 1850 US Census, Warren County, Kentucky, population schedule, District 1, page 51A, dwelling 696, family 96, Peter Penner; *Ancestry.com* (http://www.ancestry.com: accessed 16 September 2004); citing National Archives microfilm publication M432, roll 220.

[16] Warren County, Kentucky, Will Book W4, 71-72 (1 July 1864), Peter Penner; Warren County Courthouse, Clerk Warren County Court. Copied at County Courthouse in Bowling Green, Kentucky on 11 September 2014 by TC Cottrell.

[17] "Penner Cemetery," database, *Find A Grave* (http://www.findagrave.com: accessed 9 March 2011), entry for Peter Penner, 18 April 1869; citing memorial# 23893933.

[18] 1870 US Census, Warren County, Kentucky, population schedule, Greencastle, page 20, dwelling 119, family 119, Elizabeth Penner; *Ancestry.com* (http://www.ancestry.com: accessed 1 June 2008); citing National Archives microfilm M653, roll 502

[19] "Penner Cemetery," database, *Find A Grave* (http://www.findagrave.com: accessed 9 March 2011), entry for Margaret Elizabeth Alford Penner, 15 July 1879; citing memorial# 33998354.

[20] "Penner Cemetery," database, *Find A Grave* (http://www.findagrave.com: accessed 9 March 2011), entry for Margaret Elizabeth Alford Penner, 15 July 1879; citing memorial# 33998354.

[21] 1830 U.S. Census, Warren County, Kentucky, page 98, Peter Penner; *Ancestry.com* (http://www.ancestry.com:_accessed 4 February 2016).

[22] "Green River Union Cemetery," database, *Find A Grave* (http://www.findagrave.com: accessed 8 March 2011), entry for John Miller, 1888; citing memorial# 8973495.

[23] 1850 U.S. Census, Warren County, Kentucky, population schedule, District 1, page 9B, dwelling 121, family 121, Jno. Miller; *Ancestry.com* (http://www.ancestry.com: accessed 4 February 2016), citing National Archives microfilm M432, roll 220.

[24] 1870 US Census, Warren County, Kentucky, population schedule, Bowling Green, page 6, dwelling 36, family 36, John Miller; *Ancestry.com* (http://www.ancestry.com: accessed 27 December 2011); citing National Archives microfilm M593, roll 502

[25] 1880 US Census, Warren County, Kentucky, population schedule, Bowling Green, Enumeration District (ED) 225, page 69D, family 264, John Miller; *Ancestry.com* (http://www.ancestry.com: accessed 16 May 2013); citing National Archives microfilm T9, roll 444

[26] "Green River Union Cemetery," database, *Find A Grave* (http://www.findagrave.com: accessed 13 April 2016), entry for Margaret Penner Miller, 22 March 1883; citing memorial #34038452.

[27] "Green River Union Cemetery," database, *Find A Grave* (http://www.findagrave.com: accessed 13 April 2016), entry for John Miller, 22 January 1888; citing memorial #8973495.

[28] "Green River Union Cemetery," database, *Find A Grave* (http://www.findagrave.com: accessed 8 March 2011), entry for Peter Penner Miller, 1928; citing memorial# 34038910.

[29] "Green River Union Cemetery," database, *Find A Grave* (http://www.findagrave.com: accessed 8 March 2011), entry for E Dee Thacker Miller, 1923; citing memorial# 34039241.

[30] "Mount Zion Church of Christ Cemetery," database, *Find A Grave* (http://www.findagrave.com: accessed 7 April 2016), entry for George Henry Miller, 2 July 1939; citing memorial #13651455.

[31] Ibid.

[32] "Mount Zion Church of Christ Cemetery," database, *Find A Grave* (http://www.findagrave.com: accessed 7 April 2016), entry for Cletis Ray Miller, 12 February 1987; citing memorial #13651313.

[33] "Green River Union Cemetery," database, *Find A Grave* (http://www.findagrave.com: accessed 8 March 2011), entry for Albert Arthur Miller, 1898; citing memorial# 8973092.

[34] "Green River Union Cemetery," database, *Find A Grave* (http://www.findagrave.com: accessed 8 March 2011), entry for Clarence McElroy Miller, 1955; citing memorial# 40426481.

[35] "Fairview Cemetery," database, *Find A Grave* (http://www.findagrave.com: accessed 7 April 2016), entry for Clarence Sledge Miller, 25 August 1988; citing memorial #13651214.

[36] "Fairview Cemetery," database, *Find A Grave* (http://www.findagrave.com: accessed 7 April 2016), entry for Charles E. Miller, 29 March 1955; citing memorial #128695472.

[37] "Fairview Cemetery," database, *Find A Grave* (http://www.findagrave.com: accessed 7 April 2016), entry for Hester Morgan Miller, 8 February 1943; citing memorial #18695543.

[38] "Kentucky Death Records, 1852-1963," *Ancestry.com* (http:www.ancestry.com: accessed 16 April 2016), entry for Annie Bell Beck, 5 January 1921; reference certificate #2304.

[39] "Kentucky Marriage Records, 1852-1914," *Ancestry.com* (http://www.ancestry.com: accessed 16 April 2016), entry for Chas Beck and Annie B. Miller (25 March 1908).

[40] "Plum Springs Cemetery," database, *Find A Grave* (http://www.findagrave.com: accessed 13 April 2016), entry for Charles Oliver Beck, 10 July 1968; citing memorial #10023974.

[41] "Plum Springs Cemetery," database, *Find A Grave* (http://www.findagrave.com: accessed 13 April 2016), entry for Clarence Wilbur Beck, 26 June 1909; citing memorial #18184970.

[42] "Plum Springs Cemetery," database, *Find A Grave* (http://www.findagrave.com: accessed 13 April 2016), entry for Lloyd Dauno Beck, 16 May 1986; citing memorial #10489439.

[43] "Plum Springs Cemetery," database, *Find A Grave* (http://www.findagrave.com: accessed 13 April 2016), entry for Elsie Geraldine Beck, 11October 1915; citing memorial #136024546

[44] "Plum Springs Cemetery," database, *Find A Grave* (http://www.findagrave.com: accessed 13 April 2016).

[45] "Green River Union Cemetery," database, *Find A Grave* (http://www.findagrave.com: accessed 16 April 2016), entry for James Kelly Miller; citing memorial #8973488.

[46] "Green River Union Cemetery," database, *Find A Grave* (http://www.findagrave.com: accessed 16 April 2016), entry for Claude Lee Miller; citing memorial #8973181.

[47] "Green River Union Cemetery," database, *Find A Grave* (http://www.findagrave.com: accessed 16 April 2016), entry for Margery Kathileen Miller Duckett; citing memorial #13583965.

[48] "Green River Union Cemetery," database, *Find A Grave* (http://www.findagrave.com: accessed 29 January 1991), entry for Roger Lee Miller; citing memorial #13612838.

[49] "Green River Union Cemetery," database, *Find A Grave* (http://www.findagrave.com: accessed 16 April 2016), entry for Verta Louise Miller Runner; citing memorial #8976246.

[50] "Green River Union Cemetery," database, *Find A Grave* (http://www.findagrave.com: accessed 16 April 2016), entry for Claude Lee Miller.

[51] "Penner Cemetery," database, *Find A Grave* (http://www.findagrave.com: accessed 8 March 2011), entry for Albert Henry Miller, 1874; citing memorial# 40424176.

[52] "Penner Cemetery," database, *Find A Grave* (http://www.findagrave.com: accessed 8 March 2011), entry for Martha Frances Miller, 1868; citing memorial#34013049.

[53] Faye Merideth, "RE: Permission to Use Photographs," e-mail to tccottrell@earthlink.net, 8 April 2016.

[54] "Green River Union Cemetery," database, *Find A Grave* (http://www.findagrave.com: accessed 16 April 2016), entry for Ada C. Miller, 12 September 1908; citing memorial #8959648.

[55] "Mount Olivet Cumberland Presbyterian Cemetery," database, *Find A Grave* (http://www.findagrave.com: accessed 16 April 2016), entry for Raleigh C. Miller, 21 May 1917; citing memorial #36318404.

[56] Ibid.

[57] "Fairview Cemetery," database, *Find A Grave* (http://www.findagrave.com: accessed 16 April 2016), entry for Albert H. Miller, 4 February 1891; citing memorial #126607462.

[58] "Kentucky Death Records, 1852-1963," *Ancestry.com* (http:www.ancestry.com: accessed 16 April 2016), entry for Mrs. Laura Jones, 19 September 1913; reference certificate #25467.

[59] "Green River Union Cemetery," database, *Find A Grave* (http://www.findagrave.com: accessed 13 April 2016), entry for Henry Adison Miller, 19 August 1905; citing memorial #8973302.

[60] Ibid.

[61] Faye Merideth, "RE: Permission to Use Photographs," e-mail.

[62] "Green River Union Cemetery," database, *Find A Grave* (http://www.findagrave.com: accessed 13 April 2016), entry for Joseph S. Miller, 1 January 1884; citing memorial #40425775.

[63] "Green River Union Cemetery," database, *Find A Grave* (http://www.findagrave.com: accessed 13 April 2016), entry for Josephine Miller, 29 June 1897; citing memorial #40426028.

[64] "Penner Cemetery," database, *Find A Grave* (http://www.findagrave.com: accessed 9 March 2011), entry for Louisa Penner Davis, 16 March 1899; citing memorial#12309421.

[65] 1850 US Census, Warren County, Kentucky, population schedule, District 1, page 51A, dwelling 696, family 96, Peter Penner; *Ancestry.com* (http://www.ancestry.com: accessed 16 September 2004); citing National Archives microfilm M432, roll 220.

[66] "Penner Cemetery," database, *Find A Grave* (http://www.findagrave.com: accessed 9 March 2011), entry for Ashberry Vandiver Davis; citing memorial#34014423.

[67] "Penner Cemetery," database, *Find A Grave* (http://www.findagrave.com: accessed 9 March 2011), entry for Joseph Davis, 1854; citing memorial#12240240.

[68] "Penner Cemetery," database, *Find A Grave* (http://www.findagrave.com: accessed 9 March 2011), entry for Peter P Davis, 1858; citing memorial# 12240248.

[69] "Penner Cemetery," database, *Find A Grave* (http://www.findagrave.com: accessed 9 March 2011), entry for Drew C Davis, 1864; citing memorial#12240258.

[70] "Penner Cemetery," database, *Find A Grave* (http://www.findagrave.com: accessed 9 March 2011), entry for Louisa Penner Davis.

[71] "Penner Cemetery," database, *Find A Grave* (http://www.findagrave.com: accessed 9 March 2011), entry for Ashberry Vandiver Davis.

[72] 1940 US Census, Lawrence County, Illinois, population schedule, Lawrenceville City, Enumeration District (ED) 51-11, page 14A, dwelling 209, J.N. Penner; *Ancestry.com* (http://www.ancestry.com: accessed 22 May 2013); citing National Archives microfilm T627, roll 835.

[73] "Mount Pleasant Church of Christ Cemetery," database, *Find A Grave* (http://www.findagrave.com: accessed 9 March 2011), entry for Mary Malvina Penner Floyd, 10 November 1893; citing memorial #8901774.

[74] 1850 US Census, Warren County, Kentucky, population schedule, District 1, page 51A, dwelling 696, family 96, Peter Penner.

[75] "Mount Pleasant Church of Christ Cemetery," database, *Find A Grave* (http://www.findagrave.com: accessed 9 March 2011), entry for William E Floyd, 1892; citing memorial#8901801.

[76] "Mount Pleasant Church of Christ Cemetery," database, *Find A Grave* (http://www.findagrave.com: accessed 9 March 2011), entry for William E Floyd.

[77] "Mount Pleasant Church of Christ Cemetery," database, *Find A Grave* (http://www.findagrave.com: accessed 9 March 2011), entry for Mary Malvina Penner Floyd.

[78] "Kentucky Death Records, 1852-1963," subscription database, *Ancestry.com* (http://www.ancestry.com: accessed 14 April 2016), entry for John B. Floyd, reference certificate #8094.

[79] "Kentucky Death Records, 1852-1963," subscription database, *Ancestry.com* (http://www.ancestry.com: accessed 14 April 2016), entry for Annie E. Willis, reference certificate #27361.

[80] "Sand Hill Watt/Flora Cemetery," database, *Find A Grave* (http://www.findagrave.com: accessed 9 March 2011), entry for Crittendon Floyd, 1880; citing memorial#51783953.

[81] "Kentucky Death Records, 1852-1963," subscription database, *Ancestry.com* (http://www.ancestry.com: accessed 14 April 2016), entry for Clinton Floyd, reference certificate #30819.

[82] "Tennessee State Marriages, 1780-2002," subscription database, Ancestry.com (http://www.ancestry.com: accessed 14 April 2016), entry for Clinton Floyd and Etta Runner (30 April 1891).

[83] "Mount Pleasant Church of Christ Cemetery," database, *Find A Grave* (http://www.findagrave.com: accessed 9 March 2011), entry for Clint Floyd, 1892; citing memorial#8901699.

[84] 1880 US Census, Warren County, Kentucky, population schedule, Green Castle, Enumeration District (ED) 235, page 182C, dwelling 95, family 95, William Floyd; *Ancestry.com* (http://www.ancestry.com: accessed 14 April 2016); citing National Archives microfilm T9, roll 444.

[85] "Mount Pleasant Church of Christ Cemetery," database, *Find A Grave* (http://www.findagrave.com: accessed 9 March 2011), entry for America F Floyd, 1936; citing memorial# 8901657.

[86] "Kentucky Death Records, 1852-1963," subscription database, *Ancestry.com* (http://www.ancestry.com: accessed 14 April 2016), entry for Charlie M. Wilson, reference certificate #31630.

[87] "Kentucky Death Records, 1852-1963," subscription database, *Ancestry.com* (http://www.ancestry.com: accessed 14 April 2016), entry for Nancy Floyd Wilson, reference certificate #5319684.

[88] "Kentucky Death Records, 1852-1963," subscription database, *Ancestry.com* (http://www.ancestry.com: accessed 14 April 2016), entry for Charlie M. Wilson.

[89] 1930 US Census, Warren County, Kentucky, population schedule, Green Castle, Enumeration District (ED) 30, page 7B, dwelling 150, family 158, Charlie M. Wilson; *Ancestry.com* (http://www.ancestry.com: accessed 14 April 2016); citing National Archives microfilm T626, roll 780.

[90] "Kentucky Death Records, 1852-1963," subscription database, *Ancestry.com* (http://www.ancestry.com: accessed 14 April 2016), entry for Lucy Lee Floyd.

[91] 1850 US Census, Warren County, Kentucky, population schedule, District 1, page 51A, dwelling 696, family 96, Peter Penner.

[92] Warren County, Kentucky, Marriage Bond Book D, P 429 (21 September 1857), John H. Penner and Mary E. Shields; Warren County Courthouse, Clerk Warren County Court. Copied at County Courthouse in Bowling Green, Kentucky on 11 September 2014 by TC Cottrell.

[93] Michael Hansen, "RE: John S. Campbell Obituary - Kentucky," e-mail (Bremerton, Washington) to Thana White Cottrell, 10 September 2004.

[94] 1860 US Census, Warren County, Kentucky, population schedule, District No 2: Bowling Green, page 39, dwelling 268, family 268, John Penner; *Ancestry.com* (http://www.ancestry.com: accessed 16 September 2004); citing National Archives microfilm M653, roll 398.

[95] 1870 US Census, Lawrence County, Illinois, population schedule, Petty Township, Post Office Sumner, page 133A, dwelling 60, family 60, John Penner; *Ancestry.com* (http://www.ancestry.com: accessed 16 September 2004); citing National Archives microfilm M593, roll 245.

[96] 1880 US Census, Lawrence County, Illinois, population schedule, Lawrence Township, Enumeration District (ED) 189, page 1A, dwelling 7, family 7, John H Penner; *Ancestry.com* (http://www.ancestry.com: accessed 16 September 2004); citing National Archives microfilm T9, roll 224.

[97] Death of Dr. J.J. Penner, *Unidentified Lawrence County newspaper*, Lawrence County, Illinois. Original clipping found in loose scrapbook pages of Della Z Campbell Brashear, which passed to her daughter, Zalame Brashear Cottrell and then to Mrs. Cottrell's son, Taylor C Cottrell, Jr. Original pages in the possession of Mr. Cottrell, June 2004.

[98] 1900 US Census, Lawrence County, Illinois, population schedule, Lawrence Township, Enumeration District (ED) 114, page 10B, dwelling 218, family 225, John H Penner; *Ancestry.com* (http://www.ancestry.com: accessed 16 September 2004); citing National Archives microfilm T623, roll 317

[99] Death of Dr. J.J. Penner, *Unidentified Lawrence County newspaper*, Lawrence County, Illinois.

[100] "Pleasant Hill Cemetery," database, *Find A Grave* (http://www.findagrave.com: accessed 22 March 2015), entry for George Franklin Penner, 24 December 1873; citing memorial #32800613.

[101] "Penner Cemetery," database, *Find A Grave* (http://www.findagrave.com: accessed 15 July 2014), entry for Peter Wesley Penner, 25 July 1860; citing memorial # 34013225.

[102] "Penner Cemetery," database, *Find A Grave* (http://www.findagrave.com: accessed 15 July 2014), entry for Eugene Penner, 27 March 1862; citing memorial # 33998602.

[103] "Pleasant Hill Cemetery," database, *Find A Grave* (http://www.findagrave.com: accessed 22 March 2015), entry for Sarah Elizabeth Penner, 28 January 1882; citing memorial #32800673.

[104] "Lawrenceville City Cemetery," database, *Find A Grave* (http://www.findagrave.com: accessed 11 May 2013), entry for James N Penner, 1951; citing memorial # 16756379.

[105] Indiana Marriages, 1845-1920, Ancestry.com (http://www.ancestry.com: accessed 20 October 2004), entry for J. N. Penner and L. M. McCorroll.

[106] Mrs James N Penner, *Terre Haute Tribune*, Terre Haute, Indiana, 10 June 1947, page 2.

[107] Taylor C Cottrell, "Campbell-Shields Cemetery Lot Photo Survey, Campbell-Shields Cemetery, near Bowling Green, Kentucky," privately held by Taylor C Cottrell, Rockledge, Florida; Markers and plot information photographed and recorded on 31 March, 2011, by Taylor C Cottrell.

[108] Dr. Penner - Former Citizen of This County, Dies at Lawrenceville, Ind., *Unidentified Warren County newspaper*, Warren County, Kentucky. Original clipping found in loose scrapbook pages of Della Z Campbell Brashear. Original pages in the possession of Mr. Cottrell, June 2004. Hereinafter cited as Unidentified Warren County Kentucky newspaper.

[109] 1910 US Census, Vigo County, Indiana, population schedule, Harrison Township, Enumeration District (ED) 155, page 3A, dwelling 54, family 62, James N Penner; *Ancestry.com* (http://www.ancestry.com: accessed 16 October 2004); citing National Archives microfilm T624, roll 385

[110] Mary E Penner, *Terre Haute Tribune*, Terre Haute, Indiana, 27 June 1916, page 2.

[111] "Fairview Cemetery," database, *Find A Grave* (http://www.findagrave.com: accessed 8 March 2011), entry for William F Penner, 31 March 1900; citing memorial# 6479034.

[112] 1850 US Census, Warren County, Kentucky, population schedule, District 1, page 51A, dwelling 696, family 96, Peter Penner; *Ancestry.com* (http://www.ancestry.com: accessed 16 September 2004); citing National Archives microfilm M432, roll 220.

[113] 1860 US Census, Warren County, Kentucky, population schedule, Bowling Green, District 2, page 38, dwelling 255, family 255, Peter Penner; *Ancestry.com* (http://www.ancestry.com: accessed 1 June 2008); citing National Archives microfilm M653, roll 398.

[114] "U.S., Civil War Draft Registrations Records, 1863-1865," subscription database, *Ancestry.com* (http://www.ancestry.com: accessed 10 August 2014), for William F Penner (February 1864).

[115] 1870 US Census, Warren County, Kentucky, population schedule, Greencastle, page 20, dwelling 119, family 119, Elizabeth Penner; *Ancestry.com* (http://www.ancestry.com: accessed 1 June 2008); citing National Archives microfilm M653, roll 502.

[116] Warren County, Kentucky, Marriage Bond Book Q, P 383 (6 March 1880), W.F. Penner and Mrs. E.O. Lively; Warren County Courthouse, Clerk Warren County Court. Copied at County Courthouse in Bowling Green, Kentucky on 11 September 2014 by TC Cottrell.

[117] 1870 US Census, Warren County, Kentucky, population schedule, Patter, page 250A, dwelling 30, family 30, Jane J Coleman; *Ancestry.com* (http://www.ancestry.com: accessed 13 April 20-16); citing National Archives microfilm publication M653, roll 503.

[118] 1880 US Census, Warren County, Kentucky, population schedule, Green Castle, Enumeration District (ED) 235, page 184D, dwelling 133, family 133, William F Penner; *Ancestry.com* (http://www.ancestry.com: accessed 13 September 2004); citing National Archives microfilm T9, roll 444.

[119] Warren County, Kentucky, Will Book F1, 332 (23 March 1900), William Penner; Warren County Courthouse, Clerk Warren County Court. Copied at County Courthouse in Bowling Green, Kentucky on 11 September 2014 by TC Cottrell.

[120] "Fairview Cemetery," database, *Find A Grave* (http://www.findagrave.com: accessed 8 March 2011), entry for William F Penner.

[121] Warren County, Kentucky, Probate Records, 1797-1985, Vols. D, 4-6 1827-1927 - v. D, will of William F Penner, FHL microfilm 1904209, Family History Library, Salt Lake City, Utah.

[122] 1910 US Census, Warren County, Kentucky, population schedule, District No 5, Enumeration District (ED) 123, page 6B, dwelling 103, family 104, John S Campbell; *Ancestry.com* (http://www.ancestry.com: accessed 29 November 2004); citing National Archives microfilm T624, roll 505.

[123] Elizabeth O Penner Obituary Transcription, *Rootsweb* (http;//ftp.rootsweb.com/pub/usgenweb/ky/warren/obits: accessed 29 December 2004).

[124] "Penner Cemetery," database, *Find A Grave* (http://www.findagrave.com: accessed 9 March 2011), entry for Peter W Penner, 24 August 1836; citing memorial# 12309202.

[125] "Penner Cemetery," database, *Find A Grave* (http://www.findagrave.com: accessed 9 March 2011), entry for Milbern Jay Penner, 30 January 1868; citing memorial# 23894211.

[126] 1850 US Census, Warren County, Kentucky, population schedule, District 1, page 51A, dwelling 696, family 96, Peter Penner.

[127] "Kinser Cemetery," database, *Find A Grave* (http://www.findagrave.com: accessed 9 March 2011), entry for Joseph W Penner, 4 November 1935; citing memorial# 44988703.

[128] "Kinser Cemetery," database, *Find A Grave* (http://www.findagrave.com: accessed 13 April 2016), entry for Hadie Ann Cowles Penner, 11 May 1931; citing memorial# 61775642.

[129] "Kinser Cemetery," database, *Find A Grave* (http://www.findagrave.com: accessed 13 April 2016), entry for Joseph Austin Penner, 1130 January 1983; citing memorial# 61775642.

[130] 1880 US Census, Edmonson County, Kentucky, population schedule, Enumeration District (ED) 40, page 530D, dwelling 34, family 35, Ama Simmons; *Ancestry.com* (http://www.ancestry.com: accessed 13 April 2016); citing National Archives microfilm T9, roll 411.

[131] "Waxahachie City Cemetery, database, *Find A Grave* (http://www.findagrave.com: accessed 13 April 2016), entry for Peter Monroe Penner, 6 September 1925; citing memorial #50492159.

[132] "Waxahachie City Cemetery, database, *Find A Grave* (http://www.findagrave.com: accessed 13 April 2016), entry for Sarah J. Craighead Penner, 13 May 1940; citing memorial #50492215.

[133] "Waxahachie City Cemetery, database, *Find A Grave* (http://www.findagrave.com: accessed 13 April 2016), entry for Lillie Ann Penner Bevels, 23 November 1941; citing memorial #122406500.

[134] 1930 US Census, Fisher County, Texas, population schedule, Precinct 2, Enumeration District (ED) 3, page 7A, dwelling 73, family 73, G.W. Bevels; *Ancestry.com* (http://www.ancestry.com: accessed 13 April 2016); citing National Archives microfilm T626, roll 2332.

[135] "Waxahachie City Cemetery, database, *Find A Grave* (http://www.findagrave.com: accessed 13 April 2016), entry for George W. Bevels, 6 July 1972; citing memorial #122406433.

[136] "Waxahachie City Cemetery, database, *Find A Grave* (http://www.findagrave.com: accessed 13 April 2016), entry for Albert Monroe Penner, 27 May 1938; citing memorial #54725205.

[137] "Miles Cemetery," database, *Find A Grave* (http://www.findagrave.com: accessed 13 April 2016), entry for Johnnie Mae Penner Coleman, 2 February 1950; citing memorial #45771631.

[138] "Waxahachie City Cemetery, database, *Find A Grave* (http://www.findagrave.com: accessed 13 April 2016), entry for Charlie Edward Penner, 9 March 1917; citing memorial #54725152.

[139] "Laurel Land Memorial Park," database, *Find A Grave* (http://www.findagrave.com: accessed 13 April 2016, entry for Hester B. Penner Johnson, 23 August 1976; citing memorial #54725603.

[140] "Belew Cemetery," database, *Find A Grave* (http://www.findagrave.com: accessed 13 April 2016), entry for John C. Penner, 20 October 1942; citing memorial #13127393.

[141] "Waxahachie City Cemetery, database, *Find A Grave* (http://www.findagrave.com: accessed 13 April 2016), entry for Carrie Sabathna Penner, 2 September 1913; citing memorial #117403720.

[142] "Texas Death Certificates, 1903-1982," *Ancestry.com* (http://www.ancestry.com: accessed 13 April 2016), entry for John Taylor Penner (30- April 1982), reference certificate #92178.

[143] "Texas Death Certificates, 1903-1982," *Ancestry.com* (http://www.ancestry.com: accessed 13 April 2016), entry for Lester Arthur Penner (21 June 1967), reference certificate #41544.

[144] "Texas Death Certificates, 1903-1982," *Ancestry.com* (http://www.ancestry.com: accessed 13 April 2016), entry for Lester Arthur Penner (30 July 1980), reference certificate #111029.

[145] "World War I Draft Registration Cards, 1917-1918," subscription database, *Ancestry.com* (http://www.ancestry.com: accessed 18 June 2016), for Ulysses C. Penner, , Ellis County, Texas.

[146] "Belew Cemetery," database, *Find A Grave* (http://www.findagrave.com: accessed 18 June 2016), entry for Ulysses C. Penner (30 July 1980), citing memorial #13127460.

[147] 1870 US Census, Warren County, Kentucky, population schedule, Greencastle, page 20, dwelling 119, family 119, Elizabeth Penner.

[148] 1880 US Census, Edmonson County, Kentucky, population schedule, Enumeration District (ED) 40, page 530D, dwelling 32, family 33, John Flora; *Ancestry.com* (http://www.ancestry.com: accessed 13 April 2016), citing National Archives microfilm publication T9, roll 411.

[149] "Penner Cemetery," database, *Find A Grave* (http://www.findagrave.com: accessed 9 March 2011), entry for Milbern Jay Penner.

[150] 1870 US Census, Warren County, Kentucky, population schedule, Greencastle, page 20, dwelling 119, family 119, Elizabeth Penner; *Ancestry.com* (http://www.ancestry.com: accessed 1 June 2008); citing National Archives microfilm M653, roll 502.

[151] "Kentucky Marriage Records, 1852-1914, database, *Ancestry.com* (http://www.ancestry.com: accessed 13 April 2016), entry for John Flora and Polly A. Pend, 9 September 1877.

[152] 1880 US Census, Edmonson County, Kentucky, population schedule, page 530D, dwelling 32, family 33, John Flora.

[153] "Penner Cemetery," database, *Ancestry.com* (http://www.ancestry.com: accessed 13 April 2016), entry for Elizabeth F. Penner, 23 November 1840; citing memorial #23893661.

[154] "Fairview Cemetery," database, *Ancestry.com* (http://www.ancestry.com: accessed 13 April 2016), entry for Hester Taylor Penner Campbell, 25 November 1922; citing memorial #43007728.

[155] "Penner Cemetery," database, *Find A Grave* (http://www.findagrave.com: accessed 9 March 2011), entry for Josephene Penner Evans, 10 June 1862; citing memorial# 34012749.

[156] 1850 US Census, Warren County, Kentucky, population schedule, District 1, page 51A, dwelling 696, family 96, Peter Penner.

[157] 1860 US Census, Warren County, Kentucky, population schedule, Bowling Green, District 2, page 38, dwelling 255, family 255, Peter Penner.

[158] "Penner Cemetery," database, *Find A Grave* (http://www.findagrave.com: accessed 9 March 2011), entry for Josephene Penner Evans.

[159] "Mount Olivet Cumberland Presbyterian Cemetery," database, *Find A Grave* (http://www.findagrave.com: accessed 8 March 2011), entry for Calvin B Penner, 14 September 1928; citing memorial# 36381663.

[160] 1850 US Census, Warren County, Kentucky, population schedule, District 1, page 51A, dwelling 696, family 96, Peter Penner.

[161] 1860 US Census, Warren County, Kentucky, population schedule, Bowling Green, District 2, page 38, dwelling 255, family 255, Peter Penner.

[162] Warren County, Kentucky, Marriage Bond Book J, P 391 (21 December 1868), Calvin B. Penner and Miss Mary F. Shields; Warren County Courthouse, Clerk Warren County Court. Copied at County Courthouse in Bowling Green, Kentucky on 11 September 2014 by TC Cottrell.

[163] "Butt-Hill Cemetery" database, *Find A Grave*, entry for John Ennis, 9 August 1826.

[164] "Kentucky Marriage Records, 1852-1914," subscription database, *Ancestry.com* (http://www.ancestry.com: accessed 7 June 2008), for Calvin B Penner and Fanney Young (November 1876).

[165] 1900 US Census, Warren County, Kentucky, population schedule, Greencastle, page 3B, dwelling 52, family 52, Elizabeth Penner; *Ancestry.com* (http://www.ancestry.com: accessed 1 June 2008); citing National Archives microfilm M653, roll 553.

[166] 1910 US Census, Warren County, Kentucky, population schedule, Magisterial District 1, Enumeration District (ED) 3, page 8B, dwelling 89, family 89, Calvin B Penner; *Ancestry.com* (http://www.ancestry.com: accessed 1 June 2008); citing National Archives microfilm T624, roll 504.

[167] 1920 US Census, Warren County, Kentucky, population schedule, Greencastle, Enumeration District (ED) 126, page 7A, dwelling 131, family 131, Calvin Penner; *Ancestry.com* (http://www.ancestry.com: accessed 1 June 2008); citing National Archives microfilm T625, roll 600.

[168] "Penner Cemetery," database, *Find A Grave* (http://www.findagrave.com: accessed 13 April 2016), entry for George W. Penner, 10 April 1879; citing memorial #23894112.

[169] "Kentucky Death Index, 1911-2000," subscription database, *Ancestry.com* (http://www.ancestry.com: accessed 8 June 2008), for Peter Penner (1 January 1962), volume 4, certificate 1928.

[170] "Chapel Hill Memorial Gardens," database, *Find A Grave* (http://www.findagrave.com: accessed 18 June 2016), entry for Peter Penner, 1 January 1962; citing memorial #11418620.

[171] "Green River Union Cemetery," database, *Find A Grave* (http://www.findagrave.com: accessed 8 March 2011), entry for Amanda L Penner Tatum, 29 April 1929; citing memorial #36866702.

[172] "Mount Olivet Cumberland Presbyterian Cemetery," database, *Find A Grave* (http://www.findagrave.com: accessed 9 March 2011), entry for John Wesley Penner, 30 September 1966; citing memorial# 36382055.

[173] Warren County, Kentucky, Will Book 14, P 14 (21 January 1966), J.W. Penner; Warren County Courthouse, Clerk Warren County Court. Copied at County Courthouse in Bowling Green, Kentucky on 11 September 2014 by TC Cottrell.

[174] Warren County, Kentucky, Marriage Bond Book DD, P 478 (29 January 1906), J.W. Penner and Maggie Holman; Warren County Courthouse, Clerk Warren County Court. Copied at County Courthouse in Bowling Green, Kentucky on 11 September 2014 by TC Cottrell.

[175] "World War I Draft Registration Cards, 1917-1918," subscription database, *Ancestry.com* (http://www.ancestry.com: accessed 8 June 2008), for John Wesley Penner, citing United States, Selective Service System. World War I Selective Service System Draft Registration Cards, 1917-1918. Washington, D.C.: National Archives and Records Administration. Microfilm publication M1509, Warren County, Kentucky; Roll 1653845; Draft Board: 0.

[176] "Mount Olivet Cumberland Presbyterian Cemetery," database, *Find A Grave* (http://www.findagrave.com: accessed 15 July 2014), entry for Maggie Holman Penner, 27 May 1965; citing memorial #36382154.

[177] "Mount Olivet Cumberland Presbyterian Cemetery," database, *Find A Grave* (http://www.findagrave.com: accessed 15 July 2014), entry for Elizabeth Penner, 25 December 1906; citing memorial #36381878.

[178] "Mount Olivet Cumberland Presbyterian Cemetery," database, *Find A Grave* (http://www.findagrave.com: accessed 11 May 2013), entry for Robert Brown Penner, 1 June 1945; citing memorial #36382307.

[179] "Mount Olivet Cumberland Presbyterian Cemetery," database, *Find A Grave* (http://www.findagrave.com: accessed 11 May 2013), entry for Mary Frances Penner, 31 December 1909; citing memorial #36382003.

[180] "Kentucky Death Records, 1852-1953," subscription database, *Ancestry.com* (http://www.ancestry.com: accessed 8 June 2008), for John Edward Penner (22 September 1926), certificate 24201.

[181] "Fairview Cemetery," database, *Find A Grave* (http://www.findagrave.com: accessed 11 May 2013), entry for Willie H Penner, 11 February 1990; citing memorial #12089930.

[182] "Green River Union Cemetery," database, *Find A Grave* (http://www.findagrave.com: accessed 8 March 2011), entry for Elizabeth Penner Flora, 16 August 1970; citing memorial #54994825.

[183] "Kentucky Death Index, 1911-2000," subscription database, *Ancestry.com* (http://www.ancestry.com: accessed 28 December 2011), for Edward E Flora (12 December 1966), volume 61, certificate 30139.

[184] "Green River Union Cemetery," database, *Find A Grave* (http://www.findagrave.com: accessed 15 May 2013), entry for Clarence Edward Flora, 19 June 1891; citing memorial #55094236.

[185] "Mount Olivet Cumberland Presbyterian Cemetery," database, *Find A Grave* (http://www.findagrave.com: accessed 13 April 2016), entry for Frances Young Penner, 29 September 1925; citing memorial #36381821.

[186] "Mount Olivet Cumberland Presbyterian Cemetery," database, *Find A Grave* (http://www.findagrave.com: accessed 13 April 2016), entry for Calvin B. Penner, 14 September 1928; citing memorial #36381663.

Index

Cottrell-Brashear Family Linage

Cottrell-Brashear Family Linage

Cottrell-Brashear Family Linage

Cottrell-Brashear Family Linage

Cottrell-Brashear Family Linage

www.ingramcontent.com/pod-product-compliance
Lightning Source LLC
Chambersburg PA
CBHW051725260326
41914CB00031B/1736/J